THE ECONOMICS OF EUROPEAN INTEGRATION

THE ECONOMICS OF EUROPEAN INTEGRATION

THEORY, PRACTICE, POLICY

Fourth Edition

WILLEM MOLLE

Ashgate

Aldershot • Burlington USA • Singapore • Sydney

Published by
Ashgate Publishing Limited
Gower House
Croft Road
Aldershot
Hants GU11 3HR
England

Ashgate Publishing Company
131 Main Street
Burlington, VT 05401-5600 USA

First published 1990
Reprinted 1991, 1992
Second edition 1994
Third edition 1997
Fourth edition 2001

British Library Cataloguing in Publication Data
Molle, W. T. M. (Willem T. M.), 1942–
    The economics of European integration : theory, practice,
    policy. – 4th ed.
    1.European Union 2.Europe – Economic integration
    I.Title
    337.1'42

Library of Congress Cataloging-in-Publication Data
Molle, Willem.
    The economics of European integration : theory, practice, policy /
    Willem Molle. — 4th ed.
        p.   cm.
    Includes bibliographical references and index.
    ISBN 0 7546 2188 X (hc). — ISBN 0 7546 2195 2 (pbk.)
    1. European Economic Community.   2. Europe—Economic integration—
    History.   3. Monetary policy—European Economic Community
    countries.   I. Title.
     HC241.2.M58   2001
    337.1'42—dc21   00-53601

ISBN 0 7546 2188 X (Hbk)
ISBN 0 7546 2195 2 (Pbk)

Typeset by Manton Typesetters, Louth, Lincolnshire, UK.
Printed in Great Britain by MPG Books Ltd, Bodmin, Cornwall.

Contents

PART V   CONCLUSION

List of Tables

List of Figures

Acknowledgements

In writing this book I have been supported by many, in particular students and colleagues. The book's present form owes much to students at the various universities where I have lectured, particularly in Maastricht and Rotterdam, but also at universities where I have been a guest lecturer. My students' critical comments on the text have resulted in this adapted fourth version, which should be better suited to students' needs than the previous. Many colleagues, too numerous to list here, have helped me by correcting errors in the text and by making suggestions for including new material or presenting the existing material in a different way. Their expertise in their own fields has made it possible for me to cover areas far beyond the territory I could possibly have hoped to become an expert in myself. Very valuable has been the research assistance of Eric van Rijn, who updated the various tables and has been very helpful in tracking down new material for this fourth edition.

I thank them all for their help and encouragement. Needless to say, all remaining errors and shortcomings are my responsibility.

PART I
GENERAL ISSUES

1   Introduction

Objectives

Progressive integration has been one of the most characteristic aspects of economic development in the last few decades, worldwide and in Europe, where it has found expression notably in the European Union (EU). The EU has had a direct and profound influence on the economy of member states and third countries.

Much has been written about European economic integration. In the 1950s and 1960s, the discussion on economic integration was concentrated on international economic relations, as witness the specialised books on the subject from that period. In the 1970s and 1980s, the idea of economic integration quickly spread to the economics of the sectors of economic activity (agriculture, energy, manufacturing, services, transport) and to such aspects as market regulation, macro-economic equilibrium, monetary control, regional equilibrium or social welfare. At the end of the 1980s and during the 1990s, the issue of monetary integration was central to the discussion on European economic integration. In this field and in all the other fields mentioned, the body of specialised literature has grown very rapidly to become a real avalanche in recent years.

To *students of the economic integration process per se* this abundant specialist literature is inconvenient. Indeed, as economic integration touches ever more areas of society, more and more people are confronted by the bewildering complexity of the functioning of the EU. The past decades have witnessed the publication of a fairly large number of books that try to help readers by offering a systematic analysis. Many of them focus merely on the description of EU policies, often without a critical analysis of their economic rationale and effects. Others are merely theoretical in nature, favouring a mathematical treatment of the material. The present book differentiates itself from the other titles in that it aims to:

- select the most relevant aspects and developments;
- place the wide variety of issues in a robust conceptual structure;
- integrate theoretical developments with the results of empirical research and of policy analysis;
- explain the logic of the dynamic processes;
- describe the structural features of the European economy;
- highlight the response of private companies to changes in the regulatory environment;
- depict the 'historical' developments so as to give a sound basis for the understanding of the present situation and the likely future development;
- set the European developments in the light of global developments.

Three fundamental concepts

Integration

The expression 'economic integration' covers a variety of notions.[1] It may refer to the absorption of a company in a larger concern. It may have a spatial aspect, for instance if it refers to the integration of regional economies in a national one. In this book, the expression is always used with respect to international economic relations. The *definition* of integration that is used here is the gradual elimination of economic frontiers between independent states; as a result the economies of these states end up functioning as one entity.

Economic integration is not an *objective* in itself, but serves higher objectives, both of an economic and of a political nature.

- Economic welfare. The prosperity of all participating countries is enhanced by overcoming the inefficiencies of nationally segmented economies through specialisation of production and through cooperation in policy making, the two basic elements of economic integration.
- Peace. When countries become dependent upon each other as a result of economic integration this reduces the chance of armed conflicts between them.[2]
- Democracy. If participation in a group that brings benefits through integration is made conditional on the existence of a parliamentary form of democracy, it is less likely that attempts to overthrow this system of government in a member country will stand much chance of success.
- Human rights. In much the same way, the respect for human

rights may be safeguarded if this is set as a precondition for participation in a scheme for economic integration.

In this book we will not go further into the last three objectives, which are of a political nature; we will henceforth concentrate on the economic objective.[3]

The term 'economic integration' can be interpreted in two senses. In a dynamic sense, it is the process whereby economic frontiers between member states are gradually eliminated (that is to say, whereby national discrimination is abolished), with the formerly separate national economic entities gradually merging into a larger whole. In a static sense, it is the situation in which national components of a larger economic zone function together as one entity. The dynamic interpretation is the more usual, and the one to be used in this book. Of course, the static meaning of the expression will apply in full once the integration process has passed through its stages and reached its object.

Economics

As to economics,[4] three elements will recur throughout the book. We will analyse and describe:

- theoretical principles: we will present a selection of theory most relevant to explaining the dynamics of economic processes associated with the integration of (segments of) the economy;
- empirical facts: we will describe how the various segments of the European economy have evolved under conditions of integration, using selected long-term statistical series, on the one hand,[5] and using case studies of the behaviour of the business sector, on the other;
- public policy: we will discuss why and how the EU and national governments influence the economic process with policy measures; and what effect these interventions have on wealth.

We will not deal with these elements separately. On the contrary, while dealing with different aspects of integration we will combine a brief theoretical treatment with an analytical description and with the relevant elements of policy of the subject at hand.

In all parts of the book we will finally evaluate the results of the integration processes in economic terms. To measure advantages and disadvantages of integration, use will be made of the well-known concepts of welfare economics (see, among others, Mishan, 1982).

Europe

The word 'European' refers in principle to the whole geographical entity of Europe. In practice Western Europe will be the focus of major parts of this book. Indeed, in the past, the dynamism of the integration processes there has been much greater than in the centrally planned economic systems of Central and Eastern Europe. The European Union (EU), extended since its foundation from six to nine, then to 10, 12 and 15 member states, and open for further enlargement, constitutes the core of the European integration process. For reasons of simplicity we will henceforth use the term 'European Union (EU)' to indicate for the whole period of analysis and irrespective of the prevailing precise legal situation both the group of member states and the policy system drawn up on the basis of the various treaties.[6]

During the 1990s most of the Central and Eastern European Countries (CEEC) went through a transition from a centrally planned economy to a market economy. At the same time they became increasingly involved in the process of economic integration first by participating in the Central European Free Trade Area (CEPTA), but mostly by preparing themselves for membership of the European Union. So, in many chapters, reference will be made to the situation in the CEEC.

European integration is not an isolated process: it takes place in a world in which national systems become more and more interwoven. Therefore we must keep an eye on external aspects. Speaking of labour market integration, for instance, we will discuss not only internal migration within the EU, but also migration from and to third countries, distinguishing between different groups of countries. We will give an overview of these aspects in Chapter 17 on external relations.

Organisation of the material

Part I lays the *foundations* for the rest of the analysis. First it gives the fundamental concepts that will be used in this book, such as the definition of integration. Next it gives a theoretical treatment of the dynamics of the integration process. Third, it presents an historical overview of the process of integration, which makes it easier to understand the present dynamics. Fourth, it exposes the objective, the institutional set-up and the regulating capacity of the European Union.

Part II is devoted entirely to *market integration*. It starts with separate chapters on goods and services. The chapter on goods is fairly elaborate as a vast literature makes it possible to draw up a very detailed picture. The opposite situation prevails for services; here a lack of relevant data and operational concepts preclude an analysis of the same depth and detail. The next two chapters deal with the liberalisation of the markets for production factors. In each of the chapters on labour and capital, the results of empirical studies are set on a solid theoretical basis and in the framework of the dynamic development of the European policy regimes for both production factors.

Part III is devoted to *business*. The integration of markets of products and of production factors permits entrepreneurs to make their operations more efficient. The way enterprise responds to the opportunities created by integration is analysed for five sectors of economic activity.[7] For each of them we will follow the same process. We describe first the EU regulatory framework.[8] Next we depict the sectors' development under conditions of integration, referring, wherever useful, to theoretical notions specific to the sector concerned. For each sector we will single out two branches for which detailed case studies will be presented. In these case studies we follow the same logic: description of the evolution of the regulatory framework; sketch of the development of the industry in terms of production, trade, etc; and, finally, the response of companies to their changing environment.

Part IV deals with the different *socio-economic policies* that create the conditions for a balanced growth of the EU economy. For the discussion of these policies a division into chapters has been made (inspired by Musgrave and Musgrave, 1989) into the following four objectives:[9]

- efficiency in allocation of resources, requiring mainly micro-economic policy instruments aiming at the efficient use of resources; this function comprises all policies aiming at the proper functioning of the internal market;
- stability of development, requiring mainly macro-economic and monetary policy instruments to attain such objectives as high growth rates, price stability and full employment;
- cohesion of constituent parts and redistribution of income, requiring policies that aim to ensure the cohesion of the constituent parts: in this way different social and regional groups will get a fair share in the benefits of integration should the market mechanisms fail to achieve an equitable outcome;
- external identity: at each stage of integration the union has to define itself *vis-à-vis* the Third World; its external relations range from commercial policies in a customs union up to defence in a full union.

If the first two policies are essential to gather the full benefit of integration, the third is indispensable to gaining the necessary political support from all participants in an integration scheme and the fourth to establish an international identity.

In each of the four chapters in this Part, theoretical[10] and policy[11] elements will be mixed with the results of empirical economic research.

Part V contains an *evaluation* of the results presented in Parts II to IV, together with a short presentation of the *prospects for the future development* of the European integration process.

Specification of the readership

The book addresses primarily two groups of readers. First it addresses *students* – in particular students who are following courses on European integration. In this book they will find a general introduction to the dynamics of economic integration, covering in a systematic and coherent way the areas that are most relevant, ranging from agriculture to trade, monetary matters and cohesion. However, experience has shown that the book is useful also for two more categories of students. The first of these is students of economics specialising in specific fields, such as industrial economics, international economic relations, and monetary and financial economics, who are all increasingly confronted by the European dimension of their specialisation. In this book they will find a general framework for the study of their own special area. The second category is students of business, who will find in this book much information about the changing regulatory environment of the firm, and about the response of companies to these changes.

Second, this book is written *for all those professionally interested in the economic aspects of European integration* in the widest sense, including the increasing number of people who in their professional activities are faced with questions as to the organisation and functioning of the European economy (researchers, consultants, journalists). To these professionals can be added all those who are interested in the lessons that can be drawn from the European experience for the set-up and development of regional integration frameworks in other parts of the world (Mercosur etc).[12]

The material of the book has been organised and presented to allow both groups of readers to fruitfully study individual subjects without having to go through the complete text. To facilitate deeper and more complete study starting from this text, ample references to more specific literature are given. To facilitate the access to the material presented, the book has been written in such a way that only a basic knowledge of economics is needed; the use of mathematics has been reduced to a minimum. Only basic knowledge of linear equations and their graphical representation and the essentials of regression analysis is required to understand the whole text.

Constant update

A difficulty encountered in writing about the EU is that the text needs continuous adjustment and updating. Indeed in the past the EU policy environment and the response of firms and individuals have shown a remarkable dynamism. In the past decades some really dramatic changes have occurred. One is the upheaval in Central and Eastern Europe leading to the integration of the German Democratic Republic into the Federal Republic of Germany and to the transition towards a market economy of the Central and Eastern European countries. Another is the realisation of an economic and monetary union. In the near future new, although probably less dramatic, changes are likely to occur. This fourth revised edition comes, therefore, only a few years after the publication of the third edition.

The present edition differs[13] from the previous one in that it:

- covers new developments in terms of the deepening of the EU for many policy fields, in particular the Economic and Monetary Union;
- addresses the issue of widening – that is, the association of the Central and Eastern European countries;
- integrates better theoretical elements with empirical data and policy; this has led to the deletion of two chapters, elements of which are now integrated in several other chapters;[14]
- improves the treatment of the essential feature of the book by concentrating Chapter 2 on issues related to the dynamics of the integration process;
- follows more strictly the same framework in all chapters of a similar kind in order to facilitate the comparison between different segments of the economy and between different policies;
- adds to the understanding of modern services by adding sections on Internet related services and on telecommunications;
- updates with figures for recent years the series of data that highlight the long-term trends and indicates the structural factors in the integration process;
- integrates the results of new theoretical and empirical work and gives ample references to the latest literature on the various subjects.[15]

Summary and conclusions

- Economic integration is the gradual elimination of economic frontiers between partner countries. It is a dynamic process in which the economies of partner states become more and more interwoven.
- The main objectives of economic integration are of an economic nature: for example, higher growth, hence more prosperity. Other objectives are of a political nature: for example, the reduction of the chance of armed conflicts among partners.

Notes

1   The expression 'economic integration' has become so current, that it gives the impression of a fundamental notion with a long historical background. Actually the term, or rather, its negative counterpart, 'economic disintegration', was used for the first time in 1930. In a positive sense the term does not occur until after the Second World War (Herbst, 1986).

2   Empirical support for this statement is given, for example, by Polacheck (1980) who (using data for 30 countries in the 1958–67 period) showed that doubling the trade between two countries leads to a 20 per cent decline in the frequency of hostilities. Hirsch (1981) suggests that countries feel obliged to adopt a peaceful attitude when a 'balance of prosperity' is created instead of a balance of deterrence. Moreover other authors such as Buzan (1984) stress the importance of a liberal type of economic integration for peace (or international security). As a consequence the use of armed forces to improve welfare diminishes (Rosecrance, 1984). On the other hand, security (for example, NATO) stimulates economic integration (for example, EU, OECD).

3   The first objective has been central to all stages of the deepening and widening of European integration. The second objective has notably played a role in the early days of the setting up of the ECSC and the EEC. The third has played a major role in the second round of extension of the EU with three Mediterranean countries. The third and fourth will play important roles in the next round of extension with Central and Eastern European countries.

4   The accent in this book is on economics in the narrow sense of the word. Students of business will, however, find it very useful too, as the book depicts, on the one hand, the changing environment of corporations due to the integration process and, on the other hand, the reactions of firms to this new environment (notably in Chapters 9–13).

5   Note that the statistics up to the year 1990 do not cover the regions that joined as a result of the reunification of Germany. Note also that figures are given in euros for the whole period; the values of other currencies and the predecessors of the euro (such as the ECU) have all been recalculated to form a comparable statistical base.

6   Since the entry into force of the Treaty of Amsterdam one distinguishes in legal terms the European Union from the European Community (see consolidated treaties). When referring to either one in legal terms we will indicate EU plus the article number for the part on the European Union and EC plus the article number for the article of the treaty dealing with the European Community.

7   The breakdown into sectors is based, on the one hand, on the famous Clark

(1957)/Chenery (1960)/Kuznets (1966) triad and, on the other hand, on the differences in EU policy regime. This leads to a division into five main sectors: agriculture, manufacturing, energy, services and transport.

8   As combinations of policies – for instance, trade and structural policies (Klein, 1985) – are often made for specific sectors, for such sectors different sets of objectives and combinations of instruments areas can be observed. This may lead to a situation in which some sectors are exposed to external and internal competition without receiving subsidies (allocation) or transfers (redistribution), while other sectors are sheltered from external and internal competition by generous subsidies, with considerable redistributive effects.

9   The distinction between allocational efficiency, macro-economic stability, redistributive equity and external identity, so neat in theory, is often blurred in practice in the process of political bargaining. Indeed, instruments devised to serve policies in one area are often adapted under political pressure to serve other purposes as well. A good example is allocational efficiency. The instrument of guaranteed prices, introduced to make agricultural markets function properly (see Chapter 9), can easily be used also for redistribution purposes. Another example is the use of the instruments for the regulation of financial markets to control credit in the framework of stabilisation policies. A final example is state aids for the restructuring of industries that in practice may become an instrument for permanent subsidisation of certain sectors, in order to enhance their competitiveness on external markets. Indeed, original objectives are often lost sight of as policies, including common policies, develop.

10   Questions such as: how can the integrating European market economy best be regulated, and what type of economic order and policy set-up will lead to the best outcome in terms of growth of production and welfare?

11   Questions such as: what is the policy regime that the EU has developed to deal efficiently with the problems of an integrating economic area and how should these be evaluated in economic terms?

12   The question as to which lessons can be drawn from the EU experience for other regional integration schemes is dealt with in a very accessible way by Winters (1997).

13   Contacts with colleagues and experience in teaching brought up the question whether the set-up of the book was still well adapted to students' (and other users') needs. A questionnaire was sent out to a number of teachers who use the book for their courses in the EU, in the CEEC and in Third World countries. Analysis of the results showed that the responses converged on many points. They have determined the changes described hereafter.

14   The integration of the member countries of the European Union has advanced very far over the past decades. Even the integration of the countries of Central and Eastern Europe into the European economy has already gone through the initial stages and covers aspects of the highest stages of integration (such as preparation for EMU). This means that the detailed analysis of the theoretical basis of the initial stages given in the previous editions is no longer needed. So, in the process of rearranging the treatment of the theory of the customs union over the chapters in Part II, quite a few elements from the previous editions have been deleted.

15   Some 150 references have been added to the 700-odd references that substantiated the contents of the previous edition.

2 Dynamics of the Integration Process

Introduction

For a proper understanding of the details of the process of economic integration as described in the subsequent chapters, it is essential to know a few fundamental elements about the dynamics of the integration process.

To start we will make a basic distinction between the integration of markets and of policy. The former relates to the taking away of barriers to movement of products and production factors between member states, the latter to the setting up of common policies for the Union. The integration of markets (products and production factors) and the integration of different areas of economic policy follow, in practice, a sequence of forms. We will describe these stages of integration in some detail, specifying markets and policies on one hand and objectives and instruments on the other hand.

The rest of this chapter will be devoted to the dynamics of the integration process. We will describe the essentials of the different approaches[1] that try to respond to the questions of why and how further integration develops. We make a distinction here between deepening and widening. We define deepening as the involvement of Union institutions in an increased number of policy matters. Next we go into widening, which we define as the geographical enlargement of the Union – in other words, the increase in its membership. A short summary will complete this chapter.

Two dimensions: markets and policies

Market integration

Free movement of goods and services is the basic element of economic integration. The reasons for starting with market integration are of both an economic and a political nature. Institutional economics also plays a part.

The *economic logic* is based on the clear economic advantages that can be obtained from the integration of markets. Indeed, the free exchange of goods promises a positive effect on the prosperity of all concerned. It permits consumers to choose the cheapest good, generally widens the choice, and creates the conditions for further gain through economies of scale and so on. Free movement of production factors permits optimum allocation of labour and capital. Sometimes certain production factors are missing from a place where otherwise production would be most economical. To overcome this problem, entrepreneurs are apt to shift their capital from places of low return to those, which are more promising. The same is true of labour: employees will migrate to regions where their labour is more needed and therefore better rewarded. A second argument is that an enlarged market of production factors favours new production possibilities which in turn permit new, more modern or more efficient uses of production factors (new forms of credit, new occupations and so on).

Political logic suggests following the same sequence. The reasons for politicians to start integration with goods markets are that:

- a lasting coalition between sectors demanding protection, and sectors and consumers demanding cheap imports is hard to accomplish;
- substitute instruments (such as industrial policy, non-tariff barriers and administrative procedures) can be used to intervene in the economic process;
- vital political issues like growth policy and income redistribution are guaranteed to remain within national jurisdiction.

From a political logic perspective the integration of labour markets seems also to be an obvious choice in periods of a general shortage of labour (for instance the EU in the 1960s – see Chapter 7). A tangle of national regulations on wages, social security and so on leaves politicians sufficient opportunities for practical intervention at the national level for them to accept general principles about free movement at the European level. With capital market integration the issue of direct investments seems straightforward; many politicians may hope to attract new foreign investment in that way. For other capital movements the willingness to integrate is less obvious because integration may lessen the effectiveness of critical macro-economic instruments.

Institutional economics provide a third reason to start with market integration. Market integration can proceed without much demand on institutions and policy making. The taking away of barriers can in general be easily and clearly defined, and once laid down in treaties is binding on governments, companies and private persons. There is little need for a permanent decision-making machinery. The respecting of these measures is a matter of law; any firm, person or institution may appeal to the courts if infringements damage his interest.

Policy integration

In an economy which leaves production and distribution entirely to the market, the elimination of obstacles to the movement of goods and production factors among countries would suffice to achieve full economic integration. This is not the case in modern economies which are almost invariably of the mixed type, with the government frequently intervening in the economy. In all European countries there is substantial government intervention in economic life. This is based on the role of the state in enhancing economic welfare by correcting imperfections of markets and in realising a number of political objectives (such as an equitable income distribution). The reasons for continuing economic integration with policy integration are also of an economic and a political nature.

The *economic arguments* are based on the welfare increasing effects of integrated policy making. This comes about in the following way. The objectives and forms of regulations diverge among countries owing to differences in preferences (traditions, institutions and so on). As a result of the considerable international interwovenness, the policy of one country has effects in another. If objectives of two governments are inconsistent, the policy of one country will frustrate that of the other. Policy integration may bring economic benefits as it leads to the recovery of effectiveness in policy making. It will also take away the extra cost of compliance for companies that operate internationally under a multitude of different national regulations. Therefore, as the economic integration progresses, strong impulses are given towards the integration of various segments of the national regulatory systems.

Political arguments tend to determine the speed and direction of policy integration for various reasons. First, policy integration is often based on vaguely defined obligations requiring public institutions to take action. Such obligations leave ample room for interpretation as to scope and timing. They may, moreover, be reversed if the policy environment changes. Second, the polity and the bureaucracy of the member states are the more unwilling to give up their intervention power the more such elements as employment or budgetary policies (referring to expenditure on schools and subsidies, as well as revenues from taxes) are involved. Thus the conditions for the setting up of common policies in fields like social protection or monetary stability will not readily be met – let alone the conditions for the integration of policies that touch the very heart of a nation's sovereignty, like defence.

Institutional economics is a third factor influencing the dynamics of policy integration. The aim of policy integration is the creation of a common policy framework that creates equal conditions for the functioning of the integrated parts of the economy. Common policies require common institutions. These need to be stronger, the larger the competences of the Union and the higher the complications of the various packages of common policies.

Stages[2]

Markets

Goods and services   Progression may be summarised as follows:

- Free-trade area (FTA). All trade impediments such as import duties and quantitative restrictions are abolished among partners. Internal goods traffic is then free, but each country can apply its own customs tariff with respect to third countries. To avoid trade deflection (goods entering the FTA through the country with the lowest external tariff) internationally traded goods must be accompanied by so-called 'certificates of origin', indicating in which country the good has been manufactured. This enables customs officers at frontiers between member countries with different outer tariffs to determine whether duties or levies are still due (on goods originating from a third country) or whether the merchandise originates from another member state and can therefore be imported duty-free.
- Incomplete customs union (ICU). As in the free-trade area, obstacles to the free traffic of goods among partner countries are removed. Moreover one common external tariff is agreed upon, which does away with the certificates of origin at internal borders. Once a good has been admitted anywhere in the customs union, it may circulate freely. However, with respect to some categories of goods and services, barriers continue to exist.
- Customs union (CU). All obstacles to internal free movement are abolished without exception as to category of product or type of barrier. A common external tariff is implemented.

Production factors   Two stages may be identified:

- Incomplete common market (ICM). Its first building-block is an (incomplete) customs union. Moreover there is internal free movement of significant segments of labour and capital. Various options as to the relation with third countries may be chosen: different national regulations (comparable to the FTA) or a common regulation (comparable to the CU). Combinations of common policies (for instance, for labour) and national policies (for example for capital) *vis-à-vis* third countries are possible.

- Common market (CM). This consists of (1) an internal market: that is, fully free internal movement of products (goods and services) and of production factors (labour and capital); and (2) common external regulation for both products and production factors (so this definition encompasses a CU).

Policy

Economic   There are three forms of integration of economic policy:

- Economic union (EU) implies not only a common market but also a high degree of coordination or even unification of the most important areas of economic policy; as a minimum these comprise those that are associated with the CM, such as market regulation, competition and industrial structure; next come those that are related to the MU, such as macro-economic and monetary policies; and finally there are those that refer to the more social aspects, like redistribution policies and social and environmental policies. Towards third countries common policies are pursued on trade, production factors, economic sectors, monetary stability and so on.
- Monetary union (MU). The currencies of the member states are linked through irrevocably fixed exchange rates and are fully convertible, or one common currency circulates in all member states. Capital movements within the union are free. One may also distinguish a form of incomplete monetary union, whereby the exchange rates of the currencies of the member countries are pegged to a reference currency. So the exchange rates are fixed but can be adapted if needed. These forms are potentially unstable because doubts may arise as to the credibility of the arrangement in times of crisis.
- Economic and monetary union (EMU) combines the characteristics of the economic and the monetary union. The latter implies quite a high degree of coordination of macro-economic and budget policies. In view of the close interweaving of monetary and macro policies, integration evolves mostly simultaneously for both policy fields.

Other   Two further aspects of integration policy should be considered:

- Political union (PU). Integration is extended beyond the realm of economics to encompass such fields as anti-crime policy (police) and foreign policy, eventually including security policy.
- Full union (FU). This implies the complete unification of the economies involved, and a common policy on many important matters. For example, social security and income tax are likely to come within the competence of the union. The same holds true for macro-economic and stabilisation policy; this implies a budget of sufficient size to be effective as an instrument of these policies. The situation is then virtually the same as that within one country. Hence some form of a confederation or federation will then be chosen.

Forms

Instruments

All forms of policy integration require permanent agreements among participating states with respect to procedures to arrive at resolutions and to the implementation of rules. In other words, they call for partners to agree on the rules of the game. For an efficient policy integration, common institutions (international organisations) are created. All forms of integration diminish the freedom of action of the member states' policy makers. The higher the form of integration, the greater the restrictions on and loss of national competences and the more power will be transferred from national to Union institutions.

The following *hierarchy of policy cooperation* is usually adopted:

- *Information*: partners agree to inform one another about the aims and instruments of the policies they (intend to) pursue. This often induces partners to change their own policies in order to achieve a more coherent set of policies for the group. However, partners reserve full freedom to act as they think fit, and the national competence is virtually unaltered.
- *Consultation*: partners agree that they are obliged not only to inform but also to seek the opinion and advice of others about the policies they intend to execute. In mutual analysis and discussion of proposals the coherence is actively promoted. Moreover they learn from each others' experiences (best practices) and can exert some peer pressure in case of undesirable

developments. Although formally the sovereignty of national governments remains intact, in practice their competences are affected.

- *Coordination* goes beyond this, because it commits partners to agreement on the (sets of) actions needed to accomplish a coherent policy for the group. If common goals are fixed, some authors prefer the term 'cooperation'. Coordination often means the adaptation of regulations to make sure that they are consistent internationally (for example, the social security rights of migrant labour). It may involve the harmonisation (that is, the limitation of the diversity) of national laws and administrative rules. It may lead to convergence of the target variables of policy, such as the reduction of the differences in national inflation rates). Although agreements reached by coordination may not always be enforceable (no sanctions), they nevertheless limit the scope and type of policy actions nations may undertake, and hence imply limitation of national competences.
- *Unification*: either the abolition of national instruments (and their replacement with union instruments for the whole area) or the adoption of identical instruments for all partners. Here the national competence to choose instruments is abolished.

Relation between stages and instruments

There is a certain relation between the stages of integration and the instruments of policy integration mentioned above, in the sense that, in the early stages, the less binding instruments of integration will be applied. On the way to a common allocation policy, member states may begin by consulting one another with respect to certain elements (systems of value-added tax, the structure of tariffs, for example), to end up with the full unification of value-added tax rates and so on. Between the two stages, harmonisation may be practised. Parallels can be found in external policy. A free-trade area may start with consultations on the level of the external tariff, may next review the advantages of harmonisation of the structure of tariffs and may end up with unification by the adoption of a common external tariff (which turns the free-trade area into a customs union).

Another option is the distinction within one policy area between cases calling for integration and others for which partner-state competencies are maintained. Examples are the fixing of a common external tariff while maintaining partner competence with respect to quotas *vis-à-vis* third countries. So long as the balance between gains and losses of a particular transfer of competence remains doubtful, the lower degrees of integration, like consultation, are likely to be preferred, in line with the principle of subsidiarity (see the following section). As soon as the benefits of further integration outweigh cost, the next higher degree of integration will be tried out.

Each step towards further integration depends on a complicated evaluation of advantages and disadvantages by a set of actors under specific institutional circumstances. Therefore policy integration will vary in extent, nature and combination of elements of allocation, stabilisation, redistribution and external policies according to the prevailing practical political circumstances; *there is no theoretical optimum blueprint for the intermediate states between the FTA and the FU.* As a consequence the transitions between stages are fluent and cannot always be clearly defined. The first stages, FTA, CU and CM, seem to refer to market integration in a classical *laissez-faire* setting, the higher stages (EU, MU, FU) to policy integration. In practice, however, the former three stages are unlikely to stabilise without some form of policy integration as well (for instance, safety regulations for a FTA, commercial policy for a CU, or social and monetary policies for a CM).

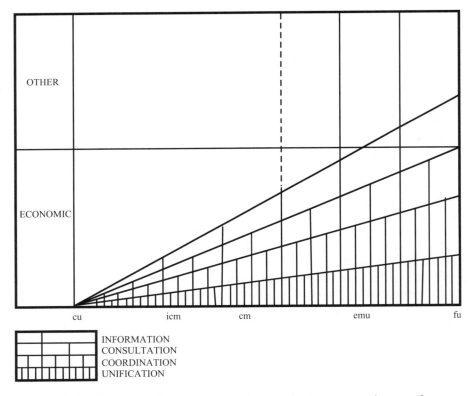

Figure 2.1   Distribution of competences between nation and union in several stages of integration

As one moves through the various stages of integration, more and more competences of the member states will be handed over to the union (implying a loss of national autonomy). We can schematise the dynamics of integration as follows (see Figure 2.1). First this applies only to economic areas, next also to non-economic ones (like culture, social areas, defence). Moreover the intensity with which the union is involved will increase (from consultation to unification).

Dynamics of deepening

Cost-benefit approaches

Progress towards further integration depends on the proof that the gains from each individual step towards integration will outweigh the cost. The basic notion of the approach of the cost-benefit analysis is that major decisions are based on the well-understood interest of the parties involved. In this view decisions to integrate the economies of member states are based on the net advantages that the members of the group can draw from this integration. So the potential members of an integration area all make their calculations and, on the basis of the outcome, make a 'rational' choice.

Over the years, economists have developed a toolbox to identify first and to quantify next the cost and benefits of each step of integration. They have combined insights from welfare economics and trade theory and later welfare economics and aspects of monetary theory. The types of cost and benefit change as one moves to higher stages.

Gains will come, in the first instance, from better allocation of resources (market integration). They come, in the second instance, from enhanced competition and innovation that stimulates economic growth. In other words, firms can operate in a larger market and under more favourable conditions, permitting them to produce at lower cost and obtain better starting positions to compete on global markets. The basis for a systematic analysis of this phenomenon has been laid by customs union theory (notably Viner, 1950), that tries to determine the welfare implications of the merging of markets (see Chapter 5).

Costs of integration will come first from the adaptation to new circumstances (short-term) – for instance, from the reinsertion of the labour made redundant by international competition. In the higher stages of integration gains come from the increased effectiveness of common allocation, stabilisation and redistribution policies (see Chapters 14–17). This positive effect of policy integration stems from the decrease in the cost of policy delivery (economies of scale), the increase in its effects (credibility) and, finally, in the decrease in the

Box 2.1   Reasons for centralisation

Competencies should be handed over to the next higher level of government (for example, from a nation to the union) for five main reasons:

- Transaction costs. The diversity of rules in a decentralised system may make it costly for private actors such as firms and owners of production factors to know what the best options are. Assigning this competence to a higher level of government may bring more uniformity, hence more transparency and lower cost.
- Economies of scale. For the production of public goods and policies there exists an optimal scale much in the same way as for private goods and services. Policy competencies should be given to the layer that can provide the lowest cost, given the level of output. An example is monetary policy, which is better organised by a union central bank than by a loosely coordinated group of independently operating local central banks.
- Spill-overs. There are cases where outsiders – that is, non-residents – may benefit from, or have to bear the cost of, actions of the insiders of a specific jurisdiction. For example, if the pollution of a firm in country A is carried by the wind to country B, country B incurs a high environmental cost, while country A has the economic benefits. In such cases the matter needs to be dealt with by a higher authority. If not, the spill-over of important cost or benefit elements to other areas will lead to inefficiencies – that is, to, respectively, an over- or undersupply of public goods (such as clean air). As integration advances, spill-over effects are likely to increase in importance, and hence more competencies need to be transferred to the union level.
- Credibility. In many cases countries have a stimulus to enter into cooperative solutions for common policies (common advantage) but may also have a stimulus to break them (free-rider). Although the choice of the latter is diminished by the fear of retaliation, many may be seduced into selecting this option for short-term policy reasons. The market will put little faith in the effectiveness of cooperative policies. So the better solution in these cases is to hand over the competence to the union level.
- Insurance. If parts of an integrated area are subject to macroeconomic shocks that have a particularly high impact in one or a few of them, there is scope for the pooling of risks. Transfers within a centralised system may be most efficient, as there is no market for macro-economic insurance.

transaction cost for business (see also Box 2.1). Costs come from the impossibility of meeting national preferences owing to a loss of autonomy, in terms of taxes, consumer protection, health and other matters (long-term).[3] Moreover centralised solutions to policy problems bring a reduction in the variety of solutions and hence imply increased costs in terms of loss of innovation and experimentation.

An overview of the gains and costs of common allocation policies is given in the study into the effects of the completion of the internal market (Emerson *et al.*, 1988, CEC, 1996a). An example of the cost and benefit effects of common monetary and stabilisation policies is given in the study into the effects of the Economic and Monetary Union (CEC, 1990b). An alternative set-up is to measure the growth effects of integration (for instance, Henrekson *et al.*, 1997).

Optimal decision making

Progressive integration implies the gradual transfer of policy competencies from national to Union institutions. Hence the explanation of progress lies in the reasons why a matter could better be entrusted to the Union instead of to the national state (see Box 2.1). These reasons are not specific to integration schemes; any state, be it unitary or federal, has to decide on the best way to distribute competencies over the various layers of government. The economic theories of optimal distribution of powers over different layers of government take efficiency as the main criterion.[4] The starting-point is the observation of welfare economics that a policy executed at the lowest level of government is thought most efficient because:

- differences in needs, and in preferences and so on, will be better taken into account, participation will be higher, implementation costs will be lower and the accountability of the institutions for their actions will be higher; and
- innovation and experiment will be given more latitude. Competition between jurisdictions will then sort out the best combinations of providing public goods and imposing taxes.

This economic rationale for choosing the lowest form of integration needed to achieve the goals set has its complement in philosophy and political science. In EU practice this is now generally referred to as the principle of subsidiarity[5] – the term which we use henceforth. The assignment of functions to the EU is justified if the matter passes the subsidiarity test (see Box 2.2). The growth of integration – that is, the increase over time of the number of matters that are assigned to EU level – is then determined by a bigger weight of the set of factors that determine centralisation. One such factor is market integration that engenders the need for policy integration for the same geo-graphical area (for instance, competition policy). Another factor is technical progress that increases the areas where economies of scale in government prevail and externalities occur (for instance, the envi-ronment). A final factor is the shift in societal preferences towards equity issues and hence centralised redistribution policies.

Box 2.2   The subsidiarity test

Assignment to EU level is restricted to matters that pass the subsidiarity test. This test uses two criteria:

1   Is there a need to act or can the matter be left to markets or to other bodies? A positive answer to this question can be given if public intervention at EU level corrects market fail-ures, compensates for externalities across intra-EU borders or creates economies of scale.
2   Is the least costly form of regulation chosen? The use of EU regulatory instruments of the more constraining type (har-monisation, unification) should have clear net advantages over the use of the less constraining instruments (such as information, coordination). So, before assigning tasks to the Union one should verify whether a credible cooperation of national governments is feasible and effective in reaching the goals.

In practice the application of the notions of 'optimal level of decision making' will not always come to clear-cut conclusions. It may then lead to a situation whereby the Union is responsible for certain mat-ters and the member states for other matters but a very large number of policy matters for which they have to come together to exercise authority jointly. One might call this 'cooperative federalism' (Casella and Frey, 1992). An example of a policy measure that brings eco-nomic advantages of integration, but jeopardises certain national social objectives may illustrate this. The harmonisation of taxes is considered necessary to the undisturbed movement of capital in the integration area. However, that may bring about a shift from direct to indirect taxes in some countries, so that the tax system can no longer be used to reduce income inequality. Whether the positive effects outweigh the drawbacks is uncertain. As a result, the Union and the member states may come to the essentially political decision not to centralise fully the competence in matters of taxes, but to share the responsibility, limiting integration to the coordination of those aspects of the tax system that impinge most on allocational efficiency. Similar political trade-offs, but with different outcomes in terms of integration, exist over a wide range of matters of public concern, leading to a large variety of practical solutions to integration problems.[6]

Institutional economics

Integration starts with private commercial transactions, governed by local or national rules. International transactions take place after having reached an agreement among traders on the basic rules that will govern these transactions. A more efficient solution is reached where the respective governments agree on these rules and on the way to enforce them (for example, mutual recognition of property law and rules for the applicable legal system). Governments incur costs in solving problems they have in common with others and in implementing collective action to arrive at common goals. These costs can be reduced by creating international institutions that permit concluding stable contracts between partners.

Institutional economics has two objectives. The first is to explain why international institutions are created; the central argument has been borrowed from transaction cost economics and says that dealings among governments and collective actions by governments are more efficient within the framework of an institution. The second objective is to explain why institutions, once created, develop as they do; in our case why integration proceeds and takes the form of the sequenced transfer of national competencies to the Union.[7]

The minimum requirement for a decision on joining an institution (framework for integration) to be taken is that the partners need to have a positive balance of cost and benefit. However, many more aspects enter into the decision process. This process can be modelled along the lines of *becoming members of a club* (Buchanan, 1965 and Olson, 1965). Clubs are voluntary agreements created to let the members (consumers) share in the benefits of an excludable public good. The application of the club goods idea to the EU is fraught with difficulties (see, for example, Streit and Voigt, 1997). However, under certain assumptions, one can see the provision of free access to the internal market as a club good of EU members. Another example is the EMU: the European Central Bank provides price stability for the members of the EMU only; non-EMU members and non-EU countries are excluded.

While founding a club (in our case, an integration scheme) the partners generally concentrate on one issue. In the case of the EU

making demands @ lowest level in order to achieve its goals.

that was internal free trade. In the course of the existence of a club it becomes apparent that the organisation can efficiently be used for other purposes as well (Casella, 1994). Consequently, many clubs diversify the club goods they deliver in the course of their existence. Compare, for example, the services delivered by automobile clubs: initially only information about roads and petrol stations, later all sorts of tourist information and, finally, financial services such as credit cards and insurance. In the case of the EU this has been done by using the EU framework for new subjects such as industrial policy, innovation policy and so on.

In the approaches described up until now, national states are neutral agents that make rational choices based on cost and benefit considerations in the common interest. Authors from the *public choice* school reject this hypothesis. They consider that the polity (politicians and bureaucrats) working in symbiosis with other actors (like special interest groups and voters) are not only able, but even inclined, to pursue personal goals which do not conform to the public interest. This suggests that European integration has gone beyond the level of centralisation that would have resulted from rational choices. The polity (national governments) has permitted (or even promoted) such 'excessive' transfer of regulatory powers from the nations to the EU (Vaubel, 1994).[8]

In the views just presented, the path taken by an integration scheme depends on two factors: first, given institutional conditions, on the specific constellation of political economy forces at any moment in time (Vaubel, 1986); and, second, on the types of game played by the different actors, which is dependent on the rules of the institution. Now as institutions are also the product of bargaining between actors with different interests, the constitutional economics school (Buchanan, 1987) examines the choice of constraints. Unfortunately, progress in explaining why institutions develop their rules as they do is, as yet, limited.[9]

Business economics

In using concepts from business economics countries can be regarded as producers, trying to create conditions for profitable operation in the medium and long term (continuity). The theoretical starting point is that firms, and in particular multinational firms, are a rational institutional solution to an economic problem (Coase, 1937/1988). The question is why a firm would produce certain intermediate products instead of buying them on the market. The answer is that the coordination costs within the firm are less than the transaction costs on the market (Williamson, 1985). In markets, where transaction costs are particularly high, integration of activities in one firm will be profitable. This business economics idea of introducing hierarchy within a multi-layer firm as opposed to contractual relations between independent firms is similar to the notion of institutional economics of the unification of regulation in an integration area as opposed to incidental negotiation between independent nations.

Box 2.3   Comparison of firm mergers and European integration

The *progress of integration* seen from a firm perspective is determined by the factors that determine success of cooperation and of mergers. The following factors identified for firms can be transposed to the integration of countries:

- External circumstances. The chances are better if the economies grow and can adapt easily to new circumstances: this was the case for the EU in the period up to 1973 and again in the period since 1985, when the single market initiative was stimulated by the economic recovery.
- Cultural differences and identity. The larger the differences, the larger the potential for conflicts, misunderstandings and so on. The cultural differences within the EU are very large. The success of the EU has been based on the fact that it has not gone immediately towards a full merger but to less stringent forms of integration. Indeed, the EU has integrated first the domains where cultural conflicts were likely to be small (the economic domain – in particular, manufacturing activities) leaving free the other domains where strong feelings existed about national preferences.
- Leadership. The clearer the direction of the new group, the more successful the integration. The importance of leadership in the creation and growth of the EU is often underestimated.[10] In the EU the success factor has been divided between three entities: the Commission for its independent role; the European Council for general orientation, and the Franco-German tandem.
- Organisation. A form of cooperation between firms, where partners remain in principle independent, sets high demands on the structure of organisation. The EU has been endowed with strong institutions even for limited forms of cooperation.

Extending the comparison, it could be said that the integration of countries in the EU is akin to a process of merging of firms into a larger, multinational and or multi-product group (Kool and Olie, 1997 based on Olie, 1996). The comparison between firms and states can be made for each stage of integration (see Box 2.3). The early stages of integration of countries can be compared to loose forms of cooperation among firms. The stage of the common market (in which only part of the sovereignty of countries is transferred) can be compared to a joint venture of firms, as the essential freedom to make independent strategic choices for the participants is not hampered. On the other end of the scale, a political union (federation) can be compared to a complete merger of firms.

Political economy (science)

Decisions on economic integration are not taken only on the basis of economic considerations, but are part of a much larger political process in which other considerations weigh very heavily too. Indeed, the final decision is taken by politicians on political grounds. Thus it is useful to look briefly at the contributions that political economy and political science have made to the explanation of the dynamics of integration. This is all the more relevant because a number of strands of thought in modern economics, discussed in the previous sections, have become close neighbours of political science.

The approach that has had the strongest resonance in academic and political circles is known as the *neo-functionalism theory* of integration (for example, Haas, 1958; Mitrany, 1966; also Keohane and Hoffmann, 1991) or neo-federal point of view (for example, Pinder, 1991). According to this theory the process of integration is driven by spill-overs from one policy area to another (see Box 2.4). The transfer of powers to the EU in the first field (for instance, goods markets) is based on the considerations of costs and benefits. Such integration generates adjustment needs in other fields that change the costs and benefits and leads to centralised solutions in that field too. This process is reinforced by such factors as:

- issue linkage and the need for package deals;
- the increased power of the EU institutions to influence public opinion as resources increase;
- shared understanding of the advantages of adopting certain common regimes; and
- causal connections between issues documented by expert committees (see, for example, Kahler, 1995).

Box 2.4   A functional view of the dynamics of European integration[11]

Customs union   Impulses to policy integration come from both the external and internal dimension of the free movement of products. Externally, the setting of a common external tariff and its regular adjustment to changed circumstances call for a common trade policy. Indeed, negotiations with third countries can be conducted to greater advantage by the customs union acting as an entity than by each member state on its own. Internally, the abolishing of many non-tariff barriers (NTBs) implies the harmonisation of many regulations in such widely divergent fields as taxation and safety. For the internal market to function properly, measures are also needed to prevent competition distortion. Hence the need for a common competition policy, with rules for private and public sectors.

Common market   The establishment of free movement of productive factors also gives strong impulses towards the coordination of policy. Free movement of workers requires in practice the mutual recognition of diplomas or certificates of professional proficiency and some harmonisation of measures of social security. Free movement of capital necessitates the elimination of some administrative obstacles, such as exchange control, and some harmonisation of fiscal rules to prevent capital flowing to states with a favourable tax regime. Finally the mobility of capital demands the adjustment of monetary policies (rates of exchange, interest and so on) to diminish economic disturbances caused by speculation. The creation of a common market may lead to concentrated investments in certain regions, and growing unemployment in others. Such situations call for measures of common social and regional policy. The proper functioning of the integrated market can be severely impeded by monetary disturbances. Moreover, countries with a stable currency will want to prevent countries with a depreciating currency from using their monetary policy as a means to enhance their international competitiveness. So the single market pushes towards monetary union.[12]

Economic and monetary union   The pursuit of the objectives of an EMU means that integration extends into a large number of different policy areas. A major policy is to foster favourable and stable conditions. As the free movement of goods and factors renders the economies of member states more mutually dependent, economic or fiscal measures taken by one member state become more likely to affect all others, perhaps conflicting with their policy. Because member states no longer have authority to counteract such disturbances by measures of trade or monetary policy, coordination of the macro-economic and other economic policies of member states becomes imperative.

Another line of thought that has received much attention recently is the so-called *liberal intergovernmentalism* (Moravcsick, 1993). It explains integration by the interest national governments have in handing matters over to a higher level authority in order to solve, in an efficient way, some of their domestic problems. In a sense this can be related to the views of the institutional economics school. In so far as progressive integration is felt to have gone beyond the level an economic cost-benefit analysis would predict, this can also be related to the insights of the public choice school.

Finally, we mention a third view, based on *multi-level governance.* Some explain progressive integration by the fact that, beyond a certain stage, national states are aware that they have lost so much power to the centre that they no longer have control over the integration process (Marks, 1993). Others (Chryssochoou, 1997) stress the interest of national governments confronted with high interdependency to create a 'confederal consociation' – in other words, a regime of power sharing that strikes a balance between the concurrent demands for territorial segmental autonomy and central Union authority. The fundamentals of these views are similar to those of constitutional economics; their operationalisation refers back to the arguments of the school of optimal decision making.

Widening

Cost benefit

The decision of any country to join an integration scheme is based to a large extent on the balance of the economic costs and benefits involved for that country. In the same way, the decision by the EU to adopt a new member should equally be based on an evaluation of the costs and benefits to the EU.[13]

The evaluation of costs and benefits suggests different sizes of the integration area at different stages of integration. To start with the Free Trade Area, international trade theory suggests that the best option for the integration of markets is the global one. And if this option is not feasible, customs union theory suggests the option of regional integration. Refinements of the original contributions to customs union theory and common market theory suggest that the net gains increase with the size of the union (Viner, 1950; Meade, 1955; Tinbergen, 1959; see also Chapters 6–10). However, policy integration theory comes to the opposite conclusion. The transaction cost between governments increase with the increase in the numbers of negotiators and the diversity of the paradigms in which they work. So the best option from an economic point of view is to start with a limited number of members and, once the required institutional effectiveness is secured, to enlarge the number of participants.

The costs and benefits are influenced in a number of ways of which we note two important ones:

- Geographical. The very fact that a number of countries agree to form an integration area changes the game for non-participants. The costs of staying out are different and so are the advantages of getting in (this point is elaborated in the section on institutional economics):
- Temporal. The pace at which the EU has been enlarged can be considered as very rapid, in the light of the historical experience of other integration areas. The causes of this high speed are, however, not well known (Tinbergen, 1991).

  The specification and quantification of the advantages and the disadvantages of integration can be set in a time scheme, showing for each of the (potential) participants in the scheme when each occurs. This approach to integration (Martin, 1996) allows the optimal sequencing of integration measures to be determined.

Optimal decision making

The basic idea of optimality has also been applied to the geographical aspect of integration schemes. The theoretical foundation of the *optimum integration area* approach was laid down quite some time ago. Rather astonishingly, this has not been done for the lower stages of integration (for example, free trade) but for one of the higher stages, *viz*. the monetary union. It has become known under the name of the Optimum Currency Area (OCA) approach (Mundell, 1961; for an extensive survey see Ishiyama, 1975).

In the approach one defines first the conditions necessary for the good functioning of the integration scheme. Next, one translates these in terms of criteria for membership. The approach has been applied to the EU by many authors (see Chapter 15), but the results were rather inconclusive. Recently, the approach has also been applied to the extension of the EU to include Central and Eastern European countries (De Grauwe and Aksov, 1999), giving indications about the countries that are likely to participate and those which still have a long way to go.

Applied to the case of the monetary union, OCA theory predicts that an EMU can the better be sustained: the lower the chances of asymmetric shocks to occur; the higher the flexibility of the system to adapt; and the higher the credibility of the institutions.

Generalising the concepts developed in the framework of OCA theory to all stages of integration one can speak of an optimum

Table 2.1 **Criteria for participation at different stages of integration**

Stage	Criteria
Free Trade Zone	High exchange of goods and services
	Equality of production structure
	Equality of economic order
Common Market	Equality on markets for labour and capital (prices and availability)
	Freedom of movement (migration and investment)
	Convergence of policy (e.g. taxes)
Economic Union	Effective coordination
	Comparability of institutions
	Transfer payments
Monetary Union	Stability of exchange rates
	Similarity of external shocks
	Product markets: a high degree of openness (trade) and of product differentiation
	Production factor markets: a high degree of capital and labour mobility
	Institutional development: a high degree of political integration

integration area (OIA) (see, for example, Tichy, 1992). On the basis of this idea we have identified the criteria for determining which countries would belong to such an OIA at each stage of economic integration (see Table 2.1).

The establishment of a currency union tends to push the number of members beyond the optimum size. As they admit more members, currency unions face a rising marginal cost curve, which cuts the marginal benefit curve from below. Costs and benefits will both be highest when joining with those partners that are the most suitable. Any additional partner will bring extra costs (coming from different industrial structures) but these may not be that high because the largest cost, coming from the loss of independence, has been accepted anyway. The additional partner may also bring proportional benefits. If members are myopic, the currency union may be enlarged beyond the point where the marginal cost and marginal benefit curve intersect for the group (Maloney and Macmillen, 1999).

The OIA approach, so neat in theory, is far from simple to put into practice. At all stages of integration one is confronted with two problems. The first concerns the lack of empirical foundation for a quantification of the criteria. Indeed, little basis exists to specify what the threshold level is for such criteria as a high degree of intra-union trade or of labour mobility. If one sets the threshold low, it will mean that many countries can participate. If one sets it high only a very limited number of countries can be accepted as members. The second problem stems from the parallel use of several criteria: it then depends on the weight one attaches to each of them what the end result will be.[14] Confronted with these problems, policy makers have adopted a simple solution – namely, to define rule-of-thumb criteria based on averages (see Chapter 15 for the EMU criteria).

To these criticisms of a practical nature one can add a more fundamental one – namely, the lack of empirical support when seen in the light of the dynamics of integration. Indeed, in the past, countries that did not fulfil the criteria for an OIA at the outset and were accepted as participants nevertheless proved to be able to come up to standards quickly under the influence of integration. Examples for the EU are the customs union in the 1960s, the EMS in the 1980s and the EMU in the late 1990s.

Institutional economics

Recently, a new perspective on the widening of institutions has been given. It takes its starting point in the *rationale for the formation and break-up of nations*. The central element in this line of thought is efficiency in the provision of public goods. Any model with economies of scale in the provision or financing of such goods will lead to a small number of big countries rather than to a single country because it is assumed that, beyond a certain point, decreasing returns and increasing coordination costs occur due to larger heterogeneity of the constituencies. The push towards larger countries is stronger the lower the degree of integration with third countries. The widening of an integration area can be explained by the reaping of the benefits of the larger area without being obliged to come to one state (see Alesina and Spolaore, 1997).

One of the first questions the potential members of a club needs to tackle is with whom they will form the club – in other words, how they define its optimum size and composition. The first suggestion comes, of course, from the advantages a group can have in integrating markets; the next derives from the advantages this group can draw from further integration (Casella, 1994). The optimal club size depends on the specific public good (Casella and Frey, 1992). Take the example of an Optimum Currency Area seen as a club. 'If money is viewed mainly as a means of transactions, then it is a fully non-rivalries collective good: more people using the same currency increase the benefits to the original users. In this case the optimal club size is as large as possible. However, if money is viewed as a sort of budget finance, or as a tool for stabilisation, then the optimal size of the monetary club is given by the requirement that preferences over the use of money be somewhat homogeneous within the club' (Casella and Frey, p. 644).

If the optimal club size depends on the specific public good, then all users should be divided into a complex system of overlapping clubs. Applied to integration this means that countries can join different functional integration areas. In this respect, one can see the notions of variable geometry, two-speed Europe and so on that often come up to account for flexibility in the integration process; that means that member governments choose whether or not to join certain elements of integration (Frey and Eichenberger, 1997). The higher functional jurisdictions have to compete for members and may overlap with other functional jurisdictions. The obvious advantage of this set-up is flexibility and adaptation to needs: the obvious disadvantage is high transaction costs for both private and public actors. As the rationale of institutions is to lower transaction costs this is not a minor objection. Sometimes functional clubs are merged to exploit economies of scale. In integration matters this would mean that only one organisation (for example, the EU) would exist; this would take care of the interests of its club members for a whole range of subjects, with members using, to different degrees, the various club goods offered (for example, EMU).

There are *political economy* forces at work that may accelerate the widening beyond the degree that would be indicated by mere costs and benefits to club members. This effect is based on the external impact of the creation of a club by changing the policy options of non-members. If the non-members are small with respect to the club, then setting up an alternative to the existing club may be very costly and risky (Baldwin, 1994, 1997). This will then unleash forces within the non-member country that push towards the joining of the club. For example, firms in non-member countries that are in a disadvantaged position with respect to EU firms will lobby for their country to become a member too. Their incentive to invest considerable sums of money in lobbying is the greater the more they have to deal with sunk cost. This phenomenon has led to the *domino theory* of integration: each time the weight of the core causes a non-member country to fall into the group, it increases the incentive for the remaining non-member to join. The EU has increasingly become the dominant power on the European subcontinent. In the process it has changed the relative attractiveness of the various options of the non-EU members. Both membership of alternative clubs and staying alone outside quickly became unattractive options to many non-members. In the past this has been the case for most EFTA countries (which have almost all switched from the EFTA to the EU club). At present the same is the case for CEFTA (Central European Free Trade Association). The EU club exerts such power that it is very difficult for the smaller countries of Central Europe to organise themselves into a club that can hope to provide the advantages of the EU (even without redistribution).

Business economics

The notion of firm merger applied to the widening issue also gives an interesting perspective. This may be seen as a parallel to the rationale for multinationalisation of firms by merger or acquisition (for example, Hymer, 1966; MacNamus, 1972; Dunning, 1979). From this extensive literature we have selected the view of *international restructuring* (Ruigrok and van Tulder, 1995; see also van Tulder and Ruigrok, 1997), as it relates, in an interesting way, international business to international political economy considerations (see the next section). The central element in their view is the industrial complex, defined as a bargaining configuration organised around a core firm in which the major actors are suppliers, workers, dealers, financiers and governments. Relations between the industries in the complex are characterised by their degree of dependency. The question as to which companies can create synergy by joining forces while keeping the problems of management under control is comparable to notions about the OIA and of effective club size.

At one end of the spectrum partners are independent and may decide to cooperate or compete; at the other end, the core firm has structural control over the dependent firm. National situations have given rise to five different concepts of control, each favouring a certain degree of dependency relation. At the low end of the spectrum we see the idea of flexible specialisation – independent firms working together in a network. At the high end we see Toyotism where the core firm controls its environment. Core firms with a relatively cohesive complex have generally invested heavily in well-functioning bargaining practices. Governments have favoured such more cohesive complexes, as they facilitate coherent trade, industrial and other policies on the national level. This has led to the development of specific national bargaining arenas.

Several factors have created a need for openness and have induced firms to go international. The nature of a firm's domestic bargaining area determines its internationalisation strategy. Firms that tend to favour control will opt for subsidiaries abroad that depend on coordination by international headquarters. On the other hand, firms that favour networks would do so internationally as well. Firms that go international penetrate countries that may have another regime (or bargaining arena), thereby triggering changes that may erode the cohesion of these arenas. The EU has tried to develop a new regime of its own in order to replace the weakened national arenas of its members.

Several of these notions have parallels to our problem of the widening of an integration scheme. We can develop these as follows:

- First, firms that internationalise by dependency can be compared to the enlargement of a union by the integration of a new member, whereas firms that opt for networks would be comparable to countries that develop their international relations.
- Second, firms that have grown strong by merging limit the strategic choices of their weakened competitors and force them into a dependency relation (possibly a take-over). This is a parallel to the domino theory. The more difficulties encountered by weak firms in competing, and the less their likelihood of creating a credible alternative option by teaming up with other weak partners, the more these firms will be inclined to accept a take-over bid by a larger competitor or be forced to accept any other relation of dependency.
- Third, the creation of a dependency relation between firms will entail the harmonisation of the rules for the management of the new company. This is not easy in the medium stages. It can be likened to the situation of the EU in its efforts to define a new regime starting from a number of rival national regimes, which has resulted, over the decades, in the development of its own elaborate regime, thereby altering the game for new entrants. Much in the same way as a large firm which is taking over a small one (or a series of small ones) will impose its existing organisation on the new subsidiaries, the EU imposes the obligation to adopt the 'acquis communautaire' on all its new members.

The new economy tends to bring to the mergers process a dimension that can be compared to the accelerator of other approaches. Indeed, these activities are often characterised by network economics. The quicker one can attain the status of the provider of the dominant technology for a set of activities the better are the chances of reaching a position of almost complete dominance of that sector. This means that firms do have a much increased incentive to merge, and this is enhanced by the so-called positive feedback that stems from the fact that the product becomes more interesting the more people are using it (see Shapiro and Varian, 1999).

Political economy (science)

The neo-functionalist view (that is, spill-overs from one integrated policy area lead to the integration of another policy area) can also be set up for widening. Both the potential member and the union have interest in joining. The potential member's interest is to regain credibility, as their national capacity of dealing with a number of issues is no longer sufficient to provide a good answer to the problems (see also the discussion on the domino theory). The interest of the union to respond to the application of the potential member by integrating the fringe is more of a political than an economic nature. We need but refer to the decision on the integration of East Germany into the Federal Republic. History shows that great powers have extended their influence over neighbouring areas first and integrated them next because of the need to deal with insecurity at borders (Kennedy, 1988). Similar factors play a role in the EU: the first enlargement was blocked by France in the 1960s on essentially political considerations. Security issues are currently prominent in the motivations of many EU member countries to stimulate the Eastern enlargement of the EU.

The multi-level governance view can also be extended to cope with the widening issue. Indeed, in a number of cases, incidental decisions by individual members on enlargement with another specific potential member based on political considerations are replaced by explicit rules to which all present members adhere and that are communicated to new members. Sometimes such rules are even put into the form of constitutional requirements. In practice this means that the potential member knows the criteria that must be met in order to join the club. Should it not yet meet them all, a catch-up programme can be put in place in time.[15]

Overview of the various theoretical economic approaches

Essential features

The approaches that have been discussed in the previous sections draw, from different sources, elements that can be helpful in understanding the dynamics of integration. In order to facilitate the *construction of a complete picture* we have regrouped in Table 2.2 the basic elements organised by the dimensions: theoretical foundation; deepening; widening; and accelerator.

Table 2.2 Key features of the various theoretical economic approaches distinguished

Approach/ Aspect	Cost-benefit	Optimal decision making	Institutional economics	Business Economics
Theoretical foundations	Welfare economics; Cost-benefit analysis	Optimal regime; Fiscal federalism; Theory of regulation	Institutional economics; Constitutional economics	Theory of the firm; Transaction cost theory
Deepening	Customs union theory (based on trade theory); Common market theory	Optimal level of regulation (subsidiarity)	Clubs; Public choice	Merger; Theory of multi-nationalisation
Widening	Trade (from second-best to first-best solution)	Optimum Currency Area	Optimal club size	
Accelerator	Small extra cost coupled with proportional benefits		Existing institution used for additional purpose; Domino effects; Specific interest group (polity)	Dependency on hegemon; Network economics

Complementarity and similarity of approaches

The analysis of the economic approaches to the dynamics of integration has shown that the various 'schools' do not give rival explanations. On the contrary they are rather *complementary* and there are many *similarities* between them. However, they do not yet form a consistent well-structured grand design.[16]

We can detail this remark as follows:

- Complementarity. The approach of optimal decision making makes use of the notions of the cost-benefit approach. Together they do not give the whole picture; institutional economics shows how decisions are influenced by the interests of the actors involved (public choice) and by institutional design.
- Similarity. Concepts and arguments used by the business economics approach reveal a high degree of similarity with those used in institutional economics. Yet there is a very limited degree of cross-referencing between authors of the approaches reviewed.

Major causes of the progress of integration

The review leads to a number of *conclusions* as far as the *causes of the progress* in integration are concerned.

First, the progress in terms of deepening (extension of scope) is determined in all stages by the economic advantage that can be derived from integration. For instance, integration of markets permits the reaping of economies of scale. To facilitate integration, union institutions are created because they are more effective and more efficient than national ones (lower transaction costs and cheaper delivery of public goods). Integration is further enhanced by the complex interplay of economic and political actors – trying to secure as large a share as possible of the advantages of integration and avoiding the problematic aspects of national decision making.

Second, the progress in terms of widening (extension of the geographical area) is determined to a large extent by the net advantages cited under deepening. However, here the very dynamics of the union deteriorates the relative position of the non-members. This increases their incentive to join.

Finally, there is as yet *no coherent framework to explain the development of integration systems* in general (cf. also Bhagwati and Panagariya, 1996), nor to explain the path European integration has taken in particular. For answers to the latter type of question one has to look beyond the economic approaches reviewed here. Political economy and political science will then help out (see for the political economy line of thought, for instance, in Scharpf, 1999; Marks *et al.*, 1996; Majone, 1996).

Summary and conclusions

- Market integration is needed because it improves efficiency and hence welfare. Policy integration is needed because the intervention of national governments in modern mixed open economies has lost its effectiveness.
- The main stages in the process of economic integration are the customs union, the common market and the economic and monetary union, representing the integration of, progressively, the markets of goods and services, of production factors and, finally, of economic and other policies.
- The main instruments for policy integration are consultation and the coordination (harmonisation) or unification of government regulations; the higher forms of integration require more binding instruments.
- The dynamics of integration are determined by a complex interplay of forces. Progress is dependent on the net advantages that market and policy integration produce. It is enhanced by efficient institutions. Economic factors are only one set among others. In the last instance major decisions on further integration are taken on political considerations.

Notes

1   The different approaches are to some extent complementary but tend to overlap. On the other hand there is much similarity. Indeed, the various strands of thought seem to have much more in common than they are aware of, at least if we take the limited number of cross-referencing between authors as indicative for the low degree of interconnection.
2   Many authors have used different definitions (for example, Tinbergen, 1954; Scitovsky, 1958). The definitions given here largely follow the classical work of Balassa (1961); other sources are the major reports preceding the various jumps that mark the European integration process, such as Spaak *et al.* (1956), Werner *et al.* (1970), MacDougall *et al.* (1977), Padoa-Schioppa *et al.* (1987) and Delors *et al.* (1989). See also Pelkmans (1991). Note that the definitions given here are conceptual ones that do not always correspond to the setting up of concrete integration schemes (Balassa, 1976; Pelkmans, 1980). Note also that the various stages distinguished here can be split up further: see, for example, for the CM, Pelkmans (1986) and, for the MU, Gros (1989).
3   Over the years economists have developed the toolbox to identify first, and to quantify next, the cost and benefits of each step of integration. The earlier approaches could only account for the static effects of trade changes, and their

application produced small net benefits (see Chapter 6). Later approaches also took some of the dynamic effects of trade measures into account; their application produced significant net benefits. However, even the most recent approaches have a number of disadvantages. As a consequence the quantification of the cost and benefits of integration, and notably those of the higher stages of integration, is still fraught with difficulties

4   The theory of transfer of power from nations to the union has gradually been worked out. The impetus to the exploration of this line of thought has been given by Tinbergen (1959, 1965) who elaborated the basics of the theory of optimal level of decision making. The first applications of this sort of reasoning to the reality of the EU relied heavily on the theory of fiscal federalism (see Oates, 1972; and the pioneering work by MacDougall *et al.*, 1977, Emerson, 1977 and Forte, 1977). Later various new approaches have been looked at (e.g. Pelkmans, 1982; CEPR, 1993). Only recently a consistent theory of regulation at various levels of government in integrating areas has been developed by Pelkmans (1997), particularly chapter 4.

5   In the works of classical thinkers such as Mill and Proudhon, the most commonly used term was 'principle of federalism'. It lies at the basis of the constitutions of many federations such as Germany, Switzerland and the USA. The papal encyclical *Quadragesimo Anno* (1931) introduced the term 'subsidiarity' that has since been most widely used (see also Wilke and Wallace, 1990). The EU has enshrined the principle in its constitution (Article 5 EC): 'The Community shall act within the limits of the powers conferred upon it by this Treaty and the objectives assigned to it therein. In areas, which do not fall within its exclusive competence, the Community shall take action, in accordance with the principle of subsidiarity only if and in so far as the objectives of the proposed action cannot be sufficiently achieved by the Member states and can therefore, by reason of the scale or effects of the proposed action, be better achieved by the Community. Any action by the Community shall not go beyond what is necessary to achieve the objectives of this Treaty.'

6   An example is regional policy, that is carried out in 'partnership' between European, national and regional authorities (see Chapter 16).

7   See for an excellent overview of this body of literature (set in a coherent theoretical framework) Vromen (1995); see further, for example, Pejovich (1998) for the basics of the comparative approach in institutional economics. The absence of the EU in these and other studies shows that the application of the institutionalist theory to the EU is still in its embryonic stage.

8   Excessive transfer may happen for the following reasons:

   –   a cartel of countries can exert more power *vis-à-vis* third countries;
   –   a cartel of countries can be used for passing unpopular regulation that is nevertheless considered useful by the polity as the council can bypass national parliaments and to some extent ignore voter preferences;
   –   the division of power between the EU and national authorities is blurred which permits national politicians to shirk their responsibility more easily;
   –   international collusion makes it difficult for voters to find alternatives;
   –   national politicians are likely to give away powers of other government levels and of national independent public institutions (judiciary, national bank, competition).

9   Some ten years ago Hodgson (1988, p. 273) concluded that the progress of this school was as yet limited and that conditions were not good for a change in the future in the following words: 'The concrete application of institutionalist theory to practical problems requires detailed and painstaking study of institutions and their development. At the theoretical level, such an approach implies

interdisciplinary scholarship, which is neither fashionable nor encouraged at present by the structure and goals of academia. It requires the lateral thinking that is often frowned upon by the burrowing, half-blind, mole-like specialist.' Little has indeed changed since: a more recent overview (Hodgson *et al.*, 1994) of the work by äuthors in this sub-discipline refers only in a very superficial way to international organisations. The recent book by Schmitdtchen and Cooter (1997) also gives proof of the limitations of the approach for the subject of EU integration.

10   On the occasion of the commemoration of the 40th anniversary of the Treaties of Rome I made a short survey among persons who had played key roles during different stages of the EU integration process. It revealed the critical role of political actors that I would categorise as political entrepreneurs. Under conditions of considerable uncertainties in economic social and political terms, they were convinced they were making the right choices, they were leading the way of a group of hesitant followers and finally had their views accepted by a majority of the voters.

11   In the simple view of neo-functionalism the integration proceeds more or less linearly from the initial stage of free trade area to the final stage of the political union (Haas, 1958; Mitrany, 1966). However, the theory has been developed to accommodate other development paths too. One example are spill-back processes as a consequence of ideological nationalism (Haas, 1965; Lindberg and Scheingold, 1971; Pentland, 1973) or domestic institutions (Bulmer, 1984). Another is the introduction of integration ceilings (Hoffmann, 1966 and Keohane and Hoffmann, 1991). A third sees cyclical ups and downs and an unstable equilibrium. A fourth prefers a curvilinear model in which the trend towards increased integration is reversed because in an advanced stage of integration the union can provide information about partners' preferences in a plentiful and cheap way; disposing of the need for harmonisation of rules. Wessels (1997) has recently tried to integrate several of these views in a fusion thesis of structural growth in cycles whereby the end outcome is open.

12   The thesis that market integration pushes towards monetary integration was well formulated in the EU report, *One Market, One Money* (CEC, 1990b).

13   In trying to calculate the cost and benefits of enlargement of the EU economists have coped with the same set of problems as they had while assessing the cost and benefits of deepening.

14   The recent literature on EMU illustrates the points made very well. Indeed, the various studies made by economists do not give an unequivocal answer to the question which sub-group of EU member countries would constitute an OCA (Bayoumi and Eichengreen, 1993; Bofinger, 1994; Jacquemin and Sapir, 1995).

15   The EU has clearly stated the requirements which the countries of Central and Eastern Europe have to meet in order to qualify for membership (for example, stable institutions; a well-functioning market economy and so on; see Chapter 18 for further details). This need not only apply to membership of the club as such, but also to the membership of sub-clubs. A case in point is the membership of the EMU that is not based on theoretical economic grounds but on the politically agreed and constitutionally enshrined convergence criteria of the Treaty of Maastricht.

16   We have not even found any attempt to come to such a grand design in economics similar to the attempt of Moravcsik (1998) in political science. See also Wallace *et al.* (1999).

3 Short History

Introduction

Economic integration, defined as a process of economic unification of national economies, has been going on all through modern European history.[1] Two factors have always stimulated integration:

- *Technical progress*. Mechanisation and automation of the production process have completely changed production methods. Advances in energy technology, for instance, led to the replacement of human and animal power with steam and, later, with electricity. With respect to transport, horse-drawn vehicles gave way to railways and lorries. As a result, goods can be produced and distributed cheaply in large numbers.
- *Political idealism*. Since the Middle Ages there has been virtually no period in which statesmen or philosophers did not point to the common European heritage and the necessity for more 'political' unity in Europe.[2]

In the following sections we will describe the progress of economic integration under the influence of these two factors for five periods. We will thereby concentrate on the structural adaptations of the economy and the institutional arrangements that accompanied integration. The chapter will be concluded by a brief summary.

Until 1815: a traditional world with little integration

The Middle Ages to the French Revolution

In the early Middle Ages, the European economy was marked by a great fragmentation of markets. The feudal system had made all regions almost perfectly self-supporting. Under the influence of urban development in the 12th century, interregional trade was re-established for an increasing number of goods. In the following centuries this tendency continued, bringing about an increased integration of markets of products and production factors.

The *movement of goods* – that is, trade among regions and countries – developed only slowly (Pirenne, 1927); yet up to the 18th century trade remained of limited scope, being mostly concerned with luxury goods. There were three reasons for this:

- Countless obstacles. Tolls, different weights and measures and coins, staple rights and the privileges of merchant groups hindered trade between regions and cities of the European countries. These intra-national barriers were comparable to those that prevailed until recently between European states, for national frontiers then did not have the economic function they have now: tolls were levied at bridges, town gates, locks and so on, rather than at the national frontier. In the late Middle Ages, the citizens of towns tried to obtain privileges so as to get around tolls and other trade obstacles. The resulting patchwork of privileges for various groups heralded in a way the complex systems of trade discrimination by country groups that developed in the 19th and 20th centuries.
- Primitive means of transport. On land, everything had to be hauled by waggon and pack animal. Most tradesmen preferred the cheaper transport by water: sea or river. The fleets of river barges and sea-going vessels increased steadily, but the tonnages of the vessels remained small.
- Economic policy. The aim of mercantilist policy was, first, to be as much as possible self-sufficient and, next, to achieve the highest possible export surplus. To that end, rudimentary trade and industrial policies were pursued with often very crude instruments (Gomes, 1987). Evidently the arguments for old mercantilist and modern protectionist policies are much alike.

The *movement of production factors* was also very gradually improved. The reasons differed for labour and capital:

- Labour movements used to be hampered because under the feudal system virtually the entire population, with the exception of the nobility and the clergy, was bound by law to a certain place (serfdom). Over the centuries, citizens fought for, and gained, the right to move and trade freely everywhere. Europeans were adept at long-distance searches for employment and opportunity (Canny, 1994). Later some monarchs pursued active migration policies to increase the productive and military capacity of their country.

- Capital movements were in principle free. In practice, however, the transfer of money was much hindered by the defective monetary system and the limited means to convey money from one place to another. From an early date, money traffic consisted, not only of payments for commercial transactions, but also of loans to princes to cover their military expenditure. Investments in trade, craft and (transport) infrastructure were mostly made and financed locally.

The innovations of the French Revolution

The French Revolution, a political event, was soon developed by the citizens, who became all-powerful, into an economic revolution, totally upsetting the 'feudal' economy. The following measures show clearly the essence of this revolution, *the integration of the regional and local economies into a national economy*:

- abolition of all rules impeding the free traffic of goods, instantly followed by the abolition of all seigneurial rights and serfdom;
- shift of customs duties to the outer frontiers;
- creation of quota systems and tariffs to protect national production;
- abolition of all privileges of companies and guilds, and of rules about the manner of production;
- introduction of a uniform system of weights and measures;
- introduction of new legal rules for trade;
- construction of new infrastructure.

Owing to the national character of these measures, at first economic integration increased internally but decreased externally. During the Napoleonic regime the above novelties were introduced all over the European sub-continent. Moreover the so-called 'continental system' was created, intended to make the continent independent of Britain. The ensuing selective international integration was the fruit of a politico-military concept rather than economic logic.

With the collapse of Napoleon's empire, the continental system broke down as well. Once more British goods could be sold on the continent and, given Britain's technological leadership, a whole range of new industries on the continent had to be closed down owing to British competition. That put free trade, and international integration, in a bad light. On the other hand, measures like the removal of tolls, which had fostered economic integration at the national level, were found useful and were maintained practically everywhere in Europe.

Fading concept of Europe

The late Middle Ages can be characterised as a period during which the pan-European ideas of Empire and Papacy were fading more and more, giving way to a growing nationalism. The idea of a Europe acting as a unity receded into the background, to reappear only when the common heritage was under immediate threat from outside. In concrete terms, the threat came from the Turks, steadily encroaching upon Eastern Europe. To take a European stand against them was pleaded more than once, but only when the Turks threatened Vienna was collective action taken: the Turks were beaten by a European coalition. Internal threats to peace also inspired some advocates of a united Europe. They looked for a way to avoid the internal armed conflicts which constantly ravaged Europe. Out of the long range of illustrious men who devoted themselves to the creation of some type of European federal state, we will mention only Sully, Leibniz, Penn, Bentham, Kant, von Gentz and Saint Pierre. However all their plans came to nothing and their worthy goals – avoiding the constant wars for the hegemony in Europe, frontiers or heritages, or trade privileges – failed to come about. The clearest evidence of that failure is found in the Napoleonic wars concluding this period.

1815–1870: progressive integration following the industrial revolution

Theory and policy

'Protection or free trade' had become the central theme of discussions between politicians and economists in many countries, and until the middle of the 19th century the free-traders were in the ascendency. The successful coalition of economists and politicians opened a new era of closer integration of European economic life, in which governments took conscious decisions to open out the opportunities to international trade and competition (Pollard, 1981b). Total external trade increased rapidly (see Table 3.1). Intra-European trade in this period relied strongly on sectoral specialisation, itself the result of different technologies practised in different countries. At the end of the period international trade, migration and capital movement were practically free all over Europe.

In the period from 1815 to 1870, the progress of economic integration differed according to the initial situation of the European countries.

Table 3.1   Some indicators of European[a] economic development, 1810–70

Indicator	1810	1830	1850	1870
Gross National Product per head (index 1900 = 100)	47	53	62	79
Industrial production (index 1900 = 100)	n.a.	20	33	51
Production of pig iron (MT/y)	1	2	4	10
Production of coal (MT/y)	20	29	67	180
Share of exports in GNP (%)	3	4	7	11
Share of foreign investment in GNP (%)	—	1	2	3
Railway track (× 1000 km)	—	—	24	105

Notes:
[a]   All of Europe (West, Central and East).
n.a. = not available.

Source: Bairoch (1976).

Unity   Far-reaching integration was realised by the UK. In this country the ideas of free trade were given a theoretical foundation and a political shape. Great classical economists such as Smith, Ricardo and Mill emphasised in their work that free national and international trade would lead to the greatest possible prosperity. They paved the way for political aspirations towards free trade (Gomes, 1987). Obstacles to the free movement of goods, people and capital were increasingly felt as suffocating and were gradually removed. The UK, as the leader in innovation of industrial technology, initially prohibited the exportation of machinery and the emigration of skilled workers. Nevertheless many British craftsmen went to work in other countries of Europe, often using smuggled machinery. Because the prohibition could not be enforced, the UK abolished all legal barriers to the emigration of skilled workers in 1825 and of capital goods in 1842. It moved further towards free trade with the abolition of the Navigation Acts and the repeal of the Corn Laws.

Homogeneity   In areas such as Germany, Austria and Italy, where economic frontiers were dividing a space felt to be culturally united, economic integration spelled a way to political unity. For example, Germany tackled the problem of trade obstacles by means of the *Zollverein* (theoretically underpinned by the German economist, List). Under Prussian leadership a customs union was created in 1834 and gradually expanded. It involved the abolition of all duties at inner borders, and a duty levied on the outer frontier which was low for 'European' and high for colonial goods. Gradually more and more states in central and southern Germany joined this union. The rapid industrialisation of Germany during this period contributed much to the success of this type of integration, and was itself stimulated again by progressive integration.

Diversity   It is interesting to see that integration was progressing even among countries that were clearly independent from one another. Most European countries adopted more liberal external policies.

Technology and diplomacy

While integration was clearly stimulated by industrialisation, founded on technological innovation (see, for example, Mathias and Davis, 1991) and by the ensuing fast economic growth, the rapid industrialisation marking most West European countries in this period (see Figure 3.1) was in turn fostered by progressive integration. Indeed the application of modern technology made further specialisation not only possible but also desirable (see Table 3.1).

A second important component of the 'natural techno-economic process' is the means of transport and communication and in particular the railways. The tremendous accumulation of capital required for the construction of railways was often warranted only if transport nodes and feeding points were also internationally connected; moreover, to be feasible, railway transport had to be liberalised to a high degree. River transport, too, was liberalised: the new, larger steamships called for flexible exploitation. Successive international agreements ensured free navigation on the Rhine (Central Committee for Rhine Navigation, 1815, and Mannheim Treaty, 1868), the Danube, the Scheldt and so on.

Monetary integration was also attempted in this period (Bartel, 1974). Many of the large states of Western Europe had already reached a considerable degree of internal monetary integration (as early as the 13th century, Saint Louis, King of France, introduced one single coin, the ECU, for his entire kingdom!). After the Napoleonic wars, practically every country had developed its own national currency system. International monetary cooperation was set up by the German (Holtfrerich, 1989) and Italian (Sannucci, 1989) states before unification. International monetary integration without political integration was attempted by the Latin Monetary Union, which was based on the French franc and to which the Belgian, Swiss, Italian and later the Greek and Spanish currencies were joined. All these

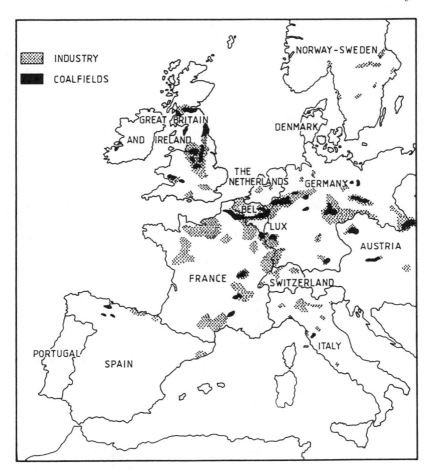

Figure 3.1   European industry around 1870

systems suffered from the lack of mechanisms obliging the participants to practise consultation and cooperation. These experiences
show that a monetary union seems to have to go hand-in-hand with
some degree of political union if it is to be successful (see also Hamada,
1985).

The form in which integration was expressed varied over the years.
International integration had always been a more or less factual process partly consolidated in bilateral agreements. This continued in the
period under discussion, for instance with the famous Cobden–Cheva-
lier free-trade Treaty of 1860, which gave French industry access to
cheaper and better coal and iron from Britain. It was copied by many
other countries for similar matters. Its importance lies in its uncondi-

tional most-favoured-nation clause, which had considerable implications for Europe-wide tariff reductions. These treaties were drawn up and implemented through the usual diplomatic channels, no permanent international institutions being created for the purpose.

Monarchist ideologies and socialist utopia

In the period after the Napoleonic wars, three initiatives of widely different inspiration were taken towards lasting peace in Europe.

- *Monarchist and anti-revolutionary.* The Holy Alliance was a bond of heads of state whose objective was to prevent revolutionary troubles in, and wars between, European states. To that end, the monarchs consulted regularly with one another, and in some instances decided to act collectively. The Holy Alliance made but little impact; the system fell apart after some time through internal conflicts and for lack of a strong institutional organisation.
- *Philosophical and visionary.* From a utopian analysis of the developing industrial society, Saint-Simon concluded that the political organisation should be left to representatives of trade and industry, in particular manufacturing industry and banks. In his view, for a satisfactory development, a peaceful international community in Europe was an absolute condition. Saint-Simon's ideas and their elaboration by the Saint-Simonists were not translated into action.
- *Republican and democratic.* The most important representative of a movement aiming to accomplish in Europe a fraternal collaboration of free peoples (Giovine Europa) was probably Manzini, the theorist of Italian unity. The movement did not have much of an impact.

Other suggestions for some form of political integration (almost invariably involving economic integration) in Europe hardly found any response at the time either.

1870–1914: stagnating integration

Depression and protectionism

Around 1870 the long period of growth came to a sudden end, in a depression which has been compared to the Great Depression of the 1930s. Many governments responded to it in a protectionist fashion. The French–German war and the Italian struggle for unity had com-

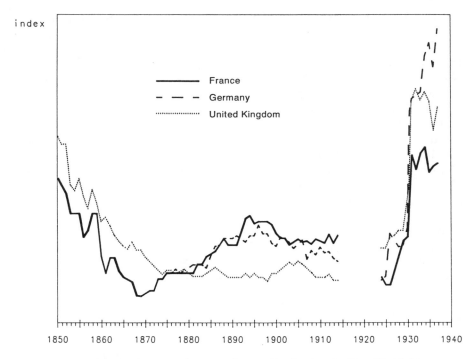

index

France
Germany
United Kingdom

1850   1860   1870   1880   1890   1900   1910   1920   1930   1940

Note: Reliable data for the years during and immediately after the First World War are not available.

Source: Messerlin and Becuwe (1986).

Figure 3.2   Evolution of British, French and German average tariff rates of protection, 1850–1938

pletely upset the situation. The powers demanding more protection for economic reasons were reinforced by a desire for autarky of mostly political and military inspiration. As a result, in many places attempts were made to curtail the existing freedoms of trade and traffic of production factors; straight tariff and subsidy wars were fought between some countries (see peak around 1890 in Figure 3.2). Having become far better organised than before, national states found themselves in a better position to impose taxes and customs duties, regulate their social affairs and pursue a protectionist, nationalist policy.

Trade in goods developed slowly, but it increased at the same rate as production, which indicates that protectionist inclinations did slow down, but not reverse, economic integration (see Table 3.2, row 5). Indeed some countries soon found out that complete autarky was an

Table 3.2   Some indicators of European[a] economic development, 1870–1910

Indicator	1870	1880	1890	1900	1910
Gross National Product per head (index 1900 = 100)	79	80	85	100	110
Industrial production (index 1900 = 100)	51	61	77	100	136
Production of pig iron (MT/y)	10	14	17	25	37
Coal production (MT/y)	180	217	328	438	574
Share of exports in GNP (%)	11	13	13	11	13
Share of foreign investment in GNP (%)	3	4	4	4	5
Ocean freight rates (index 1900 = 100)	212	180	127	100	83
Railway track[b] (× 1000 km)	105	169	225	292	351

Notes:
[a]   All of Europe (West, Central and East).
[b]   Including Asian parts of Russia.

Source: Bairoch (1976).

illusion, given the international specialisation, which had developed. Not different natural endowment, but far-reaching sectoral specialisation had become the main reason for goods trade, a specialisation based on economies of scale and technological leadership. Improved transport techniques (leading, among other things, to lower freight rates) also made for continued economic integration in Europe; the railway and canal networks proliferated during this period (see Table 3.2). However, in the construction of infrastructure, nationalist tendencies were becoming more and more manifest.

Movement of production factors, that is, of workers and capital, also remained free to a large extent during this period.

Labour   International migration mainly involved seasonal workers. Several thousands of Italians were employed in France, Germany and Austria. Some hundreds of thousands of Poles went to Germany every year, as did quite a number of other East Europeans. Many of them were employed in manufacturing industry, the mining industry or the construction trade, but many also filled the jobs in agriculture left open by the urbanising rural population. Many specialised labourers tended to move from country to country to operate special machines in regions and countries starting up new industrial projects.

Capital   During this period the financial sector developed quickly (Cassis, 1991). Europe became the banker of the world. Its total stock of foreign investment rose significantly to reach, in 1913, a level that exceeded its GDP. Annual flows amounted to more than 5 per cent of GDP in 1913. About a quarter of outgoing capital was oriented towards other European countries, one-quarter to the USA and half to the rest of the world. Banking organised itself internationally to engage in large investment projects: railways in Russia, textile factories in Silesia. As a consequence, the total foreign investment of European countries increased faster than their Gross Domestic Product (Table 3.2).

The monetary relations of all major industrialised countries were governed by the automatic rules of the gold standard. The combination of free movement of goods, labour and capital with fixed exchange rates was achieved by abstaining from an independent monetary policy (Hawtrey, 1947; Bordo and Schwartz, 1984). The increased integration was reflected by the coincidence of economic cycles across European countries (Craigh and Fisher, 1996).

The European idea

In the last part of the 19th century there were hardly any movements to promote the idea of a united Europe. Though not typically European, an important anti-nationalist movement should perhaps be pointed out, the Socialist International. This movement suggested that the popular masses had nothing to gain either from an armed conflict or from economic conflicts among capitalists of various countries. Successive versions of the Socialist International proved unable, however, to translate suggestions into a clear plan of action, let alone make the plan operational. Once more, the self-interest of national 'sections' proved the main obstacle to practical internationalisation.

The almost complete lack of utopias and proposals for concrete actions for the unity of Europe should not make us forget that most Europeans at the time under consideration continued to take the cultural unity of their part of the world more or less for granted. In spite of wide differences among nations, neither literary and artistic trends nor great spiritual movements were confined to any one nation; they were part of one common European cultural world (Duroselle, 1987) – a conception which, in economics, and especially politics, was still a long way off.

International organisation and coordination

At the turn of the century, forms of integrated policy were practised for the first time, international institutions being founded for the purpose. This was the logical outcome of increased government intervention in the economy, combined with intensified international exchange. Not surprisingly, this policy integration concerned areas directly connected with the conditions for international trade and competition.

- *Transport.* The technical standardisation of railway equipment was mainly due to the British system of measures being adopted by most states. The coordination of other elements, such as the exchange of rolling stock, the treatment of goods, time schedules and so on, was accomplished in international committees.
- *Post and telecommunication.* Among the first international organisations were the International Telecommunication Union (1865) and the Universal Postal Union (1874). Both were established to harmonise internationally all national regulations with respect to rates, procedures, infrastructure (cables) and so on. The harmonisation has contributed much to the rapid growth of PTT traffic.
- *Agriculture and fishery.* Several attempts were made at international coordination and regulation; a first, limited success was the regulation of trade in sugar (premiums being abolished). An effort was made to achieve one European tariff for foodstuffs, to protect European producers against competition, on the European market, from new producer countries.
- *Social policies.* Efforts towards integration were inspired largely by the fear that the improvement of social services and work conditions in one country would put that country at a competitive disadvantage. The abolition of slavery was among the first steps towards social policy integration: in 1890, a General Act against Slavery was signed.

Some hesitant steps were taken to bring about some coordination in other areas. However, the pressure of the techno-economic circumstances was not strong enough to make them successful.

1914–1945: disintegration

The First World War and the peace treaty

With the outbreak of the First World War, every country started to practise autarky: they reasoned that to depend economically on foreign countries makes a country vulnerable in military terms. The result was a process of disintegration. This had its effects both on markets and on policy.

- *Markets*. The first victim was international trade, which showed a steep drop, owing to government intervention. The next was production factors, their movement being more and more curtailed. Under the pressure of conscription, among other things, the free movement of individuals collapsed completely. Capital was more and more contained within national borders by a multitude of national rules. The international loans concluded during this period concerned exclusively the assistance of one government by another.
- *Policy*. The state began to interfere intensively with trade and industry, organising them for purposes of war. Because the control was strictly national, a coordinated international policy was practically impossible. Even within a political bloc, integration was shunned for fear of disloyalty of allied states. Agreements concluded between the members of each bloc covered only restricted areas. For instance, during the First World War the Allies only coordinated the use of shipping tonnage, and made some attempt at specialising production (Monnet, 1976).

The Peace Treaty of Versailles consolidated the disintegration brought about by war. The central theme of this treaty was the nations' right to self-determination. On that basis, many new states were formed in Europe, which instantly began to quarrel about frontiers, debts, minorities and so on. The result was a great length of new frontiers (some 11 000 km) with corresponding customs barriers. To support the autonomy of the national economies, most barriers were made sky-high (see the 1930–40 period in Figure 3.2). Thus the industry and transport structures were forced to adapt themselves to a multitude of small territories. Factories were built at uneconomic locations, railways rerouted, and so on.

The period up to the end of the Second World War

After the First World War some countries (notably Germany) were left with enormous debts, leading to serious balance-of-payment difficulties. These were aggravated by low prices and diminishing sales prospects on export markets. Under such circumstances, non-competitive companies, traditionally in favour of protection, grasped their chance, and the enormous unemployment consolidated the protectionist tendencies. This movement spread quickly through Europe and, as a consequence, imports were reduced to almost half the pre-war level; this in turn led to a decrease in exports as well (as illustrated by Table 3.3). An even greater decrease befell international capital movements, which fell back to about one-fifth of their pre-war level.

Table 3.3   Some indicators of European[a] economic development, 1913–38

Indicator	1913	1920	1930	1938
Gross National Product per head (index 1938 = 100)	n.a.	73	89	100
Industrial production (index 1938 = 100)	n.a.	59	84	100
Production of pig iron (MT/y)	42	22	37	39
Coal production (MT/y)	515	395	483	485
Share of exports in GNP (%)	16	9	9	6
Share of foreign investment in GNP	5	n.a.	1	1
Railway track (× 1000 km)	217	215	226	229

Notes:
[a]   Only present EC15 countries.
n.a. = not available.

Source: Calculated on the basis of figures given in OECD 1964, Bairoch (1976), Mitchell (1981).

The disadvantages of the economic disintegration were increasingly recognised and attempts were undertaken to reintegrate the economies of certain groups of states.

- *Markets*. The plan to unite in a customs union the old Habsburg states failed (Ponteroso Conference), as did a worldwide free-trade scheme in which 29 states agreed to abolish all trade restrictions within six months and never impose them again (Conference of Geneva, 1927).
- *Policy*. The League of Nations, founded by the Allies, came into operation in 1920; its object was to maintain peace in Europe. The League developed some activity in economic and social affairs (among others it created the ILO, the International Labour Organisation). However, all those initiatives hardly made an impact. In this period of general disintegration one example of effective international integration by institution building can be mentioned. The Bank for International Payments, a joint venture of the central banks in Europe, was founded in 1930 to facilitate payments, quite a feat in a period of great monetary disorder.

In the 1920s the average dependency on external trade remained virtually stable. Even that comparatively modest integration was curtailed by the depression of the 1930s. Again there was a sharp effect on both markets and policy integration.

- *Markets*. The United States' introduction of the very high Smoot–Hawley tariff in 1930 sparked off a further wave of protectionist measures in Europe, leading to tariffs of unprecedented height (see Figure 3.2) and the multiplication of the number of quotas.
- *Policy*. The most important area of disintegration was monetary policy. The gold standard, which had not worked very well during this period, collapsed (the UK left in 1931; other countries soon followed). A period of currency competition ensued, one devaluation following upon the other. All attempts to solve the crisis by international agreements failed. In other fields, too, policy integration decreased. To overcome the depression, states began to intervene even more than before in the economy, and Keynes (1936) furnished the theoretical foundation. Solutions (armament, infrastructure works) to the unemployment problem were governed by national circumstances, and the economy was often made subservient to military objectives.

The Second World War brought about some integration among members of the same political blocs. On the side of the Axis powers it was achieved by enlisting the economies of territories occupied by Germany in the German war efforts. The integration concerned not only products (agricultural as well as industrial): production factors were forcefully integrated as well (*Arbeitzeinsatz*, war loans). On the side of the Allies some integration could also be perceived: once more, production and means of transport were to some extent normalised for the sake of the war effort. The integration efforts hardly touched the other sectors of the economy, however.

The idea of a united Europe

During and between the two world wars, short-term economic thinking (the fight against unemployment) and strategic–military thinking (autarky was believed to be safer than integration) were dominant. However, some enlightened spirits began to see that nationalism only breeds economic problems and is a permanent threat to peace. The best known attempt of this period to solve the problem in a European perspective was the Pan Europe Movement, led by Coudenhove-Calergi. Although this movement aroused considerable interest, it shared with comparable activities the weakness of keeping rather aloof from the political reality of the time and being too utopian.

Initiatives towards European unity taken by leading statesmen seemed more promising. There was, for instance, the plan for a European federation which Briand, French prime minister in 1930, after consultation with the German foreign minister, Stresemann, submitted to the League of Nations. The scheme was well received, but support was soon found to be very superficial. It failed to stir the masses in any nation; nationalism had sunk too deeply in the consciousness of the average citizen. Even such weak attempts were heard of less and less in the 1930s, when fascist movements were organising themselves along blatantly nationalist lines, more and more straining international relations, and finally even trying to impose the hegemony of the Axis powers on Europe by military force. Hardly a situation to foster a true European vision.

1945 to the present: a new upsurge of integration

Europe and world policy

Integration, which had come to a halt during the war, was gradually re-established during the 1945–1955 period. First, there was a move towards free trade. The task of fostering world-wide free trade liberalisation has been entrusted to the General Agreement on Tariffs and Trade (GATT) transformed in the 1990s into the World Trade Organisation (WTO). One important instrument against the occurrence of trade disputes is the so-called 'most-favoured-nation' clause, according to which any favourable tariff which two countries accord to each other is essentially valid for all other participants in the General Agreement. The GATT/WTO has accomplished a considerable worldwide tariff decrease; many non-tariff impediments have been eliminated as well (Kock, 1969; Hoekman and Kostecki, 1996).

Next there was a move towards convertibility of currencies and free capital movements, with exchange rates pegged to the dollar. This task has been entrusted to the World Bank (IBRD) and International Monetary Fund (IMF). The combined task of these organisations was to ensure well-regulated international monetary relations (Conference of Bretton Woods). That meant fixed exchange rates between currencies. Countries that, through temporary balance-of-payment problems, found it hard to maintain these fixed exchange rates could obtain hard-currency loans. The monetary and macroeconomic coordination schemes of the IMF and the Organisation for Economic Cooperation and Development (OECD: see below) had worked well for several decades. However, in the 1970s they could no longer cope with the emerging inconsistencies, and the Bretton Woods system collapsed. The experiences of the period led to the conclusion (Padoa-Schioppa *et al.*, 1987) that free movement of goods and capital cannot be combined with pegged exchange rates and independent macro-economic policy making of member countries.

After the Allied victory, Europe was cut in two. If at first the spheres of influence of the western Allies and the Soviet Union were not precisely delimited, soon afterwards the outbreak of the Cold War led to the very sharp dividing line which went by the name of the Iron Curtain. Economic integration of European countries from the western bloc with those from the eastern bloc was thus excluded for a long time.[3] Any further integration has proceeded within each separate bloc. Some integration of the economies of Central and Eastern Europe has taken place in the framework of the Council of Mutual Economic Assistance (CMEA or Comecon), a different organisation from that chosen in the West (Kozma, 1982; Pinder, 1986; van Brabant, 1989). We will concentrate henceforth on Western Europe.

The pursuit of European unity

Already during the Second World War, the pursuit of intensive economic integration was put on a political–idealistic footing. Especially in circles of the Resistance the conviction was growing that nationalism was at the roots of the disaster which fascism had wrought in Europe and that, therefore, Europe should be rebuilt in a sphere of increased international integration, especially in economic terms. The Ventotene Manifest published in 1941 by personalities grouped around Spinelli is perhaps the best known of the ideas fostered by the Resistance. It led more or less directly to the Geneva Declaration of 1944, which confirmed the principles of an Atlantic Charter and proposed a federal solution for the whole of Europe (including Eastern Europe). For the first time the sentiments initially expressed by some members of the Resistance appeared to be attractive to large groups of people. A whole series of initiatives for European integration were fostered by these sentiments, many of which found active support from leading politicians in all West European countries. The first result was the creation of the Council of Europe, and the Union Parlementaire Européenne was the second.

Many groups continued to submit proposals and to campaign for a more far-reaching European unity. The movements varied widely in objective and organisation. International pacifism, European federalism and economic functionalism were joined, however, into one European Movement (Lipgens *et al.*, 1982). The ravages of war made it clear that Europe's only chance of survival lay in progressive economic integration. To that end some important multinational agreements were concluded and some international bodies, widely different in structure and authority, were created (see, for instance, Palmer,

Lambert *et al.*, 1968; Van Meerhaeghe, 1998). Examples are the Council of Europe, concerned in particular with cultural affairs and human rights, and the West European Union, mainly occupied with defence. Four others deal more specifically with economic integration and the Benelux Economic Union.[4] The generally felt need for economic integration soon generated a favourable climate to create, with American support, an international organisation with a widespread membership (all Western Europe), an intergovernmental set-up and a wide range of policy objectives: the Organisation for European Economic Cooperation.[5]

A limited set of countries pushed towards further integration. The UK appeared to set greater store by an Empire than a European orientation, and the British gradually withdrew from initiatives towards greater European integration. However, continental nations continued to strive for closer cooperation. This is not surprising, as most initiatives were inspired by the hope of eliminating forever the potential war threat posed by French and German differences. That political aim was to be achieved, not through unrealistic plans for complete political union, but through a strategy of gradual integration of certain functions (for example, Haas, 1958; Mitrany, 1966). These could then later be followed by other functions. The first function chosen was of an economic nature, which seemed the most practical as very good economic reasons were pushing in that direction.[6]

Two views on integration

The setting up of international institutions is needed to safeguard the durability of the integration scheme. There has been considerable debate about the degree to which national governments needed to transfer powers to such organisations. One can distinguish essentially two rival concepts:

- a *supranational* organisation, with an organ that independently executes policies and prepares decisions, and where the representatives of national governments may take decisions by majority rule; and
- an *intergovernmental* organisation, characterised by a small secretariat, and where the representatives of the national governments take decisions by unanimity.

The *supranational road* has been taken by a small group of countries creating the *European Community*, later to become the *European Union*. On 9 May 1950 the French foreign minister Schuman (inspired by Monnet) presented a plan to join together the French and German

basic industries under a European High Authority. After negotiation
the plan was accepted not only by France and Germany but also by
the Benelux countries and Italy. This success was due to the heavy
support the plan received from leading politicians (including
Adenauer and de Gasperi). The UK, having serious reservations about
its supranational character kept aloof. In 1952 the Treaty of Paris
created the European Coal and Steel Community (ECSC). The ECSC
meant to create a factual solidarity among its members based on
practical realisations in a limited field of competence. It was based
on a functional/supranational approach. The functional character
appears in the choice of the strategic sectors of coal (the major form
of energy) and steel (the basic material). The supranational character
appears in the transfer of considerable powers to the organisation in
matters of regulation of markets.

After the successful creation of the ECSC, new initiatives were
taken to extend the functions to be integrated beyond economics into
fields such as defence and foreign policy. However the ratification of
the treaties of the European Defence Community (EDC) and of the
European Political Community (EPC) eventually miscarried in the
French parliament. The pressure of those striving for further integration was then once more brought to bear of the economic function.
The choice of this avenue of functional integration seemed the more
appropriate as the sectoral limitation of the ECSC had proven to be a
serious handicap. First because the interrelations between different
sectors of the economy some of which were integrated, and others
not, caused a series of practical problems. Second and more importantly the integration of the markets of these other products could
significantly contribute to economic growth.

Studies were made (Spaak report) and negotiations started (Messina
conference) that resulted in 1958 in the Treaty of Rome. This treaty
created, on a supranational basis, the European Economic Community. The member states were the same six mentioned above, the UK
again keeping apart. With the EEC, European integration reached a
decisive stage in its development, for the Treaty of Rome set ambitious goals. In that same year, 1958, the same countries also founded
the European Atomic Energy Community (EAEC or Euratom). Since
then the EC has extended both its membership and its competences
(see next section).

The *intergovernmental road* has been taken by the other countries of
Western Europe. Under the leadership of the UK they created in 1959
the *European Free Trade Association* (EFTA). While recognising the
advantages of further integration, these countries could not, for different reasons, accept the objectives and the organisation of the Community. The objectives of EFTA were far less than those of the EC,
only a free-trade zone being established. The institutional organisa-

tion of EFTA was no other than the usual intergovernmental structure of most international organisations. Over the decades it became
clear to an increasing number of EFTA members that their interest
would be better served by joining the EC. Almost all have succes-
sively left EFTA to become members of the EC. Their accession to the
EC has been facilitated by the *European Economic Area* (EEA), a pact
signed and ratified in 1992. It merged the EC and the EFTA into a
single market with one set of regulations; indeed, the non-EU members have agreed to harmonise their legislation with the 'acquis
communautaire'.[7]

From European Community to European Union

The legal foundation of the European Community consists of the
three treaties of the ECSC, the EEC and the EAEC. Right from the
start of the latter two organisations, two of its institutions (Parliament and the Court of Justice) assumed responsibilities for the three
organisations. In the 1960s, the executive bodies (Commission and
Council) of the ECSC, the EEC and the EAEC were merged as well.
From that moment one institutional structure was in operation for
the three separate legal entities. Of these three, the EEC has come to
occupy a paramount place. Its treaty has been constantly adapted to
cope with the new constitutional needs of the dynamics of the European integration process. For example, the Single Act of 1987 provided among other things for further market and policy integration.
The Maastricht and Amsterdam Treaties formalise the colloquial name
'European Community' (Article 1 EC) and create the European Union (Article 1 EU). The latter encompasses cooperation of member
states in matters of foreign and security policy and justice and home
affairs.

Deepening   The EU has gradually extended its field of activity and
intensified its involvement in already existing common policy areas.
The first objective of the EEC Treaty (Article 3) was to create a
Customs Union and an incomplete Common Market. The next was
to create an Economic Union by setting up common policies and to
coordinate many national policies. Market integration made rapid
progress in the 1960s and the beginning of the 1970s; a customs
union was indeed quickly realised for most of the sectors of the
economy. Similar results were obtained for major parts of the labour and capital markets. Policy integration made headway, for
example with the setting up of a common agricultural and a common trade policy. The economic crisis of the middle of the 1970s
and early 1980s brought the integration process practically to a halt.
When the negative effects of this situation became evident, a new

impulse was given with the successful completion of the internal (common) market by 1992. Over the years a gradual extension of policy integration took place, based on agreements on new objectives. At some points an acceleration of this process took place. The Single Act (1987) codified the objectives of the completion of the single market, of the protection of the environment and of the improvement of social and economic cohesion. The Maastricht Treaty (1992) provides notably for an Economic and Monetary Union and for more social protection. Moreover the Treaty extends the integration process into a number of non-economic fields, such as justice and home affairs, defence and foreign policy and European citizenship. The Treaty of Amsterdam (1997) has further reinforced the role of the EU in these areas.

Widening   The number of member countries of the EU has gradually been increased (see Figure 3.3). This was the result of the success of the EU in the realisation of its objectives. When other European countries realised that they had no part in these advantages, they decided to apply for EU membership. In 1972, the UK, Denmark and Ireland left the EFTA to join the EC. In 1981, Greece was admitted, followed in 1986 by Spain and Portugal. Sweden, Finland and Austria joined in the early 1990s. Moreover Turkey, Cyprus, Malta and Switzerland have applied for membership in the period 1987–1992.

Recently the geographical perspective of the EU has been further widened by the collapse of the system of central planning in the countries of Central and Eastern Europe. The former GDR was taken into the EU when it was united with the Federal Republic of Germany in 1990. Most of the Central and Eastern European countries (CEEC) have applied for membership. Exceptions are the republics that have been created after the partition of the former Yugoslavia (apart from Slovenia) and of the former Soviet Union (apart from the Baltic States). Albania has not applied either. To facilitate transition and to prepare for membership, the EU has concluded association agreements with all CEEC applicants.

The EU has shown a remarkable dynamism. As a matter of fact its velocity of integration exceeds the speed with which other integration schemes have proceeded (for example, France, Switzerland, the USA) (Tinbergen, 1991).

Summary and conclusions

- Economic integration of Europe has been not so much an objective as a by-product of technological progress, on the one hand, and aspirations to political unity, on the other.

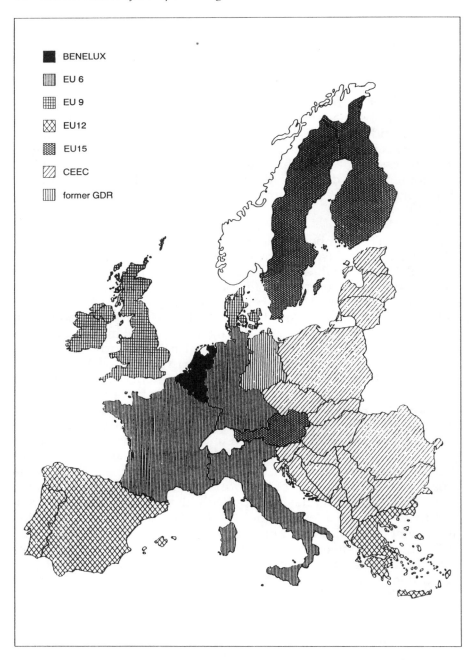

Figure 3.3   Gradual extension of the membership of the European Union

- Technical and economic factors (for instance large-scale production attended by mechanisation and automation, and the development of new means of transport such as trains and lorries) were the principal stimulus to progressive economic integration in Europe.
- Political and idealistic motives for European unity were strongly inspired by the need for peace. Their influence on practical economic integration remained slight, however. Indeed not until after the Second World War did the European idea become really effective.
- Not only can integration cease to make progress, it can also, once achieved, be reversed. Especially in times of economic depression and decline, the forces arguing against integration tend to become stronger and harder to resist. War tends to have a very negative influence on integration.
- Integration of goods and factor markets and of macro-economic and monetary policy making is most effective under strict rules and in a strong institutional setting.
- From a multitude of institutions dealing with economic integration the European Union has emerged as the most dynamic. It has extended both its fields of activity and its geographical coverage.

Notes

1   The organisation of the subject matter of this chapter has been largely borrowed from Pollard (1981a); the paragraphs concerning the 'ideology' of European unification lean in particular on Brugmans (1970); the setting of the European process in the framework of a worldwide development towards internationalisation leans on Kenwood and Lougheed (1999).
2   For a description of the changes in the perceptions of Europe in history, see A. Rijksbaron *et al.* (eds) (1987) and Wilson and van der Dussen (1995).
3   The only platform where 'integration' of East and West was still a point of discussion was the Economic Commission for Europe (ECE), a regional organisation of the United Nations. Its role has been very modest, however.
4   *The Benelux Economic Union* (1944), which joins together the Netherlands, Belgium and Luxemburg, has a long history. Unsuccessful attempts at creating a Benelux customs union had already been made in 1919 and 1932. The present agreement provides for a customs union as well as an economic union. The customs union took a relatively short time to realise; the economic union has taken more time to develop. The importance of the Benelux lies in particular in the opportunity it has given to gain experience in certain forms of integration, an experience which has often proved very useful for the European Community.
5   *The Organisation for European Economic Cooperation* (OEEC) (1948), later reorganised to become the OECD, was created to administer Marshall Aid. The OEEC aimed for trade liberalisation by the elimination of all manner of obstacles. The

OEEC further provided for some coordination of national policies, for instance at the macro-economic level and with respect to manufacturing industry and energy. The OEEC was extended and relaunched in 1961 under the new name of Organisation for Economic Cooperation and Development (OECD); at present it comprises the entire industrialised world; that is, Western Europe, North America (United States, Canada, Mexico), the Antipodes (Australia, New Zealand) and Asia (Japan, Korea).

6   See Machlup (1977) for a review of the contributions to the thinking on integration of historians (ch. 5), political economists (ch. 6), statesmen, men of affairs and men of letters (ch. 7), committee members and organisation staff (ch. 8) and economic theorists (ch. 9).

7   The EEA now encompasses, apart from the EU, Liechtenstein, Norway and Iceland; Switzerland having decided not to participate.

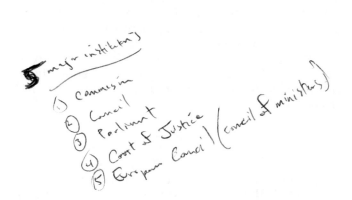

4 Institutions

Introduction

Economic integration is dependent on the legal framework that is set for it. In general one can say that strong institutions are a necessary condition for the stability and the internal dynamics of the schemes.

In this chapter we will give the essential aspects of the development of the EU system that are useful for the understanding of many of the issues dealt with in later chapters. In the next section we will present the various institutions and the original way in which they relate to each other. We will thereby refer in broad terms to their present competences.[1] Four of these institutions that form the backbone of the system merit fuller treatment, and we will describe in some detail the composition, procedures, tasks and competences of each.

The complex way in which the law- and decision-making machinery functions will then be examined. We will indicate briefly the different legal forms in use, the diversity of the decision-making processes and the dynamics of the system. Finally a section will be devoted to the budget, describing briefly the structure of expenditure and receipts and the way budgetary powers are executed, and a summary section with some conclusions will round off the chapter.

Institutional framework

Major and other institutions

The institutional system of the European Union consists of some ten different bodies (see Table 4.1 for a schematic representation). The five most important institutions of the EU are the Commission, the Council, Parliament, the Court of Justice and the European Council.[2] We will deal with these institutions in detail in the following

Table 4.1   The institutional system

Council	Commission	Parliament	Court of Justice	European Council
15 national ministers (or heads of government)	20 members	626 members	15 judges 9 advocates general	15 heads of state and of government plus president of Commission
Court of Auditors	*European Central Bank (ECB)*	*European Investment Bank*	*Economic and Social Committee*	*Committee of the Regions*
15 members	6 directors	15 governors 25 directors	222 members	222 members

sections. Five other 'institutions' exist that need some brief introduction.

The Court of Auditors (ECA)   This body examines the accounts of the Community to determine, not only whether all revenue has been received and all expenditure incurred in a lawful manner, but also whether the financial management has been sound.

The Economic and Social Committee   The ESC, composed of representatives of employees and employers, professionals and consumers, advises the Commission and the Council on their policy plans.

The Committee of the Regions   The CR also acts in an advisory capacity to Commission and Council on matters regarding local authorities and regional interests.[3]

The European System of Central Banks (ESCB) and the European Central Bank (ECB)   These have the task of maintaining price stability. To that end the ESCB/ECB define and implement the monetary policy of the EU. Moreover, they support the general economic policies of the Community.

The European Investment Bank   The EIB grants credits to business companies and governments, notably for projects of common interest to several member states that are of such a nature or size that they cannot be entirely financed by one state. Moreover the EIB can finance projects in less developed regions.

Division of power under different regimes

The institutional set-up of the EU is rather origin; has traits of an international organisation, as the kept their sovereignty and competence in essenti states are represented in the Council of Minister intergovernmental international organisations, this is the institution where final decisions are made. On the other hand, the European Union has also some obvious traits of a federal union. Its institutions exercise a *clearly defined authority* in an increasing number of areas. EU institutions are endowed with powers largely exceeding those of an intergovernmental international organisation like the OECD (with only a general secretariat to assist the ministers at their task), but falling short of those of a strong federal government (the USA).

The powers are distributed differently over its institutions depending on the subject matter at hand:[4]

- For *Community matters* (Common Market, EMU and so on) the division of competences over institutions follows to a large extent the usual division of powers existing in national states. The legislation lies with Parliament, execution with the Commission and adjudication with the Court. The Council occupies a special position in the institutional framework. It has both important executive and legislative powers. For the first function it shares powers with the Commission, for the second with the Parliament.
- For *Union matters* (common foreign and security policy and justice and home affairs) a purely intergovernmental regime exists that practically involves only the Council (with limited roles for Commission and Parliament).

The matters discussed in this book all fall under Community rules. So we will henceforth disregard the specific Union rules. The rules for Community matters are as follows.

Execution Commission and Council are jointly responsible for:

- coordinating national policies;
- issuing regulations and directives and taking decisions in Community policy areas;
- supervising the observation of the treaties and the implementation of decisions.

In practice, there is some division of work; the Council determines the strategy to be adopted, while the Commission takes care of daily

tions and controls and supervises the observation of the trea-
. The difference is one of emphasis only, for the Commission
elps to prepare Council decisions and often consults the Council or
the representatives of the national governments on the execution of
its tasks. Indeed Council and Commission perform their duties in
constant consultation.

Legislation   Contrary to many national parliaments, the European Parliament (EP) has limited legislative power. In some matters it has only
an advisory role; final decisions lie with the Council. In others it has
the power of codecision, which means that Council and Parliament
have to come to an agreement in order to put legislation into effect.

The Commission

The Commission consists of 20 members, appointed, after mutual
consultation, by the governments of the member states for a five-
year period. Each of the five largest countries appoints two members; each of the smaller countries appoints one member. The members
are chosen on the grounds of their general competence, and their
independence must be beyond doubt. Although one member acts as
president and two are vice-presidents, all members have in principle
the same powers. Decisions are made by majority vote.

Once appointed, the members of the Commission have a European
responsibility; that is to say, they must not set themselves up as
national representatives. For that reason, a member state cannot call
'its' Commissioner to account, or withdraw him. Nor can the Commission as a whole be dismissed by the Council of Ministers. However the Commission is accountable to the European Parliament, and
can be forced to resign as a body only by a motion of censure of the
Parliament. In that event, the governments of the member states
must appoint a new Commission.

To perform its task, the Commission has at its disposal an international staff (informally called the Eurocracy), for the greater part
established in Brussels. In 2000 a total of some 20 000 officials were
employed in the Commission's services, many of them engaged in
translation work (about 3000). Each member of the Commission is
responsible for one policy sector or, in more concrete terms, for the
work of one or more Directorates General (comparable to national
ministerial departments). In the course of time the role of the president of the Commission as the representative of this institution and
as the person responsible for the consistency of the actions of the
various commissioners has greatly increased.

The Commission occupies a special position in the system of the
Union. Its role is much stronger than that of the secretariat of other

intergovernmental institutions, which can only prepare decisions and implement them by delegation of authority of the representatives of member states. On the other hand it falls short of that of the government of a sovereign member state, which has full executive power, whereas the Commission shares its powers with the Council of Ministers.

The major tasks of the Commission are the initiation of actions, the execution of policies, the implementation of the budget and, finally, the enforcement of the laws.

Initiation of actions The Commission has the right of initiative; it develops new policies, proposes new regulations, directives and decisions. To fulfil its role effectively, the Commission is represented in the meetings of the Council and COREPER (see next section). The role of initiator is a highly important one, for it is that role which enables the Commission to safeguard the Community interest against the national interests dominating the Council. Admittedly the Commission is not the sole actor here. Indeed the European Council (of heads of government) has reserved to itself the initiating of major new developments.

Execution of policies Some of the Commission's executive powers have been bestowed on it by the treaties; these include the customs union, the fight against distortion of competition. Other powers have been transferred to the Commission by the Council. Indeed nearly all Council decisions contain articles which call for implementation by the Commission. However the Council tends to take a rather narrow view of the executive tasks to be entrusted to the Commission. In some cases it ties up the Commission in its executive task with some form of consultation, for instance with the so-called 'management committees' (see the following section).

Implementation of the budget This includes the operations of the so-called 'structural funds' (Agricultural, Regional, Social and Development Funds). The Commission is also authorised to raise loans to finance investments in energy, industry and infrastructure projects envisaged to help realise certain policy objectives.

Enforcement of the laws The Commission supervises the correct implementation of treaties and decisions. The authority to gather information was bestowed on it in the treaties. When the Commission finds, through an inquiry, that a company, individual or member state has violated the EU rules, it invites that company, individual or member state to explain its behaviour. If no satisfactory explanation is given, the company, member state or individual will be invited to stop the violation. In some cases a fine is imposed. Should that prove ineffective, the Commission will institute legal proceedings before the Court. Here too the role of the Commission as guardian of the Community interest is manifest.

The Council

The Council consists of one representative minister of the government of each of the member states. The composition of the Council varies with the matter in hand. In general, the Council consists of the ministers of foreign affairs of the 15 member states, but it may also consist of the ministers responsible for a specific policy field, for instance Agriculture, Transport or Finance. The Council of Ministers meets as often as it considers necessary.

The member states take the presidency in turns, for six months each. The president of the Council takes responsibility for the progress of the work of the Council. In order to safeguard the necessary continuity a troika is formed in which the past, present and future president coordinate the timing of consultations, negotiations and decisions.

On most Community matters the Council decides with a qualified majority. Depending on the size of the countries, the representatives have different numbers of votes. The total number of votes is 87. For example, the largest countries (such as Germany and the UK) have ten votes, smaller countries (such as Belgium and Portugal) have five, while the smallest country, Luxemburg, has two.

A proposal of the Commission must be supported by at least 62 votes in the Council to be accepted; in some cases these 62 votes must come from at least 10 member states. Voting by qualified majority is now the rule; unanimity is still required for voting on constitutional matters and on sensitive issues like taxes.[5]

The ministers on the Council are accountable to their national parliament and not to the EP. There is, however, a dialogue between the two bodies: during sessions of the EP time is reserved for a debate between the EP and the Council on topical subjects.

The Council has a separate staff of European officials who prepare the meetings. It is a small staff compared to that of the Commission. Important in the preparatory work is the Committee of Permanent Representatives, often indicated by the French abbreviation of COREPER. This Committee meets every week in task-oriented workgroups, in which civil servants of national departments also take part. COREPER deals with the Commission's proposals. If COREPER is agreeable to the proposal, the Council's final decision is no more than a formality. If not, the proposal is further negotiated in the complete Council of Ministers.

According to the treaties, the Council has the following roles to play:

- Coordinating the various economic policies of the member states. The Council has the 'power to take decisions'; in other words, the Council has the final say in Community legislation. In some cases it has to share this power with the EP (see below).
- Regulating the relations of the EU with other countries by treaties. In actual fact, it is mostly the Commission which acts as negotiator by the mandate given to it by the Council; the final decision is the Council's. For some treaties it needs the approval of the EP.

The European Council

Since 1975, there have been regular meetings of the European Council, which is composed of heads of government (and head of state for France) and the president of the Commission. These 'summits' (in which the foreign ministers and a member of the Commission in charge of foreign affairs also participate) take place at least twice a year. The European Council's role is to give direction to 'provide the Union with the necessary impetus for its development and shall define the general political guidelines thereof'.

In practice this means two things: first, the European Council decides on the passing into new stages of integration (for example, single market, EMU); second, it takes decisions on current policy issues that have proved too involved for the Council of Ministers. In the past the role of the European Council has much increased as an increasing number of thorny issues are transferred by the Council of Ministers to the European Council.

The European Parliament

The members of the European Parliament (EP) are elected directly for a term of five years. In most countries the election proceeds by proportional representation. There are 626 members. After reunification, Germany is by far the largest country; it has 99 seats. The other three large countries, Italy, the UK and France, have 87 seats each; Spain has 64, the Netherlands 31, Belgium, Greece and Portugal 25 each, Sweden 22, Austria 21, Denmark and Finland 16, Ireland, 15 and, finally, Luxemburg 6. Each member has one vote. The Parliament elects from its members a president and a number of vice-presidents, who together constitute the 'Bureau', the executive body responsible for the agenda, competence of committees, and so on.

From the start, EP members have grouped themselves, not by national delegations, but along party-political lines (Social Democrats, Christian Democrats, Liberals, and so on). The preliminary work of the Parliament is carried on in the parliamentary committees, which may be standing or temporary, general or special. From their members, the committees choose rapporteurs, who report on subjects to be treated in the full Parliament. Most reports contain a draft resolution, to be voted on by the full EP.

In the past the competences of the EP remained far below those of most national parliaments (see van Schendelen, 1984). The EP has striven constantly to extend its authority, on the argument that it is the only body that can make up for the democratic gaps in EU decision making. The tasks and competences of the EP have been extended gradually. In Community matters the competences of the EP are now very wide and refer to four areas: (1) decision making (legislation), (2) budget, (3) policy, and (4) control. The role of the EP varies greatly among the four; even within each area a differentiation of competences of the EP exists.

Legislation   Four different procedures exist: consultation, cooperation, codecision and assent. In the procedure of consultation (in the past the main one) the role of the EP is limited to advice. This procedure now applies to a limited number of Community matters only. In the cooperation procedure the position of the EP is strengthened, as the Council can reject amendments of the EP only unanimously. If the Council wanted to go against the EP about Commission proposals with important financial implications, reconciliation of the different standpoints would be attempted. The field in which this procedure applies covers such matters as internal market, transport, competition, environment, development aid and some aspects of social policy. The procedure of codecision applies to matters related to the internal market, framework programmes for the environment, technology and transport. Finally, assent by parliamentary approval (practically an EP veto) is required for the conclusion of treaties and for extension of the Community. Its field of application covers matters such as outline measures for cohesion and so on.

Budget   The competence of the EP is quite extensive. It can accept the complete budget or reject it. It has different powers regarding the various parts of the budget. With regard to expenditure necessarily resulting from the Treaty ('obligatory' expenditure) it can only propose modifications within the total expenditure set. With regard to other expenditure, however, it can amend the draft budget.

Policy The EP can influence the scope of EU activities; it is entitled to ask for existing policies to be extended or amended and for new ones to be initiated.

Control The powers of the EP are limited, the major aspect of control being that the Commission has to account to the EP for its actions. It does so in answer to spoken or written questions and in the discussion of its annual General Report. In the extreme, the EP can force the Commission to resign by a motion of censure. The Council is not accountable to the EP, but the two bodies are in continuous dialogue.

Court of Justice

The treaties have established an original legal order. Rights are conferred and obligations imposed directly on citizens and authorities of member states by European law; member states do not need to intervene for these provisions to take effect. On the other hand, citizens can appeal to European rules in national courts. The proper and consistent interpretation and application of European law in all member states evidently called for a supreme body to settle conflicts; this task was entrusted to the European Court of Justice. The national judge is subordinated to the European Court of Justice. The ECJ's activity concerns both the treaties and the derived legislation, that is to say, all regulations, directives and decisions (see the next section).

The Court's *composition* is of 15 judges and nine advocates general. Judges and advocates general are appointed by member state governments, by mutual agreement, for a period of six years. They must satisfy the requirements valid in their own country for the fulfilment of the highest judicial offices. They must be entirely independent and cannot be dismissed.

When a question is put before the Court, the *procedure* is as follows. First, an advocate general is appointed to prepare the decision of the Court. He analyses the matter and relates the facts to the relevant legal rules. He then publicly draws his independent and impartial conclusions, which form the basis for the consultations and judgement of the Court. Actually the Court has no legal or police staff of its own; it relies on the goodwill of all member states involved for the enforcement of its ruling. The judgement of the Court is directly applicable in all member states.

Who has *access* to the European Court? Member states and EU institutions (Council, Commission and Parliament) have unlimited access. Natural and legal persons (companies, for instance) have only limited access; they may initiate proceedings in disputes relating to such acts, or the failure to act or give compensation, of the

Commission and the Council as affect their interests directly. In a national lawsuit, too, judgement may depend on relevant European law. Individuals can request a national judge who is not sure about the interpretation of European law to demand, before pronouncing judgement, a preliminary ruling from the European Court of Justice. The number of cases brought before the ECJ has increased rapidly in line with the rapid increase in matters regulated by the EU (see Table 18.3, p. 466). To cope with the workload of relatively less important matters, the Court of First Instance was created, attached to the Court of Justice. It deals with cases that particularly concern private citizens and/or business (competition, anti-dumping, coal and steel, compensation proceedings and so on). Its verdicts are subject to a right of appeal in the ECJ.

The *subject matters* brought before the Court were concentrated in the main areas of European policy making. The action of the Court has been very important in maintaining dynamism in the process of European integration. For example, the Court has repudiated, in many judgements, any form of protectionism with respect to free movement of goods and services within the EU, and in this way the realisation of the internal market has been safeguarded. The same holds for the preservation of undistorted competition; the many disputes between the Commission (which can act against violations of fair competition, imposing fines if necessary) and companies who disagree and have submitted their case to the Court have given rise to a very extensive jurisprudence.

Laws and rules, decision-making

Legal instruments

In order to carry out its tasks, the EU makes regulations, issues directives, takes decisions, makes recommendations or delivers opinions.[6]

- A *regulation* is general in its application; it is binding in its entirety and directly applicable in all member states. This means that national legislation, if existent, is overruled by regulations; indeed European law takes precedence over national law. The national governments have no right or need to take action once a matter has been settled by a European regulation, for it is automatically valid in all member states.
- A *directive* is binding, as to the result to be achieved, upon each member state to which it is addressed, but leaves the national authorities the choice of form and methods. So, to implement

directives, action of member states is needed in the form of national laws and decrees.

- A *decision* is binding in its entirety upon those to whom it is addressed.
- Recommendations and opinions have no binding force.

The process of legislation

Decisions about regulations and directives are made by a procedure that differs according to the matter in hand (see the previous section on the European Parliament). We will only present here a very schematic view of the common features of the legislative process (Figure 4.1) in which the differences in the involvement of the various institutions according to the applicable regime have not been represented. The process can be described in broad terms as follows.

1 *Preparation*

- The Commission elaborates a planned proposal with the help of its staff; to that end work discussions are often held with committees of national experts.
- The Commission presents its opinions and outlines its planned strategy in communications to the Council and the Parliament.
- The Council and the Parliament communicate their reactions to the Commission; the Commission revises its plans, establishes its proposal and submits it to the Council and to Parliament in the shape of draft regulations or directives.

2 *First reading (consultation)*

- The proposal is discussed in the Economic and Social Committee, in the Committee of Regions and in the Parliament.
- ESC, CR, EP and Commission form their opinions and communicate these to the Council.

3 *Second reading (negotiation)*

- The Council's decision on the proposal is prepared by the Committee of Permanent Representatives (COREPER). Most of the work is done in workgroups composed of national officials, created for the purpose, in which officials of the Commission are always represented. Any amendments proposed will be submitted by the COREPER to the Council, together with the ESC and EP positions and recommendations.
- The European Parliament discusses the Commission proposals,

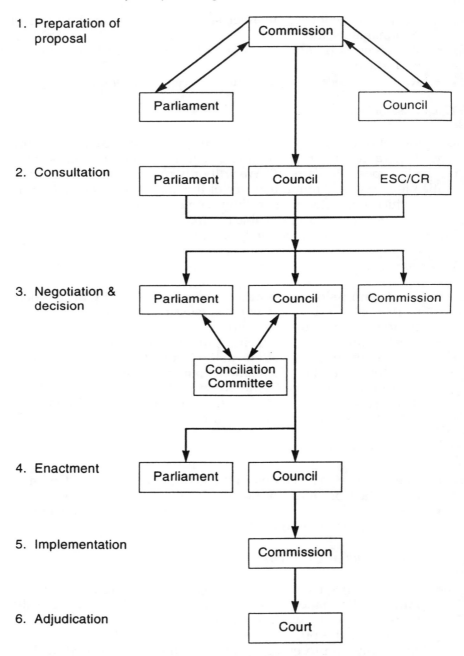

1. Preparation of proposal

2. Consultation

3. Negotiation & decision

4. Enactment

5. Implementation

6. Adjudication

Figure 4.1   A schematic view of the legislation-making process (Community matters)

the Council's position and, in cases where it has competences in the matter in hand (cooperation, codecision), negotiates with the Council in the framework of a Conciliation Committee.
- The Commission participates in this stage by adapting proposals, intermediating and so on.

4 Enactment

- Depending on the procedure followed, the Council decides about enactment (cooperation) or it elaborates a joint text, agreed upon both by the Council and the Parliament (codecision).
- The regulation, directive and so on is enacted by publication in the *Official Journal*.

The practice

The decision-making processes of the EU have determined the dynamics of the integration process. The EU institutional set-up is very conducive to international cooperation. In general national governments have an incentive to cooperate where policy coordination increases their control over domestic policy outcomes, in the sense that they create new options for policy. International organisations increase the efficiency of the multinational bargaining that leads to policy cooperation. The EU institutional set-up in general and the qualified majority voting in the Council in particular do represent very efficient forms for reducing the transaction costs of reaching cooperative agreements. Moreover, by simultaneously playing both the EU and the national political game, the governments of member states can use the legitimacy of the EU to overrule domestic lobbies, or to mobilise domestic coalitions in favour of agreements reached at the European level (Moravcsik, 1993).

However, several factors slow down the speed of decision making:

- Subjects. The EU deepened its policy integration at the moment when each of the members had set up a welfare state with government intervention in many areas. Policy integration was made a lot harder by the differences in models adopted by the various member states.
- Size. The increase in the number of actors that followed from the widening of the EU (from six to nine, to 12 and finally to 15) and the increased diversity of interests of its members make negotiations more complicated.
- Detail. There was a tendency to lay down in the European law not only the general principles but also most technical details. National officials have been insistent on this point (hence many

delays in COREPER), because their main concern was national acceptance and the consistency of national policy.

A *geographical differentiation* is often necessary to arrive at decisions. Indeed, in some cases progress can only be made by abandoning the idea of equal forms and full participation for all member states: this was the solution adopted for the European Monetary System, for the European Monetary Union and for social policy. This gives rise to expressions such as 'two-speed Europe', 'variable geometry', 'Europe à la carte' or 'flexibility'. The composition of the groups that participate in specific integration projects can be determined on the basis of the interests of each country and the efficiency of the integration process in the context of clubs (Fratianni, 1995).

The *sectoral segmentation* of the decision-making process has two effects that should be noted (Faber and Breyer, 1980). First, it tends to lead to unequal progress for different policy areas. The expert Council (of agriculture, for example) cooperates with the expert member of the Commission, seconded by his expert Directorate General, the expert Committee of the EP and with expert committees of national civil servants, after hearing experts from lobby groups. In some areas this leads quickly to results, while in other fields blockages may occur that are very difficult to remove. Next, it tends to lead to widely divergent forms of integration models for different areas (as we shall see in the next chapters), notwithstanding the efforts of the Commission and the European Council to maintain as much consistency and unity as possible.[7]

Committees

On the one hand, there is the wish to make the execution of the EU policy as efficient as possible (which implies concentration of power with the Commission). On the other hand, there is the wish of member states to keep as much control as possible on the way the implementation is done in practice (which implies some sort of involvement of the Council or the member states' representatives). The solution that has been found to this problem is the committee (Pedler and Schaefer, 1996). In some committees only experts of the Commission and of the member states are represented, in others experts from special interest groups or from the academic world are called upon too. In the past there has been a proliferation of committees; the number of those that appear in the budget exceed 300, but at least as many exist financed in less easily traceable ways. Committees have become very important elements in the EU policy-making process (van Schendelen, 1998).

After their function in the policy process one distinguishes several *types of committee*, the most important of which are:

- advisory (for example, internal market policy). The Commission determines the agenda, voting is with simple majority, and the Commission has only to take the opinion of the committee into account: it is not binding;
- management (notably used in the field of agricultural markets, see Chapter 9). The Commission proposes; the conclusions of the committee are not binding on the Commission. However, if the Council finds a qualified majority for an alternative proposal, the Commission has to execute the alternative;
- regulatory (harmonisation of national rules – for example, technical standards, see Chapter 14). The Commission can only take action on the basis of the positive advice that the committee has formulated with a qualified majority.

The number of people taking part in committees is estimated to exceed 20 000, only counting full members. This is several times the number of policy civil servants of the Commission (numbering some 5000).

Lobby groups

European decision making involves not only EU institutions, but many more (see, for example, Keohane and Hoffmann, 1991). These range from national ministries via government agencies to industry associations, professional organisations and individual firms. They generally act as lobby groups. Lobbying is best defined as the informal exchange of information in order to try to influence the decisions of public authorities (van Schendelen, 1993). With the growth of EU powers, firms, organisations, regions and so on increasingly realised that the EU could have a considerable influence on their vital interests. They realised that they should try in turn to influence EU decision making so as to make sure that their interests would be taken into account. Indeed EU lobbying has increased considerably, for different reasons (Pedler and van Schendelen, 1994):

- Growing regulatory authority: the areas in which the EU has acquired authority have gradually increased (including the internal market, economic and monetary union). Moreover the areas in which the Council decides with qualified majority have been stepped up considerably, which implies that national interest groups could no longer count on their national representations to block decisions that would harm their interests. To safeguard these interests it became necessary to try and influence all the stages of the European decision-making process.

- Discretion over spending considerable funds: the increased attention that the EU gives to aspects of economic and social cohesion has given rise to a considerable European redistribution from rich to poor regions. Being eligible for EU structural funds can make a big financial difference for a local authority infrastructure development. The same is true for a firm that may be eligible for funding of part of its research and development under a EU programme.

These developments have led to the increase in both the number and size of lobby groups that evolve around the EU institutions, notably Commission and Parliament (see Table 18.3, p. 466). It has been estimated (Anderson and Eliassen, 1991) that in 1990 there were up to 3000 lobby organisations and almost 10 000 lobbyists; their numbers have been growing considerably since.

Budget

General

The EU budget reflects the intermediate position the EU takes between a traditional international organisation and a federal state. The cost of international institutions is almost invariably paid from member states' contributions, each country paying a fixed percentage of total expenses. Most international organisations only incur staff and household expenses, larger outlays for special programmes being taken care of by those member states wanting to participate. With the European Union, things are different, on two essential counts. On the expenditure side, the EU has the cost of the large programmes it executes. On the receipts side, the EU has its own resources. These are pre-federal traits. The budget of a national state is generally of a considerable size, owing to the important financial consequences of many of its socio-economic policies. The EU differs from a national state in the following respects.

Allocation   With the relatively limited EU budget divided among a long list of programmes in different fields, only limited influence can be exerted on most segments of the economy, like transport, banking and so on. However the increased amounts spent on items like innovation do exert a significant influence on target groups. Agriculture, which devours huge sums, is traditionally the only field in which EU policy influences in detail developments in markets of a whole range of products.

Stabilisation   The EU budget is not an instrument of macro-economic policy; the treaty stipulates that the revenues and expenditure shown in the budget shall be in balance. That means that the EU's macro-economic policy stretches only to the coordination of the corresponding policies conducted by the member states. Moreover the total weight of the EU budget (a little over 1 per cent of EU Gross Domestic Product, against some 40 per cent of GDP in some member states, total EU budget being about 2 per cent of national budgets) is too low for an effective macro policy.

Redistribution   Although the expenses on EU regional and social policies have increased considerably over the past years, both in absolute and in relative terms, the redistributive power of the EU budget is still very limited if compared to national budgets (which include income tax and social security payments).[8]

Receipts

The EU has its own funds, but, unlike most federal and confederal structures, the EU cannot itself levy taxes, as it has no fiscal sovereignty. Its revenues consist essentially of EU claims on fiscal and para-fiscal levies and other receipts of the member states.[9] The EU's own resources consist mainly of the following (the figures mentioned are shares in total receipts, 2000 budget figures):

- *Customs duties* (14 per cent) are levied from products imported from outside the EU. The member state levying these duties will often be the one most favourably situated for importation into Europe, which is not necessarily the one for which the goods are destined (think, for instance, of German imports through the Dutch port of Rotterdam). In such a case, to allocate the duties to one member state seems unjust, so, from 1971, they have flowed into the EU treasury. They have decreased over time as external tariffs of the EU have been lowered continuously (see Chapters 5 and 17).
- *Agricultural levies and contributions* (1 per cent). Special types of import levies are the variable agricultural duties levied at the outer frontiers of the EU to adjust the price level of imported produce to EU prices. Duties and contributions are levied from internal EU produce as well, to control production and thus limit the need for financing from the Agricultural Fund. Once more, logically these levies accumulate to the EU. The levies

have tended to decrease over time as the EU has become increasingly a net exporter of agricultural produce (see Chapter 9).
- *Value-added tax* (36 per cent). A uniform basis has been established for value-added tax in all member states. A fixed percentage (at present 1.0) has to be transferred to the EU. Value-added tax was introduced in 1960 to replace fixed national contributions.
- *GDP-related income* (48 per cent). Since 1988 each member state pays a certain percentage of its GDP to the EU budget; this percentage is fixed every year. The relative importance of this revenue source has increased constantly. With GDP as indicator the contributions to the EU budget tend to take relative wealth levels of each member into account, thereby limiting the need for redistributive measures on the expenditure side.[10]

Expenditures

In the past, the total EU budget has shown a substantial real increase. It was needed primarily to cope with the expansion of the existing policy area (agriculture) and the introduction of new ones (cohesion, for instance). The major categories are (2000 budget figures):

- *Agriculture and fishery* (44 per cent). This category used to absorb a very large portion (two-thirds) of the total budget, mainly through the European Agricultural Fund's outlays for guaranteed prices. A series of decisions have been taken to control agricultural outlays with the effect that their relative share has considerably decreased (see Chapter 9).
- *Structural adaptation* (35 per cent). Expenditures to reinforce social and economic cohesion have assumed increasing weight over the years. Much of the outlay is financed from the so-called 'structural funds', like the European Regional Development Fund and the Social Fund (see Chapter 16).
- *Internal* (6 per cent). The programmes of major policy fields like energy, manufacturing industry, transport and research fall into this category. No large funds have been created; the amounts are spent directly on programmes (see Chapters 10 to 13).
- *External* (5 per cent). Under this heading falls development aid. In addition the European Development Fund (EDF) grants credits to developing countries (see Chapter 17).
- *Running costs* (5 per cent) consist of cost of staff, offices, travel, and so on. Some 5 per cent of costs fall under the category of miscellaneous expenses.

The procedure

The budget is established by an involved procedure,[11] the main steps of which, in Community matters, are as follows.

1 Preparation

- The Commission establishes a preliminary draft budget, taking into account the guidelines of the Council and the Parliament, and submits it to the Council of Ministers.
- The Council goes into consultation about the preliminary draft, amends it if necessary and turns it into a draft budget (acting by qualified majority). The draft is then sent to the European Parliament.

2 First reading

- The Parliament discusses the draft budget. It can only propose modification to the Council as far as the so-called 'compulsory expenditure' is concerned: that is to say, expenses springing from the legal commitments of the EU towards third parties (farmers enjoying guaranteed prices, developing countries with which cooperation agreements are in force, and so on). The European Parliament can amend the budget as regards so-called 'non-compulsory expenditure': that is to say, outlays associated with, for instance, regional development. If no amendments are proposed by the EP, the budget is adopted. If on the contrary the EP votes proposals for change, the procedure moves into its next stage.

3 Second reading

- The Council of Ministers receives the draft budget with proposals and amendments for a second reading. It must reach a qualified majority to adopt or reject the amendments and modifications proposed by the Parliament. The Council is fully competent to reject EP modifications with respect to compulsory outlays. Decisions on that score are final. If it rejects the amendments with respect to non-compulsory expenditure, the draft budget is again forwarded to Parliament, together with a report on the deliberations.
- Parliament deals with the second reading of the budget. It may reinstate the amendments rejected by the Council, acting by majority of the members and three-fifths of the votes cast. At the end of the second reading the Parliament may reject the budget.

- To avoid such conflicts, smooth the procedures and take the increasing influence of Parliament into consideration, a conciliation procedure between Parliament, Council and Commission has developed.

4   Adoption

- After a final round of negotiations between Council and Parliament, in which the Council decides on compulsory and Parliament on non-compulsory expenditure, the president of the European Parliament signs the budget, thus formalising its adoption.

Major issues

The budget procedure is subject to continuous criticism. There are four major points on which improvements are sought.

Responsibility   The budget authority of the EU is vested in the Council of Ministers and in the European Parliament. The Commission is involved only in the proposition of a draft budget. Conflicts that result from this situation are now largely resolved in the so-called 'consultation procedure'. The Parliament tries to have the final responsibility in budget matters.

Discipline   Many decisions bearing on expenses are made in a fragmented way, by specialised Councils of Ministers (for instance, of agriculture). Moreover some decisions of the Commission entail expenses. Many expense categories (such as the Agricultural Guarantee Fund) depend on market and monetary developments. The Council of Ministers draws up the framework for the budget. The Commission is responsible for making sure that policy measures that entail expenses are financed within the limits set by the Council.

Equity   The contribution to and the receipts from the budget are not in equilibrium for each member state. Some are net contributors, others net beneficiaries. This is felt to be acceptable in so far as rich member states fall into the first and poor member states into the second category.

Controls   The execution of many European policies demands the participation of member states, which makes the control function of the budget difficult to accomplish. The European Court of Auditors, charged with the control of expenditure and revenues and endowed with powers of investigation with regard to EU institutions as well as national administrative bodies, reports every year on the most important deficiencies, amongst them fraud. To remove their causes has proved extremely difficult, but should be improved in future by specific measures.

A recast of the institutional set-up

Causes for change

The European Union is committed to a further expansion in the future. In the coming decades it will integrate the countries of Central and Eastern Europe. Moreover it will have to cope with an increasing number of policy areas (for instance, security). The present set-up has been devised for a small group of countries (originally six) and a limited task (a Common Market). In the past it has been regularly adapted to cope with an increase in the number of members and with an increase in the EU competences. However, these have been of a limited size. Most observers do agree, that the present institutional set-up is inadequate for meeting present demands and are convinced that it is incapable of coping with the circumstances that will prevail after the imminent enlargement. The simple question then is how the Union can operate effectively when it has 30 members. How will it maintain its decision-making capacity and its cohesion so that the process of furthering European integration can continue? An Intergovernmental Conference has been convened in order to devise an adequate institutional set up for the enlarged EU. The Commission has made a set of proposals (EC, 2000) and the summit of Nice (of December 2000) has produced a text of which we will give here the essential elements.

Size and composition of the institutions

The functions and powers of each institution, and the balance between the institutions, have been maintained. However, the composition of each institution will be changed as of the year 2004. The Treaty of Nice fixes the number of seats (European Parliament) respectively the numbers of members (for instance Committee of the regions) and the weight of the votes (Council of Ministers) for each member country and for each candidate country. At each accession the composition of the institutions will be adapted according to these prefixed numbers. The situation for the EU27, which represents the situation where the present 15 members will be joined by all 12 candidate members, will look as follows:

- The European Parliament will have 732 members. Its composition has been changed so as to better reflect the size of the population of the different member countries (for instance 99 seats for Germany; 72 for the UK, France and Italy; 50 for Spain and Poland; 17 for Austria and Bulgaria).
- The size of the European Commission will be limited to one per member state. However, at the moment the Union will count 27 members, the size of the Commission will be fixed at a lower level than 27 by the Council. The Council will then also determine a system whereby the nomination of members of the Commission will rotate over the member states. The Commission shall be composed in such a way that it reflects the geographic and demographic reality of the member countries of the Union as a whole.
- The Court of Justice. There shall be one judge per member state. The Court of First Instance shall take care of more of the workload.
- The Court of Auditors. The tasks of the Court have been enlarged to cope with a number of new problems.
- The Economic and Social Committee and the Committee of the Regions will both have a maximum of 344 seats, whereby the largest member states will have 24, the medium sized member states 12 and the smallest five seats.

An effective decision-making process

It is vital for the smooth operation of the enlarged Union that the large differentiation in decision-making processes is streamlined. The Treaty of Nice has not adapted the realm of *qualified majority voting in the Council followed by a co-decision procedure for legislative decisions*. This would however have been justified. Indeed voting with qualified majority in most areas of policy is necessary because unanimity would place a very heavy strain on decision-making with almost 30 members. Moreover, the procedure of co-decision would do most justice to the democratic principles on which the Union is founded.

The *system of weighted votes in the Council* has been adapted. In the past the qualified majority threshold – the minimum number of votes required as a percentage of the total – has always been just above 70 per cent. It implied that a majority of the member states did agree to the proposal. The setting of the weights of the votes of each member state has been a source of vehement discussion. In order to avoid discussions on weighting at each round of enlargement, the number of votes has been fixed for each member state and each candidate member state. The number of votes is modulated as a function of population size. The large member states have 29 votes, the smallest three votes.

The new rules for qualified majority voting are somewhat more involved than the actual ones as they involve three criteria:

- the simple majority of member states (two thirds if the Council does not act on a proposal of the Commission);
- representing 170 votes from the total of 237 of the present 15 members and 258 of the 345 votes in the case of 27 member states;
- representing 62 per cent of the population of the Union (a complementary rule that a member country may invoke).

Summary and conclusions

- A strong institutional set-up safeguards the continuous development of the integration process.
- The usual division of powers in a state is partly to be found in the EU in the sense that, for Community matters, legislation is with Parliament, execution with the Commission and adjudication with the Court. The Council does not fit very well in this scheme as it has both important legislative and executive powers.
- Decision-making procedures in the EU are rather involved and differ according to subject area. In the past this has sometimes led to some sluggishness, but means have been found to provide an efficient and rapid decision-making procedure.
- The budget of the EU is relatively small. Notwithstanding that, it serves important allocation, very limited stabilisation and considerable redistribution purposes. The EU has its own financial means.
- The EU has to adapt its institutions and streamline its decision-making processes in order to continue to function effectively after further enlargement.

Notes

1 These competences have developed gradually; we will not refer to that evolution here, but come back to some relevant aspects of it in various chapters dealing with specific subjects.
2 Until 1967, the three Communities (ECSC, EEC and Euratom) had separate executive bodies (Commissions and Councils); the two other institutions (Parliament and Court) had decided to act for all three Communities. In 1967, a treaty merged the executive bodies of the three Communities as well.

Although institutions were merged, treaties were not. Indeed the merged bodies have continued to act according to the legal rules and procedures valid for the individual communities, as the matter in hand required. That situation has long been considered unsatisfactory and plans have been made to merge the treaties into one, with a single set of legal rules. The Treaty on European Union went a long way in integrating the various legal set-ups. The Treaty of Amsterdam has finally resulted in a consolidation of the various set-ups.

3   The strong institutional set-up of the regional representation is a consequence of the growing importance of sub-national government through decentralisation in many member states.

4   Usually one distinguishes between three pillars, whereby Union matters are divided between two pillars. For our purposes this distinction is not relevant as the economic impact of these policies is very limited.

5   In the past, unanimity was often tried. The Single European Act established that many decisions about the internal market, regional policy, and research and technology could be taken by qualified majority. The Treaties of Maastricht (1992) and Amsterdam (1997) have enlarged these areas. For an economic analysis of voting rules, see Mueller (1989), especially page 105.

6   These are the terms used by the EEC and Euratom; we will disregard the slightly different terms used by the ECSC for practically the same notions.

7   How serious the damage to consistency could be is illustrated by the outcomes of past negotiations concerning agriculture. In the 1970s and early 1980s, decisions repeatedly went against the principles of the EU, violating the unity of the market, exploding the financial frameworks and jeopardising the integration reached in other areas (monetary, for example). Even a kind of legal restraint imposed by the ministers of finance on the agricultural ministers met with no success.

8   Aid to developing countries (Lomé), to the CEEC (Tacis and Phare programmes) and to the Mediterranean countries (MEDA programme) constitute the reflection in the budget of the external policy of the EU (see Chapter 17).

9   Several proposals have been made to give the EU a 'fifth resource; one that is not tied to member states' contributions'. This would give the EU its own tax base. The Commission has analysed the pros and cons of several options, such as carbon tax; corporate tax; and seigniorage of the European Central Bank (CEC, 1998a). None has as yet been adopted.

10   A correction mechanism decreases the total contribution of the UK; the financing of these forgone receipts is made proportionally by the other member states (for proposals for simplification see CEC, 1998a).

11   For a thorough treatment, see CEC, 1993d.

PART II
COMMON MARKET

5 Goods

Introduction

The centrepiece of most integration schemes is the integration of goods markets. In this chapter we describe first in a theoretical way how markets evolve when barriers to movement are torn down. Next, we will describe the way in which the EU has realised the integration of the markets for manufactured goods of its member countries.

In the first section we treat some basic theoretical concepts and we will define and specify the advantages of integration, the barriers to trade and the reasons for protection. Next we will turn our attention to the way the EU has regulated the free movement of goods between its member states. We will also pay some attention to the external trade relations of the EU, although the main discussion of this point will be presented in Chapter 17.

The main body of the chapter will be devoted to a close analysis of the changes in the geographical as well as the product structure of the internal and external trade of the EU under the influence of integration. Having thus dealt with the quantity aspect of trade, we will next turn to the price aspect, finding out whether or not prices have converged under the pressure of integration.

Finally, we will indicate how liberalised goods movements in Europe have affected welfare and economic growth. As usual, the chapter will be rounded off with some conclusions and a summary.

Some basic theoretical concepts

Motives for obstacles

Many countries have protected their domestic producers from foreign competition by introducing obstacles to free trade (see Chapter

3). Protection against third countries is mostly achieved by *import restrictions*. From the extensive literature we have distilled the following arguments for such measures:

- Strategic independence. In times of war and supply shortages, a country should not depend on unreliable sources in other countries as far as strategic goods are concerned.
- Nurturing so-called 'infant industries'. The idea is that young companies and sectors which are not yet competitive should be sheltered in infancy in order for them to develop into adult companies holding their own in international competition.
- Defence against dumping. The healthy industrial structure of an economy may be spoiled when foreign goods are dumped on the market at prices below the cost in the country of origin. Even if the action is temporary, the economy may be weakened beyond its capacity to recover.
- Defence against social dumping. If wages in the exporting country do not match productivity, the labour factor is said to be exploited; importation from such a country is held by some to uphold such practices and is therefore not permissible.
- Boosting employment. If the production factors in the union are not fully occupied, protection can turn local demand towards domestic goods, so that more labour is put to work and social costs are avoided.
- Diversification of the economic structure. Countries specialising in one or a few products tend to be very vulnerable; problems of marketing such products lead to instant loss of virtually all income from abroad. This argument applies to small developing countries rather than to large industrialised states.
- Easing balance-of-payment problems. Import restrictions reduce the amount to be paid abroad, which helps to avoid adjustments of the industrial structure and accompanying social costs and societal friction (caused by wage reduction, restrictive policies, and so on).

Pleas for *export restriction* have also been heard. The underlying ideas vary considerably. The arguments most frequently heard are the following:

- Strategically important goods must not fall into the hands of other nations; this is true not only of military goods (weapons) but also of incorporated knowledge (computers) or systems.
- Export of raw materials means the consolidation of a colonial situation; it is hoped that a levy on exports will increase the

domestic entrepreneurs' inclination to process the materials themselves. If not, then at any rate the revenues can be used to stimulate other productions.

- If exported goods disrupt foreign markets, the importing country may be induced to take protective measures against the product and a series of other products; rather than risk that, a nation may accept a 'voluntary' restriction of the exports of that one product.

Categories of obstacles to free trade

Obstacles or trade-impeding factors fall into two categories, tariffs and so called 'non-tariff barriers', or NTBs.[1] They can be described as follows:

- Tariffs, or customs duties or import duties are sums levied on imports of goods, making the goods more expensive on the internal market. Such levies may be based on value or quantity. They may be in fixed percentages or variable amounts according to the price level aspired to domestically.
- Levies of similar effect are import levies disguised as administrative costs, storage costs or test costs imposed by the customs, and so on.
- Quantitative restrictions (QR) are ceilings put on the volume of imports of a certain good allowed into a country in a certain period (quota), sometimes expressed in money values. A special type is the so-called 'tariff quota', which is the maximum quantity which may be imported at a certain tariff, all quantities beyond that coming under a higher tariff.
- Currency restrictions mean that no foreign currency is made available to enable importers to pay for goods bought abroad.
- Other non-tariff impediments are all those measures or situations (such as fiscal treatment, legal regulations, safety norms, state monopolies or public tenders) which ensure a country's own products' preferential treatment over foreign products on the domestic market.

Why do away with protection?

Classical international trade theory teaches us that protection has important negative effects on prosperity[2] and that the best way to avoid these negative effects is for all the countries of the world to adopt perfect free trade. The advantages of free trade are:

- more production and more prosperity through better allocation

of production factors, each country specialising in the products for which it has a comparative advantage;
- more efficient production thanks to scale economies and keener competition;
- improved 'terms of trade' (price level of imported goods with respect to exported goods) for the whole group in respect of the rest of the world.

Why a customs union?

Countries, finding progress on the score of worldwide trade liberalisation too slow, try to adopt as a second-best strategy[3] a geographically limited form of free trade, as represented by a customs union. Recall that a customs union implies free trade among partners, but protection of the entire union against the rest of the world. So we move from a situation in which country A operates tariffs against all other countries to a situation in which it applies tariffs to third countries only and not to country B.

The *theory of customs unions* is relatively recent[4] (see Machlup, 1977). It relates to the gains and losses incurred by the establishment of such unions. In economic terms, the creation of the CU is warranted only if the former outweigh the latter. In political terms, it is feasible only if the advantages and disadvantages are fairly distributed among partners.

The effects of a customs union between countries A and B are best studied by making a distinction between trade creation, trade diversion (Viner, 1950) and trade expansion (Meade, 1955). We can explain these effects as follows:

- *Trade creation* will occur when trade between partners A and B increases. In country A, demand will shift from the expensive protected domestic product to the cheaper product from the partner country, implying a shift from a less efficient to a more efficient producer.
- *Trade diversion* will occur when imports from the efficient or cheap producer 'world market' are replaced by imports from a higher-cost (or less efficient) producer, namely, the 'partner country'. That country's products can be sold more cheaply in country A than world market production, because the CU imposes a protective tariff on imports from W, while leaving imports from the partner country free.
- *Trade expansion* will occur because the lower market price in A stimulates total domestic demand, which will be satisfied by foreign trade (either from the partner or from the world market).

For a better understanding of the nature and volume of these three effects, let us take a close look at Figure 5.1, which gives the situation for country A on the left-hand side and for country B on the right. We assume that the supply from producers in the rest of the world is fully elastic at a price level p_w. The corresponding supply is represented in the diagrams by the horizontal line S_w. Assume that, as a high-cost producer, country A enables its industry to capture part of the home market by introducing a fairly high tariff. Country B, on the contrary, produces at rather low costs, and needs only a low tariff to make sure that its producers can cover the entire internal demand. Assume now that countries A and B form a customs union which establishes a common outer tariff t^*, the average of the tariffs of countries A and B. Once the customs union is established, supply and demand in the area will settle at a price p_{cu}. Now, country A will buy all its imports (BE) from the partner country, p_{cu} being lower than p_{w+t^*}. Production in country A will be O_aB. Country B, for its part, produces the quantity O_bE', of which $B'E'$ (equal to BE) in excess of its home demand (O_bB'); B exports this quantity to the partner country.

What, then, are the trade effects of the creation of this customs union? The effects differ according to the initial situation (see Table 5.1). Let us take the two cases of protection and free trade of the previous section as examples.

- *Country A*. If protection marks the initial situation of country A, a positive development occurs. A new trade flow (BE) occurs between partners, of which CD is trade diversion; it replaces the imports that used to come from other countries in the world. Trade creation is BC and trade expansion DE. On balance, trade has increased in our example ($BC + DE$ being larger than CD) and international specialisation has intensified accordingly. Starting from free trade for country A, a negative development occurs. Trade actually diminishes by AB on the producer side and by EF on the consumer side. Moreover BE is diverted from the lower-cost world producer to the high-cost partner country.
- *Country B*. Starting from free trade, the introduction of a common tariff stops the trade that existed between B and W, which implies negative trade creation ($-A'B'$) and expansion ($-B'X$) as less efficient home producers take over from more efficient world producers. Starting from a situation of protection in B, a customs union does not give rise to trade effects (but for the exports $B'E'$), as there were no imports from the world anyway.

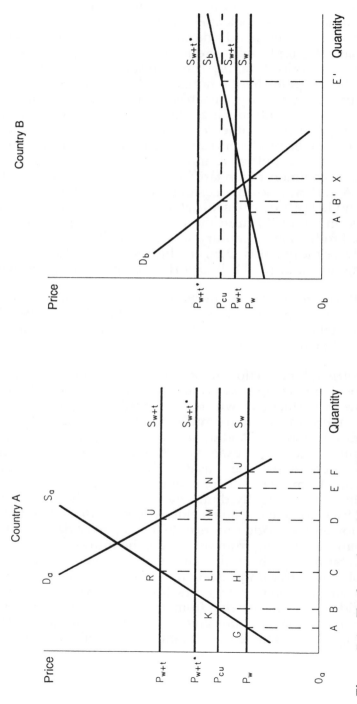

Figure 5.1 Trade and production effects of a customs union, countries A and B

Table 5.1   Trade effects of a customs union, countries A and B

Effect	Starting situation			
	Free trade		Protection	
	A	B	A	B
Creation	−AB	−A′B′	BC	*
Expansion	−EF	−B′X	DE	B′E′
Diversion	BE	*	CD	*

Note: * Not applicable.

Welfare effects of a customs union

What are the advantages and disadvantages ensuing from the customs union and the tariff? On the one hand, trade diversion tends to make production less rational, which is a disadvantage. On the other hand, trade creation and trade expansion make production more efficient, which is advantageous. To get an idea of the magnitude of the effects, consider Figure 5.2, starting from protectionism. We assume that the price for the customs union is p_{cu}.

- *Country A.* The advantages on the production side (trade creation *BC*) are represented by the triangle *KRL*. This indicates that the saving on production cost equals, on average, half the difference in costs between home production and that in country B ($p_{w+t} − p_{cu}$), leaving economic resources available for other purposes. On the consumption side (trade expansion equal to *DE*) the advantages are represented by the triangle *MUN*. The disadvantages for country A are represented by the square *HLMI*. For the amount of trade equal to *CD*, which has been diverted, production inputs have been higher than necessary. In our example the establishment of a customs union produces a net advantage for country A.
- *Country B.* The disadvantages are on the consumer as well as the producer side. The consumer gets less quantity for more money; his loss is indicated by the horizontally shaded little triangle *VXU′*. On the producer side, there is a production loss indicated by the horizontally shaded triangle *R′ZW*. The producers in B will of course enjoy a net gain.

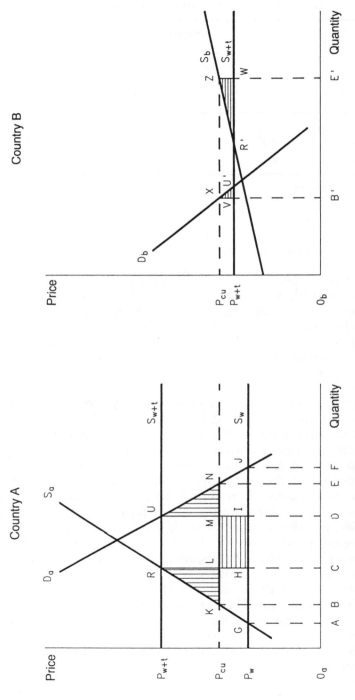

Figure 5.2 Welfare effects of a (trade-diverting) customs union

Alternative cases can be imagined in which the profits or the losses are heavier. If, for instance, the only effect is trade expansion, there will be larger net advantages, as can be shown by a slight variation of the former example. Assume the supply curve of country B is equal to that of the world. The net effect of a customs union between countries A and B will be positive, in fact the reverse of the negative one found for country A passing from free trade to protectionism (Figure 5.1). We can vary the differences between p_{cu} and p_w and the gradient of the supply and demand curves in such a way that the trade diversion exceeds trade expansion, so that the establishment of a customs union produces a net disadvantage to the world as a whole.

The present examples have a number of limitations. First, they refer to only one product. To judge the economic desirability of a customs union by its static effects, the profits and losses for all products involved need to be calculated, under consideration of the specific circumstances obtaining for each. Next, they treat only tariffs. The production and welfare effects of non-tariff barriers differ from those of tariffs, but are quantitatively at least as important.[5]

Modern analysis based on mathematical models shows that regional integration unambiguously benefits the member countries and hurts the outside country (Olofsdotter and Torstensson, 1998).

The incidence of positive and negative effects

Various factors influence the occurrence of positive and negative effects of a CU.

- *The production structure.* Two countries can be complementary or competitive. Viner (1950) pointed out that, with complementary production structures the advantages of a customs union cannot be very important. If, on the contrary, the production of either country is a potential competitor of the other, specialisation along the lines of inter-industry trade is probable and the advantages are likely to be relatively important (as with, for example cars of different makes).
- *The size of the union.* The more numerous and the larger the countries participating in the CU, that is, the larger its share in total world trade, the better the prospects for division of labour and the smaller the risk of trade diversion (Viner, 1950; Meade, 1955; Tinbergen, 1959).
- *The level of the tariffs.* As the initial tariffs of the trade partners are higher, the attendant inefficiencies will be worse and the welfare effects of the abolition of tariffs greater (Viner, 1950; Meade, 1955). On the other hand, the introduction of high

common external tariffs against third countries will reduce the positive effect.

- *Transport and transaction costs.* The increased trade has to be realised physically, for which efficient transport is required. Failing that, the transport costs will replace the tariffs as an obstacle to further specialisation. For that reason, customs unions tend to be concluded between contiguous countries (Balassa, 1961). Transaction costs between linguistic areas tend to be higher than within such areas.
- *Flexibility.* The advantages are smaller if production bottlenecks prevent the full accomplishment of advanced specialisation and the corresponding reallocation of production.
- *Terms of trade.* Importing countries united in a customs union can enforce lower supply prices on the world market (for instance, by trade restrictions or bargaining power). In this way they may improve their terms of trade (export price divided by import price). The increase in the members' welfare would then be accompanied by a loss in non-members' welfare (Petith, 1977).
- *Improved technical efficiency.* An economy that is subject to new competitive pressures will try to improve its production methods. This will lead to a lowering of the supply curve of domestic producers, in turn leading to welfare increases exceeding the static welfare increases described in the previous section. The dynamic advantages are larger the higher the industrial interwovenness of a country (Balassa, 1961).
- *Economies of scale.* For many production processes average cost decreases with the increased scale of production. Integrated markets permit the taking advantage of such low-cost production (see, for examples, Chapter 10). Countries with domestic production of industries subject to economies of scale are likely to benefit from integration (Krugman, 1980).

EU regime

Rationale and principles

The advantages from free trade predicted by theory have incited the founders of the EU to adopt very clearly *the principle of the free internal movement of goods*. This is expressed in the Treaty (Article 23 EC) in the following words:

> The Community shall be based upon a Customs Union, which shall cover all trade in goods and which shall involve the prohibition be-

tween member states of customs duties on imports and exports and of all charges having equivalent effect.

By this definition, the freedom of movement within the EU extends to goods from third countries for which, in the importing member state, the administrative conditions have been met, and the (common) customs tariffs, or measures of equal effect, settled by the importing member state (Article 24 EC).

Gradual elaboration of a common policy

In the 1960s the most important targets as to the liberalisation of goods trade among the original six member countries could be realised.

- *Import duties and levies* of equal effect in force between member states could be abolished a year and a half earlier than foreseen in the Treaty (July 1968).
- *Quantitative restrictions and measures of equal effect* among member states were also eliminated, most already in the early 1960s.
- A number of NTBs were abolished, partly under the impulse of the Commission's action programmes, partly as the result of verdicts of the Court of Justice.

In the 1970s and 1980s the new member states – both those which joined in 1972 (the UK, Ireland and Denmark) and those which joined in the 1980s (Spain, Portugal and Greece) – have abolished all quotas and tariffs in intra-EU trade during a transition period of several years. However, the removal of many NTBs proved very difficult as they were closely related to national regulations set up to pursue important objectives of public policy. Examples include the differences between member states in:

- levels and structure of indirect taxation (as on tobacco and liquor);
- technical standards set for the protection of the worker, the consumer and the general public (for example, for pharmaceuticals);
- the consequence of the external policy (national quotas for textile products);
- national industry-oriented government procurement policies (such as those on telecommunications, computers and defence equipment); and
- administrative stipulations for such diverse matters as statistics and crime.

During the 1985–2000 period the Commission took a bold approach to end the fragmentation of important segments of the European market for goods (and services). Its White Paper on the completion of the internal market (CEC, 1985d) proposed doing away with all these remaining barriers by 1992 by abolishing the controls at the internal frontiers. The so-called 'Single Act' (CEC, 1986a) laid down these objectives in a treaty and gave increased powers to the institutions of the EU to pass all necessary legislation to reach them. This programme has since been executed and a huge number of regulations and directives have been adopted, with the result that the single market for goods is now practically completed (see also Chapters 10 and 14). Note that the accession of Austria, Sweden and Finland in the middle of the 1990s could be realised without special rules as their trade with the EU had already been liberalised in the framework of the European Economic Area (see Chapter 3).

External situation

In line with the definition of the customs union (Chapter 2) the Treaty (Article 23 EC) obliges the member states of the EU to adopt 'a common customs tariff in their relations with third countries'. At the end of the transition period, the *common external tariff* (CET) came into force.[6] For the CET the arithmetical average of the duties applied in the various countries was to be taken as the basis. The national tariffs were gradually adjusted to that CET as the mutual tariffs were broken down. France and Italy in particular had to adjust themselves to freer trade, while the other member states had to introduce more protection against third countries.

The level and structure of the CET have been adapted several times under the influence of a drive for *world-wide liberalisation of trade* relations. This has taken place in the framework of negotiations on tariffs and quotas of the General Agreement on Tariffs and Trade (GATT) (the so-called 'Dillon round' of 1960–62, the Kennedy round of 1964–7, the 'Tokyo round' of 1973–9 and the 'Uruguay round' that was completed in 1993). The EU support for this reduction was based on the Treaty (Article 131), that commits the EU 'to contribute in the common interest to the harmonious development of world trade, the progressive abolition of restrictions on international trade, and the lowering of customs tariffs'.

Apart from the general negotiations mentioned, the EU has negotiated trade privileges with certain groups of countries with which it wants to keep up *special relations*. The most advanced agreement is the Free Trade Treaty with the countries in Western Europe that are not EU members. Furthermore agreements have been made to allow other groups of states privileges in their access to the EU market (Chapter 17, dealing with the EU's external policy, will discuss these agreements in some detail).

The CET system applies in general to all manufactured products. It does not apply to agricultural products: the agricultural market of the EU is protected by a separate system of variable levies on imports and subsidies on exports (export restitutions) for variable quantities of produce (Chapter 9 will explain the details of that system).

Trade patterns

Relative importance of total foreign trade

International goods trade is essential to the economies of EU member states, as is illustrated by the figures of Table 5.2, representing the relative importance of goods trade in gross domestic product.[7] First, the table shows that the *trade–GNP ratio*, indicating the degree to which a country participates in international goods trade, depends on two factors:

- *Size of economy*: for large countries, the value of goods trade (average of imports and exports, including intra-EU trade) amounts to about one-fifth of their GDP, while for smaller countries with an open economy (The Netherlands, Belgium and Ireland) the percentage rises to some two-thirds;
- *Level of development*: low-income countries like Greece (moreover historically weak in goods trade, having always applied itself to the export of services) and Spain and Portugal show relatively low figures, high-income countries like Sweden show high figures.

The figures show further very clearly that, in almost 40 years, the international integration of the economies of the EU member states by the exchange of goods has considerably increased (on average from 16 to about 25). This was realised mostly in the period 1960–1980: after that period growth levelled off.

Finally the table shows that the high increase in the trade–GDP ratios is notably due to the increase in *intra-EU trade*, itself the result of the progressive integration of the goods markets of the EU. The involvement of the EU as a whole in trade with the rest of the world has not suffered from this intra-EU dynamism; indeed the ratio for the extra-EU trade stayed more or less on the same level over the whole period. The orientation of trade changed over the period under discussion. In 1960, trade was relatively more oriented towards

Table 5.2 Percentage share of goods imports and exports[a] in total GDP of member states (current prices), 1960–2000

	1960 imp	1960 exp	1970 imp	1970 exp	1980 imp	1980 exp	1990 imp	1990 exp	2000[c] imp	2000[c] exp
Germany	14	16	16	19	23	24	23	26	22	25
France	10	11	13	12	20	17	19	18	20	21
Italy[b]	12	9	14	12	22	17	16	15	18	20
Netherlands	38	34	39	35	45	43	44	46	41	46
Belgium/Lux	34	32	43	44	57	51	58	57	59	63
UK	18	15	18	16	22	22	23	19	22	19
Ireland	34	23	38	24	55	42	46	52	60	71
Denmark	30	24	27	20	29	24	24	26	25	26
Spain	6	6	13	6	16	10	18	11	25	19
Portugal	19	12	22	13	32	16	37	24	33	22
Greece	17	5	16	5	22	11	24	10	25	9
Austria	n.a.	n.a.	24	19	31	22	31	26	32	30
Sweden	n.a.	n.a.	21	20	27	24	24	25	30	37
Finland	n.a.	n.a.	24	21	30	27	34	20	27	33
EU15 (average)	16	15	18	17	24	22	24	23	25	25
Intra	6	6	10	10	13	13	15	15	15	16
Extra	10	9	8	7	11	9	9	8	10	10

Notes:
[a] The exports of goods comprise all (national or nationalised) goods carried permanently, free or against payment, from a country's economic territory abroad; for imports, a similar definition applies.
[b] Upward correction of GDP in the mid-1980s.
[c] 1999 figures.

Source: European Commission, *Statistical Annex of European Economy*, No. 68 1999, Tables 38, 39, 42, 43.

third countries than to the countries that are now part of the EU15. In 1970 already, this situation was reversed; in line with theoretical expectations, integration has led to intra-EU trade increasingly out-weighing extra-EU trade.

The openness with respect to third countries used to be much higher for the EU than for the other major trade partners in the world, the USA and Japan. However, the gap between the EU and the USA has closed over the past decades. In that period, the USA has switched from a relatively autarkic economy connected to its large size to an economy that is more dependent on the rest of the world as a result of the liberalisation of trade, the globalisation of production and intensified specialisation. For the smaller Japanese economy, one would have expected a degree of openness higher than that of the EU and the USA. The opposite is true, however. This is notably due to the low level of imports into Japan (CEC, 1992a). In recent years the openness of the Japanese economy has also increased; for exports it is now at about the same level as the EU and the USA.

Internal trade among member states of the EU

The member states of the EU trade more among themselves than with third countries. We know from a previous section that the creation of a customs union may divert, or create, trade flows. Despite measures taken to prevent large-scale shifts (EFTA/EU custom tariff agreements), trade-creating and trade-diverting effects were experienced at the moments of the formation and enlargement of the EU. Figure 5.3 (adapted from Italianer, 1994) gives an illustration of these effects. It shows the development over time of trade between the successive old and new members of the EU.[8]

Since 1960, for the six original member states, the EU share in trade has risen considerably faster than trade with other countries. Trade among the six original EU member states between 1958 and 1972 (the year of the extension with the UK, Ireland and Denmark) had increased ninefold, while goods trade with the rest of the world grew by a factor of three. In the same period the importance of the EU as a trade partner increased with respect to two of the three new member states (trade with Denmark declined).

After 1972, the year of *the first enlargement*, the picture changed somewhat. The trade of the six original member states with the three new ones increased very fast between 1972 and 1978, showing an effect of integration. However, EU6 trade with third countries grew even faster in the same period, as a consequence of the oil price increase. Trade between the original six between 1972 and 1985 was less dynamic, owing partly to the effect of the oil crisis and partly to some relative trade diversion to the three new member countries. For

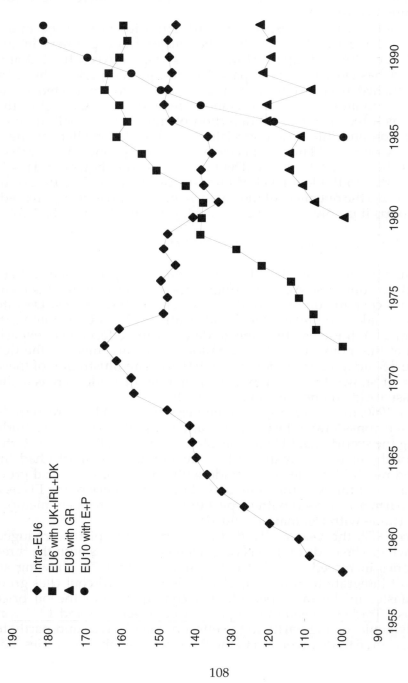

Figure 5.3   Impact of accession on trade

the candidate members, Greece, Spain and Portugal, however, the relative importance of the EU to their foreign trade remained fairly constant during the 1960s and 1970s.

The *post-1985* period is marked by three major events:

- *Second enlargement*. The effects of the integration of the three Mediterranean countries in the EU economy are rather mixed. The integration of Greece has not been very successful in trade terms. On the contrary, the integration of the Iberian countries has entailed a very dynamic expansion of intra-Union trade, certainly helped by the marked decrease in oil prices.
- *Completion of the internal market*. In the 1985–95 period, the growth of intra-EU trade has been particularly dynamic.
- *Third enlargement*. The growth of trade with the three member countries that joined in the early 1990s (Austria, Sweden, Finland) is not given in Figure 5.3, as the integration effects have been spread over a long period marked by continuous trade liberalisation between the two groups of countries.

Geographical pattern of internal trade

The geographical structure of internal trade in the present EU of 15 member states is marked by large flows between some pairs of countries and much smaller flows among others (Table 5.3). By far the largest trade partner (accounting for almost one-quarter of the total) on the import as well as the export side is Germany. This country is the largest exporter to and importer from all other EU member states, with the exception of Spain (France), Ireland (UK) and Portugal (Spain). On the trade balances of all member states, the exports to and imports from the other members are of the same order of magnitude and fairly equilibrated. The same (approximate balance of imports and exports) is largely true even of the bilateral trade flows, as appears from a pair-wise comparison of columns and rows.

Has the integration process changed the trade orientation of the member states? This has been analysed with the help of a linkage procedure clustering countries by their trade orientation in different reference years by Peschel (1985, 1999). The 1955 pre-EU situation predicted neither the formation of the EU6 (Italy, Germany, France and the Benelux belonging to different blocs) nor that of EFTA (whose member countries also belonged to different clusters). Actual integration did not change that picture very fast: by 1975, the nucleus of the EU (though without Germany) shows up but EFTA had not yet emerged. Only in 1981 did trade figures begin to reflect the institutional arrangements: a central cluster is clearly visible, made up of

Table 5.3 Intra-EU15 trade (billion euro) by country, 1998

From \ To	GER	FRA	ITA	NET	B/L	UK	IRL	DEN	SPA	POR	GRE	AUS	SWE	FIN	EU15[a]
Germany	·	51	34	39	28	35	4	8	17	5	3	21	9	5	256
France	50	·	26	16	24	25	3	2	22	4	1	3	4	2	181
Italy	36	26	·	9	8	14	2	2	11	2	3	5	3	1	120
Netherlands	42	16	8	·	20	17	2	2	5	1	1	2	4	2	123
Bel/Lux	29	25	8	22	·	14	2	1	4	1	1	1	3	1	113
UK	33	24	13	19	13	·	13	3	9	3	1	2	6	3	143
Ireland	6	3	1	2	2	14	·	—	1	—	—	—	1	—	31
Denmark	9	2	2	3	1	4	—	·	1	—	—	—	5	1	29
Spain	15	19	9	4	4	8	1	1	·	6	1	1	1	1	71
Portugal	5	3	2	1	1	2	—	—	6	·	—	—	—	—	21
Greece	2	1	2	1	—	1	—	—	1	·	·	—	—	—	10
Austria	23	3	5	2	1	2	—	—	1	—	1	·	1	—	39
Sweden	10	4	2	4	3	6	1	4	2	—	—	1	·	3	40
Finland	5	2	1	2	1	3	—	1	1	—	—	·	4	·	20
EU15[a]	265	179	114	125	106	145	28	26	79	23	11	37	42	19	1198

Note: [a] Totals may differ due to rounding.

Source: Eurostat, *External and Intra-European Union Trade, Monthly Statistics*, 1999.

the member states of EU9, to which Greece and Spain were already associated but from which Denmark was still keeping apart.

The development towards a stronger clustering of all EU countries has been going on since; in 1990, only two small sub-clusters subsisted (France–Spain and UK–Ireland–Norway) (Poon and Pandit 1996).[9] By 1997 the process seemed completed as the whole of the EU shows up as a distinct cluster; although with three sub-clusters: 1) the core; 2) the British Isles; 3) the Nordic countries (Peschel, 1999).

The dissolution of the Comecon group and the opening up to world trade of the CEEC has profoundly changed the situation of these countries. The change shows up in the data: by 1997 all CEEC had dissociated themselves from the former USSR cluster. However, their trade integration with the EU had not yet progressed sufficiently far so as to let them join the EU cluster.

External trade of the EU, by partner

The EU15 is the world's largest trade partner. Over the past decades, exports and imports of the EU (without intra-EU trade) amounted to some 20 per cent of total world exports and imports, so trade of the EU has increased at about the same pace as total world trade.

Table 5.4 shows the relative importance of EU trade with groups of third countries (without intra-EU trade). Owing to data limitations it is split up in two parts. For the period 1960–80, the data refer to the EU12, so give the situation as if that grouping had existed all over the period. For the 1980–98 period, the data refer to the EU15. Taking the change in statistical basis into account, one observes that, for the whole period 1960–98, trade relations were much closer with one group than with others. This is due to a number of factors, such as attraction (highly developed economies), friction (distance, see also the next section) and policy (see Chapter 17). Let us look briefly at each of the different *categories of countries*.

Paramount among trade partners of the EU are the countries in the western industrialised world. Within that group, the small bloc of countries that formed EFTA held a large and increasing share in the EU12 trade. This feature can be explained by their high income-level, their small distance from the EU and the absence of trade barriers (the EU has concluded a free-trade arrangement with these countries). The high figures for the USA and the increasing ones for Japan reflect not only the economic power of the two countries, but also the high level of intra-industry trade among highly developed economies.

The developing countries have a more modest and since 1980 a decreasing share. Within that group the associated African (ACP)

Table 5.4 Geographical distribution (in percentages) by groups of countries, of extra-EU15 trade in goods, 1960–98

Country (group)	Imports EU12 1960	1970	1980	Imports EU15 1980	1990	1998	Exports EU12 1960	1970	1980	Exports EU15 1980	1990	1998
Industrialised	49	51	44	39	52	48	46	53	45	38	51	44
EFTA	15	17	17	10	13	11	22	25	26	16	15	11
United States	20	22	17	18	21	21	14	18	13	14	21	22
Japan	1	3	5	6	12	9	1	3	2	3	6	4
Rest of OECD	12	8	5	5	6	6	10	7	4	6	8	7
Third World	47	43	49	52	38	38	48	40	47	50	39	38
Mediterranean	7	9	8	9	10	8	13	10	13	15	12	12
ACP	10	9	7	8	5	3	9	8	8	9	5	3
OPEC	9	8	19	20	5	2	3	6	4	10	6	4
Latin America	9	8	5	6	6	4	8	7	6	5	3	5
Asia	8	5	7	7	12	20	10	7	7	7	11	13
Other Third World	12	9	10	3	1	1	15	10	16	4	2	1
Former centrally planned	5	6	7	10	10	14	5	7	8	12	10	17
CEEC	3	4	3	4	5	10	3	5	4	7	6	13
USSR/CIS	2	3	4	5	5	4	2	3	4	5	4	4

Source: Eurostat, *External trade, Statistical Yearbook; External and intra-European Union trade, Statistical Yearbook*, various years.

countries and Latin America lose ground, the ACP notwithstanding their privileged access to the EU market. The Asian countries gain considerable market share, which is due to their competitive advantage in many labour-intensive industries. The position of OPEC improved dramatically as a result of the increases in oil prices of the 1970s, to decrease as dramatically since 1980 with the fall in oil prices.

The centrally planned economies accounted for only a small portion of the EU12 trade (just under 10 per cent), reflecting to a large extent a deliberate choice by their governments to keep trade with the West to a minimum. About 10 years ago that strategy was hesitantly changed. The position of the CEEC has improved remarkably in recent years as the result of several factors: their rapid transition to a market economy, their proximity to the EU, and their free trade with the EU (in view part of their future accession (see Chapter 17)).

External EU trade, by commodity groups

The type of commodity[10] internationally traded by the EU[11] has changed quite significantly in the period of the past decades (Table 5.5). The change in the structure of *EU import trade* reflects the shift away from the heavy dependence on other parts of the world for raw materials and energy towards inter-industry trade in manufactured products. Not visible in the table is the steep increase in the money value of energy imports that occurred in the 1970s and 1980s (see Chapter 11), an effect that had been expunged by 1990. On the *export side*, manufactured products, with machinery and transport equipment in the lead, are observed to account for about three-quarters of total exports, a share which has gradually increased over time.

Is the pattern of specialisation reproduced in Table 5.5 also indicative of the sectors for which the EU is most competitive on international markets? Indeed the EU is generally considered strongest in capital-intensive industries (where wage costs are less relevant) and in knowledge-intensive products (for which other countries do not always have the qualified labour).

In the 1970–90 period, the EU used to specialise rather in medium technology products and to hold a neutral position in low technology products (OECD, 1987a). For the products of the former categories (motor vehicles, wireless and television sets, office machinery, other machinery) the competitive position of the EU on its own market has been gradually eroded (Jacquemin and Sapir, 1988; CEC, 1993b). This deterioration of the EU's position was thought to be caused by a segmented home market. To remedy that situation, two types of action were taken: an industrial policy specifically aimed at stimulating innovation (see Chapter 10) and a policy focusing on the

Table 5.5   Distribution of the EU's[a] foreign trade by commodity group, in percentages, 1960–2000

Commodity group	Imports		Exports	
	1960	2000	1960	2000
Food, drink, tobacco	25	7	9	6
Energy products	16	11	4	2
Raw materials	26	6	4	2
Chemicals	4	8	10	13
Machinery, transport equipment	10	37	37	47
Other manufactured products	17	29	33	28
Miscellaneous	2	2	3	2
Total	100	100	100	100

Notes: [a]   1960: EU12, 2000: EU 15: estimates based on figures for 1999.

Source: Eurostat; various statistics; *External Trade, Statistical Yearbook*, External and intra-European Union trade, various years, Luxemburg.

improvement of market conditions (see Chapter 14). In recent years these policies seem to have had a positive effect, although the position of the EU in certain areas are still reason for concern (CEC, 1999a).

Explanation of spatial trade patterns

Some 'traditional' approaches

Trade theory puts a heavy accent on comparative advantage. In practice, the concept is rather difficult to work with, however. Prices and availability of factors are not easy to integrate in our framework with export and import structures. The suggestion has been made (Balassa, 1977) first to analyse the so-called 'revealed comparative advantage' (RCA) and then relate that RCA to relative cost. However systematically relating these RCA indices for the EU to explanatory factors proves too difficult.

Trade patterns may also be influenced by trade impediments. Among these we find structural factors as well as government and private distortions. Tariffs occupy a preponderant place in integration theory. Distance has also been cited in that respect. Distance-bridging transport has a clear effect on aggregate trade flows (Linnemann, 1966; Aitken, 1973). This is also the case in the EU on the disaggregate level of manufacturing industries (Bröcker, 1984). We will come back to the integration effects of tariff cuts in the last part of this chapter. In recent times the study of goods trade has tended to focus on other aspects, highlighting the role of industrial organisation (see Chapter 10), technology and so on.

Intra-industry specialisation

Contrary to what some had expected, the further opening up of the national markets for manufactured goods by the integration schemes of the EU and EFTA and the liberalisation in GATT has not produced specialisation among countries along the lines of traditional trade theory. According to this theory one country will specialise in one good, for instance steel, and the other in other goods, for instance port wines, on the basis of comparative advantages. On the contrary, at the beginning of the 1960s it became clear that the specialisation occurred *within sectors*, with, for example, both countries producing cars, but of different types: 'The more similar the demand structures of two countries, the more intensive potentially the trade between these two countries' (Linder, 1961).

Trade liberalisation in Europe has been accompanied by considerable increases in the extent of intra-industry trade (IIT). This was the case for all member countries of the EU6 in the 1958–77 period (Balassa, 1966, 1975).[12] It was equally the case for all member countries of the EU9 in the 1970–87 period (Buigues *et al.*, 1990).[13] It was finally the case for the EU15 during the period up to 1997 (CEC, 1996a; CEC, 1998). The increase in IIT is particularly striking for the traditionally less developed member states (Portugal, Spain and Ireland) which reflects the reorientation of their production towards higher value added activities.

Several factors can explain intra-industry trade. The first is scale economies; if there is much product differentiation and a wide range of products, each country will produce only a limited sub-set (such as the trade in cars produced in different European countries). Technology is another factor; if R&D produces a rapid turnover of products protected by patents, each country will specialise in different segments of the market (pharmaceutical products are a case in point). Moreover the strategies of multinational companies lead to flows of intermediary goods among plants (for example, parts and components of cars) and the delivery of final goods in their distribution systems (Caves, 1982).

Now *is the observed growth of IIT also due to integration?* A set of studies would suggest so. In the 1959–80 period, intra-EU, intra-industry trade grew more rapidly than total EU intra-industry trade (Greenaway, 1987). In addition, the level of IIT in Western Europe was positively influenced by the factors just cited and negatively by increasing distance and differences in culture (Balassa and Bauwens, 1988). There is clear econometric evidence that the cancellation of border formalities in the framework of the single market programme has contributed importantly to the growth of intra-industry trade. Some other factors such as returns to scale and foreign direct investment did also have a significant influence on IIT growth in the 1985–93 period (CEPII, 1996). Finally, the convergence of national industrial structures is an important factor which is itself dependent on integration (see Chapters 9–16).

Technology

Modern theory of trade tends to look towards technological and industrial factors for the explanation of trade patterns. The idea is that the level of innovation determines the quality of the product, which in turn determines its competitive position on external markets. This leads to specialisation: some countries specialise in high-tech goods, others in low-tech goods; the latter are generally believed to create less value added.

Within the EU, countries show a wide variation in innovation efforts, the pattern being that R&D per head is highest in the relatively

Table 5.6   National strengths in intra-EU trade by price/quality range, 1994

Country	Price/quality range		
	Low	Medium	High
Germany			+
Ireland			+
France		+	+
UK		+	
Netherlands		+	
Belgium/Luxemburg		+	
Denmark		+	
Spain	+	+	
Greece	+		
Italy	+		
Portugal	+		

Note: + = a positive 'contribution to the trade balance' of the price/quality ranges.

Source: CEPII (1996).

rich countries and very low in the relatively poor ones. Differences in a country's innovative capacity have been found to influence significantly their trade performance in high-tech products (Soete, 1987).

High innovation leads to a strong competitive position in high-quality products for which higher prices are paid on international markets. For a given product one can distinguish three categories: low (unit values more than 15 per cent below EU average); high (unit values more than 15 per cent above average) and medium (between high and low). Over the past 15 years the dispersion of unit values in intra-EU trade has grown, which means a stronger specialisation of member countries over the quality spectrum (CEPII, 1996). The general picture based on exports and imports is given in Table 5.6.

The table clearly indicates different country groupings. Germany has a comparative advantage for products in the high price/quality ranges; some other northern countries (like the UK and the Benelux) only in medium price/quality ranges; and southern countries (like Italy and Portugal) only in the low price/quality ranges.

Price differences

Evolution of differences over time

The degree of integration can be measured not only by the growth in the exchange of goods but also by the degree of convergence reached by their prices in the various countries of the EU. Under the law of one price, undistorted markets would result in completely equal prices, and trade would reflect the location of demand and the location of the lowest-cost producers. However, owing to transport costs, collusion practices, tariffs and taxes (in particular value added taxes and excises), prices do differ from one (sub-) market to another.

To compare price levels in different countries is a hazardous undertaking. To be meaningful, such a comparison should be made between products which are not only available in all the countries surveyed but also representative of all the national (and regional!) consumption patterns. This is not easy as the size of the EU and the many differences in historical origins within its borders give rise to a great variety of consumption patterns. Notwithstanding these constraints, a number of interesting studies have shed some light on the effects of the integration process.

For the initial *period of integration 1958–72* (Glejser, 1972) a comparison of the prices before (1958) and after (1970) the creation of the EU did not give very conclusive results; out of 36 products, 15 showed a tendency towards greater disparity and 21 a tendency towards convergence.

Table 5.7   Price dispersion (coefficient of variation) in the EU9*, by product group, 1975–93

		1975	1980	1985	1990	1993
Consumer goods	taxes excluded	16	19	18	19	17
	taxes included	21	20	19	20	18
Equipment goods	taxes excluded	14	13	13	n.a.	n.a.
	taxes included	14	13	13	12	13

Note: n.a. = not available.
*   Less complete data for EU12 and 15 show larger dispersion but similar developments over time.

Source: Eurostat; Emerson *et al.* (1988, p. 120); CEC (1996a).

The evolution of prices for the *period 1975–85*, broadly speaking the period between the first enlargement and the second, is given in Table 5.7. The figures reveal two major features:

- Price levels differed appreciably from one member state to another, more so for consumer goods than for investment goods. Indirect taxes, which in the period of study varied considerably among countries for the same product, were responsible for a significant share of the total price differences. However, even net of indirect taxes, prices differed considerably.
- The evolution of the dispersion of prices shows a slight tendency towards convergence over the period 1975–85. This picture is different for different sub-groups. In those sectors where there are non-tariff barriers, price dispersion has tended to increase in the period 1975–85 (+ 5 per cent). Price differences narrowed appreciably in the sectors more open to EU competition (– 24 per cent). However, there remained a large potential for price convergence; indeed an analysis applied to a specific sample of products showed the price dispersion within Germany to be half that in the EU (Emerson *et al.*, 1988).

The figures for the *1985–97 period* show the effect of two major aspects of integration:

- Widening: the price structures of Spain, Portugal and Greece did show a very clear convergence with those in the rest of the EU (Hoeller and Louppe, 1994; CEC, 1996a).
- Deepening: the completion of the internal market has brought increasing competition for a large range of products, which in

the last part of the period has brought convergence of prices for tradeable goods to the level found in the US (Rogers *et al.*, 2001). (See Chapters 10–13 for specific cases.) Little or no price convergence could be observed for the categories of goods that are subject either to different tax regimes or to significant regulation and hence NTBs (CEC, 1996a).

The opening of markets alone is unlikely to lead to complete price equalisation: numerous factors cause price differences between countries as well as, indeed, within countries. That is the case of, for example, transport costs on account of different distribution networks, of quality on account of regional and cultural differences in taste and of margins on account of differences in competitive pressures.

Welfare effects

Effects on member countries

To calculate the trade and welfare effects of integration, methods varying in sophistication have been applied.[14] One of the most common indicators with which to measure the effect of integration is the intensity of trade among partners (see Table 5.3). However growing mutual involvement of that kind cannot be considered a good sign of the progress in integration as the indicator captures a large number of other effects as well (Lloyd, 1992). More sophisticated methods have been developed to analyse the trade and welfare effects of progressive integration of goods markets (Waelbroeck, 1976). These methods are essentially an exercise in completing the accounting frameworks with data about, for instance, cost differences, supply and demand elasticities, trade flows, tariffs and consumption by good category in the countries participating in the customs union. At the time of the creation and successive enlargements of the EU, various attempts were made along these lines.[15]

Let us first look at the *trade effects*. For the first period of the EU6, from 1955 to 1969, the period of eliminating high tariffs, some estimates amounted to a doubling of trade in comparison to a situation without EU. The first enlargement that created the EU9 has been estimated to produce a 50 per cent rise in trade between the UK and the EU. A survey of the results of computations of the trade effects of the creation of the EU in the 1960s and 1970s (Mayes, 1978) showed that trade creation has amounted to between 10 and 30 per cent of total EU imports of manufactured goods. Trade diversion is on the whole estimated much lower, at between 2 and 15 per cent. Agriculture is an exception to the general picture; considerable trade diversion occurred for this sector. The second enlargement creating the EU12 was thought (in an *ex ante* study) to be of limited importance, given the low initial tariffs. As it coincided with the completion of the internal market, we should rather look for the combined effect of the two. Substantial trade creation has been found; over the 1985–93 period intra-EU import market shares increased by at least 3 per cent in average sectors and by 8 per cent in sectors sensitive to competition (Allen *et al.*, 1996).

The next step is the calculation of *income effects*. The income effects of the dismantling of tariffs were in the order of magnitude of 1 per cent of GNP (see the pioneering study by Verdoorn (1952) for a European Free Trade Area, and the studies by Johnson, 1958; Miller and Spencer, 1977; Balassa, 1975 for the EU). The studies cited have a number of drawbacks. Many use simplified methods to avoid data problems. Most studies, moreover, confine themselves to manufactured goods, leaving agriculture largely out of account. Finally, and this is a major objection, none of these studies has properly come to grips with such dynamic effects of goods market integration as economies of scale, efficiency or learning by doing. The dissatisfaction with the static models stimulated work along new lines.

In some (Marques-Mendes, 1986a, 1986b) a macro model is used to calculate the effects of changes in trade and in terms of trade. The percentage growth of GDP actually observed can be split into a part due to the EU and a residual part. The effects of the EU6 appear to be quite substantial, particularly for the smaller countries (which is in line with the suggestions made by Petith, 1977), much larger anyway than the effects calculated by the Vinerian type of study discussed earlier. The effects of the EU9 present quite a different picture. Of course the period differs from the preceding one in many respects. At the start of the EU9 most tariffs were lower than at the time of creation of the EU6; besides, a profound need for economic restructuring was recognised, energy prices were on a steep increase, trade balances were adversely affected and new protectionism was becoming generally accepted.[16] Macro models applied to the single market programme find an initial effect of some 1 per cent of GDP, but all dynamic effects could not be heeded in the short time periods analysed (see Chapter 14). Recently a new approach has been tried (Henrekson *et al.*, 1997) that concludes that integration in Europe has indeed spurred growth rates by some 0.6 to 0.8 per cent a year.

In others, micro-economic studies were made, better suited to deal with the dynamic effects. One (Owen, 1983) estimated that the effects of the opening of the European markets in the 1960s on increased competition, economies of scale and restructuring of firms have increased prosperity with some 40 to 100 per cent of the additional trade involved, or some 5 per cent of GDP.

Effect of the EU Customs Union on trade with third countries

The formation of a customs union also affects the patterns of trade with third countries. The taking away of the internal barriers in the EU has been a catalyst for the reduction of external barriers as well (Hufbauer, 1990; Messerlin, 1992).

The effects of the *formation of the EU6* on trade with third countries differ by good category (Sellekaerts, 1973; Balassa, 1975). Particularly large positive trade-creation effects occurred for machinery, transport equipment and fuels, and negative ones for food, chemicals and other manufactures. The EU formation caused a significant trade gain for associated less developed countries and somewhat lesser positive trade effects for the UK and the USA. By contrast, net trade-diversion effects occurred for the other developed countries and the centrally planned economies; very small negative effects could be observed for the other EFTA and other LDC groups.

The effects of the *first enlargement* on trade partners (Kreinin, 1973) were found to be largely trade-diverting; they were heaviest for the group of other developed countries (approximately 20 per cent) and somewhat less heavy for the LDCs (approximately 15 per cent). The effects of the *completion of the internal market* for goods on the trade partners of the EU were very diverse. For the group of EFTA countries the analyses (Haaland, 1990; Norman, 1991; Lundberg, 1992) all indicate significant increases of EU/EFTA trade, notably of the inter-industry type, going hand-in-hand with substantial welfare gains. For the group of LDCs the conclusion of an overview of studies (Koekkoek *et al.*, 1990) is that the trade effects of 1992 *vis-à-vis* developing countries are more likely to be positive than negative. Overall there has not been any trade diversion. On the contrary, trade with third countries has actually increased, which is in a sense plausible as it is easier to penetrate a market with one regime instead of a patchwork of 15 regimes (CEC, 1996a). The effects of the *third enlargement* of the EU with three former EFTA countries (in other words of the European Economic Area) on third countries were found to be very positive for all trade areas of the world (Haaland 1990; Haaland and Norman, 1992; CEPR, 1992). The magnitude of the effects is different for different countries: highest for EFTA, average for the EU and small for third countries.

The effects of the *accession of the Central and Eastern European countries to the EU* have recently been estimated using a global applied general equilibrium model (Baldwin, François and Portes, 1997). Under the base scenario they show that the extension is marginally beneficial for the EU (some 0.2 per cent of GDP) and very beneficial for the CEECs (some 1.2 per cent increase in GDP). In a less conservative scenario the authors also take into account that the accession of the CEECs will considerably decrease the risk for investors. If this would bring the risk level down to the Portuguese level, then the benefits for the East will go up to 20 per cent of the income.

Summary and conclusions

- The integration of the economies of EU countries through the exchange of goods has greatly increased over the period 1950–95 and their mutual involvement has increased more than their involvement with third countries.
- Specialisation took the form, not so much of each country concentrating on a specific sector, but of specialisation within sectors (intra-industry trade).
- The prices of most goods tended to converge, in line with theoretical expectations.
- Trade creation has on the whole been considerably greater than trade diversion; on balance, the EU appears to have contributed clearly to the efficient allocation of production factors in the world.
- Where the EU was externally open (manufacturing), the welfare effects were positive; where it was externally protected (for example, agriculture) the effects were negative.
- Integration has entailed only limited static welfare effects; the great advantages of the EU have been found in its dynamic effects following the improvement of its terms of trade and its competitiveness on internal and global markets.

Notes

1   Non-tariff barriers are very common, because international agreements forbid countries to have recourse to tariffs. The negative effects are similar to those of tariffs; see, for instance, Krauss (1979); Greenaway (1983). For a more thorough treatment of voluntary export restraints (VERs), see Jones (1984).
2   The arguments for protection and the (lack of) economic basis for them have been extensively studied in the literature. We refer here only to the authoritative work of Corden (1971, 1974), the handbook by Caves and Jones (1984), the case studies by Meyer (1973), the political economy approach of Frey (1985), the inventory of the OECD (1985c) and the European study of new protectionism by Page (1981).
3   The superiority of unilateral tariff reduction and hence of a world of free trade over customs unions has been shown by Cooper and Mansell (1965) and Johnson (1965).

4   Nonetheless classical economists occupied themselves quite frequently with the problems of preferential trade agreements. The creation of the German *Zollverein* in the 19th century gave rise to a theoretical debate on the advantages and disadvantages of protection, yet the subject of economic integration remained embedded in a more general economic analysis. International economic integration actually only became a separate object of economic thinking after the Second World War (Viner, 1950). Since then, the literature on the subject has accumulated, not least because the post-war integration processes greatly stimulated profound theoretical studies (Tovias, 1991).

5   See for a detailed treatment of these effects previous editions of this book.

6   The introduction of a CET is insufficient to guarantee the efficient working of the customs union. For that purpose, the customs procedures as well as the practices of separate customs administrations have to be harmonised as much as possible. In line with the Treaty obligation the member states have proceeded, before the end of the transition period, to the approximation of their legal and administrative customs regulations.

7   Naturally one should keep in mind that the goods trade is given at production value and GDP value added. On the other hand, GDP also comprises some activities which do not enter into the international commercial circuit. For lack of basic data, the ratio has not been corrected for these influences.

8   More detailed statistics specifying exports and imports and individual members show that the tendencies that have been given in the graph for groups of countries do apply in general also to all its members, excluding the possibility of a statistical artefact. More detailed material specifying manufacturing imports by product (Jacquemin and Sapir, 1988) corroborate the findings as to the integration effects.

9   The analysis was carried out with a somewhat different methodology focusing on developments at the world level. The clustering of countries on the basis of these world trade data suggests the emergence of a large block centred on the EU to which also belong Central and Eastern Europe and Africa.

10   A major shift in the pattern that is not revealed by the table concerns agricultural produce. Although agricultural imports increased considerably in the period analysed, their relative share dropped steeply, and by 1990 was on a level with exports. That development is closely tied up with the common agricultural policy, to be described in Chapter 9.

11   The figures given here for the EU12 are not available in a comparable form for the EU15. Fragmentary information permits us to say, however, that the figures presented are likely to be representative for both the structure and the development of the commodity trade of the EU15 too.

12   The question of how to measure and explain IIT has received much attention in the literature (see among others, Balassa, 1986; Grubel and Lloyd, 1975; Tharakan, 1983; Greenaway and Milner, 1986; Kol, 1988).

13   Similar results for the EU in Greenaway (1987). Information for EFTA countries shows the same tendency, but at a lower level; for CMEA the indices are lower (Drabeck and Greenaway, 1984). The EU results are also corroborated by Bergstrand (1983), who calculated IIT indexes for the years from 1965 to 1976 for the four large EU countries; he found that, on average, in three-quarters of the sectors he analysed IIT had increased, sometimes considerably (30–50 per cent).

14   For a brief review of methods and outcomes, we will borrow from the surveys made by, in particular, Verdoorn and Schwartz (1972), Balassa (1975), Mayes (1978) and El-Agraa and Jones (1981).

15   See, for example, Krauss (1968), Williamson and Bottrill (1971), Resnick and Truman (1975), Balassa (1975), Miller and Spencer (1977), Petith (1977), Viaene

(1982), Grinols (1984), Winters (1985) and Jacquemin and Sapir (1988). Note that many of the methods and definitions used by these authors are not directly compatible with the theoretical conception of the CU.

16   In later chapters we will take up the other effects of integration, such as mobile production factors and/or common policies. For instance, the effect of stable exchange rates on the volume of trade will be taken up in Chapter 15, on monetary policy.

6   Services

Introduction

Over the last decades the importance of services in the economy of
the EU has increased dramatically (see Chapter 12). Trade in services
has increased also; both intra-EU trade and trade of the EU with the
rest of the world. So the discussion that follows is well warranted.

Like the previous chapter the present one will go first into a few
basic concepts; although in many aspects services can be thought of
as comparable to goods, they nevertheless reveal some specific characteristics that call for preliminary elucidation. Next we will consider
the EU regime. This is of particular relevance because the EU has
played a crucial role in the process of both internal (internal market
programme) and external (GATT /WTO round) liberalisation of trade
in services.

The specific patterns of trade in services will be described in the
next section with the help of statistical series, detailing the structure
by area and by branch of activity. As trade in services is much less
well documented than trade in goods, the description will be much
less complete with regard to the length of the time series, the detail
of products and the coverage of geographical areas. This is even
more so with respect to the prices and the welfare effects of service
trade, so we can only devote very short sections to each of these
problems. The chapter will be concluded by a short summary of the
main findings.

Basic (theoretical) concepts

Motives for obstacles

Traditionally the markets for services are segmented. Many reasons
are given to justify such obstacles to free trade in services. Most of

the obstacles are allegedly drawn up to *protect consumers*. A few examples from different sectors may illustrate this.

- In banking and insurance, regulation serves to limit the risk of insolvency through surveillance of private operators by (semi-) public organisations (central banks, among others). Since foreign suppliers are hard to control, access to the national market is barred to them.
- In air transport, the safety of the passenger is the main concern. Standards are accompanied by mutual import controls in the form of landing rights.
- In communication and energy (electricity), services are regulated to protect consumers from unfair pricing by a natural monopolist.
- In medical services, the interests of the patient are protected by the enforcement of standards for the qualifications of personnel (medical doctors and so on).

Although the arguments for consumer protection are valid, they do not necessarily have to lead to trade protection; indeed other policy measures can be devised with the same effect for the safety and health of consumers while leaving international competition free.

Many other obstacles overtly aim at *protecting national companies*. There are several reasons to do so:

- strategic importance: an example is maritime transport, where international trade is restricted by a complex system of cargo reservation; a national merchant navy is thought to be necessary in times of war to provide the country with essential goods;
- economic policy: the control of macro-economic policy (through the banking system);
- enhancing national prestige (civil aviation);
- control of key technologies (telecommunication);
- safeguarding cultural values (movies, television).

However, even if consumer protection is the official reason for this protectionist regulation, in practice the real reason is often that domestic firms want to be sheltered from international competition.

Obstacles

The forms in which the free trade in services is impeded cover a wide spectrum. Many of them are fairly comparable to those that hinder goods trade.[1] However, as the value of a border-crossing service is harder to control than that of a good, tariffs are seldom practised, and restrictions on the trade in services are mostly of the non-tariff type. Moreover, because the provision of some types of service across the border involves direct investments, a set of restrictions to entry of markets is relevant too.

Trade in services can be hampered by the following instruments:

- quantitative restriction, notably on domestic consumption[2] (for instance, advertising, air transport);
- shares of markets reserved for home producers (for example, for movies);
- subsidies (for instance, in construction);
- government procurement (for instance, construction, data processing);
- currency controls on transfers to foreign countries for services provided;
- restrictions on the qualifications of manpower required to perform certain services (legal, medical);
- technical requirements for capital goods (transport, for example);
- customs valuation problems for goods required to perform services (for instance, plumbers' tools).

Entry restrictions on a profession or restrictions on setting up in business are the second category of barriers. These can take the following forms:

- restrictions on the right of foreign firms to set up or take over subsidiary companies;
- exclusion of foreign firms from certain types of activity;
- discriminatory performance requirements;
- selective taxation;
- restrictions on the transfer of profits.

Advantages

Markets that are segmented tend to be inefficient. Hence there is a drive towards doing away with obstacles and liberalising trade. The theoretical foundations of the integration of service markets are largely akin to those of the trade in goods. In practice there is much difference. Indeed, the analysis based on differences in factor endowments of different countries has not given very rich results for services (see, for a review, Landesmann and Petit, 1995). Alternative approaches, involving aspects of industrial organisation theory, are giving more promising results. These refer to notions such as economies of scale and scope and transaction cost. High transaction cost means that sourcing from abroad is expensive and that local provision (probably foreign direct investment) will be important.

The standard arguments for the integration of service markets are similar to the ones for goods markets (see the survey in Messerlin, 1993 and Chapter 5).

- Higher international specialisation raises the efficiency of re-source allocation and hence income. In other words, consumers will have more choice and the products produced and consumed will be better matched.
- Economies of scale and scope will be better exploited (for instance, in banking through spreading risks; in consulting by using international databases). So cost to consumers will go down.

As with goods, the liberalisation of international trade in services alone does not suffice to integrate markets. Most of these markets have been regulated for several reasons (to protect consumers, for example) and a certain degree of harmonisation of the rules is necessary to avoid distortions. In much the same way, competition rules must be enforced and the relations to third countries defined.

Forms of integration

The integration of service markets (the taking away of the obstacles to trade) proceeds in ways that are in agreement with the characteristics of this sector. We distinguish three types of international transaction.[3] For each type of transaction we will consider service markets to be integrated if the following obtain:

- Cross-border supply. No spatial move of either producer or consumer is needed because the service is rendered through trans-border flows of information. Integration is considered to exist if a consumer in country A is free to contract a service (for instance an insurance policy) with a company in country B.
- Consumption abroad. Consumers of one country move to producers in another country to receive the service offered. Personal services (such as staying at a seaside resort), education (such as a student studying abroad) and retail services (such as British people shopping in Paris) are cases in point. Integration exists when consumers can move freely abroad to obtain a service.
- Production abroad from home base. Producers of one country move to a foreign country to provide their services there. Managing a construction site, a plumber fixing a problem in a house

across the border, or a teacher giving guest lectures, are cases in point. Integration exists if the provider can render the service freely to a client abroad.

A fourth type named 'commercial presence' can be distinguished. It is 'establishment-based trade', which occurs when service providers create a permanent subsidiary in the importing country in order to produce and sell the service, parts of which will have to be imported (compare direct investment (DI)-induced trade in goods!). There is quite a difference between the liberalisation of the setting up of an establishment and of cross-border provision of services. The former maintains the coexistence of different national regulations, whereas the latter implies a direct competition between the various services produced under divergent rules. The four modes are of different importance; it has been estimated that the first takes about 40 per cent; the second mode about 20 per cent, the third only 2 per cent and the fourth the remaining 38 per cent of total world trade in services (Karsenty, 1999).

The transaction costs involved in international service trade are often considerable, and not all services are susceptible to economies of scale. Hence, even without restrictions, services tend to be traded less than goods. The proximity of the supplier to the customer being of crucial importance for many services, the creation of a foreign establishment by a direct investment is a solution that is more often chosen for services than for goods. However, as technological progress in telecommunications lowers the transaction costs, integration according to one of the three models described may be expected to intensify, particularly for the third category of transactions.

EU regime

Rationale and principles

The advantages of liberalisation that apply for goods also apply to services (see the previous section). So there is a case for the integration of service markets. The EU has recognised these advantages and has enshrined free trade in services in the Treaty of Rome. The Treaty reflects awareness of the wide variety in products of the service branches. The general definition of services (Article 50 EC) reads: 'activities normally provided for remuneration in so far as they are not governed by the provisions relating to freedom of movement for goods, capital and persons'. They include in particular activities of an industrial or commercial nature and those of craftsmen and professions. For all these activities the Treaty stipulates two freedoms:

- to provide services (Article 49 EC) a company of member country A can provide services in member country B without having an office there;
- to set up an establishment: that is, companies (or persons) of country A wishing to set up an establishment (that is, a legal entity with, in general, premises, staff and so on) in member country B are free to do so under the same conditions as are laid down for the nationals of the country of establishment (Article 43 EC).

There are a few exceptions to this general freedom:

- activities which are connected with the exercise of official authority are excluded completely;
- medical and pharmaceutical professions: here liberalisation depends on coordination of the conditions for their exercise in various member states;
- transport services are governed by another title of the Treaty;
- banking and insurance services: as they are closely connected with movements of capital, their liberalisation will be effected in step with the progressive liberalisation of capital.

So one can say that the Treaty considers that services and goods can be subjected to the same type of general rules for liberalisation of markets: this irrespective of whether the service is provided by cross-border trade or by establishment.

Gradual elaboration of a policy

In the lengthy negotiations carried on to substantiate the freedom to provide services, the equivalence of qualifications proved one difficult point, another being the way in which governments had organised certain markets (or sanctioned private groups to organise and protect them). The general result was that some foreign penetration through subsidiaries had occurred in several service markets, but that very little progress towards liberalisation via cross-border trade had been made. Conflicts occurred between countries and cross-border operators. The country where the service was delivered claimed the right to supervise that service or subject it to licensing. The cross-border operator maintained that compliance with the rules of his home country was sufficient.

In a set of famous rulings in such conflicts the Court of Justice has clarified the meaning of freedom of services. The Court has ruled that a service lawfully provided in one member country can in principle also be freely provided in another member state. The common element in the rulings was the consideration that governments have to demonstrate clear reasons of public interest before imposing requirements on a foreign trader over and above those fulfilled to receive a permit from his home authorities, or duplicating qualification checks already performed at home. When applying these principles to insurance, for example, governments may regulate to make sure that individual private consumers do not get confused by the (lack of) coverage from an insurance policy imported from abroad. On the other hand, corporate clients of insurance companies need less regulation of this type because they are often very competent buyers.

The ruling of the Court has in principle liberalised all services connected with agriculture, manufacturing, craft and trade (commerce).[4]

But in its verdicts the Court indicated that there should be a balance between liberalisation and harmonisation. The Commission has worked on liberalisation/harmonisation programmes for several service sectors. Two examples may give an idea of this process.

- In *professional services* (lawyers and auditors, engineers and so on), strong national corporations either had themselves regulated the profession (allegedly in the interest of the consumer) or were subject to detailed government regulation concerning both the access to the profession and the type of products supplied. The instrument used to regulate access is the specification of qualification requirements (diplomas, for instance). The EU has been working on the mutual recognition of diplomas, but for a long time progress has been extremely slow and cumbersome and, apart from a framework directive on the recognition of university degrees, little has been achieved (Pertek, 1992).
- *Financial services* (banking and insurance) are regulated on a national basis to permit prudential control of the soundness of the undertakings to make sure that they will be able, for instance, to pay the client at the moment a life insurance comes to term. The harmonisation of these rules has been extremely involved, but has finally been realised in the form of several Directives (see case study in Chapter 12).

However the Commission has found that this process was too slow and, when successful, ran the risk of leading towards too detailed European regulation. So, while proposing the liberalisation necessary for the completion of the internal market in services, a new approach was followed. This *new approach* consists of three elements:

- free service delivery, through either cross-border trade or the setting up of an establishment;

- a 'single licence' system with mutual recognition: that is, service providers operating under the licence of member state A can work in member state B, the latter recognising the quality of member state A's surveillance system;
- a minimum of EU-wide harmonisation in the form of common EU rules on the crucial features of the behaviour of service providers, on the one hand, and on the control system of member states, on the other.

An example of such regulation is the proposal to facilitate the *cross-border trade in services* (CEC, 2000b). This proposal tries to find a solution to the problem exposed in Chapter 7 that non-EU nationals that are lawfully established in one of the member states do not have the right to work in other EU member states. This causes all sorts of problems and is in fact not in conformity with the way in which the internal market for goods and capital has been given shape. The Commission now proposes: (1) the right of service businesses established in the EU to provide services in another member state using non-Community staff who are lawfully established in one of the EU member countries; and (2) the right of self-employed workers from non-EU countries, who are lawfully established in a member state to do business in the whole EU. To facilitate these operations the Commission proposes an EU 'service provision card' to be issued by the home country.

Another recent initiative in the regulation of services tries to give an answer to a technological challenge. The fast increase of *Internet-related services*, notably e-commerce made a new directive of the EU necessary in order to develop the potential of the internal market to the full. In line with the new approach sketched above, the directive states that any firm engaging in e-commerce has to comply with the rules of the country where it is established. This has to be a real establishment; a mere server would not be sufficient. The directive stipulates next that, in all member states, electronic contracts must be recognised. The directive finally gives rules for the accountability of intermediaries, the so-called Internet service providers. The most important aspect of this latter rule is that providers cannot be held responsible as long as they have no information about illegal activities or information on their net or server. With the further development of e-commerce it is likely that more rules will be needed to cope with problems of privacy, safeguards of rights (industrial property) and so on.

External situation

Contrary to the situation for goods, the Treaty is silent as to the organisation of an external policy in matters of services. As a conse-

Box 6.1   The Internet

Throughout modern history the growing integration of the world economy and technological development have created the need for governments to set up international organisations to regulate the international aspects of the use of the new technology. This has been the case, for instance, for the railways and for telecommunications (see Chapter 3). The typical form of such organisations was an intergovernmental agreement on technical standards, cost and revenue sharing and so on. Compliance was guaranteed by the national governments that had become members of the organisation.

The Internet has not developed in the same way. Its regulation has emerged largely bottom-up, meaning that its rules are the result of consensus building among its users. The process of policy formation on the Internet is largely carried out by the *Internet Engineering Task Force (IETF)* which functions as an on-line community of interested parties and is in charge of developing technical standards such as communication protocols.

So far, this original decision-making process has proved to be remarkably robust, notwithstanding its inherent flaws. However, there are signs that this may not be sufficient in the future. The problems that arise are multi-faceted. On the one hand there is the increasing risk of commercial or special interest groups taking over control of certain parts of the net. On the other hand there is the growing concern about the inability of governments to safeguard certain public goods (such as a reliable legal system for dispute settlement) or their capacity to tax international and national transactions on an equal basis.

The problem is particularly acute with the property of Internet names and numbers. Indeed, there are a very high commercial interest involved in the possibility of using company and brand names on the net. In order to cope with these problems the *Internet Corporation for Assigned Names and Numbers (ICANN)* has been created. It is a hybrid form of an on-line community (such as IETF) and a real-world government structure. It comprises accredited organisations such as the World Intellectual Property Organisation, and national governments have a voice via a governmental advisory committee. This structure has yet to prove its effectiveness.

The European Union, just like national governments, is aware of these problems. However, it has not yet established a clear position with respect to the future development of the Internet.

quence the external regime for a large number of services was in fact not a common one, but a set of national ones. Indeed, each country had regulated the industry on a national basis and maintained an external regime *vis-à-vis* both EU partners and other countries to protect its industries from foreign competition.

Three factors have changed this situation in the last two decades. First, the pursuit of an internal market in services has considerably changed the outlook for the external regime. Second, in the framework of the GATT/WTO the EU has worked on the GATS, the General Agreement on Trade in Services. This agreement sets rules and creates a framework for basic fair trading principles such as non-discrimination. Individual signatories, among them the EU, pledge market opening in a wide range of service branches. For some branches special provisions have been made, as for financial services, telecommunications and sea and air transport.

GATS is not of the same inspiration as the single market. The latter tries to do away with all remaining barriers in one go, and to create a new competitive situation. The former has listed the present barriers, evaluated the problems they create, has drawn up an inventory of the potential for liberalisation by each of the negotiating partners, and finally has worked out an agreement on a reduction of protection. The more partial and segmented approach of GATS is the result of the great diversity of preferences of the national governments that take part in the GATT/WTO negotiations.

The third new factor is the emergence, in recent years, of the Internet which facilitates the global exchange of information and the creation of many new services generally called e-business or e-commerce. The development of the Internet has taken place almost without any international intergovernmental regulation (see Box 6.1).

It will be some time before the EU manages to set up a consistent external regime for services from these rather dispersed elements. It takes the standpoint that most new Internet-related services have to fall under the GATS as well.

Trade patterns[5]

Relative importance of trade in services

Services are to an increasing extent traded internationally. However this is more pronounced in absolute than in relative terms. We distinguish between two sub-periods. For the period *1960–80* we can only analyse the trends with data on 'invisibles' that encompass, besides services, such items as income from investment. The trend these figures reveal is very common among all EU member

Table 6.1 **Percentage share of service imports and exports in total GDP of member states (current prices), 1980–2000**

Country	1980		1990		2000	
	Import	Export	Import	Export	Import	Export
Germany	4	3	3	6	5	4
France	3	5	4	5	5	5
Italy	2	4	4	5	5	5
Netherlands	7	8	6	8	12	13
Belgium/Lux.	8	11	13	16	13	14
UK	3	6	4	5	6	7
Denmark	4	8	6	9	15	7
Ireland	6	5	7	6	8	8
Spain	3	6	2	7	5	9
Portugal	4	8	3	9	6	6
Greece	—	5	4	7	7	8
Austria	7	14	7	14	14	15
Finland	4	8	5	3	6	5
Sweden	4	6	6	5	5	5
EU15	4	5	4	6	8	8
Intra	3	3	3	3	5	5
Extra	1	2	1	3	3	3

Source: Statistical Annex of *European Economy*, June 1996, EC; Table 6.1; Eurostat, *Eurostatistics*, January 2000; some estimates (for instance, year 2000 figures based on extrapolation of 1990–99 figures).

countries and shows that service trade has an increased share in GDP.

For the 1980–2000 period, there has been a somewhat slower growth of integration (see Table 6.1). Some countries appear to specialise in services. If we compare the intra-EU cross-border trade of services with that of goods (Table 5.1, p. 99) in the same period, we see two features. First, the transactions in services appear to be relatively small (less than one-third of those in goods). Second, the increase of the service trade, notably in the recent period, has been much faster. One explanation for the low level is that in services the internationalisation process has proceeded much more by establishment-based competition, rather than in terms of cross-border trade-based competition (Messerlin, 1993; see also the sections on direct investment in Chapter 8). The explanation for the strong increase in recent years is to be found in the institutional and technological changes that have had a big impact on many services (see Chapters 12 and 14). We refer here in particular to the influence of the internal and external liberalisation programmes. The *internal market programme* started in 1985, but the actual liberalisation of the various markets of branches of the service sector has taken quite some time. However, the effects are becoming visible: indeed the intra-EU trade share in total trade in services did go up for all member countries. Moreover, the intra-EU trade did go up for most service branches in the course of the second half of the 1980s (Messerlin, 1993) and after some stagnation in the first part of the 1990s picked up recently.

The *worldwide drive for liberalisation* of trade in services got off the ground only in 1993 with the GATS agreement, so in future we may expect a relatively faster growth of extra-EU trade.

Main trading partners

The EU had a surplus on its balance of trade in services over the whole 1980–99 period (Table 6.1). This surplus is, however, a relatively small percentage of total trade in services (the figures for 1980 and 1990 in Table 6.1 exaggerate the difference, as the result of rounding). The exports and imports of total services by the EU are not only fairly balanced for the total extra-EU trade, but they are also very balanced for the various (groups of) trading partners (see Table 6.2, taking account of the statistical error margin). The large surplus the EU had in 1980 with the Third World (notably ACP countries) has disappeared since and the same is true for its deficit with EFTA. The similarity in the patterns of exports and imports is typical for services; it does not appear for other types of current account transactions.

The table also shows that the EU trade in services has always been geared very much more to the industrialised countries than to developing countries (the same structure that obtains for goods: see Table 5.4, p. 112). The main trading partner for the EU in services over the past 20 years has been the USA (much larger than for goods). The paramount place of the USA in EU services trade can be explained by the weight of its economy and the importance services have in its branch structure (notably services such as software and audiovisual productions). Exchanges with the EU have, moreover, been enhanced in the past decades by the considerable drop in the cost of transport, of telecommunications and of information processing. EFTA was second for services, while it occupied the first place for goods because of the free trade arrangement with the EU and its geographical proximity. Its relatively low weight and the persistence of trade barriers in services explain the difference between its position in goods and in services.

Table 6.2 Geographical distribution (percentages) by groups of countries, of extra-EU trade in services, 1980–2000

Country group	1980		1990		2000	
	Imports	Exports	Imports	Exports	Imports	Exports
Industrialised	66	57	69	68	59	60
EFTA[a]	25	19	24	24	14	15
USA	30	28	33	31	35	34
Japan	2	3	4	6	4	6
Other[b]	8	7	8	7	6	6
Third World	31	39	27	29	29	28
ACP	10	16	5	8	4	2
OPEC	6	9	5	6	4	5
Other	15	14	17	15	21	21
Other (ex state trading)	4	4	4	3	12	12
Total	100	100	100	100	100	100

Notes:
[a] In 1998 only Norway, Switzerland, Iceland and Liechtenstein.
[b] Australia, Canada, New Zealand and Turkey.

Source: Eurostat, *Geographical Breakdown of Current Account, EUR12*, 1980–90, Luxemburg, 1993; for 2000-figures (EU15), own estimates based on New Cronos data.

Trade in services by branch

The structure of the external trade in services by sector of activity (see Table 6.3) has remained fairly stable over the 1980–2000 period. Transport and tourism were by far the most important items in terms of exports as well as imports. Over the whole period the EU has had a net surplus on its balance of trade in services. The main contributors to that surplus have changed over time. Around 1980, exports of almost all branches were slightly in excess of imports. Around 1990, tourism stood out somewhat more. By then the EU was attracting more foreign tourists than it sent (a difference, more or less, of 15 million a year). Moreover, banking and business services showed good performances. The specialisation on the latter branches has been accentuated in recent years. The surpluses of the branches of financial services (banking) and of business services (engineering, software, accounting, management consulting) would appear to reflect their strong competitiveness on world markets. A negative balance existed for audiovisual services and software, where the USA

Table 6.3   Extra-EU trade in services, by branch (milliard euro), 1980–98

Category	1980		1990		1998	
	Exports	Imports	Exports	Imports	Exports	Imports
Transport	27	25	46	44	60	57
Sea freight	11	11	15	17	22	25
Air freight	1	1	3	1	4	3
Air passenger	5	4	10	9	17	12
Other	10	9	18	17	17	17
Travel and tourism	14	13	34	29	61	62
Other	30	22	55	43	116	104
Construction	6	3	6	3	12	7
Merchanting	4	5	7	9	12	12
Banking and Insurance	3	2	11	6	18	9
Communication	1	1	2	3	4	5
Business	8	4	12	8	43	39
Computer and information					6	4
Films, TV	0	0	1	1	1	4
Other	8	7	16	13	20	24
Total	71	60	135	116	237	223

Source: Eurostat, *International Trade in Services*, various years, 1980–90 EU12, 1998 EU15.

has a very strong competitive edge. For other services, including services related to transport, commerce, technology and intra-firm transactions, the EU situation was fairly balanced.

The relative importance of external trade in the total of the branches is still limited. For most sectors the share of trade in total turnover is between 2 and 6 per cent; somewhat higher figures (10 per cent) can be found for specialist services such as computer and information, while only very specialist services such as R&D consulting come up to shares of around 80 per cent. Of course, sea and air transport are by nature very much oriented to external trade as well.

In recent years there has been an explosive growth of electronic commerce, or the trade in services on the Internet. This explosive growth is expected to continue for some years in the future. As yet only rough estimates are available on the magnitude and geographical pattern of this type of trade. These estimates show that US based companies had some 50 per cent share in this trade in 1999. The EU is expected to catch up in the coming years (see Chapter 12). Most of this commerce is e-business (inter-company trade). Its composition in terms of the traditional sectors cannot be given for lack of a statistical basis.

Price differences

The comparison over time and space of prices for typical services is a rather complicated operation. In the past a few attempts have been made for specific products; the scanty evidence produced showed that the lack of integration that has characterised service markets until recently tended to maintain considerable price differences.

Recently some better information has become available, showing that in the 1985–93 period prices converged somewhat as a result of the 1992 liberalisation programme (CEC, 1996a). Similar information about the 1993–6 period shows a continuation of the cautious trend towards convergence for services in general and most service branches. This convergence has been much less general and much less pronounced than in manufacturing (see Chapter 12 for more details).

Welfare effects

There are no comprehensive empirical studies that permit us to evaluate the trade, let alone the welfare effects of decreased protection, in services. The reason for this is that the conceptual and statistical basis for such studies is very weak. For example, the estimation of 'ad valorem' equivalents of restrictions to trade in services is very difficult, and hence the economic cost of these restrictions cannot be established. This is contrary to the case of goods, where welfare cost of protection and welfare benefits of liberalisation have been estimated on several occasions.

There are numerous examples of firms that have increased their exports or imports of services to or from other EU member states following the internal market programme. However, the increase is moderate if compared to manufacturing (CEC, 1996a). There is also substantial evidence of increases in efficiency due to liberalisation. However it has not been possible to calculate either trade or income effects on this basis.

For a large part the argument that trade liberalisation leads to positive welfare effects rests on the assumption of increased (potential) competition. It is here that some caution is needed. Indeed, in many cases where liberalisation went hand-in-hand with deregulation, an initial period of enhanced competition was followed by a period of concentration of firms, leading to a situation of limited oligopolistic competition. So a prudent policy of regulation and of enforcement of competition rules is needed (see Chapter 14).

Summary and conclusions

- Until recently many service markets have been protected from foreign competition by a variety of instruments; often the official reason was the protection of the consumer, but in practice the consumer has often borne a high cost while the producer has mostly profited.
- International trade of services is relatively limited. This is partly due to protection. It is also partly due to the need for proximity of producers and consumers that induces firms which undertake internationalisation to prefer the setting up of an establishment in the country to cross-border trade.
- The EU has liberalised the internal trade in services; this has been accompanied by a mutual recognition of home country supervision and a minimal set of EU regulations.
- The effects of liberalisation have started to become visible in terms of increases in cross-border trade and direct investment; however the deficient data situation precludes as yet any conclusion as to price convergence and positive welfare effects.

Notes

1   A detailed description of these trade barriers is given in OECD (1981b, 1983a, 1984a, 1985b, 1986a).
2   These measures are favoured by many policy makers, for several reasons. First, they are particularly well suited to being applied in times of economic downturn, to increase the effectiveness of stabilisation policies. Next, their protectionist impact is independent of substitution between foreign and domestic producers. Finally, their enforcement is often done through the involvement of agencies in which domestic producers are represented.
3   Following Bhagwati (1987a) and the WTO/GATS (see the following section) typology.
4   The Court has also clarified the role of competition on service markets by ruling that the relevant EU rules apply fully to the service sector. This is in respect of both firms that set prices (such as airlines) and governments that influence quantities (for example, public procurement).
5   To measure trade in services is quite a complicated proposition. For a service incorporated in an information carrier, for instance a consultancy report, the international transaction can in principle be recorded the moment the report passes the frontier. In cases where either the consumer (a student who studies abroad) or the producer (a professor who teaches abroad) travels from one country to another the transaction is difficult to register. To overcome such difficulties, most international service transactions are registered only at the

moment the payment is made (through the records of the central banks). The criterion for the international export of a service is then that it be paid for by a person resident or a company established in a country other than the home country of the producer. As a consequence of these recording problems most statistics on trade in services are very deficient. Consistent series over a long time period are not available. For this reason we have to limit ourselves here to relatively short series.

7   Labour

Introduction

Under certain conditions, the creation of a common market entails movements of labour which in turn have a levelling effect on the price of labour (the wages). In this chapter we will describe in some detail how these two phenomena have taken shape in practice with the integration of the labour markets of the EU member countries.

We will start the discussion with the presentation of a few *basic concepts*, such as the definition and specification of barriers to movement and the forms and advantages of integration.

Next we will devote a section to *regulation*. Each country has tried to regulate the labour market with a complex whole of national legislation and administrative rules and practices and multinational or bilateral agreements. The EU has first of all ensured unrestricted migration for work reasons within its border to nationals of member states. Next it has gradually increased its regulating of aspects of social policy that influence the functioning of labour markets.

The *exchange of labour* among member states through international migration is the subject of the following section.[1] Although labour is much less mobile than goods and capital, labour migration is an important phenomenon.[2] In this section we will give the results of studies that have tried to explain movements of labour to and in the EU.

Next we will turn to the development of the *price of labour* under the influence of integration. After a theoretical treatment of the question we will examine with empirical data how far wages in the member states of the EU have actually adjusted to the new conditions. Finally, we indicate both in a theoretical and an empirical way the *welfare effects* of migration. A brief summary of the main findings concludes the chapter.

Some basic concepts

Motives for impediments

Traditionally the international movement of workers has been subject to many obstacles. Opponents of the free movement of production factor labour justify such measures by arguments, which are mostly directed against immigration. The following arguments against immigration are frequently heard:

- pressure on wages at equal demand, additional supply leads to lower prices;
- increase in unemployment: demand remaining the same, additional supply expels existing supply;
- rise in government expenditure: foreigners are supposed to need costlier social provisions (education and housing, for instance) and to make more demands on social security than nationals;
- societal disruption: cultural differences tend to disturb the social equilibrium;
- regional disparities: labour tends to move to concentrations of economic activities;
- balance of payments deterioration: via increased remittances;
- high cost of recruitment, travel, management, personnel services and so on.

On the other hand, arguments are also raised against emigration, such as:

- loss of human capital essential to the development of the economy;
- depopulation of certain regions, causing waste of societal capital;
- opportunity cost of forgone output.

Developed countries rarely inhibit emigration, but for developing countries there may be valid arguments to do so.

Restrictions

To control the international exchange of labour, most governments use permits as a tool (comparable to quantitative restrictions in the exchange of goods), forbidding all immigration without a permit. The permit may be accompanied by all kinds of restriction, sometimes defined so sharply that in practice no immigration is feasible.

The mere abolition of such permits does not mean that factor markets are integrated. There are, indeed, several ways to impede migration of workers; they can be divided into the following categories.

- Access to functions and professions. This can be limited by direct conditions stipulating, for instance, that foreign nationals cannot be lawyers. It can also be done in a subtler way, as with the setting of professional demands which foreigners cannot satisfy (for instance because foreign certificates are not recognised); or by making public labour exchange services accessible to a country's own nationals only.
- Accommodation conditions. To accept a job, a person must have accommodation. A residence permit for foreigners can be refused or made hard to get. Restrictions can also be imposed on obtaining residential accommodation or schooling for children, and so on.
- Financial disadvantages. These can be created, for instance, by imposing higher taxes, or charging premiums for social security without granting rights to benefits. Finally the transfer of earnings can be restricted (foreign currency).

Advantages of integration

The advantages hoped for from the free movement of labour (that is to say, the integration of labour markets) depend on the type of exchange chosen. In general terms, the following advantages are expected from permanent migration:

- for supply of labour (employed persons) a better chance to capitalise on their specific qualities;
- for those demanding labour, better possibilities of choosing a technology with an optimum capital/labour ratio from the management point of view;
- levelling of differences in production cost as far as they were due to the compartmentalisation of the labour market.

In the case of temporary migration, a distinction must be made between advantages to the emigration country and those to the immigration country (Scott, 1967; Kindleberger *et al.*, 1979; MacMillan, 1982).

- Emigration countries expect three major advantages: (1) to ease their unemployment situation (and lower the budgetary cost of unemployment benefits); (2) to ease their budget and balance-of-payments problems through remittances; and (3) to improve the quality of the labour force (return migrants having acquired skills abroad).

- Immigration countries hope to gain a direct production effect: by adding foreign workers with skills that are scarce to their own manpower in places where investments require it, they are able to make the most of their own capital stock and indigenous manpower. Sometimes the advantages are manifest only in times of cyclical highs, but they may also be of a more structural nature. Immigration may also have a redistributive welfare effect: the larger labour supply lowers the wage rate of the indigenous labour force; the additional income is shared by capital and foreign labour (see the separate section on welfare effects later in this chapter). Moreover the pressure on inflation is diminished because of relaxation of labour scarcity.

The profitable effects of international migration may well be distributed unevenly between sending and receiving countries. In politics, the voices pleading restriction are often louder than those pleading full freedom. The outcome is often free movement of labour within a common market, but a policy of restriction towards third countries. This is the more likely as the common market is supplemented by some form of redistribution mechanism which could offset the potential negative effects of emigration for the less developed member countries (see Chapter 16).

Forms of integration

There is free international movement of employed persons if (1) nationals of one member state may unrestrictedly look for and accept a job in another, and (2) self-employed people from one member state are free to settle in another member state to exert their profession or activity.

There are as yet no generally accepted notions to capture the various *forms* in which the labour market may be integrated, but here, too, a distinction can be made along the lines of free trade area and customs union made in Chapter 2. In both a free labour movement area (FLMA) and a labour market union (LMU), employed persons are free to accept a job in any of the partner countries. However, in the FLMA, participant countries are free to establish their own conditions with respect to third countries, while in the LMU that competence is transferred to the union. In the former case, therefore, employed persons from third countries admitted to one member state would not automatically have the right to move freely into other member states. With the fully integrated labour markets in a union, this last limitation does not exist. Full labour market integration means, indeed, that among partner countries (all) restrictions are abolished. But to achieve real integration, measures of positive integration are needed as well. Such positive integration will mostly be realised by coordinating labour market and employment policies, as well as social policies and taxes.

EU regime

Rationale and principles

The EU has adopted the principle of free movement of workers within the area of the EU. The treaty works out the principle of non-discrimination differently for employed persons and persons practising an activity on their own account and responsibility.

- *Workers* are persons performing work in an employment situation against payment. The freedom of movement shall entail the abolition of any discrimination based on nationality between workers of the member states as regards employment, remuneration[3] and other conditions of work and employment (Article 39 EC).
- *Self-employed* or *independent persons* are those who exercise an economic activity in their own interest and on their own responsibility. Member state nationals have the right to set up businesses abroad (agencies, branches, subsidiaries, self-employed) on the same conditions as those laid down for its own nationals by the law of the country where the establishment is effected (Article 43 EC).

All sectors of the economy are affected, with one exception: this freedom shall not apply to employment in the public sector (Article 39.4 EC) and activities which in that state are connected, even occasionally, with the exercise of official authority (Article 45 EC). Given the prominent place which the government now occupies in the economy of many member states, manifest in the large shares of workers with a civil servant or equivalent status in total employment, large portions of the labour market could thus be excluded from free migration. However the Court of Justice has pronounced clearly in several verdicts that such an interpretation would be contrary to the intention of the Treaty.

Gradual elaboration of a common policy

By the end of the transition period (1970), a free market for labour had been realised for most activities. This was the result of two actions. One was the application of the fundamental principles of the free movement of salaried workers and of the free establishment of independents by the Court of Justice. The second were the efforts made by the Commission to harmonise related issues. However, for a large number of professions, problems continued to exist, springing from different qualifications required for access to their practice in different countries (see Chapters 13 and 14). Other activities, too, continued to encounter difficulties in actual practice. Some of these difficulties can be explained by deeply rooted cultural differences, others are of a legal or administrative nature.

The Commission has tried to reduce the remaining obstacles as much as possible by further harmonisation of the rules. This was given impetus by the programme for the completion of the internal market that created a completely free internal labour market by 1992 (see Chapter 14). These harmonisation programmes covered such matters as social security, residence permits, diploma recognition, work conditions, health and safety conditions and so on. Another initiative has been to set up a European clearance system (CEC, 1992b). This network of consultants in different member countries (often housed in the labour exchanges) electronically exchanges data about job opportunities and working conditions in order to make the European labour market more transparent. The *objective* of all these measures is to create the conditions for facilitating the efficient functioning of the EU labour market (see CEC, 1997a).

Wages

Neither the (original and amended) Treaty nor the relevant regulations and directives contain rules about wages.[4] This implies that the remuneration discrepancies that exist among countries are accepted; indeed wages remain a matter of concern of national contractual parties. Wage differences are due to several types of differences between EU countries, such as industrial structure, productivity and supply factors. Moreover institutions are different, and so are the attitudes of trade unions and of employers' organisations, the legal frameworks in which they operate and their respective bargaining strengths (CEC, 1967; Seidel, 1983; Ferner and Hyman, 1992).

In the future the EU may have some influence on wage formation. The legal base for this has been developed in the framework of the building up of a 'Social Europe'. Now, if management and labour so desire, their dialogue (in other words, negotiations) may lead to contractual relations. Up to now this framework has not been used for wage negotiation. The argument against Europe-wide wage formation is that it will lead to inflexibilities and regional unemployment. Indeed, in many European countries, the drive of labour unions towards nationwide bargaining has made regional differences in wages disappear and thus widened the regional differences in unemployment. As the same tendency would manifest itself on the European scale, most parties involved (trade unions, employers' organisations and governments) in high- and low-wage countries alike agree that wage formation should for some time remain a national issue.

External relations

The notions of free trade area and customs union can be transferred from goods trade to the movements of production factors, also as regards the frontiers between the EU and third countries. While the EEC Treaty clearly lays down the external regime for goods trade, it is silent on the movement of persons. Neither do the regulations and directives implementing the Treaty give common rules about the treatment of nationals of third countries (CEC, 1979a). The EU regime has not changed much over time: the relevant elements of it can be described as follows.

Workers Member states may extend the advantages they have to give to workers from other EU member states also to workers from third countries. For the latter, the advantages are restricted to the member state involved; the other member states are not obliged to apply them as well.

Independents Nationals of third countries are subject to the rules each individual member state cares to issue. The fact that they are established in one member state does not give them the right to establish in other member states.[5]

Apparently, as far as the movements of active persons are concerned, the EU resembles a free trade area rather than a customs union. Obviously such a situation is difficult to maintain as physical frontiers are abolished (see Chapter 14). For that reason attempts are made to work out a common admission policy for workers and independents (and other non-active immigrants) from third countries, coupled with a free movement in the whole EU for all those who have been legally admitted in one of the member states. However, as neither the Single Act nor the Treaty on the European Union, nor any international organisation[6] regulated these points, the matter is still left to the discretion of the member states (see Chapter 17). The Treaty of Amsterdam commits the EU to elaborate common rules within a period of five years. The accession countries in Central and Eastern Europe have not obtained free movement of labour (unlike the situation for trade where a full liberalisation is realised in the period preceding accession).

International exchange of labour (migration)

The six original member states (1958–73)

In the first decade after the Second World War, international migration of labour in Western Europe had been on a small scale. In the 1950s, Italy provided about half the supply of migrant labour, while Switzerland and France were the greatest demanders. Moreover France received significant numbers of immigrants from North Africa.

From 1958 onwards, the *intra-EU free movement of labour* has been gradually introduced among the six original member states. In the period between 1958 and 1973, the labour market was tight in all member states except Italy. That was one reason why the number of foreign workers originating from other EU member states remained, in general, limited. Only Italians migrated north in numbers (Table 7.1). Notwithstanding increasing demand, the numbers of Italian migrants did not grow very much over time, for two reasons. First their labour was increasingly needed back home owing to the growth of the Italian economy. Second the intra-EU wage differences were gradually reduced as a result of the catching up of the Italian economy.

The EU member countries have extended their recruiting efforts *outside the EU* in order to provide the booming economies of the northern member states with the necessary labour. They set up recruitment bureaus in the countries of origin, that often took upon

Table 7.1   Foreign workers[a] in EU6 (first work licences[b]), 1958–73

Period	1958–61	1962–65	1966–69	1970–73
Total (×1000)	273	595	565	751
of which EU (%)	60	36	30	26
of which Italy (%)	49	32	26	21

Notes:
[a]   Algerians in France not counted.
[b]   In 1968, abolished for workers from EU countries.

Source: KEG, *DGXV Beschäftigung ausländischer Arbeitnehmer* (V264/76-D), several years, Brussels.

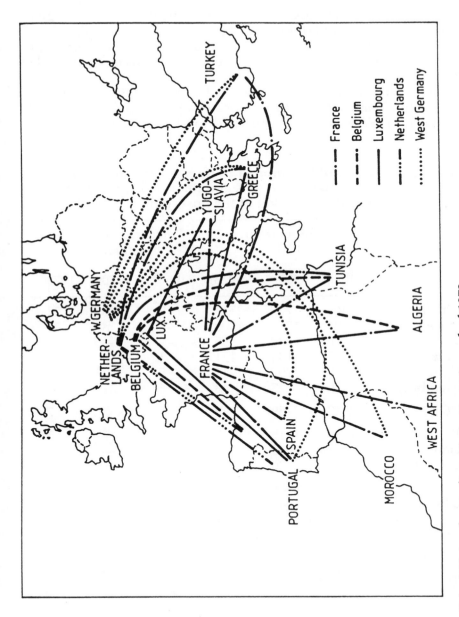

Figure 7.1   Bilateral recruitment agreements, end of 1973

themselves the organisation of transport, medical checks and housing. This means that the size and direction of the flows was ultimately determined by policy. Figure 7.1 shows the principal bilateral recruitment agreements existing at the end of 1973, and hence gives an idea of the direction of migrant flows around 1973. It also shows that, at the time, Western Europe and the southern and eastern flanks of the Mediterranean indeed formed one large market for unskilled labour.

The ensuing migration flows were of considerable *size* (Böhning, 1972), actually much larger than indicated by the figures of Table 7.1. Indeed most work licences were valid for a short period only. The

Table 7.2   **Estimate of the number of foreign workers in the member states, 1960–73, and their relative importance in the labour market of the host country**

	Absolute figures (1000s)			Percentage of labour force		
	1960[a]	1970[a]	1973[b]	1960[a]	1970[a]	1973[b]
Germany	461	1727	2519	2	6	11
France	1294	1584	1900	6	8	11
Italy	20	30	55	—	—	—
Netherlands	47	134	121	1	3	3
Belgium	170	257	211	5	7	7
Luxemburg	20	27	43	16	21	35
EU6	2012	3759	4849	3	5	7
UK	1233	1815	1751	5	7	7
Ireland	1	2	2	—	—	—
Denmark[c]	15	30	36	1	1	2
EU9	3261	5606	6638	3	6	8
EU15[d]	n.a.	6000	7000	3	5	6

Notes:
[a]   Labour force.
[b]   Dependent workers.
[c]   Given the free movement of labour existing between Denmark and Sweden, Norway and Finland, these figures have to be corrected upward.
[d]   Estimates for total: intra + extra EU12. Figures are rounded. Figures for Spain, Portugal and Greece are very low.

Sources: 1960 and 1970: United Nations (1979, p. 324). For Italy, Denmark and Ireland: national statistics and estimates.
1973: KEG, *Beschäftigung ausländischer Arbeitnehmer*, various years, Brussels.

holders of such licences, mostly unmarried, unskilled workers, used to arrive at workplaces in Western Europe, stay for a period of two years and then return to their home country. Around 1970, nearly one million migrants entered the EU, but about the same number returned home. Taking into account migration to other European countries, such as Sweden and Austria, and to a lesser extent the UK, we observe in Western Europe, in that period, a yearly gross migration of between two and three million people. In the flows, cyclical patterns can be perceived (Kayser, 1972; Moulaert and Derykere, 1982).

In the period 1960–73, *foreign labour was essential to the economy* of European receiving countries. In the original six member states the number of foreigners on the labour market rose between 1960 and 1973 from approximately two million to nearly five million (Table 7.2).[7] In 1970, in five of the six member states (Italy being the exception) an average 7 per cent of total labour supply came from third countries, against some 3 per cent in 1960. For certain sectors the dependency was actually much greater; in particular the metal industry, construction and some service sectors (catering) attracted much foreign labour in this period (Bhagwati *et al.*, 1984). Immigration enabled the EU to keep activities within its borders which otherwise would have had to relocate outside the EU (entailing outward direct investment flows) (see Chapter 8).

The first enlargement (1973–81)

In 1973, the UK, Ireland and Denmark became members and from that year onward the free mutual exchange of workers could be extended across the nine member states. Let us first see what the situation was at that moment with respect to the interpenetration of labour markets of the nine member states (see Table 7.2) and then see how migration has developed over the 1973–81 period.

The *intra-EU migration* consisted of three categories. The first refers to a hard core of workers stationed abroad by multinational companies and international organisations. The second type refers to emigrated Italians, already discussed in detail in the previous section (about one million). The third type refers to Irish emigrants (almost half a million of them), traditionally destined for the UK; that kind of emigration had already been regulated by bilateral agreement before 1973 (Böhning, 1972; Sexton, *et al.*, 1991). Together these groups amounted to some 3 million, so the degree of integration of the EU labour markets in 1973 was still quite modest (3 per cent).

The workers from *third countries* in the nine member states can be split according to their origin into three groups.

- *Greece, Spain and Portugal.* The destinations of their emigrants show very clear patterns: practically all Portuguese were staying in France, most Spaniards in France but also some in Germany; by far the most Greeks were employed in Germany, a very small proportion in the UK. Emigration was highly important to these three countries. In 1973, 19 per cent of the labour force of Portugal, 9 per cent of the Greek and more than 4 per cent of the Spanish were employed in the EU9.[8] Salt (1976) mentions that migrants had transferred to their home country sums that equalled 24 per cent of imports for Greece, 9 per cent for Spain, and as much as 37 per cent for Portugal.
- *Other Mediterranean countries.* Turkey and Yugoslavia were important emigration countries in 1973 (each accounting for 0.6 million emigrants). Workers from these countries were employed almost exclusively in Germany (Turks to a lesser degree in the Netherlands). Emigrants from North West Africa (Algeria, Morocco and Tunisia) were rather selective as to their destination, being oriented almost entirely to France and to some extent to the Benelux.[9]
- *Other countries.* A small proportion of this group were citizens of third countries who work for multinational companies or international organisations (Americans, Japanese and other nationalities). Another limited part of this group was formed by foreign workers from Central and West African countries. The main body was formed by the approximately one million foreigners staying in the UK. Most immigrants into the UK come from Commonwealth countries. For many of them the status of foreigners, in the legal sense, is far less clear than for other immigrants. For that reason, the figure of about one million Commonwealth immigrants resident in the UK should be looked upon as merely indicative.

Let us next look at the changes that occurred in the *1973–80 period* (Table 7.3). The first enlargement in 1973 coincided with the end of a long period of stable growth in Western Europe. The changed economic situation in the host countries led to a drop in GDP; many companies got into difficulties and the tension on the labour market rapidly diminished. Governments of immigration countries started to pursue restrictive admission policies *vis-à-vis* citizens of non-EU countries (Hammar, 1985) and actively to stimulate return migration (Böhning, 1979).[10] Moreover schemes were developed to stimulate the assimilation or improve the integration of workers settled more permanently (that is, whose families were resident in the host country) (Council of Europe 1980, 1983; Castles and Kosack, 1985; Edye, 1987; CEC, 1985a).

Table 7.3   Estimated total number of foreign workers (millions) in the EU15, by country of origin and percentage share in total labour force, 1973–2000[a]

	Area	1973	1980	1990	2000
Intra-EU	Total EU15	3.3	2.6	2.4	2.9
Extra-EU	Mediterranean	2.2	2.1	2.3	n.a.
	Other	1.6	1.6	2.0	n.a.
	Total of third countries	3.8	3.7	4.3	5.2
Total	World	7.1	6.3	6.7	8.1
Share in total Labour force (%)	Intra+Extra-EU15	6	5	5	5
	Extra-EU15	3	3	3	3

Note:
[a] In interpreting the magnitude and the evolution over time of the data presented one should keep in mind that their statistical basis is sometimes very weak and moreover very different over time. Figures for 2000 are estimates.

Sources: KEG, *Beschäftigung ausländischer Arbeitnehmer*, 1975 and 1982, Brussels; OECD (1992); see also Eurostat (1985, 1987, 1997); *OECD Labour Force Statistics*, various years.

The developments and measures described above have led to a drop in the number of migrant workers in the EU. This decline varied in size for different groups of country of origin, depending on the degree of integration (Table 7.3).

- *EU partners.* The figures indicate an integration effect; that is to say, migration diminishes as free trade grows.[11] For instance, on balance, 200 000 Italians working in other member states returned home in the 1970s once free trade among the EU countries had led to accelerated growth, more employment opportunities and better wages in their home country. Other countries too – such as Belgium and the Netherlands – registered a drop in the number of citizens employed in another EU member country. It is also possible that, in times of economic depression, both workers and employers tend to prefer their own labour market. The increasing number of British employed abroad in the 1970s may have been the initial effect of the UK workers' progressive integration in the common labour market, clearly helped along by economic (push factor) motives. Moreover, given the widespread knowledge of the English language, the social distances may well be shorter for English workers than for workers from other member states.

- *The three new member states*. The steep drop in the number of workers from Greece, Spain and Portugal employed in the rest of the present EU can be attributed to changes in admission policy in the receiving countries. Total return migration amounted to almost half a million (about 200 000 Spaniards, 100 000 Portuguese and 150 000 Greeks).
- *Other Mediterranean countries*. Here the restrictive policies have had less effect. Between 1973 and 1980, the numbers of Yugoslavians had decreased considerably, but those of North Africans and Turks had increased.
- *Third countries*. The doubtful measurement of the remaining group (UK) does not permit a clear-cut conclusion.

The *spatial patterns* of European international migration have been subjected to studies using different approaches. Some were mostly theoretical (for example, Mueller, 1980). Others concentrated on the motives of individual migrants and employers (for instance, OECD, 1978). Yet others focused on phenomena well known from interregional migration analysis (for instance, Klaassen and Drewe, 1973; Heijke and Klaassen, 1979). A model has also been set up that combines elements from these studies with factors suggested by integration theory, international sociology and modern political economics (Molle and Van Mourik, 1988, 1989a). The test of this model confirmed that international migration to and in Western Europe is influenced to a large extent by push factors (low earnings and the lack of job opportunities in the sending country); pull factors (availability of jobs and better pay in the host countries); friction factors (cost of movement, cultural differences between LECs and LICs); and finally immigration-restricting measures in receiving countries. Less straightforward is the outcome with respect to the hypotheses concerning degrees of integration (capital markets and goods trade). Other empirical investigations show that there is no clear correlation between the movement of goods and of people (OECD, 1992). The available evidence (when viewed in the light of the debate on substitution versus complementarity) suggests three things:

- Labour movements have to some extent been a substitute for goods movements (low-skilled labour maintaining certain productions in high-wage countries).
- The movement of goods and capital has been a substitute for labour movement (low migration, high trade flows; see also direct investment, Chapter 8).
- No evidence of complementarity has been found.

Second and third enlargement and the opening up of Eastern Europe (1981–99)

Intra-EU migration has shown little variation over time in recent years (Table 7.3). In the 1985–90 period there seems to have been a slight drop. There are several factors to explain this evolution (CEC, 1991b). First, the enlargement of the EU with three Mediterranean countries coincided with a new impetus to European economic growth given by the internal market programme. The economic restructuring of the most advanced member countries that ensued diminished the pull factors for migration, as the demand for low-skilled jobs declined. Second, the access to the EU markets and the increased confidence of both domestic and foreign investors in the three new member countries (see next chapter) diminished the push factors: the large increase in investment and an accelerated growth of GDP increased domestic employment opportunities and wages.

In the nineties, migration within the EU picked up again. This may be the effect of larger numbers of employees of MNF and international organisations that are the result of a stronger interpenetration of the economies of the enlarged EU (see Chapters 14 and 18). However the figures in Table 7.3 show very clearly that the freedom to move within the EU does not in itself bring about substantial migration; on the contrary, it seems that labour is rather immobile between EU member countries. The main reasons are cultural differences, increasingly similar employment situations, and lack of harmonisation of professional and vocational qualifications and of social security and tax regulations. This situation is likely to continue in the future. Indeed the experience of the Nordic countries shows that migration flows stay very small notwithstanding very limited cultural and language differences, harmonisation of social security and a long-standing integration of labour markets (Fischer and Straubhaar, 1996). We do not expect that the introduction of the euro is going to change that situation. Neither the pull nor the push factors seem to be significantly influenced by EMU.

The number of immigrant labourers from *third countries* into the whole EU increased in the 1980s and 1990s (Table 7.3). The causes of this increase differ within sub-groups:

- *Third countries of the Mediterranean basin.* These countries continued their sending of people and hence workers to the EU. Return migration, notwithstanding policy measures, remained low. On the contrary, again notwithstanding policy measures, immigration continued, mainly in the form of family reunion and illegal entrance. The main explanatory factor of this development is the push factor: low income and low employment possibilities due to a very dynamic population growth and a lagging economic growth in the home countries.

- *Other third countries*. The developing countries of Latin America, Asia and sub-Saharan Africa have started to send people to the EU in significant numbers. Although often occurring officially on political grounds, this increasing migration appears in practice to be motivated by economic reasons, or a combination of both.
- *Central and Eastern Europe*. These economies have been going through a painful adjustment process, from a regime of central planning to that of market orientation. In that process large numbers of workers, many of them highly skilled, have been made redundant. Many have tried to enter the EU to find a job, but actual numbers who have succeeded are limited due to the prevailing restrictions.

These migratory flows are very different from the ones that prevailed in the 1960s, for several reasons. First, they concern more sending countries over a much wider geographical area. Second, they concern more receiving countries: southern European countries that up to the mid-1980s had almost no immigration have become in the past decade the host countries of millions of third country immigrants. Third, recent migrants often go to the tertiary sector instead of the secondary one; large numbers of migrants tend even to enter the informal, sometimes even illegal, labour market (Pugliese, 1992). Fourth, the causes of migration tend to become more complex (intertwining of political, security and economic factors), leading to increased pressure. Finally, the conditions for integration in the LIC have deteriorated (lack of job opportunities and increasing cost of social integration).

As a consequence of the upsurge in migratory pressure on the EU, voices grew loud in the call to severely *limit immigration* into the EU.[12] In practice, the governments of all member countries have now resorted to a policy of restriction of immigration. Notwithstanding a clear convergence of national policies with respect to their targets and their instruments, it has not yet been possible to produce a common EU policy (see previous section).[13]

Wage structures

Movement and movement cost, price convergence

The effects of the integration of factor markets can be illustrated by comparing situations without and with migration of labour (Lindert,

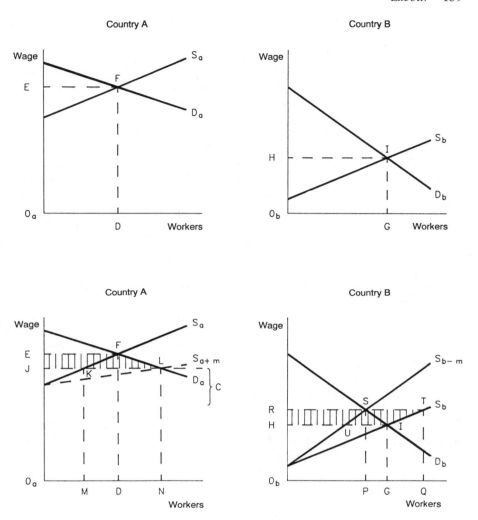

Figure 7.2   Integration of factor markets, price convergence

1986). That is done in Figure 7.2, where the upper part of the graph indicates the situation without, and the bottom part the situation with, migration. We have assumed that the world consists of two countries, A and B; the situation for A is depicted on the left-hand side, that for B on the right-hand side. The situation on the labour market is given by the upward-sloping curves S_a and S_b representing labour supply, and the downward-sloping curves D_a and D_b representing demand for labour. Together they determine the price of labour (wages) and the number of workers employed.

In the non-integrated situation, in which the labour markets of countries A and B are separate, that is, without migration (upper part of Figure 7.2), the supply and demand conditions in country A lead to high wages and those in country B to low wages. Two national labour markets with such different wage levels can be kept separate only by dint of control measures, for instance 'permits' or restricted access to professions.

In the integrated situation such barriers are removed (bottom part of Figure 7.2). Now workers of country B will move to country A where they earn a higher income. As movement entails costs, both in economic and psychological terms, this will not lead to the complete equalisation of wages. We assume these costs to be equal to C. The inflow of migrant labour into country A pushes the wages down, which leads to a lower quantity supplied domestically (O_aM) and a higher quantity demanded domestically (O_aN). The difference (MN) indicates the number of migrants from country B in country A. In country B the opposite occurs: the higher wages lead to a lower quantity demanded (O_bP) and an increased quantity supplied (O_bQ); the difference (PQ) indicates the number of migrants from country B to country A. The number of out-migrants of country B (PQ) is of course just equal to the demand for foreign labour created in country A (MN). The new curves of domestic labour S_{a+m} and S_{b-m} demonstrate the consequences.

Average wages: convergence or divergence?

In the previous section we described a mechanism that was limited to the openness on the labour markets. The international integration of goods markets does change the rather simple situation described above. The classical way in which this has been analysed is with the theory of the equalisation of factor returns (generally called Heckscher/Ohlin/Samuelson models; see Chipman, 1965–66 for a review). These models say that the change in demand for production factors that follows international specialisation will lead to an equalisation of wages. This means that goods movements may actually be a substitute for factor movements (Mundell, 1957). However interesting from a theoretical point of view, this approach is not very helpful in practice, as the assumptions on which it is based are rarely realised (Markusen, 1983). So let us look at alternative approaches that bear more resemblance to reality. These show, that *product market integration influences wages* through a number of channels (Andersen et al., 2000):

- Competitive pressures. The more integrated the economy is in international product markets, the more wages will converge to those of partner countries because of the need to stay competitive. This is *a fortiori* the case when firms have the freedom to move their production facilities to other countries.

- Cost of exporting. Where the taking away of barriers to trade permits local firms to export and does not induce foreign firms to enter the home market, wages may actually increase. Where firms from both countries enter the markets, it is unclear in which way wages will move.

- Foreign direct investment. The possibility of setting up plants in other countries and the reduction of distance cost may induce firms to split production vertically. Stages requiring lower qualified labour may then be located in low-income countries, with stages requiring highly skilled labour locating in high-wage countries. Depending on the relative changes of the demand and supply of labour in both types of country, the effects may be both convergence and divergence of wages.

- Institutions. Intensified international competition may induce labour unions and governments to accept structural reforms leading to more labour market flexibility. In general, wage restraint is highest in cases of either very centralised or very decentralised wage bargaining. Openness of product markets permits the entry of firms that have no allegiance to existing labour institutions. Depending on the initial situation this may lead to more divergence or more convergence.

The uncertainty in theoretical terms as to the outcome of the process of product and production factor integration has led to the development of two schools of thought (Molle and van Mourik, 1989b):

The *convergence school* is of rather neo-classical inspiration. It supposes that markets do work efficiently. Migration will bring equalisation of wages. Even in the absence of factor movements, the openness of product markets will induce the partners on the labour markets to align their wages to productivity. And productivity in low-wage countries will gradually increase due to catching up effects in which innovation plays an important role. Multinational firms will transfer technology and management practices to low-wage countries, thereby increasing the capacity to sustain higher wages. National governments of these countries will match this with investments in training of labour and infrastructure.

The *divergence school* maintains that the conditions for equalisation mostly do not obtain. Movement of labour tends to be restricted by factors like spatial and cultural distance and by institutional factors. Even in a customs union, trade can be impeded by collusive practices, transport costs, multinational firms monopolising new technology, and so on. The technological advance of certain countries implies that they will always select the new products with high value added as soon as they come on the market, abandoning products as soon as their value added drops and no longer sustains high wages. Thus the wage gap that accompanies the technology gap is not only perpetuated, but even accentuated. The liberalisation of European goods and factor markets was feared to have such an agglomeration effect (Giersch, 1949; Seers *et al.*, 1979, 1980).

The answer to the question, which one of these two schools actually holds the truth depends on *empirical research*. Rigorous testing of the alternative views used to be very difficult because of deficient data (Tovias, 1982; Gremmen, 1985; van Mourik, 1987). Some early analyses of the effects of European integration (Meyer and Willgerodt, 1956; Fisher, 1966; Butler, 1967) did indeed show a certain convergence of wage levels. For the founder countries of the EU, a considerable degree of international convergence of wages was found for the 1964–89 period (van Mourik, 1989, 1993). This convergence is primarily due to Italy's catching up with its partners in terms of productivity. For the period 1970–2000 the increased integration of goods markets of the EU member countries did indeed show a (cor)relation with wage convergence (Andersen *et al.*, 2000).

There are still wide differences in average wages among the countries of the EU. On the whole they are highly similar to the international differences in GDP (see Table 16.2, p. 403), with mostly high figures for the countries in Northern Europe, and low ones for the Mediterranean states. There are several reasons that explain why the convergence of wage levels is not complete. One is based on the limitations of *factor market integration.* The imperfect factor mobility among countries; an idea of the relatively limited migration among the member countries of the EU has indeed been given in the previous section. That lack of mobility is not only an international phenomenon: it also obtains on the national level among regions, sectors of activity and occupational groups.[14] Differences in pay may also spring from restrictive practices, based, for instance, on trade union power, on government regulations issued under pressure of certain groups or on employers' practices that disfavour persons of a certain race or gender. The second reason has to do with *other aspects of integration.* The catch-up process of backward countries is indeed one of long duration. The restructuring of both the industrial base and the labour supply does take time as it implies many detailed decisions on the micro level. Lack of integration (for example, on service markets) may slow down the pace at which such decisions are actually taken.

Industry wages: effect of openness

The industrial structure of wages shows a high degree of *similarity* in the different European countries, despite large differences among them in trade union practice, availability of manpower, relative importance of the sector in the total economy and so on (Butler, 1967; Bouteiller, 1971; Saunders and Marsden, 1981).[15] That similarity is due to branches having the same characteristics as to skill, occupation, sex, capital/labour ratio, firm size and so on in different countries (Vassille, 1989).

Moreover the structure shows a high degree of *stability* through time because the determinant factors are stable through time (Lebergott, 1947; Reder, 1962; OECD, 1965, 1985c). Although over time the ranking of industries tends to remain the same, there seems to be a slight tendency of convergence towards the mean.

The question may be asked how far the increased *openness to trade* has influenced this structure. Empirical evidence for seven EU countries and five more OECD countries (Oliveira Martins, 1994) suggests two effects: first a negative effect on relative wages for industries with a low product differentiation; second a positive effect in industries with a high product differentiation and large scale economies. The first outcome is predicted by traditional trade theory, the second by modern trade models with imperfect competition.

Welfare effects

Distributional effects

The welfare effects of the migration caused by the joining of markets are also illustrated by Figure 7.2. They are fairly intricate and apply to both workers and employers in country A and country B (for a review, see Table 7.4).

Workers from country A lose area *JEKF* because their wages are forced down. (For that reason, many trade unions in developed countries are against immigration.) On the other hand, workers remaining in country B gain from out-migration; there is less competition for jobs, which raises the wage rate from O_bH to O_bR. The gain is the producer surplus above the new supply curve (*HRSU*). The migrants also gain: they earn a higher income in A than they would have in B. However account should be taken of cost factor C. So the gain is the area above the old supply curve S_b and below the new one S_{b-m} (*USTI*).

Employers in country A gain considerably: the area *JEFK* is redistributed to them from workers, while the area *KFL* is a net gain. In

Table 7.4   Welfare effects of integrated production factor markets

Category	Country	Gains	Losses
Workers	A	*	*JEFK*
	B	*HRSU*	*
	B to A	*USTI*	*
Employers	A	*JEFL*	*
	B	*	*HRSI*

Note: *   Not applicable.

country B, on the contrary, employers are losers: they have to pay higher wages and hence lose profits. Of their consumer surplus (employers are demanders of labour!) they have to hand over area *HRSU* to workers remaining in the country, and area *USI* to migrants.

Countries A and B are clearly in different positions. The receiving country A has a net gain (*KFL*). The sending country B, on the contrary, has a net loss *USI* (difference between employers' loss and workers' gain). The migrants gain also: *USI* and *STI*. So the net gain to the world is *KFL* and *STI*; the distribution of welfare among countries depends on the allocation over countries of the gains to migrants.

The quantification of these effects in practice has not always been simple. The effect of increased returns to capital for France was calculated at between 1.2 and 2.2 per cent of GNP in 1971 (MacMillan, 1982). For Germany, employers' incomes have been estimated as being some 10 per cent above the level they would have had without immigration (see studies cited in Spencer, 1994). The effects of immigrant labour on wages of local workers are rather equivocal: some find negative effects (Haisken-De New, 1996), others find no effects (Pischken and Velling, (1994) and yet others even positive effects (Winter-Ebmer and Zweimueller, 1996). This confusion may be due to differences in the effect on branches: indeed for Germany it was found (Haisken-De New, 1996) that one needs to distinguish two cases. First is the case where one can presume that there is complementarity between foreign and native workers (branches with a high foreigner share); here migration has had a positive effect on native workers. Second is the case where the foreigners seem to compete with natives (branches with a small share of foreigners); here the effect on native wages has been negative.

Other effects on labour-importing countries

The most important welfare effects of migration have been enumerated in the first section of this chapter. Their quantification starts with the *static direct production effect* – in other words the increase in GNP as a result of the employment of immigrant workers. Case studies indicate that this effect is limited; in France, for example, immigrant workers, forming about 7 per cent of the French wage-earning labour force, contributed about 5 per cent of French GNP in 1971 (MacMillan, 1982). The contribution of migration to the economic growth of EU countries amounted on average to only 0.05 per cent (Askari, 1974); more recent studies for Germany come up with higher figures (Spencer, 1994).

The *dynamic effects* of labour migration to LICs are less well known (Böhning and Maillat, 1974) and there is much dispute even over the question whether the effects are positive on balance. Let us look at the different categories.

As to the *macro-economic effects*, some note a positive development because immigration, by taking away certain bottlenecks in the economy, has led to a permanently higher growth rate of GNP (UN/ECE, 1977, Zimmermann, 1995). Others note a negative effect: they argue that migration has prevented the economies of the LICs from adjusting structurally to the new global conditions in comparative advantages (see Box 7.1).

As to the effects on *public finance*, there is some confusion too. Some have pointed out the negative aspects like the presumably high cost of social services for immigrants (schools and so on). However there is no evidence that active immigrants' demands on social (security) and public services (schools, hospitals and so on) exceed systematically their contributions, the results of many studies do not produce a consistent picture (Blitz, 1977; Bourguignon *et al.*, 1977; Löffelholz, 1992; SER, 1992; Spencer, 1994). However other studies show that, if one takes into account the cost of the second generation unemployed immigrants, the balance is rather negative.

On balance, labour-importing countries seem to have benefited from immigration;[16] this benefit is larger in periods of labour shortages and smaller in periods of considerable unemployment such as the 1990s. On the basis of these findings, many experts now plead in favour of a more selective or strategic immigration policy: letting in persons of working age with the required skills and keeping out all persons for whom the cost–benefit balance is likely to be negative (for example, Zimmermann, 1995) (see the final sub-section of this section). Ideas to implement such a policy through an immigration tax seem rather far removed from political realism and practical operability.

Box 7.1   Industrial restructuring and (selective) immigration

Firms operating in high-wage countries in sectors losing their comparative advantage may try to postpone structural adaptation by finding ways to cut costs. Labour costs can be cut only if labour can be imported and effectively paid lower wages than those prevailing in other sections of the industry. In Figure 7.3 (adapted from Bhagwati, 1982) *OS* represents the real wages of the domestic labour in country A, which is threatened by low-cost competition from outside. *OL* represents the lower, fixed real wages at which foreign labour can be imported to execute the parts of the production process that have lost their comparative advantage. *SHR* is the marginal product curve of the labour that is permitted to immigrate (immigration quota *OJ*) given the input of domestic capital and qualified labour. The output in country A is then *SHJO*, of which only *OLHJ* accrues to foreign workers and the rest, *LSH*, to domestic capitalists. The latter effect makes the policy welfare-improving to the labour-importing country.

So, if the internal labour market can be effectively segmented, capitalists and the unions of the remaining domestic labour of the industry in question will bring pressure to bear on the government to import labour and thus postpone the restructuring of the sector. In view of the net welfare gain of *LSH*, governments will be inclined to accept such a policy for economic reasons (being pushed in the same direction for electoral reasons as well). However, if competition from foreign producers increases, the cost reduction that was made possible by the immigration policy is likely to become insufficient to keep up the production in country A. Industrialist pressure groups will then cry for protection, supported by both domestic and immigrant labour. Should this not be granted, the restructuring problem is aggravated, notably so if the immigrant labour, having become redundant, will not return to their home country nor find alternative jobs in the host country.

Effects on labour-exporting countries

The emigration of part of its labour force has both significant advantages and costs. These can be identified for three different categories. The *loss of part of the labour force* may not have had a very negative effect on total welfare creation in so far as it concerned unskilled

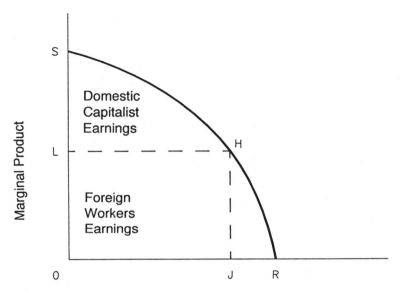

Figure 7.3   Labour import in sunset industries

unemployed persons. However it is different for the outflow of skilled workers (Sexton *et al.*, 1991). As a substantial proportion of the emigrants have received more education than the average workers in the LECs, the loss of manpower through emigration is likely to have had a negative effect on LECs' welfare. Temporary emigrants are supposed to have acquired *increased skills* while working abroad. However, once they have returned, the enhanced quality of human capital seems to have had little positive effect on the economies of LECs, for two reasons. On the one hand, the inability of LECs to offer sufficient employment opportunities to returning skilled workers has led to a net loss of human capital. On the other hand, returning migrants are generally disinclined to accept low-status jobs and frequently set up unprofitable service trades (Papadimetriou, 1978). Such factors have contributed to the rather negative welfare effects of policies that stimulated return migration (Dustmann 1996).

Migrants remittances count as a possible third positive effect of labour export. They amount to a considerable proportion of the LECs' GNP and in the short run constitute a very convenient means of financing deficits on the balance of trade. The long-run effects of remittances on the LECs' economy are limited, however, because on the whole they have been used for investment in houses and consumption purposes rather than for productive capital formation (Keely and Tran, 1989).[17] The increased consumption they have made possible has caused substantial price and wage increases and contributed to the misallocation of resources in LECs. And sometimes they have led to an overvalued currency. The transfer of savings, which also seemed promising, has proved rather disappointing in terms of investments in the emigration country, for too much money has been invested for purposes that are not directly productive.

Interesting from a theoretical point of view, but difficult to implement, are proposals to compensate LECs for the negative effects of emigration by introducing an *emigration tax* (Bhagwati, 1987b) and to transfer financial means to LECs through an International Labour Compensatory Facility (for example, Kennedy Brenner, 1979).

Summary and conclusions

- Politically the EU holds as a fundamental principle that nobody must be forced to submit to the socio-cultural and legal adjustments involved in international migration within Europe, and that ideally everyone should find sufficient work in his own country. Thus, unlike the situation on goods markets, the further integration of labour markets is not meant to entail large migration flows.
- The degree of interpenetration of EU labour markets (number of foreign workers divided by the total number of employed) is less than 2 per cent. This suggests that goods and capital movements have largely been substitutes for labour movements.
- Intra-EU migration is limited because of the taking away of barriers to goods, services and capital movement, the limited differences in wages compared to the cost of living, and the persistence of differences in culture and institutions such as social security systems.
- The fairly wide wage discrepancies prevailing among EU member states at the start of the integration period have decreased considerably since, which is in line with expectations fostered by the convergence school.
- Occupational and industrial wage structures are very similar in the various member countries, and change only very gradually.
- Most migration comes from third countries. The welfare effects of these movements are not clear. The elaboration of a common EU policy in this matter is a complicated and difficult process as it touches sensitive areas such as internal security.

Notes

1 The definition of movement of labour refers to persons residing and working outside their home country; frontier zone workers are therefore generally excluded. Although they also reflect the integration of labour markets, their motives are different from those of actual migrants.

2 In Western Europe, labour has always been on the move (see, for instance, Winsemius, 1939; Lannes, 1956); the movements were often inspired by political motives. The migration wave just after the Second World War comes immediately to mind; examples for the 1960s and 1970s are the repatriation of French people from North Africa and of Portuguese citizens from Angola and Mozambique, while very recently emigration from the war-ridden former Yugoslavia is a case in point.

3 Non-discrimination does not mean that wages in the different member countries have to be equal, but that there shall be no difference in the remuneration of workers of different nationalities working in the same establishment and country. Before the Treaty of Rome was drafted, there had been a discussion about the need to harmonise wages and the other elements of manpower cost firms have to pay (such as social security contributions, holidays and fringe benefits) prior to the internal liberalisation of labour movements. Most of those participating in the debate did not recognise such a need, however. The basic idea of the founding fathers was that wages were to be determined in the process of national bargaining between trade unions and employers.

4 The EEC Treaty did, however, prescribe equal pay for men and woman. In 1972 the gap between the principle and practice was still very wide (Saunders and Marsden, 1981). On average, the hourly earnings of women were about a quarter lower than those of men. Most of this difference was not due to wage discrimination but to the fact that men and women do different work. This in turn could be explained by factors such as less skill, lack of seniority, inappropriate age and more part-time work (Kottis, 1985). The men–women wage differential decreased over *the period 1950–83* (Schippers and Siegers, 1986).

5 The right to establish in the entire EU does apply of course also to persons who are nationals of a member state but who reside outside the EU; and to workers with an EU nationality who want to set up independent business in another member state.

6 International organisations, such as the International Labour Organisation (ILO), the OECD and the Council of Europe have each assumed a coordinating role; however, this is by no means comparable to the competences of an organisation like GATT in the field of trade. Note that the absence of a common EU policy has been remedied in part by a convergence of national immigration policies; most member countries are now fairly restrictive, limiting immigration with a panoply of instruments; some have concluded agreements with their neighbouring countries (non-EU members) to help them to put their policies into effect, such as administrative procedures.

7 In interpreting these data, keep in mind that they should be corrected upwards because of the considerable clandestine migration going on. Some have estimated illegal migration at that time at certainly no less than 10 per cent.

8 These national figures obscure even higher figures for certain regions: in some regions of Portugal, up to half the male labour force appeared to have emigrated to Northern Europe in 1973. In interpreting these data one should, moreover, keep in mind that all three countries are traditional emigration countries for other destinations than the EU: Iberians particularly to South America, Greeks to Australia and the USA (UN, 1980; Bernard, 1978).

9   The volume of the North African presence in the EU around 1973 is probably underestimated in the statistics used owing to the fact that at one time Algerians were admitted to France without working or residence permit. Some observers estimate the number of employed North Africans resident in France during this period at more than one million.

10   To stimulate return migration, measures of four types were introduced (Lebon and Falchi, 1980): (1) return premium to the person involved; (2) aid for setting up in business to person involved; (3) subsidies for professional training to the home country; (4) development aid to projects to home country.

11   Very few authors have tried to test this hypothesis quantitatively, although the subject has been debated for a long time (see, for instance, Meyer and Willgerodt, 1956; Mihailovic, 1976).

12   See Eurobarometer of various years that report that a majority of EU citizens are in favour of a policy of severely restricting immigration. The economics of the policy are discussed in Böhning, 1993; OECD, 1993a; Siebert, 1994.

13   The typical policy now is to stimulate integration into society for migrants already residing in the country and to restrict new immigration to persons who can fill in positions on the labour market that otherwise would not have been profitable. Active policies for stimulating return migration are not considered, as these are difficult to implement. However, making clear from the outset to new immigrants whether their stay is permanent or temporary is welfare improving (see Dustmann, 1996). This policy should be complemented by a policy of aid to the labour sending countries, so as to restrict push factors (Molle *et al.*, 1992; Molle, 1996).

14   Impediments to movement are many and manifold; they encompass personal choice, capacities and discrimination. Personal choice is reflected in the different amenities going with certain jobs, which may offset pay differences, and in the unwillingness of certain people to pay for the retraining required to move to a better occupation, or to change their place of residence. The capacity factor shows up in the personal qualities (intelligence, skill and so on) needed for certain jobs and limiting the number of possible entrants. Movements may also be impeded by opaque markets and by the high cost of gathering information.

15   It was even similar in the liberal Western and the centrally planned Eastern European systems (for example, Redor, 1992).

16   This is also the experience of the USA, as noted in the studies of Simon (1989) and USDL (1989); later studies, such as Borjas (1995) and Friedberg and Hunt (1995), show more contradictory effects.

17   See also, for the Maghreb countries, the contribution by Garson in OECD (1994a).

8 Capital

— Short term capital

Introduction

Capital markets reveal many special characteristics that cause their integration to differ in practice profoundly from the way other markets are integrated, notwithstanding the basic theoretical similarity to, for example, labour market integration. To prepare this difficult ground we will start with a short description of the *basic concepts* of integration of capital markets, including of course the various barriers to movement, the advantages and so on. Next a brief sketch of the European *regulatory environment* in which capital liberalisation proceeds will be given.

The remainder of the chapter will be a description of the changes in the structure of international capital market transactions by private enterprises. We make a distinction between direct investment and long-term loans. Patterns and volume of *direct investment* in Europe have been profoundly influenced by integration.

Next we go into the present patterns of other international capital movements from and to the EU, discussing two important indicators of the degree of integration, namely, the volume of international transactions, and the equalisation of interest rates that is, of the price of capital. A short section on the *welfare effects* of capital market integration and a brief summary of the findings complete the chapter.

Some basic concepts

Motives for impediments

Arguments for restricting capital movements are based mostly on the disadvantages associated with long-term capital drain-offs (Cairncross, 1973; Swoboda, 1976; Mathieson and Rojas-Suarez, 1994).

171

The most frequently heard reasons for governments to feel they should impede the *exporting* of capital are the following:

- Bloodstream of the national economy. Capital drain-offs will reinforce the economies of other countries to the detriment of the country's own economy (for instance, there is less domestic investment, so the government receives less tax on the ensuing revenue).
- Loss of currency reserves. This jeopardises the ability to meet other international obligations; this is particularly relevant when the balance of payment is in disequilibrium and authorities are trying to prevent changes in the exchange rate.
- Internal equilibrium – an argument mainly associated with the price of capital. A large outflow of capital may compel a high rate of interest when a low rate would be recommendable for the development of the national economy.
- External equilibrium. Capital outflow may lead to currency devaluation even though the rate of exchange, as judged on other criteria such as the current account, is not unbalanced. In that way, the nation might be forced into more expensive imports and imported inflation.
- Lack of confidence of international markets in policy measures of politically unstable countries. In order to maintain as much as possible the effectiveness of their fiscal and monetary policies, governments of these countries need the capital control instrument.

Rather paradoxically, arguments are also raised against the *importing* of capital, such as the following:

- Capital is power; therefore capital in foreign hands means loss of authority over one's own economy.
- Disturbance of the internal and external equilibrium: a large inflow of capital may entail a lower rate of interest than the monetary authorities think adequate for internal equilibrium.

Finally there are arguments pleading against *both the importing and the exporting* of capital:

- Disturbance. We have already pointed out the disturbances that may be the result of exporting short-term capital. Capital imports can be disturbing in cases where they are of a speculative nature, that is anticipating changes in the rates of interest and/or the exchange rates of currency.
- Perversity: free movement of long-term capital does not lead to

optimum allocation, but to concentration in countries with a large market where capital is already in abundant supply, while states with smaller markets are deprived of capital.

The experience with controls both on inflows and on outflows has shown them in the long run to be ineffective instruments for preventing structural adjustments to the balance of payments. Modern technology and the development of 'offshore' international capital markets make it very difficult to make restrictive instruments effective even in the short run (Edwards, 1999). The arguments for fighting speculative capital movements, on the contrary, are on the whole economically sound (speculation leads often to overshooting); for that purpose other instruments may now be more effective (see Chapter 15, on monetary policy).

Forms of impediments

We can distinguish three groups of instruments to restrict the importation and exportation of capital (whether or not speculative), (compare Woolly, 1974; Schulze, 2000).

Market-oriented instruments   These resemble tariffs in goods trade, as they influence the price of capital:

- lower (even negative) interests on foreign deposits, caused by taxes on interest or deposits, or otherwise.

Administrative and legal instruments   These instruments are comparable to quantitative restrictions and non-tariff barriers:

- securities: trade may be impeded by reserving the right to hold stocks and bonds to persons or institutions of a given nationality and restricting non-residents' purchases of domestic securities; moreover restrictions may be placed on domestic investment and pension funds investments in foreign securities;
- bank deposits may be hindered by a ceiling on deposits kept by foreigners or, alternatively, by restrictions on residents' deposits in foreign countries.

Other instruments   These may include the following:

- currency restrictions: authorities allotting only limited amounts of foreign currency for given capital transactions; taxes or levies on the acquirement of foreign currency; split-currency markets, with a more (or less) favourable rate of exchange for current payments than for capital transactions;

- tax withheld on foreign investment, or heavier taxes on foreign profits than on domestic ones;
- profits and interests transfers may be hindered by an obligation to reinvest in the host country all profits made with foreign capital, and by committing exporters to return as soon as possible (for instance, within five years) any capital drained off abroad.

Advantages of integration

Integration of capital markets is aspired to because it:

- diminishes the risk of disturbances such as tend to occur in small markets;
- increases the supply of capital, because better investing prospects mobilise additional savings, the investor being free to choose the combination most favourable to him in terms of return, solidity and liquidity;
- enables those who are in need of capital to raise larger amounts in forms better tailored to their specific needs;
- makes for equal production conditions and thus fewer disturbances of competition in the common market.

Forms of integration

The movement of the production factor 'capital' can be considered free if entrepreneurs can satisfy their need for capital, and investors can offer their disposable capital, in the country where conditions are most favourable for them.

Once more a parallel can be drawn with free trade areas and customs unions. A free-capital movement area (FCMA) would then be a zone within which capital can move freely, each state making its own rules with respect to third countries. In a capital market union (CMU), on the contrary, there would be a common policy concerning the union's financial relations with third countries.

The integration of capital markets can be defined first of all as the removing of constraints on foreign exchange, of discriminatory tax measures and of other obstacles. This is the so-called 'negative integration'. Since capital is highly mobile and apt to go where the returns are highest, positive integration will also be needed; that is, the integration of capital markets by coordinating or harmonising the rules which govern their organisation and functioning, such as prudential regulations for bank credit, payments, and so on. Given the interwovenness of the capital market with monetary policy, a certain integration of monetary policy, and coordination of the monetary relations with third countries, would be implied.

EU regime

Rationale and principles

The liberty of capital movement as laid down in the Treaty of Rome was limited to *the extent necessary to ensure the proper functioning of the Common Market*. That restriction indicates that member states did not aspire to fully free movement of capital as an object in itself. The reason is that member states dared not give up the right to restrict external capital flows, because they needed the instruments for the effective control of internal macro-economic and monetary developments (OECD, 1979, 1982c). Moreover full freedom of capital movement was hard to reconcile with the selectivity implicit in the measures of fiscal policy, investment stimuli and so on of many member states. As a consequence, the provisions of the EEC Treaty for freedom of capital were not directly applicable, unlike those for goods and labour. Indeed the Treaty did not enjoin upon the Community the creation of a veritable European capital market.

The Treaty of Rome permitted the following *restrictions* of capital movement:

- 'Domestic rules governing the capital market and the credit system' could be applied by member states but only in a non-discriminating way; in other words, member states had to treat residents of other EU nationalities on the same footing as their own residents.
- 'Loans for the direct or indirect financing of a member state or of its regional or local authorities [were not to be] issued or placed in other member states unless the states concerned had reached agreement thereon'.
- 'If movements of capital [caused] disturbances in the functioning of the capital market' the Commission after consultation with the Monetary Committee could authorise member states to undo the liberalisation introduced since the creation of the EU.
- Balance of payments problems could justify capital movement restrictions.

However, member states had committed themselves to the readiness to *go beyond the degree of liberalisation* of capital movements prescribed by the Treaty, in so far as their economic situation, in particular the situation of their balance of payments, so permitted. Indeed efforts made towards the progressive liberalisation of capital movements have been made ever since the EU was founded, but up to 1987 they did not result in agreements reaching beyond the stipulations of the Treaty.

Directives of 1960–62

With respect to capital movements as well, the Treaty is a framework agreement, setting out some general principles to be complemented later by further rules. Such rules were drawn up at an early date (1960–62) in the shape of two directives, which distinguish three groups of transactions by the degree of liberalisation:

- *Fully free.* This category encompassed such transactions as direct investment (making capital available for an establishment abroad), the purchase of real estate, short- and medium-term trade credits, personal transactions like repatriation of earnings and former investments, and the acquisition by non-residents of quoted stocks in another member state. The liberalisation of this group rested on the direct connection with the free movement of goods (short- and medium-term trade credits), of employees and self-employed (personal transactions) and the right to free establishment (direct investments and investments through participation in capital stock).
- *Partly free.* This group comprised the issue and placing of shares listed on the stock market of a member state other than the one where the placing body resides; the acquisition of non-quoted shares by those not resident in the same country; shares in investment funds; and finally long-term trade credits. For this group, capital movement was only partly liberalised.
- *No obligation to liberalise* existed with respect to such short-term transactions as the purchase of treasury bonds and other capital stocks and the opening of bank accounts by non-residents. The reason why the principle of free movement was not applied to these transactions is that they may be of a speculative nature and therefore a cause of disturbance. Full and irrevocable liberalisation of these transactions could not be achieved while certain conditions were not fulfilled.

So the EU was at its start rather an incomplete common market, the situation on the capital market resembling, in terms of goods market, rather a free trade area for selected products than an encompassing customs union. In the mid-1960s, a team of experts reported on the prospects of further liberalisation and integration of markets (Segré *et al.*, 1966). Between 1966 and 1986, many concrete proposals were made, but in practice nothing was achieved. The causes are involved but in the main associated with the conviction of many governments that restricting capital movement is an essential instrument for an effective monetary policy.

Progress in deregulation and liberalisation

Although the integration of financial markets by EU regulations ceased to progress in the 1960s (Philip, 1978), actual integration has not stopped since. On the contrary, some member states (Germany, the Netherlands, Belgium and the UK) have proceeded with the liberalisation, not only for transactions with partners, but also for transactions with third countries. Others, like France and Italy, went on controlling many capital movements in spite of partial liberalisation. The same was true for the countries, which considered themselves in transition (since joining), such as Greece, Spain and Portugal.

Many and varied have been the proposals made to improve the working of the European capital market (for example, Verrijn Stuart *et al.*, 1965; Segré *et al.*, 1966). In the 1980s, the attitude towards international capital transactions shifted gradually but significantly (Lamfalussy, 1981) in favour of deregulation and liberalisation. What *determinant factors* brought this change about?

- External position. The improvement of the balance-of-payments position of many European countries permitted them to abandon capital controls.
- Poor efficiency of instruments. Governments had realised that restrictions on external capital movements often just delay structural adaptations of the economy that will be necessary anyway in the end and may become more costly if put off. (OECD, 1980, 1982a).
- General tendency to deregulate national financial markets. The progressive abolition of restrictions was stimulated by the experience in many countries with the negative effects of distortions created by such intervention of the public sector in the market.
- Technological innovation. The telecommunication and automation revolution has greatly reduced the information and transaction costs of the financial sector. Information on financial markets anywhere in the world is now instantly available anywhere else.
- Competition from largely unregulated 'offshore' markets. To avoid the problem of regulated home financial markets, a large unregulated international financial market had developed that

proved increasingly efficient in coping with investors' and borrowers' needs.

Recent measures for liberalisation

Inspired by the worldwide trend to liberalise capital markets and by the will to complete the internal market (Chapter 14) also for capital (CEC, 1986e), the EU decided to realise a free European capital market by 1992 (June 1988 directive). Capital movements between member countries have been *fully liberalised*. At the same time the movement of capital between the EU and non-EU countries was gradually liberalised. The Maastricht Treaty has codified the free internal and external movement of capital (Article 56) in the following words: '*Within the framework of the provisions set out in this chapter, all restrictions on the movement of capital between member states and between member states and third countries shall be prohibited.*'

The freedom of movement between member states is subject to a certain *regulation*, though. The Treaty (Article 58) permits member states to maintain regulations that differentiate between 'tax payers who are not in the same situation with respect to their place of residence or the place where the capital is invested'. Moreover member states are allowed:

- 'to take all requisite measures to prevent infringements of national law and regulations in particular in the field of taxation and of the prudential supervision of financial institutions or
- to lay down procedures for the declaration of capital movements for purposes of administrative or statistical information or
- to take measures which are justified on grounds of public policy or public security'.

Examples of the latter may be tax evasion and consumer protection.[1]

Improving the conditions for a proper functioning of European financial markets; harmonisation

To be effective, capital market integration cannot be limited to removing barriers; it also needs the creation of transparent markets and the harmonisation of the conditions enabling investors and creditors to be informed about the quality of foreign financial products. From the many measures taken by the EU in this respect we present three by way of illustration.

Taxes   Differences in tax levels may distort the market as they may induce investors to locate in countries which offer the highest tax-adjusted profit rates (OECD, 1991). This applies notably to corporate taxes and to taxes on the revenues of capital (deposits, for example). We will come back to this point of harmonisation of taxes in Chapter 14.

Company law Direct investors (for a takeover), investors in stock (for portfolio purposes) and subscribers to foreign companies' loans want to be able to judge the solvency and profitability of the company in question. A series of directives on company law have been adopted and more are in preparation. They concern the obligation to publish annual accounts according to certain specifications, minimum capital requirements, the qualifications of company auditors, national and international mergers, and the creation of a European company.[2]

Financial intermediaries A saver who places his deposit with a foreign bank wants to be reasonably sure that the bank is trustworthy, and the same is true of an investor in so-called 'open-end' funds. The directive of 1977 ('European Banking Law') lays down uniform criteria for admission to the banking trade and for the prudential control of banks in all member countries. Other directives determine the information banks have to give in their annual reports, the definition of the term 'own funds', and the application of common solvency and liquidity ratios, and even the specification of certain financial products (mortgages, for instance).[3]

External situation

The attempts made by the European Commission to liberalise capital movements in Europe are in line with more general efforts in the same direction made by other international bodies. At the world level, the International Monetary Fund (IMF) is the framework for such efforts. At the level of the industrialised world, it is the Organisation for Economic Cooperation and Development (OECD) that has stimulated free capital movement (OECD, 1968, 1982b, 1995a, 1995b).

The external policy of the European Union with respect to capital movements has changed over time. The Treaty of Rome does not set an objective for capital movements with third countries. Unlike the case for goods (where the Treaty established as a basic principle the greatest possible freedom with respect to traffic with third countries), the Treaty only urged member states to coordinate their capital movements with third countries (see Chapter 17).

The Maastricht Treaty has, however, installed a very clear principle for the common policy in matters of capital movement with third countries. Indeed the principle is that external movements need to be fully free, like internal movements. The reason is that many countries that had liberalised their capital transactions 'erga omnes' (with respect to all other countries, partners and third countries alike) while a common European policy did not yet exist were not prepared to reintroduce restrictions towards third countries under a new common policy.

The policy of openness to third countries is not one of *laissez-faire*, though. Indeed according to the Treaty the EU may regulate the movement of capital to or from third countries involving direct investment (including investment in real estate establishment), the provision of financial services or the admission of securities to capital markets (Article 57). The EU may even adopt restrictions on the freedom of capital movement with third countries if in exceptional circumstances movements of capital threaten to cause serious difficulties for the operation of the Economic and Monetary Union (Article 59).[4] Finally the EU promotes the adoption of liberal policies by third countries as well, so as to obtain symmetry in its external relations.

Direct investments; the logic of international production

Different forms of capital movement with free trade and protection

The theory of international capital is not a sufficient base for a study of the effects of a common market on capital movements. The reason is that very often international capital transactions are not made as portfolio transactions, but in the form of direct investments (DI). Typically direct investments are internal to the company involved but external to both countries where they operate. DI mostly involves the transfer not only of capital but also of other resources, such as technological know-how, management and marketing skills. Now it is the expected return on the total of the transferred resources rather than on the capital per se that is the rationale for firms to engage in direct foreign investment. Several approaches have been tried to explain DI (Carson, 1982) welded together into an eclectic approach that has provided a fertile basis for further analysis (Dunning, 1979, 1980, 1988, 1993). The principal hypothesis of that approach is that a firm will engage in foreign direct investment if three conditions are satisfied:

- it possesses net *ownership advantage vis-à-vis* firms of other nationalities in serving particular markets. These ownership advantages largely take the form of the possession of intangible assets – a technological lead, for instance – which are, at least for a period of time, exclusive or specific to the firm possessing them;

- on the assumption that the previous condition is satisfied, it must then be more beneficial to the company possessing these advantages to *internalise its advantages* through an extension of its own activities than to externalise them through licensing and similar contracts with foreign firms;
- once these conditions are satisfied, it must be profitable for the firm to utilise these advantages in conjunction with *locational advantages*, consisting of at least some factor inputs (including natural resources) outside its home country; otherwise foreign markets would be served entirely by exports and domestic markets by domestic production.

Assume that capital movement for direct investment is free between two countries; the type of DI will vary according to whether or not trade in goods is free as well (Dunning, 1980; de Jong, 1981, among others). We can distinguish two types of foreign direct investments dependent on the situation with respect to goods trade:

- *Protection.* If country A operates trade impediments, firms from B that want to export to A need a comparative advantage superior to the level of the tariff equivalent of country A's trade barrier. This advantage may be based on superior production technology, on the exclusive right to use a patent for the product, or, more generally, on better management or entrepreneurial skills. Exporting firms of country B who judge their advantage real but inferior to the tariff, and firms of B unwilling to have their profit margin taxed away by the tariff, will consider setting up production in country A. This necessitates a direct investment of country B in country A. Many governments are keen to attract direct investment to further their country's development. Firms in B will invest in A to be able to serve the markets of A. Such investments (often called 'tariff-jumping' investments) are based on product differentiation and tend to be substitutes for trade.
- *Free trade.* Many firms following a strategy of growing through product specialisation opt for operation on several markets, wanting to export to foreign markets from their home base. However this may not always prove the optimum solution, as production in other countries may be less costly. Within the market area, a location will be chosen for each plant that is optimal in view of the prevailing market conditions and other locational determinants such as transport cost, taxes and so on. To cash in on the advantages of international division of labour

within the firm (such as scale economies and use of factors in different countries), the type of direct investment that could be called 'optimum location seeking' will then be preferred. After production is started, international trade will develop. Some countries will specialise in one good, other countries in others. Often the direction of the investment is contrary to the direction of trade; that is, the export of capital goes hand-in-hand with the importation of goods, and vice versa.

The abolition of tariffs is not a sufficient reason to stop the first type of direct investment. Indeed even in a customs union other barriers may persist that are equally important impediments to trade; these may include poor access to government contracts or the obligation to comply with national technical norms that compel firms to keep in close contact with national authorities (see Chapters 2 and 14). In some cases the type of foreign direct investment that actually occurs is difficult to tell from the observed pattern. On the one hand, firms may have production facilities in a series of countries to jump trade impediments in those countries. On the other hand, they may do the same in a situation of free trade because consumer tastes vary among countries, and technical factors do not push towards production on a very large scale.

Capital movements under conditions of integration

The creation of a common market implies the liberalisation of capital movement, including foreign direct investments. The pattern and magnitude of direct investment flows depend on the characteristics of a country. The more the firms in a country show entrepreneurial competitiveness (related to ownership advantages) the higher will be outward DI, as these firms will want to cash in on their advantages by investing abroad. The higher the locational attractiveness of a country, the higher the inward DI, as firms will have advantages in producing there rather than elsewhere (Sleuwaegen, 1987).

The DI flows will be affected by integration, as the different measures of goods and factor market integration affect firms in member and third countries in a different way (Yannopoulos, 1990) and hence will lead to different strategic responses of firms to their new production environment.

- *Intra-union*. The creation of a common market by the liberalisation of goods and factor movements leads to a restructuring of the economies of the partner countries and to an increase in trade. This is partly based on the static trade creation and expansion effects and mainly on the dynamic effects of economies of scale and innovation. This increased specialisation entails a profound reorganisation and rationalisation of production and obliges firms to redefine their international investment strategies. The combined effect of the opening of goods markets and of capital markets will lead to an increase in DI of the optimal location type. The pattern of these increased DI flows will be determined by the combination of entrepreneurial and locational advantages of each country for each activity under new conditions of integrated markets.

- *Extra-union*. The trade diversion effect of the customs union formation will induce foreign producers that experience a loss in their export market to start production within the union (tariff jumping). Theory moreover predicts that other third country producers may want to exploit the dynamic growth effects caused by integration and decide to set up activities within the union (in other words, integration has enhanced the locational attractiveness of the union) (Motta and Norman, 1996). In both cases incoming DI increases, while imports decrease. This does not mean that external trade decreases too, as the union producers may have gained competitiveness on world markets and start exporting. The effect of market integration on outgoing direct investment is not certain. On the one hand, one may expect an increase, as the growth effects of integration may permit many union firms to obtain new entrepreneurial (ownership) advantages that they will want to exploit in third countries. If the relative position of a location in a union country deteriorates relative to a third country, an increase in DI may follow. If, on the contrary, the union performs better than third countries, a decrease of outgoing union DI may be the result.

So it is not possible a priori to say whether trade and DI are substitutes or complements.

Vertical organisational split: DI stimulates trade

International trade and international movement of production factors, at least of capital, should not be considered in isolation, as they tend to be different reflections of the spatial organisation of the production process by private firms. The pattern is shaped by such factors as prevailing technology (which provides the potential for economies of scale), availability and price of factors of production at different locations, the location of demand and the structure of markets, and corporate organisation (see, among others, Helpman and Krugman, 1985; Rugman, 1982).

Table 8.1   Characteristics of companies during the life-cycle of a product

	Introduction	Expansion
Sales	Small	Fast growth
Products	Very diversified	Few competing concepts
Innovation	Very high product innovation	High product innovation Increasing attention to process innovation
Structure	Few suppliers in separate markets, joint ventures, innovation, monopolies	New entrants Deconcentration, licensing
Competition	By adapting products to needs of specific clients, pioneering	Imitative improvement Price competition
Profit/loss	Initial losses; also incidental profits	Considerable profits
Jobs	Little employment, highly qualified	Fast growing number of jobs, decreasing qualifications
Capital/ labour ratio	Labour-intensive processes	Intensification of capital input
Location of production	Developed (central) areas	Intermediate areas
Markets	Regional and national markets	Increase of exports; growing imports from partner countries

Saturation	Fall
Slow growth	Stagnation and decline
Standardised	Only brands different
Low product innovation; accent on process innovation	Absence of innovation
Strong tendencies towards concentration and oligopolies, concerted practices, mergers	Restructuring cartels; diversification through takeovers of young firms in markets with good prospects; splitting up of firms
Product differentiation High promotion cost	Cut-throat competition, rationalising Collusion
Decreasing profits	Increasing number of companies with loss
Beginning decline in job numbers, simplification of tasks	Large-scale reductions in jobs
Large-scale investment in capital-intensive processes	Reduction of labour through closure of the most labour-intensive plants
Low-cost areas	Third-world countries
High interpenetration of markets; third-country competition on home markets	High pressure of imports from third world

The modern multinational firm can be seen as a *functionally differentiated organisation* (NEI/E&Y, 1992). It will internationally orient its investments by looking for optimal locations of its various functions. Headquarters will be located in central cities with good international communications. R&D facilities will be located in an environment that will stimulate innovation through contacts between researchers and the quality of the living environment. Distribution will be located at places from where relevant market areas can best be serviced. Production facilities again follow their own logic, to which we will devote more attention.

An interesting model permitting the combination of some of these elements in a simplified view of the determinants of the *location of production* is based on the product life-cycle theory. This theory distinguishes four stages in the life of each product: (1) introduction, (2) expansion, (3) saturation, and (4) decline. At each stage in this cycle, the companies that produce them show differences in size, profitability and so on; the markets are differently structured and competition takes on different forms; and the division between capital, labour inputs and returns also displays wide variation. A schematic view constructed from indications in the work of various authors (developing the fundamental work of Vernon 1966, 1979) is given in Table 8.1.

Many elements of this framework are relevant to the process of integration. A common market may speed up innovation and enforce changes in industrial structure (see Chapter 10); it may sharpen competition (see Chapter 14) and thus lead to economies of scale, cost reductions, product improvement and a better export potential (see Chapter 5). New producers are potential competitors on the mass markets, and by innovation and imitation they will speed up the passage through the life-cycle described above.

But it is the bottom part of the table that indicates how the use of differentiated production factors and the location of production and trade take shape internationally. The continuous process is set going by a technical change inspiring the development of a new product. At the first stage of its development this product will need close contact with existing customers, located in developed countries. At the second stage, it will still require special skills to produce and a strong market potential to sell; this means that the production will be located in developed areas where it generates a high value added and sustains high wages. At the maturity stage, margins will fall and, to cut costs, the production will be relocated to areas where wages are lower. The richer countries will change over to new products that are still at an earlier stage of development.

Here again a common market is likely to influence the process. First the larger market will offer prospects to specialist producers who would not have been viable in smaller, nationally segmented markets. Next it presents a sufficient diversity in production environments, thereby offering better opportunities for the location of firms in the course of the expansion and saturation stages. Finally it makes it possible to find locations to accommodate within its territory the production of articles at the final stage of their life-cycle, and thus postpone the moment of delocation of these activities to third (-world) countries.

The models described here tend to predict a strong flow from the rich capital-intensive countries to the less well-to-do countries that have much cheap labour. These flows of FDI tend to create trade.

Horizontal organisational split: FDI limits trade

In a situation where there are clear ownership and internalisation advantages of a firm (for example, an insurance firm that has a very good reputation, a strong brand name, skills in the management of risks and cheap access to international capital) and where that firm is confronted with high transaction costs (Dunning, 1988) there will be no advantage in concentrating production in one office. Firms will then develop a network of offices and undertake the more FDI the higher their transaction costs. (Modelling work in this spirit has recently been done by Brainard, 1993, and Markusen and Venables, 1995.)

Even in the presence of a single market, the FDI will be of the 'tariff-jumping' type, transactions cost related to distance having an equivalent effect to tariffs. Such FDI is not trade creating. It is of the horizontal type, whereby two-way relations may develop: firms from A investing in B and firms from B investing in A. It can be expected that this type of FDI will grow more the more the integrating countries converge in wealth.

Some stylised facts on FDI

Some structural features

The *definition* of international direct investment (DI) is: the transfer of capital by a company in one country to another country to create or take over an establishment there which it wants to control.[5] DI of some significance is a relatively recent phenomenon: it is since the 1960s that DI has rapidly gained importance. Stocks of foreign direct investment around the world have grown four times faster than global GDP and three times faster than global trade in the same period. Growth was particularly fast in the second half of the 1980s and in the 1990s. Most

DI finds its origin in one of the three major economic areas of the world (USA, Japan, EU). The growth of the FDI activity of the EU has been particularly vigorous (see bottom line of Table 8.2).

The *geographical pattern* of the flows of DI from and to the EU reveals some interesting characteristics (see Table 8.2). Contrary to what one would expect from their relative levels of integration, the DI interactions between the EU and third countries have for a long time been larger than those among the member countries themselves. Despite the increased trade and policy integration within the EU (see Chapters 5, 14 and 17), DI flows with third countries grew much faster in the 1970s and early 1980s than those among EU countries. However, from the middle of the 1980s, that situation changed; apparently the internal market programme stimulated intra-EU DI growth. Since the middle of the 1980s intra-EU DI outweighs extra-EU DI (see also de Menil, 1999).[6] The high growth of EFTA at the end of the 1980s and at the beginning of 1990s can be attributed to the wish of industrial and service groups from the then still EFTA countries already to avail themselves of the opportunities of the completed internal market (Baldwin *et al.*, 1996).[7] Extra-EU DI is very important, both in absolute and in relative terms. Indeed, by the end of the 1980s, the EU had become by far the largest outward investor in the world. The very high upsurge in recent years of European FDI in the world reflects a globalisation strategy on the part of many European firms. For many European multinational firms the setting up of a worldwide network starts with a strong position in the USA market (see the case studies in Chapters 10–13).

The *sectoral pattern* of outward DI shows that manufacturing and services have about equal shares, the much smaller remaining share being taken up by energy. Inward DI shows a completely different pattern; here some two-thirds go to services and one-third to manufacturing, so that energy is hardly significant. Within both outward and inward DI the dominant branch is financial services. The structure of intra-EU DI strongly resembles the picture of incoming DI in the EU, with services again accounting for nearly two-thirds. This high share reflects two features of the service sector: first its dominance in all advanced economies; second the difficulty of trading its products: so DI is the only way to supply foreign markets.

The *relative share* of foreign direct investment in total investment (Gross Fixed Capital Formation: GFCF) is small. DI flows within the EU (EDIE) accounted for no more than 1 per cent in the 1970s, for 3 per cent since the mid-1980s and for more than 5 per cent recently. The increase has been triggered by the increase in integration. Extra EU DI (FDIE) flows have remained at some 2 per cent over the 1980s and 1990s. The stock of total FDI in the EU GDP has gradually risen from 6 per cent in 1980 to 12 per cent in 2000.

Table 8.2 Direct foreign investment flows of EU12 by major partner (billion current euro), 1969–98

Origin or destination	1969/73 I	1969/73 E	1974/78 I	1974/78 E	1979/83 I	1979/83 E	1984/88 I	1984/88 E	1989/93 I	1989/93 E	1994/98 I	1994/98 E
EU	8	8	13	13	20	20	55	55	175	175	327	327
World	14	13	20	28	29	58	45	116	113	117	218	398
USA	7	2	9	9	13	31	10	83	42	54	137	198
Japan	—	—	—	—	1	1	4	1	14	1	9	5
EFTA	—	—	—	—	n.a.	n.a.	19	6	32	14	37	41
As a % of GFCF*												
EDIE	0.9		0.8		0.8		1.6		3.3		5.1	
(FDIE+EDIF):2	1.4		1.5		1.7		2.3		2.2		4.8	

Notes:
I = inflow into the EU.
E = outflow from the EU.
* five-year averages.
GFCF = Gross Fixed Capital Formation; EDIE = European Direct Investment in Europe; FDIE = Foreign Direct Investment in Europe; EDIF = European Direct Investment Abroad.

Source: Eurostat: several issues of *Balance of Payments*; *European Direct Investments 1984–93, EU Direct Investment Yearbook 1999: Quarterly National Accounts*, Luxemburg; 1969–93: EU12, 1994–98 EU15; (some estimates).

External relations

The role of the EU in international DI has changed with time. From a net recipient in the 1950s and 1960s, the EU proceeded to a balanced situation around 1970 and since then has increasingly accentuated its role as a net direct investor, to become the largest direct investor in the world. The main explanation of this trend is the increased availability of funds and the growing capacity of EU firms to organise international production. The pattern of DI flows is dominated by the flows between countries of the industrialised world. The relations with other groups of countries, such as third-world countries, are less important in quantitative terms (see Table 8.2).

The structure of *inward* DI has for a long time been dominated by the USA; over time, Japan has become more important, while recently some other players (like Korea) have come on the scene.

- *USA*. Direct investment flows from the USA to the EU in the 1960s and 1970s sprang mostly from American companies, which capitalised on their ownership advantage in technology and management by conquering a portion of the growing European market. Because that market was liberalised internally and protected externally, local production (that implies direct investment) was preferred to exporting from existing production facilities in the USA. This direct investment was of the 'tariff-jumping' type. The export of capital was all the easier because during this period the USA had a strong currency and no balance-of-payment problems. Many authors have tried to assess the effect of the creation of the EU on US direct investment in Europe (USDIE). This effect is visible in the differential development of US direct investment in the UK (before it joined the EU) and in the countries on the continent that were EU members. In the 1950–58 period, the growth rate of US DI was almost equal in the two areas. Between 1958 and 1973, the UK growth rate was half the EU's; after 1973, the two rates became equal again (Whichart, 1981). The first econometric analyses (Scaperlanda, 1967; d'Arge, 1969; Scaperlanda and Mauer, 1969) showed considerable doubt about a possible effect of European external trade protection on the pattern of USDIE; they stressed the importance of the access to the EU market. However later analyses (for instance, Schmitz, 1970; Schmitz and Bieri, 1972; Lunn, 1980) showed that the tariff jumping (the external tariff) and the global diversification strategy (market size) were both important determinants. In the early and middle 1980s, USDIE had been of limited size: US firms concentrated on consolidating, rationalising and expanding their European operations

(Graham, 1992). Since 1987, there has been an upsurge in USDIE triggered by the single market (Aristotelous and Fountas, 1996). USDIE is now clearly of the market development type; the geographical orientation of USDIE within the EU is significantly influenced by a series of variables such as different factor endowments (Morsink, 1998; Clegg and Scott-Green, 1999) and the differences in taxation between EU countries (Devereux and Griffith, 1996).

- *Japan*. The reasons for the large DI by Japanese firms in the EU are rather diversified (Thomsen and Nicolaides, 1991; Ozawa, 1992): we find the localisation strategy based on leads in the product and production technology, on economies of scope and on product differentiation. Other factors are financial strength, the 1992 programme and fears of a protectionist stand by the EU (Buigues and Jacquemin, 1994). The latter factor has remained a strong consideration even after the lowering of the EU tariff barriers notably due to the threat of EU anti-dumping actions (Belderbos, 1997). This suggests that JFDIE has remained largely of the tariff jumping type (see also Barell and Pain, 1999). The geographical orientation within the EU is very much a function of the type of activity; the high level of technology involved in the products make Japanese firms often choose central locations in the EU (Clegg and Scott-Green, 1999).

- *Other*. Some of the newly industrialising countries have begun following the same strategy as Japan. Hong Kong, Taiwan and Korea have become net outward investors. Investing in the EU is not an easy task for companies from these countries, due to high transaction costs and competitive constraints. However, the attractions of the presence in the large and diversified EU market, aloof from anti-dumping threats, and of the access to technological innovations are strong motives for overcoming these difficulties (Fujita *et al.*, 1997).

The structure of *outward* DI is quite different.

- *USA*. During the 1980s, the USA became the main destination (Sleuwaegen, 1987). This European DI in the USA (EDIUS) springs from the wish of many European companies to profit from the possibilities offered by the American market for the development of a product at the 'growth stage', when the European market was still too fragmented. Now many European entrepreneurs believe they need a foothold in the three main centres of the world: EU, USA, Japan (see, for instance, OECD, 1987c). The first European companies to follow that strategy were based in countries without balance-of-payment problems that relaxed or abolished capital market controls with respect to third countries at an early date. First among these countries was the UK, followed by Germany and the Netherlands. Now other EU countries have joined in as well (France, for example). This has resulted in a rapid increase in EDIUS (Graham, 1992), which was particularly vigorous in recent years.

- *Japan*. The importance of Japan as a destination for European DI is still very limited, owing to the (perceived) difficulties of successful competition with the local public–private interest coalitions.
- *Central and Eastern Europe*. Since the transition, FDI from the EU to the CEECs surged to some 15 billion euro a year at the end of the 1990s. EU FDI in these countries accounts for about 80 per cent of their total FDI. The motives for EU firms to invest in the CEECs vary by type of activity. On the one hand, some firms (for example, in the food industry and in insurance) have moved in to capture local markets; others (such as textile, machinery or automobiles) are more of the efficiency seeking type. The geographical orientation within the CEECs is very uneven; countries that have proceeded most rapidly along the road of preparing for membership generally attract most FDI (Bocconi, 1997).
- *Other*. This is a very diversified group, among which are many developing countries. In recent years the share of this group has increased rapidly as a consequence of the growing involvement of EU firms in the countries of Central and Eastern Europe on the one hand and the newly industrialising countries, and other emerging markets, such as developing Asia, on the other. In both cases EU firms have recognised the potential of the local markets and the possibilities of exporting to the EU from those locations (see Fujita *et al.*, 1997).

Intra-European relations

Internal direct investment flows have been completely free in the EU since the 1970s. On theoretical grounds we may expect that direct investments will increase as soon as companies become convinced of the advantages of selecting optimum locations within an enlarged market area (a 'free trade' type operation). In line with this, we see a rapid *growth over time* of intra-European direct investments. In the 1966–70 period, DI by companies from one of the original six member states in other member states than their home country (EDIE) increased by 63 per cent (Pelkmans, 1983). That finding is corroborated by the observation that in the same period the number of subsidiary companies of multinationals in the EU rose from 340 to

774 (Francko, 1976). In the period 1970–83, double-digit percentage growth continued. However the real boom for EDIE came after 1985, when EDIE doubled about every two years under the impetus of the 1992 programme (CEC, 1996a). This is again in line with the optimum location hypothesis, as the taking away of the many remaining non-tariff barriers has a similar effect to the taking away of tariffs. Indeed the single market effect was highest in branches where NTBs used to be largest (such as insurance) (CEC, 1996a). An analysis of the importance of DI in the total investment shows fairly low values (Table 8.2). This low percentage in terms of flows does obscure the fact that the accumulation of such DI over the years now makes for considerable percentages of production of each of the EU countries controlled by firms from other EU (or third) countries. Increasingly this no longer applies exclusively to large multinationals but also to small and medium-sized companies.

The *industry pattern* of EDIE is very stable over time (1984–98). The service sector is increasingly dominant (accounting now for more than two-thirds); the manufacturing sector comes in second place (accounting for the remaining one-third); the EDIE of other sectors like agriculture, energy and construction is insignificant. Within the service sector, the branch of finance and insurance takes the lion's share (see the case study in Chapter 12 for more details). Much of this investment is made as part of the creation of a geographically diversified production and distribution network. The most active manufacturing firms are to be found in the branches of electronics and electrical equipment and chemical products. Other evidence (for example, Cantwell and Randaccio, 1992) shows that this is largely of an inter-industry type; for example, manufacturers of country A invest in country B, and vice versa. The liberalisation of markets and the privatisation of companies in branches such as energy, telecommunications and so on have revealed a considerable need for international rationalisation of these industries. As a consequence FDI in these industries has risen explosively in recent years.

The *geographical pattern* of the flows of DI among EU countries (EDIE) is fairly constant over time (see Table 8.3). The table invites three remarks. First, the structure of the EDIE flows is dominated by the relations between the countries in the core of the EU (mainly Germany, France, UK and Italy); the underlying material shows that these are often made up of two-way flows of comparable size, indicating a considerable interpenetration. Second, there is a flow of considerable importance from the core to the periphery (mainly Spain, Portugal and Greece). Third, the flow in the opposite direction is fairly small. The net flow of capital towards the less developed EU countries confirms that jobs are indeed going to the people, although formerly people also used to go where the jobs were (see previous

Table 8.3   **Geographical distribution (%) of direct investment between groups of member countries of the EU, 1980–98**

	1980–84	1984–88	1988–92	1993–96	1997–98
Core to core	77	80	71	79	49
Core to periphery	20	16	22	16	29
Periphery to core	3	4	5	3	11
Periphery to periphery	—	—	2	2	11

Source: Morsink, 1997; based on Eurostat and OECD statistics and a number of unpublished sources, 1980–96 EU12, 1997–98 EU15: Eurostat: *EU Direct Investment Yearbook 1999*.

chapter). The accession of Spain and Portugal to the EU (CEC, 1988a) has triggered important DI flows from the core countries (Petrochilos, 1989; Buckley and Artisien, 1987; Durán-Herrera, 1992; Simões, 1992). Apparently the concentration effects which the divergence school had feared (Chapter 16) have not materialised. The patterns also suggest that there is a complementarity between goods and capital movements, whereas there is rather a substitution between capital and labour movements (in comparison with the results of Chapters 5 and 7). Since most EFTAns joined the EU the picture has changed considerably. Most EFTAns are peripheral countries from a geographical point of view. They are very active in FDI both in the traditional core and in other EFTA countries. Hence a strong change in relative shares in the last column of the table.

An *explanation of the pattern* of these EDIE flows reveals several determinant factors. The financial strength of a country proves very important: the largest EDIE flows occur when the country of origin shows a net financial resource and the receiving country a high borrowing requirement. More specifically the strongest influence was found to come from the ownership advantage (high R&D leads to high outward DI, and vice versa); intermediate influence comes from factors like market size (+), transport cost (−), trade intensity (+) and exchange rate volatility (−). The trade intensity factor indicates that integration of goods markets stimulates that of capital markets, and highlights the point that EDIE is of the optimum-location rather than the tariff-jumping type. The exchange rate variable indicates that monetary integration, creating stable exchange rates, is likely to influence the EDIE flows positively. Finally some other factors did influence EDIE in a limited way: for example, differences in culture and taxation (Morsink and Molle, 1991; Morsink, 1997).[8] Other studies suggest that the level of real wages (unit labour cost) is a very significant variable: low wages tend to attract incoming FDI and high wages tend to stimulate outgoing FDI (Hatzius, 2000).

Direct investment through takeovers

Companies that have decided to expand production and/or distribution in other countries than their own have a choice between creating a new subsidiary company or taking over an existing foreign company. The latter strategy has the advantage of immediate access to markets whose specific characteristics are known to the local management. Such a takeover often takes the form of a (public) offer to buy all existing shares. This does not make the operation a portfolio investment (see next section) because the essential motive for the transaction is to obtain control of the company.

While by the EU regulations this type of DI transaction is completely free in principle, in practice it is not. In many countries (legal) measures (like the possibility of issuing preferential shares that limit the power of other shareholders in the Netherlands) or the involvement of banks (Germany) or the state (France) in the capital protect companies from such takeovers. The fact that some member states have a free market for companies (the UK, for one) while in others (Germany, France) restrictions tend to take a long time to be fully lifted, clearly illustrates that the integration of capital markets in the EU is not yet complete.

The different national regimes have important consequences for the strategy of firms. This is revealed by the differences in performance judged by the criteria 'growth of turnover' (sales) and 'profitability' (Table 8.4). Evidently companies under a 'liberal' regime (UK, USA) were forced to maximise profits, whereas companies in countries with a 'sheltered' regime (like Germany and Japan) could be satisfied with lower profit margins and would systematically aim at market power through maximising their sales. The efforts of the EU to create a truly free capital market in Europe, where all national differences in shelter from takeovers would disappear, are not yet completed. Hence the national differences in firms' profit figures have not yet flattened out, as is evidenced by the profitability figures given in the right-hand columns of the table.

The differences between the national rates of return on investment as indicated by this small sample did also show up in a larger harmonised data set of some 1400 manufacturing firms from ten different countries of the EU (de Menil, 1999). Among the economic factors, that explain these differences we find capital intensity (the higher this ratio the lower the rate of return). Among the regulatory environment factors, protection against dismissal of employees took a paramount place (the higher the protection the lower the return on

Table 8.4   Growth and profitability (%), 1979–98

Country	1979–88[a] Growth of sales	1988[a] Tax-adjusted profit rate	1994[b] Net profit: turnover	1994[b] Net profits: own funds	1995[c] Profits: stock-holders' equity	1998 Profits: stock-holders' equity
Germany (FRG)	80	4	2	6	14	10
France	51	4	2	8	15	9
UK[d]	45	9	7	16	24	14
EU	n.a.	n.a.	3	7	11	8
USA	48	10	5	16	24	19
Japan	190	4	1	3	6	−5

Notes:
[a]   20 companies of each country showing fastest growth.
[b]   All manufacturing.
[c]   Average figure for the eight largest companies of each country in top 500 list.
[d]   UK/NL firm (Unilever): 27 for 1991; 30 for 1998.

Sources: 1979–88: De Jong (1989); 1994: CEC (1996); 1995 and 1998 own calculations based on Fortune Top 500.

assets). Next came competition policy (the less stringent the policy the higher the rate of return). Unfortunately, the hypothesis of protection against takeovers was not tested. So we may conclude that, in the early 1990s, real capital market integration in the EU still had a long way to go.

Long- and short-term loans: some theory

Liberalisation of movement of factors; full price equalisation

The integration of factor markets will lead to better allocation of capital. This can be illustrated by a neo-classical static two-country diagram (there is no influence from the rest of the world). In Figure 8.1, the horizontal axis gives the stock of capital. The sloping curves *AD* and *BE* indicate the level of production that can be obtained at each size of input of capital assuming a certain input of the complementary production factor. The curves of country B mirror those of country A, so that one picture describes the effects of integration on both countries (see Grubel, 1981). The effects of integration of markets for production factors (on the assumption that goods markets

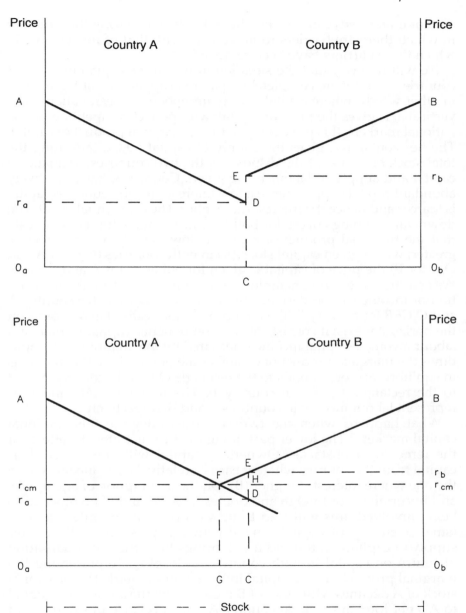

Figure 8.1 Integration of factor markets, price equalisation

are not integrated) can now be illustrated by comparing the situation in which there are barriers to movement with that of integration, in which these barriers have been removed.

We will first consider the situation in which the capital markets of countries A and B are completely separated (upper part of Figure 8.1); in other words, where capital is fully immobile between nations. The vertical axis gives the price of capital; with perfect competition on the national markets, this price is equal to the marginal product of capital. The horizontal axis gives the supply of capital (O_aO_b, indicating the total stock of capital at the disposal of the two countries), demand of capital and supply of labour being given. Country A has a relatively abundant capital supply, hence a low interest rate; in country B capital is scarcer and hence the interest rate higher. The differential is *ED*. The downward-sloping curves for both country A and country B indicate that the marginal product of capital is lower as the capital stock is greater; with a given capital stock (K) in both countries (O_aC for A and O_bC for B) the price of capital is given for either: r_a for A and r_b for B. We assume there is no unemployment. From this picture the distribution of income can be derived. Total output is O_aADC for country A and O_bCEB for country B (the total production realised at all points on the horizontal axis; it consists of two components: capital income and labour income). Capital income (measured by the quantity of its input times the marginal product of capital at the point where the market is in equilibrium) corresponds to the rectangle O_ar_aDC in country A, and to the rectangle O_bCEr_b in country B. The triangles r_aAD and EBr_b represent labour income in countries A and B, respectively.

What happens when the two countries integrate their national capital markets? The lower part of Figure 8.1 illustrates the effects of the removal of obstacles. Owners of capital will now move their capital from the country where it earns a relatively low income (A) to the one where interest is higher (B). On the assumption of equal risks and uncertainty for foreign and domestic assets and of no other costs being involved, this will lead to upward pressure on interests in A (smaller supply of capital) and downward pressure in B (greater supply of capital). In the end it will bring about the full equalisation of return on capital in both countries at level r_{cm} (representing the marginal productivity of capital in the common market). The capital stock of A declines while that of B increases by the amount *GC*, equal to A's net foreign asset. So country A will specialise in savings and country B in investment.

Even if there are no differences in factor prices between the two countries, the removal of controls is likely to favour a better allocation of resources. On capital markets, different liquidity preferences in the two countries will cause the importing of long-term capital and the exporting of short-term capital in A, and the reverse in B.

The removal of internal constraints

In the previous section we assumed full employment, at the national level, of the two production factors, labour and capital. However that assumption is unlikely to be fulfilled in reality. In small segmented markets specialised labour will be hard put to find sufficient demand for its services, or the necessary capital with which to complement prevailing technological know-how. So in small segmented markets both the supply of and the demand for factors of production may be constrained, with negative effects on production and welfare. By taking away controls on the international movement of capital, both supply and demand can assert themselves, and an efficient allocation of all specialised factors of production will come about.

The 'trade' effects of removing the constraints on the capital market are illustrated in the upper part of Figure 8.2, which gives the supply and demand curves for capital. The supply of capital comes from savers, its demand from investors. Controls on capital imports and exports are making the capital market of country A inefficient. The financial products provided by the banking sector in A being inadequate, potential investors and savers refuse transactions, which implies that some capital remains idle; this is indicated in the figure by *AB* (given demand), investment and hence savings being limited to the amount *OA*. The price for the investor, or the borrowing rate, is *OI*, and the lending rate for savers is *OG*. The spread between the two, *GI* or *FD*, is the margin taken by banks for their intermediate role. This margin can be that high because banks are protected from foreign competition. This creates a 'monopoly', permitting banks to earn a monopoly rent of *GIDF* (quantity *OA* times the margin *GI*). Assume now that controls on international capital movements are abolished and thus all inefficiencies in the markets removed. Fear of new entrants from abroad taking away profitable markets will induce banks in the home country to propose new products, better adapted to the wishes of both savers and investors. This will bring additional supply and demand on the market. Let us assume provisionally that the resulting rate of interest (*OH*) is just equal to the interest rate abroad. Both savings and investment will now expand to *OB*.

There is an important gain to society as a whole. First investors increase their 'consumer surplus' by the area *HIDC*. Next savers increase their 'producer rent' by the area *GHCF*. Of their monopoly rent *GIDF*, banks lose *HIDE* to investors and *GHEF* to savers. This leaves a net gain to society equal to the triangle *FDC*.

The effects of partial liberalisation are different. Under such conditions, the liberalisation of financial markets is unlikely just to balance out home supply and demand at the prevailing world market price.

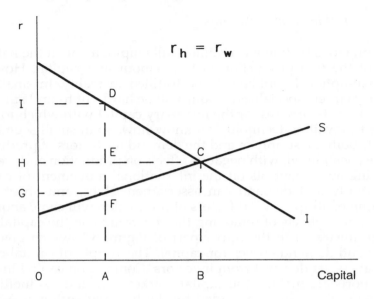

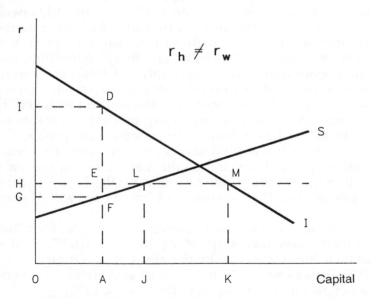

Figure 8.2   Welfare effect of capital market integration through deregulation

The lower part of Figure 8.2 represents the situation where the world interest rate OH is lower than the domestic equilibrium rate without international exchange. Now controls may affect only capital out-flows, leaving inflows free, or alternatively, may affect only capital imports, leaving exports free. Let us analyse the effects of either case on the situation $r_w < r_h$.

In a situation of free outflow and controlled inflow, savers will take the opportunity of getting higher returns on the foreign market (OH) than on the domestic market (OG), and expand their supply to OJ. Under this pressure, domestic banks will have to diminish their margins from GI (= FD) to HI (or ED) to acquire the necessary capital (OA) for making the transaction with the domestic investors. The remaining supply AJ is invested abroad (either directly by savers or indirectly by banks). This will give rise to an inflow of interest pay-ments equal to the area $AELJ$. The 'rent' of savers increases by the area $GHLF$, of which $GHEF$ is gained at the expense (transfer) of the banking sector's monopoly rent, and FEL is the net welfare gain to society.

In the situation of free inflows and controlled outflows, the same reasoning applies. In the closed domestic market, investment was constrained by savings to OA. In the new situation, foreigners will acquire equity (portfolio investment) or companies (direct invest-ment) and get higher returns than on the world market. That inflow will take total investment up to OK instead of OA, the quantity AK being imported, which entails payment of interest on foreign debt corresponding to the area $AEMK$. Investors find their 'surplus' in-creased by the area $HIDM$, of which $HIDE$ is at the expense of monopoly 'rents' of financial intermediaries (that is, a transfer) and the triangle EDM is the net welfare gain.

A liberalised capital market has positive effects on economic growth (welfare effects) despite a possible initial deterioration of the balance of payments (from the equilibrium in the upper part of Figure 8.2 to the deficit of $JLMK$ in the lower part of Figure 8.2). However, if the imported capital is used to create production units, the output of exportables may expand, compensating for the deficit in interest payments.

International exchange of capital: some figures

Relative importance of foreign capital

Under the influence of the liberalisation of capital markets, investors have started to increase their investments abroad. The international interwovenness of EU capital markets has grown considerably in the

Table 8.5   Foreign assets/liabilities and foreign portfolio investment, stocks (% of GDP[a]) EU15, 1982–97

	Capital			Stock		
	1982	1990	1997	1982	1990	1997
Germany	40	60	70	0	10	20
France	60	60	90	n.a	10	20
Italy	30	40	70	0	10	30
Netherlands	90	140	170	10	30	60
Belgium	130	200	230	10	30	60
UK	130	180	260	10	40	80
Denmark	n.a.	90	120	n.a.	30	50
Spain	30	30	70	0	0	20
Austria	60	60	80	10	10	30
Sweden	50	70	130	0	10	70
Finland	30	50	80	0	10	40
USA	30	40	70	10	10	30
Japan	20	60	50	10	20	20

Note: [a]   Rounded to the nearest ten.

Source: NIESR (1996), OECD, *Main Indicators*, various years, IMF, *International Financial Statistics*, 1999.

past decades. This is evident from the growth of the two indicators given in Table 8.5 (average of foreign assets and liabilities as a percentage of GDP and average of the stocks of incoming and outgoing foreign portfolio investment).

We observe a number of interesting *features and trends*. First, both indicators show all over the study period and for all countries a substantial increase. Second, the ratios for total foreign capital are significantly higher than those for foreign stock: the difference is explained to a large extent by foreign direct investment (for details, see previous sections). Third, some countries like the UK and the Netherlands that have disposed of controls relatively early do indeed show a higher degree of international integration than other countries like Germany or Italy. Some of the countries of the latter group seem, however, to be catching up, as the growth of their ratios over time is higher than for the former group. Fourth, the EU countries are on average much more open than major third countries, like the USA or Japan.

This increased integration goes hand in hand with a structural adaptation of the capital market and of the various financial centres of the EU (Seifert *et al.*, 2000).

Quantity exchanged

The development of capital market integration might ideally be measured by the size of the loans that were contracted between savers and
investors in different countries, much in the same way as the development of the goods market integration is measured by the trade in
goods between different countries. Unfortunately there is no good
statistical record of such transactions.

One indicator often employed is the correlation between the domestic savings and investments. The weaker this relation, the higher
integration. EU integration has progressed on this score, as there is
evidence that this indicator decreased over time (CEC, 1998b).[9] The
same is true for the integration of the five most advanced accession
countries from Central Europe in international capital markets. Their
capital market liberalisation measures have borne their fruits as is
evidenced by a ratio of openness that is similar to that of the southern member countries of the EU. At the same time, differences in the
structure of the two groups remain. Portfolio flows are less important for the Eastern European countries than for Southern Europe
today, but already have a higher share than in the latter countries
prior to their accession (Buch, 1999).

Another indicator is the size of trans-border transactions of bonds
and stocks. As an illustration of the very fast growth of such transactions we have given in Table 8.6. figures for three major member
countries of the EU.

Table 8.6   **Trans-border transactions (residents with non-
             residents) in bonds and stocks as a percentage of GDP
             for selected member countries, 1975–98**

Country	1975	1980	1985	1990	1995	1998
Germany	5	7	33	57	172	334
France	—	5	21	54	187	415
Italy	1	1	4	27	253	640

Source: BIS.

A third indicator is the figures on international capital transactions
(IMF or Eurostat) taken from the balance of payments statistics. These
are rather deficient in quality, but their analysis permits us to highlight three features. First, there is considerable volatility over time of
both portfolio and other categories of investment. Second, substitut-

ability between these two categories, as large decreases of one often go hand-in-hand with equally large increases of the other. Third, an impressive magnitude that increases considerably over time; flows of the size of considerable percentages of GDP are increasingly common. Contrary to what we found for direct investment, the time and geographical pattern of these recorded flows does not show much relation to economic fundamentals. These conclusions do not change even after the putting of the largest and politically most sensitive parts (short-term capital) into the perspective of trade flows. Also they are not related to capital controls.[10]

'Euro' markets

Until 1990 the integration of long-term and short-term capital markets in the EU had made very little headway owing to the restrictions imposed on capital movements by a number of member countries. Failing the integration by direct dealing between member countries, a different type of integration has developed in which both countries deal with a third party. This has been done through the so-called '"Euro" markets', a misleading term because it actually refers to offshore capital markets falling outside the control of any monetary authority. These markets, almost non-existent in the early 1960s, developed tenfold in the 1970s and again in the 1980s (Johnston, 1983; Kane, 1982).

The success of the Euro*bond* (denominations other than the currency of the country where they are issued) market was based on an inconsistency in regulation. Governments tended to limit the access of foreign issuers of bonds to their national markets, but their control of domestic investors purchasing foreign bonds was less stringent or non-effective.

The Euro*currency* market (short-term) thrived on the difference in interest levels on deposits: lower than national ones for borrowers and higher than national ones to lenders (Levi, 1981; Dufey and Giddy, 1981; Clarke and Pulay, 1978).

Although little is known about the origin and destination of capital on these markets, the Bank for International Settlements (BIS) has estimated that Western Europe in the 1980s held a share of some 40 per cent in total demand. Most transactions on the bond and currency markets used to be denominated in US dollars.

Since its introduction, the euro (see Chapter 15) has fundamentally changed the situation. In 1999 the total volume of emissions in euro-denominated bonds was, for the first time, significantly in excess of the volume of dollar-denominated bonds. The reason for this high growth is primarily the efficiency of the market that has developed in euros – a large and deep market that has replaced the segmented markets in the former EU currencies. The second reason is the very high demand of the corporate sector in the EU for bonds, stemming from the need to finance the upsurge in mergers and take-overs (see Chapter 14).

Price convergence

Interest rate parity

A first way to study the equalisation of prices is to see whether there is a movement towards parity of interest rates for comparable financial products in different national markets. A distinction is thereby made between assets with a short- and with a long-term maturity. Differences in interest rates between countries stem mostly from two causes. First, there is the difference between supply and demand, a factor that should disappear with the taking away of barriers to international financial transactions in the framework of the integration of capital markets. Second, there is the inflation differential (related to the likely change in exchange rates: see Chapter 15), a factor that should only disappear with monetary union. In addition, there is a set of factors such as the quality of the debtor, the differences in reserve requirements of financial intermediaries, fiscal regime, transaction costs in thick or thin markets, monetary unrest, and so on.

The development of national interest rates[11] over the period 1960–2000 shows marked differences by sub-period, regime and maturity (Figure 8.3). Let us first analyse *sub-periods*. For both the short- and long-term rates, a certain tendency of convergence can be observed for the period up to 1973. The monetary unrest that was created by the first and the second oil crises increased the divergence again. From the mid-1980s to 1993 convergence has again prevailed; notably due to the success of the stabilisation of exchange rates. Under the influence of the monetary turmoil of 1993 a new upsurge of divergence occurred. However, in recent years convergence has prevailed again. Let us next turn our attention to *regimes*. We note that, since the early 1980s, the level of divergence was much lower for the five core countries of the Exchange Rate Mechanism (ERM) of the European Monetary System (EMS) (see Chapter 15) than for the other EU countries (both EU7 and EU14). Similar figures for the most recent years of the evolution of the differences between the interest rate levels of the countries that form part of the EMU also show a very clear convergence (see also Chapter 15). If we finally turn to the aspect of *maturity* we note that for short-term rates the amplitude of the effects is very marked over time, while it is rather cushioned for long-term rates.

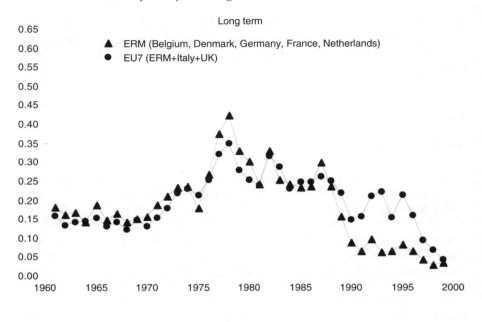

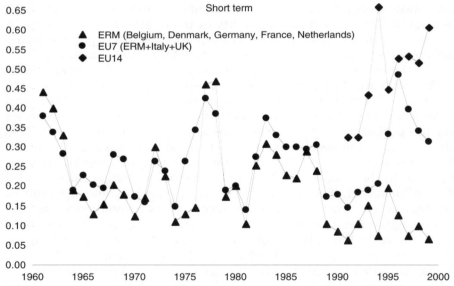

Note: Divergence: unweighed coefficient of variation.

Sources: 1960–85: Mortensen (1992); 1985–2000: own calculations, based on IMF, *Financial Statistics*; Eurostat, *Money and Finance*, several years.

Figure 8.3   Divergence of interest rates between groups of member countries, 1960–2000

The *potentially determinant factors* of the evolution over time of the differences between countries in the price of capital were given at the beginning of this chapter as we discussed the reasons for capital controls. In an empirical test for the 1974–93 period (Lemmen and Eijffinger, 1996), only three of them were found to be of relevance to explain the 'closed interest rate differential' of 11 EU countries. The most relevant factor was inflation; out of line inflation puts pressure on a weak currency; governments wanting to avoid realignment and not willing to raise interest rates for domestic policy purposes (such as growth, debt burden) will then use capital controls to prevent capital from seeking higher returns abroad. The second factor was the instability of governments; indeed political instability limits the confidence of international investors in government policies, and capital controls are then needed to prevent capital movements that would make it even more difficult to pursue an effective policy. Finally capital formation also had a certain influence, indicating that countries with high investment needs are more apt to resort to capital controls.

With increasing capital liberalisation (both internal and external), the relationship between the interest rates on international, EU and national markets becomes increasingly close. However there are still many imperfections, and hence no full convergence of prices.

Returns to stock

A second way to study price convergence is by looking at the return to investment in equity. The indicator of return chosen here is the dividend yield plus the rate of change in the prices of equities in different national stock markets. An analysis of the evolution over the 1975–95 period (NIESR, 1996) shows the expected effect of EU and global integration. The European integration prevails as correlation between the London market and those of other European countries were generally higher in the 1990s than they were in the 1970s. Global integration is important too, now, as evidenced by the present quite high correlation between the UK and the US markets. Note that the latter correlation is not as high as that between the UK and some European stock market yields. The increase in integration of the EU markets is also highlighted by the finding that the correlation between the two large continental markets, France and Germany, and the markets of their neighbours are much higher than between these two markets and the USA.

Welfare effects

Some theory

The analysis of the *welfare effects* of capital restrictions (and of the removal of such restrictions) are rather complicated (see, among others, Phylaktis and Wood, 1984). The welfare effects of integration can be described with the help of Figure 8.1. They are different for different groups and hence lead to distributional disputes. Let us look first at the *distribution over countries*. Total welfare will increase for both country A and B by the following process. The net domestic product of country A declines by *GFDC*, its net national product, composed of the domestic part O_aAFG and the investment income earned abroad, *GFHC*, increases by *FHD*. The net domestic product of B increases by *GFEC*. As *GFHC* must be paid to A, the net gain for B is the triangle *FEH*. The total net gain arising from the better allocation of capital through integration corresponds for both countries to the triangle *FED* (*FHD* in A and *FEH* in B).

The distribution of income between the *main functional categories* (wage income versus capital income) changes when the factor markets are integrated. In country A the part of total income that accrues to labour is reduced in favour of the part that accrues to capital owners (by $r_a r_{cm} FD$), whereas in B the share of labour increases at the expense of owners of capital (by $FEr_b r_{cm}$). This explains why trade unions tend to welcome incoming investment, but are opposed to domestic investment abroad, even if it leads to a higher aggregate income. Of course that effect will come about only if markets function properly; that is, if the wages are adjusted downward. If not, the result may be more unemployment, leading to reduced production, which the growth of capital income may fail to compensate in the short run.

The welfare effects of *foreign direct investment* are similar to those for capital flows as described in Figure 8.1. By shifting labour demand across countries, FDI raises the wage in the host country (B) and lowers the wage in the source country (A), thereby raising profits of source country firms at the expense of host country firms. The extent of cross-ownership of firms and the relative supply of skilled labour alter the impact of FDI on welfare (Glass and Saggi, 1999).

Integration is bound to change government revenue springing from the taxation of international capital. If country B taxes foreign assets, a proportion of the area *GFHC* remains in B. If it exceeds the net gain of A (the triangle *FHD*), country A will suffer a net loss from opening up its capital market while country B had not done so completely (Grubel, 1974).

Empirical estimates of effects

The empirical evidence on the welfare effects of the integration of European capital markets is very thin. This may be due to the absence of a clear-cut objective; indeed the markets of EU countries were to be only partly integrated among themselves, and the attitudes of EU member countries towards world integration were rather negative. Let us briefly review the situation with respect to the three main categories.

The few studies that have analysed the effects of free internal flows of *European direct investment* have been limited to the employment effects in both source and destination countries. The latter seem invariably to have benefited from DI. The effect on the former varies from negative, when exports from the home bases are replaced, to positive, when the penetration into a foreign market actually increases home employment (Buckley and Artisien, 1987). More generally, FDI will be low where unit labour costs are too high compared to competing locations; this may be responsible for welfare losses due to high unemployment. The opposite will be the case for countries where wages have been relatively low (given a certain productivity level) (Hatzius, 2000). To our knowledge, no comprehensive studies have been carried out on the welfare effects of DI in the EU.

An estimate of the welfare effects of the integration of short-term and long-term capital markets made along the theoretical path indicated by Figure 8.1 resulted for the EU as a whole in a benefit of 1500 million ECU (Price Waterhouse, 1988).

Summary and conclusions

- The objective of European capital market integration was initially fairly limited and for a long time remained practically restricted to direct investment; only lately has complete internal and external freedom of capital movements been installed.
- Direct investment in the EU has expanded considerably. The intra-EU pattern of DI shows a net flow from the 'core' (northern) member states towards the 'peripheral' (southern) member states, which should lead to more convergence of wealth levels (see Chapter 16).
- Long-term and short-term loans were for a long time contracted on segmented markets. An alternative to European integration has developed with the growth of the practically unregulated offshore markets. With increasing liberalisation, the national markets in the EU countries have tended to align with these 'world' markets.

- The welfare effects of the integration of European capital markets are largely unknown as far as DI and portfolio investment are concerned. However, for short-term and long-term loans, it was shown that considerable benefits can be gained through integration.

Notes

1 The EU has not obliged member states to notify such measures. However the OECD has done so. It has published the reservations made under each code by individual member countries (OECD, 1995a, 1995b, 1995c). An evaluation of the reservations made by EU member countries shows that the reservations with respect to internal EU moves are very few. They are concentrated in a few countries, such as Germany, Portugal and Italy (NIESR, 1996).

2 These directives guarantee that certain minimum rules are respected by all companies. The EU rules are stricter for companies listed on the stock exchange than for others. The directives establishing them concern the minimum requirements for listing, the information to be given with the application for listing (prospectus) and after admission (half-yearly reports). Other directives of interest concern the issue of prospectuses, insider trading and public takeover bids. A case in point are the new rules (issued in 2000) on the obligation of firms that want to take over a company to bid for all the shares in order to protect the interests of minority shareholders.

3 Harmonisation has not always been easy, owing to differences in the legal status of certain intermediaries, different traditions of prudential control and deep-rooted differences in culture (such as the opposition between the British view of finance as an independent industry and that of some continental countries of finance as an activity that should be placed at the service of the real economy).

4 Reservations with respect to third countries are more numerous than those with respect to internal flows. The ranking of the EU member states by openness is identical for external and internal liberalisation (NIESR, 1996).

5 Or in the IMF definition: 'an investment that is made to acquire a lasting interest in an enterprise operating in an economy other than that of the investor; the investor's purpose being to have an effective voice in the management of the enterprise'.

6 The European integration effect on FDI has also been found by de Menil (1999); his model showed intra-EU FDI to be far higher than could be expected on the basis of the influence of the usual variables of a model of intra-OECD FDI.

7 In future one may expect that the flows between the former EFTAns and the EU12 will be more equilibrated, as the regime for the two has changed; this is implied by the results of a simulation model reported in Baldwin *et al.*, 1996.

8 A first exercise in Morsink and Molle (1991) has been elaborated by Morsink (1997). The results on the various variables of the model used are confirmed by Mortensen (1992) for the rate of return on capital, by Devereux and Freeman (1995) for the real rate of interest and the tax wedge between the home and host country and by the studies summarised in CEC (1996a) for the ownership advantage and the trade variable. The results for most variables are also confirmed by de Menil (1999) but for the influence of the exchange rate. Pain and Young (1996) found that differences in taxation had a significant influence on the direction of intra-EU DI from British and German firms.

9   The balance between national savings and investment (assuming that there is more integration the less the correlation between domestic investment and savings in a set of countries) was used as an indicator of integration already by Feldstein and Horioka, 1980. The empirical testing of this approach proved beset with such difficulties that the approach was considered less suitable for measuring the progress of financial integration (Lemmen and Eijffinger, 1993). This was again confirmed by the inconclusive results of Armstrong *et al.* (1996). So one has to work with other indicators.

10 This question, particularly relevant for integration studies, may be answered by comparing the size of the flows of the countries that have practised such controls with the figures for countries that had a liberalist regime. The pattern one would expect is that flows in countries with controls would be smaller than in countries without. More specifically, as controls were mostly meant to restrict capital outflows, one would expect the outflow to be smaller than the inflow for countries practising controls. However, as neither of the two expected features could be found in an analysis of the data, the conclusion can be drawn that capital controls were rather ineffective (Gros and Thygesen, 1998).

11 In the past, several methods have been used (Frankel, 1989) for measuring the degree of capital market integration.

Short-term interest rates have been analysed by Van den Bergh *et al.* (1987), who estimated the interdependence between the development of short-term interest on Euromarkets and internal markets. The results for the 1970s show very little integration. In the 1980s, on the contrary, the markets of Germany, the UK, the Netherlands and Belgium became highly integrated, whereas the integration of the Italian and French markets remained poor. Real interest rate (RIR) parity among countries has not been found in empirical studies (Mishkin, 1984a, 1984b; Mark, 1985a, 1985b; Gaab *et al.*, 1986; Caramazza, 1987).

Long-term real interest rates on international markets are much less documented than short-term ones. One reason is that comparable financial instruments on Euro and domestic capital markets are hard to find. Following Fukao and Hanazaki (1987), we have estimated the significance of real interest rate differentials between Germany and five other EU countries. We have made a distinction between the pre-crisis period (1963–73), with low inflation and fixed exchange rates, the 1973–9 period, when monetary disturbances occurred and capital controls abounded, the 1980–86 period, when international capital movement controls were abandoned or relaxed in many countries, and the period 1987–91, when these trends gained momentum. The analysis shows that in the first period only small differentials occurred (index 94). In the second period the differences were fairly large, in particular for the UK and Italy (index 81). After the relaxation of capital controls, the differences became very small (index 92 in 1980–86).

PART III
SECTORS OF ACTIVITY

9 Agriculture

Introduction

The integration of the markets for goods generally refers implicitly only to manufactured goods. However the advantages of integration do apply to the integration of agricultural produce markets too. Therefore the EU has decided right from the outset to also integrate agricultural markets.

In the first section below we will discuss in detail the principles of EU agricultural policy. The next section will give a summary description of the development of the agricultural sector under conditions of integration, detailing production levels, trade, production structure, concentration of firms and so on.

We will then give, with the help of three case studies, an idea of the workings of different EU regimes: guaranteed prices, bonuses and quota.

The principal system operated for a long time by the EU is neither the only one feasible nor the best one from an economic point of view. The disadvantages of some characteristics of the EU regime will be pointed out clearly in the last section, where we will give an evaluation of the welfare effects of the CAP.

To round off the chapter, a brief summary of the main findings will be given.

EU regime

Rationale and principles

National governments have often regulated agriculture strongly. They tended to pursue four objectives: first to protect farmers from the uncertainties of price developments; second, to make sure the country would be able to feed itself (security of food supply); third, to maintain the viability of small family businesses; and, fourth, to attain spatial planning objectives, such as maintaining a specific regional balance. To protect farmers from foreign competition and from large price fluctuations (see Box 9.1) many countries have established a policy of market control for agricultural products.

In many integration schemes agriculture has been excluded from the free traffic of goods (for example, EFTA), because the costs of adaptation were perceived to be higher than the advantages of integration. The EU has decided to integrate agriculture right from the outset. The economic motive was the strong association of the agricultural sector with the rest of the economy: differential prices for agricultural produce, affecting the cost of raw materials as well as

---

Box 9.1   Unstable markets

Agricultural markets tend to be unstable – much more than, for instance, manufactured goods markets. The causes are as follows. On the demand side, agricultural products are vital necessities and so have a very low price elasticity. On the supply side, the vagaries of the weather may cause large fluctuations in production volume. Coupled with inelastic demand, this leads to large price fluctuations. The very many suppliers, by reacting simultaneously to price signals, may boost fluctuations even further. Indeed farmers are small producers compared to the size of the market. They tend to react to price changes without taking account of the underlying demand and supply changes.

An illustration of the inability of agricultural markets to achieve equilibrium is the so-called 'hog-cycle', which owes its name to the German economist Hanau, who was the first to analyse the phenomenon with respect to the pig market. Figure 9.1 presents the relevant supply and demand curves. Suppose there is a sudden rise in demand (from D_1 to D_2); supply fails to adjust (it takes some time for pigs to be born and become fit for slaughter). As a consequence, the price rises to p_3 instead of p_2, which would be the new equilibrium price at which the equilibrium quantity OC would be sold. Producers considering the high price p_3 to be the long-term measure will extend the supply of pigs from OA to OB. However demanders are not prepared to digest so much supply at that price, so that the price will drop to the p_1 level. Many producers now decide not to produce at this price; fewer pigs are raised, supply is after some time limited to OA, after which the cycle can start anew.[1]

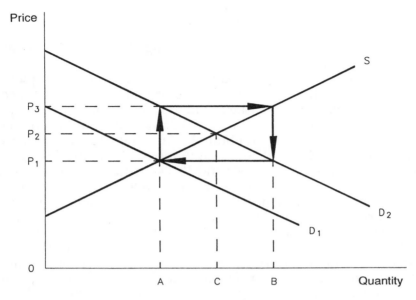

Figure 9.1 Disequilibria in agricultural markets: hog cycle

labour cost (through food prices), lead to differential costs in other sectors and may thus disturb competition. The political motive was that, as a counterweight to the prospects the common market opened to German manufacturing industry, equivalent chances had to be created for French agriculture.

The *objectives of the Common Agricultural Policy* (CAP) (Article 33 EC) are:

- to increase agricultural productivity by promoting technical progress and the optimum use of production factors;
- to ensure a fair standard of living to the agricultural community by increasing their per capita income;
- to stabilise markets;
- to assure the availability of supplies;
- to ensure reasonable consumer prices.

The editors of the Treaty, realising that objectives were to some extent conflicting owing to the conflicting interests of consumers and producers, tried to give some indication of priority by the order of the points of this Article. From the position of points 1 and 2, to improve the income prospects of the producers is clearly the primary aim. We will see in subsequent sections that this has had very important consequences.

Gradual development of common policy[2]

During the 1960s and 1970s, the Treaty obliged the EU to elaborate a common agricultural policy. In 1958 a conference of expert representatives of the member states was convened in Stresa to plot the main lines of such a policy. Two kinds of policy were found necessary: one for controlling markets, and the other to improve the structure of agricultural production. The results of the Stresa conference enabled the Commission to submit the first drafts fairly soon, and as early as 1960 the Council could on that basis issue the first regulations. In the course of the 1960s and 1970s the EU agricultural policy was elaborated. In line with the principles adopted, income support was the prime aim. Hence there has been a tendency under the market policy to set very high guaranteed prices. Moreover generous support has been given to improving production structures. Together this has led to considerable overproduction. In turn, overproduction caused problems with taxpayers (in view of the very high budget outlays) and with trade partners (due to the negative effects of EU-subsidised exports). So it became clear that the policy had to be reformed.

In the 1980s a number of changes were introduced that combined liberalisation and interventionist measures.[3] The central element was the dissociation of market policy and income policy. The objective of the market order policy is to create stable and efficient markets; this implies the use of the *price instrument* for clearing the markets, maintaining some form of market regulation to stabilise prices.[4] At the end of the 1980s, the EU timidly set out on the road indicated by these proposals by introducing a system of so-called 'stabilisers' (for example, for cereals and oil seeds). They implied an automatic reduction in the intervention price in cases where the production exceeded a certain ceiling. The second element was to compensate the farmers for their loss of income by direct income support. This took away many of the welfare losses that the CAP had created for consumers (both final and intermediate) and for third countries, while limiting the losses for the taxpayer (see the final section on welfare effects).

At the beginning of the 1990s a more fundamental change was made. The McSharry plan introduced considerable cuts in guaranteed prices (some 30 per cent for cereals), quotas for the production of milk, and a set of other measures to limit overproduction and budget outlays.[5] The reform introduced a system of direct payments to farmers in order to offset the impact of the cuts in guaranteed prices on producer incomes.

The factors that, in the past, have made it possible for the EU to set up and maintain such a costly system against economic rationale have recently been eroded. Moreover, new factors have emerged that have induced the EU to reform the CAP fundamentally (CEC, 1995a).

- A need to *reduce budget outlays* and welfare losses. The need to observe the criteria about budget deficits for entering the Economic and Monetary Union (see Chapter 15) have convinced political decision makers and even representatives of agricultural interests that the policy of market control could no longer be based on guaranteed unlimited sales at high fixed prices.
- A change in the *external situation*. In the past there has been little achievement by international organisations in the regulation of world markets for agricultural products (production and trade).[6] However, in 1994, the GATT/WTO agreed on a programme for the worldwide liberalisation of trade in agricultural products. They implied the replacement of all non-tariff protection by tariffs,[7] the subsequent reduction of these tariffs by some 36 per cent, the reduction of subsidised exports by 36 per cent and, finally, the reduction of total support to the agricultural sector by 20 per cent.
- The enlargement of the EU by a number of *Central and Eastern European countries*. The agricultural sector in these countries is very important. (Associated countries' production is about one-third of the present EU's production.) Moreover their present prices are very low compared to the EU level. If the CEEC brought their agricultural production capacity up to present EU productivity levels, a considerable increase in production would ensue, exceeding by far the consumption levels of the enlarged EU.

In the framework of the *Agenda 2000* a new reform has been agreed. This continued the 1992 reform (CEC, 1998b) and comprises:

- the setting of a fixed ceiling for the budget outlays in the coming five years;
- the reduction of the market support prices[8] (ranging from 15 per cent for cereals to 20 per cent for beef);
- the maintenance of the quota system for milk;
- the increase in the levels of direct income support.

These reforms are very likely to be continued along the lines of reducing support prices, first because the EU has accepted the principle that the CAP is subject to the new WTO constraints (Tangermann 1999) and, second, because the imminent enlargement of the EU urges action.

Policy of market control

The common European policy of market control has been based on three *principles*,[9] important enough to be discussed in detail.

- *Unity of the market* implies, first, the free internal traffic of agricultural products (that is to say, no customs tariffs, quotas and so on). Given the special structure of agriculture, it also implies the setting of one price for the whole market and the protection of the outer frontiers. Finally, it implies harmonisation of national instructions with respect to health control, veterinary care and so on, and supervision to prevent certain, mostly national, measures from distorting competition.
- *Priority for EU's own products.* The needs of the market are in the first instance provided for by European production; only if that is insufficient will imports be resorted to. Should the world market price be above the EU price, the system provides for a subsidy to be paid on imports to avoid upward pressure on the internal price level, and for a levy to be imposed on exports, to prevent the EU production from seeping away abroad.
- *Financial solidarity* among member states. A policy of market control yields (levies) as well as costs money (restitutions, storage costs and so on). All payments are made into and from the European Agricultural Guidance and Guarantee Fund, Guarantee Division (EAGGF). Because in general the returns from levies on agricultural produce are not sufficient to finance all costs, the European Agricultural Fund is fed additionally by the EU's other own financial means (see Chapter 4).

The common market regulation is not the same for all products. The three most important types of market control system operated by the CAP are the following:

- *Outlet guarantee/intervention price.* This type of scheme guarantees a minimum price at which intervention agencies will buy up any domestic supply, the quantities involved being stored and sold when the market situation is favourable. It applied to by far the greater part of production – namely, cereals, sugar and dairy products. There were broadly similar market schemes for pork, fruit and vegetables, and table wine, but they put the emphasis on storage and processing support rather than on an automatic sales guarantee at fixed prices.[10]
- *Quota.* In order to restrain production to levels that cover about internal consumption while nevertheless paying high support prices an intervention in quantities is necessary. Right from the

start of the CAP such production quota have been introduced for sugar, continuing in fact the quota systems that were operated by a number of member states for this product. Since the 1980s the system has also applied to milk.

- *Bonuses*. For some products, for instance those for which international agreements allow no protection at the border, a system of subsidies on the value of the produce is sometimes applied. Such a system allows domestic production to be maintained at high producer costs, consumer prices being kept low nevertheless. It is applied, for instance, to oilseeds. Producers of olive oil, too, are given support in proportion to their production volumes. In other cases, subsidies by hectare, number of cattle and so on are offered.

These different schemes have widely divergent welfare effects, depending on the domestic price level and the differences between the domestic guaranteed prices and the world market prices (see the three case studies hereafter).

Structural policy

If the EU policy of market control was worked out rather rapidly, things were different as far as structural policy was concerned. Given the pluriform production conditions and national regulations, until the early 1970s the Commission practically confined itself to some coordination of the member states structural policies. The impulse towards a genuine European structural policy for agriculture was given by the so-called 'Mansholt Plan' (CEC, 1968). Some relevant decisions were made around 1972, and from then on this policy has been gradually extended. At present it comprises three main elements: support to management, improvement of trade channels for agricultural produce and reduction of regional differences. The long-term aim of structural policy is to enhance the productivity of agricultural enterprise, an aim that derives directly from the first objective of agricultural policy (Article 33 EC). The main aspects of the structural policy as it has been pursued over the past decades are as follows:

Support to management means first of all supporting investments aimed at technical progress, interest subsidies and investment subsidies being the instruments wielded. Improving educational and training possibilities for agricultural workers is another form of support. Rational management is stimulated by support to senior owners of marginal establishments willing to close shop, and infrastructural measures such as improvement of the water economy, reallotment schemes and so on. Finally the building up of a network of consulting agencies (able to give advice on widely diverging matters associated with conducting an agricultural business) has been stimulated.

Improving sales channels and processing of agricultural products is indispensable to a well-functioning agricultural sector. In that connection the EU provides subsidies to improve the performance of dairy factories, slaughterhouses, packing establishments for fruit and vegetables, wine-bottling establishments, auction rooms, cold-storage warehouses and so on. Furthermore the EU can make funds available for producer groups ('cooperations') with a view to reinforcing the farmer's position in his negotiations with customers.

At the end of the 1990s the structural policy received a new impetus from the set-up of a European *rural development policy*. This puts the accent more on sustainability in environmental terms, on the diversity and quality of the production and on the social fabric of the rural areas (CEC, 1998b).[11]

The EU measures sketched above are not the only ones to be taken to improve the European agricultural structure. The main responsibility is still with the member states, as is apparent from a comparison of expenditures incurred by the EU and the national budgets.

The costs of the European structural policy are paid from the EAGGF, Guidance Division. In practice this often means that the EAGGF finances a certain proportion of a programme's total costs. That proportion is on average small in so-called 'strong' areas, but may be as high as 65 per cent in so-called 'weak' areas. The Guidance Division has considerable sums at its disposal, especially when seen in comparison to the expenditures of the EU for other sectors of economic activity.

Sketch of the sector

The sector as a whole

From the fact that agricultural policy is the EU's most elaborate policy area and has always been the focus of interest, one might presume that this sector is the most important in the EU economy. That is not true, however. Admittedly in the past agriculture was the most important sector of the economy, but gradually industry and, later, services have developed, reducing agriculture to a relatively modest position. Table 9.1 shows the steep drop in the relative significance of agriculture in the EU economy over a period of 50 years.

At the moment, about 2 per cent of total GDP is produced by the agricultural sector, with only 5 per cent of total active population of the EU still employed in agriculture, figures which in 1950 were six times as high. In the 1950s, the shares of agriculture differed widely

Table 9.1 Percentage share of agriculture in total GDP and total employment of the EU15, 1950–2000

Indicator	1950	1960	1970	1980	1990	2000
GDP	12	8	6	4	3	2
Employment	30	21	13	10	7	4

Sources: GDP: Eurostat, OECD, *National Accounts*, various years; Molle *et al.* (1980). Employment: 1950–70 Molle *et al.* (1980); 1970–98 OECD, *Labour Force Statistics*, various years, some estimations. Figures for 2000 are estimates based on 1998 figures.

among the countries of Europe. While in Italy, France and other Mediterranean countries such as Spain, Portugal and Greece the sector was still very important, in the UK it was very modest. The differences, though still there, have shrunk in the course of time.

The main cause of the relative reduction of the agricultural share in the economy is the low income elasticity for food products. Indeed, as incomes rise, people tend to spend a smaller portion on food. Typical income elasticities in the EU are between 0.1 and 0.3 only, and for some products elasticity is even negative (see, for example, Hill and Ingersent, 1982). Because the cost of food is increasingly made up of such industrial activities as processing, packaging and presentation, the share of agricultural products in the economy is even smaller than the elasticities seem to imply.

Sub-sectors

The broad sector of agriculture hitherto referred to falls into some important branches: (1) arable farming (cereals); (2) livestock farm-

Table 9.2 Percentage share of selected product groups in the total production value of EU agriculture, 1974–97

Product		1974	1980	1990	1997
1	Cereals (mainly wheat)	12	12	11	9
2.1	Dairy (mainly milk)	19	19	18	18
2.2	Meat (mainly beef and pork)	31	32	30	30
3	Vegetables, fruit, olives	13	14	15	15
4	Wine	4	5	6	6
5	Other	21	18	20	22

Source: CEC, *The Agricultural Situation in the EU*, Brussels, various years, 1974–80 EU9; 1990 EU12; 1997 EU15.

ing (meat, milk, dairy products); (3) horticulture (vegetables, fruit, flowers and so on); (4) viniculture; (5) forestry (timber); and finally (6) fishing.[12] Each of them can be sub-divided into product groups. Table 9.2 highlights the relative importance of the meat and dairy sectors in the total. It also indicates the stability of the shares of all the groups through time. Only in recent years can the decline of the cereals sector be observed.

Size of farms

The structure of the agricultural market is characterised by almost perfect competition on the side of supply. Table 9.3 gives an indication of the number of suppliers, in this case the number of farms. The picture is not complete, very small holdings (often run as side activities) not being included.

National and EU measures to improve the structure were among the causes of a rapid decline in the number of establishments in the past 35 years, by more than 40 per cent. Table 9.3 also shows that small farms in particular have been closed down or taken over, or have had their land put to another use. In the countries of the original EU6 smallholdings dominated, while in the UK and Denmark there were more large farms. The share of small farms (between one and 10 hectares) dropped by some 8 per cent (of a shrinking total!) over the whole period. In the last few years the decline has been slowing down, owing to, among other things, the worsening prospects of employment outside agriculture. As a result of the developments described, the average farm size almost

Table 9.3   Development of the number and size of farms (agricultural establishments), EU10[a]

	1960	1970	1980	1987	1993
Number of holdings larger than 1 ha (thousands)	8 100	6 600	5 500	5 000	4 500
Share of holdings smaller than 10 ha in total area of holdings of over 1 ha (%)	70	66	63	62	63
Average size of holdings (ha)	11	14	16	17	20

Note:
[a] No comparable figures available for EU15.

Source: Eurostat, *Yearbook of Agricultural Statistics*, various years; *Statistical Yearbook*, various years; some estimates.

doubled between 1960 and 1993 (consistent figures for more recent years are not available).

There are large differences between the EU member countries in average farm size: in 1987, when in the EU 50 per cent of the farms fell into the category from one to five hectares, in Greece, Portugal and Italy the corresponding figure was still around 70. Moreover in these countries the average number of hectares per employed person was less than half of the EU average.

Domestic production and world markets

Where domestic production is below the equilibrium levels of domestic supply and demand the self-sufficiency ratio (SSR) is below

Table 9.4   Self-sufficiency ratio[a] of the EU for selected agricultural products, 1960–96[b] (index)

Product	1960	1973	1974	1981	1985	1996
Wheat	90	111	103	117	122	117
Rye	n.a.	105	94	103	112	116
Barley	84	113	106	114	133	116
Maize	64	67	58	66	84	93
Potatoes	101	102	100	101	102	101
Sugar	104	116	91	135	125	100
Vegetables	n.a.	97	93	97	107	n.a.
Fresh fruit	n.a.	82	80	83	86	n.a.
Citrus fruit	n.a.	41	42	43	74	n.a.
Wine	89	101	99	102	104	109
Cheese	100	102	102	107	108	107
Butter	101	118	101	120	129	109
Powdered milk	139	191	208	411	348	232
Beef	92	85	92	105	106	116
Veal	n.a.	104	104	101	112	n.a.
Pork	100	99	101	101	102	106
Poultry	93	100	103	109	105	109

Notes:
[a] Bear in mind, in interpreting the SS-rates, that many of them are much too low, because the EU includes in demand the quantities which it has been forced to sell on the internal market to low-grade users and at special prices.
[b] 1960–73: EU6; 1974–81: EU9; 1985: EU12; 1996: EU15.
n.a. = not available.

Sources: Eurostat, *Basic Community Statistics; Yearbook of Agricultural Statistics; Statistical Yearbook Agriculture; Supply Balances; Animal Production* and *Crop Production; Quarterly Statistics; The Agricultural Situation in the EU,* various issues.

100. On the other hand, where domestic production exceeds domestic demand the SSR is above 100. The surplus production must be sold in world markets; as the price there is lower than the domestic price, subsidies are necessary. These tend to distort world markets, with considerable welfare effects for third countries, both importers and exporters.

For the period since 1960, Table 9.4 indicates the SSR for a set of important products. Before the enlargement of 1973, the EU increased its self-sufficiency for many products to a considerable degree, in some cases by more than 100 per cent. The first enlargement entailed a drop in self-sufficiency for the EU9, due mostly to the UK's position as a large importer of many agricultural products. Since then, however, the production of practically all commodities has grown considerably. By 1984, the EU had again become a net exporter of many of the products mentioned in the table. The extension of the EU to 12 countries did not affect this situation very much because agriculture is an important sector in these Mediterranean member countries too. The extension of the EU to 15 countries in the 1990s has changed this situation only marginally. However, some of the policy changes started to have their effects during that period (note the decreases for sugar and powdered milk).

Case study 1: guaranteed prices for cereals

Regulatory framework

The common market organisation for cereals was created in 1962. It was based on intervention and external protection. Intervention consisted basically of the setting of an intervention price at which producers could sell unlimited quantities. External protection was based on variable levies and restitutions to compensate for the difference between world market prices and domestic prices. The way in which this scheme of market control works and the effect it produces on various internal (national or EU) guaranteed and world market prices is shown in Figure 9.2. Here S_{com} is the EU supply curve, which runs rather a level course, implying that a price increase causes a somewhat more than proportional production rise. D_{com} is the demand curve, drawn as rather precipitous, in concordance with the inelasticity of demand for most agricultural products. We can now distinguish four cases corresponding to the four prices in Figure 9.2.

- The price on the world market is p_1, at which price any quantity wanted can be obtained (fully elastic supply). In an entirely open economy, domestic production will now become OA, do-

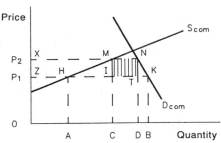

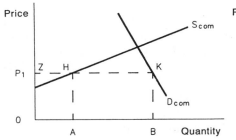

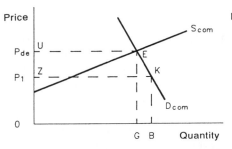

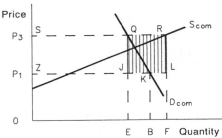

Figure 9.2   EU market regulation system for major agricultural products (guaranteed prices)

mestic demand *OB*, and a quantity *AB* will be imported, every-thing at the price p_1. The domestic agricultural production is low in that case; so are consumer prices. Government subsidies do not apply, so the taxpayer is not asked for a contribution (left-hand upper part of Figure 9.2).

- At a guaranteed price p_2, domestic production will rise to *OC* and demand drop to *OD*. On the quantity imported, *CD*, an import levy of $p_2 - p_1$ will be imposed to make prices on the world and EU markets equal. That yields $CD \times (p_2 - p_1)$ in tariff revenue, the shaded area *IMNT* in the right-hand upper part of Figure 9.2. The consumer is worse off: he consumes less at higher prices (consumer loss *ZXNK*, deadweight loss *TNK*). The farmer's gross return, achieved in one transaction, namely

through selling to the intervention authority, will amount to
OXMC. The area *ZXMH* represents an extra producer rent transferred to farmers from consumers (*HMI* deadweight loss).

- The price p_{de} implies domestic equilibrium between supply and
  demand. The rise to this level can be done without creating
  surpluses and without involving public budget expenses to be
  borne finally by the taxpayer, albeit at a cost to consumers (left-
  hand lower part of Figure 9.2).
- At a price p_3, the situation changes profoundly, however. Demand will drop to *OE*, entailing an additional loss in consumer
  surplus. As supply rises to *OF*, market authorities have to buy
  up a quantity *OF – OE* at price p_3. That quantity has to be sold
  on the world market, which implies an export subsidy (or 'res-
  titution' in EU jargon) of the difference between the guaranteed
  price (or intervention price) p_3 and the world market price p_1.
  The amount is *JQRL*, which is charged to the taxpayer. The
  gross return to the farmer, achieved in one transaction through
  the selling of production to the intervention authority, will
  amount to *OSRF* (right-hand lower part of Figure 9.2).

Since among the objectives of agricultural policy farmers' income
has pride of place, it is hardly surprising that intervention prices
have been set as high as possible. In the 1980s, when it became
apparent that the system could no longer be upheld, several measures were taken to curb production. One such measure was the co-
responsibility levy, a sort of price cut in case production exceeded a
threshold level. In recent years prices have been lowered and the
variable import levy has been replaced by tariffs. Moreover, elements
of income support along the lines of the system indicated in case
study 3 have been introduced.

Branch characteristics

Arable crops (of which wheat is a part) account for some 40 per cent
of the agricultural land area and for the largest part of the budget
outlays of the Agricultural Fund. The main problem is the high price.
This has its roots in the systems operated before the creation of the
EU. In 1964 wheat prices were much higher in Germany than in
France and somewhere in between in other EU member countries.
Because of the German position, the EU price finally resulting was
well above the average of all other countries. EU prices were thus set
well above world market level (p_3 in Figure 9.2); on average EU
prices have been almost double the world market ones over the years
1970–90. This does not mean, however, that European consumers
have paid twice as much for their bread as they would have done

without the CAP price system. As a matter of fact, prices on the world market have been heavily influenced by the EU system that dumped goods on the world market, bringing down prices there.

In recent years prices in Europe have been lowered and hence European exports have dropped. As a consequence, prices on the world market have recovered. The usable production in the EU (*OF* in Figure 9.2) is about 200 million tons, of which 170 is for local consumption (*OE*). Some 30 million tons are exported (*EF*). Consumption does not rise very fast; the only category that could be expanded in a significant way is the feedstock for the meat sector. However, in order to make EU cereals competitive in this market segment, prices would have to come down much further. To add to the difficulties, production still has a tendency to rise. One reason for this is the continued increase in productivity (in the past 40 years productivity has more than doubled).

Case study 2: production quotas – milk

Regulatory framework

EU production of milk has for quite some time been regulated on the basis of price support. However, when in the early 1980s surpluses rose very quickly and the co-responsibility levy proved ineffective to restrain production, the quota system has been introduced for this large sector (Petit *et al.*, 1987). The system involves the fixing of maximum production levels for each country and, within each country, setting a maximum authorised production level for every farmer (for more details see CEC, 1997a). The advantage of quota schemes is principally to reduce budget cost. This is illustrated by Figure 9.3. At an intervention price of p_3, production will be at *OF* and demand at *OE*, the difference between the two being exported with a subsidy of $p_3 - p_1$ (intervention price minus world market price) at a cost of *JQRL* to the budget. Introducing a quota system that limits total quantity to *OW* for the whole of the EU limits the budget cost to *JQTU* (horizontally shaded in Figure 9.3). It also eases the strain on external relations because the quantity exported to world markets is reduced by *WF*. However, under this quota system, the loss of consumer surplus remains at *ZSQK* (the same as before in Figure 9.2), of which *JQK* is deadweight loss. The deadweight loss on the producer side diminishes by about *UYRL*; as some of the most inefficient producers will continue to produce their quota while some efficient producers have to cut down, the exact amount depends on the share each group has in the quota.

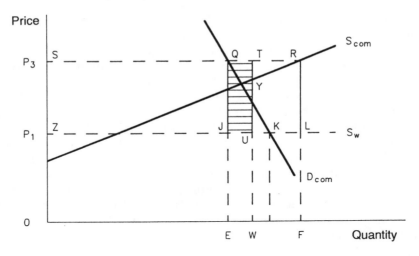

Figure 9.3   The effect of quotas

Branch characteristics

The milk market is specific in the sense that virtually all milk is sold from farms to a relatively small number of processing plants. This feature allows production to be controlled at the individual farm level. Had this market structure not prevailed in the milk sector, it would have been almost impossible to uphold a quota system. It also allows support measures to be taken on the level of dairy products such as cheese and butter. This support can be recalculated in terms of the raw material, milk. The same is true for the device that is used to limit foreign producers' access to the EU market. That used to be the variable import duty and is now (since the GATT/WTO round) a tariff. Between 1995 and 2000 this tariff ($p_3–p_1$ or TU in Figure 9.3) has been reduced by 36 per cent.

Up until the introduction of the quota system *milk prices* have been increased at a high rate (about 8 per cent a year in the 1973–84 period). Since then, the rise in prices has slowed down considerably and is now less than 1 per cent. So the line SR in Figure 9.3 does not move upwards any more (and, given inflation, even lowers slightly in real terms).

Demand is roughly stable. However, that is not to say that market equilibrium has been reached. On the contrary, at the end of the 1990s there was still considerable *surplus production*. Subsidised exports (represented by *EW* in Figure 9.3) amounted to some 10 million tons. 'Promoted consumption' (a form of surplus disposal that has pushed the demand curve to the right) has been estimated at another

10 million tons. Together, these surpluses represent some 15 per cent of total production.

Evaluation of the system gives a mixed record (Tangermann, 1984; CEC, 1997a). In terms of the prime target set (which was to curb budget outlays) the system has performed satisfactorily. In 1998 outlays for the milk sector were less than 10 per cent of total agricultural market support compared to 30 per cent in 1980. However, on other scores the evaluation is less favourable. First, there is the continued excess production (*QT* or *EW*). This is partly due to the continuous rise in *productivity* that compensates the rationalisation of the sector (at the end of the century the production in kilos per cow was double that in 1960). Second, there is the very heavy administrative burden of the system. A third factor is the fossilisation of the existing market situations and the blocking of entry by newcomers. Moreover, farms holding production authorisations claim rents that are not economically justified. Finally, existing producers benefit from windfall gains provided by the sale, rent or lease of quota. As the higher values of quota have also had an upward effect on land prices, alternative uses of land have been frustrated.

Unfortunately, these negative aspects will persist for some time as the system's complete abolition is not predicted until the year 2006.

Case study 3: bonuses – oilseeds

Regulatory framework

The third type of market regulation to be dealt with is the bonus system. During the years in which the common agricultural policy had to be set up, international acceptance could only be obtained at the cost of the EU agreeing to have a very low level of external protection for oilseeds. So, given these external constraints, a system of deficiency payments was put in place for the main oilseeds – namely, rapeseed and sunflowerseed.

Its use has been extended in the 1990s to many other products (notably cereals), often as a complement to the systems described in the two previous sections. A variant of the system used to be applied, among other countries, in the UK, where it was known as the scheme of *deficiency payments*.[13] Figure 9.4 illustrates the working of this scheme.

- At a price p_1 (world market price) (upper part of Figure 9.4) demand will be *OB* and domestic production *OA*. The consumer enjoys high quantities *OB* at a low price and the government's (taxpayers') resources are not tapped.

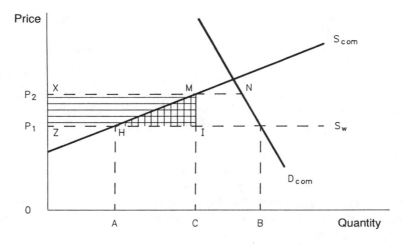

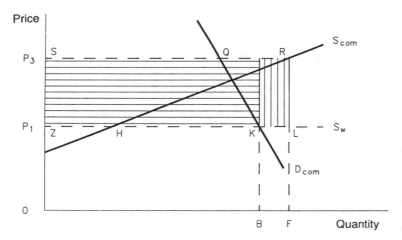

Figure 9.4   Alternative market regulation systems (deficiency payments)

- A country wanting to boost its own production will grant farmers a kind of subsidy by unit of produce (upper part of Figure 9.4). A subsidy of $p_2 - p_1$ will entail a domestic supply of OC and imports of CB. The price remains low for all consumers: p_1. The taxpayer contributes $ZXMI$. The farmer's gross return consists of two parts: the market part $OZIC$ and the subsidy part $ZXMI$. Even less costly is a system that is related not to the production volume but to the difference in cost and revenue. With such a system, based on information on production cost of groups of farms, producers in the OA range would not receive any subsidy, producers at point C the full subsidy $p_2 - p_1$, and producers in the AC range a subsidy that would be just sufficient to cover their cost. Costs to the government (taxpayer): the triangle HMI.

- Because with this system farmers' income support and price policies remain largely separate, a pressure strong enough to push up the price to p_3 (through subsidies in the order of magnitude of $p_3 - p_1$) is not likely to build up easily; should it happen nevertheless, the subsidy would work out as a production subsidy for the OB part and as an export subsidy for the BF part (see lower part of Figure 9.4).

The EU policy differentiates according to size of farms, type of region, products and so on (for instance, tons per hectare for cereal producers, on livestock numbers for beef producers).

Branch characteristics

The production of oilseeds has increased tenfold over the period 1970–91, as a consequence of an expansion of the cultivated area and a very high increase in productivity. Expenditure to the budget increased in line with production. In order to limit budget problems (and thus production) the system has been made subject to maximum guaranteed amounts. Demand has developed also and has been able to easily absorb this increased production. Even imports have grown in absolute terms. So, in terms of Figure 9.3 the EU situation can best be represented by the upper part of the figure (with the exception of rape oil).

Welfare effects

The common agricultural policy has a very controversial record. On the one hand, it has realised its objectives on many points. Internal markets have been stabilised. Farmers' incomes have increased at about the same rate as those in the rest of the economy (see Table 9.1). Production has grown rapidly, ensuring a continuous supply. On the other hand, it has created enormous problems. The attempt to keep up agricultural incomes by boosting the price levels has led to a large overproduction: surpluses, which could only be disposed of at

Table 9.5   Outlay (in 1000 million euro) on the European
             Guidance and Guarantee Fund for Agriculture, 1970–
             2000

	1970[a]	1980[a]	1990[b]	2000[b]
1 Guarantee	2.0	11.2	29.2	36.6
2 Guidance	—	0.4	1.6	4.3
3 EAGGF	2.0	11.6	30.8	40.9
4 Total budget	2.4	16.8	49.1	92.0
3 as a percentage of 4	88	70	63	40

Notes:
[a]   Average figures for five-year periods around reference years: accounts.
[b]   Average figures for the years around reference year: budget.

Source: CEC, *The Agricultural Situation in the Community*, various years; *Financial Forecast for the EU 2000–2006.*

very considerable cost. So the evaluation of the CAP, even on its own stated objectives, is that it has only in part been effective and in total extremely inefficient (Winters, 1990). The evaluation of the CAP on wider economic criteria shows many additional negative points. Paramount among them are the considerable welfare losses which the CAP has created.

A first group of losers in the EU are the *consumers*, because they pay more for their products than necessary. A second group of losers in the EU are the *taxpayers*. If consumers pay too much for products they need, taxpayers pay for production nobody really wants. The total cost incurred by these groups can be estimated with the help of the analysis of the total outlay for agriculture (Table 9.5).[14] The cost of the CAP to the EU *citizen* has been estimated (Kol and Kuypers, 1996; OECD, 1996) to amount to some 400 euro per person; of which about 250 euro come from the consumer and some 150 euro from the taxpayer.[15] These transfers are very important indeed if we compare them to the average disposable income for a family in the EU.[16]

A third group of losers is composed of *third countries*, many of them developing countries. In so far as they are net exporters, they have faced two problems: first, poorer prospects of exporting to the EU; and, second, lower revenues from their sales to world markets because of dumping by the EU. The predicament is serious, for it has brought the EU into conflict not only with developed countries like the USA (about cereals, for example) but also with developing countries which depend very much on the revenues of their exports (of sugar, for example) to pay their imports (Hine, 1992).[17] Thus the beneficial effects of EU development policy (see Chapter 17) have been partly undone by the detrimental external effects of the CAP (Zietz and Valdés, 1986). On the other hand, the complete abolition of the EU protective system would favour the LDCs as a group only slightly. One reason is that the recovery of world market prices is to the detriment of the many LDCs who are themselves importers of food (Tims, 1987). Some doubts prevail about the stability of the recovery of world market prices (Valdés and Zietz, 1995) and hence also about the net effects of the EU policy change on the LDCs as a group.

Next, there is the constraint on growth due to the *misallocation of production factors and resources.* Agriculture and the industry producing inputs for it are using up resources that could have been better employed elsewhere. Biotechnological industries have had difficulties developing, among other reasons because their input prices were too high (sugar, for instance).[18] A considerable area of agricultural land, which could have been used for other products (wood, for instance, which is in very short supply in the EU) or for nature reserves, is tied up in useless production. In some countries, the high product prices have even led to the further extension of agricultural land at the expense of ecologically valuable areas like woodlands. Moreover, the large claims agriculture makes on the budget frustrate the development of other EU programmes. Finally, efficient allocation is seriously harmed, as the CAP has been found to be very susceptible to *fraud.*

Apart from the cost of the CAP, agriculture brings with it other costs – for example, from complementary national support schemes. The total of these outlays amounted in the mid-1980s to some 3 per cent of GDP; as a result of restrictive measures it is now some 1.5 per cent of GDP. If we compare this with the total contribution of agriculture to GDP (Table 9.1), one sees how large the distortions in allocation are. Indeed, on average some 50 per cent of agricultural production values stemmed from subsidies. For the three products of the case studies these figures amounted to respectively 47 per cent for wheat, 63 per cent for milk and 52 per cent for oilseeds. For some products this figure went up as high as 90 per cent (OECD, 1996).

Summary and conclusions

- While under the EU regime a liberal spirit predominates, in the sense that market forces are to take care of the orientation of production and the price mechanism is to play its full role, the sector of agriculture has been set apart and is in fact intensely regulated.

- Heavy pressure has been brought to bear by the farmers – the directly interested – to create mechanisms for the transfer of money from both consumers and taxpayers to themselves. This has given rise to large welfare losses. The codification of rules in the Treaty of Rome has made it extremely difficult to realise on the political level what should have been done on economic grounds.
- The restructuring of the CAP started with the decision of the Council (of April 1986) to stop the raising of agricultural guarantee prices and even to reduce some of them, together with its refusal to adopt more quota systems.[19]

Notes

1   In its pure form the cyclical movement only occurs if the gradients of the demand and supply curves are equal. If the gradient of the demand curve is steeper than that of the supply curve, the system is explosive; that is to say, it progressively removes itself from the equilibrium; if the supply curve has a steeper gradient than the demand curve, the system converges (cobweb theorem).

2   Over the years the policy has been elaborated in untold regulations, directives and decisions. See, for a detailed account of this policy, Ingersent and Rayner (1999).

3   Measures of structural policy have to be revised as well, as the present policy tends to stimulate production in the long run. New measures of structural policy should aim at improving the quality of products rather than increasing productivity. Finding alternative products is the aim of a last group of measures.

4   Proposals in this direction have been made by Koester and Tangermann (1976), Heidhues *et al.* (1978), van Riemsdijk (1972), Meester and Strijker (1985) and Tarditi (1984).

5   Much in the same way as the sugar regime, the milk system had been set up as provisional but proved to last a long time.

6   Admittedly international agreements have been drawn up for certain products, aiming at some control of their world markets, so liable to great fluctuations through speculations and other causes. Such control schemes tend to be specialist in their orientation – to one product – and weak in their institutional structure. The Food and Agriculture Organisation of the UN is concerned in particular with worldwide aspects of food supply. The OECD's concern (for example, OECD, 1987d, 1996) has been of a coordinating nature (exchange of information and cautious adjustment of policy).

7   To give an indication of the external protection of the EU, 'tariffs' on wheat and beef were at some point some 150 per cent; on dairy and sugar some 300 per cent.

8   This is in line with earlier calculations about the size of the price cut to come to market equilibrium (CEC, 1994a, 1995a, Tangermann, 1995).

9   Another principle introduced by the Treaty is that agricultural production is largely exempted from the rules for competition that govern all other product and service markets (see Chapter 14).

10   There is a variant of this regime that uses only *limited free price formation* with

the world market screened off. This type of scheme has been introduced for certain kinds of fruit and vegetables, flowers, eggs and poultry meat. These products do not count as basic foods and often have a short production cycle, which is why guarantee prices are not judged necessary and constraining the imports by levies and restrictions is thought sufficient.

11 For an analysis of the economics of the various proposals of the new EU rural policy see Mahe and Ortalo-Magne (1999).

12 The fishery policy of the EU has some very distinctive characteristics. Interested readers are referred to Holden (1994).

13 Such payments can be compared with production subsidies for industrial products, because they serve a protectionist aim: to increase home production. As farmers have taken them as income-support schemes instead of production-support schemes, the political debate is now transferred to income policies for farmers, although such schemes are practically non-existent for other socio-economic groups in Europe. For a detailed study of the effects of various schemes of income support to farmers, see OECD (1983b).

14 Relative expenditure on agriculture could go down as the EU has increasingly assumed new responsibilities that entail budgetary costs (regional policy, technology, environment and so on) that have increased the total budget outlays faster than outlays for agriculture.

15 The total cost to the taxpayer is not the only bone of contention; the distribution of the tax burden is another one. We recall that the burden of the budget is shared equally by the member states (see Chapter 4). The benefits of the CAP, however, tended to go to member states with a high national SSR (Strijker and de Veer, 1988). In some studies attempts have been made to measure these redistributional effects of the budget (Buckwell *et al.*, 1982; Koester, 1977; Rollo and Warwick, 1979). The group of states with low national SSRs being relatively poor, large compensation amounts needed to be paid out to them, which upset the budgetary balance of the EU. If market disequilibria in agriculture could be avoided, the distributional problems would be much easier to handle.

16 They are also important when seen from the perspective of supply: in 1995, the average yearly subsidy per farmer (full time equivalent) amounted to some 15 000 ECU.

17 It has been estimated that the so-called 'Cairns group' of countries (composed of Argentina, Australia, Brazil, Canada, Chile, Colombia, Fiji, Philippines, Hungary, Indonesia, Malaysia, New Zealand, Thailand and Uruguay), who have a comparative advantage in agricultural production, have missed in this way some 50 per cent of their potential revenue from exports (Tyers, 1994).

18 An example is Western Germany. For this country it was estimated that the liberalisation of the agricultural sector would entail some 3 per cent extra growth and a considerable increase in employment.

19 Another interventionist strategy introduced by the EU is to regulate quantities in order to limit the use of the production factor, land. One option used is to pay the farmer for not using his land; crop-specific measures are a variation on the same theme. One such measure which has already been in operation for some time is that the area under viniculture is not allowed to expand.

10 Manufacturing

Introduction

The industrial sector is at the heart of most integration schemes as these tend to begin with the integration of the market for manufactured goods. However this market integration is to be followed by policy integration. Indeed, given the importance of the industrial sector for the growth of the economy, most countries pursue a national industrial policy. As this may lead to distortions in the common market, a European framework is needed.

The way in which the EU has regulated industrial integration will be discussed in the next section.[1] Next, we will give a concise description of general industrial development under conditions of international integration (highlighting such aspects as specialisation, concentration and firm structure). This will be followed by case studies of the dynamics of three selected branches of industry (steel, white goods and motor cars). To complete this chapter we will devote a section to price convergence. In the final section we will recall briefly the most important features of the analysis.

EU regime

Rationale and principles

The development of the manufacturing industry is very important for the welfare of a nation, leading many governments in the past to pursue policies to foster industrial development. The theoretical justification for such policies (which is also applicable to other sectors) are to be found both in the failure of markets and in the failure of government interventions in other areas (see Chapter 14). There existed several *national models* of industrial policies,[2] with varying levels of effectiveness.

239

- The Mediterranean model relied very heavily on state intervention, public enterprise, support to national champions and so on.
- The Anglo-Saxon model is based on stimulating competitiveness by more general measures such as low tax levels and deregulation.
- The Rhineland model favours public–private cooperation and networks of companies and public institutions to favour sustained growth.

The European integration process has taken away the instruments with which national governments furthered industrial development through state intervention, whichever model they applied. The common commercial policy has taken away the instrument of external protection; the European competition policy has done the same with instruments such as state aids and government procurement, while the completion of the internal market policy took away the instruments for setting technical standards. The capacity for national industrial policies is further eroded by internationalisation and technical progress that leads to an increase in scale; indeed the scale of many new projects (as in aeronautics) is now such that it goes far beyond the capacity of one national state.

In order to cope with market failures there is a case for an EU industrial policy. In this way it is possible to recover at the European level the capacity to intervene that is lost at the national level. However, for quite some time it has been unclear how such a policy had to be shaped given the large differences between member countries with respect to the objectives and instruments. After some hesitation the EU agreed, in the 1990s, on the principles of an EU industrial policy.

The *objectives* of the EU policy (Article 159 EC) are:

- speeding up the adjustment of industry to structural changes;
- encouraging an environment favourable to initiative and to the development of undertakings – particularly small and medium sized enterprises;
- stimulating cooperation between firms;
- fostering a better exploitation of the industrial potential of innovation, research and technological development policies.

Market control policy: prices and quantities

The EU market for industrial products is in principle governed by the play of market forces. The EU does not regulate the prices and quantities. Although from time to time proposals have been made to give the Commission or the national states the authority to make such interventions, the practice has gone in a different direction. Price controls, where they still existed, were abandoned. There is of course some indirect influence of EU and national governments on markets. One example is competition policy: both the ECSC and EEC Treaties give ample power to the EU to prevent companies taking action affecting trade negatively within the EU or abusing dominant positions (Chapter 14). Another is external trade: foreign producers have access to the EU market, subject to the rules of the Common Commercial Policy (see Chapter 17). These permit different import levies being imposed for different products, which implies a certain element of price regulation. However, such policies do not constitute market intervention in the proper sense.

There is one exception to this rule. The ECSC Treaty permits a far-reaching market regulation policy for the steel sector, allowing certain interventions in prices and quantities such as minimum prices, national production quotas, import restrictions and so on (Article 61). In the past these powers have only been used in very particular instances (see the special case study later in this chapter) and have not been very effective. As the ECSC Treaty will expire in 2002, this instrument is no longer relevant.

Structural policy

The *legal basis* of the EU industrial policy is defined in the various treaties. The ECSC Treaty endowed the Commission with ample powers for the preventive control of investments and financial support for projects improving the structure of the steel sector. The EEC Treaty nowhere mentions an industrial policy in the sense of setting the course for and stimulating structural development of the manufacturing sector (contrary to agriculture and transport). The designers were of the opinion that such a policy was not called for: healthy competition would keep prices low for the consumer, ensure the suppliers' efficient use of production factors and guarantee the continuous improvement of the quality of the product.

However, in due time, a mere competition policy was found insufficient to achieve certain desired changes, and a European structural policy for industry was contemplated (CEC, 1970; Toulemon and Flory, 1974). The uncertainties as to what would come under the heading of such a policy has caused quite some confusion.[3] In practice, however, it is clear that the following *policy instruments* were gradually developed (Hall, 1986; Franzmeyer, 1982).

- *Sectoral policy*. In the 1970s, the pressure of the old industries (like steel and textiles) confronted by restructuring led to some involvement of the EU. Later attention shifted to key technology industries (Buigues *et al.*, 1995).[4]

- *R&D stimulation.* In the 1980s and 1990s growth industries obtained support for the stimulation of technological innovation via large multi-annual programmes financed by the EU. They applied to such fields as telecommunication equipment, information technology, new materials and biomedicines. To avoid problems with European competition policy, all schemes address the so-called 'pre-competitive' stage of technical development. Afterwards each company is at liberty to exploit the results of these common R&D efforts to develop and market its own products.[5]
- *Technical standards and norms* are often used as effective protection against foreign competition. They are equally used to achieve certain social objectives, such as curbing pollution, and protection of consumers or people in employment. The EU has tried steadily to harmonise such norms at the European level to facilitate low-cost production and thereby enhanced competitiveness on EU and global markets. However regulation at the EU level is but rarely used as an instrument to further innovation (as with car exhaust gas!) or to protect indigenous firms.
- *Government procurement* is frequently used to stimulate the development of certain products especially in sectors of advanced technology. The EU tries to achieve an effective application of this instrument of industrial policy at the European level (by permitting minimum local content requirements and preference for EU firms in national and local public procurement procedures). Owing to the limited size of the EU budget and hence of EU public procurement, the instrument has little potential for EU industrial policy.
- *Trade policy.* In recent years the so-called 'strategic trade policies' have again attracted much attention from politicians and academics. Although the EU practice contains many elements of this (Buigues *et al.*, 1995), there is no deliberate industrial development-oriented external trade policy (see Chapter 17, on external relations).

After much experimentation with industrial policy elements the EU has decided that it would have a formal industrial policy. The Commission in its memorandum 'European Industrial Policy for the 1990s' (CEC, 1991d) mainly opted for a non-interventionist approach. It rejected the direct subsidisation of production and/or exports and put the accent on policies that aim *to create good conditions for improving the competitiveness of EU industrial firms*. In this category fall the good functioning of the internal market, the early adoption of new technologies by user industries, the facilitation of cross-border intra-EU cooperation, and so on. This policy has a constitutional basis in the Treaty on European Union (Article 157 EC).

The Commission may use the following *instruments to improve competitiveness*:

- Promoting cooperation between member states and exchanging best practices.
- Supporting specific actions. Many of these are of the type gradually elaborated in the past, such as support to R&D programmes for information and telecommunication in the framework of the development of 'e-Europe' (see also Chapter 18).
- Improving the regulatory and institutional environment of firms. This aspect has recently attracted much more attention than in the past. This is reflected by the studies of the Commission (for example, CEC, 1999a) and of scholars who judge the horizontal policies of the EU (such as allocation, monetary, social and so on) in terms of their contribution to competitiveness (Lawton, 1999).

Sketch of the sector

Development of branches

Historically manufacturing industry grew out of craft, which in the beginning could hardly be separated from agriculture and trade. For a long time, manufacturing industry remained a relatively small sector. The great industrial revolution of the 18th and 19th centuries, involving thorough mechanisation and entailing scale enlargement and concentration, changed the picture drastically. In the first half of the 20th century, manufacturing industry grew into the most important sector in the economy of developed ('industrialised') countries, larger than agriculture and services.

In the post-war period, the manufacturing sector became one of considerable importance to the economy of the EU countries, as Table 10.1 shows. Although its relative importance has declined since 1970 in favour of the service sector, the manufacturing sector still accounts for about one-fifth of total employment and wealth creation in the EU.

The development of this large sector is the result of diverging developments of its constituent branches. These again are dependent on the development of their major products.[6] The latter tend to follow a certain pattern that is called the 'product life-cycle'. It begins with an innovation, or rather an invention followed by an innovation.

Table 10.1   Percentage share of manufacturing in total GDP and total employment (EU15), 1950–2000

	1950[b]	1960[b]	1970	1980	1990	2000
GDP[a]	n.a.	40	36	33	27	21
Employment	29	32	33	27	24	19

Notes:
[a]   Inclusive of mining, public utilities, energy (approximately 4 per cent).
[b]   1950–60; EU12; 2000 estimates based on the extrapolation of the 1990–99 figures.

Sources: GDP: OECD, Eurostat: *National Account Statistics*, various years; Employment: 1950–70 NEI FLEUR database; 1970–2000 OECD *Labour Force Statistics*, various years.

These processes give rise to whole new groups of products, which frequently coincide with branches of manufacturing industry. The economy is therefore often divided into new or growth industries and stagnating ones. The result of these dynamic processes is that the importance of branches within total industry tends to vary considerably over time.[7]

A picture of the long-term growth and decline of manufacturing branches in the EU economy is given in Table 10.2 (presenting em-

Table 10.2   Employment (millions) in manufacturing by branch (EU15), 1950–2000

	1950	1960	1970	1980	1990	2000
Ferrous and non-ferrous ores and metals, other than radioactive	1.5	1.9	1.9	1.4	1.0	0.9
Non-metallic minerals and mineral products	1.9	2.3	2.2	1.9	1.6	1.4
Chemical products	1.4	1.9	2.3	2.1	2.0	2.0
Metal products, machinery, equipment and electrical goods	6.6	9.4	11.0	10.6	10.6	8.8
Transport equipment	2.9	3.6	4.1	3.5	3.0	2.3
Food, beverages and tobacco	3.6	4.2	4.1	3.7	3.5	3.0
Textile and clothing, leather and footwear	8.3	7.8	6.6	5.0	3.6	2.8
Paper and printing products	1.7	2.2	2.5	2.5	2.5	2.1
Products of various industries	3.2	3.5	3.7	3.8	3.9	3.1
Total	31.1	36.8	38.4	34.5	31.7	26.4

Sources: NEI: FLEUR-data; Eurostat: various sources; estimates based on national statistics and EC, *Panorama of Industry*.

ployment figures, the only indicator for which long time-series could be made comparable in some detail). The metal industry (ranging from basic metals to transport equipment) is by far the largest sector. The table also indicates that employment in all sectors of manufacturing industry has declined in absolute terms since 1970. Much can be explained by improved productivity:[8] in terms of production (gross value added) many sectors have at least remained stable or have grown.

In some industries the drop in employment due to technical progress and competition from Third World countries started early, especially in such traditional industries as textiles and clothing. Their share in total manufacturing employment fell between 1950 and 1999 by about two-thirds. By contrast, chemicals and metal were obvious growth industries in the period 1950–70: their shares increased considerably. The figures are totals only and hide important developments at the sub-branch level. (For example, in recent years branches such as informatics and telecommunication equipment have shown considerable growth.)

Size of European firms

In the world rankings, most European firms fall outside the top 20; these rankings are dominated by US and Japanese firms. Size is mostly measured by turnover (sales), but employment is another

Table 10.3   The ten largest manufacturing[a] firms based in the EU15 (private ownership, worldwide employment, thousands), 1970–98

	Name	Country	1970	1980	1990	1998
1	Daimler	Germany	150	190	370	440
2	Siemens	Germany	300	350	370	420
3	Volkswagen	Germany	190	230	270	300
4	Unilever	UK/NL	340	320	300	270
5	Philips	Netherlands	370	340	270	230
6	Fiat	Italy	190	220	300	220
7	Bosch	Germany	120	120	180	190
8	Peugeot/Citroën	France	80	250	160	160
9	Bayer	Germany	100	180	170	150
10	Renault	France	160	230	160	140

Note: [a]   Excluding financial trusts and energy.

Source: *Fortune*, several issues.

much used indicator. Ranked by employment, the largest European firms give the display shown in Table 10.3.

The table shows three interesting features:

- *Branch.* The largest firms are concentrated in very few branches: transport equipment (5) and electric machinery and equipment (3).[9]
- *Country.* Germany is very well represented on the list, with five firms; in relative terms that is also true of the Netherlands. However, most EU member countries do not show up on the list at all.
- *Rank.* During the 1970–98 period, the composition of the list of the six largest firms in the EU did not change at all and the list of the largest 12 very little. However, after 1985, more drastic changes occurred as the result of, among other things, mergers (Daimler-Benz) and worldwide restructuring (Philips, Unilever).

Specialisation, economies of scale and location

The EU was conceived to bring about a better allocation of resources through specialisation and large-scale industrial production. Notably in manufacturing, economies of scale are very important (see, among others, Pratten, 1988) and, therefore, an analysis of the effects of the formation of the EU on production, direct investment and marketing is in order. Strategy and internal organisation of multi-product, multinational companies differ under different trade and direct investment regimes (see Table 10.4).

Table 10.4 Production and trade patterns of multinational, multi-product companies under different trade regimes

Trade regime	Location of production units for each product	Dominant part of firm
Free trade	one plant (usually home base)	production and export
Protectionism	numerous plants (one in each major national market)	national companies
Integration	limited number of plants (at good locations)	matrix of national and product organisations
Free internal market	one plant (optimal location)	international product divisions

Philips is a good example of a firm that has experienced these changes in environment. Box 10.1 describes how its strategy has evolved over time (Muntendam, 1987; Teulings, 1984).

Box 10.1   Philips: expansion and adaptation to regime changes

Taking advantage of the *liberalist trade environment* from the first decade of the 20th century, Philips rapidly increased its production of lightbulbs and other products, such as radio sets and domestic appliances. As early as 1910, Philips had established sales companies in 18 European and eight other countries of the industrialised world. Most were supplied by the home base, built for low-cost, large-scale production.

In the 1930s, the surge of *protectionist measures* (see Chapter 3) compelled the company to change its strategy thoroughly. It switched to the exploitation of ownership advantage. Its direct investments became of the tariff-jumping type (see Chapter 8). First, assembly lines for each of the major products were set up in every individual country in whose market Philips was well established. Next, national Philips companies were created, which became responsible for the production and local marketing of all Philips products. Quite naturally these national companies, having to gear their production to local taste, also acquired responsibility for product development. Conditions during and after the Second World War reinforced the system of geographically decentralised combined production and selling units.

In the 1960–90 period, characterised by the *opening of the EU markets,* all national companies were integrated in a centralised international system based on product division. This reflects a direct investment behaviour of the optimal location type (see Chapter 8). The major plants, which used to produce a whole array of products, were now made to specialise in only one or two products.

Recently this European strategy of specialisation and product division has been been given a worldwide dimension under the impetus of global trade liberalisation.

Concentration

The creation of a large integrated market area like the EU will entail an increase in average firm size and a higher concentration in national and EU markets (Pryor, 1972; Scherer, 1974). There is evidence that this has indeed already happened. An early EU study (CEC, 1974) showed for the EU6 that in 1962, in 13 out of 46 sectors of activity, the four largest firms had a market share of over 50 per cent; by 1969, the number had gone up to 18 out of 46. In the same period the situation in the UK (not a member) did not change. Other measures, such as the top eight, 30 and so on, convey the same message: their share in total output increased significantly in the 1960–75 period (Jacquemin and de Jong, 1977; Locksey and Ward, 1979; de Jong, 1987).

The same is true for the top 50. After a hesitant start in the early 1960s, the 50 largest companies increased their shares in the output of the total manufacturing sector from 15 to 30 per cent between 1965 and 1980, accounting in 1980 for about one-fifth of the sector's total employment. The next-largest 50 accounted, in 1980, for another 10 per cent of jobs and 15 per cent of output (Geroski and Jacquemin, 1984). In the early 1980s, the concentration of manufacturing seems to have been more or less stable. The 1992 process has had some influence on further concentration in manufacturing; for the average industry the C4 index, showing the share of the top four companies in total sales of the branch increased between 1987 and 1993 by two to three percentage points. As expected, the most significant increases have taken place in industries that used to be subject to regulation (related to public procurement and to food processing) or are at the moment subject to rapid market changes (technology-intensive industries). Industries where advertising, brand name and marketing are dominant features have tended to concentrate on their national markets rather than on the EU market (CEC, 1996a).

An interesting question is how the large European manufacturing firms perform in comparison with their American and Japanese counterparts. In 1980, the EU and the USA had comparable numbers of firms in *Fortune*'s Top 100 (19 and 23, respectively), while Japan had only a few (Geroski and Jacquemin, 1984). Their relative performances, however, were very different. European firms compared poorly to their competitors. Their outputs by employee and their profitability ratios were much lower than those of their American sisters. Their productivity was much lower than that of their Japanese sisters. This conclusion points to a significantly lower cohesiveness in European industrial and market structures, possibly due to cultural, legal and political differences among the member countries of the EU. This situation has convinced decision makers of the necessity for the 1992 programme to do away with a large number of such barriers to better performance (see Chapter 14). The EU-wide restructuring that followed, accompanied by worldwide restructuring, has changed the situation. By 1998, the EU had more firms (12) in the top 100 than either the USA (11) or Japan (10).

Price effects of integration

The analysis of the evolution in the *differences in prices* made in Chapter 5 revealed that convergence has been observed over the 1975–93 period for the whole category of consumer goods. In the 1985–93 period this tendency towards convergence can be observed for all major sub-groups too (CEC, 1996a). Additional information indicates that the decrease was highest for the groups for which initial dispersion was highest. This is in line with what one would have expected from integration theory. In more recent years the tendency towards price convergence has continued (CEC, 1999b). For manufacturing as a whole, the price dispersion index decreased between 1993 and 1996 from 15.4 to 10.5. There is still quite some room for further price convergence as the average ratio of dispersion in the EU is significantly higher than the ratio for the US. Table 10.5 gives an overview of the situation and of the main trends for the most important branches of manufacturing. Note that the remaining price dispersion is related to branch characteristics such as low import penetration and excise duties (beverages) or government regulation (pharmaceuticals). By contrast, mature markets, such as for white goods (see the case study), show very low price divergence.

Table 10.5 Level and evolution of price dispersion by product group (EU15), 1985–96

	Initial situation	Trend towards convergence (1985–96)
Food	Average	Average
Beverages	Very high	Small
Textiles	High	Strong
Clothing, footwear	Average	Strong
Pharmaceuticals	High	None
Non-metallic products	High	Very strong
Metal products	High	Slow
Machinery	Average	Average
Radio, TV etc.	Low	Strong
White goods	Low	Slow
Transport equipment	Average	Average
Equipment goods	Low	Average

Source: DRI as given in CEC (1996a); CEC (1999b).

Case study 1: domestic appliances

Regulatory framework

The EU has opened up the markets for industrial products that have previously been subject to considerable protectionism. This regime change has had important implications for industries that are subject to economies of scale. An establishment which can produce larger quantities more cheaply than smaller ones, and is constrained in its outlets by a market of limited size, does profit from the extension of the market offered by a customs union (Corden, 1972a). Figure 10.1 can help us to analyse the effect of 'economies of scale'. In this figure, D_a and D_b are the (identical) demand curves for countries A and B, and D_{cu} their common demand curve. S_w is the world supply curve; once more we assume a perfectly elastic supply. Contrary to the demand curves, the supply curves are not the same for countries A and B, country A producing, on average, at higher cost than country B. In both countries the cost decreases as the production increases in volume (definition of 'economy of scale').

We can analyse trade effects for situations of free trade, protection and integration.

- Free trade appears to be the most advantageous option: at price p_w, countries A (left-hand upper part of Figure 10.1) and B (right-hand upper part of Figure 10.1) both import their total demand (OQ for either) from the world market.
- Protection has drawbacks for welfare. If countries A and B both close their markets, in other words adopt a policy of autarky, country A consumes OL at price p_a, country B consumes OM at price p_b. Evidently, to prevent the national producer from making monopolist profits in this case, the tariffs must not be higher than $(p_a - p_w)$ for country A or higher than $(p_b - p_w)$ for country B (see the discussion of made-to-measure tariffs in Corden, 1972a). The total demand in countries A and B would be $O_aL + O_bM$, appreciably less than the $O_aQ + O_bQ$ in the case of free trade.
- Integration, through the formation of a customs union between countries A and B, has different effects depending on the choice of the common external trade policy it wants to adopt. Suppose that this customs union decides to close its own market to competitors from the rest of the world. Evidently in that case, represented in the left-hand bottom part of Figure 10.1, demand in the union could be $O_{cu}R$ at a price of p_{cu} and a customs tariff of $p_{cu} - p_w$. The implication is that country A would take care of the entire production, production in country B being discontinued. The effects of trade creation, diversion and ex-

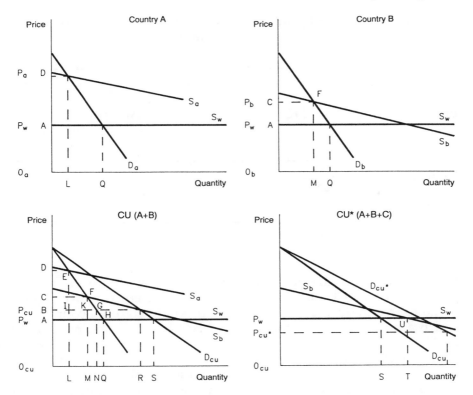

Figure 10.1 **Economies of scale in production for individual countries A and B and for customs unions of A and B and of A, B and C**

pansion of this CU are in line with the definitions given earlier, albeit that account has to be taken of the slope of the supply curves.

What are the *welfare effects of the customs union of A and B* that protects itself against external competition by a tariff of $p_{cu} - p_w$ in comparison with a state of autarky of both country A and country B and with a state of free trade? (See Table 10.6 for an overview.) Compared to the case of autarky, consumption in country A becomes *ON* instead of *OL*, an advantage equal to *BDEG*. Part of it, namely *BDEI*, is the cost-cutting effect of the economies of scale, equalling trade creation O_aL; the other part, the triangle *IEG*, is trade expansion (*LN*). For country B, consumption becomes *ON* instead of *OM*; the advantage is *BCFG*, of which *BCFK* represents the cost-cutting effect, which equals trade expansion (*MN*). This example shows once more

Table 10.6   Trade and production effects of a customs union under conditions of economies of scale, countries A and B

	Initial situation			
Effect	Free trade		Autarky	
	A	B	A	B
Creation	*	*	O_aL	*
Expansion	$-NQ$	$-NQ$	LN	MN
Diversion	$O_{cu}N$	$O_{cu}N$	*	*

Note: *   Not applicable.

that, to promote trade between partner countries, an external tariff has to be set which just protects the most efficient producer. Compared to free trade, the customs union produces for both countries A and B a negative trade contraction of NQ and a trade diversion of $O_{cu}N$.

For the customs union to be an advantageous alternative to overall free trade, the prices of the world producers must be equal to or higher than those of country B. That would be so if a third high-cost country C with a domestic market at least the size of ST joined the customs union (the case depicted in the right-hand bottom part of Figure 10.1). The considerable advantage of such a large market achieved by the customs union is that it enhances the international competitiveness of the union. Indeed this enlarged customs union enables the producer in country B to diminish his costs so as to deliver the good at price $p_{cu}{}^*$. As this price is below p_w, he can start to export his product to the world market. This will permit the customs union to abolish the tariff $p_{cu} - p_w$, which leads to a further trade expansion and creation in both countries A and B.

Do 'economies of scale', as described above, justify the creation of a customs union? That depends in the end on the net effects for the union as a whole, and the distribution of benefits and cost over partners. In our example, a customs union seems favourable on balance. However the losing partner A is likely to demand compensation in terms of money transfers from country B, or to try and achieve a better starting-point than country B for other products, so that their manufacture can be concentrated in country A.[10]

Industry characteristics

The domestic appliance industry in general and the refrigerator industry in particular show in an interesting way how market integration sharpened competition, forcing European manufacturers to respond with progressive international specialisation (see Maillet, 1977; Mueller, 1981; Owen, 1983; Stopford and Baden-Fuller, 1987; Bianchi and Forlai, 1993). The manufacture of refrigerators has flourished greatly in the last four decades. From a luxury item in the possession of only a few families, the product has become standard household equipment with a very high degree of market penetration (practically 100 per cent in the more highly developed West European countries).

The post-war period was characterised by stability, demand characterised by isolated national markets and supply by restricted national oligopolies. In the late 1950s, Italian industry, by combining some major innovations in the production and product technology with the standardisation of the product range of refrigerators, achieved enormous economies of scale. Considerable national concentration occurred in Italy in the early 1960s.

The 1960s were a period of great turbulence. The market of the other EU countries had been opened as a consequence of the liberalisation of internal EU trade. The cost advantage achieved by mergers enabled the Italian producers to penetrate very quickly the markets of the other EU countries and even the market of the UK (which until 1973 was not an EU member). Table 10.7 gives an idea of the magnitude of the effect: by 1972, the Italians had captured over two-fifths of the German and British markets and two-thirds of the French.

Company structure

Producers in the other European countries responded in three ways to the challenge of the Italians. Some tried to merge with other producers in their home countries to form a company of the size required for successful competition. Others decided to give up the refrigerator market altogether, concentrating on other products. Yet others stopped their domestic production but stayed in business by taking shares in Italian firms. The process was the same in all major European countries where companies had been shaken up by Italian competition. The French firms Thomson-Houston, Hotchkiss-Brandt and Claret merged to form Thomson-Brandt; firms like Frigidaire and Arthur Martin, who did not join in, had to withdraw. The German firms Bosch and Siemens merged, and so did AEG-Linde-BBC; again, several firms withdrew from the market. The UK was not at the time a member of the EU; in its protected market three domestic

Table 10.7 Production of and trade in refrigerators (1000 units), 1958–72

	Germany 1958	Germany 1972	France 1958	France 1972	UK 1958	UK 1972	Italy 1958	Italy 1972
Production	1 550	1 700	580	500	360	1 110	500	5 400
Exports	n.a.	470	n.a.	50	n.a.	190	n.a.	3 900
Imports	n.a.	870	8	890	n.a.	580	n.a.	30
from Italy	n.a.	710	n.a.	600	n.a.	n.a.	n.a.	—
Imports/consumption (%)	3	40	1	65	—	42	5	2

Note: n.a. = not available.

Source: Owen (1983), Maillet (1977), Mueller (1981), additional estimates.

producers merged in the late 1960s to form BDA; others left the trade. Dutch Philips stopped its own production but took over Ignis, while AEG acquired a one-fifth stake in Zanussi. Still others continued only as commercial operators, leaving production to (Italian) large-scale producer firms. The three largest Italian producers (Ignis, Zanussi and Indesit) together accounted for more than three-quarters of Italian production by the mid-1970s. The additional sales thus realised enabled them to achieve further scale economies and thus to displace (other) competitors.

A second period of stability (1972–82) occurred after this period of turbulence in the EU market, both in terms of products (decrease in growth) and competitive positions of firms. Firms used their mastering of national distribution channels to split production and commercial control. As a consequence, price differences between EU countries developed. From the early 1980s, a new period of restructuring started. Stagnating demand and increased capacities put a pressure on price. The 1992 programme was to take away barriers to access to foreign markets. A new wave of concentrations followed, in which the Swedish firm Electrolux took a leading role. As a consequence the share of the four largest companies (the C4 index for all domestic appliances) was raised from 20 in 1964 to 50 in 1976 and 60 in 1988.

In the 1990s a similar development occurred on the world level, with some very large companies (Whirlpool, Electrolux), having taken over a number of competitors, competing for world markets (Bianchi and Forlai, 1993).

Case study 2: steel

Regulatory framework

The regime for the steel sector differs from that of all other branches, as we said in the previous section on regulation, by virtue of the special powers the Treaty of Paris has bestowed on the Commission to stabilise markets and restructure the industry. In the past the Commission used this competence to overcome the 1975–80 crisis in this sector. In the mid-1970s, the Commission negotiated a programme of voluntary restriction of output by all producers. This was no longer sufficient when the crisis deepened in the early 1980s. After declaring a state of 'manifest crisis', the Commission regulated directly both quantities and prices in the steel sector (by the power given under Article 58). Quantities were controlled by introducing a system of production and supply quotas by country and by company for a large number of products. In setting the quotas, the position on the market as well as so-called 'restructuring aspects' for efficient companies were taken into account. Prices were directly set (by virtue of Article 60) through so-called 'price lists'. Not only producers but also traders were included in this system (Article 95). A close check was kept to ensure that the prices declared were indeed identical to the prices actually charged. The practical implication was that the European market broke down into national markets, largely fed by national production (as witnessed by the stabilisation of intra-EU trade during this period). To complement these measures the Commission has negotiated Voluntary Export Restraints with among others Japan and Eastern European countries. It was in turn confronted with import restrictions on EU steel by the US.

The economic appraisal of the crisis management of the EU is not very positive; adaptation has taken a very long time, welfare costs have been very high (Oberender and Rüter, 1993) and innovation has been retarded (Moore, 1998). This is one reason why it is unlikely that these special powers will be used again in the future. The second one is that the ECSC Treaty expires in 2002 and its duration is unlikely to be extended. This means that the steel sector will come under the normal rules of the EU.

Salient industry characteristics

Technological change has determined the development of the European steel industry to a large extent. It has pushed the industry towards the use of large-scale integrated plants or of small-scale specialised plants (see Table 10.8). The 1950s were marked by the disappearance of many small plants and firms. Between 1950 and 1980, one observes a tendency towards concentration of basic steel production in a limited number of plants of (very) large scale. After the crisis of the late 1970s, many of the smaller and some of the

Table 10.8   Number of steel plants, by size category (Mt/y), in EU15, 1960–95

Capacity	1960	1970	1980	1990	1995
0.5–2.0	64	70	39	31	26
2.0–5.0	7	18	29	25	25
over 5.0	—	1	8	4	4
Total	71	89	76	60	55

Source: Own estimates based on *Iron and Steel Works of the World*, Metal Bulletin Books, London/New York, several issues.

medium and largest plants were closed. Other very large plants were scaled down to medium size.

Continued technical progress in all parts of the industry leading to ever larger economies of scale increased the necessity for *concentration of firms*. In the period up to the Second World War, concentration had taken the form of vertical integration (coal, iron ore, iron and steelmaking, and metalworking). Since then, horizontal concentration has dominated the restructuring process (see Table 10.9).

Table 10.9   Output (Mt/y) of the largest EU15 steel-producing firms,[a] 1980–2000[b]

Company	Country	Mt/y EU output		
		1980	1990	1998
Usinor	FR	3		
Sollac	FR	9	18	
Sacilor	FR	3		
Cockerill	B	4		43
Sambre	B	3	4	
Arbed	LUX	5	4	
Sidmar	B	3	4	
British Steel	UK	8	14	21
Hoogovens	NL	5	5	
Thyssen	GER	12	11	
Krupp[b]	GER	5	3	16
Hoesch	GER	5	4	
Ilva/Riva	ITA	14	12	14

Notes:
[a] With a European crude steel output of over 6 Mt/y in 2000.
[b] Estimate.

Source: International Iron and Steel Institute; websites of major producers.

In the period of continuous growth between 1950 and 1974, capacity was expanded in line with demand. EU firms were competitive on the world scale (reflected in net exports; see Table 10.10). The process of adjusting to the enlarged competition triggered by the new large ECSC market established after 1952 resulted in increased intra-industry specialisation among European firms (Adler, 1970) and intra-EU trade gradually expanding (Table 10.10).

Table 10.10   Some characteristic data on the EU15 steel industry, 1950–2000

	1950	1960	1974	1980	1990	2000*
Employment (1000)	787*	1 031	991	843	444	284
Capacity (effective (Mt/y))	n.a.	108	210	234	197	198
Crude-steel production (Mt/y)	51	105	181	152	149	161
Consumption (Mt/y)	44	92	158	123	120	141
Intra-EU trade as a percentage of consumption	n.a.	10	18	26	37	47

Notes: *   Estimate based on preliminary data and extrapolation of figures for 1990–99.

Source: OECD: *The Iron and Steel Industry; The Steel Market and Outlook*. Eurostat: *Iron and Steel Yearbook*, various years.

In the period of economic crisis (1974–85) the total production of crude steel in what is now the EU15 dropped by 20 per cent (see Table 10.10). A considerable overcapacity (capacity-utilisation level in the 1980s approximately two-thirds) was the result, and the industry had to restructure in depth, closing down the older plants and laying off hundreds of thousands of employees. However, microeconomic as well as social factors spoke against the reduction. Given their very high fixed costs, firms were prepared to make drastic price cuts to stay in the market. When that strategy threatened to make some of them go bankrupt, governments moved in with subsidies to maintain employment. In the EU9, these amounted to a total of some 50 milliard euro for the 1979–86 period. They have led to the de facto nationalisation of large parts of the industry (in 1990, over 80 per cent in the UK, France and Denmark; over 60 per cent in Italy, Belgium and Luxemburg).

A normalisation of the situation occurred in the second half of the 1980s. Market integration was re-established gradually, one product group at a time, and was completed by the end of the decade. As a consequence of rationalisation and specialisation, employment was cut to less than half the 1980 level, capacity was reduced by some 20 per cent and integration of markets has increased (which means firms have become less oriented towards their home markets) (see Table 10.10).

By the end of the 1980s a new crisis hit the industry as a result of the changes in Eastern Europe. The increased competition of Central and East European (CEEC) firms on both home and export markets of EU firms forced the latter into a new round of rationalisation and the laying off of substantial parts of the workforce (about 50 000 to 100 000 after 1990). The Commission has taken the necessary measures for an orderly process of restructuring by the exchange of information between industrialists and a trusted representative of the Commission and by taking protective measures against imports (for example, agreements with CEECs).

In recent years demand has picked up again, production has followed and as capacity had roughly remained constant the utilisation levels have improved considerably. Market integration has also increased considerably as witnessed by the indicator intra-EU trade as a percentage of consumption. This has, however, not resulted in a stabilisation of employment. On the contrary, the drive towards competitiveness and the technological changes have led to a very large increase in productivity and hence a considerable drop in employment.

Company structure

We can distinguish a few stages in the process of the restructuring of the industry in response to changing technological demands and economic integration. The key element in all these stages is further concentration. This is in line with the predictions of industrial economics with respect to mature industries (see de Jong, 1993b).

At the beginning of the 1950s, the situation of the European steel industry was marked by the existence of a large number of firms, tending to be linked (via financial groups) to other firms in the same sector, located in the same region. There was hardly any international integration. Some Belgian capital had penetrated into companies of the Lorraine district; the Dutch blast furnace company Hoogovens controlled the German firm of Hörder, and the Luxemburg and Saar industries were to some extent controlled by French and Belgian capital. International trade in iron and steel was limited. After the creation of the ECSC in 1952, competition soon made further concentration imperative.

In the 1960s, concentration followed a *regional pattern*. Evidently such technical factors as economies of scale, transport costs and labour force adaptations induced firms to join efforts with firms close by rather than with firms in other countries. First, concentration of firms occurred at a local level (Liège, Sambre and Dortmund, for example). Next the concentration movement was extended to operations on a larger spatial scale. In France, the government stimulated the formation of regional groups: Usinor in the north and Sacilor in Lorraine; similar developments took place in the Ruhr area. Likewise, in Spain, Ensidesa regrouped firms in the Asturias, and Altos Hornos companies in the Viscaya district. Arbed integrated steel firms in the Luxemburg/Saar/Lorraine/Flanders area into what became practically the only international steel company in Europe; later Estel merged the German Hoesch group with Dutch Hoogovens in another international regional grouping.

The next round of horizontal concentrations assumed a *national dimension*. In Italy, the large financial holding of the state (Finnsider/Ilva) assured a lively interest in the development of the national steel industry. In the UK, the nationalisation of the steel industry led to a concentration of three-quarters of national steelmaking capacity in British Steel. In Belgium, France and Germany, the crisis of the mid-1970s induced the governments to step in with very substantial aid, given in exchange for a certain measure of control of the developments that invariably led to concentration on the national level. Usinor and Sacilor in France merged creating a company covering almost the whole of national steel production. The international Estel group fell victim to nationalist pressure (the German Hoesch group was forced to participate in a 'German' restructuring). The tendency towards concentration of firms on a national basis was practically completed in the early 1990s with the Krupp–Hoesch–Thyssen mergers in Germany, and the regrouping by RIVA of a number of smaller private Italian companies followed by the merger of RIVA with the privatised parts of ILVA.

Further concentration was bound to have an *international character*. Two major international mergers have recently been realised. The first is between Usinor (F), Arbed (L) and Acelaria (SP). This merger was preceded by an association of the two latter companies, and by the take-over of Coquerill/Sambre (B) by Usinor. The second one was the merger of British Steel with Hoogovens, creating CORUS. In this way the number of large steel companies has been reduced from 13 in 1980 to only four now. Each of these giants produces more than 13 million tons, more than double the capacity of the largest companies in 1995.

Next to these giants there exist a limited number of medium-sized companies and a fairly large number of smaller producers. Under the former category we can cite Voest Alpine from Austria and SSAB from Sweden. The steel industry in the accession countries is dominated by a number of medium-sized producers such as Nova Huta in Poland or Sidex from Romania. Given their position on an extended EU market some further concentration may be expected in the future.

Notwithstanding the numerous horizontal mergers, the *concentration ratio* in the EU as a whole for quite some time did not rise very high. In 1980 the four largest companies accounted for about 29 per cent (C4) and the eight largest (C8) for about 43 per cent of total steel production of the EU15. In 1995 this was hardly higher; in that year the C4 stood at 30 per cent and the C8 at 47 per cent (see Table 10.9; see also Oberender and Rüter, 1993). So it seems that, in the 1980–95 period, the merger process principally served the objective of rationalisation and not the reinforcement of market power. Since the recent upsurge of international mergers this situation has, however, dramatically changed. In 1998 the C4 stood at 50 and the C8 at 67 (and even at 52 and 69 had the capacity of HKM (50 per cent owned by Thyssen) been included).

Case study 3: cars

Regulatory framework

The regulations of the EU concerning the automotive sector apply to three areas: taxation, external trade and technical standards. Harmonisation of *taxes* has not very much advanced. Major differences do indeed persist with respect to three types of taxation. Purchase taxes range from low levels in Germany to almost 200 per cent in Denmark. The annual circulation tax differs from 100 to 1000 euro largely in function of the choices made with respect to motor fuel taxes (see Chapter 16).

Another important part of the regulation of the automotive sector is *external trade*. Some member states have over a long period maintained protectionist measures against third country producers. Italy, for one, restricted its imports of Japanese cars to 2300 a year, a quota dating from before the foundation of the EU. France has had, since 1977, a bilateral agreement with the Japanese government to restrict the Japanese share in the French market to 3 per cent. Finally British and Japanese associations of car manufacturers have voluntarily agreed to restrict the Japanese share to 10 to 11 per cent. Such VER (CEC, 1983a; OECD, 1987e) have led to physical checks of all cars at some intra-EU borders. These barriers have been removed in the framework of the 1992 programme. At the same time, an EC-wide arrangement with Japanese exporters has been made, that ran to the end of the century. As from the year 2000, external protection with QR no longer exists.

A final important element of regulation is *technical harmonisation*. The myriad technical regulations that national states had established seriously hindered international trade. Technical standards have been harmonised with the 'EC Whole Vehicle Type Approval System'. EU regulations range from very important ones, such as emission standards and noise levels, to very mundane ones, such as towing hooks. The Commission is pursuing its harmonisation efforts between EU and non-EU countries in order to facilitate global production strategies of firms (for a description of the policy process on automobile regulation see McLaughlin and Maloney, 1999).

Industry characteristics

The *overall trade position vis-à-vis the outside world* is characterised by both substantial exports and imports (see Table 10.11). The export performance of the EU has stagnated since the end of the 1970s, while producers from third countries have considerably increased their presence on EU markets. The European industry, while falling behind on export markets mostly in favour of the Japanese, has been able to retain much of its home market, partly thanks to important protectionist measures. However, against all kinds of impediment, the Japanese managed to capture as much as 13 per cent of the market in 1990, from a negligible beginning in the years when the EU was established (both imports and local assembly).

Table 10.11   **Production and consumption of, and external trade in, cars in the EU (millions), 1960–98**[*]

	1960	1970	1980	1990	1998
Production	4.8	10.2	11.4	13.2	14.5
Imports	n.a.	0.2	n.a.	1.7	1.9
Japan	(—)	(0.1)	(0.9)	(1.2)	(0.9)
Exports	1.1	1.8	n.a.	2.7	2.5
Consumption	3.7	8.5	10.3	12.2	13.9

Notes: *   Data on production, imports, etc. are not fully consistent.

Sources: As for Table 10.8, Owen (1983), Maillet (1977), Mueller (1981), additional estimates; JETRO, *White Paper on International Trade*, 1960–90 EU12, 1998 EU15.

The *interpenetration of markets in the EU* is indicated by the share of the three largest producers in total sales on their national home markets. This indicator has the advantage of taking into account the growing openness of the EU countries both to producers from other EU countries and to producers from third countries (Owen, 1983). Table 10.12 shows the – foreseeable – considerable and consistent decrease of the indicator between 1960 and 1998 for the four largest member countries of the EU.[11]

   In the 1950s, international trade in cars was low, as it was hampered by high tariffs (20 to 40 per cent), by the intervention of governments in car production, the difficulty of creating dealer networks

Table 10.12 **Shares (%) of the three largest national producers in home-market sales, 1960–98**

Country	Companies	1960	1970	1980	1990	1998
Germany	VW, GM, Ford	79	66	59	54	52
France	Renault, Peugeot, Citroën	82	70	67	61	57
Italy	Fiat, AR, Lancia	90	72	63	53	39
UK	BL, GM, Ford	79	76	57	55	39

Source: *Tatsachen und Zahlen; Automotive News*, various years. ACEA: *Autodata*; AID, 1996; additional information from the companies' homepages.

abroad, and so on. Scale economies are very important in the car industry, probably even more so for parts than for final goods, so there is ample impetus for scale-driven exports. Indeed large producers can use their savings on cost to penetrate foreign markets. To stop such inroads into their home markets, producers of other countries are forced to take up exporting as well. In the 1960s and 1970s, this determined the intra-EU pattern of trade (Owen, 1983). The importance of scale economies in competitive markets (see Figure 10.1) is illustrated by the relative performance of French producers, which deteriorated every time their unit cost went out of line with that of their German competitors. The effect thereof in terms of change in market shares became larger the higher the penetration of the two countries in each other's markets.

The trade structure of the finished product hides the *international trade in parts* (Hudson and Schamp, 1995). For example, the final assembly of the Ford Escort model took place in the UK and Germany, but its parts were provided by factories in 11 EU countries, as well as the USA, Canada and Japan (Dicken, 1986). A highly developed European industry for components is an asset to the EU car industry (Salvatori, 1991; Bongardt, 1993).

Table 10.13 gives an idea of the evolution of the *production of the most important car manufacturers by country of location*. The smaller producers, most of whom lost their independence in the past, have been left out. The table indicates five main features:

- the steep increase in production between 1960 and 1986 and the more modest growth since that date;
- the stagnation in production in the United Kingdom in the first period;
- the remarkable growth of Spain, where many firms have established production facilities (Hudson and Schamp, 1995);

Table 10.13   Production (in thousands), by car manufacturer in the EU15, 1960–98

Country	Company	1960	1986	1998
Germany	VW/Audi	740	1 780	2 200
	GM (Opel)	330	900	1 050
	Ford	190	560	520
	Daimler-Benz	200	590	850
	BMW	60	430	640
France	Renault	430	1 300	1 190
	Citroën/Panhard	280		
	Peugeot/Talbot	190	1 470	1 370
	Simca[a]	220		
	Fiat	—	—	20
	Smart	—	—	20
Italy	Fiat (AR/Lancia)	690	1 650	1 370
	Peugeot	—	—	20
Belgium*	Ford	n.a.	260	320
Netherlands	Volvo	n.a.	120	160
	Mitsubishi	—	—	90
UK	BMC-Rover-BMW	450	400	470
	Ford[b]	340	350	340
	GM (Vauxhall)	130	160	280
	Rootes (Peugeot)[a]	120	80	70
	Nissan	—	—	290
	Honda	—	—	110
	Toyota	—	—	170
Spain	VW/Seat	n.a.	320	740
	Renault	n.a.	230	460
	Ford	n.a.	260	300
	GM	n.a.	300	450
	Peugeot/Citroën	n.a.	170	250
Sweden	Volvo	n.a.	290	80
	Saab (GM)	n.a.	110	110

Notes:
[a]   Merged first with Chrysler, later with Peugeot.
[b]   Including Jaguar.
*   Not included are the assembly plants in Belgium producing some 800 000 cars per year.

Source: *L'Argus de l'automobile*, various years; ACEA, *Autodata*; AID, *Car Yearbook*.

- the rise in the assembly plants of Japanese firms located notably in the UK; and

• in the recent period, the stagnation of France and Italy and the vigorous growth in Germany.

Recently international specialisation has increased further; in order to cut cost, parts of production were transferred to low-cost EU member countries (like Spain and Portugal) and even lower-cost Central and Eastern European countries.

Appreciable differences between *car prices* have persisted for various reasons. First, car manufacturers by their control over dealers have been able to fix different prices on different national markets. Second, taxation differs; heavy tax pressure has led to low net prices in Denmark: companies selling there were forced to reduce pre-tax prices in a country with such a very heavy tax burden on cars (Murfin, 1987). Third, national import restraints (VER, QR) matter: high penetration of foreign cars has led to low prices in Greece and Belgium. Fourth, alignment with prices of the major national producer and a market protected by driving on the left (few parallel imports) has led to high prices in the UK, where producers prefer greater benefits from limited sales volumes to higher market shares at lower prices (BEUC, 1982; Gual, 1993).

The Commission has tried to do away with this price discrimination between countries by favouring the possibility of parallel imports (Rule 123/85). Exclusive rights for sales networks are accepted, but consumers have the right to go and buy a vehicle in any other EU country. Some small firms specialise in this trade. Car manufacturers have to accept normal obligations of guarantee and so on for these cars. As a result of these measures, price differences have decreased markedly in the 1990s, notably for small and medium-sized cars, as here competition between manufacturers is fiercest (CEC, 1999b; CEC, 1999c).

Company structure

In the *1950s and early 1960s*, the European volume producers were national champions in the sense that most of their production facilities were concentrated in one country, were controlled by capital from their home country and very often enjoyed government support. Standing up to international competition was often only possible with government assistance for restructuring of operations and development of new products. The European volume producers concentrated on family cars with idiosyncratic national styles, which meant that they were oriented towards their national markets.

In the *1960s, 1970s and early 1980s,* under the pressure of the US firms pursuing their concept of global industry, styles and technology converged into one rather homogeneous product, which could be sold both on national and foreign markets. Notably Ford and GM built up their German and British subsidiaries by rationalising on a European level their product ranges. More than before, attention was on minimising unit cost of development and production by large production series. In the face of increased competition, a tendency to concentrate along national lines prevailed, smaller firms being gradually absorbed by the larger ones (Fiat acquired Alpha Romeo and Lancia, Volkswagen acquired Auto Union, British Leyland resulted from a merger of UK companies, Citroën acquired Panhard). The only major attempt at an international take-over by a European firm (Citroën being acquired by Fiat) failed and, after considerable intervention by the French government, Citroën was finally merged with Peugeot.

By the *end of the 1980s* a new group of players came to the European market. Japanese car firms, which until then were satisfied with exporting to the EU, started to build production and assembly facilities in the EU (Nissan since 1986, Toyota in 1992, and Honda in 1993, all in the UK) and to take shares in European companies, as with Mitsubishi (Netherlands). The total capacity of these plants amounted to some one million by the end of the decade.

Owing to the effects of the 1992 programme (Salvatori, 1991) that removed a number of obstacles in the field of taxes, technical standards and import restrictions, concentration has been enhanced again. Concentration was further enhanced by the creation of the European Economic Area (see Chapter 17), the transition of Central and Eastern European economies and increased Japanese imports. Volkswagen (Germany) acquired Seat (Spain) and Skoda (Czechoslovakia), Renault has taken a large share in Revon (Dacia of Romania) and tried to make a deal with Volvo (Sweden) that was finally taken over by Ford, BMW acquired the Rover group and GM took a large stake in Saab.

The confidence that European car manufacturers have in their regained strength has led them to internationalise on a global scale. We can cite here first the recent merger of Daimler Benz with Chrysler and the large stake this new group has taken in Mitsubishi; second, the take-over of Nissan by Renault and, third, the expansion of Volkswagen in China and Brazil.

In 1998, five of the ten largest European manufacturing firms (and six out of 11) were in the automotive sector (see Table 10.3). This shows the importance of economies of scale in that industry. Consequently the concentration of firms in European car manufacturing is fairly high. From Table 10.10 we can calculate that the four largest producers accounted for about 50 per cent of total production in 1960 and somewhat less than 60 per cent in 1998. In the same period the C8 increased gradually from about 80 to about 90 per cent.

Summary and conclusions

- The EU industry has gone through a process of profound structural change. New sectors of activity have developed (electronics), older ones (shipbuilding) have faded out. This has caused the creation of many new jobs and new firms, on the one hand, and the loss of many jobs and firms, on the other. It has also meant the relocation of activities within and outside the EU.
- The creation of the EU has not affected all sectors in the same way; some have responded quickly and are now characterised by firms with European dimensions and much intra-industry trade; others have been kept sheltered by various types of government intervention. This situation has recently changed as the completion of the internal market (the 1992 programme) has torn down the remaining obstacles to free internal trade of goods and the free flow of production factors.
- As far as industrial policy is concerned, the attitude of the EU is fairly non-interventionist; market forces, regulated by competition policy, are supposed to take care of the process of change. However the EU does stimulate the renewal of industry by positive action in the field of innovation (R&D).

Notes

1 Manufacturing is also subject to coordination efforts of other international organisations. The developed ('industrial') countries have formalised their international industrial cooperation in the OECD. Since its foundation, this organisation has carried out comparative studies, collected statistics of various sectors and compared national policies with respect to industry (and technology). The integration achieved in that way is limited, however. This is even more so for UNIDO (United Nations Industrial Development Organisation), which stimulates industrial development in third-world countries by exchanging information and supporting projects.

2 Industrial policy is not well defined; some authors adopt a narrow definition, others a very broad definition, encompassing parts of macro policy, trade policy, competition policy and so on. We have chosen to define industrial policy as the set of government measures aimed directly at firms from the manufacturing sector with the objective of enhancing their development and their structural adjustment to new conditions of worldwide competition. To that end, young sectors are stimulated, the conditions of mature sectors guarded, and old sectors assisted in their restructuring.

3 See, for a discussion of the relations between the EU industrial policy and other EU policy fields, Buigues *et al.* (1995); see the same publication for the

application of such policies to the steel and the motor industries, two of the case studies presented in this chapter.

4   Company regrouping is an instrument that has often been used by governments that have large stakes in the capital of manufacturing firms, or have other ways of putting pressure on private firms. At the EU level the use of this instrument would imply that the Commission would favour the creation of large European companies that would be more capable than their smaller predecessors to face the competition of non-European firms on internal as well as external markets. In the early days the EU (CEC, 1970) tried to help companies to acquire a sufficient size of operations by stimulating mergers. Since the late 1980 such ideas have been abandoned and the EU considers that the best tool to promote such a larger scale is the safeguarding of fair trade in an internal market under good competition conditions (Schwalbach, 1988; Helg and Ranci, 1988).

5   This public–private cooperation is of great value to those who have to take decisions with long-ranging impacts in both government and industry, particularly in a period of fast technical progress and much uncertainty about the external environment. Accelerated technological progress and changes in the international environment have made good insight into possible medium- and long-term developments not only more necessary, but also harder to achieve. The Commission is active in carrying out prognoses and pilot studies providing information as well as scientific and technical documentation. Another matter worth mentioning is that some successful cooperative associations of industries in various member states have been accomplished (with the coordinated support of some governments) with the aim of making certain products ready for marketing. Airbus, the European consortium for the construction of civil aeroplanes, is a well-known example; Ariane, a group of companies concerned with space travel, is another.

6   These branches are distinguished by their different products and production processes. Most of them can be clearly delimited, as with foodstuffs, electronics and furniture. With some modern activities, however, the differences are steadily becoming vaguer. A case in point is informatics, a sector comprising classical industrial production (such as cables and equipment for telecommunication), less classical industrial activities like the graphic arts, as well as a large number of traditional service sectors such as libraries, telecommunication and so on.

7   See, for a general discussion of the relation between sectoral growth, life-cycles and industrial policy, de Jong (1993a).

8   The quantitative side of employment change hides the technological progress of the last few decades, which has radically changed the production apparatus and the qualifications of the workforce. The large numbers of blue-collar factory workers have been replaced more and more by the grey and white collars of those concerned with management, research, control, checking, sales and organisation, working in offices, showrooms and laboratories.

9   Had the list been extended, the next company on it would in 1998 again have been a transport equipment company (BMW from Germany) and an electric equipment company (Alcatel from France).

10   Imperfect competition may change the distribution of the effects over the customs union partner and third countries. If the supply curve of third country producers is not fully elastic, but also subject to increased returns, the decrease in third country exports to the CU due to the increase in the internal competitiveness of customs union producers depicted in Figure 10.1 will lead to an increase in the cost level of these producers and hence a further loss of their competitiveness on third markets (Venables, 1987).

11   In each of the large countries given, a home producer was present. That is not

always the case for smaller member states. Hence the relative share of imports in the smaller countries was much greater than for the four larger countries. As Hocking (1980) has shown, the negative relation between the size of the home market and the volume of imports diminished in the 1960s, but still persisted to some extent into the mid-1970s, some 15 years after the formation of the EU.

11 Energy

Introduction

The EU has from its very beginnings pursued the integration of energy markets. The regime it has created is described in the next section. It is a complicated one, because it needs to take account of the different ways in which all member states intervene in the energy markets and in the structure of the energy sector.

The next section sketches the changes, which in the 1950–98 period occurred in European energy markets (consumption, production and prices). The fourth and fifth sections treat the integration of certain markets in more depth; oil and electricity have been chosen as examples. In both case studies we will describe the EU regime, the development of the branch and the strategic responses of the major firms. A section with some conclusions will complete the chapter.

EU regime

Rationale and principles

Energy is essential to economic development. Without the ample supply of energy the present levels of welfare would not be possible. The control over energy supplies has always been a matter of concern for governments.

In an integration scheme, the equal access to energy is of great economic importance; as energy is a major input in many other productions, non-integrated energy markets coupled with integrated goods markets would lead to distortions. It is also of much political importance as the interdependency on strategic commodities may be the best guarantee for peace.

The *objectives of the Common Energy Policy* have been remarkably stable over time as far as their essential characteristics are concerned (CEC, 1988b, 1992c, 1992d, 1995b, 1999d). These are:

- *security of supply* which aims to minimise risks and impacts of possible supply disruption on the EU economy and society;
- *competitiveness* to ensure low-cost energy for producers and consumers; the most important instrument is to enhance the working of market forces;
- *environmental protection* which is integrated in both energy production and energy use to safeguard sustainable development.

These objectives have been elaborated differently over time in view of the changing external conditions.

Gradual development of policy

In the 1950s the EU energy policy started with development of a coal policy by the ECSC, followed by the set up of a common policy for the nuclear sector by the EAEC. Since then a coherent energy policy has gradually been developed on the basis of the three treaties.[1]

In the 1960s, it was recognised that the situation in the energy field lacked balance. Since then, the Commission has submitted a series of proposals for a more coherent EC energy policy. The 1962 Memorandum on Energy Policy was followed in 1968 by a 'First Orientation to a Common Energy Policy'. It reflected the fundamental problems of the EU energy position and established the principles of EU policy, namely to ensure supply at the lowest possible price, with due regard to the specific structure of the energy sector. A common market for energy products and coordination of the member states' energy policy were to be the means. This led to the decision of the European Council in 1972 to develop a coordinated energy policy.

The *1973–1985 period* is marked by the two energy crises, in 1973 and 1979, that showed that the EU was confronted by three major problems (CEC, 1981a).

- Insecurity of supply. The EU was dependent for a large part of its energy on foreign oil. The cutting of supplies was used as a weapon by some producers for strategic as well as economic reasons (d'Anarzit, 1982).
- Instability of prices. Fluctuations in the price of crude oil and the exchange rate to the dollar (see Figure 11.1) had caused huge disturbances of the European economy in general and the energy sector in particular.
- Disequilibrium on the balance of payments. Between 1973 and 1981, the oil bill of the EU had multiplied by eight (in dollars), despite a simultaneous decline of net imports by some 40 per cent.

Source: CEC (1986f, 1996b).

Figure 11.1   Import prices of energy

The very divergent national responses to the 1973 crisis (virtually disintegrating the common energy market) made the EU painfully aware of the need for further action. This was reinforced by the second oil crisis of 1979. In a series of communications from the Commission to the Council, the former progressively worked out the objectives and implementation of its policy. A central element of the EU policy is to render consistent the objectives and measures of energy policy as pursued by national governments. To coordinate the programmes of member states (Lucas, 1977, 1985), the Commission organised periodical surveys of member states' energy policy schemes (for example, CEC, 1982c).[2] The EU agreed on two common targets to improve the security of its supplies and the competitiveness of its energy sector. The first one was to diminish the ratio between the growth of energy consumption and the growth of GNP. The second one was to reduce the share of oil and stimulate the use of solid fuels and nuclear energy both in primary energy consumption and in electricity generation. The success of this policy, and the breaking up of the OPEC cartel, meant that, in the mid-1980s, the price of energy fell considerably, which changed fundamentally the market conditions and permitted the reorientation of the EU energy policy.

In the period 1985–2000, major developments shaped a new framework for each of the three major objectives for EU energy policies. The first was the drive towards the completion of the internal market in order to enhance competitiveness. Traditionally the markets for the different fuels are very heavily regulated on a national basis, and some of them (electricity, gas) were traditionally monopolies. As a consequence the European market was very segmented. The new objective to create a competitive market with a pan-European regulatory framework implied a major restructuring and liberalisation of important segments of the sector. The second new development was the increased concern with the environment. Indeed one of the major causes of air pollution is the burning of energy sources with a high carbon content, so the objectives of the policies became more oriented towards the limitation of consumption, and towards less polluting sources (CEC, 1992d, 1995b). This objective has recently been reinforced (CEC, 1999d) as the EU has accepted higher targets in this field both internally (Treaty of Amsterdam) and externally (Kyoto conference). The third development concerned the security of supply. The EU will increasingly be dependent on imported energy and the opening up of the Eastern European countries with their very important energy reserves has provided a new opportunity. A European Energy Charter has been signed between the EU and the CEEC to expand the infrastructure and subsequently the trade in energy between the two areas. This has fundamentally changed the external dimension of the EU energy policies (CEC, 1992e, 1999d).

Market regulation

The Commission has laid down, in regulations and directives, rules for the markets of different energy products. An important impetus has come from the completion of the internal market for energy products, whereby the causes of distortions on the EU market for energy, such as differences in taxes on energy products, national monopolies, government interventions and protective national procurement, are taken away. The EU activity may be grouped under three headings.

Security of supply   To avoid the type of problem that occurred during the oil crises, member states are committed to maintain minimum stocks of oil and, in times of supply problems, to introduce a rationing scheme for these stocks (Directives 68/414/EEC and 98/93/EC).

Transparent markets   Member states are committed to inform and consult the Commission on the development of prices and domestic and foreign supplies in the different sub-markets (oil, gas and so on).

For example, the conditions and prices of home deliveries, of imports and exports are published (Directive, 1990) and the market situation is discussed regularly on the basis of the Commission's quarterly reviews.

Access to markets   In the electricity and gas markets the monopoly power of the companies controlling the distribution networks has for a long time barred the access of efficient producers to potential clients. The EU is now in the process of realising the internal market for all remaining energy products too (see the case study on electricity).

Structural policy

The objectives of the common energy policy (CEP) cannot be realised without a certain restructuring of energy production, consumption and trade. The following measures of structural policy are in force in the framework of the CEP.

Stimulating EU production
- nuclear energy (financing by EAEC);
- coalmining (ECSC financing and regulation);
- alternative (permanent and renewable) sources: subsidies to research projects and demonstration programmes).

Saving energy
- loans to manufacturing industries applying new technical procedures.

Supervising restructuring
- coalmining (ECSC powers) for capacity reduction;
- oil refining: supervision of the reduction of capacity by exchange of information, contacts and negotiations with industry representatives.

Sketch of the sector

Employment and value added

Energy is a collective term for many types; a common distinction is that between primary and secondary energy. Primary energy springs from a variety of sources. Historically human and animal muscle power, wood, wind and water (tides and rivers) were important. In more modern times fossil fuels have come to the fore (coal, oil, gas). Since the Second World War, nuclear energy has developed fast. Recently other forms of energy have regained interest, in particular the so-called 'renewable resources', like sun radiation, tidal waves, hydropower and biomass. Because primary energy sources are not always easy to use, they are converted into secondary ones, such as coke and gas from coal, petrol and liquefied petroleum gas (LPG) from crude oil. Some of these are converted a second time for the generation of electricity in coke- or oil-fired power stations.

The energy sector is composed of primary energy production (such as coalmining) and by secondary energy production and distribution (for example, electricity generation and oil refining). Each count for less than 1 per cent of total employment, which means that the entire energy sector represents about 2 per cent of total employment. In terms of gross value added, the percentage is about 3 per cent higher because of the relatively high productivity and the large contribution the sector makes to government revenue. Although the sector does not represent a large part of total economic activity, we give it a separate treatment because of its strategic importance.

Total consumption of primary energy

The 1950–73 period was characterised by high and stable economic growth (on average almost 5 per cent a year). Total energy consumption in the European Union increased very fast too (ratio between the increase of energy consumption and that of GNP was on average about one during the whole period).

The 1973–82 period started with some events, which were to exert a strong effect on the entire consumption pattern. For one thing, the oil price, practically stable until then, rose almost fourfold. For another, the continuous supply of oil became uncertain as some oil exporters put an embargo on oil exports to certain consumer countries. An economic recession was the result, with, in 1975, the first decline of GNP and of energy consumption since the Second World War. The high price of oil induced its replacement by other sources of energy, as well as measures to diminish consumption by energy saving. In 1979 there followed the second oil shock, again multiplying the oil prices by almost four. It was the main cause of an actual drop in energy consumption. As the increase of GDP during that period was very low, the elasticity of demand was negative.

In *the 1983–98 period*, with economic growth accelerating and prices of energy decreasing drastically, demand for energy picked up again too.

Consumption by primary energy source

Consumption has developed differently for the various primary energy sources,[3] as Table 11.1 illustrates. Certain trends can be discerned throughout the period 1930–97, such as the fall in the share of coal

Table 11.1 **Percentage shares of primary energy sources in total energy consumption (Mtoe), EU15, 1930–97**

	1930	1937	1950	1960	1973	1980	1990	1997
Coal	95	90	83	63	23	23	22	16
Oil	4	8	14	31	61	51	44	42
Gas	—	—	—	2	11	15	17	21
Electricity	1	2	3	4	5	11	17	21
Total	100	100	100	100	100	100	100	100

Source: OECD, *Energy Statistics, Energy Balances, Oil Statistics*, various years; OECD (1966, 1973)

(from a very dominant position), the rise and subsequent fall in the share of oil and the continuous rise of the shares of (natural) gas and primary electricity (comprising hydraulic power and nuclear energy). The table shows that there is some differentiation between sub-periods as far as the development of oil is concerned. In the period from 1950 to 1973, consumption switched fast from coal to oil. This trend reached a turning point in 1973: as a result of the considerable increase in oil prices and subsequent policy measures, the share of oil decreased from 1973 onward. Since 1985, there has been a steep fall in oil prices due to the breakdown of the OPEC cartel, which halted the decrease in the share of oil in total energy consumption in the EU.

The determinant factors behind the substitution of one energy source for another are costs, consumer convenience and availability; of course, the latter two can also be translated into costs. The important switch from coal to oil in the post-war period is due to the divergence of their relative prices. While high labour costs of production and transport made coal more and more expensive, the consumption prices of oil could be reduced thanks to its capital-intensive production and the economies of scale achieved in conversion and transport (Eurostat, 1974).

The steady rise in the share of gas in total consumption has been due in particular to its convenient use in many installations and to the fact that it is more and more produced in the consumption areas. Finally the share of primary electricity has steadily been growing as a result of the high growth of demand for electricity and the stimulation of hydro- and nuclear energy. Other primary energy sources, such as wood, wind, sun and animal force, are still of very limited importance in quantitative terms; the high costs and/or great inconvenience to consumers have been the main delaying factors in their development.

Conversion of primary into secondary energy

Primary energy sources are not always convenient to users, which is why they are converted into secondary ones. *To convert energy costs energy.* On the one hand, oil refineries and coke ovens use energy to feed the production process. On the other, the return of thermal power stations is rather low: energy escapes through cooling into the water and through chimneys into the air. The cost of these conversion processes is justified by the higher efficiency in production, transport and consumption of the users of secondary energy. The primary sources differ widely in the extent to which they are converted into secondary energy. About one-half of all coal is converted, mostly in power stations, with a small proportion in coke factories. Brown coal is converted almost entirely into electricity. Crude oil is fully converted into oil products, of which a portion, in particular fuel oil, is processed further in electric power stations.

Table 11.2   **Percentage shares of energy sources in the consumption of European power stations (calculated on the basis of a conversion in oil equivalent), 1950–97**

	1950	1960	1970	1980	1990	1997
Solid (coal)	71	67	51	47	37	31
Liquid (oil)	1	7	24	22	11	7
Gas	—	1	5	7	7	9
Nuclear	—	1	4	11	36	48
Hydro	28	24	16	13	9	5
Total	100	100	100	100	100	100

Note: [a]   1950–90 EU12; 1997 EU15; differences between series for EU12 and EU15 for earlier reference years negligible.

Source: OECD, *The Electricity Supply Industry in Western Europe,* various years; CEC: *Panorama;* OECD, *Energy Balances of OECD Countries,* Paris 1999.

Apparently, then, many primary energy sources are ultimately converted into electricity. The relative volumes of the various primary energy sources utilised for the generation of electricity have changed over time (Table 11.2) under the influence of a combination of factors, such as the relative price (coal versus oil) and government policy (decrease of oil and increase of nuclear power for strategic reasons).

Production and import

Along with the consumption pattern of energy in Western Europe, the pattern of production and import, and hence the *external dependence*, have greatly changed (CEC, 1996b). The first change came when coal, a predominantly domestic energy source, was replaced by an imported one, oil. More and more coal was imported as well, because the West European mines could not compete with foreign ones. As a result, the dependence coefficient of the EU, defined as the share of net imports of energy in total energy consumption, rose rapidly (from just 1 per cent in 1930 to 7 per cent on the eve of the Second World War, to 15 per cent by 1950 and to 66 per cent in 1973: EU12 figures). The oil crisis of the early 1970s opened European eyes to the risk of such a development. Since then extensive schemes have been carried out to make Europe less dependent on foreign energy, notably oil: schemes to boost national production as well as reduce consumption. The policy has produced the desired effect: the external dependence coefficient of the EU15 was down to 42 per cent in 1985. Between 1985 and 1992, it went up again, to almost 50 per cent, as a consequence of the fall in imported oil prices; since then it has oscillated around 47 per cent. Let us look rather more closely at the individual energy sources.

Crude oil   The EU's own production was practically negligible in 1950. In the 1985–95 period, the EU15 produced some 30 per cent of its total oil consumption (of which the UK had the lion's share[4]). By becoming increasingly self-supplying, Western Europe diminished its total dependence on foreign oil. Moreover it reduced strategic risks by drawing oil from an increasing number of supplying countries. In the early 1960s, four Middle Eastern countries, Iran, Iraq, Kuwait and Saudi Arabia, still accounted for three-quarters of the oil supply to Western Europe. By 1970, their share in European imports had been reduced by half, and this dropped further in the course of the 1970s because new producers, in particular in North and West Africa, but also in Mexico, had joined the traditional Middle Eastern oil suppliers to Europe. In the 1980s, it was Norway and in the 1990s the CEEC that grew in importance. Figure 11.2 gives an idea of the geographical pattern of Western European crude oil imports.

Solid fuels   Traditionally Western Europe produced its own coal and, throughout the 1950–97 period, the largest producer countries in Western Europe were the UK and Germany, with France, Spain and Belgium following at some distance. The production in the rest of Western Europe was negligible in comparison. In the 1950s, no more than about 5 per cent of total demand for coal needed to be im-

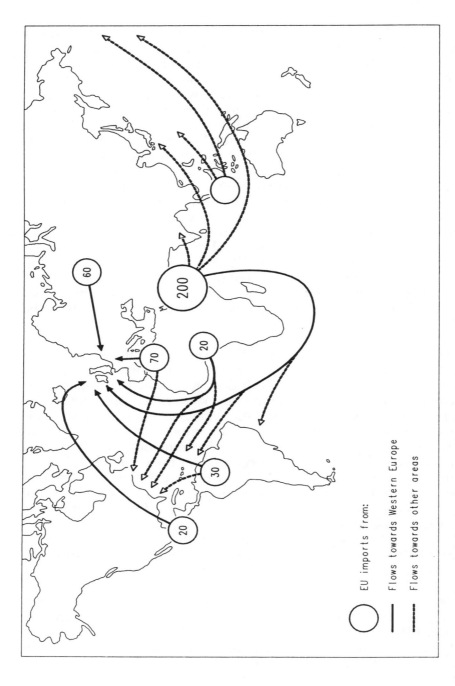

EU imports from:

Flows towards Western Europe

Flows towards other areas

Figure 11.2   Flows of crude oil towards the EU (Mtoe), 1990

ported. In the 1960s, the average percentage was 10. By 1994, when the consumption of coal had picked up again, the EU15's dependence on imports had risen to some 35 per cent. Most imports came from the USA and Poland. For a long time, coal extracted in EU countries was able to hold its own against oil and imported coal only with the help of supporting measures. Now coal is of limited importance; only Germany is a producer of significant size (90 Mtoe per year). Notwithstanding substantial aid to the remaining coal industry, its present position is very weak. The future of coal is rather bleak, as it is the most polluting in terms of carbon content; an agreement on a carbon tax would penalise coal very heavily.

Natural gas   The production in the EU has grown to become quite important (particularly in the Netherlands, and later on also in the North Sea (UK)). In Western Europe outside the EU, Norway is another large producer and recently (liquefied) natural gas has begun to be imported (LNG by tanker from North Africa, NG by pipe from Eastern Europe, the latter accounting for 45 per cent of total EU imports).

Other   Among the other sources of energy, nuclear is of particular importance. Because uranium can be stocked, the fiction is often maintained that nuclear energy is a domestic source of energy; that uranium has to be imported into Europe is overlooked. As for such alternative primary sources as hydro-power and wind, the EU is by definition independent of imports; given their small scale, we need not pay further attention to them here.

Consumption by category

To analyse the consumption pattern,[5] we distinguish three main sectors: industry, household/commerce, and transport. The relative position of these consumer categories in total consumption was rather stable throughout the 1950–80 period (see Table 11.3). Industry invariably took first place, with a share of more than 40 per cent. It was followed closely by household/commerce, with a share of some 35 per cent. Transport invariably came in third position. In the 1980s and 1990s, the share of industry has fallen, to the benefit of transport.

Industry   The iron and steel sector is the largest consumer. Coke and coal (for blast furnaces) are in the lead, but other energy sources, especially electricity, are steadily gaining in importance. A second very important sector is that of chemical products, in particular the petrochemical industry, which uses mainly oil products and gases. Note that the consumption of industry also comprises non-energetic

Table 11.3   Final domestic consumption of energy (including for non-energy purposes) in the EU15, by consumer category and secondary energy source (%), 1950–97

	1950	1960	1970	1980	1990	1997
Industry (incl. non-energy)	41	47	47	41	37	34
Household/commerce	40	35	35	36	35	37
Transport (incl. bunkers)	19	18	18	23	28	29
Total	100	100	100	100	100	100

Sources: OECD, 1987g; OECD, *Basic Statistics of Energy, Energy Balances,* various years.

consumption, for instance of naphtha as a raw material of the petrochemical industry. Non-energy consumption increased significantly as the petrochemical industry grew in importance (Molle and Wever, 1983). The industrial consumption of coal has declined fast since 1960, while that of all other energy forms has been rapidly increasing. This cannot be attributed entirely to the developments in the steel and chemical industries described above, for most sectors of other industry show the same tendency.

Household, commerce   Household consumption has accounted for half to two-thirds of the entire category's consumption over the whole period. The development of the various energy forms offers a striking picture: after a rise in the 1950s, coal was practically eliminated in the 1960s, obviously because it was inconvenient to the user. Electricity and gas, on the other hand, have grown fast, as did oil until the decline prompted by the oil crises.

Transport   Haulage is by far the largest consumer group, accounting for more than half of the category's total consumption. Moreover its share has steadily increased over time. The demand of the haulage sector is almost entirely for oil products, which is also by far the most important source of energy for air and water transport. Electricity is almost completely and exclusively used for rail transport; coal has lost most of its former important position in shipping and rail transport to oil and electricity.

Prices

Under conditions of integration one generally expects a convergence of prices. We can analyse the *evolution of prices on EU energy markets*

Table 11.4   Evolution of price differences of selected energy products in EU9ᵃ, 1980–93

	Incl. VAT, EXCᵇ				Excl. VAT, EXCᵇ			
	1980	1985	1990	1993	1980	1983	1990	1993
Coal, coke	22	15	18	29	20	13	23	29
Motor fuels	12	11	13	9	10	9	11	10
Natural gas	35	26	36	41	31	23	33	36
Electricity	25	13	6	20	25	11	15	20

Notes:
[a]   Coefficient of variation.
[b]   VAT: value added tax; EXC: excises.

Source: CEC (1996a).

for the period since 1980 for a number of products (see Table 11.4). The figures show four important features:

- There are important differences in price among the member countries of the EU.[6] These differences reflect, apart from obvious factors such as differences in transport costs, a clear lack of market integration.
- There is no general tendency towards convergence. On the contrary, since 1985 we instead see divergence. The evolution over the 1980–85 period reflects the abrupt and large fall in the price of energy (see Figure 11.1); the subsequent increase reflects the very different reactions of countries to changes in energy markets.
- Disparity for certain fuels is much higher than for others. Determinant factors here are distances between major production and consumption sites (high for coal and natural gas, low for motor fuels) and degree of integration (low for electricity, high for motor fuels).
- Market prices are heavily influenced by taxation. A significant part of the price difference can be explained by differences in VAT and excises (see Chapter 14).

Case study 1: oil refining

Industry characteristics

Economies of scale play an important role in the refining industry. Therefore production has been gradually concentrated in a relatively small number of large plants. This led to a continuous increase in the average size of refineries during the 1950–2000 period (see Table 11.5). The restructuring process of the European refining industry has followed a distinct pattern dependent on the different stages of the industry life-cycle (Molle, 1993).

Table 11.5   Number of refineries by size class and total capacity of refineries (Mt/y), EU15, 1950–2000

Class (Mt/y)	1950	1960	1970	1980	1990	2000
0.1–1.0	60	53	31	17	6	4
1.1–5.0	11	45	81	55	28	33
5.1–10.0	—	5	30	57	40	28
10.1–15.0	—	1	7	16	14	24
15.1–20.0	—	—	5	6	5	3
Larger than 20.1	—	—	1	4	4	1
Total number	71	104	155	155	97	93
Distillation capacity	41	192	695	987	614	672
Average capacity	0.6	1.8	4.5	6.3	6.2	7.2

Source: Molle and Wever (1983); Molle (1993). Additional estimates based on *Oil and Gas Journal*.

The *introductory stage* happened shortly after the Second World War, when a large number of relatively small plants were created.

The *expansion stage* lasted from the early 1950s up to the first oil crisis in the mid-1970s. During this period, the total capacity of the refinery sector in Europe increased rapidly, in line with the strongly increased demand. Part of that growth was achieved by the expansion of existing refineries, part by the creation of new ones. In oil refining, as in other industries, growth was attended by a tremendous enlargement of the scale of plants (Table 11.5). In spite of this increased scale in plant size, there was no spatial concentration of production facilities. Throughout the period 1950–75, markets were indeed growing at an even higher rate than the optimal scale, which permitted refinery activities to orient themselves to national markets

and to spread geographically (Molle and Wever, 1983). This orientation to national markets, based on location factors like transport cost,
was consolidated by the strategy adopted by several governments to
build up their own 'national' oil industries.

The *maturity* stage came suddenly in the mid-1970s. The causes
were the dramatic increases in oil prices, which led to a slack in
demand. New investment was halted but the extension of existing
refineries and the coming on stream of new ones that had been
planned before the events added to overcapacity (see figures for 1980
in Table 11.4). Only after 1980 was it realised that the fall in demand
was of a structural nature and only then were measures taken: many
plants were closed altogether, while most others were reduced in
capacity. The pattern of these reductions was influenced less by considerations of competition between firms on integrated markets than
by the need to adapt local capacity to local demand. As Table 11.5
shows, this implied that most of the smaller refineries were closed;
some others were scaled up to reach the minimum efficient size,
while in the 1990–2000 period many of the largest ones have been
scaled down considerably. Consequently there has not been much
increase in international specialisation and trade in refinery products.

Company response

The European market for oil products is relatively competitive. The
three *largest European companies* (see Table 11.6) are also large players
on a world scale. The major groups of players[7] can be described as
follows (Molle and Wever, 1983; Molle, 1993).

Table 11.6   **Rank order of EU15 oil companies by worldwide sales
(billion euro), 1998**

Rank	Company	Country	Sales
1	Royal Dutch Shell	NL/UK	77
2	Total/Elf/Fina	France/Belgium	62
3	BP Amoco	UK	56
4	ENI	Italy	27
5	Repsol	Spain	13
6	Fortum	Finland	8

Source: *Fortune*, 1999.

Majors   These were formerly called the seven sisters (Sampson, 1977). To this group belonged, up to the mid-1970s, five American (Exxon, Texaco, Gulf Oil, Mobil Oil and Chevron) and two European companies (Shell and BP). In the turmoil of the oil crisis of the 1970s, two left the European scene: Gulf (operations taken over by KPC) and Chevron. The majors operate on a world scale and show a high degree of vertical integration. This means that they are active at all stages of the oil industry: in the exploration and exploitation of crude oil, the transport of crude and products, the refining and, finally, the marketing of the finished products. They are, moreover, active in such related activities as (petro)chemicals. In the 1990s some regrouping took place, whereby BP joined forces in Europe with Mobil, an alliance that has been dissolved recently because Mobil has been taken over by Exxon. The relative position of the original seven majors decreased quite a lot in the 1950–2000 period: while in 1950 they controlled 65 per cent of total European refinery capacity, in 2000 they were down to about 30 per cent. Among these majors Shell (EU) and Exxon (USA) occupied the most important places. At the height of its influence, Shell possessed 23 refineries in ten European countries and controlled about 20 per cent of the total refinery capacity.

State-controlled European companies   In a deliberate policy to strengthen the national position in the refinery industry with respect to the majors, a number of countries have established state-owned or state-controlled refinery companies. Most of them confine their refinery activities within the national borders.[8] They usually held a very large share of the national refining sector. Among these companies we find Total and Elf in France, ENI in Italy, Petrogal in Portugal. Other countries also had some national or semi-national companies, but their position in the EU refinery sector was relatively modest. In many countries the national oil companies were privatised during the 1990s. Some of them (for example, Total, Elf, Fina) merged and diversified their markets by expanding their operations into other countries, which makes them more like the traditional majors.

Independent private companies   Within this group two sub-groups can be distinguished: the Western European companies and the American companies. The group of Western European independents used to be composed of some medium-sized multi-plant companies and a large number of smaller companies that are mostly active on a local scale only. Many of these companies ceased to exist, because they stopped production or were taken over by larger companies (state, major or chemical companies). Their market position and resource base were often too weak to stand up to international competition.

Chemical Many products now based on petroleum feedstock used to be produced from other feedstocks. Starting from their petrochemical base, some of these companies integrated backwards, participating in or taking over oil-refining facilities. Examples are ICI, Montedison and BASF. Most of these have now limited their activities to a participation in a joint venture or have pulled out altogether.

National companies from producer countries In the 1970s the main producer states took control of the majority of world oil and gas reserves. The oil companies of these countries, such as Libya (Tamoil), Kuwait (KPC) and Venezuela (Petroven) strove for increased control of the facilities for processing, distribution, storing and marketing oil products. Some companies of producer states have moved into Europe with production and distribution facilities; in particular KPC has gained a firm foothold.

European integration has had some influence on the company structure, in that it has contributed to a certain concentration. But the main driving forces behind the company restructuring were worldwide changes in control over oil reserves and the privatisation of national companies. Up until recently the concentration was rather low: in 1995, the C3 index (indicating the share of the three largest EU companies in total sales) stood at 32 per cent. In 2000, however, the C3 (Shell, Total, BP) had risen to 80 per cent.

Case study 2: electricity

Regulatory framework

Electricity used to be considered as a public utility that did not fall under the rules of the EU. It used to be heavily regulated by national governments. In the past the Commission has sometimes tried in vain to bring the sector under the usual EU regime (for example, under the 1992 programme). In the 1990s the Commission came under increased pressure from the corporate consumers for a liberalisation of the electricity market. Indeed, large industrial users, considering they were paying too high prices, contested the monopoly power of the supplier by seeking access to the national grid in order to buy directly from other industrial producers in the same country or from a foreign electricity company. The Commission has adopted the view, that electricity is not fundamentally different from other goods for which measures have been taken to complete the internal market. Notwithstanding very fierce opposition from many national governments, it has been able to have the relevant legislation (directive (96/92/EC) adopted by the Council. This directive establishes common rules for the organisation and functioning of the electricity sector and for access to the market. It combines (partial) liberalisation and framework regulation.

The new EU regime obliges the electricity sector to maintain the *separation of production, transmission and distribution.* In principle production is free, and governments have to lay down rules under which they will authorise the construction of new electricity-generating capacity. Transmission of high voltage is entrusted to the transmission system operator. Producers supply this grid, and large industrial customers and distribution companies tap from it. Distribution system operators are entities that are responsible for the line to the final consumers. In principle these three functions are to be carried out by separate companies. However, if they are still operated by the same company, the EU obliges this company to take three basic measures: first, independent management for each function; second, full transparency of the accounts of the three parts (no cross-subsidies); and, third, appropriate mechanisms to avoid confidential information being passed by the transmission operator to other parts of the company.

The *liberalisation* of electricity supply means that production companies and customers are free to choose the partner they prefer. This freedom is introduced in stages. The first stage started in 1999 with the largest clients (consumers of more than 40 GWh a year), the next continues over the 2000–2003 period with clients in smaller-sized categories (first the category of more than 20 GWh a year, followed by the category larger than 9 GWh). By this time about 33 per cent of the total market will have been liberalised. However, as many member countries implement their programme of liberalisation more rapidly than required by the directive, a much larger segment of the EU market is likely to be liberalised by 2003.

Given the monopoly of the transmission grid operator, the liberalisation of the electricity market hinges critically on the conditions under which third parties can gain access to this grid. The EU has provided for different systems, but the most common one is now the *regulated third party access*, in which the relevant authorities set the prices at which any user can transport electricity. This system has the advantage in the short run that it excludes discrimination against competitors and in the medium term that companies can plan future electricity deals with advance knowledge of transparent tariffs.

The regime put into place by the EU has a framework character. Much has to be worked out in practice. To do so most countries have set up a *regulatory authority* for the electricity sector (independent from the electricity companies). These national regulatory bodies will carry out their role in partnership with the usual national competition authorities and the Commission as the guardian of fair competition on the EU level.

Industry characteristics

Electricity *consumption* has increased extremely fast in the last few decades. All the EU member states, in their efforts to be self-sufficient, have matched this increase in demand with a corresponding increase in the capacity of their generation plants and distribution lines. They have preferred to import primary energy rather than electric power.

Only a small percentage of total electricity production enters *international trade*; intra-EU15 trade as a percentage of EU15 final consumption increased gradually from 2 per cent in 1960 to some 8 per cent in 1994, indicating the rather low degree of integration of the sector. Exchange with third countries during this period was limited to some imports. The explanation for these low figures is that the international exchange of electricity used to be limited to the volumes that were necessary to overcome specific shortages in the power provision of a country (for example, due to maintenance of major thermal power stations, temporarily low production of hydro plants or technical difficulties). This situation is at odds with the general philosophy of the EU, which is based on the notion that the rationale for the exchange of all goods and services is comparative advantage (for theory, see Chapter 5; for clear examples, see Chapters 10 and 12). The liberalisation has not had a very high immediate impact on exchange, as adaptation of the infrastructure has taken some time.

The differences among EU countries in the *price of electricity* for typical household and industrial consumers used to be very substantial (see Table 11.4). We may give the following reasons for such differences.

- *Inefficiencies.* While markets are split and regulated to a very high degree, production is likely to be inefficient (as a result of bad allocation of resources and rent seeking). Some countries may have been better able to check such tendencies than others.
- *Policy.* In monopoly markets there is ample scope for setting different prices for different consumer categories (UNIPEDE, 1982, 1985). The public electricity companies have followed different strategies, based on the level of fixed costs of production and distribution and the possibilities of dividing these costs between different categories of users, taking account of market response and industrial, environmental and regional policy objectives.

- *Fuel mix*. In France, almost three-quarters of all electricity is generated in nuclear power stations, while Denmark's power plants are almost exclusively coal-fired. The more expensive producers were those that depended on oil or gas firing.

With the completion of the internal market for electricity, and the increase in trade in electricity that follows from this, a number of the above factors have lost importance and hence price differences have decreased. In the period 1996–99 the average decrease of prices in the EU amounted to some 6 per cent. In some countries, like Spain and Finland, the decrease was even three times as high. Further decreases can be expected as soon as the capacity for cross-border trading is sufficiently developed. (Indeed, decreases of around 30 per cent were recorded after the earlier liberalisation of the UK market).

Company structure

The liberalisation of the EU electricity market has entailed a major upheaval in terms of company structure. All companies are now redefining their strategies. They have very different starting positions. Because the European market for electric power has long been fragmented along national lines, international integration of firms has been non-existent. In many countries economies of scale and scope have induced electricity firms to organise on the national level (for instance, France where EDF controls the generation, transmission and distribution of electricity). In the UK, following the liberalisation of the market in the early 1990s, various companies were created in the course of the privatisation process, each controlling parts of the generation and transmission and distribution process. Other member countries showed highly diversified patterns as to the organisation of the supply side, mainly depending on the institutional balance between different layers of government, and on the ideological balance between public services and private initiative.

The new EU regulatory framework has had two effects. First, it obliged companies to undo their vertical integration. That means that the network for distribution to the final customer and the transmission lines has to move into independent hands. Second, it has induced companies to concentrate on an international level in order to take advantage of the potential for cost cutting that goes hand-in-hand with scale. A few moves have already been made. Electricité de France (the largest company in the EU and one of the largest worldwide) has bought London Electricity, the UK capital's supplier. In addition, it also has stakes in a number of other EU countries in some of the CEEC and in non-European countries. RWE Energie, one of the largest German producers (after having taken over power companies in the former East Germany) has acquired stakes in a Portuguese company and several companies in the CEEC. Two other major German producers, VEBA and VIAG, have merged their energy operations (VEBA had already acquired a majority stake in the Dutch EZH).

However important national differences still remain as a function of the deeply rooted differences in the industry's internal institutions and their institutional environments (Glachant and Finon, 2000).

Summary and conclusions

- The involvement of the EU with energy is based on three different treaties: ECSC for coal, EAEC for nuclear energy and the EEC for all other energy products. Gradually a common energy policy has evolved.
- For a long time the dominant energy source was coal. From the mid-1960s, oil took over the lead. Electricity, generated from various primary sources, is becoming ever more important.
- Oil markets have gone through very turbulent times, but the market partners, in particular the multinational oil companies, seem to have responded adequately by adapting and modernising the production, refining, transport and distribution systems, taking into account the integration of the European market and the linkages with world markets.
- Electricity, by contrast, is traditionally a highly regulated industry and until recently the market has remained fragmented along national lines. Electricity has grown to a prominent place in energy markets. The first steps on the path to liberalising the internal EU market have been taken and a programme to complete this liberalisation will be executed over the coming years.

Notes

1   The EU energy policy is based on three different treaties, each containing rules for specific segments of the energy sector. The *European Coal and Steel Community* (ECSC) has pursued both a market regulation and a structural policy for the coalmining sector. The High Authority's (now Commission's) first task concerns the adequate functioning of the market. In principle, free competition should govern the market process. However, in times of 'manifest crisis' or scarcity, the ECSC can intervene either directly in the prices (Article 61) or through production quotas (Article 58) and international trade (Article 74); such intervention must be applied only if more indirect measures fail. The second task of the ECSC is to pursue a structural policy. To that end the ECSC draws up indicative programmes, appraises individual investment programmes, supports invest-

ments and research, and finally supports restructuring by appropriate measures (Articles 46 to 56).

The *European Atomic Energy Community* (EAEC) has no powers as to the regulation of the market; demand is free, and for the supply of ores, raw materials and fissionable material an EU monopoly has been given to an 'Agency' created for the purpose. The EAEC's main task is a structural–political one, in which we distinguish the following elements: to develop research (Articles 4–7) – it carries on extensive research programmes in its own research centres – to disperse knowledge (Articles 14–24) and to make investments (Articles 40 and 47). Apart from supporting and coordinating, the EAEC can also participate directly in investments.

The *European Economic Community* (EEC) Treaty contains no specific stipulations for the energy sector; therefore the functioning of the (crude) oil, (natural) gas and electricity markets is left to supply and demand forces regulated by the general stipulations of the Treaty, for example with respect to competition. No structural measures for these sectors have been provided for at all either.

See, for a more complete description of the origins of the EU energy policy, for instance, Weyman-Jones (1986) or Jensen (1983).

2   From its very creation, the OECD has also paid attention to the energy problem. A relatively advanced form of international cooperation, by OECD standards, was initiated after the first oil crisis by the creation of the International Energy Agency. This agency was instructed to draw up an international energy programme; it tries to carry out this programme by coordinating the national policies of the participating states (OECD, various years). The International Energy Agency, however, goes one better: it curtails member states' elbow room by laying down uniform rules of behaviour which all member states are supposed to respect, their conduct being judged regularly, in meetings of government representatives, from detailed reports (for instance, OECD, 1987f). However with energy, as in other matters, the OECD does not have authority to enforce the policy agreed upon.

3   To be made comparable, the various energy sources (coal, oil and so on) have all been converted to the energy content of the dominant one: oil. The unit we have used is Mtoe, which stands for million tons of oil equivalent. The figures for the post-war period should be compared to the historical growth figures of about 1 per cent a year from 1930 to 1950.

4   In addition, some 25 million tons of oil were produced by Norway.

5   Contrary to the OECD definition, we count bunkers in final consumption; the OECD treats this category as exports. The categories are not defined, as in Table 11.1, in terms of primary sources, but in terms of secondary sources (after conversion: 'liquid' comprises all oil products, 'solid' coal, coke and brown coal; gas comprises natural gas as well as coke-oven and refinery gas and so on; and 'electricity' refers to power from nuclear as well as thermal power stations. Final domestic consumption is defined as total domestic production plus imports minus exports and minus the energy sector's own consumption.

6   The figures do not change very much in the case where one takes the EU15 as the basis (CEC, 1996a).

7   Some refineries are jointly owned. Examples are the refineries of Rotterdam (BP and Texaco) and Neustadt (Mobil, VEBA, Petroven). Quite a few of these joint ventures have been undertaken by an oil company and a chemical company. Examples are Erdoelchemie (BP and Bayer) and Rheinische olefinwerke (Shell and BASF).

8   Elf had a number of refineries abroad, in particular in Germany, which made it something of a multinational even before its merger with Fina and Total.

12 Services

Introduction

While the European Union has always looked upon services as an essential part of the integration process, it has taken some time for the EU to devote much attention to them. In the present chapter we propose to look into the European service sector in some detail. The pattern of this chapter is the same as that of the previous ones.

First we will give a succinct description of the European policy regime. The mix of liberalisation and regulation of the EU had to take into account the fact that major segments of the service sector have been subject to considerable national government regulation. Convinced that a socially desirable organisation of quite large segments could not be left to private enterprise, governments have even assumed direct responsibility for production and distribution, especially for services associated with the welfare state (such as social security). Other branches (such as medical services) are a combination of public and private effort.

Next we will give a description of the service sector in Europe; we will focus in this chapter on the services that can in principle be traded by private agents, thus excluding the public sector from the discussion. Transport is also left out of the present chapter; because of its special position in the European setting it will be dealt with in a separate chapter.

We will then report the results of two case studies of integration. The first one is insurance, for which integration started some time ago. The second one is telecommunications, a branch that is expanding very quickly as a consequence of the development of the information society and is transforming itself very quickly as a result of recent privatisation and liberalisation.

A summary of the findings will complete the chapter.

EU regime

Rationale and principles

The Treaty of Rome is fairly brief on services. It reflects awareness of the wide variety in products of the service branches. The general definition of services (Article 50) reads: 'all these activities normally provided for remuneration in so far as they are not governed by the provisions relating to freedom of movement for goods, capital and persons'. They include in particular activities of an industrial or commercial nature and those of craftsmen and professions. For all these activities the Treaty stipulates the freedom to:

- provide services (Article 49): a company of member country A can provide services in member country B without having an office there, and
- set up an establishment (Article 43): companies (or persons) wishing to set up an establishment (that is, a legal entity with, in general, premises, staff and so on) in another member country are free to do so under the same conditions as are laid down for the nationals of the country of establishment.

The substantiation of the freedom to provide services has dragged on for a long time, for two main reasons. One was the difficulty in defining the equivalence of qualifications, another the access to certain markets that were organised by national governments or by private groups sanctioned to organise and protect them.

In the early 1970s, several rulings of the Court in principle liberalised almost completely all services connected with agriculture, manufacturing, craft and trade (commerce). However, until 1985 quite a few problems remained regarding the service branches. The programme to complete the internal market in services brought a solution by a combination of three elements (Chapter 6): (1) liberalisation – freedom for cross-border trade in services; (2) mutual recognition of the quality of the home country's control; and (3) harmonisation – minimum sets of European regulation.

Market regulation

Apart from its efforts to liberalise intra-Union trade in services, the EU does not pursue a *market regulation policy* for the service sector. The market for services is indeed organised in much the same way as that for most manufacturing and energy activities (except steel and coal), for which EU institutions have neither responsibility nor power to intervene in prices and quantities. Service markets come under the general rules for competition (see Chapter 14), which are considered sufficient to have European markets function properly. Many service sectors are, however, heavily regulated at the national level, with government influencing important aspects such as access to markets (for example, insurance, medical services) and prices (insurance and so on). Two principles govern the EU policy for the completion of the internal market of these sectors: first, to establish a minimum European framework of basic standards; second, to let companies working under different sets of rules compete freely, thereby obliging governments to compete with each other in optimal rule setting (see Chapter 14).

Until recently there was no European *policy vis-à-vis third countries* in matters of services, in stark contrast to the very elaborate schemes operative on goods markets (Chapter 17). Under the impetus of technological change (data transmission) and under pressure from third countries, questions about external trade in services were placed on the agenda of the Uruguay round of GATT/WTO.[1] This has finally resulted in an agreement to diminish the protection in trade in many service branches.

Structural policy

Unlike agriculture, manufacturing and energy, the sectors discussed in the preceding chapters, the service sector is not subject to a European *structural policy*. There are no schemes to encourage innovation, support investments in infrastructure or production equipment, or improve human capital. This is in line with the situation we find back in the individual member countries: the private segment of the service sector is mostly left to fend for itself. There are two very important exceptions to this. The first relates to telecommunications. The structural policy of the EU for this sector of activity uses two instruments: (1) support for innovation via the large-scale technology programmes, and (2) support for infrastructure by the newly established possibility for support of trans-European networks.

The second relates to *electronic commerce and the use of the Internet*. The EU considers that the future competitiveness of its economy will be dependent on the speed with which it will be able to transform itself in a knowledge-based economy. It has set up an action programme for the stimulation of the so-called content industries (eContent). This umbrella term covers many traditional publishing products (books, periodicals and so on), radio and television, and the modern multimedia applications. This sector is estimated to account for some 5 per cent of GDP and is expected to grow at a rate of some 20 per cent a year. The action programme aims to take away the barriers to the development of a European market for these products.

One of these barriers is the multilingual character of the products that the EU market needs. By providing solutions to this problem it is anticipated that the present handicap can be transformed into an asset because it would permit the export of multilingual multimedia products to other parts of the world.

Sketch of the sector

Employment and value added by branch

Since the Second World War, the service sector[2] has rapidly advanced to assume the leadership in the total economy of the EU. With increasing productivity and low income elasticities, the shares of the agricultural and manufacturing sectors first stagnated and then dropped, making room for the quickly expanding service sector. One reason why statistics show such a large expansion is that certain functions which had hitherto been carried out within other sectors (cleaning, auditing and so on) have become independent and are thus registered as such. This phenomenon results when technically progressive services break off from manufacturing for reasons such as the broadening of the scope of products, the improvement of the quality through specialisation, or the cutting of cost by using economies of scale.

When the service sector becomes dominant in an economy and many service activities concern the handling of information rather than trade in goods, the terms 'post-industrial' or 'information society' are often used. The EU has entered that stage. Indeed the total service sector that accounted for little over a third of total employ-

Table 12.1   **Percentage share of the service sectors in EU15 total employment, 1950–2000**

Sub-sector	1950	1960	1970	1980	1990	2000
5 Construction	7	8	8	8	8	8
6 Commerce	13	14	15	16	17	18
7 Transport	6	6	6	6	6	6
8 Finance and Business	3	4	5	6	7	12
9 Community and Social	9	12	19	24	27	31
Total services	38	44	53	60	65	75

Sources: NEI, Fleur data base; OECD, *Labour Force Statistics*, various years; 2000 estimates based on recent figures from various sources.

ment just after the Second World War now accounts for almost three-quarters of employment (and also of GDP) (Table 12.1). That spectacular growth has been accomplished by a few branches; while the relative position of the construction and transport branches stagnated (the latter will be treated separately in the next chapter), trade, and notably financial services and business and community services were very dynamic. The very fast growth of community services in the 1950–80 period has been closely related to the build-up of the welfare state and the ensuing increased involvement of the public sector in society (Saunders and Klau, 1985; Rose *et al.*, 1985).

The breakdown of the service sector into branches reveals some interesting aspects (employment figures). The sub-sector of commerce consists mostly of wholesale and retail trade, the rest being hotels and such. The sub-sector of finance and business is dominated by banking and insurance, followed by business services and miscellaneous personal services. The large sub-sector of community services consists of three branches of about equal size – public administration, education, medical – and a small group of other services. For GDP, the branch composition of these service sectors is in broad lines comparable to that of employment.[3]

Europeanisation or multinationalisation of firms

The list of the largest service firms in the EU (excluding public enterprises and public and private transport companies) is dominated by firms from the telecommunications, trade and finance sectors. For each sub-sector of services, we have indicated in Table 12.2 the biggest firm (by employment), to give an indication of the intersectoral differences.[4]

Table 12.2   Service firms, largest by sub-sector, 1998

Name	Country	Branch	Employment (× 1000)
La Poste	F	Mail, package, freight delivery	288
Deutsche Telekom	D	Telecommunications	196
METRO	D	Retail trade	181
HSBC Holdings	UK	Banking: commercial and savings	145
VEBA Group	D	Trading	117

Source: *Fortune*, 1999.

Generally speaking, service firms have a considerably smaller average size than manufacturing firms. The size of firms in certain sub-branches, such as professional services or business services (marketing, legal and so on), are particularly low; concentration and multinationalisation have not yet advanced far in these branches (Rubalcaba-Bermejo, 1999).

Most firms have their home in one of the larger countries of North Western Europe; this is true for all branches. These countries have large internal markets that provide a good basis for early expansion at home and subsequent expansion abroad. Head offices of these firms are mostly in London, Paris and Frankfurt. The Southern European countries are very poorly represented. This situation has been reinforced by the completion of the internal market. In the past decades most mergers and acquisitions have indeed been initiated by companies from northern member states, often seeking to absorb companies from southern member states.

Market structures[5]

The markets for services of the EU member countries have long remained sheltered from competition, owing to lack of mobility of services across markets and firms within markets. This situation was due to three factors.

- *Natural determinants of the degree of concentration.* Among these factors we find economies of scale and of scope. For a service like telecommunications, for instance, the cost of a network determines the very high concentration; in other services large numbers of sellers appear on more diversified markets, as with hotels.
- *Barriers to entry.* Many service industries typically incur fixed costs in two types of assets: tangible (such as buildings) and intangible (such as reputation). Sunk costs in the tangible category occur, for example, in telecommunications (networks). Sunk costs in the intangible category consist, for example, in maintaining a good reputation for financial services (banks, insurance).
- *Government regulations.* These are usually divided into two categories: (1) those that affect the structure of the industry (for example, the entry of new firms) and (2) those that impinge upon the conduct of existing firms. Some branches have relatively little of both (construction, for instance), some have much of both (for example, insurance) and some are subjected to structural instruments only (for example, distribution).

Table 12.3 Market structure in services

Branch	Determinants			Degree of competition	
	Concentration	Sunk cost	Regulation	Before	After
Construction	low	low	medium	high	high
Distribution	low	low	medium	medium	high
Hotels	low	low	low	high	high
Telecom	high	high	high	low	medium
Banking/ insurance	medium	medium	high	low	medium
Business	low	medium	low	medium	medium

Source: CEC (1993c, 1996a).

For a number of service branches we have indicated the scores on these three factors in Table 12.3 (first three columns). From this information we can assess the degree of competition in each branch (last two columns): first the situation that prevailed before the 1992 programme was implemented ('before' column) and second the situation that prevailed around 1996 ('after' column).

Competition has in general increased (Table 12.3) as a consequence of the completion of the internal market; low competition has become medium and medium competition has become high. However, overall the increase in competition seems to be less strong in services than in manufacturing, reflecting the lack of implementation of the internal market programme in many domains of the service sector.

The 1992 process has led to a better *allocation*; that is, to the provision of the European consumer with service products that are better adapted to his needs at lower cost. In some branches where competition has not increased much (such as banking) these effects were not very strong. In other branches, like mobile telecommunication and logistics/distribution, the scope of services has been substantially enlarged and their price substantially reduced. This in turn has increased the possibilities for EU-wide sourcing and improved the competitive position of the branches that use these services (CEC, 1996a).

This process of restructuring has not led to big changes in the *location of production*, because of the high degree of proximity between consumers and producers that many services require. However ownership of firms has been affected, as local service providers have increasingly become parts of multinational firms or networks. This may be as subsidiaries or via cooperation agreements (association, licensing, franchising). The latter are often used by branches such as accountancy, consultancy and distribution.

The impact of the 1992 programme on *concentration* has been very different for the various branches of the service sector. Sub-sectors with relatively light regulation, such as distribution, have shown increases in concentration both at the EU and the national level. Highly regulated services, such as retail banking, have shown only small increases in EU-wide concentration, while concentration at the national level tended to increase more (CEC, 1996a).

There has been a general tendency towards *price convergence* in services over the 1985–93 period (CEC, 1996a). This convergence has continued although at a slower pace in the period 1993–96 (CEC, 1999b). However price dispersion in market services stays at levels much above those in manufacturing. The remaining price disparities are caused by a number of factors.

- *Wage levels.* Services for which international transaction cost tend to be prohibitive will be costed at the price of the local labour market inputs (real estate).
- *Regulation.* Important differences in government intervention still prevail in services like health, water distribution and so on.
- *Market structures.* Exclusive distribution systems (insurance) or access to market regulations (telecommunications) hinder the arbitrage process (CEC, 1996a).

Case study 1: insurance

Regulatory framework

Within the EU countries, the insurance industry has developed on a national basis, each national sub-market being regulated by a whole array of measures.[6] The only exception to this was the UK industry, which has always been of a highly international nature. The common market for services was scheduled by the EEC Treaty to be realised by 1970, but this has proved impossible. The Commission has tried to bring about a common European market for insurance services,[7] but for a long time has found it very difficult to convince national governments. In its *harmonisation* programme, the Commission has made a distinction between life and non-life. This principle of specialisation forbids life insurance companies to do other types of insurance, so as to protect the interests of life policyholders against considerable risks. In its *liberalisation* programme, the Commission has made a distinction between the freedom of establishment and the freedom to provide services abroad.

Freedom of establishment implies the possibility of creating a subsidiary in another member state; non-discrimination requires that such a subsidiary, a broker, or an agent be treated on a level with national companies. In the 1970s, several directives introduced this freedom of establishment (1973 for life, 1979 for non-life). The directives obliged every member state to subject all insurance business, of both local and foreign companies, on its territory to authorisation on the same conditions; as a result, all companies anywhere in the EU have come under supervision. The problem was, however, that this system tended to add to the cost for the insurer (for example, the French authorities, applying French standards, required minimum reserves that had to be franc-dominated and lodged in francs), which added to the costs of the foreign insurer. Subsequent directives have set minimum standards, to inspire mutual confidence in national regulations and to make sure that coverage would be similar (for example, in the motor insurance branch, so as to take away the need for border controls of insurance documents). In 1986, the European Court of Justice confirmed in a case of the Commission against four member states that national restrictions against foreign insurance companies were not acceptable; exceptions could be made, however, if the protection of the consumer so required.

Freedom to provide services means that, for example, a French client can conclude an insurance contract directly with the London office of an English company and is not obliged to do so with a France-based firm. This situation used to be precluded by national regulations. In line with the general sense of Court ruling in other branches of activity, the Commission had proposed several schemes for liberalisation and harmonisation; however, up to the end of the 1980s, they had all failed to gain sufficient approval from the Council to reach realisation. The reasons for this are that national regulations were well entrenched, and opposition to further harmonisation and liberalisation was quite fierce (Finsinger *et al.*, 1985). Liberalisation was only half-heartedly supported by insurance companies. Indeed the latter were often well settled behind protecting regulations even in foreign markets. In that situation the German broker Steicher went against the German regulations by arranging for insurance of his German clients directly with non-German insurers. The European Court of Justice, asked to consider the case, ruled in December 1986 in favour of Steicher, considering that corporate clients could very well be left free to choose between products of different companies at home or abroad. The far-reaching implications of that verdict were soon realised, which speeded up the discussions on the proposals for the common market for insurance in the framework of the 1992 programme. A number of directives have been agreed upon. Full freedom of insurance service provision both for the life and non-life markets was realised by the mid-1990s.

The *European legislation* covers such matters as the formation of an insurance company, the opening of branches and agencies and the subsequent supervision of technical reserves, assets, solvency margins and minimum guarantee funds. Harmonisation of these aspects is important to prevent companies from being pushed by competition into contracts that do not cover the cost of the risks involved (for a concise overview of the theory behind the regulation see Rees and Kessner, 1999). This theory does not predict that a very tight regulation is the best option. So the EU regime is rather based on a rather limited set of rules. The Commission is counting on a tendency towards spontaneous harmonisation of national regulatory systems as increased international competition of firms implicitly entails competition of the national regulations under which they operate.

The *supervision of insurance companies* is carried out by national authorities. The coordination of this supervision is an important aspect of European legislation because it is the basis for a double target: (1) to permit a company to do business in several EU countries under a single licence supervised by the authorities of the country where it has its (European) head offices (home country control principle); (2) to afford persons seeking insurance access to the widest possible range of insurance products on offer in the EU (CEC, 1992f; Carter and Dickinson, 1992; Pool, 1990). In the 1990s this regulation proved to be in need of some clarification. This was due, on the one hand, to the development of new technological possibilities, such as remote contracting via electronic commerce, and, on the other, to the need to specify the possibility of limiting liberalisation for preserving the 'general good'. The Commission has clarified these issues in a recent communication (CEC, 2000c).

In the past many governments have blocked the combination of insurance and banking in one company for reasons of consumer protection, quality of supervision and fair competition. Since the EU-wide deregulation such barriers have been lifted. Now a number of banks and insurance companies see advantages in the combined marketing of products, the organisation of access to capital, and the spreading of risks. The strategy of combining the two into one corporate structure is called '*banc-assurance*'.

Industry characteristics

The insurance business consists of two main branches, life and non-life (motor, fire and so on). The importance of both segments in the total market of the EU has varied over the past decades; in the 1990s each accounted for about half of total business. Insurance is a product for which demand is growing fast; as a result, the share of premiums in total GNP increased from 3 per cent in 1960 to 7 per cent in 1995. There is little national variation in the share of 'non-life' products in total expenditure. On the contrary, national differences in expenditure on 'life' products are fairly large, owing to differences in preferences, social security coverage and so on. There is some tendency towards convergence: in the countries with a low coverage, demand for life insurance has grown very fast in the past decades; growth has been less dynamic in mature markets.

Until recently *integration* had not developed far. The European insurance market used to be segmented into national markets. On each national market, concentration tended to be fairly high as a consequence of economies of scale and scope. The largest group typically held a 15 to 25 per cent share in the national market. In some countries (France, Ireland), a large portion of the business was covered by nationalised companies, but in most countries private firms dominated the market. In all countries, mutual-insurance companies also took a fair share of the market (CEC, 1985c).

During the 1990s a general trend towards *liberalisation* took place, in which many state owned companies were privatised. The very highly regulated German market was opened up, significantly reducing the high cost structure in that country. However, until now, two other effects that one would have expected did not happen: (1) the interpenetration of markets by cross-border trade; and (2) significant new entry into the German market. Apparently, the barriers to market access (no independent brokers, differences in legal stipulations) are still too problematic for a real internal market to develop (Rees and Kessner, 1999).

In the recent past, interpenetration of markets has been stimulated by the *multinationalisation of firms*. Firms have several motives to multinationalise by mergers and acquisitions:

- *Need to spread risks*. This can be done better by companies that have grown to a certain size and have diversified their geographical markets. Acquiring a large size[8] is not easy on small national markets, so companies have tried increasingly to get at their objective by internationalisation. As it is not easy to start branch operations in a new market from scratch, many companies have internationalised by acquisition and mergers.
- *Demand from multinational firms*. MNFs from other branches have increasingly centralised their buying of insurance services, asking for worldwide coverage of their operations by one insurance company. This factor does play its role notably in the non-life business.
- *Completion of the internal market*. This has entailed a process of restructuring of firms at the European level, and this has been facilitated by the large-scale privatisation of nationalised industries in a number of EU countries.

The *increase in multinationalisation* can be measured by several indicators. The share of foreign owned firms in the total national premium income of the 15 member countries of the EU was only between 3 and 10 per cent in the mid-1980s. It increased in the first half of the 1990s by some 13 per cent on average. The ratio of foreign premium income in total domestic income from the various European insurance companies increased more than fourfold in the same period (Rietbergen, 1999). Recent figures are not available, but the process of mergers and acquisitions described must have led to considerable further increases in these two ratios.

In the past, segmentation of national markets led to *large price differences* among EU member countries. To illustrate their magnitude: in 1985, consumers in Portugal paid nine times as much for the same life insurance policy as consumers in the cheapest country, the

UK (BEUC, 1988). Similar differences in prices were found for other categories of insurance (house, motor, fire and liability). Assuming that the average of the four countries with the lowest prices would be a fair indication of the EU price after integration, the potential for price cuts was found to amount to more than 50 per cent for Italy, 30 per cent for Belgium, Luxembourg and Spain, 25 for France and 10 for Germany (Price Waterhouse, 1988). In the 1985–96 period the price dispersion decreased significantly (CEC, 1999b). Moreover, productivity of the industry increased, implying efficiency gains to producers and consumers.

Company structure

The changes in the regulatory environment have led many companies to revise their strategies. The first is with respect to their legal form. As the founding principles of mutuals became difficult to uphold under the pressure of competition, a movement of demutualisation set in, leading to a significant rise in the market share of incorporated companies (based on shares). The second is with respect to markets. Many firms have recognised the necessity of becoming a multinational company, which has led to a frenzy of mergers and acquisitions. As a consequence, the number of companies in the EU fell by one-quarter between 1990 and 1997.

By way of example, we describe the *genesis and development of the four largest EU companies:*[9]

- AXA (F). The transformation of a small regional company into a multinational ranking first in the EU has been realised in the time span of a few decades through a series of take-overs and mergers. Initial take-overs concerned firms in the UK (Equity and Law) and the USA (Equitable). A major merger was concluded in 1996, when AXA joined forces with UAP, itself a multinational, having acquired (majority stakes in) companies like Royale Belge (B), GESA (SW), Sun Life (UK) and Groupe Victoire (F) (which included Colonia (G)). The strategy of the AXA group is to stick to insurance as its core business.[10]
- Allianz (G). This company has purchased RAS, the second largest Italian group, and a number of smaller companies in other countries. It has recently strengthened its position on its home market by acquiring complete control over Vereinte (through a swap with Münchener Re) and on the EU market by acquiring control over the major parts of the French group AGF (other elements of AGF were acquired by Generali).
- Generali (I). In the past this company has grown internationally by acquiring a series of companies. To strengthen its home

base and to ward off the possibility of itself being taken over by one of the other large EU insurers, it has made a bid for INA, the third largest insurer in Italy. Notwithstanding many relations with banks, Generali has insisted it does not want to become a *banc-assurance* group.

- ING/BBL (NL). This group is the result of a deliberate strategy of international *banc-assurance*. It has a strong position in both banking and insurance in the Benelux, as well as important insurance activities in other EU countries and in the US. Its objective is to become a major player in *banc-assurance* in all countries of Europe and the US.

During the 1990s *internationalisation by cross-border take-overs and mergers* has entailed three changes. First, the average size of the largest EU firms has greatly increased (some four times). Second, some European firms are now among the world leaders due to their global expansion. Third, the ranking of the largest EU insurance companies has been profoundly changed.

In the future it is likely that a further concentration and internationalisation of firms will occur, as there are still large rationalisation advantages that have not been realised (Dickinson, 1993; CEC, 1996c). The intentions of the major companies can give us some idea of the pattern that the process is likely to follow. Most major companies have targeted first the German market and next the markets of Central and Eastern Europe – particularly the markets of the countries that are most likely to join first (Rietbergen, 1999).

Case study 2: telecommunications

Regulatory framework

Only a short time ago telecommunications was regarded as a clear case of a natural monopoly. More than one supplier would imply the duplication of a very costly network infrastructure and hence imply a welfare loss for society. In most EU countries public telephone operators were state owned organisations which tended to cross-subsidise different services at the demand of government and privilege domestic equipment manufacturers. Technological developments have completely changed this situation. Networks for cable television or electricity distribution can now be used for telecommunication services, while satellites offer even more versatility and permit the rapid development of mobile phones. In view of these changed circumstances the national monopolies were no longer justifiable. Moreover, multinational corporate users of telecommunications services exerted increasing pressure to liberalise, as their competitiveness in world markets depended on good and cheap telecommunications. This became even more urgent with the opening up of a whole range of new services based on the Internet.

The EU has recognised that a change in the regulatory framework has become imperative. In the 1980s it decided that telecommunications were to be regarded as a market service, and hence formed part of the programme for the completion of the internal market. In addition, it has launched programmes to support European firms in the adoption of the new technologies. Examples of such programmes are RACE (Research in Advanced Communications in Europe) and ESPRIT (European Strategic Programme for Research and Development in Information Technologies). These have had a significant impact on the speed of innovation and industrial structure of the European telecommunications industry (Dumont and Meeusen, 1999). In 1993, after long hesitation, the EU committed itself to the liberalisation of the European telecommunications service sector. This went hand-in-hand with important reforms in member states (Hulsink, 1999), that have now all implemented the relevant EU legislation.[11] The move towards a liberalised EU market has been driven not only by technology but also by the global trend towards liberalisation in the framework of the GATS (General Agreement on Trade in Services: see Chapter 17).

The first step towards the setting up of the new EU regime has been to separate the regulatory functions from the operational functions. The next one was to make the operational functions subject to the usual competition policy. The third step was to specify and organise the new regulatory functions (see Eliassen and Sjovaag, 1999). The *new EU system* consists of the following elements:

- The setting up of National Regulatory Agencies (NRAs) in all member countries. These authorities are in charge of the implementation of the EU regulation and need to be independent from both operators and government.
- The specification of certain conditions under which the operators have to work. One example is interconnection, which means the linking of the facilities of different operators and providers. Interconnection is essential in safeguarding access of new providers to the existing network infrastructure. Another example is numbering. It implies that the consumer who has obtained a number with one company can keep this number while moving to another provider.

Industry characteristics

The major part of the market of telecommunication services (a total value of 161 billion euro) is still with fixed telephony (and related services such as fax which was worth some 100 billion euro in 1999). These services have a very high penetration rate among households in the EU and growth rates are henceforth relatively modest, although still very substantially above GDP growth rate levels. Recently two new services, mobile telephony and the Internet, have developed at a spectacular speed. The former (accounting for some 40 billion euro in 1999) shows average growth rates of some 15 per cent and very quickly developing penetration rates. Growth of Internet subscriptions and services is even more vigorous. Within a couple of years mobile services are expected to overtake fixed line services in terms of sales volume; the same is expected to be the case for Internet-related services with respect to voice telephony.

Price dispersion has decreased under the influence of increased competition (CEC, 1999b, 1999c): the index went down from 33 in 1993 to 20 in 1996. This tendency has since been reinforced. In some countries, prices of international and national long distance calls (markets in which competition is fiercest) have been cut by 30 per cent or more. However, prices for local calls (a market still dominated by the former monopolists) have scarcely decreased at all.

Company response

The company structure of the telecommunications industry changed very profoundly during the 1990s. Currently, the *major players* on the EU market are the incumbents (that is, the former national public telephone companies) of the major member countries. These are all very large even by world standards (they are all among the ten largest on the 1999 Fortune list). Most of these are now fully or partly privatised. Since the liberalisation movement gained momentum, a significant number of alternative suppliers have entered the marketplace. At the beginning of the 21st century the number of those who had obtained licences for nation-wide and international services exceeded 500. As a consequence the entire EU population now has the opportunity of choosing between at least two providers for these services.

This situation is far from stable. On the contrary, a frenetic movement of regrouping consisting of building alliances, cooperating in joint venture projects and, notably, *mergers and acquisitions,* has only just started. This process is not limited to the EU and the CEEC. On the contrary, companies are increasingly struggling to acquire a sufficient scale of operations to become one of the major players on the world level. This involves huge sums (in excess of 100 billion euros). Incumbent companies from one country have often started by taking over one or two such alternative suppliers to start up business in other countries than their home market. For example, Deutsche Telekom took over One2one in the UK, SIRIS in France and acquired large stakeholdings in CEEC companies (for example, Matav of Hungary). The British company Vodafone acquired the American company Airtouch and, in a very spectacular hostile bid, acquired the German company Mannesmann. Subsequent to this deal it had to sell the British mobile phone company Orange in order to comply with EU competition rules. France Telecom put in the winning bid for Orange and thus became the second largest operator of mobile phones in Europe (it had already large stakeholdings in Dutch, Danish and CEEC providers of mobile phone services). Mergers of incumbent companies from the bigger member countries have not yet taken place, but the merger movement between smaller ones has started (for example, between Norway's Telenor and Sweden's Telia (which has stakeholdings in the Baltic countries). Deals between new operators in this market are also increasingly common: for example, Dutch KPN teamed up with the Japanese giant NTT/DoCoMo. As technology in this field changes very rapidly and so do the services related to them, it is likely that this turbulence is only a beginning.

Summary and conclusions

- The EU had always considered services an essential part of the integration process, but paid little attention to it in practice. The growing importance of the sector in intra- and extra-EU trade has changed that situation, and now policies are being worked out for the liberalisation of the internal service market as well as for external trade in services.
- Many service firms have up to now been sheltered from international competition by government regulations. For that reason, little multinationalisation of firms has occurred. The sector's low degree of integration is also apparent in the fairly high differences in prices among EU countries.
- The case studies of insurance and telecommunications, branches in which economies of scale are important, show that liberalisation (both the freedom to provide services in another country and the freedom of establishment) has led to a growing interpenetration of markets and multinationalisation of firms.

Notes

1   Indeed the growing importance of services in the economy did not immediately bring about a greater interest among international organisations. For a long time, services were considered an essentially domestic sector hardly in need of international attention. Since the 1970s, however, the awareness has grown that such lack of interest has bred many protectionist measures impeding the internationalisation of service activities (Griffiths, 1975, among others). Organisations like WTO now carry services as an important subject on their negotiating agenda.

2   Unlike the situation with other sectors of activity, a definition of the service sector is difficult to give. Services are often described as a 'rest sector' encompassing the activities other than primary and secondary. Another approach focuses on the intangible nature of the output, and thus excludes, among other things, construction. Attempts have been made to overcome the problems of definition by adding such criteria as perishability and simultaneity of production and consumption, but, from the literature on the subject, such new criteria have all failed to make a distinction between goods and services, so that the line of severance between the two remains arbitrary. Statistical measurement is poor and hence also the possibility of quantitative analysis of the sector. Within the service sector, sub-sectors of activity are usually distinguished. They include such traditional ones as wholesale and retail trade, but also modern ones, like Internet services. A wide definition of the sector includes such government services as public administration and defence.

3   Comparisons between the industry figures on GDP and employment need to be made with caution, as the differences between the two indicators may be due not only to productivity divergences but also to differences in sector delineation.

4   The service sector is a very mixed bag, and because firms from different service branches are difficult to compare (turnover for commerce, gross premium for insurance, assets for banks and so on) we have opted for employment figures as the best indicator of size.

5   This section is largely taken from CEC (1993c).

6   The regulations have been made in the first instance to protect the consumer and to call for a certain prudence in the management of the resources that have been entrusted to the company. Many governments have extended that concern for the consumer into the definition of the product (prescribing certain standard clauses). Many have gone farther and have prescribed prices. It goes without saying that these measures are easily used for protection against outside competitors. A classification of such protectionist measures can be made, along several lines. OECD (1983a) made a distinction between establishment and transactions, on the one hand, and between types of different measures (tax, solvency ratio, public sector and so on), on the other. See also Ingo (1985), Carter and Dickinson (1992).

7   For a more elaborate description of the EU's initial involvement, see CEC (1985c, ch. 2); for national systems of some member countries, see Finsinger and Pauly (1986); for the programme, see Pool (1990); and for the recent situation, see CEC (1992f).

8   Large size permits companies to achieve economies of scale in the marketing of their products. Large scale also permits one to improve one's bargaining position on financial markets. In order to reap these advantages even more fully, some companies have joined forces with banks in so-called 'total finance' companies. This has been made possible by the new deregulated environment.

9   The 1999 list excludes some very large reinsurance companies, such as Münchener Re. Nor does it include Lloyd's, the British firm that occupies a very special place in insurance brokerage. Apart from the companies based in a EU member state, some Swiss companies are also very active on the EU market (for example, Zurich, Winterthur).

10   Another firm that sticks to insurance is the number 10 on the 1999 list, AEGON (NL). In the beginning of the 1980s, two Dutch companies, AGO and ENNIA, each the result of mergers between smaller companies, merged to become AEGON. The strong position on a small home market stimulated the company to go international, which it has done via take-overs in the EU and the USA (Monumental; Western Reserve Life). In 1996, AEGON US took over three insurance divisions of Providian, followed in 1999 by Transamerica Corporation. The company has also embarked upon a strategy of expansion in the EU by taking over the life insurance business of the third British company Guardian Royal Exchange.

11   A full list of the directive's decisions and recommendations has been given in the fourth report of the Commission on the implementation of the telecommunications regulatory package. The present information is rather based on the fifth report (CEC, 1999e). Note that a number of CEECs have also already begun to implement the regulatory package on telecommunications.

13 Transport

Introduction

Economic integration implies that each member state specialises in the production of those goods for which it is best equipped in terms of economic, geographic or other conditions. Specialisation within a customs union implies the spatial separation of supply and demand, and hence increased international goods transport. The increased interaction that follows from the creation of an economic and monetary union (freedom to provide services, free movement of persons and so on) leads to increased international passenger transport. How profitable integration will be depends also on the cost of transport. In that respect, transport costs are not different from customs tariffs or other obstacles to the complete free trade of goods and movement of persons. Logically, therefore, the transport sector should not be overlooked as integration proceeds.

In the following sections of this chapter, the development of the transport sector in the course of the European integration process will be analysed in much the same way as the other economic sectors in previous chapters. First, we will describe the policy regime that the EU has created for the transport sector.[1] Next some significant aspects of the development of the sector, such as production capacity, employment and firm size, will be discussed. Finally we will present two case studies. The first is on goods transport (notably by road), the second on passenger transport (notably by air). A summary of the major findings will complete the chapter.

EU regime

Rationale and principles

In the past, all *national governments* in Europe have become deeply involved in the regulation of transport markets. One argument for intervention was that, since transport services cannot be stocked up, capacity tends to be geared to peak demand. Because a large proportion of the costs are fixed, inelastic supply in periods of low demand, combined with a low price-elasticity of demand, could lead to very keen price competition. Governments felt duty bound to prevent such a situation (which is by no means typical of transport alone). Another argument is that transport requires expensive, long-lasting infrastructure for which the government is mostly responsible. Because the construction costs of this infrastructure and their recovery differ widely among transport modes (compare the railways with inland shipping and road traffic), measures are needed to restore a balanced competition. Third, the specific characteristics of railroads lead to a monopoly; and the government needed to regulate this in order to safeguard the consumers' interest. Finally, over the decades, the objectives of transport policy have increasingly become merged with other societal objectives such as cheap transport to backward regions, for certain social groups; moreover, many sectors of transport have so-called 'public service obligations'.

In view of these circumstances, it is not surprising that the discussion on the *integration of the transport sector* has been a particularly difficult one. The package that came finally into the text of the treaties[2] was based on the following principles:

- an obligation to establish a common transport policy;
- non-discrimination,[3] which puts an end to the practice of charging high prices on import destinations and low prices for export destinations;
- freedom of establishment – that is, the possibility of creating a company in another member state;
- no freedom of services – access to the market in other member states is dependent on the setting of common EU provisions;
- different regimes for different modes (see following sections).[4]

These conflicting principles sprang from considerable differences among member states in economic and geographical conditions and in conceptions of transport policy (Button, 1984; Erdmenger, 1981). Some countries (especially Germany and France) saw transport as a public service or as an integral part of the social structure, affecting the distribution of population and shaping the community's social life. They had regulated their transport sector in a very detailed way and considered that government intervention in both markets and structure was the only way to realise the social objectives of their transport policy. Others (the Netherlands and the UK) took a largely commercial view of transport; they considered that the application of market–economic principles was in the best interest of customers (shippers) and society.

All the national market-control schemes pushed up the costs for the users of transport services. If the objectives of the treaty were to be realised, national government interventions had to be partly harmonised and partly abolished. The experience in countries, which decided to deregulate their transport markets was that service improved and prices dropped, without the market being disturbed (Auctores Varii, 1983). Economically, therefore, liberalisation of the European transport market was the most desirable solution and one in line with the EU regime for the rest of the economic sectors.

Gradual development of a common policy

1960–1982: the liberalisation–harmonisation deadlock The Commission started its activities in the early 1960s with the aim of establishing a common transport market for all inland transport modes, guided by the principles of market economics and inspired by the liberal attitude displayed in the Treaty of Rome with respect to the goods trade. It was hoped that a common transport policy, replacing the various national policies, would guarantee fair competition among and within branches of transport, as well as create conditions of equal competition for other sectors in the economy, such as agriculture, manufacturing industry and commerce. In that vein, the 1962 Memorandum of the Commission proposed three *objectives*.

- Removal of obstacles created by transport and impeding the common market for goods and persons. The implementation of this first objective implied, among other things, the abolition of tariff discrimination for reasons of nationality.
- Integration of the transport market. In addition to some intra-EU liberalisation of transport services the Memorandum proposed quite detailed regulations with respect to market control, namely for tariffs, market access and so on (comparable to the market regulations in agriculture).
- Establishment of a European transport system. This concerned, first, adjusting the infrastructure to the demands of increased international exchange (frontier-crossing motorways and so on) and next the harmonisation of technical (axle load, carriage length, containers), fiscal (motor vehicle tax, petrol duty), social (driving hours) and economic (professional requirements) stipulations.

In practice these objectives and principles proved so difficult to realise that the common policy advanced at a snail's pace, and the integrated market for transport services hardly at all (see, for instance, CEC, 1973a). For many years, harmonisation was the first concern, on the consideration that no fair competition would be possible or liberalisation admissible without it. In the second half of the 1970s, the progress of the common transport policy was slowed down even more by the economic recession, the increased concern for the environment, the higher energy costs and the extension of the EU.

1982–2000: liberalisation hand-in-hand with harmonisation   Confronted with stagnation, the Commission then proposed new schemes, limiting its own involvement to laying down general principles and emphasising the harmonisation of national measures. The idea of working out a complete European regime for transport, following the pattern of agriculture, was abandoned. However the new proposals, like the earlier ones, came to nothing because of the Council's indecisiveness. In that situation, in 1982, the European Parliament, always an active promoter of a European transport policy, summoned the Council of Ministers before the Court of Justice. That this unique procedure was resorted to characterised the regrettable situation that had evolved: 25 years after the founding of the EU, and more than 15 years after the end of the transition period, still no EU transport policy had been worked out.

In its verdict the Court stated that the Council:

- is committed to regulate within a reasonable period the liberalisation of frontier-crossing transport within the EU (including transit);
- shall establish the conditions under which entrepreneurs from one member state are permitted to take part in transport in another member state;
- may, but is not obliged to, take complementary measures (in practice social, technical, environmental and other harmonisation measures).

The Court left the question of timing open by using the term 'within a reasonable period'. The Commission and the Council specified the horizon, much in line with the other aspects of the internal market (Chapter 14), as the year 1992. In the following sections we will illustrate how this liberalisation and regulation have been given substance (see CEC, 1999f).

Market order

After much hesitation and negotiation the markets for transport services are now operating under the same *liberal regime* that prevails for the other sectors of the economy. In order to let markets function properly, a set of detailed regulations specific for transport apply.

One of these applies to the *recovery of infrastructure cost*. Indeed, different systems can distort competition between transport modes as well as disturb international trade. Two conditions must be satisfied for the adequate recovery of costs: (1) correct computation of total costs and (2) correct attribution to users. Levies would have to satisfy two requirements: (1) to reflect marginal social costs and (2) to meet the demand of overall budget equality. The computation problem was solved in 1970, when the Council introduced a common system to establish the costs of road, railroad and waterway infrastructure. The attribution problem has not been solved yet. On the basis of the many studies made (see, among others, Allais *et al.*, 1965; Malcor, 1970; Oort, 1975), the Commission has submitted to the Council various proposals for directives. Notwithstanding considerable progress, the fair and efficient pricing (covering social and external cost) remains a major point of further action (CEC, 1999f).

The *external dimension* of the EU internal transport market is based to a very limited extent on common European rules; much is still dependent on bilateral deals of member states with third countries.[5] This is the case, for example, for road transport: the bilateral deals concluded by individual member states with third countries make it practically impossible for third-country hauliers to offer their services on the EU market. However price competition from companies from Central and Eastern Europe is strong on the EU–CEEC links. The same problem did not occur with rail transport, because on the continent any international transport by rail required the cooperation of nationalised companies with monopoly power. In inland shipping, the Mannheim Act applies only to riverine states of the Rhine, which means in practice that third countries (apart from Switzerland) are banned from services on the Rhine.[6] In civil aviation, national authorities regulate access to their territory for EU and third-country companies alike: a common external civil aviation policy has not yet got off the ground. The Commission considers the setting up of a common external policy in transport matters as a cornerstone of its policy. However the progress on this score is limited.

Structural policy

European structural policy in matters of transport has advanced only slowly. The policy is concerned with both transport infrastructure (generally in the public domain) and production means (in principle in private hands, in practice also to a large extent in public hands).

The first proposals made by the Commission for intensive coordination of national investments in *infrastructure* were refused by the

Council as an intrusion of the EU in national autonomy; it accepted only a consultation procedure (Gwilliam *et al.*, 1973). To that end, an Infrastructure Committee has been set up (CEC, 1979b). Since the early 1980s the Commission has sought the competence to give financial support to projects (see CEC, 1979b, 1982d, 1982e)[7] that remove bottlenecks in the networks for international transportation of goods, by road, railroad and inland waterways, and of information (telecommunication). Examples of such large-scale projects with evident European dimensions are the Channel Tunnel and the high speed trains network. Neither the planning nor the financing of such projects was a direct task for the Commission. However, as far as the latter aspect is concerned, the Commission may, since 1990, contribute its support (Regulations 3359/90).[8] With the Maastricht Treaty the setting up of Trans-European Networks (TEN) in the areas of transport has become an EU task. The aim is to promote the interconnection and interoperability of national networks as well as access to such networks. In the framework of this policy, support has been given to a number of individual projects for improvement of international transport links, to the amount of some 300 million euro a year. The TEN programme will be extended to cover the applicant countries as well.

Policy concerned with the improvement of the *production means* varies among transport modes. In railroad transport, rolling stock is subject to many national rules, but no relevant EU measures have been taken. EU measures to improve the production structure of road transport concern technical prescriptions as to axle load, brakes, permissible weight and so on. The Commission has taken some perfunctory steps towards a structural policy for inland shipping, more specifically with respect to the scrapping of obsolete ships. Regarding sea traffic, the structure-improving programmes concern measures like the setting up of a European register of ships. Air traffic regulation shows a major deficiency. Indeed a major problem for the operation of airlines in Europe is the way in which the airspace is managed. In the whole of Western Europe, 54 air traffic control centres are active, working with different computer systems and programming languages. These complicated, time-consuming and costly procedures limit the capacity of the European skies and cause considerable delays of many flights. In view of the very high losses involved, for some time European airlines have been pressing for the setting up of a 'single sky'. (Compare the USA, which, over a much larger area, has 20 centres with one system!)

Notwithstanding deficiencies, a coherent common policy for the development of the structure of the European transport sector has gradually been elaborated.

Sketch of the sector

Importance of the sector

The transport sector is of strategic importance to the EU economy, though relatively modest in terms of wealth creation and employment, accounting throughout the 1950–90 period for a very stable 5 per cent of GDP and employment. By the end of the 1990s this share had gone down a little (to 4 per cent).

The branches of the sector have developed differently. Road transport, now accounting for almost half of employment, has taken the place that rail transport occupied in the 1950s (now some 25 per cent). The relative importance of water and air transport is less, but the latter is growing very fast.

Production means

The developments of production means reflect the structural changes in European transport. Table 13.1 neatly illustrates the fast rise of road and the decline of railroad transport. The length of the railroad network dropped by 12 per cent between 1960 and 1997: the number of goods wagons fell by 60 per cent between 1970 and 1997. By contrast, the number of lorries (commercial vehicles) increased fourfold in the same period. The relation between the data for units and for capacity (or production) reveals how much the scale of transport has grown. Such developments can be observed in most branches of inland transport: road haulage, pipeline transport and in inland shipping (taking into account the increase in capacity of self-propelled craft and barges).

Case study 1: goods transport, haulage

Regulatory framework

The *regulation* of the haulage industry is dominated by qualitative standards. These are derived from social (driving hours), safety (technical check-ups) and environmental considerations (exhaust gases). In the past governments have also intervened by setting minimum prices and by regulating supply. National road transport used to be reserved for national companies susceptible to national market controls (licensing and permit systems, tariff setting, access restrictions based, for example, on expertise, finance and so on). In some countries, internal long-distance carriage was subject to licensing systems.

The *liberalisation* of the road haulage market in Europe started with international transport. To that end national trip permits (quotas)

Table 13.1   Characteristics of the inland transport system EU15, 1950–97

	1950*	1960	1970	1980	1990	1997
Road						
Motorways (1000 km)	2	4	16	31	39	48
Cars owned (× 1 000 000)	7	22	63	103	146	170
Commercial vehicles						
(× 1 000 000)	3	5	8	11	16	20
Railway						
Coaches (× 1000)	113	111	98	96	86	75
Passengers (1 000 000 p/km)	n.a.	n.a.	217	253	274	283
Goods wagons (× 100 000)	15	14	15	12	8	6
Goods (1 000 000 t/km)	n.a.	n.a.	283	287	256	238
Track total (1000 km)	163	175	171	165	160	154
Inland waterways[a,b]						
Self-propelled craft (× 1000)	n.a.	29	24	18	15	10
Dumb and pushed barges						
(× 1000)	n.a.	10	5	3	3	3
Pipe[b,c]						
length in service (× 1000 km)	n.a.	6	13	18	20	21

Notes:
*   EU12
[a]   Data indicated for 1960 apply to 1965; the last column refers to 1995.
[b]   Excluding Finland and Sweden.
[c]   Excluding DK, IR, PORT.
n.a. = No comparable data available.

Sources: UN/ECE, *Annual Bulletin of Transport Statistics for Europe*, various years; Eurostat, *Transport Annual Statistics*, various years; some estimates based on various national statistics.

were replaced by an EU system of trip authorisation with national quotas. That system could never respond adequately to the needs of a market. Many vehicles were forced to return empty.[9] So further liberalisation was undertaken. The number of EU authorisations has been gradually stepped up to become large enough for the transition to a fully free common market for international road transport (finally reached by the end of 1998).

Integration has also been realised by *harmonisation*. Regulations have been introduced for the operating conditions of international road transport in the following fields:

- fiscal: exemption from customs duties for fuel in the tanks;
- social rules: mainly concerned with hours of driving and resting;
- admission to the profession: certificates and so on for firms, and a European driving licence;
- safety: periodic inspection of vehicles, speed limits;
- environment: energy consumption, emission of exhaust gases, dangerous materials.

Industry characteristics

Under conditions of integration transport develops faster than total economic activity, as goods trade increases faster than industrial production. Intra-EU international transport has grown (in tons) faster than extra-EU international transport, which confirms the data derived from international trade statistics (Chapter 5).

The *modal split*, that is the relative importance of the various transport modes for goods transport in Europe, has undergone important changes over the past decades (Table 13.2). The major shift from railroad to road haulage is evident. Before 1960, road haulage played only a modest part in goods transport among member states, amounting to less than a fifth of railroad transport (Blonk, 1968). Now, some 40 years later, the roles are reversed: international road haulage accounts for the lion's share of inland transport. This is even more pronounced if we look at domestic transport; here haulage takes some 90 per cent of all tonnage transported (Eurostat, *Transport Statistics*).

What have been the *determinant factors* of this shift in the modal split of goods transport? The significance of the various factors such as price, speed and reliability varies with the nature of the product to

Table 13.2   Inland goods transport (in ton/km) by mode of transport (in percentages), EU15, 1970–2000

Mode of transport	1970	1980	1990	2000[a]
Road	48	56	68	76
Railroad	33	26	19	12
Inland waterway	12	10	8	6
Pipeline	8	8	6	5
Total	100	100	100	100

Note: [a]   Estimates based on 1990–98 figures.

Source: European Commission, *Transport in Figures*, 1998.

be carried. For low-value bulk goods rail and water transport are eminently suitable. Intermediary products and finished manufactures are generally carried in smaller quantities and to more dispersed destinations; here the lorry is most suitable. The latter type of product has an increasing share in the total, owing to the structural changes in the economy. Hence the rise in the share of road haulage. Regulation with regard to prices and quantities has affected the long-term change in the modal split only marginally (Voigt *et al.*, 1986). Recent liberalisation has, however, improved the position of the road haulage sector, the more so because the liberalisation of the rail freight sector has still not become effective.

Company response

International road haulage is dominated by small firms: 80 per cent of the firms have fewer than five vehicles, 10 per cent have five to 10 vehicles and another 10 per cent more than 10 vehicles. The average size does, however, grow over time and with it the degree of concentration. A relatively high share of the EU market for road transport is held by companies in the Benelux; this can be explained by the large transport flows that originate in the major North Sea ports.

The deregulation that the EU has carried through in the framework of the creation of the single market has had a number of effects (Sleuwaegen, 1993). Companies have lowered their prices for cross-border transport by an estimated 6 per cent. The greater efficiency has cut margins, as costs have grown in the same period (fuel, harmonisation: CEC, 1996a). This reduction in transport cost has further stimulated demand for road transport.

There has been a substantial *restructuring* of the sector. First, there has been a shake-out of inefficient firms. Second, there has been a concentration both at the EU level and at the national level. Third, many small firms have entered the market. Differentiation has been accentuated. On the one hand, one sees the emergence of firms that are 'architects of transport and logistics': they have invested in international networks of firms with national client access, in telecommunication and in computerised handling and tracking. They try to realise greater efficiency and to reap the economies of scale and scope that are made possible by the larger market. On the other hand, one sees the emergence of smaller companies in the role of subcontractor or of jobber. Finally a number of specialists have developed (for example, for bulk chemicals). The middle group is often quasi-integrated into larger organisations. This is an efficient form, as it achieves economies of scale without being subject to moral hazard problems related to the use of vehicles (Fernandez *et al.*, 2000).

Case study 2: passenger transport by air

Regulatory framework

The civil aviation industry is very heavily regulated. Everywhere in the world countries have pursued a national aviation policy that aims at protecting the market of the national flag-carrier(s). Governments maintain a firm grip on the air traffic market by holding controlling stakes in the stock of their national air transport company, by regulating their airspace control, by allocating landing rights and so on. Moreover national airlines often used to enjoy a monopoly on internal routes in their country of origin, which allowed them to offset profit-making activities against loss-making activities connected with their public service role of providing services to outlying areas and on low-density routes. Internationally there is a veritable tangle of multilateral accords (Convention of Chicago) and bilateral agreements governing landing rights, capacity, frequency, routes, tariffs and market sharing.

Until recently the situation that prevailed worldwide also prevailed on the internal EU market.[10] As a result of this protection and of the segmentation of markets within the EU, prices were generally too high and services not optimal.[11] This situation involved many welfare losses. Consequently the Commission has tried several times to *liberalise the intra-EU air traffic market*. This has finally been made possible within the framework of the total programme for the completion of the internal market. Liberalisation has started with interregional air transport. Next, the market-sharing agreements were loosened and intervention in prices restricted. Since 1997 full freedom to provide airline services within the EU has existed for companies from EU member states. Finally, strict rules on state aids were introduced. The internal market for airline services is still some way off. One reason for this is the limited capacity of air traffic control. Due to the multiplicity of national systems of air traffic control, capacity is lower and the costs to carriers (back-up aircraft and crew) and consumers (delays) higher than they could be under a single EU system (CEC, 2000d).

The situation with respect to *external liberalisation* is quite different. Here the whole panoply of protection based on bilateral agreements persists. Worldwide, the US government has been practically the only one to speak in support of liberalisation. The EU has not been able to make a stand on this. Whereas the UK and the Dutch governments are favourable to an 'open skies' policy, the governments of many other member states are rather afraid of the idea. The Commission has been trying to get a mandate for international negotiations, in line with the powers it has in matters of external trade relations.

However, up to now the member states have not given up their prerogatives. Consequently, the Commission has decided to challenge these open skies agreements in the Court of Justice. The international organisations that are in charge of international trade in services have for some time been studying the dossier of civil aviation, but the prospects for a successful negotiation of worldwide liberalisation seem still a long way off.

Industry characteristics

Passenger transport has grown considerably since the Second World War. In 1960, the average EU inhabitant spent 8 per cent of his total net income on mobility (purchase and use of car, moped, bicycle and so on, plus train, tram, bus and air tickets). By 1990, the percentage had risen to approximately 14. The tremendous growth of international passenger traffic is explained on the demand side by demographic growth, increasing incomes and leisure time and the integration of markets (which increased business contacts). Explanatory factors on the supply side are fast-decreasing cost due to increases in productivity (notably air) and better services (as to time, destination, luxury and so on). The explosively growing demand could be satisfied thanks to the overall adequate extension of the infrastructure: airports, motorways, fast trains and so on. Air traffic has shown the most spectacular growth of all modes. Over the 1960–2000 period, the total number of passenger kilometres flown by the major European airlines increased almost twentyfold.

The *supply structure* has changed very little over the 1960–95 period. In the dynamic growth market of civil aviation such stability could only be sustained because all major suppliers were, until recently, nationalised companies that were heavily protected against competition. The following three indicators (based on the data in Table 13.3) clearly show the extent of segmentation of markets due to considerable protection.

- *The low overall concentration of supply of European air transport.* In 1998, calculated on total world operations, the C1 index (share of largest company in total operations) was 25 per cent; C4 (share of numbers 1, 2 and 3 companies) was 69 per cent.
- *The stability in participation of companies.* In the 1970–98 period, the list showed neither new entrants nor departures, and only a few national mergers.
- *The stability of the ranking of the eight major companies.* Between 1970 and 1998, four companies did not change places at all, while two pairs changed only one place.

Table 13.3   Total passenger kilometres (1000 million) on scheduled services (international and domestic) of major international European airlines, 1960–98

Rank	Company	Country	1960	1970	1980	1990	1998
1	British Airways	UK	6[a]	16	40	66[b]	116
2	Lufthansa	Germany	1	8	21	42	75
3	Air France	France	4	10	25	37	75[c]
4	KLM	Netherlands	3	6	14	26	57
5	Alitalia	Italy	1	8	13	23	36
6	Iberia	Spain	1	6	14	22	33
7	SAS	Scandinavia	2	5	11	17	21
8	Sabena	Belgium	1	2	5	8	15
9	Finnair	Finland	—	1	2	5	11
10	Olympic	Greece	—	2	5	8	9
11	TAP	Portugal	—	2	3	7	9
12	Austrian	Austria	—	1	1	3	7
13	Aer Lingus	Ireland	—	2	2	4	7
14	UTA	France	1[d]	2	5	6	—
15	British Caledonian	UK	—[e]	1	4	—	—
	Total	EU15	20	72	165	274	471

Notes:
[a]   BEA + BOAC.
[b]   Including British Caledonian.
[c]   Including UTA.
[d]   TAI + UAT.
[e]   BUA.

Source: *World Air Transport Statistics*, several years.

The EU carriers are not very big by world standards; if companies are compared on the basis of total passengers carried (both domestic and international), many American and Asian airlines take precedence over even the larger European carriers.

The *price effects* of the liberalisation have been fairly small. Price cuts of some 15 per cent have occurred on routes with competition (CEC, 1999b, 1999c). However, the tangle of national landing rights, the problems with air traffic control and so on have led to a situation whereby, on many routes, there are still only two suppliers that can easily collude to keep prices high.

Company response

The shift in the EU attitude towards civil aviation has brought about *increased competition*. On all intra-EU connections, major airlines have now to compete with one another and with many smaller EU suppliers struggling for advantageous positions in niche markets, notably services between regional airports and between regional and major airports. Between 1985 and 1994, this shift in markets from full fare tickets for business purposes to discount fare tickets for a whole variety of purposes has pushed down the yield of airlines in real terms by almost 20 per cent. This change in conditions is bringing about great changes for all players.

All major carriers have had to *cut costs, raise productivity and improve service*. The main way of achieving this has been to reduce the labour force directly employed by the airline. Some airlines have been able to restructure successfully at an early stage (for example, BA, KLM, Lufthansa); others have been struggling for some time with the problem (for example, Air France, Iberia) and have been depending on heavy government support to recover.

The market position of the major EU airlines[12] is given in Table 13.3. The liberalisation of markets would normally entail a substantial *restructuring of the industry*, by the entry, mergers and exit of companies.

- Many new *entrants* have indeed emerged and they have put much pressure on existing companies on many connections within the EU. However, as the threshold for entry into the business of large-scale international air transport service is quite high, a major upheaval from that type of competition has not occurred.
- *Exit* of companies that used to be national flag-carriers has not occurred either. However, some of the companies that have been losing out have become more of a regional specialist (Olympic).
- *Mergers* between companies have changed in character. Between 1960 and 1995, only four mergers were recorded; all were between companies of the same country. This seemed the best option for both internal political reasons (for example, Air France with UTA and with Air Inter) and external policy reasons (the whole international system is based on bilateral deals; multinational companies are at odds with this system). International mergers between EU companies have not yet become a reality; in this category we can mention the aborted attempt to merge KLM and Alitalia.[13]

Given remaining constraints of international law and EU regulation, the response of many EU companies has been to form *global alliances*.[14] These involve typically a major EU and a major US airline, plus a number of others. Four major groupings exist, together accounting for some 60 per cent of the world traffic. One is the Star alliance, which groups Lufthansa (EU), United (US), Thai, SAS (EU) and Varig. Another one is the One World alliance grouping British Airways (EU), American Airways (US) and, among others, Iberia (EU), Cathay and Quantas. A third one is the Wings alliance of KLM/Alitalia with NorthWest/Continental. The fourth one is Skyteam regrouping Air France (EU), Delta (US) and, among others, Aeromexico. These alliances are very effective in increasing returns as they redirect traffic to the benefit of alliance members by means of code sharing, common frequent flyer bonuses, while permitting cost cuts by the exchange of slots and terminal facilities, the common use of agents and so on. However, experience has shown that they are not very stable and that switching of partners is a recurrent theme.

Summary and conclusions

- The European transport market has for a long time been very heavily regulated on a national basis and therefore much fragmented. Rulings of the Court have obliged the Council to work out a common transport policy along the same liberal lines that obtain for the rest of the economy. Liberalisation has been pursued in the framework of the completion of the internal market.
- Goods transport by road has increased much faster than industrial growth. However this growth has not yet gone hand-in-hand with international integration of road haulage firms. A number of large European logistic firms have recently been created in a process of take-overs and mergers.
- Passenger transport by air has increased very rapidly, but the company structure has until recently remained practically unaltered, evidencing the lack of competition and international integration. In recent years, intra-EU liberalisation and worldwide competition have changed this situation profoundly, leading to some mergers of EU companies and a strengthening of the linkages of major European companies with other major carriers in the world.

Notes

1   For an overview of the various texts of the EU regulation see CEC (1999f).
2   The three treaties give different stipulations for transport. The ECSC Treaty is concerned only with preventing the distortion of fair competition by tariffs for transport of coal and steel that discriminated by nationality origin/destination. For the rest, transport policy was explicitly reserved to the member states. The EAEC Treaty is not very important in transport matters. The EEC Treaty, on the contrary, provides (in its Article 3) for *a common transport policy*. The principles of such a policy are given in a separate title (V, Articles 70–80), a privilege shared only with agriculture. The modes of transport are treated differently. Remarkably the transport title as such applies only to the so-called 'inland traffic', namely transport by rail, road and inland waterway. With respect to navigation and aviation, the Treaty stipulates merely that appropriate provisions may be laid down (Article 80). Common rules for international inland transport must be laid down, as well as the conditions under which transport entrepreneurs are admitted to national transport in a member state in which they are not resident (Article 70). This shows that the right of establishment, contrary to the right to provide services, is directly applicable to transport.
3   Such tariffs were indeed practised by some countries. Just before the Coal and Steel Community was founded, coal produced in Germany was transported at tariffs up to a quarter below those for imported coal. An example of a low tariff for exports is that for French sodium salts, which paid up to two-fifths less for transport than salt destined for the domestic market.
4   The regimes for road and air transport are discussed in the next sections; some major features of the other modes of transport are as follows:
    Rail: railways' heavy investment in infrastructure has led to state-owned monopoly enterprises, to a firm hold of governments on the tariff structure, and to railroad companies' obligation to provide transport. The EU has pursued two objectives: (1) a normal price setting in commercial supply and demand situations, and (2) the abolition of subsidies. The harmonisation decision of 1965 commits member states either to reimburse the costs of charges and transport obligations foreign to the trade, or to abolish the obligations. Now governments have to conclude public service contracts with the railway companies. Railway companies are now obliged to be financially independent, and are encouraged to concentrate on the exploitation of the railways (leaving infrastructure to the public sector) and to regroup themselves internationally.
    Maritime transport is of critical importance for the EU as well, as a very large share of external goods trade is made by ship. Moreover maritime shipping regulation became particularly important when, with the joining of three new member states (two of them islands!) in 1972, some maritime shipping turned into intra-community transport. The Court has confirmed that sea navigation comes under the general rules of the Treaty. Market control in maritime shipping mostly takes the form of so-called 'shipping-line conferences': associations of shipowners active in the same sailing area, which, in economic terms, are cartels. In the framework of UNCTAD negotiations, the EU was forced not only to accept the existence of such conferences, but also to concede a certain division of the market between developed and developing countries. Admittedly provisos have been made to the effect that the division of cargoes will not be applied to intra-EU sea traffic and that all EU shipowners will have equal access to EU cargoes to third countries (Hart *et al.*, 1992).

Inland shipping was practically free when the EU was created, thanks largely to the Mannheim Convention, which guarantees free traffic on the Rhine. The economic recession of 1973 inspired associations of shipowners to enforce, through a blockade, a rotation scheme for the proportional allocation of freight on the canal systems of Holland, Belgium and France. The EU has opposed such a development, which is at cross-purposes with the Treaty. After lengthy negotiations a scheme has been adopted for the abolition of the limitation of free market access for all categories by the year 2000.

5   Some of the external aspects of the transport market are regulated by international organisations. Merchant shipping in particular has had the attention of such UN affiliates as ECE, UNCTAD and the International Maritime Organisation, and air transport that of the International Air Transport Association. European agencies concerned with transport problems are the European Conference of Transport Ministers, the OECD Transport Committee, the European Committee for Civil Aviation and the Central Rhine Shipping Committee.

6   This is still the case; after the opening of the Rhine–Main–Donau canal, ships from Central and Eastern Europe have access, in technical terms, to Western European waters but have as yet no access to Western European markets.

7   This even extends to projects in third countries (Switzerland, CEEC) as far as is essential to intra-European traffic.

8   This support to infrastructure is based on considerations of transport policy; transport infrastructure in backward regions is supported on regional–economic considerations by the European Regional Development Fund (Chapter 16).

9   In the early 1980s, an estimated 40 per cent of international road haulage had no return cargo at all.

10   See for a detailed description of the development of EU air transport policy Button *et al*. (1998).

11   For a price comparison of Europe and the USA, see, among others, CEC (1979c); Gialloreto (1988) calculated that airline operating costs in Europe were 50 per cent above those in the USA.

12   There are many more companies that provide jet services (far more than 100 in 1990). Their number has grown quickly following the recent liberalisation of intra-EU traffic. Many of the larger charter companies are actually bigger than the smaller flag-carriers in terms of the total number of passenger kilometres flown. However the overall picture is difficult to get hold of, as many flag-carriers have taken (sometimes majority) stakes in such (charter and feeder) companies operating mainly from their home country base.

13   PM Swissair, not on the list, took a 50 per cent stake in the ailing SABENA to get a foothold in the EU market.

14   See for the economics of international alliances in air transport Button *et al*. (1998) chs 5–6 and Hanlon (1999) for global airlines.

PART IV
CONDITIONS FOR
BALANCED GROWTH

14 Allocation, Internal Market Policies

Introduction

The main objective of the European Union is to enhance the allocational efficiency of the economies of the member states by removing barriers to the movement of goods, services and production factors. Moreover policies have been agreed upon to make the European market, once created, function properly. In the following sections we will describe in some detail a number of these policies.

Before we go into the specific policy areas, we will first specify some of the basic principles about government intervention in European markets. Next we will describe the EU regime in matters of allocation policies. To ensure the good functioning of the internal market, two types of policy are needed: competition and harmonisation.

Competition is the first specific policy area to which we will give attention. We will describe the economic rationale of the EU involvement with competition and the specific forms in which this policy has been elaborated over the past.

The *harmonisation* approach will be illustrated with two examples. The first concerns indirect influencing of markets through taxation. This applies both to goods and services markets (value added and excise taxes) and production factors (corporate and income taxes).[1] The second applies to the regulating of market access by defining technical norms and standards for the quality of products. Such regulation used to be a major policy instrument for governments to protect their markets. The EU policy measures needed to remove such obstacles will be reviewed in a last policy section.

All distortions of the efficient allocation take a heavy toll in welfare from the EU, and their removal has positive *welfare* effects. Some estimates of these effects will be presented, before a final section in which we present some conclusions and a summary.

Foundations

Theory of market regulation (prices and quantities)

The basic assumption of economics is that the workings of markets will bring the best outcome in terms of allocation efficiency and hence the best outcome in terms of wealth creation and growth. However, in some cases, market forces do not lead to optimal outcomes. In those cases government intervention may then correct non-optimal situations. One form of intervention uses *direct price and/or quantity controls*. These may be justified in the following cases:

- Acute scarcity may drive up the prices of products providing for basic needs, which for social reasons must be kept low. Basic economics teaches that, to prevent excess demand in such cases, the quantities need to be controlled as well. Such direct intervention was very common during and just after the Second World War (for example, for food and housing) but has now become the exception rather than the rule.
- Natural monopolies (in electricity distribution, for instance) are inclined to charge too high prices and restrict production. Such potential abuse of market power calls for regulation to keep prices at the level that would prevail under competitive conditions.
- Unstable markets (like those for agricultural products) may cause grave social problems and a fragile production structure. Governments may use instruments as guaranteed prices or selling and purchasing from public stocks to stabilise markets.
- Social considerations may lead to the setting of minimum wage levels, compulsory social security contributions and rules about equal pay for men and women in labour markets.
- External effects of the consumption of goods (health and environment, for instance) and the existence of public goods lead in some cases to the fixing of prices (for medical and pharmaceutical products and transport, among others).

Now, apart from its presumed beneficial effects, such intervention in markets also has some important negative effects. Too much regulation tends to suffocate the economy (see Box 14.1). So the instruments of *price regulation* should be carefully chosen with a view to the objective one wants to attain. In the previous chapters we have indicated that the intervention in prices has been a feature of some EU markets of products (agriculture) and some national markets of production factors (for example, wages). However, the discussion in these chapters has also made clear that the use of the instrument has decreased considerably over the integration period.

Box 14.1 Market regulation and output growth

The optimal level of regulation is difficult to find. Yet some evidence (see Figure 14.1 taken from Koedijk and Kremers, 1996) suggests that in the past a number of EU member countries have gone too far and would now benefit from deregulation. The graph gives the correlation between two rankings of EU member countries. On the vertical axis we find the ranking according to output growth during the period 1981–93. On the horizontal axis we find the ranking according to intensity of regulation. This accounts for both labour markets (for example, restrictions on being sacked, level of minimum wages) and product markets (for example, competition policy, public ownership). The chart shows that the countries with the least regulation have shown the highest growth. A more detailed analysis of these data reveals that 'excessive' regulation in product markets tended to do more harm than in labour markets.[2]

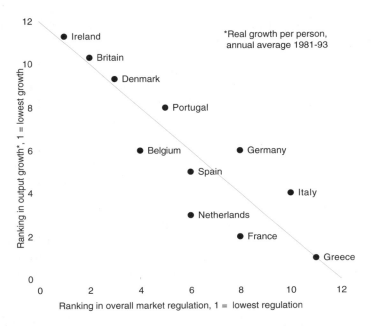

Figure 14.1 Output growth and market regulation

Nowadays intervention rather relies on such *indirect instruments as taxes and subsidies*. Governments will impose indirect taxes such as excise duties to discourage the consumption of goods with negative external effects (for instance, tobacco and liquor, on account of their harmful effect on health) while subsidising goods with positive externalities (for instance, sports facilities, cultural events and the like). Taxes and subsidies change the (relative) prices of goods. Differences in national practices of such indirect intervention can distort trade between partners. As compensatory import and export duties or quantitative restrictions are incompatible with the Customs Union, some harmonisation is called for (see the following section).

Theory of structural policies

In western-type market economies the prime task of economic development is left to private enterprise. Entrepreneurs have to compete with one another for markets and resources. Institutions safeguard the rules of the game under which this competition takes place. Governments set the rules so as to optimise the conditions for the competitiveness of firms. The question then becomes what intervention is best for the economy.

The *theoretical foundation* for the pursuit of an 'industrial' or a sectoral policy is mainly found in market failures[3] (see, for instance, Jacquemin and de Jong, 1977; Urban, 1983, Odagiri, 1986, Wolf, 1987, Chang 1996). The reasons are monopolistic behaviour, the existence of public goods, economies of scale, external effects, the cost of gathering information and making adjustments, rigidities, entry barriers and so on. To correct such imperfections and to secure an optimum situation, the government needs to intervene in the market. A classical case in point is the infant industry argument: a firm should be protected (by subsidies, for instance) from its foreign competitors at the first stage of its development, because only in that way can it grow enough to profit from economies of scale and become competitive. The costs of protection in the first period are compensated by the benefits of production reaped at a later stage (creation of private and tax revenue).

The quality of the arguments for intervention in the two strands of thought has been severely criticised (for example, Lindbeck, 1981; Eliasson, 1984). One criticism is that the cost of intervention is often overlooked, another that public authorities are generally no better equipped to evaluate future developments than are private decision makers (public sector failures).

The arguments for intervention for structural purposes apply not only to the manufacturing sector, but also to other sectors (agriculture and services) and factor markets (think, for instance, of programmes for the (re)training of workers who will be needed in certain new industries, or the retraining of workers made redundant in old industries). In the previous chapters we have described, for each sector, the way in which the national and EU involvement has developed.

Many of the instruments of structural policies tend to affect the allocative efficiency of the Union economy. An example in this field is *state aids*. Where subsidies are given for political reasons (for example, for the maintenance of employment in industries that have lost their competitiveness) resources are badly used. However, even where subsidies are given to industries for economic reasons, theory shows that this generally represents a distortion. So, the prohibition of state aids actually increases welfare for the Union as a whole (Collie, 2000). Indeed 'structural' subsidies to domestic industry can be recalculated in money values per unit of product, with an effect on importers similar to that of tariffs. For that reason, a common stance towards national measures of structural policy aid is an obvious necessity in a customs union and in an economic union. Common rules for state aids are the obvious first step; at later stages, common programmes for structural change may become a more efficient solution.

EU regime

The basic principle: a liberalised market

EU member countries entered the EU with very different traditions of state intervention in markets, be it control of prices and quantities, state responsibility for production and regulation of quality, or vigilance with respect to competition rules. Some countries – France for one – have a more interventionist tradition; others, like Germany, are more of the liberalist type (at least for markets of manufactured goods). However no EU country defended a straightforward *laissez-faire* regime, nor had any country adopted a system of rigorous central planning.

The underlying *principle* of the order of the European Union is that decisions as to production, consumption, investment, saving and so on have to be left to economic agents and that the public authorities do not intervene in the markets. Within these general European rules set for the allocation process, there is room for a competition of national rules which is supposed to sort out the policy environment that is most conducive to growth. National governments are free to adopt a more interventionist or a more liberal approach; initially a number of governments were in favour of heavy regulation; recently, however, all member state governments have opted for a more liberal stand.

When the EU order had to be worked out, it was only logical that one would steer a course between the two extreme views. Over time, the blend of interventionist and liberalist measures has varied for different sectors of activity, as the previous chapters have shown. Indeed the ECSC Treaty gave the EU institutions quite considerable powers to intervene in coal and steel markets. This instrument is no longer used, however. The EEC Treaty, on the contrary, trusted mainly to market forces for the allocation function; the Commission has no powers for intervention in markets, with two noticeable exceptions: agriculture and transport. The common policy that was elaborated on the basis of the specific treaty principles for agriculture still relies very heavily on both quantity and price controls (Chapter 9). In the area of transport, many direct influences on price and quantities (quotas) have been abolished (Chapter 13) under the pressure of recent EU liberalisation measures. That still leaves one interventionist island in the predominantly liberalist sea.

A liberalised market needs certain conditions to function properly. Paramount among them is regulation. The EU has opted for a blend of regulatory policies that comprise both competition and the harmonisation of laws of national states.

Main objective: a single market

The unity of the market is a basic principle of the EU, whatever the attitude chosen *vis-à-vis* a particular sector of activity. In defiance of the general principles, many impediments to the free movement of goods, services, capital and labour persisted up to the mid-1980s, some of which implied controls at internal borders.[4] Concern about the negative effect of these barriers to European growth increased (Albert and Ball, 1983), notably among industrialists who had to stand up to international competition on world markets. To arouse public interest, Philips' president, Dekker, in 1984 launched his Plan for Europe 1990. Following this impetus the Commission (CEC, 1985d) came up with a white paper containing the bold proposal for a consistent and comprehensive list of measures that would do away with all controls on goods, services, capital and persons at the internal borders of the EU by the end of 1992. This programme has been endorsed by the Council and was made into a treaty obligation by the adoption of the Single European Act (CEC, 1987a): 'The internal market shall comprise an area without internal frontiers in which the free movement of goods, persons, services and capital is ensured.'

The most important elements of this programme were successfully executed over the 1985–92 period, while other elements have taken some more time. The *success factors* were fourfold:

- Complete comprehensiveness: it covered all measures needed to do away with internal frontiers; the continued presence of any one reason to maintain frontier controls could be enough to keep them intact.
- A clear timetable: the target set was the end of 1992. This recalls the approach of the Treaty of Rome to the abolition of all tariffs and quotas on internal trade by the end of the transition period.
- A simplified decision-making process: the new rule required only a qualified majority for decisions on most measures needed to accomplish the internal market, instead of unanimity.
- A balance between liberalisation and harmonisation. A sector-by-sector approach, that gradually liberalised increasing segments of each heavily regulated sector, while at the same time setting framework EU rules, has removed in many instances hesitations of national governments and of the sectoral interest groups (see, for example, Chapter 11, case study on electricity, Chapter 12 case studies on insurance and telecommunications and Chapter 13, case study on civil aviation).

There are two *reasons why the internal market is not yet complete.*

- Difficulties of coming to agreement among member states about EU legislation: examples are the lack of full freedom for the movement of persons (owing to problems about safety checks, and absence of a common immigration policy) and the ailing harmonisation of taxation (see further sections in this chapter).
- Non-compliance of member states with EU legislation: the cases involve a range of single market directives including excise duties, public procurement and financial services.

In order to speed up work on the removal of the remaining problems, the Commission has introduced an annual cycle of setting of target actions and reporting on the progress of implementation (CEC, 1999j). The latter consists of a so-called Scoreboard and on reporting on for instance price convergence. The former encompasses initiatives and actions both at the EU and the national level with concrete deadlines for realisation (for instance, a directive on electronic commerce).

Competition

Theoretical foundations for regime choices

In western industrialised countries, most decisions are left to private economic actors. Market forces (including competition) are allowed to play their role and the price mechanism is largely relied upon to bring about an efficient allocation of resources. However private actors may collude to avoid competition. Indeed Adam Smith wrote, more than 200 years ago, in his famous book, *Wealth of Nations*: 'People of the same trade seldom meet together, even for merriment and diversion, but the conversation ends in a conspiracy against the public or in some contrivance to raise forces.' In these cases, he argues, prosperity is less than with free competition; monopoly spells loss of welfare to consumers. To prevent it, public authorities must take it upon themselves to intervene with competition laws and policy (Demsetz, 1982; Scherer, 2000).

There are also advocates of limitations to competition – for instance, by cartels and monopolies. Cartels, for example, would permit enterprises to finance R&D, while competition would take away the margin that is necessary for making these investments in innovation. Another argument often heard is that to beat foreign competition a sufficiently large margin has to be realised on home sales.

The balancing out of arguments pro and con has found its best expression in a school of thinking that advocates the *'workable competition'* concept. In this view an authority should be charged with the maintenance of such a workable competition in the various markets. This task used to be executed by national authorities. Their policies differed: some, like the Netherlands, used to be very lenient towards restrictions; others, like Germany, used to be fairly strict (see, for the origins of this variation in forms and their subsequent adaptation, Martin, 1999).

A set of independent national competition policies is unlikely to be sufficient for establishing a good competition regime in integration areas.[5] Indeed, if two firms in different member states agree to refrain from competing on each other's home market, national competition policy probably cannot do anything against it. Yet such agreements obviously impede the trade between member states. Some form of union competition policy is indeed needed to ensure the fair play of common market forces.

Theoretical effects of increased competition due to integration

The principal *theoretical reason for governments to pursue competition policies* (see, among others, Shepherd, 1985; Scherer, 2000) is indeed the need to avoid the misallocation resulting from:

- static inefficiency in resource allocation: a firm charging a price above the real (marginal) cost of production (because of monopolist power) keeps production and consumption below

the optimum level (with excess profits to the firm and losses to the consumer);
- reduced technical efficiency: firms producing at lowest cost under conditions of competition will begin to operate inefficiently (through overstaffing, higher wages, lack of response to new opportunities, poor management) in sheltered situations;
- dynamic inefficiency: this is an extension of technical inefficiency. To be dynamically efficient requires constant innovation in production and products.

In this way the removal of barriers to competition has similar effects to the removal of barriers to trade.[6] The technical and dynamic efficiency effects are far more important than the static ones (Geroski and Jacquemin, 1985; Pelkmans, 1984). This can be demon-

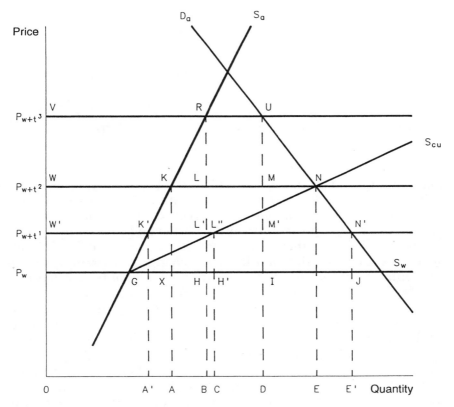

Figure 14.2   Effects of tariffs and improved technical efficiency, account being taken of the customs union supply curve, country A

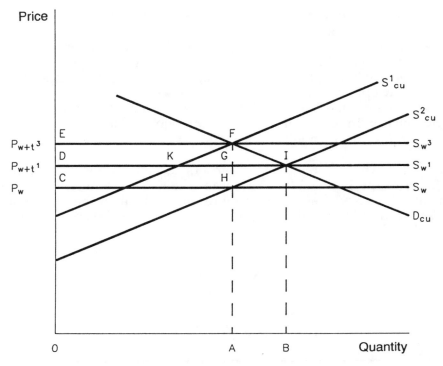

Figure 14.3   Advantages of improved (technical) efficiency

strated with the help of Figures 14.2 and 14.3. The first step in the analysis of the effects on trade and welfare can be illustrated with Figure 14.2, which reproduces the market for good x in country A. Curves S_a and D_a represent, supply and demand in country A itself (see Chapter 5 for the theoretical base). Supply from the world, fully elastic, is once more denoted by S_w. A change has occurred in the representation of the supply from country B; it is not indicated by a curve S_b here, but combined with supply S_a and incorporated in curve S_{cu}, which is valid for the entire customs union. The diagram has been drawn in such a way that the tariff t_2 is just sufficient to avoid any imports from the world market (S_{cu} cuts through N). Now suppose that, before the CU was established, country A operated a tariff of t_3. After creation of the customs union, the common external tariff will be set at t_2, and further lowering of this common outer tariff to t_1 is envisaged. Let us consider the static effects of this customs union; according to the model given in Figure 14.2, the lowering of the initial tariff from t_3 to t_2 would mean that total demand in A is now satisfied by supply from the customs union.

This implies a trade-creation effect of *KRL* and a trade-expansion effect of *MUN*, against a trade-diversion effect of *HLMI*. As the area of the latter is about equal in size to the combined areas of *KRL* and *MUN*, this customs union would be about welfare-neutral. Reducing the tariff further to t_1, triggering off an import quantity *A'C* from the partner country and *CE'* from the world market, would be highly welfare-creating, as the combined areas *K'RL'* and *M'UN'* clearly outweigh the area *XK'L"H'* (*A'C* being the trade diversion from W to B).

Now this is not the whole story. Manufacturers in A, finding themselves confronted by a great loss of sales markets (from *OB* with tariff t_3 to *OA'* with tariff t_1), rather than accept the loss will accomplish savings on production costs (Figure 14.3). As a result the supply curve of A will move down and the supply curve of the entire customs union will drop accordingly (from S^1_{cu} to S^2_{cu} in Figure 14.3). We have assumed that it dropped sufficiently to permit the customs union producers to satisfy total home demand in the CU under a tariff protection of t_1. The production and consumption effects of this drop in cost are indicated by the shift of the equilibrium point from *F* to *I*. To see the basic change in welfare effects, consider the change in cost of production of the initial quantity from *OE* to *OD* that producers have realised under the pressure of stronger competition. The cost reduction is equal to *DEFG*. This is a net positive effect and not, as in the earlier static examples, a redistribution effect of *DEFK* and a new effect of *KFG*.

Basic features of the European regime

The need for a Common European Competition Policy has been recognised right from the start; both the Treaty of Paris (ECSC) and that of Rome (EEC) contain a chapter on it. The powers in matters of competition given to the EU by the ECSC Treaty reached further than those bestowed on it by the EEC Treaty. For instance, under the former, companies wanting to merge needed the advance approval of the Commission, a stipulation that was unknown in the latter. Over time a coherent EU competition policy has been worked out. The basic features of this policy are as follows.

The *objective* of the European competition policy is to protect the competitive process, and hence the benefits of integration, by preventing distortions of the market process by either private (company) or public (national government) actions. To that end, different instruments can be used; these are given in Table 14.1. We will highlight in the following sections the three EU actions that are marked with an asterisk.

Three *institutions* have in the course of the years developed and applied the fundamental European competition rules: the Council by

Table 14.1   Major components of the EU competition regime

Concerning	Private firms or groups	Member state or public enterprise
Instruments	Cartels* (Article 81)	Anti-discrimination (Article 12)
	Dominant positions* (Article 82)	Equivalent measures (Articles 28–30) State monopolies (Article 31)
	Concentrations (Regulation 4069/89)	Public enterprise (Article 86) State aids to firms* (Articles 87–9)

its legislation, the Commission by its administrative practice and the Court by its jurisprudence.

- The Council's role is limited to the issue of regulations and directives on the general application of the rules laid down in the Treaty.
- The Commission has been given the central role. It investigates violations of the rules on its own initiative or upon receiving complaints from member states, companies, private persons or institutions. When the Commission observes an infringement, it may order it to be rectified. In many cases such actions end with the company or member state's voluntarily changing its conduct. In other cases, where the Commission finds a complaint well founded and the company does not change its conduct, the Commission can order changes, and member states are obliged to help the Commission enforce such a ruling. All firms and public institutions are committed to allowing the officials of the Commission to make any investigations it thinks necessary to gather evidence. The Commission can impose fines, which may amount to tens of millions of euros.
- The Court deals with appeals from the allegedly infringing company. Since its creation, the European Court has treated a large number of cases, and 'case law' has greatly helped to define competition law and to make clear the interpretation of the rules.

The *field of application of EU competition rules* is very wide; they apply irrespective of:

- the company's location, so they also cover companies from third countries operating in the EU;[7]
- the legal or proprietary form, which means that government companies (with the exception of public utilities) are subject to EU competition rules too; to identify possible competition distortions, the financial structure of state-owned companies must be transparent;
- the sectors of private economic activity: notwithstanding the differences in market structure, all sectors are now subject to the EU competition policy.[8]

The European competition policy is *complementary to national competition policy*; the former regards competition from the angle of interstate trade, the latter from whatever angle is specific to it. However, as in all other fields, the European competition law prevails in cases where there is a conflict between EU and national laws. Such conflicts are less likely now than some time ago, as many national regimes have been profoundly recast and have adopted the EU principles (Laudati, 1998; Martin, 1999).

Cartels (company agreements)

The first basic rule for competition (Article 81) bans as 'incompatible with the Common Market all agreements between undertakings, decisions by associations of undertakings and concerted practices which may affect trade between Member States and which have as their object or effect the prevention, restriction or distortion of competition within the common market'. The objective of this article is to prevent companies from re-establishing, by means of market-sharing agreements and export bans, less visible but equally effective barriers to trade to replace the customs frontiers that were abolished by the European Common Market for goods and services. Moreover any agreement or decision prohibited by the treaty is automatically void.

The following groups of *activities are incompatible with the EU competition rules*:

- market-sharing agreements which create protected markets, dividing the EU into sub-markets that coincide with single member states;
- price-fixing agreements of groups of firms that control a large share of the European market;
- exclusive purchase or supply agreements involving arrangements to buy only from or sell only to specified manufacturers or buyers;

- exchange of company information on cost, production and sales;
- exclusive or selective distribution agreements (the Commission's opposition to any form of restriction of parallel imports has been demonstrated in a number of cases; selective distribution arrangements are sometimes permitted if they improve the quality of the service provided, but discrimination against retailers, especially for their pricing strategies, can be severely punished);
- concerted practices whereby, without a formal agreement, partners align their policies so as to result in practical cooperation.

Exemptions can be given for:

- production and distribution: in view of a reduction of structural overcapacity of a branch, agreements can be made on the phasing out of plants, but complementary agreements that are not strictly necessary for achieving this objective remain forbidden;
- research and development: cooperative research or agreements on specialisations may favour innovation and progress.

Dominant positions

The second basic competition rule (Article 82) reads: 'Any abuse by one or more undertakings of a dominant position within the common market or in a substantial part of it shall be prohibited as incompatible with the common market in so far as it may affect trade between Member States.' Abuse of a dominant position can damage either the consumer or the competitive process. Forms of abuse include unfair pricing, exclusion or limitation of supply and discrimination among trade partners (see Box 14.2).

Box 14.2   Factual abuse of a dominant position

Hoffman-Laroche dominated the world market of vitamins in bulk (market shares of over 80 per cent). The company had passed 'fidelity' contracts with its customers, which would give it a permanent position of priority or even of exclusivity as supplier to these customers. The Commission fined Hoffman-Laroche, which thereupon appealed to the European Court. However the Court confirmed the essentials of the Commission's decision, making it clear that the dominant firm may not limit a customer's supply possibilities, nor bar the entry of new suppliers which could put a downward pressure on prices.

Firms may be tempted to acquire dominant positions by merging. Mergers and acquisitions have shown a very different dynamism during the various integration periods. In *the 1972–84 period*, merger activity stayed at a fairly low level. An analysis of the mergers among the thousand largest firms in this period (De Jong, 1993a) showed that the majority of mergers were of the horizontal type. The principal motive for such mergers was 'critical mass': to increase efficiency, obtain a better competitive position and spread R&D cost over longer series. Most mergers involved two firms based in the same country and were oriented towards the national market. Increased European integration during this period did not lead to more cross-border European mergers (Lemaitre and Goybet, 1984) because of differences in management strategies, cultural traditions, government intervention and legal practices. As a consequence, for most branches the concentration levels on the EU market remained stable during this period.

In *the 1985–2000 period*, merger and take-over activity increased very spectacularly (see Figure 14.4). This was largely due to the completion of the internal market, which incited many firms to try to acquire quickly the critical size for effective cost cutting. This has been accepted by the Commission because for many industries mergers offer real prospects of efficiency gains and access to world markets, while competition on the EU market of non-EU firms limits the disadvantages of the ensuing concentration. Indeed the share of the

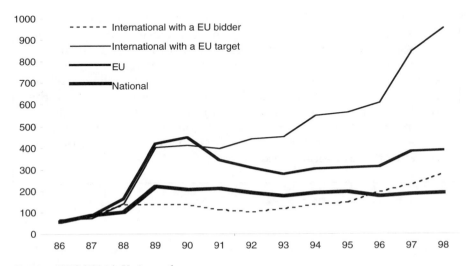

Source: CEC (1996c). Various other sources.

Figure 14.4 Mergers in the EU, 1985–98

largest enterprises in the total of a number of branches has risen substantially in recent years (CEC, 1994b).

The composition of mergers changed in this period. As to branches, mergers involved increasingly firms from service sectors (such as distribution, banking and insurance) that until then were in sheltered markets (NTB). As to nationality, the merger activity between firms within the EU has decreased relative to mergers aimed at obtaining strong positions on world markets. The latter fall into two categories: those that involve only EU-based firms and those that involve a EU and a non-EU firm. The attractiveness of the single EU market for non-EU firms wanting to acquire a position there is reflected by the very high increase in the number of mergers and acquisition operations where a non-EU firm chose as its target an EU firm.

To prevent firms acquiring dominant positions, the Commission has intensified its *monitoring of mergers* (Figure 14.4).[9] The vast majority of the notified cases obtained clearance in the first phase of examination, sometimes only after parties had offered to make changes to their original plans. Some cases have been examined more closely, of which few were actually forbidden (for instance, the merger of the truck divisions of Scania and Volvo; see also Box 14.3.)

Box 14.3   Risk of abuse of dominant position

RTL, the Luxemburg broadcasting company, Veronica, the Dutch commercial television company, and Endemol, one of the largest independent producers of television programmes in the EU had formed a joint venture (HMG) to which RTL's two Dutch television channels and Veronica's television channel were transferred. The case was submitted by the Dutch government to the EU. The Commission considered that HMG would have a dominant position in the Dutch market for television advertising and for television programmes and declared the merger incompatible with the common market.

State aid

Aid is given to correct market failures and to attain social objectives by influencing private economic decision making. However it introduces in turn distortions and hence losses to welfare for the domestic and international economy (see CEC, 1991a).[10] To avoid such distortions, the EU in principle forbids state aid. Indeed state aid to firms is incompatible with the Common Market in so far as the unfair advantage it gives to certain firms distorts trade among member states or damages competing firms (Articles 87–89).

There has been a continuous debate on the implementation of this rule. As state aid is a major instrument for national governments to intervene in the economy to pursue certain important goals of socio-economic policy, some forms of state aid must be exempted from this general principle. Consequently the Commission has defined the kinds of support that are permissible. As such it qualifies aid that aims at:

- regional development; a maximum aid level has been established by the Commission for each problem area; the aid measures have to be public and transparent;
- industrial restructuring; special guidelines have been established for certain branches like shipbuilding, steel and textiles; the Commission insists that such aid be exceptional, limited in duration and geared directly to the objective of restoring long-term viability to firms or to reducing capacity in declining industries;
- research and development enabling companies to develop products and compete successfully on the world market (see Box 14.4);
- environmental improvement ensuring as much as possible the principle the 'polluter pays';
- conservation and development of new indigenous resources of energy.

Box 14.4   Authorised state aid

SGS Thomson had designed a programme of more than one billion euro to acquire the technology of key semiconductor products. The French government planned to subsidise this R&D programme with a capital grant of some 300 million euro and submitted its case to the Commission. The Commission authorised the aid (IP/94/714), taking into account the objectives of its trade policy (limiting the considerable deficit for these products) and of its industrial policy (strengthening the position of EU firms in a sector dominated by US and Japanese firms).

To permit the Commission to implement this set of rules, plans for such aid must be submitted to the EU for prior approval. Controls have been tightened over time.

Indirect influence on prices, taxes

Some theory

In the course of time every country has set up an elaborate system of taxation for generating government revenue and for correcting undesirable effects of the working of markets. The structure, rates and exemptions of these systems reflect the history of a large number of choices about the functions of government in allocation, stabilisation and redistribution. Such systems affect the relative price of goods, services, labour and capital. In open economies these effects are transmitted to partner countries. This limits in practice the autonomy of nations in tax matters; actually, the more the economies are integrated, the more autonomy is lost.

What would be the best response by both national and EU authorities to the new situation created by further integration? (See Dosser, 1966, Brennan and Buchanan, 1980.) In line with the principle of subsidiarity (see Chapter 2), nations should be left with maximum sovereignty and flexibility in arranging their own tax systems. That has induced some to favour full competition of rules (no coordination, at best some consultation), others to favour harmonisation or even unification of tax rules (Cnossen, 1987). We will indicate the arguments in favour of and those against full competition.

Advantages   The first argument for competition is that it promotes the efficiency of the public sector. Countries will be forced to examine critically the quality of the public goods they provide and will try to provide the best service at the lowest cost to the taxpayer. The second argument is that it permits experimentation and quick adjustment. Different authorities, responsible for the operations of different systems, will react more quickly to new challenges of changes in external circumstances than large systems and will more easily try out novel approaches that may turn out more effective. The final argument is that it permits authorities to seek the lowest compliance cost by adapting the system to the exigencies and traditions of the local private sector (Cnossen, 1990).

Disadvantages   The first argument is that competition may yield a sub-optimal level of public goods because of lack of resources and the difficulty of matching taxes with the marginal benefits of public goods such as health (for example, Gordon, 1983; Zodrow, 1983). The second argument is that competition leads to solutions that frustrate equity. Inter-category equity is jeopardised because the high mobility of capital permits it to flee high-tax countries; to avoid this, countries will decrease their tax burden. So competition will result in zero capital taxation in all countries. Consequently the full burden is put on the rather immobile factor, labour. Interjurisdictional equity is put in danger because residents from a low-tax, low-public service country may use the public goods of a high-tax, high-public service country.

The balancing out of advantages and disadvantages of competition leads to two *guidelines for the coordination of taxes* in an integration area:

1   Only those taxes need be harmonised that cause a real distortion in the process of integration.
2   Agreements on minimum levels of taxes should prevent the system evolving to sub-optimal low levels of taxation.

Which taxes should be subjected to harmonisation? The answer to this question differs with the stage of integration (Prest, 1983).

Trade (FTA and CU)   National systems with different levels and structures of indirect taxation (VAT and excise duties) will lead to different prices for consumers in different national markets. That situation may encourage sales of goods from low-tax countries to residents of high-tax countries, at the cost of a loss of government revenue in the latter. To prevent this, national indirect taxation systems are usually complemented by trade controls and border adjustments of taxes. Liberalising trade entails the need for adjustment of indirect taxes.

Production factors (CM)   Differences in levels of national direct taxes, such as the corporation tax and the wage (income) tax (including social security), will lead to differences in net income position of the different actors on the capital and labour markets. To prevent both supply (savers and workers) and demand (investors and employers) moving to countries where the net situation is most favourable, border controls are used. Liberalising movements of production factors means that another way has to be found to prevent distortions in allocation. This is most relevant for capital, as it is highly mobile (OECD, 1991).

Policy (EMU)   In moving towards higher forms of integration, more and more taxes (like the income tax) become Union competences. However policy integration can proceed quite far without further harmonisation of taxes.

EU regime

The tax policy of the EU has followed the general principles indicated in the previous section. Indeed the EU tax policy has been designed and developed so as to serve the objectives of other policy fields, notably an efficient allocation (Neumark *et al.*, 1963). In line with the principle of subsidiarity, the EU tax policies have gradually developed; EU harmonisation has been applied only to those parts of the national taxation systems that caused significant distortions and inefficiencies at the EU level. The involvement of the EU with tax harmonisation has changed with the stage of integration.

Incomplete customs union　In the early 1950s, the workings of the ECSC made it apparent that the differences between member states in sales (turnover) taxes could lead to quite important distortions of the competitive positions of coal and steel producers located in different countries. The report by a study group set up to suggest solutions (Tinbergen, 1953) has actually given the basic principles on which harmonisation of this tax has been based.

Customs union　The Treaty of the EEC, basing itself on the ECSC experience, recognises the necessity of the 'harmonisation of turnover taxes, excise duties and other forms of indirect taxation to the extent that such harmonisation is necessary to ensure the establishment and the functioning of the common market' (Article 93). It forbids the use of such taxes for discriminatory practices (such as high taxes on imported goods, low ones on home-produced goods) (Articles 90–92). Although the major decisions on indirect taxes were made quite quickly, further progress proved slow.

Common market　Already in the early 1960s it was recognised that unharmonised direct taxes could distort the free movement of capital and workers, thus jeopardising the effectiveness of the European Common Market. The member states negotiated at an early stage the abolition of all double taxation of residents and firms. However until the end of the 1980s the EU had not advanced very far towards a fully free market for capital and labour; the problems of direct taxation were not considered to be urgent and received little attention.

Internal market　The white paper on the completion of the internal market identified differences in national fiscal regimes as one of the main barriers to free internal movement; it made framework proposals to see them removed (CEC, 1986g). Although much doubt was cast on the likelihood of success (fiscal matters needed to be decided with unanimity), the major decisions as to the harmonisation that was necessary to abolish border controls have all been taken. However many problems remain, so that the internal market is still not perfect.

Economic and monetary union   The EU's march along the road to an economic and monetary union has not so far necessitated a further integration of the tax systems of the member countries (Brennan and Buchanan, 1980). The Commission has defined three challenges to the taxation policy in the EU (Monti, 1996):

- stabilisation of member states' tax revenues (tax competition between member states should not lead to a race to the bottom; see section on theory);
- smooth functioning of the internal market (see preceding sections);
- promoting employment (alleviating the tax burden on the immobile factor labour (see section on direct taxes hereafter).

Indirect taxes on goods and services: value added tax (VAT)

When the EU was created, member states were operating different systems of sales (turnover) tax. The Neumark report inventoried their advantages and disadvantages. The need for harmonisation of this tax (which accounts for 12 to 20 per cent of total tax receipts and for 5 to 10 per cent of GDP in the member countries of the EU) has been quickly accepted by the member states. At each enlargement of the EU, VAT has been adopted by the new member states as part of the 'acquis communautaire'. In the harmonisation process of this tax a series of directives have set up common principles, structures and modalities of application, leaving considerable variation as to rates and specific issues.[11]

Value-added   The different systems of EU countries like the German turnover tax, the UK (wholesale) purchase tax or the French value added tax had certain common features. The French system of taxation at every level of the process, with the possibility of deducting the tax that had been paid already on inputs, had three distinct advantages. One is that it is neutral as to the degree of vertical integration of firms. The second is that it is a self-policing operation: the purchasing firm has an interest in having an invoice from its supplier certifying that the taxes on the inputs have been paid. The third is that it is a very stable and flexible source of government revenue. The essentials of the harmonised system were adopted in the 1970s and have since been elaborated.

Table 14.2   VAT rates* in member countries of the EU, 1970–2000

State	1970–74			1985–1990			2000	
	Standard (Normal)	Reduced (Essential)	Increased (Luxury)	Standard (Normal)	Reduced (Essential)	Increased (Luxury)	Standard (Normal)	Reduced (Essential)
Germany	11	5.5	—	14	7	—	16	7
France	23	7.5	33	18.6	2/7	23	20.6	2.1/5.5
Italy	12	6	18	19	4/9	38	20	4/10
Netherlands	14	4	—	18.5	6	—	17.5	6
Belgium	18	6	25	19	1/6	25/33	21	1/6
Luxemburg	10	2/5	—	12	3/6	—	15	3/6
United Kingdom	10	—	—	15	0	—	17.5	5
Denmark	15	—	—	22	—	—	25	—
Ireland	16	1/5	30	23	0/10	—	21	4/12.5
Spain	n.a.	n.a.	n.a.	12	6	33	16	4/7
Portugal	n.a.	n.a.	n.a.	17	0/8	30	17	5/12
Greece	n.a.	n.a.	n.a.	16	3/6	36	18	4/8
Austria	16	8	—	20	10	—	20	10/12
Finland	n.a.	n.a.	n.a.	n.a.	n.a.	n.a.	22	8/17
Sweden	18	3/9	—	23.5	4/12.9	—	25	6/12
EU minimum	—	—	—	15	5	—	15	5

Note: *   Rates are tax-exclusive – that is, based on selling prices before tax.

Rate categories   The differences between the EU member countries are given in Table 14.2. All countries have a 'normal' or standard rate for most goods (and services) and a reduced rate for goods that are considered essentials, like food or clothing, or merit goods like cultural services. Some countries also applied an increased rate to goods labelled as luxury goods (video-recorders, for instance). The purpose of this differentiation is to achieve some redistribution (southern member states relied more on (differentiated) VAT, northern countries more on (progressive) income tax for redistribution). The EU has decided to do away with the increased rate and to define precisely which goods fall into each of the two other categories.

Rate levels   There used to be important differences between EU member states (Table 14.2). The EU has tried to arrive at a diminution of these differences. Initially governments were not very inclined to cooperate. High-rate countries (such as France) feared that they would not be able to raise equivalent income from other sources if they lowered their VAT rates. Low-rate countries (such as Germany) were loth to raise them as they were afraid of inflationary pressures. These attitudes changed with the imperative of the internal market. The experience in countries like the USA showed that small differences between the member states do not lead to significant distortions (Pelkmans and Vanheukelen, 1988).[12] The option chosen by the EU has thus not been full unification, but the setting of minimum rates (of 5 per cent for reduced and 15 per cent for standard) with possible upward national variations. This has been considered preferable in the light of the subsidiarity principle, as it leaves member states free to operate their VAT systems in line with national social and economic policy objectives, albeit within the limits of EU regulation.[13] Convergence of rates has been minimal. Between 1985 and 2000 the spread decreased by only 1 per cent (from 12–23 to 15–25 per cent). The applicant countries (CEECs) have all introduced VAT in order to be prepared for membership (OECD, 1998a); the spread of their standard rates is limited (between 18 and 25 per cent). However, major problems do still exist with respect to the taxation of public sector bodies and so-called essential products (Cnossen, 1998).

The present system has a number of drawbacks.[14] Many proposals for improvement have been made by experts (for example, Keen and Smith, 1996). The Commission in mid-1996 made new proposals for directives with the objective of establishing a definite VAT regime before the year 2000. However, progress on this score has been very slow. Decisions in the Council have to be taken by unanimity and a number of very thorny issues have to be solved, such as (1) the reallocation of revenues among member states and (2) the harmonisation of the rates so as to simplify transactions and limit fraud. Finally modern technology poses a problem: the trade over the Internet in digital services (so-called intangibles such as a programme, a video or music that is downloaded) takes place exempt from tax. As this trade develops quickly there is an increasing risk of distortion, as the sale of a video in a shop continues to be subject to VAT.

Indirect taxes on goods; excises

Excise taxes are less important than value added tax to tax revenues of member states (6 to 12 per cent instead of 10 to 20 per cent). On the other hand, they apply to politically highly sensitive goods which, according to many, have serious negative external effects (alcohol and tobacco on health, petrol on the environment). Excises, like sales taxes, need to be harmonised. The systems of excises of the member states had many elements in common, but differed markedly as to the detailed operations (see Table 14.3). Harmonisation measures of the EU (ex Article 93) have focused on two aspects.

Table 14.3   Examples of excise taxes (euro) in EU member states, 2000

Member state	Cigarettes (per 100)	Beer (per litre)	Wine (per litre)	Pure alcohol (per litre)	Premium petrol (per litre)
Germany	7.67	0.01	0.00	1.30	0.58
France	8.64	0.03	0.03	1.45	0.63
Italy	5.54	0.01	0.00	0.65	0.58
Netherlands	6.93	0.09	0.49	1.50	0.63
Belgium	7.49	0.02	0.47	1.66	0.55
Luxemburg	5.28	0.01	0.00	1.04	0.40
UK	18.40	0.18	2.30	3.01	0.81
Denmark	12.45	0.36	0.95	3.70	0.58
Ireland	14.63	0.20	2.74	0.76	0.46
Spain	4.84	0.01	0.00	0.69	0.40
Portugal	5.69	0.07	0.00	0.81	0.49
Greece	5.69	0.01	0.00	0.91	0.34
Austria	6.67	0.01	0.00	0.73	0.48
Sweden	10.36	0.16	3.11	5.74	0.59
Finland	10.76	0.29	2.35	5.05	0.63
EU: minimum	57%	0.01	0.00	0.55	0.34

Source: CEC, Excise duty tables, 2000.

- Adopting a common definition of the products that are subject to excises: the establishment of a European list of products subject to excise taxes has resulted in three categories – tobacco products, alcoholic beverages and petroleum products. Excises on other products (for instance on soft drinks in the Netherlands) have been abolished.
- Limiting the variance of the rates applied for each product: the convergence towards a European standard has been very slow for a long time. The 1992 programme suggested a complete unification. However agreement on a fixed amount in euro for each product proved impossible to obtain, owing to political resistance on the part of several member countries. The Commission then put forward proposals for minimum rates, coupled for some products with a progressive convergence towards an EU standard.

The situation for each of the three main product categories is as follows. For *tobacco* products, some headway was made with harmonisation of the excises in the 1980s (Kay and Keene, 1987). The relation to VAT is close: the minimum excise is 57 per cent of the retail price (excluding VAT) of the most common brands (Directive 92/79). For other tobacco products a minimum excise per kilo has been agreed upon (Directive 92/80).

With *alcoholic beverages*, member states tended to tax imported products more heavily than domestically produced ones, for instance wine versus beer in the UK, whisky versus cognac in France. The Commission in its harmonisation efforts took the view that excise taxes for different products should be based on the rationale of the excise, which is to compensate for negative health effects. Hence the rate should be proportional to the alcohol content. The Court has in many cases ruled against discrimination, considering that all these products were in competition with one another and therefore must be taxed on an equal footing. The option finally chosen is minimum rates for beer, wine and alcohol (for wine the minimum rate is zero in view of the specific position of this product in southern member countries) (Directives 92/83 and 92/84).

The harmonisation of taxes on *petroleum products* has proceeded very slowly. Member countries operate widely varying combinations of sales, cars, road and fuel taxes to raise money for the covering of the cost of traffic infrastructure and the removal of negative (environmental) effects. From Table 14.3, petrol excises appear to be fairly similar in the EU. For all products (unleaded, diesel and so on) minimum rates have now been set (Directives 92/31 and 92/32).

Direct taxes, labour

The harmonisation of the taxes on the income of the production factor labour (wage tax for dependent workers, personal income taxes, encompassing also independent workers, and social security contributions) has not raised much interest in the EU up to now. This may surprise, given their quantitative importance (more than two-fifths of total tax receipts in the EU). For one thing, as we explained in Chapter 7, the free movement of labour has not created an inter-penetration of the labour markets anything like that of the goods market. The creation of the EMU is not likely to change this. Hence tax differences on labour do not cause major distortions of interna-tional relations. Furthermore, as these taxes are not levied, controlled or balanced at the internal borders, the Commission does not con-sider their harmonisation a necessary condition for the completion of the internal market in general and the integration of labour markets in particular, and has not been intent on achieving this.

There are, nevertheless, two reasons for EU action. The first ap-plies directly to the objective of safeguarding the internal labour market and concerns migrants and people who work in a country other than their country of residence. Problems such as the double taxation of the same income and the lack of coordination for indi-viduals who pay taxes in one country and social contributions in another are not removed by the existing harmonisation (see Chapter 7). The second applies to the objective of employment growth (see Chapter 16). Between 1980 and 1993, the implicit tax rate on em-ployed labour increased by about one-fifth, while the same indicator for other factors of production (mainly self-employed and capital) decreased by one-tenth (Monti, 1996). Decreasing labour cost by de-creasing the tax burden on labour should have a positive effect on employment.

Direct taxes, capital

The EU member countries operate systems of capital taxation that are quite different as to systems, rates, dividend withholding and so on. Paramount among these are the *corporate taxes* (CT). The major differences between the national CT (see Table 14.4) are the follow-ing.

- *Systems.* Half of the member states, including all the larger ones, use the imputation system, which gives shareholders cred-its on their personal income tax for the corporation tax im-puted to the dividends due to them. In the other half, widely divergent systems are in use.

Table 14.4   Corporate taxes: systems and basic rates, 1977–2000[a]

System	Country	1977	1985	1991	2000
Imputation	Germany	56	63/47	50	52/43
	France	50	50	34	33
	UK	52	52	33	30
	Italy	25	41	36	37
	Finland	n.a.	n.a.	n.a.	29
	Ireland	45	50	38	24 (10)
Classical	Netherlands	48	43	35	35
Tax credit	Spain	36	35	35	35
	Portugal	36	40	36	34
Special PT rate	Austria	n.a.	n.a.	n.a.	34
	Belgium	48	45	40	37
	Denmark	37	40	34	32
	Greece	39	49	35	35
	Luxemburg	40	47	37	30
	Sweden	n.a.	n.a.	n.a.	28

Note: [a] In many countries there is a surcharge, surtax or a local tax that makes the total rate of CT some 10 per cent higher than the rates shown here.

Sources: Cnossen (1987); Gardner (1992); Cnossen (1996); KPMG International.

- *Rates.* The statutory rate varied in 1977 from 25 per cent in Italy to 56 per cent in Germany. Since 1985, the tariffs have converged, while the average has decreased to some 35 per cent. The rates of the applicant countries of Central Europe (not shown in the table) are largely similar to the ones in the present EU (between 18 for Hungary and 40 for Slovakia).

Although they are not very important in quantitative terms (EU average about 1 per cent of total tax receipts) corporate taxes may cause important distortions, as tax differences are an important determinant in the choice of the country of investment. Low corporate taxes are indeed used by member governments to attract investment. Distortion may stem from national differences in tax incentives, double taxation (by the countries of origin and destination) of income from investment, differential treatment of residents and non-residents and of corporate investments (CEC, 1966; Devereux and Pearson, 1989; Ruding Committee, 1992; Cnossen, 1996). Tax incentives make the effective rate much lower than the posted rate. An idea of the difference between the two is given in the last column of the table. Also noteworthy is that countries with very high nominal tariffs also seem to have the largest differentials, probably to stay competitive within an integrated EU (MAAREC, 1999).

Some *harmonisation* of national tax provisions is needed, for two reasons: first, for a good functioning of the European capital market in a world of highly mobile capital; second, to avoid problems of a fair distribution of wealth due to erosion of the tax base of some member countries.[15] The history of the efforts towards harmonisation is one of many attempts and little success. Even on the necessity of defining minimum rates no agreement could be reached as yet. In the past the fierce resistance by certain member states to any attempt to harmonise capital taxes was justified by their wish to safeguard their sovereignty in this particular sensitive area.

Up until now, the same argument has been made that no agreement could be reached on the EU-wide harmonisation of the *taxation of interest* on savings deposits held in another member country than the country of residence. However, in mid-2000 an agreement of principle was reached, that provides for the following rules:

- Member countries agree that they will inform each others' tax authorities about the capital income earned by non-residents.
- If they do not do this because of their national rules on bank secrecy, they will be charged a withholding tax of at least 20 per cent.

By 2015 this information system is bound to replace the withholding system for those member countries that have adopted it. New member countries will have to immediately adopt the information system.

Access to markets, technical barriers

Some theory

Governments wish to limit market access for several reasons.

- Imperfect information makes it hard for consumers to judge the quality of goods and services, and may also spell material losses and risk to health and safety.
- Production and consumption may have external effects in the shape of costs or benefits to third parties. Environmental damage is a case in point.

To cope with such aspects, governments use various *instruments*.

- For goods, governments mostly rely on the specification of technical standards and norms with which goods must comply (for instance, safety windshields in cars).
- For services, governments tend to set minimum requirements which key persons in a profession must satisfy (for instance, pharmacists and lawyers). Continuous control of a company's financial soundness is another instrument; such prudential control is applied to financial institutions such as banks, pension funds and insurance companies, to whom the public entrusts large sums of money, sometimes on long-term contracts.
- Governments may reserve certain activities to themselves or to (state) monopolies, thus blocking the entry of other suppliers. Many social services belong to this category, along with, for instance, defence industries.

That a free market cannot be created by simply removing tariffs and quotas will now be clear. Indeed states can effectively use national standards like technical specifications to bar the importation of foreign goods, requirements for qualifications, diplomas and so on to curb the free movement of active persons and services, and prudential control of financial institutions to restrict the movement of capital. They have indeed done so in the past, with different countries having developed different requirements for quality and practices of testing the product's conformation to these requirements. Specified requirements and the ensuing technical trade barriers have often been used to protect private interest groups rather than the general public. An example is the telecommunications industry, where the requirements public companies set for the equipment they purchase were such that only domestic firms were likely to comply with them.

Technical trade barriers exist when differing national regulations (specifications of shape, construction or performance laid down or referred to in public law) and/or standards (codifications of shape, quality and so on, voluntarily agreed to) prevent the free movement of goods, or when countries impose duplicative testing and certification procedures on imported goods.

The European Union regime

Goods subjected to technical norms represent about 75 per cent of intra-EU trade. The segmentation of the EU market has for a long time compelled producers to adapt their products to a number of different sets of national norms and standards. As this situation is very costly in welfare terms, the EU has tried several approaches to do away with the differences.

Mutual recognition (some 25 per cent of intra-EU trade)   Technical specifications that are set up as measures of quantitative restriction are
prohibited (Article 28). In a number of famous cases, in which the
objective of the national regulation was clearly to protect special
interest groups in one country rather than the public interest, the
European Court has followed that view. The trendsetter was the case
of Cassis de Dijon (1979), an alcoholic product not conforming to
German liquor standards in that it contained only 18 instead of the
prescribed 25 per cent of alcohol. Another famous case was that
against the German *Rheinheitsgebot*, a prescription dating from the
16th century laying down that beer could only be made from certain
ingredients. In these and similar cases the Court ruled that a good
produced and marketed in one member country according to that
country's national specifications should in principle gain free access
to the markets of partner countries. Only in a case where a country
can prove that 'mandatory requirements' of public interest justify
higher national technical norms than those of the partner country
can obstacles to free movement be imposed.

Harmonisation: the 'old approach' (some 30 per cent of intra-EU trade)
The 'approximation of such provisions laid down by law, regulation
or administrative action in member states as directly affect the functioning of the common market' (Article 94) is a second strategy. Since
1968, when the Commission proposed a general programme of harmonisation, experts of the Commission, national administrators and
external institutions have exerted themselves to harmonise the technical standards for a large number of products, with meagre results,
however. The standards set covered only a small portion of the products for which some harmonisation was needed, small in particular
for the efforts made. The approach has indeed turned out both ineffective and inefficient (Pelkmans and Vollebergh, 1986). The poor
record was notably due to the rule of unanimity in the Council,
where agreement proved difficult to obtain as the experts tended to
aim at excessive uniformity and the specification of many technical
details. This approach has now been made more efficient and is
followed for goods where the nature of the risk is held to require
extensive and detailed EU legislation.

Harmonisation: the 'new approach' (some 20 per cent of intra-EU trade)
The new concept reflects a fundamentally different view of market
integration. From a monolithic conception of the EU's integration
process in which national legislation and powers are replaced by
European powers, the EU has turned to a pluralistic, pragmatic and
federalistic conception in which national legislation is no longer
replaced but framed in a way that respects minimum European

requirements (Padoa Schioppa *et al.*, 1987). This takes somewhat different forms for goods and services:

For *goods*, the new approach is based on mutual recognition of, and reference to, standards. Let us indicate briefly its main aspects. The directives implementing the technical harmonisation henceforth define only the essential requirements with which products must comply to circulate freely all over the EU. They refer to European standards (technical specifications) defined by the competent normalisation organisations, such as CEN, CENELEC and CEPT. Member states are obliged to notify partner countries of, and discuss with them, any plans for new national regulations, in order to circumvent later cumbersome procedures of harmonisation. All matters are decided on in the Council by qualified majority. Each member state must give free access to any product manufactured according to the European standards; restrictions based on public interest may no longer be invoked.

For *services*, the new approach is based on recognition of the quality of control in the home country. The segmentation of service markets is due to national regulations concerning products (insurance products, among others) but also to the prudential control exerted by national authorities on all establishments located in their territory. Of course this presupposes a minimum standard of surveillance.

Welfare effects

In the *early 1980s*, a few attempts (for example the one reported in Hartley, 1987) were made at quantifying the cost of the remaining non-tariff barriers and formalities at the internal borders of the EC and the other imperfections of the internal market (termed 'cost of non-Europe' by Albert and Ball, 1983). They could only provide a very limited and fragmentary view of the problem.

In the *late 1980s* the Commission tried to establish a more complete picture of the welfare gains to be obtained from the removal of the remaining obstacles.[16] In this ex-ante study a distinction was made between three types of effects:

- *Border control removal*. In economic terms, the cost of administration of both importers and exporters, and the cost of delays for transporters are similar to tariffs that impede trade.
- *Market entry and competition effects*. The short-term effect is that prices will drop to the level of the most efficient producer in the EU. The long-term effect is the further reduction of cost through enhanced innovation and learning effects.
- *Economies of scale*. As competition leads industries to restruc-

ture, closing down inefficient plants, investing in new plants and expanding output, production will become more efficient.

The total welfare gains resulting from the completion of the internal market of the EU were estimated at some 6 per cent of GDP, provided the right macro-economic policies were carried out.

In the *mid-1990s*, the Commission made an ex-post evaluation of the effects of the completion of the internal market (CEC, 1996a). It has thereby distinguished between two major effects:

- Allocation (this encompasses the three effects mentioned in the ex-ante study). The improvement of efficiency has been calculated for individual markets (for example, goods, capital) and industries (for example, manufacturing).
- Accumulation: the effect of the transformation on the improvement of the productivity of the production factors of the entire economy.

Improved allocation was shown to have led to significant reductions in price–cost margins. The 1992 programme has led to important welfare improvements as the efficiency gains more than compensated for the initial losses due to restructuring (Allen *et al.*, 1996, 1998; Bottasso and Sembenelli 2001). The total effect for the whole economy has been studied with some macro-economic models (CEC, 1996a) and found to be in the order of 1 per cent of GDP, each of the two effects accounting for about half of 1 per cent. The effect on employment is somewhat less, as a result of important productivity increases. However, as some of the medium-term effects have not yet materialised, the impression is that the growth bonus from the completion of the internal market will become significantly higher.

Summary and conclusions

- The main rationale for the European economic integration is the enhancement of allocational efficiency; the main instrument to achieve it is the liberalisation of markets.
- In addition to liberalisation measures, the EU has introduced new regulations in order to create the conditions for the proper functioning of markets, the most important being the very elaborate EU competition policy. Other European policies that have been developed concern technical norms and taxation, notably value added tax.
- In the 1960s and 1970s, the internal market remained incomplete. In the 1980s and early 1990s, a new programme suc-

ceeded in bringing about the complete abolition of all controls at internal borders on goods, services, workers and capital. This programme had substantial positive welfare effects.

Notes

1 The other side of the coin of indirect influences is subsidies. As these apply rather to production than to products, they are dealt with under competition policy.

2 As argued in Chapter 16, regulation on the labour market may actually enhance growth. Regulation brings confidence in the stability of conditions over time and thereby facilitates investment in human capital (and therefore improvement of production factors). Moreover it facilitates consultation between social partners and the government and thereby limits industrial disputes.

3 Governments intervene to smooth the continuous restructuring that marks modern economies, implying the balanced phasing out of old industries, the optimisation of the production environment of mature industries and the support for the creation and development of new activities. At the first stage of new products, public intervention may be beneficial because the market is not well informed, the risks are considered too high for the participants, or the socio-economic cost/benefit ratio is greater than one while the private one is not, or not sufficiently (externalities). At the second stage of growing product volumes, disturbances may arise from uncoordinated private decision making (overcapacities); the cost of adjusting capacities to demand levels may be minimised by government intervention. Finally, at the recession stage, the public authorities can steer the sector through the rough waters of capacity reduction.

4 National governments had three major reasons for such intervention.

- The need to comply with technical standards and norms adopted by some countries for environmental reasons or to protect consumers or workers. Related to this are the controls of movements of plants and animals to check whether they come up to national health standards.
- Different levels of indirect taxation. Goods need to be checked to establish the amount of VAT or excise duties to be levied in the country of destination.
- Public security measures, giving rise to personal checks at the internal borders (illegal immigrants, criminals, terrorists).

However the European Union itself has also contributed to the segmentation of the European Market in national markets:

- The Monetary Compensatory Amounts of the Common Agricultural Policy have for some time effectively let the unity of the market disintegrate.
- Multi-Fibre Agreement: the insufficiency of the Common External Policy has led to an elaborate system of national quotas for so-called 'sensitive' products.

5 See, for an introduction to the theory and a review of the competition policies practised by the EU countries (and a comparison with those of the USA and Japan), Shaw and Simpson (1987).

6 The same effect can be achieved, of course, by potential competition; when

existing suppliers fear that potential new suppliers have easy access to the market, they will set their prices with more care. (This contestable-market theory is elaborated by Baumol *et al.*, 1982.)

7   The external dimension of EU competition policy has recently been enlarged to the European Economic Area (so including EFTA). The association agreements with Eastern European countries also contain a section on competition. Moreover the Commission has made a cooperation agreement on competition with the US authorities.

8   In the past many branches of the telecommunication, transport, bank and insurance and energy sectors were practically removed from competition policy. Deregulation, privatisation and the opening of markets in the framework of the 1992 programme have brought them into EU-wide competition and hence under the EU competition rules. Specific rules still exist for agriculture, transport and coal and steel.

9   Preventive merger control was made possible by the 1990 Merger Regulation. A good overview of the foundations of EU merger policy in terms of economic advantages and disadvantages of mergers is given by Jacquemin (1991) and Neven *et al.* (1993); for a broader treatment, see OECD (1984b) and, for the dynamics of the international merger process in the past, see Mueller (1980) and Cooke (1988).

10   In the past, state aids in the EU have amounted to some 2–3 per cent of total GDP. This is double the Japanese level and even four times the US level. Over the past decade, the amount of state aid as a percentage of EU GDP has gradually decreased.

11   This harmonisation programme was prompted, not only by the need to remove distortions in the working of the customs union, but also by the wish to have a comparable base for the calculation of the contribution of member states to the budget (see Chapter 4).

12   For certain activities where this freedom could lead to distortions, as for companies selling directly to the client by mail, special rules have been made.

13   The need for such leeway had become clear in the 1970s and 1980s as many governments raised VAT to cope with the budget burden created by the economic crisis. In the years 1986–2000 national governments also made such moves for national political purposes. The standard rates were increased by Germany, confronted by the cost of reunification, and by Spain and other countries confronted with the need to fulfil the budget criteria of the EMU (see Chapter 15).

14   One thorny problem is the system of VAT applied to internal trade (destination principle) (see for alternatives Cnossen, 1987). Other problems refer to the goods that fall under categories of zero rating and exemptions etc (OECD, 1998a).

15   The external openness of the EC capital markets (Chapter 8) implies that not only EU but also worldwide harmonisation is called for (Giovannini, 1989; OECD, 1991).

16   The results of a series of detailed sectoral studies have been put together in three volumes: (1) a scientific report (Emerson *et al.*, 1988); (2) a volume containing the executive summaries of the detailed reports (CEC, 1988d); and (3) a more popular book, which became known as the Cecchini *et al.* (1988) Report, after the chairman of the working group.

15 Stabilisation: Economic and Monetary Union

Introduction

The progress along the road from free trade area to full union takes in the station of Economic and Monetary Union (EMU). We recall (Chapter 2) that such a union implies, on the monetary side a single currency. On the economic side policies that sustain the internal market and the monetary union. One implication of this is the need for coherence of the budgetary policies of member states.

The policy integration needed for a monetary union has mostly to do with stabilisation. The purpose of stabilisation policies is to cushion the effects of internal and external shocks to the economy. An example is the intervention of monetary authorities in foreign exchange markets when speculations tend to put these out of alignment with fundamental economic factors. Budgetary policies to soften the effects of the business cycle on economic activity are another example. The latter, however, need to be dovetailed with anti-inflationary policies in order to retain consistency with monetary policy. As integration of markets erodes the possibility for independent national policies, stabilisation is an important European policy field. We will discuss this below in the following way.

First we will go into the theoretical foundations. The main rationale for monetary integration is that it smoothens trade and investment in the EU and hence contributes to the efficient allocation of resources. Now, for such relatively small open economies as most EU member states are, the independent pursuit of stability is very difficult. We will indicate the advantages and disadvantages of different degrees of integration.

Next, we will describe the way the EU has gradually developed its economic and monetary integration. We describe the evolution from its hesitant start on a narrow legal basis to the development of the precursor of the EMU, the European Monetary System.

In the section that follows we describe the set-up chosen for the European Monetary Union and the criteria for membership. Effective monetary integration imposes constraints on national macro-economic goals. We will discuss the forms these constraints on national policy take in terms of budgetary deficits, government indebtedness and so on. The EU has set a number of criteria that its member countries have to meet in order to participate in the EMU. We will indicate what the application of these criteria has given in terms of countries that participate in EMU and those that do not.

The next section will deal with the workings of the EMU. We will discuss in particular the independent monetary policy by the ECB and the coordination of fiscal policies of the member countries.

As usual, we will end the chapter with an evaluation and some conclusions.

Some theoretical aspects

The problem: growing interdependence narrows the scope for independent policies

The creation of a customs union and a common market increases the specialisation of the constituent economies and the exchange of goods, services and production factors. As a result, the economies involved become increasingly interdependent, every country being dependent on its partner countries and affected by the developments there.[1] Interdependence has a strong bearing on the degree to which individual governments can influence the economy through budgetary (fiscal) and monetary (exchange rate) policies. For example, a budgetary policy intended to increase output by increased government spending may be ineffective if the additional purchasing power created is spent on imported rather than domestic goods. A monetary policy that restricts the money supply to keep inflation low may be frustrated by price increases of imported goods as a result of wage inflation in the partner (exporting) country. Interdependence of national economies means that developments on the national scale are apt to have spill-over effects in partner countries, each country giving impulses and feeling the impact of impulses in other countries (see Box 15.1, for example).

This situation imposes severe constraints on domestic macro-economic and monetary policies. They imply a reduced ability to control the instruments of policy (such as the domestic money supply under a regime of fixed exchange rates) and to influence policy targets (such as the level of real output, the level of unemployment and the level of inflation). Now private decision makers in financial markets are very well aware of the reduced effectiveness of policies pursued independently, so public authorities have to make considerable

---

Box 15.1   The French stimulation plan, 1981–83

When the Mitterrand government took office in 1981, it launched an ambitious plan for stimulation of the economy. Several policy measures created an expansion of consumption. The growth rate increased subsequently, by 0.2 per cent in 1981 and by 1.8 per cent in 1982. The close links between France and its EU partners resulted in spill-overs of this expansion to other countries. So much of the extra impact on demand and employment was drained away to these countries. Moreover, for domestic policy reasons, Germany pursued policies to cool off its economy. To restore internal and external equilibrium, France was forced to adopt restrictive counter-measures equivalent to a reduction in growth of at least 3 to 4 per cent of GDP. So this experiment (like earlier experiments of France and the UK in the mid-1970s) underlines the incapacity of even large EU countries to pursue isolated policies for stimulation of the economy by reflating demand. The lesson has been costly, as the effect of such independent policies was the opposite of the one intended: instead of providing a boost to growth, the ultimate outcome was a net decline in growth.

---

efforts to remain credible. If they fail, private parties will go on responding to expectations of future exchange rates, irrespective of policy intervention, thus doing away completely with whatever room for manoeuvring there was left to the public authorities. This is particularly relevant under the now prevailing conditions of generalised free movements of capital using a technological infrastructure which makes it possible to move considerable sums from one country to another almost instantly. The enormous sums that private traders can now mobilise, compared to the limited means of monetary authorities, reinforce the need for partner countries to cooperate and in this way to regain collectively the control, which they had lost individually.

The solution: coordination or unification through common institutions

The central element of the solution to the problem of loss of autonomy is, then, policy coordination or unification. This approach finds its theoretical underpinning in game theory (Sachs, 1980; Steinherr, 1984; Buiter and Marston, 1985; Hamada, 1985).[2] The general conclusion of this body of literature is that, in all types of games in which the policy of one country affects (directly or indirectly) the variables making up the other country's welfare function, better results are possible with a cooperative than with a non-cooperative attitude (Fisher, 1987).

The important question arises as to why in practice cooperation is the exception rather than the rule. Steinherr (1984) presented the following reasons for limited progress in the past with policy coordination preparing an EMU.

- *Uncertain relations between objectives and policy.* Players believe in different models of the real world (for instance monetarists versus Keynesians). Even if they agree on one basic model, the quantification of the parameters is very difficult, leaving large margins for error. Coordination can be introduced with success only if conceptual problems can largely be eliminated.
- *Absence of compensation mechanisms.* If, under coordination, country A is not worse off than before, while country B stands to reap large benefits, the scheme is unlikely to be considered a good deal by country A. Better deals may be concluded if side payments are made to countries that lose or gain but little from cooperation. If no mechanisms for such payments exist, cooperation may not be realised. If gains and losses from consecutive games tended to compensate each other, such side payments would not be necessary. However, if there is no institutional stability and hence no guarantee that the game be continued, cooperation is again unlikely to come about.
- *Rank and file.* Players (governments) are constrained not only by other players' strategies, but also by their national parliaments and pressure groups. The need to maintain a balance back home may preclude the choice of the optimum solution in Brussels. Therefore the coordination of budgetary and income policies may be harder to achieve than monetary policy. The latter is carried out largely by central banks, which in an increasing number of countries are politically independent.
- *High cost of coordination.* Negotiations can be long-winded, and conditions may change while they are going on. The adoption of compromise objectives and policies, needed because optimum policies are found unfeasible, may incur the highest costs. Indeed welfare functions are very hard to define, and the weighing of advantages accruing to one group rather than to another meets with conceptual as well as statistical obstacles.
- *Complexity.* Even in a group with a limited number of members and confining its attention to only one or two objectives, the game is already complex. The complexity increases with the number of players (geographical extension) and the number of

targets (extension of subjects to deal with). The difficulty increases further with the adding of objectives with different time horizons. So the feasibility of coordination depends critically on the limitation of the number of targets.

We can cite one more reason:

- *Lack of awareness of loss of autonomy.* Countries that have traditionally pursued an independent policy tend to be slow to realise that increased international integration erodes the effectiveness of such policies.

The conclusion that can be drawn from this analysis is that the setting up of institutions and the acceptance of common rules are important conditions for the durability and effectiveness of policy coordination.

Goals

Stabilisation is not a goal in itself. It is pursued because it brings economic benefits. For instance, limiting the effects of cyclical fluctuations by stabilising fiscal policies brings about a higher growth rate. This growth bonus occurs as short-term stability favours the process of building-up human capital and learning by doing (see for empirical proof Martin and Rogers, 2000). The principal goals for an EU stabilisation policy are threefold.

Stability of exchange rates   This first goal is derived from the higher goal of creating the stable conditions for the efficient functioning of markets. The main instrument for arriving at this goal is contained in the very definition of the monetary union: the definitive fixing of the exchange rates with the currencies of all partner countries or the adoption of a single common currency.[3] It is understood that there is full and irrevocable convertibility of MU currencies, which implies that unlimited foreign exchange is available for all international transactions among MU partners, be they related to trade, services, capital or remittances (essential for CU and CM). The goal of fully fixed exchange rates is not easy to attain, and therefore intermediate goals have been advocated. In one, the variability of exchange rates is limited to certain target zones around pivot rates. In another, a so-called 'pseudo union' (Corden, 1972b) is established, in which exchange rates are fixed but monetary policies are not fully integrated; there is no Union monetary authority, and some doubt persists about the durability of the exchange rates.

Alignment of inflation rates   This second goal is derived from the goal of stable exchange rates; indeed in the long run the exchange rate has to be adapted to changes in the inflation rates between the two countries. So, to keep the former fixed, the latter have to be aligned. The instrument used to arrive at a target rate of inflation for the whole Union is the coordination or unification of monetary and budgetary policies. Obviously, in a complete EMU with only one currency, money-supply and budgetary policies are agreed upon jointly by partners or decided by Union institutions.[4] In other words, the member states lose all autonomy in that respect. On the way to an EMU, intermediate solutions are likely to be found, that gradually reduce the divergence of inflation rates through the coordinated use of policy instruments by member states.

Alignment of budgetary deficits   In order to comply with the previous goals and to make sure that budgetary policies can still play their role as stabilisers in the economy, national fiscal policies need to be coordinated. This will effect, notably, the target variable of the budget deficit. In order to keep inflation low and differential small, budget deficits should be very limited. In order to keep some room for expansionary budgetary policies in a period of recession, without risking inflation, the budget needs to be close to balance in normal times. Coordination may take several forms. During the intermediate stage (preparing for EMU), governments retain some flexibility as to the degree of compliance with the goal, and as to the mix of instruments used. The stronger the commitment to an EMU the more closely will be the coordination of a whole series of policy elements, such as the composition of government spending and of tax and other receipts. The efficiency of the coordination process (consistent involvement of partners) and the effectiveness of its outcome (credibility in markets) depend critically on the gradual reinforcement of the regulatory and institutional set-up.

The route controversies between 'economists' and 'monetarists'

Over the past years, reaching an agreement on the way in which these two objectives of the EMU could be realised has been made difficult by the deep-rooted differences of opinion among experts about the best way forward. Although everybody agreed that the benefits of monetary integration increase, and the costs of integration decrease, with increasing interdependence in terms of goods trade (see Figure 15.1), there were differences about the point where the two lines intersect. The main dividing line was between economists and monetarists. They have different conceptions about the balanc-

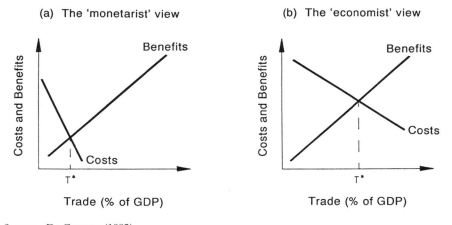

Source: De Grauwe (1992).

Figure 15.1   Two views of cost and benefits of a monetary union

ing of the cost and benefits of the EMU, notably about the cost level of integration (see Figure 15.1).

The *economists* (found in particular among German and Dutch scholars) gave priority to the harmonisation of economic policies, and considered results on that score an essential condition for further monetary integration. Their argument was that divergent inflation rates (springing from different economic policies and the incapacity to overcome rigidities in the field of wages and immobility of labour) sooner or later lead to exchange rate adaptations. If that option is not open any more, some countries may be forced into a very costly deflation which for internal political reasons they would rather avoid. The ensuing tensions will almost certainly break up the fragile systems of exchange rate stabilisation agreed upon. The economists held that the cost curve is far away from the origin (right-hand side of Figure 15.1) and hence that the full unification of economic policies must precede full monetary integration.

The *monetarists* (chiefly found among the Italians and in earlier years also among French and Belgians) defended the view that the use of exchange rates is in the long run ineffective to correct for imbalances. In this view (left-hand part of Figure 15.1) the cost curve is very close to the origin. Monetary integration (fixed exchange rates, controlled liquidity and so on) is the best way to commit national governments to take the necessary measures of economic policy to curb inflation. Their argument was that governments of high-inflation countries will not start adjusting their policies and curb the forces that tend to press inflation upwards, such as politicians (budget policy) and labour unions (wage-cost inflation), unless forced to do so by fixed exchange rates (for example, Giavazzi and Pagano, 1986).

The skirmishes between the two schools have flared up with every step taken towards further integration into an EMU. On several occasions there have been cease-fires (as with the EMS), both parties having agreed to the compromise that the two elements need to be gradually integrated in a balanced fashion.

Participation

Countries that participate in a customs union, and *a fortiori* in a common market, will come to realise that the costs of non-coordinated policies tend to increase. For one thing, the volumes of trade subject to exchange rate risks have become greater. For another, there are larger flows of capital, which tend to shy away from exchange rate risks in so far as they are of a structural nature, but tend to increase them inasmuch as they are of a speculative nature. These costs push CU partners and, even more, CM partners, to progress to an EMU eventually.

The question is then: who should take part in a scheme for monetary integration? In the literature the concept of the Optimum Currency Area (OCA) has been favoured (Mundell, 1961; see also Chapter 2). To identify the group of countries likely to form an OCA, different indicators are used that refer to the stages of integration distinguished earlier (products, production factors and policy). The most popular indicator is openness of goods markets: pairs of countries with high import or export figures in respect of their domestic consumption are good candidates for a monetary union (McKinnon, 1963). The higher the integration on these scores the lesser is the likelihood of asymmetric shocks occurring. Next follows the degree of openness to production factors (for example, Ingram, 1973). Finally comes the degree to which forms of integrated policy with respect to stabilisation and redistribution are realised (MacDougall *et al.*, 1977; Allen, 1983). The higher the mobility of the production factor labour, the more flexible real wages and the more effective the compensation mechanisms the more likely it is that the group of countries can effectively cope with whatever asymmetric shocks occur. To some (for example, Hamada, 1985) these indicators are irrelevant as criteria for EMU membership; to them a monetary union cannot be sustained without full political unification.[5]

The search for optimality for defining membership of an EMU on the basis of such criteria as openness to trade, capital and so on has been severely criticised (by Ishiyama, 1975, among others). For one thing, the scores on these criteria are often difficult to measure. For another, which criterion would be best is hard to say; even a combination is of little avail, as we do not know what weights to attach to them. Finally countries may value their independence so highly that the perceived cost of participation outweighs the advantages of integration. There is also a more institutional reason not to follow up the argument of the OCA. To be viable, an EMU must have a fairly strong institutional structure and real powers. Such a structure is unlikely to be created or sustained among countries that have not acquired some experience with the institutional set-up of less difficult forms of integration. This implies that countries already forming a CU or a CM will be the best candidates for participation in an EMU.

There is a much more fundamental reason why the OCA approach is not sufficient to decide on the participation of countries. This is that the mere participation in an EMU actually helps countries to grasp the benefits of it while exclusion from it makes the meeting of accession criteria ever more problematic. One can compare this argument to the observation we made in Chapter 6 on the participation in the customs union of countries that did not seem to be first candidates for such membership. Yet their very participation did lead, after some time, to very high levels of goods market integration. The argument that the criteria are endogenous has also been developed for the Monetary Union (Fatas, 1997; Frankel and Rose, 1998; de Grauwe, 2000); participation in an EMU actually helps countries to fulfil the conditions for its sustainability. The business cycle correlation may rise with stronger trade ties that in turn are enhanced by the stability brought about by a common currency.

Gains and losses

The question of whether to create an EMU, then, becomes a much more pragmatic one: what conditions must be met for CM partners to realise monetary integration? That depends on the trade-off between the loss of autonomy in certain policy fields and the economic advantages which integration promises, to each member individually and to the union collectively. Governments will give up autonomy in sensitive policy areas only in case they consider the gains from integration will exceed cost.[6] So the identification and quantification of gains and losses becomes the essential point of analysis for the decision to move towards an EMU (Thygesen, 1990; Gros and Thygesen, 1998; de Grauwe, 2000; Eijffinger and de Haan, 2000).

The *gains* can be summarised under three heads.

- *Efficient goods, service, labour and capital markets.* The basic reason for monetary integration is to relieve traders and investors of transaction costs; that is, exchange losses on their international transactions. The second reason is that they take away the uncertainty as to future fluctuation of exchange rates and the fear of competitive devaluations. Indeed uncoordinated policies lead to 'overshooting' in a system of flexible exchange rates, and hence to largely unnecessary fluctuations in trade, production and investment. In general stability will increase the volume of international exchanges. This in turn is likely to improve the financial services needed for payments and hence reduce transaction costs even further. The third reason is that the single currency will eliminate significant information cost and price discrimination that is based on these imperfections. So the better allocation of available resources resulting from these measures will produce welfare gains.

- *Efficient monetary system.* A MU needs far smaller monetary reserves than the group of constituent countries operating individually. For one thing, no stocks need be kept of currencies of other MU members; for another, peak demands for the currencies of third countries are unlikely to occur in all member countries at the same time. Intervention in foreign exchange markets by MU authorities is more effective than individual actions because of the increased means and the unity of purpose. Moreover, the use of the common currency by third countries provides extra benefits to the common central bank; they can actually be seen as a lowering of domestic taxes. Finally the easier management of the system will free part of the resources formerly tied up in it (both with the monetary authorities and with the banking system).

- *Faster economic growth.* The direct growth effects of the improved allocation and better coordinated budgetary and monetary policies will be complemented by some dynamic effects. These stem partly from more efficient markets (that have been discussed in Chapter 14), partly also from a better macro-economic situation (lower interest rates lead to lower budget deficits and to a lower burden on the economy).

The *cost* of monetary integration is to be measured in the loss of production and value added, employment and so on, and stems from three types of problems:

- *Changeover cost.* Both the public and private sector incur cost by the changeover from national currencies to a common currency. For both, these are in terms of adaptation of the hardware and software of administrative and financial systems. The problems are of course more acute for financial institutions than for the other segments of the economy.

- *Non-optimal policy mix.* Many governments assume that there is in the short run a certain relation between the level of inflation and the level of unemployment. Each country that used to 'choose' independently a combination of these two is now forced to accept a common inflation rate, and hence accept a different combination of inflation and unemployment. The costs involved depend, of course, on the form of the curve, the discrepancies between independent national targets and the common MU rates, the time period and so on. These costs can be reduced if partners take long enough to realise convergence of national rates for these two variables so as to realign with the Union targets that bring a definite strengthening of confidence in the long-run predictability and stability of the price level.

- *Rigidities.* Economies are regularly victims of external shocks. Some of these, that affect the whole Union in the same way, and others, that are minor and country-specific, will be easily accommodated. However a MU constrains domestic policy making in response to major country-specific shocks (as, for example, with a sudden fall in demand for a country's exports or a rise in import prices). Adjustment of the exchange rate is no longer feasible, so adjustment will have to occur in the real sector. The cost involved in that adjustment process (for example, the lay-off of production factors) will depend on the lack of institutional and social flexibility of the economy. An EMU may make this adaptation more difficult as the larger transparency of labour markets may lead to wage claims that are not in line with the new situation of international competitiveness, as indicated by cost and productivity.

So the *basic cost–benefit assessment* of monetary union has to weigh a set of micro- and macro-economic costs and benefits of very different sorts. The balance can come out differently for each participant country, depending on the structure of its economy, its past policies, its institutional arrangements (rigidities) and so on. One feature is prominent in all this, however: the cost of monetary integration in terms of the percentage of welfare (GDP) gets lower, and the benefits higher, the more open the national economy (in terms of trade and capital relations) and the more interrelated the economy in policy terms.

EU regime: from the start to the EMU

The beginnings

The Treaty of Rome is not very explicit on the macro-economic and monetary integration of Europe. It provides for some embryonic integration on this score, designed to facilitate the proper functioning of the Common Market for goods, services and production factors. The general *objectives* of the EU in matters of economic and monetary policy at its start were to ensure:

- equilibrium of its overall balance of payments;
- confidence in its currency;
- a high level of employment; and
- a stable level of prices.

To attain these objectives, three *instruments* were to be used:

- coordination of national economic policies, particularly cyclical policies;
- stabilisation of rates of exchange;
- assistance (in terms of credits) in case of balance of payments problems.

The role of the European Union in matters of monetary policy is not foreseen by the EEC Treaty but not explicitly precluded by it either. That is, however, the case for one instrument of macro-economic policy: the EU cannot pursue a budgetary policy (Article 268), as the EU outlays and receipts must be in balance every year. Should the resources of the EU fall short of needs, then member states have to put up the money; the EU cannot, like its member states, raise money by imposing taxes, nor finance spending by loaning on the capital market.[7]

Why was the Treaty so cautious in bestowing powers of monetary and economic policy on the EU? The answer to this question lies in the economic conditions of the period: the Bretton Woods system of fixed exchange rates was functioning smoothly, and the European economies were all at a stage of long-term economic growth, so that all attention could be given to short- and medium-term policies.

The creation of an intermediate stage (EMS)

While European integration was in progress it became apparent, that the coordination system had some severe shortcomings. To cope with the problems more unification than coordination seemed necessary. Several proposals for the realisation of an economic and monetary union were made. At the Hague Summit of 1969 the heads of state and government agreed in principle to the creation of an Economic and Monetary Union, and requested the Commission to work out proposals for the successive realisation of its elements – in particular a single currency.[8] However, due to the considerable monetary turmoil in the 1970s, these plans had to be shelved.

The experience of the European governments in their efforts to cope with the problems showed repeatedly that, for both small and large EU countries, macro and monetary policies had lost effectiveness. The growing awareness of the negative effects of the (lack of) macro-economic and monetary cooperation convinced more and more academic, business and political circles that further progress towards the EMU was urgently needed (see among others Albert and Ball, 1983). Indeed, only a coherent EU policy would permit partners to regain collectively the control that they had all lost individually.

In a period when economists were hopelessly divided over both the advantages of a system of free-floating exchange rates and the best road to monetary stability (see the previous section), a decision was taken by three statesmen (Giscard, Schmidt and Jenkins) to get out of the deadlock. They proposed an incomplete monetary union (see Chapter 2) as an intermediate stage to full monetary union. These ideas have been realised by setting-up the European Monetary System (EMS).[9]

The *main aim* of the EMS was to create *short-term exchange rate stability* in Europe. This has been put into practice by the creation of the European Currency Unit (ECU) and of an Exchange Rate Mechanism (ERM). The ECU was made up of parts of the currencies of all member states and so reflected the whole Union's financial identity. Each national currency contributed a certain part to the ECU. For the national currencies that participated in the ERM, reference parities (central or pivot rates) to the ECU were defined, which also defined all bilateral exchange rates between these currencies. Together they formed a grid of parities. The market value of the currencies changed continuously as a consequence of supply and demand conditions. Hence differences between the real rate and the central rate occurred.

Stability was realised by the intervention of monetary authorities on the exchange markets.[10] They let the market rate fluctuate only within certain margins. In the beginning these margins were small (for most countries 2.25 per cent above or below the central rate) but, in mid-1993, speculation forced many currencies out of these small margins, and some (like the UK pound) even out of the ERM. In order to make such speculative attacks much more costly for speculators and less costly for the authorities, the margins have been considerably widened, to some 15 per cent. In practice, however, the central banks of many countries kept much smaller margins.

The *objective of the EMS* was twofold. The first was stable exchange rates. On the whole, the system has worked very satisfactorily, producing a fair balance between flexibility (daily variations of exchange rates) and stability (central rates) (Gros, 1987; Ungerer *et al.*, 1986;

Giavazzi and Pagano, 1986). Next, more efficient markets. Intra-Union trade[11] and capital movements[12] have indeed been stimulated by the decrease in exchange rate uncertainty (note that an increase in migration is not an objective – see Chapter 7). This result is not surprising; as a matter of fact, the decrease of exchange rate volatility and *a fortiori* the creation of a monetary union has been shown to lead to large increases in trade among the participant countries (Rose, 2000).

The creation of EMU

The EMS had some inherent weaknesses. Moreover, the advantages of the scheme fell short of those of a full monetary union. Under the impetus of the successful completion of the internal market, initiatives were taken to revitalise the plans for an EMU. A committee under the chairmanship of the president of the Commission set to work and drew up a new plan (Delors *et al.*, 1989). The committee was composed of members of the Commission, of the governors of the national central banks and a number of independent experts. It was strongly supported by the business community, which had been made painfully aware of the disadvantages of the monetary disorder (AMUE, 1988). The proposal was the basis for the negotiations that finally resulted in the inclusion in the Treaty of the creation of the EMU in three stages.

- *First stage.* Realisation of full freedom of capital movements. Strengthening of the cooperation between central banks (realised by the end of 1993).
- *Second stage.* Creation of a new institution, the European Monetary Institute, as the precursor of the European Central Bank (ECB). Its main function: strengthening the cooperation between national central banks. Initiation of actions by member states to create the independence of their national central banks and to avoid excessive budget deficits (realised by December 1998).
- *Third stage.* Introduction of a single currency for Monetary Union members. This implies, first, the changeover to the euro by the banking and finance industry, followed by the rest of the economy. Next, it implies the cancelling of the legal tender status of national banknotes and coins (to be realised between 1999 and 2002).

In the debate that led to the adoption of EMU the evaluation of the costs and benefits of the operation in economic terms has played a relatively minor role. It proved very difficult to quantify the major components specified in the theoretical section. The Commission had estimated (CEC, 1990b) the benefits from lower transaction costs at some 0.5 per cent of GDP. The effect of not having an EMU on the high EU unemployment had been established (Gros, 1996) but the positive effect of EMU on growth proved difficult to quantify. On the cost side a number of studies showed that the negative effects of a non-optimal policy mix[13] and of remaining rigidities were probably lower than initially foreseen.[14]

EMU: basic features

The essential features of EMU are as follows.

- A single currency, the euro, is issued by a European Central Bank.
- Monetary policy is conducted by the independent ECB, largely along the lines of the Bundesbank. So the ECB inherits the credibility of the Bundesbank by having adopted the essentials of both its institutional set-up and its policy practice.
- Economic policy is the responsibility of the member states that have, however, the obligation to coordinate their policies (see the following section).
- Monetary relations within the EU between the members and the non-members of EMU that so wish are governed by an Exchange Rate Mechanism. This ERM has to provide exchange rate stability between the euro and the currencies of these non-EMU members. The euro has an anchor role in these relations. The central rates and the width of the band are set in mutual agreement between the ECB, the ministers of countries of the euro area, and the minister and governor of the central bank of the non-euro country. If appropriate, non-euro area member states can establish, on a bilateral basis, smaller fluctuation bands between their currencies and the euro. Supportive policy measures should be taken, including appropriate fiscal and monetary policies conducive to economic convergence.

To date, the practical use of the ERM2 has been very limited. Only two countries – Denmark and Greece – have entered into it, and Greece has left the arrangement as it has now also entered the EMU. Moreover, the major outsider is the UK; the pound sterling has deliberately been kept out of the system and, as yet, nothing has been decided either on the timing or on the conditions under which it will join the EMU. The ERM2 has, however, considerable potential importance, as it will have to provide the stabilisation of the currencies of Central and Eastern European countries in the transition period after their accession to the EU but before their becoming members of the EMU.

The functioning of the Economic and Monetary Union

Challenges to monetary and fiscal policy

The setting-up of an EMU is a unique experience and therefore the conditions for success are not very well known. The theory of EMU is not sufficiently developed to help out. So the EU has distilled from various segments of economic thinking and of policy experience a set of rules about sound macro policies that should be imposed upon participating countries in order to safeguard the conditions for a well functioning EMU.

These have been enshrined in the Treaty on European Union as the *criteria of convergence*[15] of national economic performance (Articles 104 and 121 and adjunct protocols). They make participation in EMU conditional on the member state's meeting the following criteria:

- inflation rate not higher than 1.5 per cent above the average of the three countries with the lowest inflation rates;
- budget deficits not in excess of 3 per cent of the GDP;
- government debt not in excess of 60 per cent of the GDP;
- long-term interest rate not more than 2 per cent above the rates of the three countries with the lowest inflation rates.

In the following sections we will go into more detail into these criteria, discussing the rationale of their introduction, the past performance of the EU member countries and the effect of their application on membership of the EMU.

Inflation rates

A monetary union cannot be sustained if inflation rates diverge. Indeed, as Figure 15.2 shows, in the long run higher than average inflation rates of EU countries inevitably lead to a corresponding depreciation of their currencies. The opposite is also true.[16] The conclusion is that countries need to bring their inflation rates in line (make them converge) with the inflation rates of their partner countries. However, this is not enough. Because inflation has a certain number of negative economic effects, low inflation is a desirable policy goal. So the double objective of a group of countries striving for an EMU must be to maintain low inflation rates that show only a small divergence from the EU average. Let us see how the EU countries have performed on these two scores.

First, inflation rates in the EU have shown wide differences *over time* (see Table 15.1, where the periods are given, marked by events

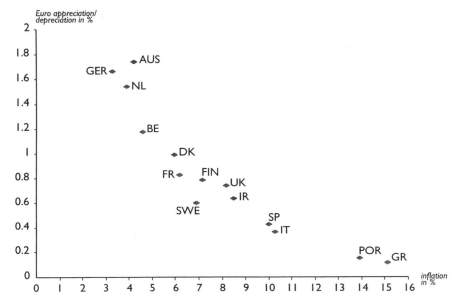

Source: Inflation data from Table 15.1 and exchange rate changes of national currencies to the euro from CEC (2000f).

Figure 15.2 Inflation and currency depreciation or appreciation, 1973–1998

that had a major influence on inflation). The economic crisis of 1973 brought about a tremendous increase in overall EU inflation. Since 1983, inflation has been cut back considerably. Many governments have indeed chosen an anti-inflationary policy. Average inflation has considerably decreased even further since 1993, when the creation of the EMU was agreed on. Since then all member countries have committed themselves to meet the convergence criteria of the Treaty. The highest figures occur now in countries where the labour market is tight (Ireland and the Netherlands).

Second, inflation rates have shown considerable *differences between EU countries* over the period 1973–92[17] and very small differences in recent years.

What are the *causes* of the large differences between EU countries in inflation rates that existed in the past and of the recent convergence? Schematically the explanations can be grouped under the following heads (see for an early overview Frisch, 1983).

Institutionalist: labour market Increase in wages beyond the increase in productivity results in a cost-push. This mechanism is most effective

Table 15.1   Average annual inflation rate (GDP price change) by country and period (%), 1960–2000

Country[a]	1960–72	1973–82	1983–92	1993–99	2000[b]
Netherlands	5.8	7.1	1.8	2.0	2.9
Germany	4.2	4.8	2.8	1.7	2.3
Austria	4.3	6.2	3.5	2.0	1.8
Belgium	3.9	7.2	3.7	2.0	3.0
Luxemburg	3.7	7.8	3.8	3.1	4.3
Denmark	6.3	10.1	4.4	1.7	2.3
France	4.6	10.8	4.5	1.5	1.7
Finland	6.3	12.0	5.4	2.2	2.9
UK	4.9	14.3	5.5	2.5	0.9
Ireland	6.6	14.8	5.5	3.1	4.6
Sweden	4.8	10.0	6.8	2.0	1.3
Italy	4.9	17.0	7.7	3.5	2.8
Spain	6.7	16.1	7.9	3.4	4.0
Portugal	3.6	17.8	15.8	4.4	3.8
Greece	3.3	17.5	16.9	8.2	3.7
EU15	4.9	11.5	5.6	2.5	2.3
USA	3.3	7.8	4.0	2.0	1.8
Japan	5.5	7.1	1.8	0.2	0.4

Notes:
[a]   Ranking by the 1983–92 performance.
[b]   Estimates by Eurostat, March 2001.

Source: Eurostat, *National Accounts, Aggregates, 1960–1985*; CEC (1996, 2000); *European Economy, Statistical Annex, Brussels.*

in countries with a fragmented labour market structure (like Italy). It is least effective in countries with a neocorporatist structure (like the Netherlands), characterised by encompassing organisations on both the employers' and workers' side that involve collective bargaining supervised by the central government (for example, Seidel, 1983; Crouch, 1985). In the 1980s the strength of this factor has decreased as trade union power has decreased everywhere, employers' organisations have obtained more flexibility and many governments have tended to withdraw from political exchange in labour markets (Ferner and Hyman, 1992). In the 1990s the collective wage bargaining systems in most EMU countries have been adapted so as to take account of the exigencies of the EMU. Although the variety of national institutional forms remains, they all take account of the need for maintaining competitiveness in a rapidly globalising world (Kauppinen, 1998).

Institutionalist: monetary   The Central Bank's high degree of independence allows it to pursue effectively an anti-inflationary policy. Indeed, the independence of, for example, the German and Dutch central banks has been found to be one of the major reasons for the good performance of these countries in matters of controlling inflation (Eijffinger and de Haan, 1996). EU countries, while striving for EMU membership have all awarded independence to their Central Banks, which has contributed to the low inflation in recent years.

Monetarist   Price increases result from expansion of the money supply beyond the increase in the total product available (Friedman and Friedman, 1980). This results in general from governments spending more than their income, which is reflected in an increase in the public budget deficit (Cameron, 1985). This largely explains the high inflation that obtained in the past in the third group of countries (such as Italy and Greece). Recent convergence to the criteria is due to the pursuit of strict budgetary policies by many countries that traditionally had large deficits. However, the qualitative aspects of the policies give rise to some worries, as several countries have reduced government consumption and investment instead of social expenditure. The balance between the two has to be improved in order to arrive at solutions that are also conducive to competitiveness (OECD, 1999).

Structuralist   Wage uniformity disregards structural differences, like the dichotomy between a sheltered and an exposed sector in the economy (Maynard and van Ryckeghem, 1976; Magnifico, 1985). In other words, the application of the fairness principle makes every branch and region follow the increase in the most productive part of the economy, notwithstanding differences between sectors (for example, manufacturing versus services) or regions (for example, London versus a provincial town) in the increase in labour productivity. Recently this factor has gained new attention in the framework of international catching up (see Chapter 16). Indeed price level convergence associated with convergence in wealth levels has contributed to observed inflation differences in the euro area (Rogers *et al.*, 2001).

Government deficit, government debt and interest rates

In economic terms it might have been sufficient to specify only the inflation criterion for membership of the EMU and leave the type of measures that are needed to come up to that criterion to individual member states. However, in a world of free capital movements, an EMU is only sustainable if the markets are convinced of the *firm long-*

Table 15.2   Nominal convergence towards EMU criteria, 1985–2000[a]

	Deficit (% of GDP)			Debt (% of GDP)			Long-term interest rate (%)		
	1985	1990	2000	1985	1990	2000	1985	1990	2000
Germany	1.2	2.0	2.1	43	44	61	6.9	8.9	5.0
France	2.9	1.5	1.9	46	47	58	10.9	9.9	5.2
Italy	12.6	10.9	2.0	82	98	112	14.3	13.4	5.3
Netherlands	4.8	4.9	0.6	70	79	64	7.3	9.0	5.2
Belgium	9.0	5.8	1.0	120	128	110	10.6	10.1	5.3
Luxemburg	–6.2	0.0	–2.0	14	7	8	9.5	8.6	5.3
UK	2.9	1.3	0.2	59	40	49	10.6	11.1	5.0
Denmark	2.0	1.5	–3.0	77	67	50	11.6	11.0	5.0
Ireland	11.2	2.5	–4.6	108	102	34	12.7	10.1	5.3
Spain	6.9	3.9	1.3	45	45	64	13.4	14.7	5.3
Portugal	10.1	5.5	1.8	71	68	54	25.4	16.8	5.4
Greece	13.6	18.6	1.9	63	95	104	15.8	23.0	6.6
Austria	n.a.	n.a.	1.9	51	58	63	7.8	8.7	5.3
Finland	n.a.	n.a.	–2.1	17	15	48	12.7	13.2	5.3
Sweden	n.a.	n.a.	–2.3	64	44	64	13.0	14.2	5.6
EU15	4.9	4.0	0.0	59	60	63	10.9	11.9	5.2

Note: [a]   Data for 2000 are estimates by the European Commission.

Source: CEC, 'Annual Economic Report for 1993', *European Economy*, no. 54, March 1993; *European Economy*, Supplement A; *Statistical Annex*, 1996; *European Economy*, Annual Economic Review, 2000; Eurostat, *Euroindicators*, 2000.

term commitment of the governments of the participating countries to sound principles of public finance. Indicators of this commitment to disciplined behaviour are a small budgetary deficit and a sustainable size of the public debt of the member states. The development of these indicators between 1985 and 2000 is given in Table 15.2.

In line therewith, the Treaty specifies two more criteria for joining the EMU: no excessive budget deficits and no excessive government debt. The concept of 'excessive' is not easy to translate into numerical values. On the one hand, one should allow governments sufficient flexibility to cope with problems of different nature; on the other, a limitation is necessary as governments will be tempted to use all the available leeway to avoid painful decisions. There is no way of scientifically determining the level at which these two criteria need to be set. So the practical solution chosen by the EU has been to set early 1990 EU average as criterion for the public debt (which should not exceed 60 per cent of GDP); consistent with this is a budget deficit of maximally 3 per cent.

The durability of the convergence achieved by the member states is reflected in the *long-term interest rate* levels. Indeed these rates are dependent, first, on the expectations of the financial markets as to the future rates of inflation in the country at hand and, next, on the solvency of its government. So a high long-term interest rate may signal a lack of policy discipline in the country in question (see Chapter 8). For that reason the EU has opted for the divergence of the long-term interest rate as an additional criterion for joining the EMU. The development of this indicator has been given in Table 15.2). In practice this criterion means that, observed over a period of one year before the examination, a member state has had a nominal long-term interest rate on its government bonds that does not exceed by more than two percentage points the rate of the three best performing member states in terms of price stability.

Which countries do participate?

At the moment when the decision about participation had to be taken (in 1998) the EU member countries were divided into two groups. In the first we find 12 EU member countries that were striving for EMU membership. In the second group we find three countries that for political reasons had decided not to join (UK, Denmark and Sweden). The countries of the first group had all made considerable efforts to meet the convergence criteria specified at the beginning of the previous section. During the 1998 examination of the performance of each member country it was clear that one country – namely Greece – did not qualify. All others did, albeit with some difficulty, meet the criteria for inflation, budget deficit, interest rate and stability of exchange rate. A number of countries were confronted with a government debt exceeding the threshold value. However, in all these cases it was considered that debt had tended to decrease sufficiently to make EMU participation possible. So the EMU started on 1 January 1999 with 11 countries participating. In the meantime Greece has qualified for membership, and Denmark and Sweden have revised their policies so that the EMU may shortly comprise all EU members except the UK.

It is interesting to compare the practice with some of the theoretical notions we presented in Chapter 2. The exercise of comparing the results of the application of the convergence criteria with those of the theory of *Optimum Currency Area* (OCA) is rather complicated. Indeed, the empirical literature does not give a straightforward answer to the question of which sub-group of EU member countries would constitute an OCA (Bayoumi and Eichengreen, 1993; Bofinger, 1994; Jacquemin and Sapir, 1995). Some agreement existed about a collection of 'core countries' (Germany, France, the Benelux countries, Austria and Denmark). For all other EU members the literature gave contradictory results. As there is no way to determine which of the criteria should predominate over the others, inclusion or exclusion tended to be rather a matter of personal judgement than the result of a scientific analysis. So one can conclude that the result of the application of the convergence criteria is not contradicted by the results of OCA analyses.

The application of the *domino theory* in matters of the EMU appears less complicated. Indeed, if so many countries have gone through much trouble to be able to take part in the EMU it is because staying outside is an increasingly costly option for several reasons. First, non-EMU countries do not benefit as much from the internal market and the single currency as EMU countries (transaction cost argument). Moreover non-EMU currencies may suffer from speculative attacks if financial markets do not believe that governments will keep their promises to avoid depreciations, cut public expenditures and keep interest rates low. This problem risks being perpetuated as weak countries outside the EMU risk being trapped in a sort of misery circle (Jacquemin and Sapir, 1995). They may have to keep real interest rates high, in order to fulfil the convergence criteria and to keep the possibility of participation open. Financial markets demand risk premiums on domestic interest rates, which increases interest payments on domestic debt stocks, which in turn increases budget deficits. The lack of credibility means that higher than necessary unemployment will have to be accepted (de Grauwe, 1996). This set of reasons explains why most CEECs are very eager to participate in the EMU after accession to the EU.

The institutional conditions for sustaining EMU

The European Central Bank: monetary policy

The design and implementation of monetary policy in the euro area is the exclusive preserve of the European Central Bank. The ECB is seconded in this task by the national central banks of the countries of the euro area. The former is primarily responsible for policy making, the latter for implementing the directives of the ECB.

The *independence* of the ECB is safeguarded in several ways by provision in the EU Treaty. The first is by the long terms of tenure that obtain for the members of its Executive Board and for its governors. Next, there is the ban on national governments' attempts to influence the ECB's and national central banks' decisions. This very strong safeguard of the ECB's independence is justified by the empirically substantiated negative relationship between the rate of inflation and the degree of independence of central banks. Finally, there is the prohibition of any financing by the ECB of national governments or EU institutions. The ECB is accountable to the European Parliament for its policy. However, to many observers (de Grauwe, 2000) the accountability of the ECB is not well organised, given the exceptional degree of independence of the ECB.

The prime *objective* of the ECB is price stability. Without prejudice to that objective the ECB shall also support the objectives of economic policy, such as sustainable growth, high employment and economic cohesion among member states. In pursuing its monetary policy the ECB will *target* both monetary aggregates and inflation. To that end it will monitor a variety of indicators such as the monetary base, price and wage changes, the exchange value of the euro and developments in assets markets.

The EU has chosen to use market-oriented *instruments* for executing its monetary policy. Among these are both cash reserve requirements and open market operations. Given the very different ways in which the national central banks from the EU countries have executed their policies in the past, there is debate about the best option for the ECB. In practice, the ECB will work out an original European monetary policy regime. A potential flaw in this system is the division of responsibility for the supervision of the banking system; this is left primarily to the national central banks.

The Stability Pact and the Excessive Deficit Procedure: fiscal policy

Under EMU the principle of fiscal autonomy of national governments is maintained. But the EU has set the scene and the rules for national fiscal policies. So, national policies have to find a balance between two concerns. The first is *flexibility*. The national budgets will be the main instrument for coping with diverse shocks and stabilising the economy. As neither the magnitude nor the type of shock can be predicted, there seems to be a need for substantial leeway for policy makers. The second is *consistency*. Indeed, strict EU constraints have to curtail internal pressures for government spending in excess of income and safeguard the continuous application of rules of sound public finance. Although the consistency criterion conflicts with the flexibility criterion, theory teaches us that national governments do nevertheless have an interest in adopting these rules in order to avoid other more difficult problems (Beetsma and Uhlig, 1999).

Overall constraints make it possible that the EU operates with a limited form of fiscal coordination and surveillance of member states' policies (Gros *et al.*, 1999). Such surveillance implies that the present and future position of each of the member states in matters of public budgets is systematically monitored by the Commission and evaluated in the framework of a set of criteria by the Council.

The form chosen is that of the so-called *'Stability Pact'* (Articles 98–104). This pact forbids EMU member states to run a budget deficit of more than 3 per cent of GDP. Countries are invited to strive for a 'close to balance budget'. The margin between balance and a 3 per cent deficit is available for counter-cyclical policies in periods of economic downturn. This is thought to be sufficient to cope with most shocks, both normal cyclical ones and other more exceptional ones (Viñals, 1994; OECD, 1999; CEC, 1999h).[18]

Transgressing the 3 per cent rule leads to the start of the *'excessive deficit procedure'*. This has two dimensions:

- Prevention. If a member state deviates significantly from the path (that is, a low budget deficit) the Council will intervene in the form of a recommendation on the policy measures to be taken in order to bring the country back on track.
- Deterrence. If the Council decides that an excessive deficit exists, and that insufficient action has been taken, it can impose sanctions. In the first instance, this sanction takes the form of a non-interest bearing deposit. The amount is 0.2 per cent of GNP and, depending on the size of the excess deficit, may be as high as 0.5 per cent of GNP. If after two years the deficit has not been reduced, the deposit can be turned into a fine. The amount of the fine is then distributed among the EMU member states that respect the criteria as a compensation for the negative effects of the lack of rigour of the defaulting member state.

Exceptions to these rules will only be made for member countries that are hit by particular large shocks (such as natural disasters): these are considered to have occurred if the economy of that member state shows a decline in one year of more than 2 per cent of GNP.

Coordination of various policies

Given the absence of the demand policies to cope with shocks and in view of the limited real wage flexibility (Berthold *et al.*, 1999) EMU must be sustained by a careful blend of policies. So the coordination between the different policy areas and the different actors becomes an urgent matter. Recently, the EU has enlarged the scope of policy coordination. It covers now three principal objectives:

- macro-economic and budgetary stability (Stability and Growth Pact)
- improving competitiveness;
- improving the employment situation (Employment Pact)

In order to improve the effectiveness of the policies that are pursued to attain these objectives, the EU has started a new coordination procedure. Major instruments in this framework are the so-called Broad Economic Guidelines which make an inventory of the structural problems and suggest policy actions, both at EU and individual member state level (see CEC, 1999i). Although these guidelines are not legally binding obligations, they can nevertheless lead to effective coordination, as they use three types of tool: first, the setting of benchmarks and the identification of best practices; second the monitoring of the progress of policy implementation and the attainment of targets; and, third, the use of peer pressure on member states that do not comply with the common stances.

Summary and conclusions

- The EU has been slow to develop coordinated (let alone harmonised) stabilisation policies. The recent ratification of the TEU has, however, set the very ambitious target of an Economic and Monetary Union.
- Stable exchange rates were the main objective of European monetary cooperation in view of the welfare gains they bring international traders and investors. The European Monetary System, with its centrepiece the ECU, has for quite some time been successful in bringing about such stability.
- With free capital movement and independent policy making of national governments, it is difficult to maintain the stability of the exchange rates. Therefore national policies need to be constrained by European rules in order to maintain the conditions for stability.
- Countries of the EU that want to participate in the setting up of the Monetary Union have to fulfil five criteria: low inflation, no excessive deficits on the public budget, not too heavy a debt burden, a long-term interest rate in line with the rates of the countries with low inflation, and no devaluation of their currency.
- Convergence towards the threshold values of these criteria did imply a significant policy effort for virtually all member countries. EMU successfully started on 1 January 1999 with 11 countries participating. The euro was introduced at the start of the year 2000.

Notes

1   Interdependence is more than openness. An open economy is dependent on the outside world, but small open economies do not necessarily have an impact on the economies of partners. Structural interdependence is notably not the only effect of integration with partner countries. To this needs to be added the effect of openness on the rest of the world. The vulnerability to shocks from outside the group (such as an oil shock) is changed under the influence of group integration, and an effective response will need coordinated action.

2   This approach has supplanted the more traditional approach to monetary integration, which started from the Phillips curve (Fleming, 1971; Corden, 1972b; de Grauwe, 1975). The latter approach was not very well suited, for two reasons: first because the relationship does not hold in the long run, and second because the approach does not take into account the policy reactions of other countries. Quite a few authors have tried to develop international macro models (Cooper, 1983). However the fact has gradually become clear that traditional economic modelling is not rich enough to capture the complex interrelationships between private and public economic agents, and in particular the role of expectations and the reactions of other countries.

3   This currency may still take different forms in different countries (Belgian and Luxemburg francs, for instance).

4   Evidently the exchange rate with all third currencies as well as balance-of-payment questions with the rest of the world will then become matters of common policy, the Union Monetary Authority controlling the pool of exchange reserves.

5   See, for an overview of the development of this theory, Kawai (1992).

6   We have already seen that similar decisions had to be taken in earlier stages of integration. Countries participating in a customs union waive the right to use tariffs, quotas and other trade instruments *vis-à-vis* their partners, and the right to decide on their own to use such instruments towards third countries. Much in the same way, partners in a common market refrain from using instruments for the control of capital flows to pursue macro-economic objectives. All partners have given up part of their competences because they reckon that the benefits of cooperation outweigh the loss of room for manoeuvre.

7   But even if the EU had been authorised to pursue budgetary policies, their effect would have been doubtful with an EU budget amounting to no more than about 1 per cent of total GDP.

8   A blueprint for such a union was the report called 'The Realisation by Stages of the Economic and Monetary Union in the Community', submitted in 1970 by a committee under the chairmanship of Werner. The Werner Report, adopted by the Council in 1971, proposed the realisation of the EMU in stages, and presented an ambitious calendar, foreseeing completion in 1980. The Werner plan soon proved an illusion. The monetary disorder of the mid-1970s made it very difficult to obtain adequate political support. While awaiting the single currency, a need has developed for a European monetary unit that does not have all the attributes of a currency. Indeed, accepting one of the member states' currencies (German mark) or a third currency (US dollar) as a vehicle for financial transactions in the EU is hard to defend politically. Therefore several forms of European units of account were developed in the past, all of which proved inadequate for the tasks ahead.

9   Over the past decades, the EU has worked out several systems to reduce exchange rate uncertainty among its members (Steinherr, 1994). The first major attempt was the 'Snake' arrangement of April 1972. The widely varying policy

responses of the European countries to the oil crisis reduced the arrangement to a small group of currencies around the DM. In 1979, the European Monetary System (EMS) started. For a description of the genesis of the EMS, see Ludlow (1982); for the basic text, see CEC (1979d) and for an elaborate description, see Gros and Thygesen (1998).

10   The *medium-term stabilisation* of the exchange rates was done by negotiations on the adaptation of the pivot or central rates. A structurally weak currency, that is a currency steadily valued at, say, around 10 per cent below the pivot rate, may need an adjustment of the central exchange rate. EMS countries have agreed not to proceed unilaterally with respect to such exchange rate changes (devaluation or revaluation), but to make them subject to negotiations among all EMS partner countries and hence to their approval. The reason is that EMS countries have recognised both the danger of countries competing with one another by successive devaluations and the detrimental effect of sudden exchange rate changes on the interest of partner countries.

11   Uncertainty in exchange rates has an influence on both imports (sudden increases in production cost through intermediate goods) and exports (sudden fall in a country's competitiveness when its own currency appreciates) (De Lattre, 1985). Although financial markets have responded with different products (forward markets and hedging mechanisms) to cover the risk of floating, short-term exchange rate volatility still entails cost. Moreover, for many risks, coverage is difficult to obtain. This is notably the case for long-run misalignments (Steinherr, 1985). So, many firms remain exposed to such financial risk and prefer exchange rate certainty to floating. There is much controversy about the thesis that the exchange rate certainty of the EMS has contributed to intra-EU trade. Some empirical econometric research gives weak (Cushman, 1983; de Grauwe, 1987), other none (CEC, 1995c), yet other very strong (Stokman, 1995) support for the thesis. Strong support comes also from inquiries among representatives of industry and commerce, which always indicate exchange rate turbulence as a major hindrance to trade (De Lattre, 1985; AMUE, 1988). It is mainly the long-run evidence that supports the case for a monetary union (Pugh *et al.*, 1999).

12   Direct investment flows between EU countries have been negatively influenced by exchange rate uncertainty (Morsink and Molle, 1991; Morsink, 1998). The same applied to foreign transactions in loans and stock (NIESR, 1996).

13   The limitation of the budget deficit was not regarded as a cost (Buiter *et al.*, 1993; Allsopp and Vines, 1996), as it was due anyway for sound economic reasons. An overview of research (Perotti, 1996) indicated that the fall in public demand can under certain circumstances be (more than) offset by a rise in private demand (Alesina and Perotti, 1995). Moreover it permits lowering of the high tax levels on labour, thus decreasing the barrier to enhanced employment (Masson, 1996).

14   There are several reasons why the loss of the exchange rate instrument was considered less costly in practice than in theory. First, a number of countries have already, over an extended period, refrained from using the instrument (for example, the Netherlands, which had a fixed exchange rate with Germany). Second, those countries that have used the instrument have found that it is not a very effective one in the long run. Third, the occurrence of asymmetric shocks in an EMU decreases (Rubin and Thygesen, 1996). Fourth, many shocks in Europe are region-specific rather than country-specific, which makes national exchange rate change an ill-adapted instrument (Decressin and Fatas, 1995). Fifth, some studies found that national monetary policies were already ineffective to cope with problems like unemployment (for instance, Erkel, Rousse and Melitz, 1995). Finally, some authors observed that many shocks in the past

had been more of a sectoral nature than of a country nature (for instance, Bayoumi and Prassad, 1995; Gros, 1996).

15   This type of convergence is also called 'nominal convergence', in opposition to real convergence, which is the reduction of the differences in wealth levels between the member states. The latter is taken up in Chapter 16.

16   These relations remain the same if other OECD countries, including the larger ones, are also taken into account.

17   We can distinguish in this period three blocs of countries:

- below average rates, inflation-shy countries, mostly in northern Europe;
- about average rates (France, UK, Ireland);
- above average rates, 'inflation-prone' or 'inflation-permissive' countries, all lying in the Mediterranean basin.

18   Somewhat larger margins may be needed for coping with very heavy shocks such as an oil crisis or to cope with shocks while being simultaneously obliged to solve major structural problems such as the decrease of a very large debt ratio or the cost of the 'greying' of the population.

16 Redistribution: Cohesion Policies

Introduction

Competitive markets (efficiency) may generate considerable inequality. Government intervention is then required to reduce this inequality by redistribution. The EU creates a need for such redistribution on the European scale. Indeed the EU's main objective is to step up efficiency and stimulate economic growth by integrating the markets of goods and production factors. The structural changes implied (relocation of economic activities, changing composition of sectoral activity) have negative consequences for certain sectors of society. The most vulnerable groups tend to be concentrated, on the one hand, in particular regions or even countries (regional dimension) and, on the other, in particular sectors of the labour force (social dimension).

The EU has taken it upon itself to redistribute funds so as to help these groups to adapt to the new situation. It considers that in this way the cohesion of its constituent parts will be improved.[1]

Cohesion has no clear definition. It is best understood as *the degree to which disparities in social and economic welfare between different regions or groups within the Community are politically and socially tolerable.* Whether cohesion is achieved is thus largely a political question. However the contribution of economics is in the study of the development of disparities and the possibilities of influencing the system in such a way so as to decrease disparities (NIESR, 1991).

In the following sections we will go into the way the EU has devised its cohesion policies.[2] The chapter is arranged as follows. In a first section we will examine the theoretical foundations. Next we will deal with regional and social policies in successive sections. For both we will follow the same approach, which consists, first, of the assessment of the major problems; second, of the presentation of the objectives of the policy; third, of its gradual development; fourth, of a critical examination of some of its major elements, in particular the

395

funds; and finally, of an evaluation of its results. The chapter will be rounded off with a brief summary of the major findings.

Some theoretical aspects

Divergence or convergence in development?

The distribution of welfare among the different partners in an integration scheme is an issue of overriding political importance. The objective is in general to stimulate poor countries to catch up with the richer ones. To that end the factors that determine the location of high income generating activities need to be influenced. One such factor may be integration. Now the answer to the question whether integration contributes towards more or towards less disparity (catching up) is not easy to answer; there are theoretical arguments that plead for and others that plead against (see Chapter 8 for the relationship of this phenomenon to wage convergence).

- *Convergence.* The neoclassical and Heckscher–Ohlin–Samuelson models lead to the conclusion that factor returns (that is, interests and wages) tend to converge when markets are opened up after the creation of a customs union and a common market (see Chapters 5 to 8). However the outcome of such models depends on many assumptions, the most important probably being that markets function properly and that there are no impediments to movements. The model based on the life-cycle of the product may also lead to convergence between the levels of development of different areas in the common market. It comes about by the gradual absorption of skills and know-how in areas benefiting from direct investment to develop production at the middle stages of a product's life-cycle. This permits them to develop gradually their own research and innovation and to upgrade the quality of the production, at the same time increasing the capacity of their productive system to sustain high wages and high profits.
- *Divergence* may occur as the effect of an initial imbalance is aggravated because investment tends to favour regions that have a technology lead, while labour tends to move to areas with the best career potential (in general already developed regions) (Myrdal, 1956, 1957; Vernon, 1966; Hirsch, 1974). This may be illustrated with the help of Figure 16.1. If the environment in country A is better for growth, as the result, for example, of a higher input in technological innovation than in country B, the curve of country A may shift upwards while the curve of

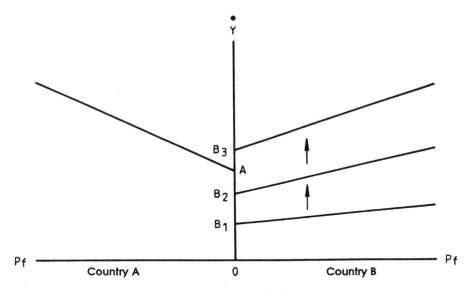

Figure 16.1   Policies for intra-Union balanced growth

country B (B_1) remains where it is. The expectation of a continuation of this trend may lead to a situation where the expected returns on labour and capital are higher in A than in B and consequently where labour and capital may start to flow from B to A (Krugman, 1979). This, in turn, may lead to further dynamic (cumulative) effects.

The debate between the proponents of the convergence and the divergence schools has acquired a new dimension with the new growth theory. Important factors in this theory are market access, human capital, technological change, international competitiveness, economies of scale, institutional efficiency and so on. Theory shows that some countries master good combinations and grow, others fail to do so and lag behind. This is irrespective of the initial situation. The effect is the synchronic occurrence of the convergence of some, and the divergence of other, countries. The outcome of the process is not determined beforehand; depending on the details, the new theoretical models can produce both convergence and divergence (see, among others, Krugman and Venables, 1995).

Foundations for intervention

Because the system, when left to its own devices, appears on many occasions to be unable to achieve a socially desirable equilibrium, governments have devised policies to bring about a more equal distribution of wealth over persons, categories and regions. Traditionally two reasons for intervention are given.

Efficiency   This argument, of an economic nature, says that measures of regional and social policy help towards the efficient allocation of resources by taking away bottlenecks and barriers to development. Total welfare increases, as resources that are badly utilised or not utilised at all will participate (better) in production. Some examples may illustrate this.

- Regional. Where labour is rather immobile, unemployed human capital will not be put to work by private investors unless conditions for a profitable operation in that region (for example, in terms of infrastructure) are met. A government programme for such infrastructure removes the obstruction to development.
- Social. A programme for the retraining of workers for taking up jobs in a new industry after being made redundant in an industry that had lost its competitive position will adapt the human capital to new conditions. Private initiative would not have taken this up.

Equity   This argument, of a socio-political nature, says that large groups of the population feel that inequality is morally unacceptable. Total welfare would increase if the inequalities between groups and regions were removed. Again we may give some examples.

- Regional. Minimum standards of provision of public goods may be set for all regions (for example, number of hospital beds per inhabitant). The government's budget then transfers the money to regions that do not have the capacity to generate sufficient revenues themselves.
- Social. Minimum personal income standards may be set. Transfer payments from the most to the least affluent can take the form of detailed schemes of social security: old age pensions, unemployment benefits, insurance against illness and so on – schemes generally associated with the welfare state. Another way is the definition of basic social rights of workers, including minimum standards for the quality of occupations (safety, health, hours of work, length of paid holidays and so on) and industrial relations (such as collective bargaining, strikes and employee co-management) (Kolvenbach and Hanau, 1988).

The above arguments indicate why government intervention for cohesion purposes is needed. They do not say how much redistribution is needed to obtain the policy goals. To give an answer to that question one needs to make detailed economic calculations, on the one hand, and political trade-offs, on the other (Okun, 1975; Padoa-Schioppa *et al.*, 1987).

Why are Union[3] redistribution policies necessary?

Countries participate in integration schemes because they expect welfare gains from them. However there are also costs involved in progressive integration that may be unevenly distributed. These are different for the various stages of integration.

Customs union   The internal liberalisation and the development of a common foreign trade policy deprives member states of the trade policy instruments by which they had supported activities of certain social groups or of regionally concentrated industries. In the process of specialisation, resources are set free that need to adapt to other occupations. This often entails the loss of expertise, costs of moving and so on. For some countries the benefits may take a long time to materialise, whereas the adjustment costs occur immediately. For others, gains may be quick to come about, while the costs are limited. In other words, costs and benefits may be very unequally distributed among countries.

Common market   The problems are aggravated when the free movement of production factors is introduced, and labour and capital begin to flow to the regions offering the best locations for investment. Now production factors may not always move in such a way as to bring about a better equilibrium. Capital in particular tends to move to those areas that have already secured the best position. Labour may move from low-wage to high-wage countries, but that may entail high social and personal cost. So these movements aggravate the risk of an unbalanced development.

Economic and monetary union   The setting up of an EMU further curtails the instruments available to national states. They are losing, for example, the possibility of influencing the equilibrium with partner countries by exchange rate and monetary policies. In an EMU this requires the moving of production factors (Giersch, 1949; Williamson, 1976; Molle *et al.*, 1993). Furthermore, with the progress of harmonisation, especially on the industrial and social planes, national instruments lose much of their implicit power to control regional developments.

Countries that find incomes sinking below those of others may be inclined to opt out. Although solidarity with integration schemes is not marked solely by immediate economic gains, for some countries the absence of such gains may become a political factor important enough to inspire compensation schemes.

Claims for redistribution are generally restricted to participants in schemes of social cooperation for mutual advantage. This has important consequences. Since such schemes coincide traditionally with nation states, claims can be made only by citizens of the specific state involved. Because for participants in economic integration schemes the boundaries of cooperation tend to extend beyond the national framework, it is logical to extend distributional justice to citizens of all member states of the union.[4]

The effects of integration on regional equilibrium may be both positive and negative. Much depends on the initial situation, the capacity of regions to adapt, the growth effects of integration on all regions and so on (see, among others, Williamson, 1976; Vanhove and Klaassen, 1987, ch. 6; Molle, 1990).

What form could international redistribution schemes take?

The need for redistribution changes as integration reaches higher stages. Higher-stage integration in general means stronger institutions. It also means a stronger solidarity between the constituent parts of the integration area. These factors largely determine the type of instrument that can best be used for international or interregional redistribution schemes (see Table 16.1).

During the *lowest stage of integration* (preferential trading agreements, free trade areas) redistribution is often absent from the policy toolkit, for three reasons: the embryonic character of the institutional set-up, the lack of solidarity among constituent parts and the lack of agreement about the way compensation has to be calculated. If these barriers can be overcome, the next step is a simple system of compensation; payments are made to member states that do not benefit from integration (for example, because trade diversion leads to higher cost to the consumer); contributions are made by member states that are net gainers.

Redistribution in the *higher stages of integration* may use two types of transfers. The first is interpersonal. Income is generated by, for example, progressive income taxes, which means that the rich pay more than the poor. The spending of these funds may be concentrated to benefit most the disadvantaged segments of the population, for example, in the form of social security benefits. The second type is interregional. Poor regions may receive more from the central state to finance their programmes than their contribution to central government income.

Schemes for the international/interregional redistribution of resources under medium and higher stages of integration (customs

Table 16.1 Forms of redistribution at different levels of integration

Instruments/ Integration	Low PTA/FTA	Medium CU/CM	High EMU	Full FED
No action	0			
Expenditure:				
Compensation	*			
Specific purpose		*	*	*
General purpose			*	*
Receipts:				
Compensation	*			
Contribution		*	*	
Taxes			*	*
Social Security				*

union, economic and monetary union) differ as to the combination they use of income instruments (tax, social security) and expenditure instruments (grants, programmes) (MacDougall *et al.*, 1977).

The *highest forms of integration*, like federations, will use the income instruments dealing directly with the individual; these are most effective as federal powers over income taxes and social security are substantial and the federal budget represents a considerable portion of GDP.

During *the medium forms of integration* (customs union), redistribution occurs rather through the expenditure instruments involving different layers of government because (1) expenditure can be tailored to specific needs (including compensation of negative integration effects) and (2) governments are generally reluctant to let unions decide on interpersonal redistribution matters. There are two main ways to handle the redistribution of funds through the expenditure side of the union budget (Musgrave and Musgrave, 1989).

General-purpose grants take the form of block payments from the union to a member country. The underlying philosophy is one of needs. These have to be evaluated for each individual state against a standard for public-sector programmes and the capacity of the member state to finance them. The union has no control over the actual use of the funds thus transferred, which thus risk being used in a way not expedient to structural improvement.

Specific-purpose grants, not having the same drawback, are the most common. Here the union decides on the type of programme that should be set up and to which it is prepared to give financial aid. Its inspiration is of the utilitarian type: such grants are considered to lead to optimum welfare in the long run, because they lead to a better allocation of available production factors to whole sections of the economy.

Structural policies

Redistribution schemes should be designed in such a way as to help along (or alternatively to do the least possible harm to) the achievement of the targets of allocation and stabilisation policies. This implies that they must help to create a viable base for future-oriented economic activities. Examples of this type are financial aid programmes for specific social groups, designed to retrain workers who have become redundant because of the structural changes of the economy due to integration. While such schemes are mostly short-term, others are of a structural nature. An example of the latter is a programme for the improvement of the infrastructure in regions that are far below the average level of development, aimed at creating the conditions required for self-sustained regional growth.

The rationale for and the equalisation effect of such structural policies are illustrated by Figure 16.1. Suppose income growth ($\dot{y}$) is determined completely by increases in production factor availability and productivity, together called p_f. Suppose further that country B is not only a slow-growth but also a low-level income country (OB_1), while country A is not only a fast-growth but also a high-level income country (OA). To make income levels in the Union converge, the curve of country B has to move upwards, with the intercept moving from point OB_1 through OB_2 to OB_3, which is beyond point OA (the structural growth in country A).

Disparities between nations and regions

Assessing the national disparities

The disparity in regional wealth levels is to a large extent determined by the disparities that exist between the countries of the EU (row 3 in Table 16.2). Some member states are relatively poor: GDP per head levels in Greece and Portugal stood at about 50 per cent of the EU average in the 1990s. The underlying factors, such as resources, the level of schooling of the labour force, the access to markets and, in particular, the social and economic institutional infrastructure, are national rather than regional characteristics. So the improvement of national factors is an important condition for the catching up of the lagging countries and, subsequently, regional cohesion.

Table 16.2   Indices[a] of regional disparities of wealth in EU15, 1950–90

		1950	1960	1970	1980	1990
1	disparity among regions	0.124	0.100	0.079	0.058	0.057
2	disparity among countries	0.096	0.080	0.063	0.043	0.040
3	2 : 1 in %	77	80	80	75	70

Note: [a]   Theil indices of Gross Regional Product by head of population based on exchange rates.

Source: Molle *et al.* (1980); Molle (1990): additional estimates based on various Eurostat and national publications.

The objective of the EU is the *constant improvement of the living and working conditions of the European peoples* and reducing the differences between the various countries. In practical terms this means, first, the fostering of economic growth for all countries and, second, the convergence of wealth levels among member countries. The EU has achieved these two targets.

Growth   The average growth of the Gross Domestic Product for the countries that now make up the EU15 was almost 3 per cent a year over the second half of the 20th century. The pace was different in different periods. First there was a long period of high and stable growth (4 per cent a year) that lasted up to the first oil crisis. This coincided with the first extension. Next there was a period of adjustment, with low growth (less than 2 per cent a year); the end of this period coincided with the second extension. Finally the period from 1985–2000 has shown somewhat more dynamism (a growth rate of 2.5 per cent a year).

Convergence of wealth[5] (see Table 16.3)   Immediately after the Second World War, some of the countries now making up the EU15 were rather poor (Portugal, Greece and Spain, to a lesser extent Italy, and initially also Germany) while others (Belgium, Denmark, the UK and France) were relatively well off. Differences in wealth in 2000 were much less marked than those in 1950. Indeed, much of this divergence had already disappeared in the 1950–80 period. This was due on the one hand to higher than average growth rates for member countries with an income level below the EU average. On the other hand, growth in Belgium and in the UK was below average (Kaldor,

Table 16.3　**Development of GDP/P (EU15 = 100), for the 15 EU member countries, 1950–2000[a]**

Country	Level (index)				
	1950 euro	1990 euro	2000 euro	1990 PPP	2000 PPP
Germany[b]	93	125	111	116	106
France	136	111	106	109	101
Italy	71	101	89	102	99
Netherlands	100	100	111	100	113
Belgium	166	104	106	105	111
Luxemburg	201	149	191	150	180
UK	140	89	113	99	102
Denmark	153	132	142	104	117
Ireland	81	71	112	74	114
Spain	35	69	67	77	82
Portugal	35	37	49	61	76
Greece	30	43	52	58	67
Austria	58	109	112	105	112
Sweden	170	142	122	108	103
Finland	114	143	110	102	101
EU15	100	100	100	100	100

Notes:
PPP = purchasing power parities.
[a]　Estimate.
[b]　In 2000, inclusive of former DDR.

Source:　*OECD National Account Statistics*, several years; Eurostat, *National Accounts (ESA) Review*, several years; *Statistics in Focus 1996/5*. National figures on GDP made comparable with exchange rate figures; EC, *European Economy*, No. 70, 2000, Tables 8 and 9.

1966; Hudson and Williams, 1986; Boltho, 1982). A case to highlight is Ireland which has successfully fought its way into the league of above average countries over the past decades. However, a quite important deficit in wealth level still persists for the three Mediterranean countries that joined in the 1980s.

The *causes of convergence of national wealth* within the EU are complex. Integration has played a major part with respect to several determinant factors. We distinguish between the following.

Markets: production structure

- *Goods.* Market access for products is an essential prerequisite for growth. The dynamic effects of the liberalisation of international trade in goods appear through the structural adaptation of firms. Access to markets has resulted in the catching up of low-income countries. Illustrative in this respect is the Italian white goods industry which was capable of exploiting its innovation advantages through the access it gained to the markets of other member countries (Owen, 1983). The completion of the internal market has favoured growth in the cohesion countries (Spain, Portugal, Greece and Ireland); the GDP of this group was in 1993 some 10 per cent higher than it would have been had the pre-1987 growth trends continued (CEC, 1996d).
- *Labour.* When the EU was formed a substantial migration of labour took place from the poorer countries in the south to the richer countries of northern Europe (see Chapter 7). After some time, return migration occurred. Internal migration in the EU has since been on a relatively low level. Labour migration has therefore not contributed very much to convergence.
- *Capital.* The most important category of capital movement in this respect is direct investment (DI). An analysis of the flows of DI in the EU does indeed show that these contributed to convergence: the 'poorer' member states are net importers of DI, while the 'richer' member states are net exporters (Chapter 8). This investment, triggered by European integration and accompanied by the transfer of technical and managerial skills, has helped the catching-up process.

Policies: production environment

- *Infrastructure.* This is one of the major determinant factors for growth (OECD, 1995d, 1995e). Large EU funds have gone into infrastructure improvement (transport, energy, telecom). Recently this aspect has received more attention with the setting up of the Trans-European Networks (see Chapter 13).
- *Institutions and regulation.* Individuals and firms with similar interests tend to group together to obtain advantages for themselves at the expense of other groups of society, or of society as a whole (Olson, 1983). By their collective action, special-interest groups reduce overall efficiency and hence aggregate income and growth.[6] Integration introduces new competitors that challenge the positions created prior to the integration by special-interest groups. Collusion of firms under sanction of the government becomes more difficult, trade union power in

sheltered industries is diminished by competition from outside, and so on. The access to the EU has had a very clear influence on the relatively high growth figures of France in the 1960–73 period (Hennart, 1983), of Ireland in the 1973–85 period and of Ireland, Spain and Portugal in recent years (CEC, 1996d).

Assessing the regional problems[7]

The European Union shows a considerable diversity in regional situations. For many regions these do not give rise to particular concern at the European level. For others they tend, however, to become particularly difficult, resulting from deficiencies in the infrastructure, production sector, labour-force qualifications and so on. The considerable differences in economic development between member countries, and between the regions of each of these countries, have a negative effect on cohesion. To approximate the development of cohesion, one can follow over time the development of indicators on the *disparity between member countries and regions*. Examples are the level of income per capita, the productivity per working person, and the availability and accessibility of jobs, environmental goods, cultural infrastructure, leisure activities and so on.

The disparity in income per head among the European regions is generally accepted as the key indicator of cohesion. The 10 most favoured regions in the European Union are three times 'richer' than the 10 'poorest' (measured in GDP per head,[8] but also by level of infrastructure, capital endowment and so on). This difference will increase very considerably with the imminent eastern extension of the Union.

The disparity between all European regions decreased considerably over the period of analysis (first row of Table 16.2; results confirmed by other studies such as Barro and Sala-I-Martin, 1991). This tendency towards convergence also prevailed in all major EU countries (Molle and Boeckhout, 1995; Sala-I-Martin, 1996).[9] However, from the end of the 1980s onwards, the tendency came to a halt, and recently disparities between regions have even tended to increase (CEC 2001).

The *causes of this decrease in disparity* can be found to a large extent in the decrease in the differences in wealth between countries (rows 2 and 3 of Table 16.2; see next section). On the regional level, the most important causal factors have been the following:

Market

- Goods:[10] the impact of market integration on regions has been studied notably in the framework of the final part of it, that is the completion of the internal market. Most studies have emphasised the diversity of the sectoral and regional effects (Molle, 1990, Bachtler and Clement, 1992; CEC, 1996d).

- Capital: direct investment has gone from central to peripheral areas of the member countries (see Klaassen and Molle, 1982).
- Labour: the migration of workers was rather neutral in most countries.

Policy

- Regional policy: aid to problem regions has stimulated growth there; after integration more resources have been made available (see subsequent section).
- The creation of the welfare state: the provision of such welfare services as schools, hospitals, transfer payments and social security systems has strengthened the economic base of the less affluent regions (Molle, 1986). Here integration has not yet had much influence (see section on social policy).

The ranking of European regions by their level of prosperity evidences a remarkable stability. Indeed, throughout the 1950–2000 period, the 'peripheral' regions of Mediterranean countries were always in the lowest positions, while some urban regions in northern Europe were consistently at the top. Only two significant shifts in the first half of this period are recorded: (1) all German regions moved strongly upward; and (2) all regions of the UK and Belgium fell back.

Regional policy

Policy objectives

The unequal distribution of welfare over regions has obliged both national and European authorities to intervene. To obtain maximum effect, the European regional policy is conducted in cooperation with the member states; indeed EU regional policy is not a substitute for, but a complement to, the national regional policies. The *main objective* of European regional policy is twofold:

- to improve the situation in existing problem regions. Many regional problems are very deep-rooted and hence require structural policy actions that are maintained over several decades.
- to prevent new regional disparities that could result from structural changes in the European and world economy. Some of

these are due to integration, others are the result of the continuous changes that occur in technology, in environment, in social values and in world politics.

The *arguments* for the EU regional policy follow the theoretical ones we have indicated before:

Efficiency   The economic argument for a European regional policy has been central in each of the stages of its development. An example from the crisis period of the late 1970s may be illustrative in this respect. The lack of alternative activities in 'steel regions', where substantial cutbacks in employment were necessary, has induced certain member states to give heavy support to the established industry, to which other member states responded by threatening to close their frontiers to these subsidised products. Now that would mean a direct violation of the founding principles of the EU (free market and international specialisation), so the lack of an effective regional policy to help the regions develop new activities put the very functioning of the EU in jeopardy.

Equity   The social argument for European regional policy has only gradually come to the fore. Until the mid-1980s, neither the social dimension (see, for instance, Vandamme, 1986) nor the public support for a fiscal contribution to assist regional development in a different EU member country had developed much (CEC, 1980). The EU now puts more emphasis on social and human aspects as necessary complements to purely economic ones.

Gradual development

The European regional policy has developed gradually under the influence of progressive deepening and widening. The major stages, that follow in practice the theoretical model of Table 16.1, can be described as follows:

- *1955–75*. Regional imbalances were already being debated at the Messina Conference. The fathers of the EU were well aware of the regional problems; this is evident from the preamble of the Treaty of Rome, according to which the member states were 'anxious to reduce the differences existing between the various regions and the backwardness of the less favoured regions'. In spite of warnings by academics (such as Giersch, 1949) that European integration spelled problems for certain regions, the EEC Treaty made no provisions for a European regional policy in the proper sense. However, during the functioning of the

Common Market, such problems did indeed arise (for example, with coal and steel regions like Wallonia).

- *1975–85.* The northern enlargement of the EU increased the regional imbalances. The UK, afraid of losing out to its continental competitors, on the one hand, and of an unfavourable distribution of receipts from and payments to the EU budget, on the other, had obtained in the negotiations of accession an assurance that a European regional policy would be set up. This was realised in the second half of the 1970s. Large sums of money were put into a distribution scheme using specific-purpose grants as the instrument (CEC, 1985h).

- *1985–93.* Two factors caused a further stepping up of the regional policy efforts. The first was the drive towards more allocative efficiency through the completion of the internal market. The second was the enlargement with three less developed new member states. To improve the economic and social cohesion in a wider and deeper EU, the resources devoted to cohesion were doubled, the target groups restricted, the procedures improved and the instruments refocused (CEC, 1990a).

- *1993–2000.* Similar factors played a role in the 1990s. Deepening concerned the setting up of the EMU and coping with international developments like the further decrease of external trade protection (Uruguay round). To deal with the EMU effect, a cohesion fund was set up (with a gradual shift of specific purpose to general purpose grants). Widening concerned notably the integration of the new German *Bundesländer*. The extension with three EFTA countries did not constitute a major new challenge for EU regional policy, given their relative wealth. To deal with these new challenges, the resources devoted to structural adaptation have been stepped up again.

- *2000–2006.* The future enlargement of the EU with a number of CEECs will considerably increase the demands on the EU budget for cohesion. That implies that the present funds need to be better used. To that end the new regulation of the Structural Funds (1260/1999) first limits the number of objectives and targets.[11] Moreover, the regulation improves the institutional set-up: each member state has to designate one managing authority that is responsible for supervising the implementation. Finally, the financial control system has been tightened.

Summarising these developments we may say that the EU set out without sufficient authority in regional matters, that it has gradually acquired the necessary instruments, and that now the regional element occupies a prominent place among the European policy areas.

Coordination between the EU, nation states and regions

All countries in Western Europe have taken up regional policy in the course of the past decades. They have developed a panoply of instruments, that can be divided into two groups. The first group applies to people: they concern mainly financial support to persons willing to move house (now practically abandoned everywhere). The second group applies to economic activities. They cover, first, financial benefits (loans, grants and so on) meant to encourage locating investment in certain regions, and second, the large category of instruments improving the location conditions in certain regions (roads, ports, industrial sites, training of workers, public utilities, innovation and so on) (Yuill *et al.*, 1999).

National governments have gradually learned to take a European view on regional problems. Actually what from a national point of view may seem a grave problem justifying a substantial money outlay may seem trifling from the EU point of view. So the first task of the EU was to define the priority regions on the European level. The second task was to prevent governments from outbidding one another with subsidies, which would mean in practice that the richer member states would be able to match any package allowed to the less well off ones. The EU has put a ceiling on aid levels in each type of problem region: that is, the bigger the problems, the higher the ceiling.

Because the regional policy of the EU is complementary to that of the member states, national and EU measures need to be coordinated. Once that need had been recognised, the regional programme was introduced as a policy instrument (for example, CEC, 1979e, 1984d). Its purpose is to give substance to the principle of partnership by organising the involvement of all competent organisations at the regional, national and European level. There are three stages in this programming.

- *Preparation.* In most cases a so-called 'Single Programming Document' is prepared. This co-production of a member state, a region and the Commission has three elements. First it sets out the strategic choices of the regional and central authorities in the light of an analysis of the problems. Next it identifies the areas for priority action, the financial resources and the forms of assistance (Community Support Framework). Finally it details the concrete activities for each priority action in the various regions (operational programmes) and their likely impact on objectives (*ex ante* evaluation).
- *Implementation.* The authorities of the member states and the regions ensure the implementation (one authority has to be

designated to manage the whole programme). Monitoring committees in which the regions, member states and Commission are represented supervise the execution of the programmes and make a mid-term evaluation (see for methods CEC, 1999k).
- *Ex post evaluation.* After the execution of the programme an evaluation has to be made; this has to indicate how far the results obtained correspond to the targets set (see, for a critical comment, Bachtler and Michie, 1995).

For the smooth coordination of more general issues between the EU and the member states other committees have been installed. The Committee of the Regions permits the EU to hear directly the opinion of the lower layers of government.

The role of the European Regional Development Fund and other structural funds

For effective help to regions in distress, the EU must have financial means. After several attempts the EU obtained in 1975 the necessary finance with the creation of the European Regional Development Fund (ERDF).[12] The tasks of the ERDF (CEC, 1977, 1990a) are to grant subsidies to stimulate investment and promote innovation in economic activities and develop the infrastructure in regions designated as European problem areas (see Figure 16.2). Eligible for investment support in these regions are those activities which are already receiving aid from the member state in question or one of its agencies; the EU intervention is indeed meant to complement such aid.

The problem regions tend to fall into two main types.

- *Lagging regions (objective 1).* Many of these regions are traditionally backward, have failed to develop sufficient manufacturing or service industry and are still oriented to agriculture. Especially in southern member states, agriculture is often not very productive. This type of region is generally characterised by a peripheral situation, a deficient infrastructure, a meagre endowment with business services and a lack of skilled labour with a good industrial and service tradition. Below-average GDP per head is a main indicator of problems here; regions with a GDP less than 75 per cent of the EU average are eligible for aid.
- *Regions of industrial decline (objective 2).* Many of these regions played a leading role at a certain stage of economic development, specialising in one or other sector. They have landed in difficulties as production conditions for these sectors changed. This type of region is generally marked by inadequate infrastructure and by serious problems in old industrial areas. They

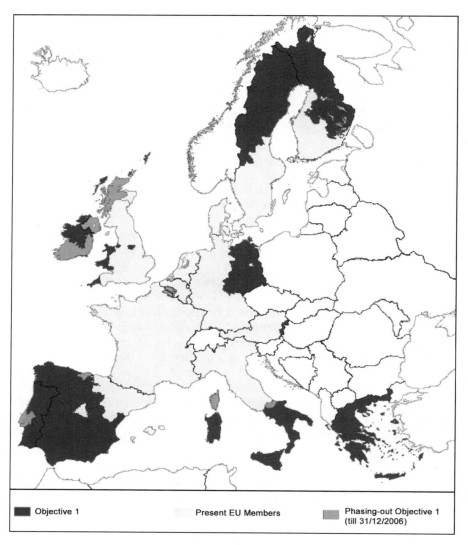

Figure 16.2   Regions qualifying for ERDF aid

often have a highly specialised manpower whose skills are, however, at odds with modern requirements. High unemployment is the main indicator of distress here. Regions are eligible for aid if their unemployment rate is higher than the EU average, their percentage share in agriculture of industrial employment is higher than the EU average, and there is a sudden drop in this employment.

The ERDF works together with three other structural funds, so termed because their efforts are oriented towards the improvement of the production environment. These are the European Social Fund (ESF, see following sections), the Agricultural Fund (EAGGF, Guidance Section; see Chapter 9) and the relatively small Fishery 'Fund'. The aim is to combine the efforts of these funds.

The total *size* of the structural funds devoted to regional development has been gradually stepped up with the increasing needs of the less advantaged regions and the increasing accent on cohesion. For the first 10 years (1975–84) it amounted to some 1000 million euro a year. In the transition period from 1985 to 1993 it was stepped up gradually to some 10 000 million a year. For the period 1994–99, resources averaged more than 25 000 million euro a year. A further increase is budgeted for the period up to 2006 (see Table 16.4). The structural funds are fed by the EU budget.

Table 16.4 Structural funds, distribution of aid by objective, 1989–2006

Objective		Funds involved	Billion euro		
Code	Name		1989–93	1994–99	2000–06
1	Backward (incl. Ex GDR)	ERDF, ESF, EAGFA	43	102	136
2	Industrial decline	ERDF, ESF	9	22	23
3	Labour market	ESF	8	15	24
	Total		60ᵃ	139	183

Notes: ᵃ   Plus some 5 billion euro for Community initiatives.

Source: CEC, *Reform of the Structural Funds 2000–2006*, Brussels, 1999.

The *distribution over regions* of the structural funds favours in particular the main problem regions (see Table 16.4). Objective 1 (structural difficulties) regions received about 75 per cent of the resources available for some 25 per cent of the EU population. Objective 2 (industrial conversion) regions are rather dispersed geographically; here some 15 per cent of the resources were spent in regions representing some 18 per cent of the EU population. The effect of this is that the financial means of the funds are attributed in such a way as to strongly favour low-income countries (two-thirds of the funds go to Spain, Portugal, Greece, Ireland, and southern Italy).[13]

The *distribution over the type of project* of the funds has changed considerably. In the late 1970s and early 1980s, the bulk (80 per cent) of the resources was used to assist investment in basic economic infrastructure (transport, telecommunications, water, energy). Since then, resources devoted to productive investment in industry and services have increased significantly, and the same holds for projects that improve the business environment and develop human resources (CEC, 1991a, 1996d). The accent on various categories differs from country to country.

Coordination of EU policies with a regional impact

The different policies of the EU should reinforce each other, or at least should not be contradictory. This implies two actions. First, while carrying out regional policy (for example, with infrastructure projects), due account should be taken of such matters as social and environmental policy objectives; the Structural Funds Regulation does indeed make aid conditional on compliance with a number of such other policy objectives. Second, European policies should not have an adverse effect on regional equilibrium.

The different EU policies (such as agriculture, trade, energy and monetary) have different and often contradictory effects. At the end of the 1980s, the combined effects of the major EU policies tended to be more positive for the non-assisted areas and more negative for problem regions of long standing in southern Europe (Molle and Cappellin, 1988). In the debate on cohesion effects of other policies, the following three receive particularly attention.

- Agriculture. The CAP (which consumed the lion's share of the EU budget and involved the largest redistribution of income among European citizens) mainly benefited the 'rich' regions (Henry, 1981; Franzmeyer *et al.*, 1991). Since the 1992 reforms (see Chapter 9) most 'cohesion' countries seem to benefit increasingly from the CAP (CEC, 1996d, 2001).
- Internal market. One of the main preoccupations of the EU has always been the competitiveness of its economy. The single market programme has been of outstanding importance in this respect. The effects of this programme are difficult to dissociate from those of simultaneous developments (like the accession of Spain and Portugal) and of the support by the Structural Funds. However most studies show that the effects have been rather positive (CEC, 1996a, 1996d, 2001).
- Economic and Monetary Union. EMU entails some new adaptation problems for the backward regions (Molle *et al.*, 1993). In order to fight these a 'Cohesion Fund' was created (of 3 billion

euro a year) that finances infrastructure developments in the Mediterranean countries to support them in meeting the demands of the stability and Growth Pact (see Chapter 15).

Some problems come up quite suddenly as the result of EU policy changes. Take the case of an agreement on the external trade in textiles. More openness for imports can spell problems for regions that have specialised in textiles. The EU has the possibility of reacting relatively quickly to such adverse regional developments, including regions other than those given on Figure 16.2. Indeed a certain part of the structural funds is not spent under the Community Support Frameworks, but is used for so-called 'Community Initiatives' (CI, that used to claim 10 per cent of the total resources are now down to 6 per cent). Of particular importance are INTERREG, which emphasises the transborder, trans-national and interregional dimension, and URBAN that has as its objective the economic and social conversion of urban areas.

Evaluation

How effective is regional policy in realising certain objectives, such as growth of employment and decrease in disparity? The question has three aspects.

The choice of the EU as to the *system* seems to be a good one. Indeed the allotment of aid in the form of specific-purpose grants in the framework of Community Support Frameworks seems to be more efficient than a system that would operate with block grants. Moreover the reform of 1989 concentrated aid to specific problem areas and improved the procedures and hence the workings of the system. Finally the system takes due account of aspects of allocational efficiency and policy consistency. Indeed transfers were carefully aimed at meeting the objectives (Gordon, 1992).

The *effectiveness of the operational efforts* is not easy to establish. Evaluation studies of individual projects and programmes suggest that the specific policy targets are generally met (CEC, 1996d). The more general targets such as decrease in disparity seem also to have been met: regional aid is supposed to have added an extra percentage point to the growth of the cohesion regions.[14]

The answer to the question of *efficiency*, that is whether the EU would have attained these positive effects using fewer resources, is much more critical. The organisational and administrative costs of the present system are very high. The way to improvement may be to apply better the subsidiarity principle and leave more to the member states: this would involve a trimming of the flows to and from the richer member states (see the advantages of decentralisation proclaimed by the fiscal federalism school).

Social policy

Assessing the social problems

The EU is confronted by many social problems. Since the beginning of
the 1980s *unemployment* overshadows all the other social problems in
Europe. The development of overall unemployment is shown in Figure 16.3. Until the mid-1980s, it increased considerably as a consequence of the two crises in the 1970s. Unemployment declined in the
second half of the 1980s under the impetus of the upswing related to
the completion of the internal market. In the beginning of the 1990s it
significantly increased again. This overall picture assumes greater significance if we look at some structural differences (Table 16.5). Unemployment is particularly concentrated in many countries of the
periphery of the EU (Spain, Italy, Greece, Finland) and in the new
Bundesländer. The EU is much less effective in securing employment
than both the USA and Japan (see Figure 16.3). By the end of the 1990s
many member countries had witnessed a rapid decrease in unemployment; some have actually experienced labour shortages. This is the
positive effect of the growth of the economy, itself spurred by a combination of EU and national policies (see Chapters 14 and 15).

There is a set of *causes* for the rise in European unemployment.
First, there have been a number of adverse developments: in particular, movements in the terms of trade and the effects of counter-
inflationary demand policies (Modigliani, 1996). Second, these shocks

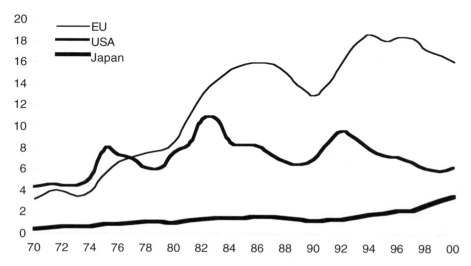

Figure 16.3   Evolution of unemployment (millions), 1970–2000

Table 16.5   Indicators of social disparity in the EU, 1980–2000

	Unemployment[a] (% share; year 2000)			Expenditure on social protection per head (thousands 1985 euro)[b]		
	Total	Men	Women	1980	1990	1996
Germany	9	8	10	3.7	4.1	4.7
France	10	9	12	3.1	4.0	4.6
Italy	11	9	15	1.8	2.9	3.2
Netherlands	3	2	4	3.5	4.2	4.3
Belgium	9	7	11	3.1	3.5	4.3
Luxemburg	3	2	4	3.1	4.3	5.8
UK	6	6	5	2.1	2.8	3.7
Denmark	4	3	5	3.8	4.7	5.8
Ireland	6	6	6	1.4	1.8	2.4
Spain	15	11	22	1.0	1.5	1.8
Portugal	4	4	5	0.4	0.7	1.1
Greece	11	7	17	0.5	1.2	1.4
Austria	4	4	5	n.a.	3.6	4.3
Sweden	6	7	6	n.a.	6.0	6.1
Finland	10	9	11	n.a.	4.4	5.4
EU	9	8	11	2.4	3.2	3.8

Notes:
[a]   Beginning of 2000 except for Greece (1998).
[b]   Eurostat, *Social Protection, Expenditure and Receipts: 1980–1996*, Luxemburg, 1999.

Source: Eurostat.

have had a large impact because of the low responsiveness of the European labour market (Balakrishnan and Michelaci 2001). This poor functioning of the European labour market is thought to be due to rigidities coming from 'over'-regulation. Third, there are propagation mechanisms that lead temporary shocks to have persistent effects (Bean, 1994; Layard *et al.*, 1991; Heylen and van Poeck, 1995; OECD, 1994b). And, last but not least, unemployment is due to the excessively rapid growth of the cost of labour. There is a chain of causes here. The increase in cost of labour is caused by the growth of the taxes on labour. These in turn are a consequence of the shift in the tax burden from capital and goods taxes to labour. This comes about because tax competition (see Chapter 14) shifts the burden to the most immobile factor. And the rise in labour cost has induced firms to substitute capital for labour (Daveri and Tabellini, 2000).[15]

Differences in *the level of social protection* are a second major problem. Over the years the richer countries of the EU have developed an elaborate system of protecting their citizens in general and their workers in particular against loss of income due to unemployment, sickness, accidents and so on. Moreover legislation protects workers against hazards at their workplaces. These systems are much less well developed in the less well off member countries. (An indication of the differences in levels is given in Table 16.5.) In the member states that have high social standards (1994 figures ranging from 3.6 to 5.8), labour cost will be higher than in states with low standards (1994 figures ranging from 0.9 to 3.1). This has given rise to the accusation of *social dumping*: employment will be lost in the former and won in the latter because firms faced with losses in market shares will relocate to low-cost, low-protection locations. Those demanding protection against this social dumping can neither use the instruments that apply to goods and service markets (free movement), nor those of a macro-economic nature (a devaluation is precluded by the monetary union). So, they advocate countering a downward pressure upon social conditions by setting for all member states minimum wage levels, social provisions and health and safety standards.[16]

We will go further into the remedies for these two problems in the following sections, where it will be seen that the major EU policy instrument against unemployment is the Social Fund, and against social dumping the harmonisation of national social security systems.

Gradual development of policy

European social policy is a complement to national social policies. Social policy is closely associated with, and may even encompass, labour market policy, which addresses issues like unemployment but also education, training and working conditions. It is generally defined to include also the fight against problems such as poverty, social exclusion and illness (Hantrais, 1995). The promotion of social cohesion requires the reduction in disparities, which arise from unequal access to employment opportunities. Many other social problems are aggravated by the unemployment problem, so it is only logical that the EU has placed the fight against unemployment at the centre of its policy actions.

The *objectives and actions* of the European Social Policy have changed as the EU has moved into higher stages of integration (Degimbe, 1999).

Beginnings (1952–74)   The experience of the ECSC proved profitable when the social policy paragraphs of the EEC Treaty were devised.

While the countries of Europe were still discussing the need for economic integration, the need for a complementary social policy had already been recognised (ILO, 1956). However the preparatory discussions for the Treaty of Rome did not produce a clear-cut view on such a policy, so that the relevant Treaty articles form rather a mixed bag. For a long time the situation has been characterised by a dichotomy between aims and means. Indeed the aims set are broad and ambitious (Article 136): 'the member states agree upon the need to promote improved working conditions and an improved standard of living for workers, so as to make possible their harmonisation, while the improvement is being maintained'. However the instruments provided are not very specific; the 'improvement is largely to be achieved through the beneficial effects of the Common Market'. The same dichotomy of aims and means is found in Article 137. The first part of this article states that the Commission's tasks are to promote close cooperation in a very widely defined social policy field. The second part of the same article allows very limited means to realise these tasks: the Commission is asked to undertake studies, arrange consultations and so on.

More initiatives (1974–85)　As a reaction to the deterioration of the economic situation, the Council agreed in 1974 to an action programme for social policy. Objectives were the improvement of living and work conditions, codetermination of workers and full employment. It proved very difficult to move forward. At the end of this period some bits and pieces of social legislation had been passed, but the overall situation of a limited practical involvement of the EU in social policy matters had not changed. Up to the mid-1980s EU social policy has in practice mainly dealt with two subjects:

- the Social Fund, which has the task of 'rendering the employment of workers easier and of increasing their geographical and occupational mobility' (Article 146); this was meant to ease the adaptations made necessary by the Common Market;
- coordination of social security systems (Article 42) to secure freedom of movement for workers; workers who migrate from one national system of social security to another need protection to safeguard their rights, but that does not necessarily mean that the systems themselves need to be changed; further harmonisation of social security systems may be envisaged (Articles 136–137).

Social Charter and Single European Act (1986–92)　The discussion assumed a different perspective when the plans for the single market were set up (CEC, 1988c). There was much concern that the increase in economic efficiency would entail considerable social problems, for two reasons. First, the adaptation to new circumstances would lead to unemployment. Second, the competition from low-wage countries that also have low social protection would lead to an erosion of the high social protection in the richer countries. (In this respect the argument of social dumping was often advanced.) So the Commission, the Parliament and the ESC asked for minimum standards to be applied throughout the EU. As existing international agreements, such as the ILO Convention,[17] proved inadequate, the EU set up its own Social Charter of fundamental social rights of workers. This covers aspects such as working conditions, freedom of movement, social protection, collective bargaining, worker participation, health and safety, and so on. The rights listed in the Social Charter are often qualified so as to take account of national practices. Unfortunately the subjects treated are a very mixed bag and do not fall into coherent categories of objectives. Notwithstanding this, real progress on their realisation has been made: most of the programme has been implemented (Addison and Siebert, 1994).

The Treaties of Maastricht and Amsterdam (1993–)   The Social Protocol of the TEU (commonly referred to as the Social Chapter) has considerably broadened the scope of the action of the EU in the social field (minimum hours of work per day, social security, health and safety requirements and so on). The concern for subsidiarity has meant that the Protocol expressly excludes certain areas from EU involvement (wages, strikes and so on). An innovation is that the Protocol provides for a direct consultation of the social partners which may give a new impetus to the activities of the Economic and Social Committee, which up to now have not been of much consequence (CEC, 1993d). The Treaty of Amsterdam introduces the possibility of a European policy to promote employment. This will take the form of guidelines for national policies. Any action has to take into account two other objectives: sustainable development (environment) and equal opportunities between men and women.

European Social Fund; instrument for employment creation

The original objective of the European Social Fund (ESF) is to increase the occupational and geographical mobility of workers in the EU, thus serving both an allocational purpose (to increase the efficiency of the European labour market) and a redistribution purpose. This was to be achieved mainly through vocational retraining and resettlement allowances, but aid could also be granted for the benefit of workers whose employment was reduced or temporarily suspended as a result of conversion. The fund was to be administered by the Commission, assisted by a committee of representatives of governments, trade unions and employers, an arrangement that is still valid. The tasks of the fund have been continuously changed under the influence of new political demands and new economic and social circumstances. Four periods can be distinguished (Collins, 1983; Degimbe, 1999), marked by major reforms.

1958–72 (EU6). In this period the ESF was almost entirely devoted to enhancing the allocational efficiency of the EU labour market; in other words, occupational mobility. In the period considered, 97 per cent of the fund's resources went into the financing of vocational training or retraining schemes. Only a minor portion (10 million euro) of the total amount of 320 million euro of grants paid in this period were channelled into schemes for resettlement, for the purpose of stimulating geographical mobility. The reasons are not hard to find: the shortages on the labour market were already calling forth large external immigration flows. Nothing was done to encourage conversion, mostly because member states could not agree on the type of project that would be eligible for aid.

1973–83 (EU9). In this period, the financial scope was gradually increased from some 250 million euro to 1500 million euro. The fund was able to contribute up to 50 per cent to the training and related costs of programmes for specific target groups. In this period the redistribution objective overtook the allocation objective. Indeed half the fund's money went to the less developed regions. In that realm, the European Social Fund worked alongside the ERDF, the latter helping to create job opportunities, the ESF helping the labour force to acquire the skills needed for the new jobs. Almost 30 per cent of the grants paid by the ESF were used to improve employment prospects for young people, because much of the burden of rising unemployment appeared to be shouldered by the young.

1983–88 (EU12). The fund's volume was increased to 2500 million euro in 1986. First priority was given to young people: 75 per cent of the fund had to be spent on their education, training and initial hiring. In allocation of the fund's resources, emphasis was placed on the redistribution towards the most distressed regions; 45 per cent of total ESF aid accrued to the following: all regions of the three poorest countries of the EU (Greece, Portugal and Ireland), the Italian Mezzogiorno and large parts of Spain.

1988–present. The structural funds have been integrated (Agricultural Guidance, Regional and Social). For the Social Fund part, the main objective set was developing high quality employment (objective 3 in Table 16.4), in particular by promoting the reinsertion of the unemployed in jobs and the development of human resources (also in innovation, technology and so on).

The European Council has on several occasions declared that the fight against unemployment is the *number one priority* of the EU. The member states should assume the primary responsibility for taking policy actions. Such policies, usually called Active Labour Market Policies, aim at improving the functioning of the labour market by enabling persons to take on new job opportunities, by developing skills of employees and by keeping the potentially unemployed in contact with the labour market. Unfortunately, the effectiveness of such policies is rather uncertain (Martin, 1998). The EU task is two-fold:

- setting frameworks and guidelines for the improvement of con-ditions (for example, improvement of the working of the inter-nal market, investment in human capital, switching of the tax burden from labour to other taxes, consistent monetary and macro policies) (Modigliani, 1996);
- support from the structural funds to programmes specifically aimed at employment improvement.

By way of example we describe here two major Community Initia-tives (CI) for the development of human resources that have been in operation during the 1994–99 period:

- EMPLOYMENT, consisting of four interrelated programmes to promote the labour market chances of women (NOW); of the disabled (HORIZON); of people under 20, especially those with-out basic qualifications (YOUTHSTART); the INTEGRA pro-gramme concentrates on actions against social exclusion;
- ADAPT, for adjustment to structural change, as with the infor-mation society.

It was estimated at the start that, under these two CI, more than a million people would receive training or other support to improve their job prospects in an increasingly competitive EU labour market (CEC, 1996d). For the 2000–2006 period the set-up has been recast and a new initiative called EQUAL will take over. It will promote new means of combating all forms of discrimination and inequalities in connection with the labour market through trans-national coop-eration.

Social protection

In the debate on social protection, broadly two views can be distin-guished: the 'economic or liberalist' and the 'social progress or regu-lators' view (Holloway, 1981; Dearden, 1995, Brown *et al.*, 1996).

In the *economic view*, the social security systems need only be harmonised as far as necessary for the proper functioning of the Common Market. In modern times this view has been reformulated to limit the harmonisation of labour market legislation to what is clearly needed to safeguard the fair competition within the internal market. The EU should favour a competition between rules and refrain from any major policy action.

In the *social progress view*, the EU is more than a common market, and has the clear task of enhancing welfare. This view has led to claims for standards to avoid a downward spiral and even to claims for upward alignment, eliminating at least the gravest shortcomings of the systems in certain member states. Proposals for a redistribution from the rich to poor member countries by means of a European Social Security Fund have been put forward, too, but owing to the obvious lack of political support they have not been realised.

The outcome of the debate between economists and social progressionists has changed over time. Initially the economists won. The Commission, which had associated itself with the social progress approach, was forced, in 1966, to adopt the economic line advocated by all member states. This line was followed during the period 1965–90. In the 1990s, things changed. The European Social Charter established that any citizen of the EU is entitled to adequate social protection, including social security; the determination of the level and form is, however, to be arranged by each member state.[18] The white paper of the Commission on European Social Policy (COM 9433) presented competitiveness and social progress as complements. On the one hand, factors like a highly developed social security system and the stability of labour market institutions are considered to strengthen investments in human capital and to lead to a motivated labour force. On the other hand, long-term productivity growth has also to be based on increased competitiveness on world markets; such growth in turn is a necessary condition for the further improvement of social protection.

The debate between the advocates and opponents of *EU-wide standards* is still going on (OECD, 1994c). The argument of the 'regulators' is that EU standards prevent the negative effects of a downward spiral in social protection occurring. Such negative effects are of two types: first, serious social problems may lower productivity; second, labour market institutions may become less efficient as the positive external effects of regulation are forgone. The argument of the 'competition school' is that standards restrict the functioning of markets. This also has two aspects. First, standards increase the cost level of the below average income member states, which restricts their chances of competing successfully on product markets, which in turn increases the possibility of their becoming dependent on transfer payments (for example, De Molina and Perea, 1992). Second, EU standards increase the rigidity on labour markets, which is one of the major causes of unemployment (see previous section).

A general conclusion as to which approach is the best is not possible; case-by-case solutions will have to be found (Bean *et al.*, 1990; Addison and Siebert, 1994). The EU standards that are set should be formulated as a set of common objectives and not as a set of common procedures (Brown *et al.*, 1996).

Evaluation

Up to the end of the 1980s, European social policy consisted mainly of (1), a set of rules defining the rights of migrant workers to social security benefits, (2) a loose cooperation in the form of exchange of information on other aspects of social policy, and (3) a means of redistributing European funds among member countries for the re-training of workers in the poorer regions. The various elements of this stage of European social policy have drawn mostly unfavourable critiques (Laffan, 1983; Steinle, 1988) which argue that, at best, the ESF has served the redistribution of European money, but failed to attain any specific Community objectives (allocation function).

In the 1990s, the social policy of the EU has been extended. The EU has engaged considerable resources in its fight against unemployment, its first policy priority. The effectiveness of this policy cannot easily be evaluated in general terms. However, many of the instruments used come under the heading of Active Labour Market Policies whose effectiveness was found to be rather ambiguous (OECD, 1993b; Layard *et al.*, 1991). The recent increase in EU harmonisation of national social protection measures is too recent to be subjected to evaluation. In qualitative terms one may, however, conclude that they have realised a number of social improvements; others have occurred as the outcome of the spontaneous evolution of economic realities and the convergence of national interests on specific points.

Summary and conclusions

- The most important policies carried out by the EU to improve internal cohesion through the redistribution of wealth are regional and social policies. The instruments used for both reflect the wish of the EU to make these policies conducive to more allocational efficiency as well.
- Growth rates of GDP have diverged quite a lot in the EU, but, as the below average income countries generally grew faster, GDP levels have converged, which was one cohesion objective.

The determinants of the differences in growth among countries are as yet insufficiently known to assess correctly the role of demand and supply factors and that of increased integration.

- Regional policy's objective is a decrease in disparity. Notwithstanding a gradual decrease over the past decades, considerable differences in wealth remain. The effect of the Regional Fund on that development is uncertain. European integration has helped to diminish the disparity in national wealth, and that is a major determinant of regional disparity.
- Social policy has ambitious objectives: in practice the essential features of the policy are (1) a redistribution of resources through the European structural funds for the fight against unemployment and (2) the harmonisation of a large variety of labour market regulations.
- Evaluations of the effectiveness of both policies are fairly critical; although the redistribution effect in budgetary terms is certain, the contribution to growth of employment and wealth appears to be unsatisfactory.

Notes

1   EU involvement has developed gradually. In the 1950s and 1960s, a hesitant start was made. Real political commitment to a European regional and social policy was achieved at the 1972 Paris Conference of the European Council. In the following 15 years the policies were given shape and substance. With the adoption of the Single European Act (Article 158), confirmed by the Maastricht Treaty, cohesion by redistribution has become a constitutional obligation: 'In order to promote its overall harmonious development, the Community shall develop and pursue its actions leading to the strengthening of its economic and social cohesion.'

2   There is some lack of precision in the use of the words 'cohesion', 'convergence', 'regional', 'redistribution' and 'structural'. Cohesion has been defined at the beginning of this chapter. Cohesion policy aims at decreasing the disparity between regions and social groups, in other words at making wealth levels converge to a EU mean. The main instrument for attaining this objective is redistribution of financial resources. The EU has created several funds to that end. They are called structural funds because they stimulate notably the improvement of the economic structure of problem regions and groups. In that respect one also speaks of structural policies.

3   The fundamental ideas of different schools of thought on redistribution have been used for the setting up of international union redistribution schemes (Findlay, 1982).

4   The consequence of such limiting of claims to a well-delimited sub-set of the world, be it the nation or the union, is that international transfers to third countries have more in common with acts of charity than with distributional justice. We have included development policies among the external policies (Chapter 17) as they are considered by the EU as independent policies and not as an external dimension of internal redistribution. The case of the aid to

potential member countries in Central and Eastern Europe is on the borderline between the two.

5   In the jargon of the European Commission, this is also called 'real convergence' as opposed to 'nominal convergence'. The latter applies to macro-economic indicators like inflation and is relevant in the context of the criteria for joining the EMU (see Chapter 15).

6   Such distributional coalitions also reduce the rate of economic growth because they slow down a society's capacity to adopt new technology and to reallocate resources in response to changing conditions. Moreover they raise the level and complexity of regulation and government intervention in markets, diminishing still more the capacity to adapt. The more a society accumulates special-interest groups and collusions, the lower its rate of growth. The relevance of this theory to the EU is best illustrated with some country situations. The post-war economic miracle of Germany is explained by the fact that the Nazis broke the influence of many special-interest groups, and the allied powers did away with the influence of many others (large industrial trusts). The slow growth of the UK up to the mid-1970s, on the other hand, is attributed to that country's long-term stable evolution, giving rise to a dense network of powerful special-interest groups, such as trade unions and the upper-class establishment (Murrell, 1983).

7   From the beginning, the Commission has reported on the regional situation and regional developments in the Community (CEC, 1961, 1964, 1971, 1973b, 1981b, 1984c, 1987b, 1991c). Recently it has broadened its scope and now reports on cohesion (CEC, 1996d).

8   Turbulence on exchange rate markets does influence disparity figures quite a bit. When the GDP/P figures are made comparable with purchasing-power parities instead of exchange rates, one observes two differences: first, the disparity figures are reduced by about half; second, the decrease in disparity since the turbulence of the 1970s is very limited. Another indicator of regional disparity is unemployment. As it appears to be highly concentrated in the same regions that also show a low GDP/P level we have not detailed unemployment here.

9   See for further details about the time and regional patterns of convergence in the EU the various contributions in Vickerman and Armstrong (1995).

10   An important role has been played by the gradual shift over a long period of high value added economic activity towards low-income countries and regions. As a result, the branch structure of the regions and countries of the EU has become much more similar over time (Molle, 1997).

11   For a comparison of the new situation with the one prevailing in the previous period see (CEC 1999)* http//www.info.regio.cec.eu.int/wbdoc/docgener/guides/compare/info.en.pdf

12   For a description of the proposals for the ERDF see CEC (1969); for the creation of the fund, see Talbot (1977), for the first restructuring CEC (1981c) and for a review of its performance in the first ten years the EU brochure (CEC, 1985g).

13   The efforts of Ireland have brought such welfare increases that the country no longer qualifies as an objective 1 region.

14   Several methods have been used to define and measure effects of *the operational efforts* in terms of the attainment of the two major policy objectives.

  • *Employment.* The simplest approach to measure the effect of regional policy in terms of employment is to add up all persons that one observes as being employed in activities that have been supported. But the question is how much of that employment would have been created anyhow, without support. The most sophisticated method is to develop a model intended to isolate the effects of regional policy from 'normal' development. However the general conclusion from the latter type of studies is that the effect of regional policy measures on employment is very hard to measure (Molle, 1983; CEC, 1996d).

- *Decrease in disparity.* The actions of the structural funds are concentrated on the improvement of the supply side, in other words of the growth potential of the problem regions. Most of the support is given to infrastructure and manpower. This is justified, as the improvement that companies want to see in backward areas is largely of the type of physical infrastructure and human resource improvement (IFO, 1989). Empirical work by de la Fuente and Vives (1995) showed that ERDF spending on public infrastructure and education in backward regions of Spain (the largest beneficiary of such spending) had accelerated growth of these regions by up to two percentage points, and diminished the disparity in productivity between Spanish regions by some 5 per cent, which represents one-third of the observed decrease. Similar conclusions can be drawn from the analysis of the aid given to Ireland. As Bradley *et al.* (1995) show, the European aid has resulted in an initial acceleration of the growth of GDP per head of 1 per cent per year; after some years, the growth bonus becomes much higher, because the supply-side effects take some time to materialise. By adding an extra percentage point to the growth of the below average regions, regional aid has indeed contributed to a decrease of disparities on the European level. Other analyses of the supply-side effects of regional policy were less conclusive (CEC, 1996d).

In macro-economic models putting their accent on the demand side of increased spending by the structural funds, the effects show up as significant (CEC, 1996a).

15 In Chapter 14 (Box 14.1) we found that the distortions on the labour market in terms of regulation were less harmful for growth than distortions on product markets. In terms of distortions due to taxes the opposite seems to be the case.

16 There is a parallel with the need for setting up minimum levels of taxation and technical and environmental norms in the single European market; see Chapter 14.

17 Convention no. 102 of the International Labour Organisation (adopted as early as 1952) commits ratifying states to certain minimum standards for social security systems. For Europe, these standards were raised somewhat in 1964 when the Council of Europe adopted the European Code of Social Security (IEE, 1978).

18 This is in line with the fundamental features of the present EU; as a pre-federation it does not have the power to use income tax and social security benefits for redistribution purposes. These instruments remain the domain of the member states. So other instruments (specific-purpose grants) are used for redistribution, while social security is only harmonised to the extent that is needed for creating the conditions for other policies.

17 External Relations

Introduction

Integration schemes need to define rules not only for their internal functioning, but also for their external relations. Owing to the high degree of worldwide economic interdependence, each member country has developed a whole panoply of relations with third countries. The higher the stage of economic integration, the smaller the scope for independent action by member countries. Indeed a matter which has been regulated internally by the Union cannot be treated in external international relations without the participation and consent of the Union. In the next section we will go into these fundamental principles and also describe the international institutional setting in which the European regime has evolved.

As the EU is based on a customs union, trade policy will receive ample attention below. Two sections will be devoted to the common external trade policy, one to the objectives and instruments and the other to the specific relations with different groups of trading partners. The EU is developing from a customs union via an economic and monetary union into a political union, which means that other matters than trade are the object of gradual integration and are thus becoming the concern of the common external policy. The final section of this chapter therefore briefly reviews labour and capital movements, international economic and monetary coordination and development aid, and will also touch upon external policies less associated with economic issues, such as foreign and defence policy. Some general conclusions will round off the chapter.

General issues

Dynamics of integration

The setting up of common policies is more efficient than the pursuit of independent policies by member states if the common policy produces better results with less effort than independent ones. This will often be the case in international matters, where the power relations between the various partners determine in part the outcome. The scope of the common external policies is determined by the stage of the integration process.

A *customs union* lays the basis for a common external policy by setting up a common commercial policy. It generally covers both a common external tariff and rules on the common use of non-tariff barriers to prevent member countries using such instruments to obtain supplementary competition advantages for their industry. As international trade in goods and services is welfare-improving, customs unions have an interest in pursuing a policy of openness towards third countries (trade leads to a better allocation of resources and the competition of imports has a disciplining effect on domestic supplies). However strategic considerations may nevertheless induce trade blocks to use trade impediments (for example, accepting provisionally some protection for some industries to get sufficient political support for the liberalisation of most other industries' trade).

A *common market* will entail common policies in the fields of labour and capital. For labour, the abolition of internal border controls for workers, and *a fortiori* for all persons, will induce a common policy for immigration from third countries. It will likewise create a need for the harmonisation of other policies (such as crime prevention and social security). For capital, a similar reasoning applies: the liberalisation of movements between members will imply capital flowing into the whole of the common market through the country that gives the easiest access to capitalists of third countries; a common stance is therefore necessary.

An *economic and monetary union* also brings a need for an extension of the scope of external policy. Let us take just a few examples for illustration. In terms of allocation policies, foreign firms need to know whether they have to comply with the rules on competition and whether they qualify for financial support of technological innovation by one of the EU programmes. The setting up of a monetary union requires a common exchange rate policy, whereas a common external redistribution (aid) policy may be required to enhance the effectiveness of the various efforts.

Financial flows

The importance of the categories of an economic union's external relations can be derived from its balance of payments, which is the financial record of its transactions with the rest of the world. These transactions include current ones concerning merchandise, services and so on, as well as long- and short-term capital transactions. We have rearranged the headings in the statistics of the current account of the European Union to fit the general organisation chosen earlier in this work; the results are given in Table 17.1.

Table 17.1 **Percentage share of categories in total external payments of the EU[a]; average of assets and liabilities,[b] 1970–98**

	1970	1980	1990	1998
Merchandise	67	64	64	64
Services (commercial)	20	19	18	18
Labour (inc.)	1	1	1	—
Capital (inc.)	12	16	17	18
Current account (CA)	100	100	100	100

Notes:
[a] 1970–80: EU12; 1990–98: EU15.
[b] Figures of assets being very much like the liability figures for all headings, we have preferred this presentation to the more common one of net figures (assets minus liabilities).

Source: Eurostat, *Balance of Payments, Geographical Breakdown*, Luxemburg 1993; IMF, *Balance of Payments*, Washington, various years.

A few brief comments on the results are in order. The first is that the structure of the external transactions has been fairly stable through time. The prominence of merchandise exports is striking; they accounted for about two-thirds of total current transactions. This justifies the considerable attention we will devote in the next sections to the external trade in goods of the EU. Services occupy a modest place in comparison. Among the payments associated with production factors, the returns on capital invested abroad are growing in importance; the payments made by and to the EU for labour (earnings from work and remittances by emigrant workers and so on) are very small in comparison. Next to these current account transactions there are those of the capital account, whose total volume, as a matter of fact, is by far the greater. This justifies an ample discussion of the involvement of the EU in world policies on stabilisation and development.

International institutional setting

The process of European integration takes shape in the framework of a rapid globalisation of economic activities. As a consequence there is an increasing need for international institutions to set the policies to accompany these developments. However these have developed to very different degrees according to the subject. Most is done for the basic element of integration, trade, very little for other elements such as allocation policies and macro-economic and monetary policies (van Meerhaeghe, 1998).

Trade relations (manufactured goods) have for a long time (1950–95) been regulated by GATT, the General Agreement on Tariffs and Trade. In 1995, the WTO, the World Trade Organisation, took over the responsibilities of GATT. It has, moreover, been given responsibility for trade in services, agricultural products and ideas (intellectual property) and for trade-related investment measures. All member countries of the EU were contracting parties to the GATT and are now members of its successor, the WTO. The *essential functions* of the WTO are as follows.

- Administering and implementing the multilateral and plurilateral trade agreements. Central to this set of rules of conduct for international trade has been the so-called 'most-favoured-nation clause'. It means that any advantage affecting tariffs or other trade regulation instruments which is granted to one of the members must immediately be granted to all other members as well. Exempt from this rule of non-discrimination are arrangements with the objective of creating a free trade area.
- Providing a forum for multilateral trade negotiation. Members have agreed that changes in trade policy, such as the imposition or raising of tariffs, the setting of quotas and so on, cannot be decided unilaterally by one national government, but must be subjected to international negotiation. That rules out unilateral increases in protection which might lead to retaliation and tariff wars, and at the same time provides countries prepared to make concessions in the direction of free trade with a lever to obtain similar concessions from other nations (reciprocity).[1]

WTO conducts regular reviews of members' trade policies and practices. Unresolved disputes between signatories are brought before a panel of independent experts for conciliation and adjudication.

Production factors are much less well covered by international institutions. Some consultation on capital transactions is done by the OECD, and was in earlier days in the framework of the IMF. For labour markets, the ILO has done relevant work on labour standards, while both the OECD and the ILO have worked on migration issues.

Policy coordination, again, has been done in the OECD. This organisation has covered the whole range of subjects discussed in this book, from policy coordination for economic sectors to stabilisation. Regular work on worldwide monetary coordination has been done by the IMF, which has the task of monitoring and promoting the stability of the international financial system. Relevant in terms of macro-economic and monetary policy coordination has been the G8, the yearly summit meetings of the heads of government of the eight largest economic powers in the world (Hajnal, 1989; Blommestein, 1991).

EU regime

The competence of the EU as to external relations has been gradually expanded over time. The original Treaty bestowed on the EC only the competence to deal with external trade matters. The expansion of the EU competence to *other economic policy areas* than trade has been a source of multiple conflicts between the Council and the Commission, many of which have been submitted to the Court. The consequences of the case law of the European Court can be summarised as follows (Schwarze, 1987):

> The implied powers (of the EU) to conclude treaties with third countries does exist when: a) the Community holds the respective internal power and b) the treaty is necessary for the attainment of any objective recognised by Community law. This concept has become known as the principle of parallel powers whereby the Community's treaty making powers are congruent with its internal competences in any given field.

In practical terms this means that the European external policy has been extended by new subjects as integration progressed through the stages we distinguished in Chapter 2 (see also Molle and van Mourik, 1987; Ward, 1986). The increased weight of the EU implies that it will have to take increasingly into account the effects of internal policies on third countries (including agriculture, and also the internal market; see Borner and Grubel, 1992; Redmond, 1992). In the course of time the Commission has taken action in such economic matters as civil aviation, distortion of competition and monetary stabilisation.

The choice of *instruments* of external policy integration for the EU will depend on the advance of internal policy integration. With external policies that are a complement to a clearly defined internal union competence, unification of instruments may be the answer (for instance, a common external customs tariff for a customs union). In areas where powers are not yet clearly vested in the 'union', for example when countries of a common market strive for some stabilisation of the exchange rates of their currencies internally, the definition of the stance towards third countries will be carried out by consultation or coordination among member countries. The instruments that are used for the reaching of agreement with third countries will depend on the international institutional framework – negotiations in WTO for trade, but consultation and information in G8 for macro policy.

Trade policy: a fan of instruments

Principles and objectives

The EU *trade regime* is based on a number of theoretical principles. Indeed, the literature on external trade relations indicates the importance of a regime of openness as most conducive to growth (for example, Giersch, 1987). Indeed the possibility of imports and the rivalry of foreign firms that have made direct investments put the local producers under constant pressure, leading to more dynamism than would occur in a country with a closed economy. The EU practice is meant to be in line with these theoretical recipes.

The preamble of the Treaty of Rome already states the desire to 'contribute by means of a common commercial policy (CCP) to the progressive abolition of restrictions on international trade'. The Treaty (Article 27) gives the following motives:

- the need to promote trade among member states and third countries;
- the possible improvement of the competitive capacity of undertakings;
- the avoidance of competitive distortions in finished-goods markets, related to supplies of raw materials and semi-finished goods;
- the avoidance of serious disturbances in the member states' economies, while ensuring the growth of production and consumption within the EU.

The common commercial policy (Article 133) covers not only tariffs but other trade instruments as well. So all powers regarding changes in tariff rates, conclusion of trade agreements, export policy, the achievement of uniform liberalisation, and anti-dumping or countervailing duties are within the competence of the EU institutions. Nevertheless the mixed nature of their economies caused member states to use independently all sorts of instruments on the borderline of trade policy, which has given rise to lengthy competence battles between the Commission and member state governments. Over the years a trade policy practice has been worked out that uses fairly complicated procedures and a very elaborate panoply of instruments (CEC, 1993b).

Common External Tariff

The Common External Tariff (CET) of the EU was established for each category as the arithmetic average of the tariffs applied by the member states. Thus the first CET reflected the whole history of the trade relations of all member countries. The EU has effectively worked towards free trade, as the Treaty of Rome had enjoined upon it (in its Article 131). The EU wishes 'to contribute, in the common interest, to the harmonious development of world trade, the progressive abolition of restrictions on international trade and the lowering of Customs tariffs'.

Some major reductions in the CET have been made in the framework of GATT negotiations. The so-called 'Dillon round' of 1960–62 and the subsequent 'Kennedy round' of the mid-1960s cut the tariffs by about half. A further tariff cut of some 30 per cent of the 1978 level was agreed upon during the so-called 'Tokyo round' of the mid-1970s. The recent Uruguay round has resulted in yet further cuts. Consequently the general level of tariff protection of the EU is now very low, about 4 per cent on the MFN level. For many manufactured products the EU tariff actually applied is now nil or negligible. Moreover the dispersion has become very narrow; only very few tariffs on manufactures exceed 11 per cent.

Until the recent Uruguay round, these reductions applied to industrial products only. The dismantling of the EU protective system for agricultural products has started only recently.

Non-tariff barriers

Less visible than tariffs but no less effective as instruments of trade policy are the so-called 'non-tariff barriers' (NTBs). In line with its policy objectives (internal obligations set by the Rome and subsequent treaties; external obligations set by international agreements like the GATT/WTO) the EU has tried over the years to *free its external trade from NTBs*. Let us analyse the progress for three forms of NTB.

- Many *quotas* applied to imports from non-EU members date from pre-EU times. Although the Treaty of Rome had allowed member states to retain such quotas, the Commission has been pushing to dispose of them. Other quotas have been introduced over the past decades with the objective of protecting so-called 'sensitive sectors'.[2] The completion of the internal market made national quotas impractical as border controls were no longer permitted. As a result, all national ones have now been removed; the few remaining are EU-wide quotas.
- *Voluntary export restraints* (VERs) (by one exporting country) and *orderly marketing arrangements* (OMAs) (multilateral voluntary restraint agreements) existed outside the GATT framework, and were therefore, from a political point of view, more expedient than quotas. They have been widely used. In the WTO Agreement on Safeguards, the EU has done away with these 'grey area' measures.
- *Technical regulations.* The internal EU rules on mutual recognition have had an external liberalisation effect as well (see Chapter 14). Indeed, a product imported from a non-EU country that is legally marketed in one of the member states, because it comes up to the technical specifications of that country, has free access to the other member states as well.

Anti-dumping protection against unfair trade practices

In their attempts to conquer a new export market, firms sometimes adopt the strategy of first selling at a loss in foreign markets to force local producers out of business, and afterwards raising their prices to very profitable levels. The practice is known as *dumping*. GATT/WTO rules allow the importing country to take protective measures against such practices, in particular to impose anti-dumping duties which level off the difference between the selling prices the dumping firm charges in its home and export markets. GATT/WTO rules require that such measures be taken only if it can be shown that (1) imports have increased substantially, (2) there is a substantial price difference between home and export prices of the exporter, and (3) the imports cause material injury to the home producers.

These GATT/WTO rules have inspired the EU anti-dumping regulation (Regulations 2423/88; 3283/94; 384/96).[3] The *procedure* is as follows:

- a complaint is lodged by (groups of) firms directly concerned; the regulation indicates in detail what information the Commission requires;

- verification by the Commission of the information given by the complaining party;
- if a dumping margin is found to exist and if injury has been done, the Commission may either accept the exporters' offer to adjust prices and/or subsidies, or, if the adjustment is insufficient, impose a duty.

Anti-dumping investigations have grown over the past 20 years. In 1999, the EU initiated some 32 anti-dumping actions; in 11 cases provisional measures were taken; in ten cases definitive duties were imposed, while no cases were reported where price undertakings were agreed between the EU and the exporter. By the middle of 1999, some 183 EU anti-dumping measures were in force (WTO, 2000). The geographical pattern of anti-dumping measures has changed over the past years. Those against the former communist countries have fallen, while those against the newly industrialising countries (NICs) have increased. The cases where anti-dumping duties have been applied represented only a small percentage of total EU imports (Tharakan, 1988; Messerlin, 1988; CEC, 1993b).

Liberalisation versus protectionism

There are sound economic arguments for the abolition of all protective measures. Theoretical analyses and empirical analyses (Chapter 5) have, indeed, shown that trading partners obtain net welfare gains from getting rid of protective measures. In the case of the EU, a recent study has shown that the total cost of its trade protection measures could amount to as much as 7 per cent of its GDP (Messerlin, 1999). Large welfare benefits have also been found in studies on the effects of the various GATT/WTO rounds of trade liberalisation (see for an overview François *et al.*, 1996). Now, if economic considerations plead so convincingly against the use of protective instruments, why have they been so widely used? The reasons are of a political economy nature.

- The negative effects of liberalisation on welfare in terms of jobs lost is not easy to determine, yet in many people's eyes the unemployment in certain sectors is directly attributable to trade.[4] Claims for protection were found to be higher as (1) the industry is more concentrated corporately or regionally, (2) the historical levels of protection are higher, (3) the industry is better organised, and (4) the macro-economic performance (including the balance of payments) is weaker.
- The positive effects of liberalisation are more general and diffuse and hence less visible. Export industries and consumers

have no interest in protection. However, in contrast to the sectors demanding protection, they tend to be poorly organised and have little influence.

Adjustment costs are only a small part of the total benefits (for a survey see Matusz and Tarr, 1999). Nevertheless the former tend to carry more weight than the latter. Politicians anxious to be re-elected, whatever their ideology, tend to listen more to the slogans of well organised pro-protection pressure groups than to the pleas of anti-protectionists (Caves, 1975; Frey and Schneider, 1984; Baldwin, 1984, Weiss, 1987). The state will only override the pro-protection interest groups if considerations of international relations carry enough weight (Borchardt, 1984). This is the case under international agreements that liberalise trade across the board: a country that gives special protection to a specific group risks the revocation of the agreement, which puts in jeopardy the advantages of free trade for all other groups. So under such schemes it is unlikely that the political pressure of special interest groups will be strong enough to override the general interest.

Trade policy: differentiation by area

A hierarchy of trade relations

EU external trade relations are governed by GATT/WTO rules, notably the most-favoured-nation (MFN) rule. However there have been strong pressures on the EU to use the loopholes in the GATT system and discriminate in practice between (groups of) countries. This has resulted in special advantages being given to specific groups of countries with which the EU wanted to retain special relations. Table 17.2 gives a summary idea of the highly differentiated system that has evolved. It gives at the top of the hierarchy, or pyramid (Mishalani *et al.*, 1981; Hine, 1985; Pomfret, 1986) the arrangements for which relations are closest, while it gives at the bottom the relations for which most protection persist.

We will detail this overall picture for each group in the following sections. We will thereby analyse how far this discrimination has had the effects that were expected of it. From the vehemence of the political debate on changing the clauses of discriminatory arrangements, the advantages accruing to their beneficiaries do seem to be well worth while. However, in practice, the discrimination is seen to be hardly effective, owing to the low level of tariffs, on the one hand, and the high level of uncertainty as to prices and exchange rates, on the other.

Table 17.2 The hierarchy of EU trade relations

Countries concerned	Form of relationship	Share[a] in EU external trade (%)	Population (millions)
EFTA	Free trade area; incomplete common market	11	12
Central and Eastern Europe	Association	12	130
Mediterranean	Mixed[b]	10	230
ACP[c]	Special one way preference[d]	3	580
Other Third World	Generalised preference[d]	25	4000
US, Japan, CIS, etc.	Most favoured nation	38	850

Notes:
[a] See Table 5.4; 1998 imports and exports divided by two.
[b] Customs unions, free trade areas, reciprocal and non-reciprocal (one-way) tariff preferences.
[c] African, Caribbean and Pacific countries.
[d] One-way (non-reciprocal) preferences: the EU reduces/eliminates its tariffs on imports from the partner country but obtains no reciprocal (reverse) concessions on its exports; generalised preferences apply to all developing countries, special preferences to a selected group.

EFTA (other Western Europe)

EFTA countries have paralleled the members of the EU in the liberalisation of their internal trade in manufacturing goods. In 1966, some years ahead of schedule, their free trade area was successfully established. That quick success was helped by the generally good economic environment, as well as by the limitation to manufactured goods only; the agricultural sector was left out entirely. The relations between the EU and the EFTA have been very deeply influenced by the fact that, at regular intervals, groups of EFTAns joined the EU.

At the end of the 1960s, the UK and three other EFTA member countries decided to leave EFTA and apply for EU membership. A major problem arose: trade among former free trade partners risked being greatly disturbed by the trade barriers still remaining between the EU and EFTA.[5] The solution chosen was that of a large European free trade area, of which the EU is the core. In this way, full free trade in manufactured goods in Western Europe took effect in 1977; as in EFTA, agricultural goods were excluded from the arrangements. As a consequence, trade relations between the EU and EFTA intensified throughout the 1960–85 period (Table 5.4).

In the mid-1980s, a similar problem arose. Once again the EU was joined by some EFTAns. The completion of the internal EU market tended to have a negative effect on the remaining EFTA countries. The solution found has been to make the EFTA–EU relations even closer; this has increased EFTA–EU trade relations (see Table 5.4) and improved welfare in the EFTA group (Norman, 1989, 1991).

In the early 1990s, a third group of EFTAns joined the EU. Although the economic weight of the remaining EFTA is now very small, the group is nevertheless very important for EU trade; they come third after the USA and the CEECs (see Table 5.4).

So the conclusion may be that EFTA has benefited from free trade with the EU; this is in line with the theoretical notions on the effect of free trade areas among highly developed countries (see Chapter 5).

Central and Eastern Europe

The trade relations of the EU with the countries of Central and Eastern Europe have seen revolutionary changes over the past, due to two factors: first, the change of economic system that these countries have implemented since the turn of the decade; second, the acceptance of the CEECs as candidate members by the EU. As a consequence the CEECs have moved from the bottom to the top of the EU trade hierarchy. Let us briefly look at both the old and the new situation.

Up to the end of the 1980s, the CEE countries had centrally planned economies. Most of them were not contracting parties to the GATT (Lopandic, 1986). Trade among Council of Mutual Economic Assistance (CMEA or Comecon) member countries was conducted in the form of barter, and that is the form which had become dominant in East–West trade as well. As trade was a matter of the state in CMEA countries, most East–West trade was based on bilateral cooperation agreements between individual EU and Comecon member countries. Consultation between the EU and the CMEA was difficult: the EU has found itself compelled to set the conditions for imports from Comecon countries unilaterally, in the form of import quotas, which were revised every year, again unilaterally.

It is not surprising that, under such conditions, trade relations did not develop much (see Table 5.4). It may even surprise that the deterioration of the relative position of CMEA exporters as a consequence of the proliferation of EU preferential trade agreements with

various groups of other countries had not resulted in an actual decrease of EU–CMEA trade (Yannopoulos, 1985).

Since 1989/90, the EU has assumed a new responsibility for the
CEECs.[6] It has concluded with each of them bilateral association
agreements (so called Europe agreements) that have an important
trade component. Over the past years the EU has abolished tariffs
and quantitative restrictions on its imports from the CEECs of almost
all industrial products. Exceptions exist for some ('sensitive') products for which special arrangements have been concluded. Over the
coming years the situation for these products needs to be clarified
and trade liberalised so that a new distribution of production based
on comparative advantages can be sorted out. The CEECs have agreed
to schemes that gradually liberalise their imports from the EU; some
of these schemes actually foresee a complete abolition of barriers by
the year 2001, so as to be ready for early accession. Trade in agricultural goods is subject to reciprocal preferential treatment.

The European trade regime has become very complicated because
the bilateral agreements of the EU with the CEECs are complemented
by a host of bilateral agreements among the CEECs and by some
multilateral agreements among CEECs (notably CEPTA, the Central
European Free Trade Area). This discriminatory system is highly
inefficient. Several options exist to get rid of the set-up, differing in
the degree of integration and the number of countries involved. A
quick integration of the CEECs into the EU would involve only a
small number; a generalised free trade agreement for only industrial
goods could cover the whole of Europe (Sapir, 2000).

Now that the CEECs have moved up the EU trade hierarchy, EU–
CEEC trade is expanding very rapidly, a trend that is likely to continue in the future. At this moment the welfare effects of this change
in trade relations are not well known, but one may expect them to be
as positive as those of earlier enlargements.[7]

Mediterranean countries (mainly North Africa and Middle East)

In the period 1960–85, the EU trade relations with Mediterranean
countries were of a special nature (Shlaim and Yannopoulos, 1976;
Pomfret, 1986) for several reasons. The first is that some European
countries in the Mediterranean region had applied for EU membership, and agreements were concluded with them to regulate relations during the waiting time. The second is that some North African
countries used to have colonial ties with one of the EU member
countries and wanted to maintain the special trade relations that
had been established. Yet others wanted to obtain advantages on
the EU market similar to those their neighbours had obtained. The
EU gave way to the strong political pressures for preferential treat-

ment, the form chosen depending on political aspirations, on the one hand, and GATT limitations, on the other. As the GATT rules allowed such preferential treatment only as the precursor of a genuine free trade area or customs union, many trade agreements between the EU and the Mediterranean countries were made to fit that framework. When after a while that method proved difficult to continue, the EU made efforts to put the agreements on a more uniform basis (Pomfret, 1986). That, together with the second enlargement of the EU with Greece, Spain and Portugal, has simplified the picture.

For the period 1985–95, the following categories of bilateral agreements with the countries of the southern and eastern shores of the Mediterranean[8] existed:

- *Cooperation agreements* with the Maghreb (Morocco, Algeria and Tunisia) and Mashreq (Egypt, Lebanon, Jordan and Syria) countries and with the former Yugoslavia. The parts concerned with trade were in the form of a one-way preference scheme, which means that these countries had tariff-free access to the EU market for industrial goods and preferential access for agricultural commodities. The EU has settled for an MFN treatment of EU goods on the home markets of these countries. For some sensitive goods the imports into the EU were limited by quotas or import ceilings. The advantages of the trade agreement with the EU should not be overestimated: for limited quantities these countries already had tariff-free access by their generalised system of preference (GSP) status.
- *Association agreements,* possibly leading to full EU membership, with Turkey, Cyprus and Malta. Under these agreements, these countries have obtained tariff-free access to the EU for manufactured goods. These agreements aspired to a full-fledged customs union, which has recently been realised between the EU and Turkey.
- *A free trade agreement,* on the principle of full reciprocity, with Israel.

The Mediterranean countries appear to have been able, in the last 30 years, to increase their share in EU imports considerably, while their share in EU exports has stagnated, which is an indication of their improved position *vis-à-vis* the EU and other countries exporting to the EU (see Table 5.4). The preferential access to the EU market has brought substantial gains for these countries (Pomfret, 1986). For the EU itself, the economic effect of its Mediterranean policy seems to be small. GSP countries seem to have suffered from the policy's trade-diversion effects.

Recently the EU has made proposals to recast the relations with the countries of North Africa and the Middle East in the form of so-called 'Euro-Med-Agreements', together forming a vast free trade area for most manufactured goods and a zone of preferential and reciprocal access for agricultural products. A number of such agreements have in the meantime been concluded (Tunisia, Morocco). The beneficial effects of these agreements for the Mediterranean countries are supposed to stem partly from trade and partly from the locking in of the effects of structural reform (for example, Hoekman and Djankov, 1996).

The Lomé Convention (Africa, Caribbean, Pacific)

Right from the start, the EU has taken over the responsibility for easy access of producers of the former French colonies in sub-Saharan Africa to the EU market. After the UK had joined the EU, the schemes were extended to the former British colonies, whose economic structure resembles that of the associated states. The present scheme applies to some 70 so-called ACP countries, including practically all countries in sub-Saharan Africa and some few, very small countries scattered across the Caribbean and Pacific areas.[9] The main provisions of the present scheme are the following.

- *Tariff preferences* are fairly generous for ACP countries; indeed almost their entire exports have access to the EU market free of any tariff or quota.[10] In that sense the ACP countries have a better deal than the other developing countries (GSP, see below), which are sometimes subject to formal and informal quantitative restrictions.
- *MFN*. The EU tariff preferences are non-reciprocal; the agreement stipulates only that the ACP countries grant imports from the EU the same favourable treatment that is allowed to the most favoured developed country.
- *Agriculture*. ACP exports to the EU of products coming under the CAP receive, within some quantitative limits, a reduction of the levies, which the EU puts on many agricultural imports.

The *effects* of the whole series of Lomé-type agreements have been disappointing for ACP countries, not least because they have failed to prevent their share in the total EU imports from halving over the past decades. The early association agreement has had as its main effect to produce windfall gains (due to higher export prices) to exporters in ACP countries of some 2.5 per cent of the 1969 export value; no diversion of EU imports to associated countries could be found (Young, 1972). The first Lomé convention produced small trade-creation effects for its participating countries, and even smaller trade-diversion effects (from Latin American countries to ACP). The ACP countries have not benefited from the extension of the EU; their losses on EU6 markets were hardly offset by their gains on the UK market (Moss, 1982). The experience of the 1980s and 1990s is not any better; notwithstanding some success stories of export growth and diversification, the overall picture is bleak. The main reasons for this poor performance are armed conflicts, lack of initial endowments and absence of stable institutions and sound policies (realistic and stable exchange rates, good governance, reduced trade protection) (CEC, 1996e).

In future the value of the Lomé preferences stands to decline further as a consequence of multilateral liberalisation, pre-accession agreements with the CEECs and the other EU-centred preferential trade agreements (for example, the Mediterranean).

Generalised system of preferences (GSP) (Latin America and Asia)

The wish to do something about the problems of developing countries[11] in general has been the motive for the EU to establish preferential trade relations with this group of countries. The UNCTAD adage 'trade instead of aid' has been important in this context. The European system of preference (GSP) has the following distinctive features (Hine, 1985; Langhammer and Sapir, 1987).

Status   The GSP is not a uniform world system, applied in the same way by all developed countries; on the contrary, the EU, the USA and others have created their own systems, albeit broadly on the same principles. The EU version of GSP is autonomously granted to a number of beneficiary countries. As it is not an agreement concluded between two or more parties after negotiations, the EU can unilaterally decide to change it or even withdraw it completely.

Instrument   The scheme offers a tariff preference: in general, goods coming under the GSP are imported into the EU tariff-free, whereas non-GSP countries face the full Common External Tariff. There is no reciprocity, EU exports to GSP countries receiving MFN treatment.

Product coverage   The GSP is confined to semi-manufactured and manufactured goods and excludes agriculture.[12] For a list of sensitive goods,[13] it used to be limited to sometimes fairly restricted quotas. The new EU GSP that came into force in 1995 abolished tariff quotas and ceilings. A critical look at the product structure reveals that the products that are of most interest to GSP countries have received the least benefits.

Countries selected   The GSP is in principle available to all developing countries, but the EU has specified those to which it agrees to give GSP status. In practice, some countries coming under the GSP, such as ACP and Mediterranean countries, prefer other, more advantageous schemes; that leaves Latin American and Asian countries as the most important beneficiaries.

'Graduation'   Although the GSP was initially a non-discriminatory scheme, in practice it has developed into a highly complicated and selective arrangement. Indeed the trade advantages are differentiated according to the level of development of the country involved (low for relatively highly developed) and the type of goods traded (for example, low for relatively high tech).

The *evaluation* of the effect of the GSP on EU–LDC trade starts from an analysis of the penetration of LDCs into the EU market. For quite a few branches of manufactured products (such as textiles and clothing) the picture is positive. For others (food), market shares have stagnated (see Table 17.3). The impact has been different for different sub-periods. By the mid-1970s GSP had led to a trade expansion of some 15 per cent of all eligible exports; trade diversion was slight (about 2 per cent) (Baldwin and Murray, 1977).

Table 17.3   **Market penetration by imports from LDC into the EU[a] (in percentage of apparent domestic consumption), 1970–97**

ISIC	Category	1970	1980	1989	1997
31	Food, beverages	4	5	6	5
32	Textiles, clothing	3	9	17	20
33	Wood and wood products	2	4	5	3
34	Paper, publishing	0	1	1	0
35	Chemical and rubber	1	3	10	8
36	Non metallic mineral prod.	0	1	1	6
37	Basic metals (steel)	5	5	6	6
38	Metal products (machinery)	0	2	3	6
39	Other	17	41	64	48
3	Manufacturing	2	3	6	7

Note: [a] 1970–80: EU9; 1989: EU10, EU12 without Ireland and Luxemburg; 1997: EU14, EU15 without Luxemburg.

Source: Kol (1987). For later years additional calculations are based on: OECD, *Foreign Trade by Commodities*, vol. 1, various years; OECD, *Indicators of Industrial Activity*, various years; and OECD (1995), *Database for Industrial Analysis, 1975–1994*.

The welfare gains of the GSP differed by area. For the beneficiary GSP countries, gains amounted to some 2 per cent. The EU registered a loss of about 0.5 per cent. Third countries had lost no welfare as far as the manufacturing sectors were concerned, but about 1 per cent in agriculture (Davenport, 1986; Langhammer and Sapir, 1987). In the late 1980s and early 1990s, the effect of the tariff preferences was very small as a consequence of two factors: first the multitude of controls for sensitive products, and second the decrease of the preference margin as a result of the decrease in MFN tariffs. For the future the latter factor may increase in importance, the EU envisaging to conclude free trade agreements with a whole spectrum of countries at the same or at a lower level in the EU trade pyramid. Cases in point are the successor states of the USSR and the members of integration schemes like Mercosur (South America) and NAFTA (North America).

Most-favoured-nation (MFN) (USA, Japan and others)

There is a group of countries with which the EU has established trade relations on the basis of the most-favoured-nation treatment. To this group belong all non-European industrialised countries. Among these, the USA and Japan take pride of place, while others, like Australia, are less important to the EU. We have already indicated that trade among GATT/WTO partners has been considerably liberalised in successive rounds of tariff reductions.

The trade relations with the *USA* have for a long time been strained over the CAP. In the latest GATT/WTO negotiations the EU and the USA have agreed to a fair amount of liberalisation of trade in agricultural products. In the same way substantial progress has been made in the liberalisation of the trade in services.

The trade relations of the EU with *Japan* have been strained for one major reason, namely the considerable deficit on the commercial balance between the two. While in 1970 the trade balance was still practically in equilibrium, in the early 1990s EU exports to Japan covered only 30 per cent of its imports from that country. According to some observers, Japanese exporters owe their success to the protection of their own market, quickly achieving profitability and economies of scale there, and then invading other markets, including the EU market, with low-cost products.

From trade to foreign policy

Production factors

The EU has been given distinct powers in external trade matters (negotiations with the Commission, treaty with the Council) and the previous sections have given an idea of the complex system that has evolved. There is nothing comparable for the external relations engendered by the Common Market. Contrary to the situation in goods trade, the EU lacks external identity with respect to both labour and capital movements. The competence of the EU and the national governments with respect to production factors (already touched upon in Chapters 7 and 8) are different for labour and capital.

For *labour* the EU resembles a free trade area. There is full freedom of internal movement for EU nationals. External relations with respect to the movement of both workers and non-active persons from third countries are governed by unilateral policy measures of individual member states and by bilateral agreements that each of the individual member countries has concluded with third countries. Member states have worked out administrative rules for controlling immigration of non-EU citizens. As these controls cannot be perfect, countries are confronted with illegal immigration. The EU has recently committed itself to work out a common policy towards immigration (permanent stay) and a common visa policy (temporary stay), which would bring the EU in line with the definition of Common Market in this area also. Unlike the situation for trade, there is no institution on the world level that is empowered to deal with migration matters, so the EU is likely to proceed by unilateral rules or bilateral agreements with the most concerned third countries. The rules that apply now are as follows:

- *European Economic Area.* The EEA Treaty stipulates that the present internal EU rules on freedom of movement will be applicable over the whole EEA area for nationals of all EU and EFTA countries; additional rules for third country nationals.
- *Central and Eastern Europe.* The association agreements between the EU and the CEEC liberalise the movement of workers to the extent that this is conditional for the transformation of the CEEC economies (for example, specialists and managers). For the rest it is regulated by bilateral agreements.
- *Other.* There is some coordination of member states' immigration policies (both for workers and others); however this has not yet resulted in a common policy, and progress is likely to remain slow.[14]

Restrictive measures do not take away the 'root' causes of migration, which means that the pressure on the EU will continue. To step up the effectiveness of the restrictive immigration policy, two types of complementary measures are taken. The first, with a short-run objective, concerns the introduction of a clause in the cooperation agreements the EU concludes with the countries on the southern and eastern borders of the EU: (1) to take back their citizens who are expelled from the EU because they have no permit to stay; and (2) to take responsibility for sending back to their home countries those citizens of third countries having passed illegally into the EU through the territory of the country in question. The second, with a long-term objective, is the improvement of the conditions in the sending countries: hence the importance of aid programmes like Phare and Tacis for the CEECs and like MEDA for North Africa (see next sections and Molle, 1996).

For *capital*, external free movement has practically been realised by the mid-1990s; some EU countries maintain specific types of capital controls in view of specific internal policy objectives. Much of the integration in capital markets was not achieved by EU countries among themselves (see Chapter 8), but by individual EU countries with the offshore capital markets. The efficiency of these markets required that the full liberalisation of the EU capital market be accompanied by a policy of external openness of EU countries 'erga omnes'; that is, free movement towards partner and third countries alike. Indeed the capital-diversion effects of any EU-wide control would have been too costly to be acceptable for countries that had already opened up to the rest of the world. The Maastricht Treaty installed such an EU policy of complete openness towards third countries for capital transactions; it permits, however, some restrictions in the form of safeguard measures. The EU policy of external openness is based on a unilateral decision; there is no GATT/WTO type of international agreement concluded for capital transactions. The agreements that the EU has concluded with its partners hardly mention capital movements, and in cases where they do (for example, the EU–Med programme) the relevant clauses do not seem to have much effect in practice.

Economic policies

Clearly the gradual development of the EU identity leads to a definition of a common EU policy *vis-à-vis* third countries on all matters that follow from the internal development of the Economic and Monetary Union. However in the past little progress has been made with the external dimensions of the *various policies* that define an economic union.

Allocation policies are hardly coordinated with third countries. The noteworthy exception is competition policy. With the increase in globalisation and the rise of giant multinational firms that span the globe there is an increasing need for the coordination of competition decisions. Cases in point are the control of mergers that can impede fair competition on both the EU and the US markets. It seems as if, for the time being, there is an informal understanding of EU and US institutions. Formalisation of bilateral approaches and a multilateral approach (through the WTO) are now under discussion (see also Chapter 18).

A special form of unification of internal market policies applies to the EFTA and the CEECs that adapt their legislation in such a way that it becomes compatible with the EU rules on the internal market. Farthest advanced along this road are the *EFTA* countries. The EU has concluded an arrangement with EFTA countries that implies the implementation of the *acquis communautaire* by EFTA, with flanking policies in the fields of social affairs, transport, R&D and environmental protection. The European Court of Justice has been made competent to settle any disputes according to common rules. The *CEEC* have in the meantime embarked on similar programmes to adopt the 'acquis' in the framework of their accession to the EU; progress is as yet very uneven (see the next section and Chapter 18).

Monetary and fiscal policies

Stabilisation policies, if coordinated internationally, have the same type of advantages as was pointed out for internal EU coordination (Chapter 15). Such global coordination is progressing only slowly, however. The EU involvement in the work of the groups charged with coordinating the macro and monetary policies (the Group of Seven largest developed countries) is increasing. The need for coordination and stabilisation of exchange rates on the world scale is most acute for the stabilisation of the key currency, the US dollar. The variations in the dollar/euro exchange rate (see Figure 17.1) were particularly wide in the 1970s and 1980s, leading to conflicts between the USA and the EU. Since the introduction of the euro the exchange rate has again shown significant variability. Currently, the determinants of these changes are only ill-understood, and few models have been able to heed the past let alone predict the future (Rogoff, 1999). However, differences between countries in government spending and productivity levels (growth) are important next to monetary variables (Helleman and Hens, 1999). Taken in a historical perspective the present euro/dollar exchange rate volatility does not seem to be very great.

The creation of the euro changes the relations of the EU to the outside world because the euro has a certain potential to become an

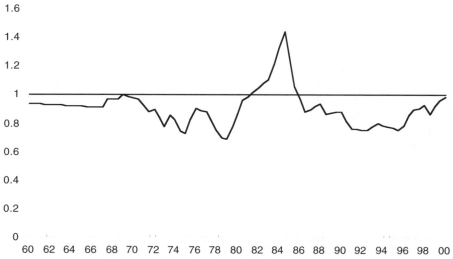

Figure 17.1   Dollar/euro exchange rate over time

Table 17.4   Private and public functions of an international currency

Money function	Private sector use	Public sector use
Means of payments or medium of exchange	*Vehicle currency* used to settle international trade and to discharge international financial obligations	*Intervention currency* used in foreign exchange markets and currency used for balance of payments financing
Unit of account (numeraire)	*Quotation currency* used to denominate international financial instruments and to invoice foreign trade transactions	*Pegging currency* used in expressing exchange rate relationships and as an anchor for other currencies
Store of value	*Investment currency* used to denominate deposits, loans and bonds	*Reserve currency* used as international reserves by monetary authorities

Source: Hartmann (1998).

international currency. In fact, the US$ fulfils the role of an international currency. The various functions that are implied are given in Table 17.4.

Having a dominant international currency offers the country concerned both political and economic benefits. On the other hand, there are also significant costs (Eijffinger and de Haan, 2000). In the past, the balance between the two was such that Germany has not been willing to let the deutschmark take on the functions of an international currency. As long as the British pound and the CEEC currencies have not become part of euro the potential for the euro to take on the various functions described in Table 17.4 outside the realm of the relations of the euro zone with third parties seem to be rather limited.

Aid to development

The EU and its member states have both a moral obligation and good economic reasons to cooperate to achieve a better distribution of wealth at the world level (legally enshrined in Articles 177–188). Indeed the gains from international trade of the EU may be unevenly distributed among the EU and its partners. As trade issues are closely related to development issues and trade policy is a common EU policy, there are good reasons for a common EU development policy too. This point had already been recognised by the Treaty of Rome. The scope of EU aid to development was initially limited to the associated ACP countries, but later other countries became eligible for EU aid too. The EU aid in the form of grants is complementary to that given in the form of loans by both the EU and the EIB, the aid given on a bilateral basis by the individual EU member states, and to the aid given on a multilateral basis by other donors (for example, World Bank).[15]

The distribution of EU aid over countries has changed over time as a function of changing geopolitical circumstances. Traditionally, aid has been concentrated on the ACP countries but, recently, more attention has been given to the Mediterranean countries (including Palestine). Aid to the other countries in Africa, Latin America and Asia is smaller in size, although it is growing fast for some – for instance, for South Africa). Given its relative importance, we will detail the situation for the former group of beneficiary countries further (see, for a more thorough treatment, Cox and Chapman, 1999).

The total amount of the *aid to ACP countries* is some two billion euro a year, financed from the European Development Fund (EDF). Most of the aid is given in two basic forms:[16]

- *Investment.* The EDF provides loans and grants to facilitate investment in infrastructure, both of an economic type (roads, ports, water) and of a social type (hospitals, schools, information and trade-promotion institutions) and to productive investments in agriculture, mining, industry and energy. Investment is also promoted by loans from the EIB.[17]

• *Stabilisation of export earnings.* If the value of an ACP country's exports to the EU drops by more than a certain minimum percentage, the EU compensates for the loss with a transfer of money. The STABEX mechanism for agricultural and the SYSMIN system for mineral products apply only to products contributing substantially to the country's total export earnings. The schemes give only temporary support, cushioning the first shock rather than compensating losses in the long run.

The evaluation of the EU development policy *vis-à-vis* the Lomé countries produces a mixed picture. In general, EU aid does not seem to have been less effective than other aid schemes (Hewitt, 1984). EU-commissioned evaluation reports have generally concluded that financial and technical cooperation matches both the objectives of the donor and the needs of the recipient countries. Effectiveness is found to be relatively high, notably as regards infrastructure and social projects. However the poor state of the institutions and ill-devised economic policies have in many of the recipient countries been major constraints in raising living standards and the level of development (CEC, 1996e).

EU development policy towards the *Mediterranean countries* has gradually come off the ground. Many Mediterranean countries receive aid in various forms from the EU. The MEDA programme, which is destined for the eastern and southern Mediterranean region, is the principal one. It makes about one billion euro a year available. Approximately half this amount is spent on aid to structural adjustment, development of private enterprise and the improvement of production factors. The other half is available for projects in technical and social infrastructure.

During the 1990s the EU diversified its aid in terms of recipient countries. There is some 1 billion euro a year available for aid to countries in *Asia, Latin America and South Africa.* The reason for this greater attention is largely of a political nature.

Aid to transition and accession

European aid to countries in transition from a centrally planned economy to a market economy is of recent origin. The major programme is Phare (originally an acronym for Poland and Hungary Action for the Restructuring of the Economy; now applicable to all CEECs that are candidate members of the EU). Similar programmes exist for the NIS (newly independent states or the successor states of the former Soviet Union and Mongolia). The major programme is Tacis, an acronym for Technical Assistance to the Commonwealth of Independent States).

The size of the budget for implementing the pre-accession strategy is very considerable (more than 3 billion euro a year after 2000). The Tacis programme is smaller in size, accounting for some 1 billion euro a year. Additional financial support comes from the European Investment Bank and from the European Bank for Reconstruction and Development (for more details on aid to CEECs and NIS see Cox and Chapman, 1999).

The basic objective of the *Phare programme* is now to prepare the beneficiary countries for EU membership. Its basic features are:

- funds are offered as non-reimbursable grants and not in the form of loans;
- projects eligible for support must enhance (1) the process of reform (for example, privatisation), (2) the build-up of technical infrastructure (transport, telecommunications) and social infrastructure (institutions, public administration, social services and health), (3) the development of private enterprise (agriculture, energy), (4) the improvement of human capital (training), and (5) conditions for sustained growth (environmental protection);
- recipient countries need to propose the relevant programmes for EU support; the EU, however, often provides technical assistance, studies and so on, to set them up.

In order to step up the *effectiveness* of the aid to the CEECs, the EU has assumed the role of coordinator of the support of both EU and third countries' aid to them (G24). As the programmes have only recently really come off the ground, it is too early for an evaluation of the effectiveness in welfare terms of the EU policy in this field.

Foreign policy

External *policies for non-economic areas* have gradually become a EU matter for two reasons. Third countries increasingly tended to look upon the Union as one political entity and expect a common EU stand on a large variety of diplomatic issues (such as human rights in China, or peacekeeping in former Yugoslavia). Moreover, the member states have increasingly become aware of the fact that coordinated foreign policies tend to increase the effectiveness of individual member states' actions (for instance, in the fight against terrorism). This led in the 1960s to regular meetings of the Ministers of Foreign

Affairs of EU countries regarding diplomatic questions. In the 1970s, the European Political Cooperation (EPC) was created as an inter-governmental 'institution', not linked to the EU framework, and work-ing essentially through information and consultation. The centrepiece of the EPC was the commitment to consultation with partners before adopting final positions or launching national initiatives on all im-portant questions of foreign policy common to EU member coun-tries, and to the joint implementation of actions. Over the years the cooperation has steadily intensified and its scope has continually broadened. The work of the Conference of Ministers was comple-mented by meetings of the Political Committee (high-ranking civil servants) and expert groups. The dissociation of the EPC from the normal EU institutions was increasingly felt as a problem. This led, first, to the regular participation of the president of the Commission and the Commissioner for External Relations in the EPC conferences. Next the EPC was formally hooked onto the EU institutional frame-work by the Single European Act, without much alteration to its objectives or its intergovernmental features. The Treaty on European Union has brought the intergovernmental work on foreign policy under the EU umbrella. As external economic and diplomatic issues are closely intertwined, the Presidency and the Commission have to ensure the consistency of the two policies.

How important is this common foreign policy in *economic* terms? Two sides of the problem can be distinguished in this regard:

- The use of economic instruments by third countries to pursue non-economic foreign policy objectives may directly affect the European internal market or endanger the security of supplies to the EU. An example was the selective oil embargo of Arab states against some EU countries in the 1970s. Sometimes the EU has used sanctions (for instance, against South Africa), or imposed export restrictions on strategically important goods.[18]
- Progress towards further integration by completing the inter-nal market implies common foreign policy measures. A case in point is the common visa policy for foreign visitors, which has become necessary now that the controls of persons at internal borders have been abolished.

Security (defence) policy

A particularly important matter in the context of a European external policy is defence. The history of this starts right from the birth of the EEC. One of the major objectives envisaged with the creation of the EU was to contribute to a durable peace; however its pursuit was to be made by economic means, not by military ones. We may bring to mind that, after the failure of the European Defence Community in the 1950s, European defence matters were treated in international bodies such as NATO (North Atlantic Treaty Organisation) and the WEU (Western European Union). Most of the 15 EU member states (the exceptions being Ireland, Sweden, Finland and Austria) are members of both NATO and the WEU. The WEU was created by the Treaty of Brussels in 1954 to strengthen peace and security. In the past attempts have been made to merge its institutional structure with that of the EU. That has been only partly realised by the Treaty on European Union; but the WEU is indeed considered an integral part of the development of the European Union. Like foreign policy, the defence policy is carried out in an intergovernmental way. The EU will request the WEU to elaborate and implement decisions and actions of the EU which have defence implications (Article 17).

Summary and conclusions

- The EU is based on a customs union; in practice its external relations are mostly trade relations. However its progress towards economic and monetary union has drawn other areas, such as immigration, international capital and monetary matters, into the domain of EU external policy. Moreover the EU has recently integrated a number of non-economic elements in a full-dress EU external policy.
- A complicated system of trade advantages, differentiated according to specific groups of countries, has been drawn up. Although this system has some of the economic effects hoped for and has been established for political reasons, it would seem advisable to simplify it considerably.
- The common commercial policy uses a spread of instruments to regulate trade and protect EU industry. However the EU has consistently moved towards greater liberalisation of world trade and, apart from agricultural matters, is fairly open to third country suppliers.
- The external relations implied in the establishment of the Common Market (labour capital) and the Economic and Monetary Union (for example, currency policy) give a growing identity to the EU in matters of foreign policy.
- Foreign and security policies are coordinated with economic external policies.

Notes

1   The GATT has engaged the contracting parties in some major rounds of inter-national negotiation, in the course of which substantial reductions of tariffs and other barriers to trade have been realised. Empirical analyses of the wel-fare effects of these liberalisation measures (see, for the Tokyo round, for exam-ple, Deardorff and Stern, 1981; Whalley, 1985) have shown that these are mostly positive for all partners (EU, USA, LDCs, NICs and so on).

2   Sensitive sectors are composed of low-technology manufacturers, using rela-tively standardised, labour-intensive production technologies, the very sectors in which LDCs have been gaining increasing comparative advantage. Para-mount among them is the textile and clothing sector. Under the Multi-Fibre Arrangement (MFA), negotiated between the EU and the principal textile-exporting developing countries, the latter have agreed to a voluntary restric-tion of their textile exports to the EU. In practice, the MFA had deteriorated into a scheme by which the individual EU member countries had fixed the quantities of textile products they will import from each separate exporting country. The abolition of the MFA was calculated to lead to considerable wel-fare increases (Koekkoek and Mennes, 1988), so the recent measures of liberali-sation should lead to a positive impact.

3   The new *WTO Agreement* concluded with the Uruguay round provides for greater clarity and more detailed rules in relation to the method of determining whether a product is dumped, the procedures to be followed in initiating and conducting anti-dumping investigations, and the methods to determine whether dumped imports cause material injury to a domestic industry. The new *EU regulations* have also introduced more detailed rules which greatly improve the predictability of the law. They require anti-dumping decisions to take into account all interests, including those of users and consumers.

4   In the EU it was found that other factors are much more important in explain-ing unemployment (see Dewatripont *et al.*, 1999).

5   Several factors have influenced the outcome. The first was the general conviction that the introduction of new trade barriers would be harmful to all concerned, but particularly to the remaining EFTA members, which are greatly dependent on the enlarged EU. Harm could be circumvented only by installing some form of free trade area among all concerned. The remaining EFTA countries were unable to join the EU for reasons of foreign policy (neutrality, lack of democ-racy). A customs union was out of the question: the EU clearly stated that it was not prepared to share its responsibility for trade matters in the framework of the CCP with countries that were not full members. The formula chosen for this FTA was that of bilateral agreements between the EU and individual EFTA countries.

6   We distinguish between three groups of countries. The first consists of the countries west of the former Soviet Union, plus the Baltic countries and Slovenia; they are dealt with in the remaining part of this section. The second group consists of the successor states of the Soviet Union; they now come under the MFN category. The third consists of countries for which the relations still have to be defined (Albania) or are suspended for political reasons (former Yugosla-via). We disregard the latter group here.

7   Another comparison that may be more relevant is that with NAFTA, the North American Free Trade Association. This scheme also integrates countries at very different levels of development. Large gains are expected for all participants in this scheme.

8   The relations with non-EU Mediterranean countries on the European shores come under the CEEC heading.

9 The ACPs are neither a political group nor an economic entity: ACPs as a group exist only in the framework of relations with the EU for historical reasons. So it seems as if the group might better be split up into three sub-groups, the countries of each sub-group joining strong regional integration schemes in their own geographical area.

10 Access is granted for goods which can be shown to originate for more than 50 per cent of the value added in the country itself, in other ACP countries, or in an EU country.

11 Developing countries participating in world trade face several problems.

- In the developed countries, demand for agricultural products is growing only slowly because of the low income elasticity of food, while the share of indigenous production is increasing owing to support schemes and increased productivity; world markets are distorted by dumping and export subsidies to agricultural production in the developed world. Prices tend to fluctuate very heavily around a downward trend.
- On non-agricultural commodity markets, a similar situation prevails: economic growth is now accumulating to the less material and energy-intensive activities. These markets, too, are highly unstable: prices, and hence export earnings, tend to fluctuate very much.
- On markets for manufactured products, developing countries face protective tendencies on the part of developed countries, because the very competitiveness of their new industries threatens the viability of the older sectors in developed countries.

12 For agricultural products, the EU record has been negative. The CAP has repulsed external suppliers from the EU market and it has thrown its huge agricultural surpluses on the world market with almost unlimited subsidies. This has driven developing countries out of their traditional home and export markets, and caused a steep drop in world market prices, and hence in the export earnings of developing countries (see, for instance, Matthews, 1985; IBRD, 1985).

13 For a list of so-called 'sensitive products' (goods whose increased imports would cause serious damage to certain European producers) quotas were set on a national basis, both on the EU (importer) side and on that of the exporters. Davenport (1986) reports that the EU GSP involved some 40 000 different EU-wide and bilateral quotas and ceilings. Moreover some products, such as textiles, which were ruled by the Multi-Fibre Arrangement (MFA), were completely excluded from the application of the GSP.

14 On many detailed points, such as visas, passports, asylum seekers and so on, some form of coordination has existed for some time on the basis of concerted practices of the national administrations.

15 Redistribution policies towards third countries are hardly the subject of coordination on the world level either. This adds to the difficulties of many recipient countries in devising consistent programmes of development. In order to improve consistency and to help developing countries with their structural reform, equilibration of the balance of payments and the establishment of sound public finance, the EU provides macro financial assistance in the form of loans.

16 There are two more forms worth mentioning:

- *Structural adaptation.* See previous note.
- *Food aid.* The provision of food to people in areas struck by acute famine is taken from the EU stocks (or surpluses from the farm policy; see Chapter 11). Recently an evaluation study of independent experts concluded that the 'impacts of EU programme food aid have been, on balance,

marginally positive, but its provision has involved very high transaction cost suggesting the need for radical changes to improve effectiveness and efficiency' (Clay *et al.*, 1996).

17   The EIB can only help to finance profitable projects.
18   For the limited effectiveness of economic sanctions, see Hufbauer and Scott (1985), van Bergeijk (1987) and Kaempfer and Loewenberg (1992).

PART V
CONCLUSION

18 Evaluation and Outlook

Introduction

The objective of this book has been to present an economic analysis of the process of European integration. To that end we described in the first part the conceptual basis, the historical roots and the institutional framework of integration. In the second part we discussed the theoretical foundations and empirical dynamics of the customs union and common market, with at their centre the freedom of movement of goods, services, labour and capital. The changes in the organisation of economic activity in the various sectors of the economy under the influence of economic integration occupied the central place in this book. As freedoms cannot flourish nor economic sectors develop unless government creates the proper conditions, a discussion of the policies pursued with these goals in mind complemented the book.

At the end of this analysis of separate segments, a more general view of the dynamics of the whole process of European economic integration seems in order. To measure the progress of integration we will make a distinction between indicators of a more economic nature, such as the share of trade in total GDP, and the more policy-oriented indicators, such as the limitation of power of nation states in different segments of economic policy. As economic integration is to be instrumental to the attainment of higher goals, we will evaluate its contribution to the growth and the distribution of welfare and to a number of non-economic objectives of integration.

The economic integration of Europe is a process of long duration that is far from being completed. In the future, integration will enter new fields and become more intensive in the fields already covered. In the last sections of this chapter we will look ahead. For both deepening (the new areas of competence for the EU) and widening (the geographical extension of the EU) we will sketch the likely developments and their economic impact for a selected range of issues.

A more projective and speculative approach characterises this outlook, unlike the rigour with which we have presented the theoretical and empirical results in all previous parts of the book. As usual a short summary completes the chapter.

Progress of integration; economic indicators

Quantities

A usual way to measure the progress of integration is by looking at the evolution of the quantities traded or exchanged. For goods and services this is done in practice by measuring the extent to which the production of one country is consumed in another. In much the same way, the advance of integration on the markets for production factors can be assessed by the change in the extent to which the labour and capital of one country are put to work in another. Both indicators have been employed in the detailed analysis of the preceding chapters. Table 18.1 combines the dispersed results.

For *goods and services*, the figures leave little room for doubt. By 2000, EU countries had become far more integrated with their partners than in 1960. The integration of the EU in the world economy has not suffered from this dynamism; the ratio of extra-EU imports and exports to GDP for goods and services remained more or less stable during the study period. Looking specifically at the goods trade, we observe that the orientation of trade has changed under the influence of integration. In 1960, trade in goods was more oriented towards third countries than to (potential) partner countries, whereas in 2000 intra-EU relations largely outweighed the extra-EU ones. For services, intra-EU trade has always been of the same order of magnitude as extra-EU trade. The increase in internationalisation is visible for both intra- and extra-EU trade; the latter, of course, reflects the growing importance of the world economy (for example, transport, insurance) for EU producers and consumers.

For *labour*, the figures indicate that only a small percentage of labour in EU countries is of foreign origin, and that this percentage has been very stable over the last decades. The average percentage share of labour from other EU member countries in the total labour force of the member countries of the EU oscillated within a narrow band around 2 per cent between 1960 and 2000. For workers from outside the EU, the level is rather low, too. A steep increase in the 1960s was followed by a levelling off in the 1970s and 1980s. (Another increase in recent years is not visible in the figures due to rounding.) In interpreting this indication of limited integration, one should remember that massive migration flows were never an objec-

Table 18.1   Growth of market integration in the EU15 (goods, services, labour and capital) (%), 1960–2000

		1960	1970	1980	1990	2000[e]
Customs Unions						
Goods[a]	Intra	6	10	13	15	17
	Extra	9	8	10	9	10
Services[a]	Intra	1	2	3	3	4
	Extra	1	1	1	2	3
Common Market						
Labour[b]	Intra	2	2	2	2	2
	Extra	1	3	3	3	3
Capital DI[c]	Intra	n.a.	1	1	3	5
	Extra	n.a.	1	2	2	5
Capital income[d]	Intra	n.a.	—	1	2	n.a.
	Extra	n.a.	1	2	3	n.a.

Notes:
[a]   Average of imports and exports as a percentage share of GDP; EU15; 1960 estimates.
[b]   Non-nationals as a percentage of total labour force.
[c]   Direct investment; four-year averages. Average of imports and exports as a percentage share of Gross Fixed Capital Formation; 1960–90: EU12.
[d]   Income from investments abroad as a percentage of GDP; 1970–80: EU12.
[e]   Estimates based on an extrapolation of 1990–98 figures and some additional information.

Sources: Goods: Chapter 5; services: Chapter 6 plus some estimates based on balance-of-payments data; labour: Chapter 7; capital: Chapter 8, plus some estimates based on balance-of-payments data.

tive of the EU. On the contrary, the movement of capital to, and the differential growth of, the economies of poor member countries were intended to keep intra-EU migration in check (see Chapter 7), while national admittance laws regulated immigration from third countries.

For *capital*, the quantities exchanged can only be studied for direct investment, figures for other forms of capital movement not being available. Within the EU, foreign direct investment has been fully liberalised since the 1970s. Although its volume increased considerably in the past decades, its share in total Gross Fixed Capital Formation (GFCF) is still modest. EU countries used to be less oriented to their partners than to third countries; this was due as much to heavy EU investment activity abroad as to foreign (third country) investment in EU countries. However in recent years the interrelations among EU countries have been developing much faster than those with third countries and now outweigh extra-EU relations. Here the effect of the single market is visible.

Another indicator of the integration of capital markets is the income received from investment abroad (both DI and portfolio). The figures available show a very fast increase for both external and internal EU relations. The increasingly global character of capital markets is reflected in the relative importance of the extra-EU relations with respect to the relations among EU countries themselves.

Prices

The progress of integration can also be measured by the convergence of prices for the same goods and services and production factors in the various countries of the EU. However the international comparison of prices is beset with difficulties, both of a methodological and a statistical nature. The few figures available are reviewed hereafter (Table 18.2).

Table 18.2   Price convergence for goods, services and production factors, 1975–95

Indicator	1975	1980	1985	1990	1995
Customs Union[a]					
Consumer goods					
(tax-inclusive)	21	20	19	20	18
(tax-exclusive)	16	19	18	19	17
Equipment goods					
(tax-inclusive)	14	13	13	12	13
(tax-exclusive)	14	13	13	n.a.	n.a.
Common Market[b]					
Capital[c]					
Long-term interest rate	20	23	23	14	24

Notes:
[a]   Index of dispersion (see Chapters 6 and 7); the lower the indices the higher the integration. EU12, 1995–93.
[b]   Data on wages not available (see Chapter 9).
[c]   Divergence indicator (see Chapter 10) of the long-term interest rates; the lower the indicator the higher the integration. EU7. Value of the indicator in the 1960–70 decade: 15.

Goods   There was little overall convergence of the prices of consumer and equipment goods in the 1975–90 period. More detailed material shows that this is the result of two opposing trends: in branches open to competition, prices tended to converge, while they diverged for branches with many NTBs. The internal market programme has led to stronger competition for an increasing number of branches; in the figures for the most recent period, the 1992 effect is visible in the decreasing value of the disparity indicator (Chapter 5).

Services The few data available for the period up to the end of the 1980s show considerable price differences and no tendency towards convergence, which is in keeping with the limited integration of this sector. As a result of the 1992 liberalisation programme, prices have converged somewhat in recent years (Chapters 6 and 12).

Wages The price of labour appears to have shown a gradual convergence. However the measuring of this trend is not very easy, while it is even less easy to identify the integration effect (Chapters 7 and 16).

Capital Prices on the markets for short-term and long-term loans have shown about the same tendencies over the past integration period; the amplitude of the changes has been higher for the short term than for the long term. There was some convergence up to 1973. The turbulence of the first oil shock brought a clear divergence. From the mid-1980s to 1993, capital prices converged again, under the influence of the stabilisation of exchange rates in the EMS and the measures of liberalisation of capital movements by many countries. Under the influence of the monetary turmoil of 1993, divergence occurred again. Recently, owing to the creation of the EMU, convergence has been observed (Chapters 8 and 15).

Progress of integration; policy indicators

Institutions; growth of operations

Looking at the European Union as an organisation, we can measure the progress of integration in several ways. The most obvious indicator is the increase in the *number of members*. Indeed widening has been a distinct feature of the dynamics of the EU. Membership has increased at almost regular intervals, from six to 15.

A second indicator of integration that visualises growth, even to the casual observer, is the *number of people* involved in the EU policy-making machinery (input). We give evidence for three groups (Table 18.3). *EU civil servants* employed by the Commission and other EU institutions form the core. Their number has rapidly increased; for example, with the Commission, from 1000 to 24 000 between 1960

Table 18.3   Growth of activity of those involved in EU operations, 1960–2000[a]

Indicator	1960	1970	1980	1990	2000
Permanent civil servants					
($\times$ 1000) of Commission[b]	1	5	11	17	24
Committees[c]	n.a.	70	150	300	1 000
Number of lobby organisations[d]	167	309	410	3 000	n.a.
Official Journal (pages $\times$ 1000)	2	12	26	35	55
Judgements of the ECJ[e]	6	30	90	180	230

Notes:
[a]   Estimate based on extrapolation of figures for 1990–99.
[b]   Sources: CEC (1986i); CEC General Reports; *Official Journal* (several years); Eurostat; own estimates.
[c]   Estimates based on Falke (1996) and van Schendelen (1998).
[d]   In 1990 trans-national producer and professional groups were estimated at some 700; new lobby groups at some 2300; the 3000 groups totalling some 10 000 lobbyists (Anderson and Eliassen, 1991).
[e]   Yearly average of periods (e.g. 1970 = 1961–70).

and 2000 (in the same period, the total number of civil servants in the countries of the EU15 rose from 4 million to about 9 million).

National civil servants and experts can be found in the first ring around this core. Their increased involvement is reflected by the figures on the growth of the number of committees; their number exploded during the 1990s as a consequence of the Commission's increased involvement in many detailed issues of a large number of policy areas. This growth is the more marked as the number of meetings of each committee has also increased. The same holds for the meetings of the Council of Ministers, of its working parties and of other institutions such as the European Parliament.

Interest groups form the outer ring of this system. In the 1960–85 period, new lobbyist groups were regularly established, and older ones increased their efforts to influence European policy and decision making by extending their membership and consolidating their presence in the centre of EU decision making. The first to be set up were transnational interest groups in the industrial, commercial and professional spheres. From 1965 to 1985, the rate of increase was rather low. From 1985 to 1990, a new upsurge in the growth of lobby groups occurred under the impetus of the single market. Alongside the growth of the traditional ones, many new lobby groups have appeared on the scene (local authorities, extra-EU interest, and so on).

The *yearly production of the EU institutions* (output) can be measured by two indicators: the number of pages of the *Official Journal* and the number of judgements of the Court. The figures show the rapid and continuous growth of output between 1960 and 2000. Difficult to measure is the growth of the volume of preparatory work that precedes the actual publication of policy measures: expert studies, committee reports, white papers, communications and so on.

Subject matters; the movement to higher stages

There are sound economic as well as political reasons to start economic integration with goods markets (customs union), continue with production factors (common market) and conclude with intensified policy integration (economic and monetary union). In that view, the progress of economic integration in Europe can be measured by the stage it has reached at different points in time. Remember, however, that the stages are not strictly successive in the sense that the lower ones have to be fully realised before the higher ones can be tried for. Rather, as remarked earlier (Chapter 2), progress in the higher stages is a condition for the full realisation of the lower ones.

The *Customs Union* was to be realised before the end of the 1960s. The evidence from internal and external trade in goods (Chapters 5, 10 and 17) shows that for large parts of the economy (manufactured goods) that objective has indeed been realised quickly. However services and some other sectors have remained protected for a long time (Chapters 6, 12 and 17). For these sectors the CU has also been implemented in the framework of the 1992 programme (see Chapter 14). Apart from relics (such as rail transport) this programme is now completed and hence the CU can for all practical purposes be considered as fully realised.

The *Common Market*, implying the abolition of obstacles to the free movement of capital and workers, is an old target. Progress on it has been fairly rapid for large parts of both the labour and capital markets (see Chapters 7 and 8). However until recently, large sections of both remained excluded. The 1992 programme has almost completely abolished the remaining barriers. Some exceptions persist, such as the lack of freedom to move between member countries of extra-EU immigrants and the lack of a common external regime of the labour market.

The *Economic and Monetary Union* became an objective of the EU in the 1970s. Before that time, a number of common policies had been adopted and the coordination of monetary policy had been prepared. Notably the creation and successful operation of the EMS paved the way for the creation of the EMU.

With regard to *full economic union*, in the past, work started on a number of subjects engaging the EU in an even closer integration than that implied by the CM and the EMU. The EU has penetrated fields such as environmental, foreign and defence and science policy: the Treaties of Maastricht and Amsterdam have set the framework for further future developments in these areas.

Instruments: the shift of competence from national to European institutions

All progress of integration tends to curb the freedom of action of the member states' policy makers. The more use is made of higher instruments from the hierarchy, from information via consultation and harmonisation to uniformity (Chapter 2), the more the autonomy of the member states will be limited and the further integration has apparently progressed. The progress in policy integration made since the EU came into existence is indicated in Table 18.4.

Before we go into that, let us recall that the situation for the *four freedoms* – of goods, services, labour and capital – is very clear: from the outset their regimes were fully uniform. In principle the member states ceded from the start all relevant authority to the EU. Important limitations have for some time existed for services and capital. Indeed large segments of the service sector were practically unaffected by European integration until the 1992 programme. Until 1990 capital movements were only liberalised as far as was necessary for the functioning of the Common Market.[1]

Allocation covers policies that aim at the proper functioning of the common (internal) market, including those that try to improve the structure of productive activity. Right from the start, competition policy was harmonised, some would say even partly unified. Although the scope of the European competition policy has since been broadened and the intensity with which it is pursued stepped up, the situation of the division of competences has remained virtually unchanged. For fiscal, technical and related internal market policies, a timid start with consultation was soon followed by partial harmonisation efforts (for example, for value added in fiscal matters). The EU accepted very early responsibility for a limited part of structural sectoral policy (agriculture, and coal and steel) but, for most sectors, integrating efforts of industrial policy have not passed beyond the stage of consultation. In the 1980s, some large-scale European supply-side programmes were implemented (Esprit, Monitor and so on), for which harmonisation seems to be an apt description.

For *stabilisation* policies – mostly monetary and macro-economic – consultation was foreseen right from the start.[2] In the 1970s and 1980s, consultation was broadened to cover also growth policy. The EMS, created to stabilise exchange rates, can be regarded as a form of

Table 18.4 Synoptic view of the development through time (1960–2000)[a] of the degree[b] of policy integration,[c] by activity area[d]

Field of action	1960	1970	1980	1990	2000
Allocation					
competition	U*	U*	U*	U*	U*
fiscal	C*	H*	H*	H*	H*
technical	C*	H*	H	H	H
structural	C*	C	C	H	H
Stabilisation					
monetary	C	C	H*	H*	U
macro + budgetary	C	C	C	C	H*
growth policy	I	I	C	C	H*
Redistribution					
regional	I	C	H*	U*	U*
social	H*	H*	H*	H*	H*
External					
trade: goods	U	U	U	U	U
trade: services	I	C	H	U*	U*
prod. factors: labour	O	I*	C	C	C
prod. factors: capital	I*	C	H	U	U
development aid	U*	U*	U*	U*	U*
foreign/defence	O	O	I	C	C
Other					
environment	O	I	C	H	H
home/justice	O	O	O	I	C
physical planning	O	O	O	I	C

Notes:
[a] The first column presents the situation at the moment of birth of the EU; the last column describes the recent situation; the middle columns describe the situation just before the first and second extensions.
[b] O means that there was no EC involvement; I = Information; C = Consultation; H = Harmonisation and U = Unification.
[c] Evidently, each situation is liable to be characterised differently by different observers; we think, however, that the table gives a fair overall picture.
[d] The asterisk indicates that only part of the policy field is affected by the indicator given; for that part the highest form is indicated.

harmonisation. EMU brings with it a uniform monetary policy and the harmonisation of macro and growth policies.

In *redistribution*, we have distinguished between regional and social policies. The EU started in 1958 without a clear idea about regional policies.[3] By 1973, a consultation procedure had been put into practice. With the creation of the European Regional Development Fund (ERDF), national regional policies were subjected to European harmonisation; with the extension of the scope of the ERDF, partial unification seems the more adequate characterisation. For social policies, the situation is different; the European Social Fund (ESF) was created right at the start of the EU, and there has been considerable development since. Notwithstanding this extension, we indicate partial harmonisation even for 2000, as some very important fields, such as social security, remain largely unaffected by the integration process.

External policies cover a whole array of policies, from trade to defence. The common trade policy (implying uniformity) has been quickly realised for goods, but for services it has only recently come off the ground. External policies for production factors were absent in the 1960s; some coordination began in the 1970s. Recently a common policy for capital was decided on (full external freedom). A part of development aid has been uniform right from the beginning, but the better part of it remained in national (uncoordinated) hands. In the 1980s, some consultation on diplomatic and defence matters started (EPC); although this policy has since received new foundations, we think that 'consultation' is still the adequate label for the present practice.

Other policies that were non-existent in 1960 have become the object of EU consultation and harmonisation, cases in point being, respectively, environment and home and justice affairs. For many more policies the stage of information has started recently; we give physical planning as an example of a whole array of very diverse policies.

Summarising, we find that the use of higher instruments clearly increased over time. Between 1960 and 2000, the number of H scores rose from 1 to 7, the number of U from 3 to 5, while the number of uncoordinated areas diminished (0 scores going down from 5 to 0), I scores from 4 to 0.

Objectives and results

Economic growth and equal distribution

Economic integration is not an end in itself but is pursued to realise faster economic growth, that is, wealth improvement. The income effects of market and policy integration of the EU have been substantial. We can summarise the various empirical studies, reported on in the previous chapters, as follows.

For *product markets* the effects have been calculated mostly for manufactured goods, leaving agriculture, energy and services largely out of account. The combined effects of better market entry, increased competition, more innovation, quicker learning and economies of scale amounted to several per cent of GDP.

For *labour markets* the welfare effects spring in particular from the immigration of people from third countries, as migration among EU countries has on the whole been on a low level. The effects of the employment of immigrant workers are not well quantified. Some believe that immigration, by removing certain bottlenecks from the economy, has led to a permanently higher growth of GNP; others point out that immigration has prevented the economies of the EU from adjusting structurally to the new world conditions in comparative advantages.

For *capital markets* the empirical evidence on the welfare effects of integration is very thin, and differs from one sub-market to another. For direct-investment flows, attention has been limited to employment effects. These seem invariably positive for the host country, but for the home countries vary from negative (when exports from the home bases are replaced) to positive (when the DI facilitates penetration of a foreign market, thus enhancing activity at home as well).

For *common policies* the situation as regards the welfare effect is rather unclear. Although the study of individual policies shows in general positive net effects, the quantification of the growth and welfare effects of the integration of policies (like macro and monetary policies in the framework of the EMU) is still not satisfactory.

A major objective of the EU is to achieve a balanced distribution of this wealth. In other words, the EU strives for a harmonious development of the European economy by reducing the differences in wealth among the various countries and regions. It implies the pursuit of policies leading to higher than average growth rates for low-income countries and regions. The EU has managed to come closer to this objective. Indeed a comparison of the growth figures of the individual member countries with the EU average shows two things: first, that many of the countries that had below average incomes in 1950 have grown at a more than average rate; and, second, that countries that were rich at the outset grew at a below average speed. So in 2000 there was more equality than in 1950. The access to the EU is believed to have had a marked influence on the high growth figures of Italy in the 1960s and of Spain and Portugal in the late 1980s and the early 1990s. For the latter countries this market integration went hand-in-hand with the transfer of considerable amounts of money from the structural funds. The identification and quantification of the effects of improved allocation and redistribution on differential growth of member states are still deficient.

Beyond economics

Economic integration is first and foremost a device to enhance economic growth. However it is also a method for attaining some non-economic objectives. In recent European history (see Chapter 4) two such objectives have been paramount:

- *Peace.* Countries that are very dependent on one another will not enter easily into an armed conflict.
- *Democracy and human rights.* Attempts to overthrow this order will have little chance of success in an integrated framework that makes membership conditional on respect of these values.

The three objectives – growth, peace and democracy – have had different weights in the setting up and extension of the institutions that in the past have given form to European integration. The Benelux Economic Union only pursued economic objectives, the EU strove for both growth and peace, while EFTA's objective was only growth. The first extension of the EU had only an economic target, whereas for the second both the growth and the democracy argument were used. The latest enlargement with three EFTA countries set only an economic objective. For the future extension with CEEC all three arguments will be very relevant. Political scientists agree that the EU has attained its non-economic objectives.

Pattern of development

The objectives of the EU can be detailed in terms of stages of integration. The gradual stepping up of ambitions and development of their realisation over time has been summarised in Table 18.5.

Looking at the overall process of deepening and widening, we may conclude that the EU has needed in the past about 14 years to forge strong links between the members of a group, working towards the attainment of a well-defined objective. This turned out to be the basis on which a new extended group could start work on a higher objective (for example, EU12 working towards the realisation of the internal market). However, if we analyse the process in rather more depth, we see that there are intermediate steps, too (1952 for the ECSC; 1967 for the first, unsuccessful, negotiations with the UK; 1981 for the accession of Greece; 1993 for the accession of three EFTAns).

If we extend this dynamism with the same periodicity from the past to the future, we come up with the prediction that both deepening and widening will proceed. Deepening will lead the EU to create an EMU by the year 2000 and a political union at some point in the

Table 18.5   The process of deepening and widening of European integration

Deepening	Widening					
	1944 Benelux	1958 EU6	1972 EU9	1986 EU12	2000 EU15	200? EU??
ICM		*	*			
CM				*	*	*
EU	*			*	*	*
MU					*	*
PU						*

next century. Widening will result in a first round of extension with CEECs between 2004 and 2007 and a second one somewhat further into the next century.

Success factors

From the various strands of literature we have distilled the following general factors that have conditioned in the past the success of progressive integration.

Unity of purpose   The EU started with a limited number of members around the strong axis of France and Germany. The risk of dilution was limited as extensions were few, occurred only after considerable periods of internal strengthening, and new members were only admitted on the condition that they accepted the 'acquis communautaire' of the past and the new objectives for the future.

Limited diversity   Differences in levels of development between the members are not very large by world 'standards'. All EU countries belong, indeed, to the category of (highly) developed countries. As a consequence, one could start without intra-EU financial transfers, always a bone of contention, and continue with a redistribution scheme that kept transfers at a relatively low level. This set-up has made it possible to continue to work on programmes for improving allocational efficiency (for instance, the completion of the internal market) and macro-economic stability (for instance, EMU) without the discussion being distorted by distributional issues.

Safety mechanism against reverse developments   The integration of markets, once achieved, cannot be rejected by a member state. Safeguards are the whole EU legal system and the heavy cost that a breakaway would inflict on business that has organised itself on the assumption of durable and reliable access to markets, complemented by common policies.

Institutional strength   The powers of the EU to make laws on the basis of qualified majority voting that are, moreover, directly applicable in all member states have permitted this supranational organisation to function relatively effectively and efficiently. The institutional set-up of the EU has reduced very significantly the cost of bargaining, that is of reaching cooperative solutions to political problems in areas where national policies have lost effectiveness.

Operational flexibility   The EU has a diversity of regulatory forms. In many cases the directive is used. This permits much flexibility as to the way in which national authorities actually implement EU regulation in their legislation. If needed, the EU has temporarily permitted exceptions to general rules – for example, with longer transition periods for Mediterranean countries to comply with the rules of the internal market or environmental policy. In some cases it has even permitted the opting out of certain members for whole sections of its activity (as with the UK for the Social Chapter).[4]

Conditions for major progress

Specific accelerations of the integration process have occurred when a set of conditions was fulfilled. We make here a distinction between deepening and widening.
   Success with *deepening* depended on the following conditions:

- clear-cut objectives that can be easily understood by large sections of society (for example, removal of all barriers for the completion of the internal market; one market, one money for EMU);
- tangible gains; felt directly by influential interest groups like big business and supported by independent assessments or by academics (as with the studies on the cost of non-Europe for the benefits of the 1992 programme);
- coherent action for realisations, with a timetable and a clear distribution of roles for the various actors (Commission, industry associations and so on; see white paper (CEC, 1985d) and subsequent work programme for '1992').

The process of *widening* has deliberately started from a narrow base. Extension came on three conditions:

- excess of economic advantages over cost (an acceleration of the growth of GDP offsetting short-term restructuring cost);
- taking away of political barriers (for example, lack of democracy and human rights in Mediterranean countries);
- limited strain on the functioning of the EU (no renegotiation of the 'acquis communautaire'; limited budget outlays; institutional continuity).

Failures

The EU has not only had successes. On the contrary, its past performance also shows some important failures in respect of things that the EU has done and should not have done. The two principal examples were reported in earlier parts of this book. They are both related to allocation:

- For a long time the EU has tended to *over-regulate* the economy. It has changed its approach only with the advent of the internal market programme, focusing now on subsidiarity.
- The regimes for *agriculture* (and for some time, to a lesser extent, those for steel, energy and transport) have occasioned considerable distortion in markets, leading to inefficient redistribution, to persistent large losses of welfare and to international tensions.

One is tempted to define another category of failures – namely, things the EU has not done and that it should have done. This is a much more difficult nut to crack, as it implies the identification of a number of integration measures that would have had large welfare increases yet have not been realised or have not been realised in due time. Many things come to mind in this category, such as: the incomplete tax harmonisation leading to tax evasion and fraud; the non-existence of a European corporate statute, which prevents firms from organising themselves efficiently; the late integration of the service sectors and so on. However, the evidence for these examples is less clear than for the previous category and furthermore the losses incurred by not acting seem to be less important than the losses related to the EU acting wrongly.

The major *reasons* for failures (doing things wrongly) were as follows:

- The EU has started out as an experiment that could neither use historical examples, nor a solid theoretical base to guide its actions.
- The special constitutional standing of a number of regimes for specific sectors, coupled with a sector-specific bureaucracy, made

them resistant to change even after conditions had changed radically.

Future deepening

Foundations

The theoretical foundations for the explanation of the EU's past dynamism, as reflected in the growth of intra-EU trade and investment and the considerable increase in its scope of competences, have been given in Chapter 2. The most encompassing concept in this respect is the idea of spill-over. This concept starts from the benefits that can be had from trade integration by using to the full the advantages of economies of scale, dictated by technology. Once markets have been opened, integration spills over into other areas, as one economic function is related to others. For example, common policies are needed as they enhance the effectiveness of market integration. This economic interpretation of the progress in integration needs to be complemented by factors from political science in order to formulate a full explanation of the specific forms that integration has adopted.

In the past a projection into the future of the subjects that integration would cover could be based on this notion of movement through principal stages, and this approach has indeed permitted us to correctly forecast three major developments: first, the completion of the internal market by 1992 (Molle, 1985); second, the successful set-up of the economic and monetary union by the end of the last century, and, finally, the increased weight that redistribution policies have taken in total EU activity during the 1990s (Molle, 1989). With hindsight this appears to be the single logical outcome of a long-term course of events. However, at the time of writing these issues were highly controversial.

As the EU has arrived at the highest stage of integration short of the full economic union, the approach of the movement through stages can no longer be used to predict how integration will move on. We can, however, predict two rather general features of this process:

- European regulation will cover an increasing number of detailed subjects from a very wide array of economic policies. The form that this integration will take depends on the specific configuration of the political forces of the principal players involved in the field at hand; no grand design is likely to emerge from this.

- For the regulation of these subjects the less committing instruments will be selected. Indeed, the EU has understood the advantages of subsidiarity and has set on a course of using coordination rather than unification.

In the beginning of the 1990s there was a very considerable variety of opinions about the way in which the EU had to develop its different dimensions (Jacquemin and Wright, 1993). At the beginning of the new millennium, the EU has again adopted a clear major strategy (Lisbon summit). This strategy consists in the building of a dynamic economy that is competitive in the world and that makes the best use of the potential offered by the electronic (or digital) revolution. Much of the development will be related to knowledge-intensive activities that will shape the information society of tomorrow. This will be done through the elaboration of an action plan for e-Europe that will cover such actions as the stimulation of access to cheap modern communication infrastructure and the improvement of the conditions under which e-commerce and Internet-based activities will flourish.

In the following sections we will present for each dimension of integration (policy area) the elements that are likely to present major challenges to policy makers in the near future.

Allocation; market policies

The integration of markets, the hard core of European integration, is in need of further development. The *business community* is much in favour of the further move from a single to an integrated market. The latter differs from the former in the sense that it has done away with most of the national differentiation of consumer preferences and regulation. This would enable corporations to realise important efficiency gains by selecting optimal internal and external organisational forms; that is, the configuration of their own activities and those of their suppliers as if they were in a market like the USA. There is one exception, the labour market, where the business community is strongly in favour of national responsibility (Jacquemin and Wright, 1993).

From the standpoint of the *public authorities*, in charge of creating the conditions for a good functioning of the internal market this implies a shift in attention. In the past it concentrated on the elaboration of a common legal framework. Now it concentrates on the systematic support for the structural reform of the (national) markets for products and capital by the benchmarking of each others' performances, the selection of the best practices and the exertion of peer pressure to implement the necessary changes.

There are three points that seem to be relevant to develop further:

- *Competition policy.* The role of the EU as a guardian to the fair play of market forces will gain in importance in an integrated market for several reasons. First companies increasingly want to deal with only one single EU instead of with several national and Union authorities. Second, there are important issues to be cleared up, such as limitation of state aids and equality of access to corporate control. Finally the international dimension of competition policy has become much more important in a rapidly globalising world.
- *Intervention in markets.* In the past the number of areas where governments intervened directly in the functioning of markets (prices and quantities) or in the access to markets (public companies) has rapidly decreased. Some pockets of interventionism still exist, of which agriculture is the main problem, given its important negative effects on consumer wealth, on cohesion, and on external relations. Further action needs to be taken to complete the internal market for services (notably of financial services and network services) and to create the conditions for the enhanced development of 'e-Europe'.
- *Taxes.* The competition of national systems is likely to tend towards a non-optimal solution in matters of corporate taxes. A shift away from labour-based taxes towards other parts of the tax base is needed in order to provide the conditions for employment growth. A solution has to be found for the erosion of the VAT base due to the increase in trade in intangibles over the Internet, such as the downloading of videos, music, programmes and so on.

The challenge for the authorities assumes a much broader dimension if we put allocation policies in the context of the optimal model of European society. The ingredients are, on the one hand, rivalry, deregulation and hence flexibility in order to gain international economic competitiveness. On the other hand, it takes participation, consensus, redistribution and stabilisation to arrive at a harmonious social development. Finding a good blend of these elements is a major task for the next decade.

Stabilisation: the need for better coordination

The major challenge to the EU is to *implement successfully the EMU* while at the same time *improving the employment situation*. This calls for a package of policies that are well coordinated both vertically and horizontally – vertically in the sense that national and EU policies need to be consistent and horizontally in the sense that monetary (expansion of money supply, interest rates), fiscal (reorientation of public expenditure) and labour market (wage restraint) policies need to be consistent. The present EU coordination mechanism already covers a large set of policies (see Chapter 15). We do not expect this number to increase much, as the positive effects of the increase in consistency may well be offset by the negative effects of the lack of flexibility. In this respect, a case can even be made for the streamlining of the present procedures.

A second issue that needs to be seen is whether there is a need for additional stabilisation mechanisms. The present adjustment mechanisms are supposed to be able to cope with the most important shocks to the system. Many observers do think that there is no need for increased stabilisation and that time and events will have to show where the present set-up still needs improvement.

Redistribution: towards more cohesion

The European cohesion policies will face a number of new challenges in the near future. These are, on the *economic* side:

- *EMU.* The creation of the MU may generate additional problems for the current problem regions. Increased competition may increase the need for support, while the capacity for providing such support is constrained by the Stability and Growth Pact.
- *Central and Eastern Europe.* The opening up of the EU market to the CEEC (in a perspective of eventual widening) has far-reaching consequences for the patterns of trade, tourism, technology transfer, direct investment, labour competitiveness and international aid. This entails two types of challenges. First, some of the industries of the less well developed regions of the present EU may be hard hit by the new industrial specialisation patterns that will result. Second, the accession of new member states in Central Europe will increase the intensity, complexity and variety of the regional problems that have to be faced.

On the *social side*, quite a number of problems exist that also put cohesion in jeopardy; the overriding one is unemployment. Other problems are the increasing ageing of the population, the high level of long-term unemployment, social exclusion and lack of integration of immigrants. There is a growing need to step up social infrastructure and to care for the socially disadvantaged groups, notably in urban centres.

In order to *combat these increased problems*, several types of EU policy measures need be taken:

- *Improving efficiency.* The present system is very involved and realises effects at fairly high cost. New ways need to be found to step up effects, while at the same time limiting the increase in resources.
- *Spatial concentration.* The efforts of the EU need to be refocused on the major problem regions of an enlarged EU. Current member countries should take care of the lesser problem regions.
- *Combating social exclusion.* The problems that specific categories of the population face may make the whole society less efficient.

External relations: fortress or crossroads?

The European Union was created with two objectives in mind: to establish the conditions for durable peace and to enhance the economic development of Europe. Right from its start it has been aware that promoting 'integration' with non-member countries would serve the same objectives at the world level. Notwithstanding the progress made in the past, this world-wide integration of the EU is far from complete. For the future the major challenges present themselves as follows.

The external *trade* relations of the EU have, first of all, a sectoral aspect. These are dominated by the EU commitment to a positive outcome of the new WTO negotiations (the Millennium round). For products of agriculture and the service sector, further progress on liberalisation is needed. Next, they have a geographical aspect. The progressive liberalisation of the trade relations with Central and Eastern Europe and their integration into a single framework (Sapir, 2000) is of paramount importance; then come the relations with the Mediterranean countries, where trade is conducive to stability. Finally the EU should favour relations with other regional integration schemes that are a good basis for the improvement of worldwide trade relations.

With respect to *production factors*, the EU is not likely to change its policy a great deal. Capital movements are now completely free. They are likely to increase in nature as FDI over larger geographical areas are likely to increase with further progress of globalisation. For labour movements, the present situation of nationally regulated and increasingly restricted access is likely to continue in the near future. In time, however, the logic of the completed market will push towards making uniform the external dimension of the labour market, which means European immigration laws. It is unlikely that the

European Union will open up again for large-scale external migration. This implies, however, that the EU will not accept any international regime that would strive to liberalise labour movements worldwide. Indeed, the welfare effects of such a scheme are highly controversial (Grubel, 1994). Hence a need for the EU to intensify its efforts to improve trade possibilities and step up its development assistance as instruments to alleviate the employment and wage situation in third countries.

For *common economic policies*, however, substantial changes are on the cards for the near future. As the range of matters treated within the EU expands, so does the need to discuss them externally. The globalisation trend also pushes other major players to seek discussion of these matters on a global level. So the EU will increasingly be asked to cooperate in the elaboration of the global economic regime. Multilateralism will then become more important than bilateralism.

The future will be dominated by the increase in *globalisation*. This will mean that, for a large number of subjects, the optimal area for regulation is no longer the EU or the national state (in the case of the US, for instance). Optimal regulation areas will increasingly correspond to the whole world. Seen in this light, the present global regime seems to be rather embryonic and inadequate for the increased demands that will be put on it. Indeed, there is no unified institutional framework but a rather disparate set of organisations and agreements (see Preston and Windsor, 1997). Major elements are the World Trade Organisation and the International Monetary Fund. Other international organisations exist but are of less relevance to our subject.

The logic of this set-up can be related to the balance between economic advantages and political cost. The WTO has concentrated on trade issues and aspects that are immediately related to it. This is in line with the theoretical insight that the first level of integration should apply to the integration of goods markets since clear advantages can be had here, while government power in essential domains is not lost. The IMF is responsible for stable monetary relations. This is in line with the insight that trade and investment relations are facilitated by stable monetary conditions.

The question then becomes in what way *the global regime is likely to develop*. Our hypothesis is that *the way in which the EU has developed in the past may give some indications as to the path that the world system may follow in the future*. To that end we refer back to Table 18.4.

We see there that the policy integration of the EU has in first instance covered aspects of *allocation policies*: policies that facilitate the good functioning of markets – particularly those of goods. The case of the EU agricultural market order is so blatantly a failure that we do not even need to check whether it merits finding its counter-part on the global level. However, the early set-up of a common EU competition policy seems to be replicated worldwide. Indeed, the case for the setting up of such an international (multilateral) compe-tition policy is strong (Meiklejohn, 1999), although there are as yet many obstacles to its realisation, among which the inadequacy of the existing institutional framework (WTO) is not the least. A compelling case can also be made for the setting up of an investment regime (such as the multilateral agreement on investment project of the OECD) even if the political circumstances have aborted the latest set-up. Finally, more work can be expected on the scores of technical norms and standards and government intervention in services such as landing rights.

Integration can go a long way without necessitating common *stabilisation policies*. So we do not expect that, in the foreseeable fu-ture, the need will occur for a considerable strengthening of the present system. Further coordination can be expected with the G8 and the IMF, gradually expanding and refining their toolkit.

Redistribution policies are typically only feasible in cases where the solidarity among the members of an integration area has far ad-vanced. On the global level this is not likely to be the case in the foreseeable future. The present situation, with bilateral donors and a number of multilateral donors (such as the World Bank) seems to be adequate to accommodate the need for redistribution also at the levels of global integration we expect for the near future.

Finally, a number of policies that do accompany the whole inte-gration process, such as *environment or technology*, will be subject to global regimes. In the environmental field a considerable effort to set up a global regime has already been made, and we expect this devel-opment to continue with an increasing number of specific problems being attacked by multilateral agreements. For non-economic poli-cies such as safety, police and so on, globalisation may take more time to come to effect.

Future widening

Economic foundations

The *theoretical foundations* for the explanation of the widening of an existing framework of regional economic integration have been given in Chapter 2. We distinguished there between a number of approaches. The theoretical concept that has received most attention is the *opti-mum integration area* (OIA). It suggests that countries that have reached among themselves a certain degree of exchange, and show a certain degree of convergence of policy, can participate, whereas countries that do not fulfil such criteria should be excluded from participation. In practice, however, it proved rather difficult to implement this theory, for a number of reasons already given in Chapter 2. The solution has been to translate the discussion on the criteria into a discussion about cost and benefits. For countries that are part of the OIA the benefits will in general outweigh the cost; the opposite is the case for countries that are not part of the OIA. Incidentally this economic balancing does not fully determine the outcome: many political arguments may come into play and may even overshadow the economic ones in the final decision.

In the *past* the decisions about the enlargement of the EU have been taken in a manner that is in line with these theoretical foundations (see previous chapters). Indeed, economic studies have produced evidence of the advantages of enlargement for both the EU and the accession countries. In those cases where political arguments have tipped the balance in favour of the decision, the very functioning of the EU (market and policy integration, including the participation of old and new member countries in EU redistribution schemes), has made it possible for countries to come up to the requirements. This finally tipped the balance of advantages and disadvantages, not only in political but also in economic terms. These advantages have been influenced by such factors as the increase in the efficiency of firms of the new member countries in having direct access to the European internal market. Staying out proved to be costly, which induced firms in non-EU countries to lobby for accession. This phenomenon described by the domino theory of widening proved to give a quite adequate view of the process.[5]

The *future of widening* is probably mostly determined by the view of the theory of clubs (see Chapter 2). As a matter of fact the EU, as the dominant organisation, is capable of setting the rules and the criteria for membership. It then negotiates with the candidate countries the modalities of their access to the EU. To each individual country the decision is taken on the basis of the net effect of the economic and political benefits. The major task is to integrate the countries of Central and Eastern Europe. Here the domino theory comes to mind again. Indeed, for the CEECs the alternatives to membership of the EU are not very attractive; this applies both to a stand-alone situation and to the participation in an alternative club.[6] Accession of such a large group of countries would certainly strengthen the club in terms of economic power; however, it would need quite a few adaptations on the institutional side to make sure that it will continue to function properly (see the final section of Chapter 4).

Political conditions

The EU has always been open for membership of other democratic countries in Western Europe. In the past widening has been decided on a case-by-case basis. The need to accomplish the historic task of integrating the CEECs into the EU called for *a more systematic approach*. In 1993, the European Council therefore defined the economic and political conditions a candidate country has to fulfil in order to qualify for membership. Defining such principles has a number of interrelated advantages. First, it enhances the predictability of the EU position. Second, it improves the efficiency of the efforts of the candidates to transform their economies. Third, it guides the EU in designing together with the candidates the programmes of aid.

The *requirements for EU membership* are as follows:

- stability of institutions guaranteeing democracy, the rule of law, human rights and respect for the protection of minorities;
- existence of a functioning market economy, as well as the capacity to cope with competitive pressure and market forces within the Union;
- ability to take on the obligations of membership (adopt the acquis communautaire), including adherence to the aims of political, economic and monetary union.

Further extension does not only require adaptation from the candidates; the EU itself has to adapt, too. This implies that the EU should prepare itself institutionally for coping with an increased number of difficult issues, and with an extended and more diversified group of member countries.

A closer look at the economic criteria

The first of the economic criteria is about the *functioning market economy*. Whether this is achieved is judged on the answer to a number of questions; the most important of which are:

- Are market forces allowed to play their role? In other words, is there freedom of economic actors to set prices and to trade freely?
- Have obstacles to the entry of new firms and to the exit of existing firms (bankruptcy) been lifted?
- Is there an effective legal system that sets rules for the fair play of market forces, such as property rights, and is there an effective system to enforce compliance?

- Has macro-economic stability – that is, low inflation, a low budget deficit and a sustainable position of the balance of payments – been achieved?
- Is there a sufficient consensus about the main orientations and principles of the major policies?
- Is there a developed financial sector that permits savings to be channelled effectively into productive investment?

The second criterion is about *competitiveness*. A country is thought to be competitive if it has a positive score on the following sub-criteria:

- *Trade integration into the EU*. If the country exports to the EU this can be taken as a proof of competitiveness. Of course, the sectoral composition needs to be taken into account – that is, exports should come from the manufacturing and service sectors and not only from the natural resource sectors.
- *Balanced composition of firms in the economy*. The past dominance of state firms should have been brought to an end by successful privatisation. Moreover, small and medium-sized enterprises must have developed.
- *Good health of the private sector*. Indicators of health that can be used are the growth of output, the rate of investment, the degree of innovation and the profitability of operations.

A number of additional criteria that are *conditions for competitiveness* are also used. They are more of a qualitative nature. The most important ones are:

- *Production structure*. Are those types of intermediate product that are essential for many activities – such as energy, capital, telecommunications and so on – available?
- *Production environment*. Is there an adequate provision of infrastructure, of education, of R&D and of environmental services?
- *Institutions*. Are matters of competition, corporate governance, investment and so on well-regulated and are there organisations that can effectively implement them? Cases in point are, for instance, the markets for securities and a competition authority. In general, however, the efficiency of the whole public administration should be judged.

Meeting the criteria: from outside or inside?

The catching up of the applicant countries with the EU is complicated by two factors: first, the completion of the transition to a market economy on the part of the applicants; and, second the simultaneously progressing of the EU towards a very high stage of economic integration.

There are two *models* of coping with this problem of the moving target.

- Gradual participation in ever more aspects of the integration process without formal membership. This model has actually been offered to the CEEC by the EU and is now being implemented under the term 'pre-accession strategy'.
- Rapid membership and long transition periods. This option has been advocated by many applicants, which think that this would be the best way to accelerate growth and change and to safeguard the democratic system. However the EU is very reluctant to choose this model, because the German reunification has shown how high the cost would be in a case where a country that does not belong to the OIA is nevertheless integrated in an accelerated way.

The road the CEEC must follow in catching up with the integration process in the West is a long one. The first part of this road is being covered according to the first model. The benchmark for the end of the first part is likely to be the capacity to meet the exigencies of the internal market. The second part of the road will then be made according to the second model, so meeting the exigencies of aspects of the economic (for instance environment) and monetary union (for instance the introduction of the euro) may then be done as members of the EU.

Central and Eastern Europe: progress on the road to membership

Almost all Central and Eastern European Countries (CEECs) have applied for membership and are striving for closer integration with Western Europe. There are large differences between the present EU and the various candidate countries (see Table 18.6). Unemployment is in general higher in the CEECs than in the EU; GDP per head is much lower; the structure of the economy is still much more oriented to agriculture and less to services; and the number of Internet connections is much lower. These differences are much more prominent for some of the CEECs than for others. Many of the indicators are actually in line with the level of development indicated by the GDP/P figures. Note that for almost all candidate countries trade is now mainly oriented to the EU.

The Commission has regularly analysed the performance of all candidate countries in meeting the criteria for membership.[7] Five of the CEECs (Poland, Hungary, the Czech Republic, Estonia and

Table 18.6   Basic economic indicators for candidate countries in Central and Eastern Europe in 1998

Candidate country[a]	Pop[b]	Unemployed[c]	GDP/P[d]		Structure labour force[e]			Trade		Internet[h]	FDI/P[i]
			CP	PPP	Agri	Industry	Service	E/I[f]	EU/T[g]		
Slovenia	2	8	44	68	12	39	49	90	67	91	100
Czech Republic	10	7	24	60	6	41	53	92	63	64	150
Hungary	10	8	20	48	8	34	58	90	69	73	170
Slovakia	5	13	17	46	8	40	52	82	53	26	60
Poland	39	11	18	36	19	32	49	60	67	26	120
Estonia	1	10	16	36	10	33	57	68	57	131	200
Lithuania	4	13	13	31	21	27	52	64	4	23	110
Romania	23	6	8	29	40	29	31	70	61	6	50
Latvia	2	14	12	27	19	16	55	57	56	33	150
Bulgaria	8	16	7	23	26	31	43	86	47	7	40
EU15	380	9	100	100	4	23	73	*	*	143	*

Notes:
a   By order of GDP/P (PPP).
b   Millions.
c   % of labour force (ILO definition).
d   CP: current prices; PPP: purchasing power parities.
e   % of total employment.
f   Export as a percentage of imports.
g   Trade with EU as % of total trade (I+E:2).
h   Internet communications per 1000 inhabitants.
i   FDI (incoming) per head of population (euro) yearly average 1996–98.

Source: Eurostat (2000) *Statistical Yearbook on Candidate and SE European Countries*, Luxemburg.

Slovenia) have in the meantime made such progress that negotiations with them have already made quite some headway (accession negotiations take place with each candidate country separately). For the early entrants it will be necessary to agree on many details of the internal market 'acquis' and on transition periods for those sectors of the economy where the EU integration has in the meantime proceeded further (such as the EMU). For the more backward CEECs, negotiations are at a more preliminary stage and longer periods will certainly have to be taken into account before membership becomes feasible. If, to some, these time periods appear too long, it is worth keeping in mind that the entrance of the southern EU members in the 1980s was only realised some ten years after their political revolutions, and in those cases no economic revolution was necessary.[8]

What would be a *realistic timetable* for the various stages? This depends, on the one hand, on the internal restructuring of the EU itself (institutions, agriculture and so on) and, on the other, on the speed with which the CEECs will be able to meet the criteria. To fulfil the criteria at the internal market level, the CEECs will have to make considerable progress with respect to liberalisation of the movement of goods and factors, and with economic, legal and institutional reform. Critical in this respect is the freedom of movement of persons. The EU wants to preclude large migration flows from the CEECs to the present EU. In an internal market that would only be possible where the differences between the richest and the poorest participant do not exceed the ones that exist in the present EU. To arrive at this situation, the CEECs that are now the most developed would, over the coming years, have to register a growth rate considerably in excess of that of the EU. This is not unrealistic; in the recent past some of them have already demonstrated similar growth rates. So, evaluating all factors, the first CEEC members of the EU may be expected to gain entry in the years 2004–2006.

Central and Eastern Europe: common efforts for preparation of membership

The pre-accession strategy of the EU consists of the following elements:

- Accession partnerships. They set out the key short- and medium-term priorities to be met in order to prepare for membership. They also indicate the financial assistance available from the EU (presently over 3 billion euro) in support of these priorities and the conditionality attached to that assistance.
- Europe Agreements institutions. At regular intervals a systematic examination is made of each candidate country's progress. To that end committees and sub-committees have been set up.

- National programmes. These specify the resources and the time-table foreseen for the adoption of the 'acquis'. In addition to the agreed partnership priorities, most applicant countries have defined their own priorities for accession.
- Participation in Community programmes. This allows the accession countries to become familiar with Community policies and working methods. (All candidate countries do participate now in such programmes – particularly in the field of vocational training, energy, environment and so on.)
- Financial and expert assistance. As the pace of integration accelerates, the EU has decided to double its pre-accession assistance to over 3 billion euro a year. Traditionally this assistance has been given through the Phare programme, which focused on investment in infrastructure, on institution building and on the adoption of the 'acquis'. From 2000 onwards the Phare programme will be joined by two new instruments (see also Chapter 17 'External Relations').

EFTA/Mediterranean

In the past a number of non-economic factors such as neutrality and the loss of autonomy have stopped *EFTA* countries such as Switzerland and Norway from becoming EU members. These perceived high costs in political terms were not offset by the relatively small net economic benefits that could be expected from membership. This trade-off between economic and political factors is not likely to change much in the immediate future, so we will not pay further attention to it.

A similar trade-off of political and economic arguments has to be made by candidate members like *Cyprus* and *Malta*. However, here the decision has finally been to apply for membership. The effect of their accession is of marginal importance to the EU economy, so we will not pay further attention to it here either.

The case of *Turkey* is different. The EU committed itself a long time ago to the likelihood of its full membership. In 1987, Turkey applied officially for membership. However progress has not been made, for two reasons. The EU considers that the situation in Turkey with respect to human rights is far from satisfactory, which precludes negotiations on membership. Also some political currents in Turkey seem to be in favour of a Middle Eastern rather than a European integration. It is unlikely that this situation will clear up in the immediate future.

Summary and conclusions

- Integration has made considerable progress in Europe in the post-war years. That is evidenced by many indicators: economic ones, such as the interpenetration of markets and the convergence of prices, and policy ones, such as the fields covered, and the strength of instruments used by EU institutions.
- Integration has reached its objectives: peace and democracy have been safeguarded, and wealth has increased while the distribution of wealth has improved.
- New objectives have been set for future economic integration. In terms of deepening, the most important goals are: (1) the completion of the Economic and Monetary Union and (2) the making of a competitive Europe in the electronic age, characterised by new economic sectors (such as e-commerce) and new infrastructure (such as the Internet). In terms of widening, the most important goal is the integration of the countries of Central and Eastern Europe.

Notes

1   Although the freedoms were not immediately implemented, we have considered a U to be the best for 1960; a U also for 1990, notwithstanding some rudiments of national discretion.
2   The EEC treaty refers to coordination, but the standard term, 'consultation', describes more adequately the situation that prevailed during this period.
3   Although the EEC Treaty set regional equilibrium as a common objective (as there was a few of the negative side-effects of EU allocation policies), the practice of the formative years of the EC was one of information (see Chapter 6).
4   This practice, that has developed over the past, has been enshrined as a constitutional right by the Treaty of Amsterdam. It permits groups of member states to use the EU institutions framework for forms of closer cooperation.
5   A preliminary empirical test of the domino theory has been done by Sapir (1997) with the help of a gravity model estimated for the period 1960–92. His results clearly show that EFTA members have been urged to join the EU due to loss of competitiveness.
6   Only Russia and its associated states may hope to be able to present a credible alternative to the EU. The participation of the CEECs in agreements with the EU gave them the perspective of joining the club, offering CEEC governments a commitment which helped them to implement reforms that otherwise would not have come through, due to time inconsistencies. This applies both to economic reforms such as the liberalisation of the trade regime and political reforms such as democratisation (Fernandez, 1997). The modern conditions under which the global trade system functions tend to enhance the pressure on CEECs to join the EU (Ethier, 1998). For instance, multilateral free trade has diminished tariff protection, which makes transport cost more important and hence regional cooperation more interesting. Moreover, the high mobility of capital means that small differences between the locational quality of countries can

cause big differences in the choice of multinational firms in the location of their investment. As FDI is of the utmost importance for growth in CEECs, showing that reforms are effective and irreversible by joining the Union is a very important factor.

7   Reports on the progress of reform and on the implementation of the 'acquis' are given in CEC (2000e). Up to date information on the enlargement process can be obtained from the web site of the Commission: http://europa.eu.int.comm. enlargement/index.htm

8   There are political reasons that may speed up this timetable. One is the need to avoid unrest on the Eastern borders of the EU, which may be a recurrent factor if economic growth expectations take too long to be fulfilled.

List of Abbreviations

ACP	African, Caribbean and Pacific Countries
BEUC	Bureau Européen des Unions de Consommateurs
BIS	Bank for International Settlements
CAP	Common Agricultural Policy
CCP	Common Commercial Policy
CEC	Commission of the European Communities
CEEC	Central and Eastern European Countries
CEN	Comité Européen de Normalisation
CENELEC	Comité Européen de Normalisation Electronique
CEP	Common Energy Policy
CEPT	Conference Européenne des Postes et Télécommunications
CET	Common External Tariff
CI	Community Initiative
CM	Common Market
CMEA	Council of Mutual Economic Assistance (Comecon)
CMU	Capital Market Union
CNIR	Covered Nominal Interest Rate
CU	Customs Union
COREPER	Committee of Permanent Representatives
DI	Direct Investment
EAEC	European Atomic Energy Community (Euratom)
EAGGF	European Agricultural Guidance and Guarantee Fund
EC	European Community
EBRD	European Bank of Reconstruction and Development
ECA	European Court of Auditors
ECB	European Central Bank
ECE	Economic Commission for Europe
ECJ	European Court of Justice
ECSC	European Coal and Steel Community
ECU	European Currency Unit
EDC	European Defence Community
EDF	European Development Fund
EDIE	European Direct Investment in Europe
EDIUS	European Direct Investment in the US
EEA	European Economic Area

EEC	European Economic Community
EFTA	European Free Trade Association
EIB	European Investment Bank
EMCF	European Monetary Cooperation Fund
EMI	European Monetary Institute
EMS	European Monetary System
EMU	Economic and Monetary Union
EP	European Parliament
EPC	European Political Community/Cooperation
ERDF	European Regional Development Fund
ERM	Exchange Rate Mechanism
ESC	Economic and Social Committee
ESF	European Social Fund
EU	European Union/Economic Union
FCMA	Free Capital Movement Area
FDIE	Foreign Direct Investment in Europe
FED	Federation
FLMA	Free Labour Movement Area
FPC	Foreign Profit Creation
FPD	Foreign Profit Diversion
FRG	Federal Republic of Germany
FTA	Free Trade Area
FTL	Full Truck-loads
FU	Full Union
GATS	General Agreement on Trade in Services
GATT	General Agreement on Tariffs and Trade
GDP	Gross Domestic Product
GDP/P	Gross Domestic Product per Head of Population
GFCF	Gross Fixed Capital Formation
GJ	Gigajoule
GNP	Gross National Product
GSP	Generalised System of Preference
HFL	Dutch Florin
IBRD	International Bank for Reconstruction and Development (World Bank)
ICM	Incomplete Common Market
ICU	Incomplete Customs Union
IIT	Intra-Industry Trade
ILO	International Labour Organisation
IMF	International Monetary Fund
ISIC	International Standard Industrial Classification
LDC	Less Developed Country
LEC	Labour-Exporting Country
LFTL	Less Than Full Truck-loads
LIC	Labour Importing Country

LMU	Labour Market Union
LPG	Liquefied Petroleum Gas
MCA	Monetary Compensatory Amounts
Mecu	Million ECU
MFA	Multi-Fibre Arrangement
MFN	Most Favoured Nation
MNC	Multinational Company
MNF	Multi National Firm
MU	Monetary Union
Mt/y	Million (1 000 000) tons per year
Mtoe	Million (1 000 000) tons of oil equivalent
NATO	North Atlantic Treaty Organisation
NG	Natural Gas
NIC	Newly Industrialising Countries
NORDEL	Nordic Electricity
NTB	Non-Tariff Barriers
OCA	Optimum Currency Area
OECD	Organisation for Economic Cooperation and Development
OIA	Optimum Integration Area
OMA	Orderly Marketing Arrangements
OPEC	Organisation of Petroleum Exporting Countries
PTA	Preferential Trade Agreement
PTT	Post Telegraph Telephone
PU	Political Union
QR	Quantitative Restrictions
R & D	Research and Development
RIR	Real Interest Rates
SDR	Special Drawing Right
SEA	Single European Act
SSR	Self Sufficiency Ratio
TEU	Treaty on European Union
TRIMS	Trade-related Investment Measures
TRIPS	Trade-related Intellectual Property Rights
UCPTE	Union for the Coordination of the Production and Transmission of Electric Power
UK	United Kingdom
UNCTAD	United Nations Conference on Trade and Development
UNIDO	United Nations Industrial Development Organisation
UNIR	Uncovered Nominal Interest Rate
UNO	United Nations Organisation
USA	United States of America
USDIE	US Direct Investment in the US
VAT	Value-Added Tax
VER	Voluntary Export Restraint

| WEU | Western European Union |
| WTO | World Trade Organisation |

Bibliography

Addison, J.T. and Siebert, W.S. (1994), 'Recent developments in social policy in the new European Union', *Industrial and Labour Relations Review*, vol.48, no.1, pp.5–27.

Adler, M. (1970), 'Specialisation in the European Coal and Steel Community', *Journal of Common Market Studies*, vol.8, pp.175–91.

Aitken, N.D. (1973), 'The Effect of the EEC and EFTA on European Trade; a Temporal Cross-Section Analysis', *American Economic Review*, vol.63, pp.881–91.

Albert, M. and Ball, R. (1983), *Towards European Economic Recovery in the 1980's*, European Parliament Working Documents 1983/84, Luxemburg.

Alesina, A. and Perotti, R. (1995), 'Fiscal expansions and fiscal adjustments in OECD countries', *Economic Policy*, vol.10, pp.205–48.

Alesina, A. and Spolaore, E. (1997), 'On the number and size of nations', *Quarterly Journal of Economics*, pp.1027–56.

Allais, M., Duquesne de la Vinelle, L., Oort, V.J., Seidenfus, H.S. and del Viscoro, M. (1965), 'Options in Transport Policy', *The EEC Studies*, Transport Series no.4, Brussels.

Allen, C.B., Gasiorek, M. and Smith, A. (1996), *Competitiveness, impact, and the quantification of trade creation and trade diversion due to the MSP* (background study to CEC, 1996b), Brussels.

Allen, C.B., Gasiorek, M. and Smith, A. (1998), 'The competition effects of the Single Market in Europe', *Economic Policy: a European Forum*, pp.441–86.

Allen, P.R. (1983), 'Policies to Correct Cyclical Imbalance within a Monetary Union', *Journal of Common Market Studies*, vol.21.3, pp.313–27.

Allsopp, C. and Vines, D. (1996), 'Fiscal policy and EMU', *National Institute Economic Review*, pp.91–107.

AMUE (Association for the Monetary Union of Europe) (1988), *European Business and the ECU*; results of a survey carried out by FAITS et OPINIONS among 1036 business leaders in the European Community with the help of the ECU Banking Association and the European Commission, Paris.

Anarzit, P. d' (1982), *Essai d'une Politique Pétrolière Européenne*, Editions Techniques et Economiques, Paris.

Andersen, T., Haldrup, N. and Soerensen, J.R. (2000), 'Labour market implications of EU product market integration', *Economic Policy, a European Forum*, vol.30, no.2, pp.107–33.

Anderson S. and Eliassen, K. (1991), 'European Community Lobbying', *European Journal of Political Research*, vol.20, pp.173–87.

Arge, R. d' (1969), 'Note on Customs Union and Direct Foreign Investment', *Economic Journal*, vol.79, pp.324–33.

Aristotelous, K. and Fountas, S. (1996), 'An empirical analysis of inward foreign direct investment flows in the EU with emphasis on the market enlargement hypothesis', *Journal of Common Market Studies*, vol.34, no.4, pp.571–83.

497

Armstrong, H.W., Balasubramanyam, V.N. and Salisu, M.A. (1996), 'Domestic savings, intra-national and intra-European Union capital flows, 1971–1991', *European Economic Review*, vol.40, pp.1229–35.

Askari, H. (1974), 'The Contribution of Migration to Economic Growth in the EEC', *Economica Internazionale*, vol.27, no.2, pp.341–5.

Aubrey, B. (1984), '100.000 Travailleurs Frontaliers', *Economie et Statistique*, no.170, pp.13–23.

Auctores Varii (1983), 'Issues and Experience of Transport Regulation Reform', *International Journal of Transport Economics*, vol.10, no.1–2.

Bachtler, J. and Clement, K. (eds) (1992), '1992 and regional development', special issue of *Regional Studies*, vol.26, no.4, pp.305–419.

Bachtler, J. and Michie, R. (1995), 'A new era in EU regional policy evaluation: The appraisal of the Structural Funds', *Regional Studies*, vol.29, no.8, pp.745–52.

Bairoch, P. (1976), *Commerce Extérieur et Développement Economique de l'Europe au XIXe Siècle*, Mouton, Paris.

Balakrishnan, R. and Michelacci, C. (2001), 'Unemployment dynamics across OECD countries', *European Economic Review*, vol.45, pp.135–65.

Balassa, B. (1961), *The Theory of Economic Integration*, Irwin, Homewood, Illinois.

Balassa, B. (1966), 'Tariff Reductions and Trade in Manufactures among Industrial Countries', *American Economic Review*, vol.56, pp.466–73.

Balassa, B. (ed.) (1975), *European Economic Integration*, North-Holland/American Elsevier, Amsterdam.

Balassa, B. (1976), 'Types of Economic Integration', in F. Machlup (ed.), *Economic Integration, Worldwide, Regional, Sectoral*, Macmillan, London, pp.17–31.

Balassa, B. (1977), 'Revealed Comparative Advantage Revisited: an Analysis of Relative Export Shares of the Industrial Countries 1953–1971', *The Manchester School*, pp.327–44.

Balassa, B. (1986), 'Intra-Industry Trade among Exporters of Manufactured Goods', in D. Greenaway and P.K.M. Tharakan (eds), *Imperfect Competition and International Trade*, Wheatsheaf, Brighton, pp.108–28.

Balassa, B. and Balassa, C. (1984), 'Industrial Protection in the Developed Countries', *The World Economy*, vol.7, no.2, pp.179–96.

Balassa, B. and Bauwens, L. (1988), 'The Determinants of Intra-European Trade in Manufactured Goods', *European Economic Review*, vol.32, no.7, pp.1421–39.

Baldwin, R. and Murray, T. (1977), 'MFN Tariff Reductions and Developing Country Trade Benefits under GSP', *Economic Journal*, vol.87, pp.30–46.

Baldwin, R.E. (1984), 'Trade Policies in Developed Countries', in R.W. Jones and P.B. Kenen (eds), *Handbook of International Economics*, vol.I, North-Holland, Amsterdam, pp.571–621.

Baldwin, R.E. (1994), *Towards an Integrated Europe*, CEPR, London.

Baldwin, R.E. (1997), 'The causes of regionalism', *CEPR Discussion Paper*, no.1599, London.

Baldwin, R.E. and Venables, A. (1995), 'Regional Economic Integration', in G. Grossman and K. Rogoff (eds), *Handbook of International Economics*, vol.III, North-Holland, Amsterdam, pp.1597–1644.

Baldwin, R.E., Forslid, R. and Haaland, J.I. (1996), 'Investment creation and diversion in Europe', *The World Economy*, vol.19, no.6, pp.635–59.

Baldwin, R.E., François, J.F. and Portes, R. (1997), 'The cost and benefits of eastern enlargement: the impact on the EU and central Europe', *Economic Policy: A European Forum*, vol.24, pp.127–76.

Barrell, R. and Pain, N. (1999), 'Trade restraints on Japanese direct investment flows', *European Economic Review*, Vol.43, pp.29–45.

Barro, R.J. and Sala-I-Martin, X. (1991), 'Convergence across states and regions', *Brookings Papers on Economic Activity*, no.1, pp.107–182.

Bartel, R. (1974), 'International Monetary Unions, the 19th Century Experience', *Journal of European Economic History*, vol.3, no.3, pp.689–723.

Baumol, W.J., Panzar, J.C. and Willig, R.D. (1982), *Contestable Markets and the Theory of Industry Structure*, Harcourt Brace Jovanovich, San Diego.

Bayoumi, T. and Eichengreen, B. (1993), 'Shocking aspects of European Monetary Integration', in Francisco Torres and Francesco Giavazzi (eds), *Adjustment and Growth in the European Monetary Union*, Cambridge University Press, Cambridge, pp.193–229.

Bayoumi, T. and Prassad, E. (1995), 'Currency Unions, economic fluctuations and adjustment: some empirical evidence', *CEPR Discussion Paper*, no.1172.

Bean, Ch. (1994), 'European Unemployment: A Survey', *The Journal of Economic Literature*, vol.32, no.2, pp.573–619.

Bean, Ch., Bernholz, P., Danthine, J.P. and Malinvaud, E. (1990), *European labour markets: a long-run view*, CEPR Macroeconomic Policy Group, Centre for European Policy Studies, Brussels.

Beetsma, R. and Uhlig, H. (1999), 'An analysis of the Stability and Growth Pact', *The Economic Journal*, vol.109, pp.546–71

Belderbos, R.A. (1997), 'Antidumping and tariff-jumping: Japanese firms' DFI in the European Union and the United States', *Weltwirtschaftliches Archiv*, vol.133, no.3, pp.419–57.

Bergeijk, P.A.G., van (1987), *The Determinants of Success and Failure of Economic Sanctions, Some Empirical Results*, Development and Security, Groningen.

Berglas, E. (1979), 'Preferential trading theory: the n commodity case', *Journal of Political Economy*, vol.87, pp.315–31.

Bergstrand, J.H. (1983), 'Measurement and Determinants on Intra-Industry International Trade', in P.K.M. Tharakan (ed.), *Intra-Industry Trade: Empirical and Methodological Aspects*, North-Holland, Amsterdam, pp.201–55.

Bernard, P.J. (ed.) (1978), *Les Travailleurs Etrangers en Europe*, Mouton, The Hague.

Berthold, N., Fehn, R. and Thode, E. (1999), 'Real wage rigidities. Accommodative demand policies and the functioning of EMU', *Weltwirtschaftliches Archiv*, vol.135, no.4, pp.545–72.

BEUC (1982), *Report on Car Prices and Private Imports of Cars in the EC Countries*, BEUC 105892, Brussels.

BEUC (1988), *Term Insurance in Europe* (Report nr. 51/88), Brussels.

Bhagwati, J.N. (1982), 'Shifting Comparative Advantage, Protectionist Demands and Policy Response', in J. Bhagwati (ed.), *Import Competition and Response*, University of Chicago Press, Chicago, pp.153–95.

Bhagwati, J.N. (1987a), 'Trade in Services and the Multilateral Trade Negotiations', *The World Bank Economics Review*, vol.1, no.4, pp.549–69.

Bhagwati, J.N. (1987b), 'International Factor Mobility', in *Essays in International Economic Theory*, vol.2, edited by R.C. Feenstra, MIT Press, Cambridge, Massachusetts.

Bhagwati, J.N. and Panagariya, A. (1996), 'The theory of preferential trade agreements: historical evolution and current trends', *AEA Papers and Proceedings*, vol.86, no.2, pp.82–87.

Bhagwati, J.N., Schatz, K.W. and Wong, K. (1984), 'The West German Gastarbeiter System of Immigration', *European Economic Review*, vol.26, pp.227–94.

Bianchi, P. and Forlai, L. (1993), 'The domestic appliance industry; 1945–1991', in H.W. de Jong (ed.), *The Structure of European Industry*, 3rd edn, Kluwer, Dordrecht, pp.171–202.

Blitz, R.C. (1977), 'A Benefit–Cost Analysis of Foreign Workers in West Germany 1957–1973', *Kyklos*, vol.30, pp.479–502.

Blommestein, H.J. (ed.) (1991), *The Reality of International Policy Coordination*, North-Holland, Amsterdam.

Blonk, W.A.G. (1968), *Enige Aspecten en Problemen van het Goederenvervoer tussen de Lidstaten van de Europese Economische Gemeenschap, met Name ten Aanzien van de Kwantitatieve Beperkingen en Kwalitatieve Belemmeringen*, Born, Assen.

Bocconi (University of) (1997), 'EU foreign direct investments in Central and Eastern Europe', mimeo, Milan.

Bofinger, P. (1994), 'Is Europe an optimum currency area?', *CEPR discussion paper series*, no.915, Centre for Economic Policy Research, London.

Böhning, W.R. (1972), *The Migration of Workers in the UK and the EC*, Oxford University Press, London.

Böhning, W.R. (1979), 'International Migration in Western Europe, Reflections on the Last Five Years', *International Labour Review*, vol.118, no.4, pp.401–15.

Böhning, W.R. (1993), *International Aid as a Means to Reduce the Need for Emigration*, ILO/UNHR, Geneva.

Böhning, W.R. and Maillat, D. (1974), *The Effects of the Employment of Foreign Workers*, OECD, Paris.

Boltho, A. (ed.) (1982), *The European Economy; Growth and Crisis*, Oxford University Press, Oxford.

Bongardt, A. (1993), 'The Automotive Industry; Supply Relations in Context', in H.W. de Jong, (ed.), *The Structure of European Industry*, 3rd edn, Kluwer, Dordrecht, pp.147–70.

Borchardt, K. (1984), 'Protektionismus im historischen Rückblick', in A. Gutowski (ed.), *Der neue Protektionismus*, Weltarchiv, Hamburg, pp.17–47.

Bordo, M. and Schwartz, A. (1984), *A Retrospective on the Classical Gold Standard*, NBER, New York.

Borjas, G.J. (1995), 'The economic benefits of immigration', *Journal of Economic Perspectives*, vol.9, no.2, pp.3–22.

Borner, S. and Grubel, H. (1992), *The European Community after 1992; Perspectives from the Outsiders*, Macmillan, London.

Bottasso, A. and Sembenelli, A. (2001), 'Market power, productivity and the EU single market programme: evidence from a panel of Italian firms', *European Economic Review*, vol.45, pp.167–86.

Bourguignon, F., Gallast-Hamond, G. and Fernet, B. (1977), *Choix Economiques liés aux Migrations Internationales de Main d'oeuvre; le Cas Européen*, OECD, Paris.

Bouteiller, J. (1971), 'Comparaison de Structure Inter-industrielles de Salaires dans les Pays du Marché Commun', *Annales de l'INSEE*, no.8, pp.3–24.

Brabant, J.M. van (1989), *Economic integration in Eastern Europe; a handbook*, Harvester Wheatsheaf, New York.

Bradley, J., O'Donell, N., Sheridan, N. and Whelan, K. (1995), *Regional Aid and Convergence, Evaluating the Impact of the Structural Funds on the European Periphery*, Avebury, Aldershot.

Brainard, S.L. (1993), *A simple theory of multinational corporations and trade with a trade-off between proximity and concentration*, NBER working paper, no.4269.

Brennan, G. and Buchanan, J.M. (1980), *The Power to Tax, Analytical Foundations of a Fiscal Constitution*, Cambridge University Press, Cambridge.

Bröcker, J. (1984), *Interregionaler Handel und ökonomische Integration*, Florentz, Munich.

Brown, S., Button, K. and Sessions, J. (1996), 'Implications of Liberalised European Labour Markets', *Contemporary Economic Policy*, vol.14, no.1, pp.58–69.

Brugmans, H. (1970), *L'idée Européenne 1920–1970*, De Tempel, Brugge.

Buch, C. (1999), 'Capital mobility and EU enlargement', *Weltwirtschaftliches Archiv*, vol.135, no.4, pp.629–56.

Buchanan, J. (1965), 'An Economic Theory of Clubs', *Economica*, vol.32, pp.1–14.

Buchanan, J. (1987), 'Constitutional Economics', *The New Palgrave*, Macmillan, London.

Buchanan, J.M. (1968), *The Demand and Supply of Public Goods*, Rand McNally, Chicago.

Buckley, P.J. and Artisien, P. (1987), 'Policy issues of intra-EC direct investment; British, French and German multinationals in Greece, Portugal and Spain, with special reference to employment effects', *Journal of Common Market Studies*, vol.26, no.2, pp.207–30.

Buckwell, A.E., Harvey, D.R., Thomson, K.T. and Parton, K.A. (1982), *The Cost of the Common Agricultural Policy*, Croom Helm, London.

Buigues, P. and Jacquemin, A. (1994), 'Foreign direct investments and exports to the European Community', in M. Mason and D. Encarnation (eds), *Does Ownership Matter? Japanese Multinationals in Europe*, Clarendon Press, Oxford.

Buigues, P., Jacquemin, A. and Sapir, A. (1995), *European Policies on Competition, Trade and Industry*, Edward Elgar, Aldershot.

Buiter, W., Corsetti, G. and Roubini, N. (1993), 'Excessive deficits: sense and nonsense in the Treaty of Maastricht', *Economic Policy*, April, pp.57–100.

Buiter, W.H. and Marston, R. (eds) (1985), *International Economic Policy Coordination*, Cambridge University Press, Cambridge.

Butler, A.D. (1967), 'Labour Cost in the Common Market', *Industrial Economics*, vol.6, no.2, pp.166–83.

Button, K.J. (1984), *Road Haulage Licensing and EC Transport Policy*, Gower, Aldershot.

Button, K.J., Haynes, K. and Stough, R. (1998), 'Flying into the future: Air transport policy in the European Union', Edward Elgar, Cheltenham.

Buzan, B. (1984), 'Economic Structure and International Security; the limits of the liberal case', *International Organization*, vol.38, pp.597–624.

Cairncross, A. (1973), *Control of Long-Term International Capital Movements*, Brookings Institution, Washington.

Cameron, D.R. (1985), 'Does Government Cause Inflation? Taxes, Spending and Deficits', in L. Lindberg and C.S. Maier (eds), *The Politics of Inflation and Economic Stagnation*, Brookings Institution, Washington, pp.224–79.

Canny, N. (ed.) (1994), *Europeans on the Move; studies in European migration 1500–1800*, Clarendon Press, Oxford.

Cantwell, J. and Randaccio, F.S. (1992), 'Intra-Industry Direct Investment in the EC, Oligopolistic Rivalry and Technological Competition', in J. Cantwell (ed.), *Multinational Investment in Modern Europe*, Edward Elgar, Aldershot, pp.71–106.

Caramazza, F. (1987), 'International Real Interest Rate Linkages in the 1970s and 1980s', in R. Tremblay (ed.), *Issues in North American Trade and Finance*, North American Economic and Finance Association, vol.4, no.1, pp.123–50.

Carson, M. (1982), 'The Theory of Foreign Direct Investment', in J. Black and J.H. Dunning (eds), *International Capital Movements*, Macmillan, London, pp.22–58.

Carter, R.L. and Dickinson, G.M. (1992), 'Obstacles to the Liberalisation of Trade in Insurance', *TPRC*, Harvester Wheatsheaf, London/New York.

Casella, A. (1994), 'Trade as an engine of political change: a parable', *Economica*, vol.61, pp.267–84.

Casella, A. and Frey, B. (1992), 'Federalism and clubs; towards a theory of overlapping political jurisdictions', *European Economic Review*, vol.36, no.2/3, pp.639–46.

Cassis, Y. (ed.) (1991), *Finance and Financiers in European History 1880–1960*, Cambridge University Press, Cambridge.

Castles, S. and Kosack, G. (1985), *Immigrant Workers and Class Structure in Western Europe*, Oxford University Press, London.

Caves, R.E. (1975), 'Economic Models of Political Choice: Canada's Tariff Structure', *Canadian Journal of Economics*, vol.9, pp.278–300.

Caves, R.E. (1982), *Multinational Enterprise and Economic Analysis*, Cambridge University Press, Cambridge.

Caves, R. and Jones, R. (1984), *World Trade and Payments*, 3rd edn, Little, Brown, Boston, Massachusetts.

CEC (1961), *Document de la Conférence sur les Economies Régionales*, vol.II, Brussels.

CEC (1964), *Reports by Groups of Experts on Regional Policy in the European Economic Community*, Brussels.

CEC (1966), *The Development of a European Capital Market*, Segré Report, Brussels.

CEC (1967), *Critère à la Base de la Fixation des Salaires et Problèmes qui y sont liés pour une Politique des Salaires et des Revenus*, Brussels.

CEC (1968), *Mémorandum sur la Réforme de l'Agriculture dans la Communauté Economique Européenne*, Agriculture 1980, COM 68/100e, Luxemburg.

CEC (1969), *A Regional Policy for the Community*, Brussels.

CEC (1970), *De Industriepolitiek van de Gemeenschap*, memorandum van de Commissie aan de Raad, Brussels.

CEC (1971), *Regional Development in the Community: Analytical Survey*, Brussels.

CEC (1973a), Communication from the Commission to the Council on the Development of the Common Transport Policy, COM (73), Brussels.

CEC (1973b), *Report on the Regional Problems in the Enlarged Community* (Thomson Report), COM 73/550, Brussels.

CEC (1974), *Third Report on Competition Policy*, Brussels.

CEC (1977), 'The Regional Policy of the Community, New Guidelines', *Supplement 2/77 to Bulletin of the European Communities*, Luxemburg.

CEC (1979a), *Etude Comparative des Conditions et Procédures d'Introduction et d'Accès à l'Emploi des Travailleurs de Pays tiers dans les Etats Membres de la Communauté*, Brussels.

CEC (1979b), 'A Transport Network for Europe, Outline of a Policy', *Supplement 8/79 to Bulletin of the European Communities*, Luxemburg.

CEC (1979c), 'Air Transport, A Community Approach', *Supplement 5/79 to Bulletin of the European Communities*, Luxemburg.

CEC (1979d), *The European Monetary System: Commentary Document*, European Economy no.3, Brussels.

CEC (1979e), 'The Regional Development Programmes', *Regional Policy Series*, no.17, Brussels.

CEC (1980), *The Europeans and their Regions*, internal EC document DG XXVI no.9, Brussels.

CEC (1981a), *Energy Strategy to be Adopted by the Community*, Brussels.

CEC (1981b), *The Regions of Europe: First Periodic Report*, Brussels.

CEC (1981c), *Proposal for a Council Regulation Amending the Regulation (EEC)*, no.724/75, establishing a European Regional Development Fund, Brussels.

CEC (1982a), *The Competitiveness of the Community Industry*, Brussels.

CEC (1982c), *Review of Member States' Energy Policy Programmes and Progress towards 1990 Objectives*, Brussels.

CEC (1982d), 'Experimenteel Programma betreffende de Vervoersinfrastructuur', COM 82/828 def., Brussels.

CEC (1982e), 'European Transport, Crucial Problems and Research Needs, a Long Term Analysis', *Series FAST*, no.3, Brussels.

CEC (1983a), *Commission Activities and EC Rules for the Automobile Industry 1981–1983*, COM 83/633 final, Brussels.

CEC (1984c), *The Regions of Europe; Second Periodic Report on the Situation and Socio-economic Evolution of the Regions of the Community*, Brussels.

CEC (1984d), *Les Programmes de Développement Régional de la Deuxième Génération pour la Période 1981–1985*, Collection Documents, Brussels.

CEC (1985a), *Migrants in the European Community*, European File 13.85, Brussels.

CEC (1985c), *The Insurance Industry in the Countries of the EEC, Structure, Conduct and Performance* (S. Aaronovitch and P. Samson), Documents, Brussels.

CEC (1985d), *Completing the Internal Market*, Cockfield White Paper, Brussels/ Luxemburg.

CEC (1985g), *The European Community and its Regions; 10 Years of Community Regional Policy and the ERDF*, Luxemburg.

CEC (1985h), *Main Texts Governing the Regional Policy of the EC*, Collection Documents, Brussels.

CEC (1986a), 'European Act', *Supplement 2/86 to Bulletin of the European Communities*, Luxemburg.

CEC (1986e), *Programme for the Liberalisation of Capital Movements in the Community*, Brussels.

CEC (1986f), *Bulletin of Energy Prices*, Luxemburg.

CEC (1986i), *Directory of European Community Trade and Professional Associations*, 3rd edn, Brussels.

CEC (1987a), *Treaties Establishing the European Communities*, abridged edn, Luxemburg.

CEC (1987b), *Regional Disparities and the Tasks of Regional Policy in the Enlarged Community* (Third Periodic Report), Brussels.

CEC (1988a), 'The Catching-up Process in Spain and Portugal', *European Economy* Supplement A, no.10, Brussels/Luxemburg.

CEC (1988b), *Major Results of the Survey of Member States' Energy Policies*, COM 88/ 174 fin, Brussels.

CEC (1988c), *La Dimension Sociale du Marché Intérieur*, Rapport d'Etape du groupe interservices présidé par M.J. Degimbe, Brussels.

CEC (1988d), 'Research on the "Cost of Non Europe" – Basic Findings', vol.1; *Basic Studies; Executive Seminaries*, Brussels.

CEC (1989), *European Community Research Programmes; France, work programme 1978– 1981*, Status 1989, DG XII, Brussels.

CEC (1990a), *Guide to the Reform of the Community's Structural Funds*, OOPEC, Luxemburg.

CEC (1990b), '"One Market, One Money", an Evaluation of the Potential Benefits and Cost of Forming an Economic and Monetary Union', *European Economy*, no.44, Brussels/Luxemburg.

CEC (1991a), 'Fair Competition in the Internal Market; Community State Aid Policy', *European Economy*, no.48, pp.13–114, Brussels/Luxemburg.

CEC (1991b), 'Immigration of Citizens from Third Countries into the Southern Member States of the European Community', *Social Europe*, Supplement 1/91, Brussels/Luxemburg.

CEC (1991c), *The Regions in the 1990's; Fourth periodic report on the social and economic situation and development of the regions of the Community*, OOPEC, Luxemburg.

CEC (1991d), 'European Industrial Policy for the 1990s', *Supplement 3/91 to Bulletin of the European Communities*, Luxemburg.

CEC (1992a), 'The Degree of Openness of the Economies of the Community, the US and Japan', *European Economy*, Supplement A, no.4, Brussels/Luxemburg.

CEC (1992b), *Social Europe*, 2/92, Luxemburg.

CEC (1992c), 'Social Security for Persons Moving within the Community', *Social Europe*, OOPEC, Luxemburg.

CEC (1992d), 'Energy policies and trends in the European Community', *Energy in Europe 20*, OOPEC, Luxemburg.

CEC (1992e), 'Energy policies and trends in the EC; focus on the East', *Energy in Europe 19*, OOPEC, Luxemburg.

CEC (1992f), 'A Common Market for Services', vol.I, *Services Completing the Internal Market*, Brussels.

CEC (1993a), 'The economics of Community public finance', *European Economy*, Reports and Studies, no.5, Luxemburg.

CEC (1993b), 'The European Community as a World Trade Partner', *European Economy*, no.52, Luxemburg.

CEC (1993c), 'Market Services in the Community Economy', *European Economy*, Supplement A, no.5, pp.1–11, Luxemburg.

CEC (1993d), *European Social Policy; options for the Union* (green paper), OOPEC, Luxemburg.

CEC (1994a), 'EC agricultural policy for the 21st century', *European Economy*, no.4.

CEC (1994b), 'Mergers and acquisitions', *European Economy*, Supplement A, February, Brussels.

CEC (1995a), *Agricultural situation and prospects in the Central and Eastern European Countries*, working document, Brussels.

CEC (1995b), *An energy policy for the EU* (white paper), Brussels.

CEC (1995c), 'The impact of exchange rate movements on trade within the single market', *European Economy*, no.4.

CEC (1996), 'Financial situation of industrial enterprises', *European Economy*, supplement 4.

CEC (1996a), 'Economic evaluation of the internal market', *European Economy*, Reports and Studies, Luxemburg.

CEC (1996b), 'Energy in Europe', *1996 Annual Energy Review*, special issue, Luxemburg.

CEC (1996c), 'Mergers and acquisitions', *European Economy*, Supplement A, no.7, Brussels.

CEC (1996d), *First cohesion report*, COM (96)542 final, Luxemburg.

CEC (1996e), Green paper on relations between the European Union and the ACP countries on the eve of the 21st century; challenges and options for a new partnership, COM 96, 570, Brussels.

CEC (1997a), 'CAP 2000 working document: situation and outlook, Dairy sector', http://europa.eu.int/comm/dg06/publi/cap2000/dairy-en/dairyen.pdf.

CEC (1997b), *Commission Action Plan on the Free Movement of Workers*, COM 586, Brussels.

CEC (1998a), *Financing the European Union: Commission Report of the Operation of the Own Resources System*, Brussels (DG 19).

CEC (1998b), *The CAP Reform: A Policy for the Future*, COM 98.158 final/.

CEC (1999a), *The Competitiveness of European Industry*, COM1999.465, Luxemburg.

CEC (1999b), 'Market integration and differences in price levels between EU member states: study 4 in EU economy 1999 review', http://europa.eu.int/comm/dg02/document/ggreview/ctent.pdf

CEC (1999c), 'Economic reform: report on the functioning of Community product and capital markets', Brussels, http://europa.eu.int.comm/dg15/en/update/econ/cardiffen.pdf

CEC (1999d), 'The shared analysis project; economic foundations for energy policy', http://www.shared–analysis.fgh.de/pub-fr.htm

CEC (1999e), 'Fifth report on the implementation of the telecommunications regulatory package', http://europa.int/comm/dg13/5threp99-eng.pdf

CEC(1999f), 'Guide to the transport acquis', http://europa.eu.int/en/comm/dg07/enlargement/guide2acquis/en.polf

CEC (1999g), 'The common transport policy; sustainable mobility, perspectives for the future', http://europa.eu.int/en/comm/dg7/ctp-action-prog/documents/en.pdf

CEC (1999h), 'Budgetary surveillance in EMU; the new stability and convergence programmes', *European Economy*, Supplement A, no.3.

CEC (1999i), 'Broad Economic Policy Guidelines 1999', *European Economy*, no.68.

CEC (1999j), *The Strategy for Europe's Internal Market*, COM (1999) 624, final/2, Brussels.

CEC (1999k), *Better Management through Evaluation: Mid Term Review of Structural Fund Programmes: Objectives 1 and 6 (1994–1999)*, Brussels.

CEC (2000a), *Adapting the Institutions to Make a Success of Enlargement*, COM 2000.34, Brussels.

CEC (2000b), 'Single market: two proposals to facilitate the cross border provision of services', http://europa.eu.int./comm/internal-market/en/services/services/53.htm

CEC (2000c), 'Insurance: Commission clarifies concepts of freedom to provide services and general good', http://europa.eu.int/comm/internal-market/en/finances/insur/genralgood.htm

CEC (2000d), 'Air transport', http://europa.eu.int/comm/transport/themes/air/english/at2en.html

CEC (2000e), *European Economy: Supplement C: Economic Reform Monitor*, Brussels (see also http://europa.eu.int/comm/economy-finance/document/eesuppc/eecidxen.htm).

CEC (2000f), 'Convergence report 2000', *European Economy*, no.70.

Cecchini, P. *et al.* (1988), *The European Challenge 1992*, Gower, Aldershot.

CEMT (1985), *Trends in the Transport Sector, 1970–1984*, Paris.

CEPII (1996), *Intra- versus inter-industry trade flows inside the EU due to the internal market programme* (background study for CEC, 1996b), Brussels.

CEPR (1992), 'Is Bigger Better? The Economics of EC Enlargement', *MEI* Series 3, London.

CEPR (1993), 'Making Sense of Subsidiarity; How much Centralization for Europe?', *CEPR/MEI* series 4, London.

Chang, H.J. (1996), *The Political Economy of Industrial Policy*, Macmillan, London.

Chenery, H. (1960), 'Patterns of Industrial Growth', *American Economic Review*, vol.50, pp.624–54.

Cherif, M. and Ginsburgh, V. (1976), 'Economic Interdependence Among the EEC Countries', *European Economic Review*, vol.8, pp.71–86.

Chipman, J.S. (1965/66), 'A Survey of the Theory of International Trade', *Econometrica*, part I, vol.33, no.3, pp.477–519; part II, vol.33, no.4, pp.685–761; part III, vol.34, no.1, pp.18–76.

Chryssochoou, D.N. (1997), 'New challenges to the study of European integration: implications for theory building', *Journal of Common Market Studies*, vol.35, no.4, pp.521–42.

Claassen, E.-M. and Wyplosz, C. (1982), 'Capital Controls; some Principles and the French Experience', *Annales de l'Insee*, no.47/48, pp.237–77.

Clark, C. (1957), *Conditions of Economic Progress*, Macmillan, London.

Clarke, W.M. and Pulay, G. (1978), *The World's Money; How it Works*, Allen and Unwin, London.

Clay, E., Dhiri, S. and Benson, Ch. (1996), *Joint evaluation of European Union programme food aid, Synthesis report*, ODI, London.

Clegg, J. and Scott-Green, S. (1999), 'The determinants of FDI capital flows into the EC: a statistical comparison of the USA and Japan', *Journal of Common Market Studies*, vol.37, no.4, pp.597–616.

Clout, H. (1986), *Regional Development in Western Europe*, Wiley, Chichester.

Cnossen, S. (ed.) (1987), *Tax Coordination in the European Community*, Kluwer, Deventer.

Cnossen, S. (1990), 'The Case for Tax Diversity in the European Community', *European Economic Review*, vol.34, pp.471–9.

Cnossen, S. (1996), *Reform and harmonisation of company tax systems in the European Union*, OCFEB RM9604, Rotterdam.

Cnossen, S. (1998), 'VATs in CEE countries: a survey and analysis', *De Economist*, vol.148, no.2, pp.227–55.

Coase, R. H. (1937/1988), 'The nature of the firm', *Economica*, vol.4, pp.386–405;

reprinted as chapter 2 in: Coase, R.H. (1988), *The Firm, the Market and the Law*, University of Chicago Press, Chicago.

Collie, D.R. (2000), 'State aid in the European Union: the prohibition of subsidies in an integrated market', *International Journal of Industrial Organisation*, vol.18, pp.867–84.

Collins, D. (1983), *The Operations of the European Social Fund*, Croom Helm, London.

Cooke, T.E. (1988), *International Mergers and Acquisitions*, Basil Blackwell, Oxford.

Cooper, C. and Mansell, B. (1965), 'A new look at customs union theory', *Economic Journal*, vol.75. pp.742–47.

Cooper, R.N. (1983), 'Economic Interdependence and the Coordination of Economic Policies', in R. Jones and P.B. Kenen (eds), *Handbook of International Economics*, North-Holland, New York.

Corden, W.M. (1971), *Theory of Protection*, Clarendon, Oxford.

Corden, W.M. (1972a), 'Economies of Scale and Customs Union Theory', *Journal of Political Economy*, vol.80, no.1, pp.465–75.

Corden, W.M. (1972b), 'Monetary Integration', *Essays in International Finance*, no.93, Princeton University, Princeton, NJ.

Corden, W.M. (1974), *Trade Policy and Economic Welfare*, Clarendon, Oxford.

Council of Europe (1980), *European Migration in the 1980s, Trends and Policies*, Strasbourg.

Council of Europe (1983), *The Situation of Migrant Workers and their Families; Achievements, Problems and Possible Solutions*, Strasbourg.

Cox, A. and J. Chapman (1999), *The European Community External Cooperation Programmes: Policies, Management and Distribution*, Overseas Development Institute, London.

Craigh, L.E. and Fisher, D. (1996), *The Integration of the European Economy*, Macmillan, Basingstoke, St. Martin's Press, New York.

Crouch, C. (1985), 'Conditions for Trade Union Wage Restraint', in L. Lindberg and Ch.S. Maier (eds), *The Politics of Inflation and Economic Stagnation*, Brookings Institution, Washington, pp.105–39.

Cushman, D.O. (1983), 'The Effects of Real-Exchange-Rate Risk on International Trade', *Journal of International Economics*, vol.15, pp.45–63.

Davenport, M. (1986), *Trade Policy, Protectionism and the Third World*, Croom Helm, Beckenham.

Daveri, F. and Tabellini, G. (2000), 'Unemployment and taxes: do taxes affect the rate of unemployment?', *Economic Policy: A European Forum*, vol.30, pp.47–104.

Dearden, S.J.H. (1995), 'European Social Policy and Flexible Production', *International Journal of Manpower*, vol.16, no.10, pp.3–13.

Deardorff, A. and Stern, R. (1981), 'A disaggregated model of world production and trade; an estimate of the impact of the Tokyo Round', *Journal of Policy Modeling*, vol.3, no.2, pp.127–52.

Decressin, J. and Fatas, A. (1995), 'Regional labour market dynamics in Europe', *European Economic Review*, vol.39, pp.1627–55.

Degimbe, J. (1999), *La politique sociale Européenne*, Institut Syndical Europeen, Brussels.

Delors J. et al. (1989), *Report on the Economic and Monetary Union in the European Community*, CEC, Brussels.

Demsetz, H. (1982), *Economic, Legal and Political Dimensions of Competition*, North-Holland, Amsterdam.

Devereux, M.P. and Pearson, M. (1989), 'Corporate Tax Harmonisation and Economic Efficiency', *Report Series*, no.35, Institute of Fiscal Studies, London.

Devereux, M.P. and Freeman, H. (1995), 'The impact of tax on foreign direct investment; empirical evidence and the implications for tax integration schemes', *International tax and public finance*, vol.2, pp.85–106.

Devereux, M.P. and Griffith, R. (1996), 'Taxes and the location of production: evidence from a panel of US multinationals', *IFS Working Paper*, 14–96, London.

Dewatripont, M., Sapir, A. and Sekkat, K. (eds) (1999), *Trade and Jobs in Europe: Much Ado About Nothing*, Oxford University Press, Oxford.

Dickinson, G. (1993), 'Insurance', *European Economy/Social Europe*, no.3, pp.183–210.

Dosser, D. (1966), 'Economic Analysis of Fiscal Harmonisation', in C.S. Shoup (ed.), *Fiscal Harmonisation in Common Markets*, Columbia University Press, New York.

Drabeck, Z. and Greenaway, D. (1984), 'Economic Integration and Inter-Industry Trade, the CMEA and EEC compared', *Kyklos*, vol.37, pp.444–69.

Dufey, G. and Giddy, I.H. (1981), *The Evolution of Instruments and Techniques in International Financial Markets*, SUERF, Tilburg.

Dumont, M. and Meeusen, W. (1999), 'The impact of the RTD policy of the EU on technological collaboration: a case study of the European telecommunications industry', in W. Meeusen (ed.), *Economic Policy in the European Union, Current Perspectives*, Edward Elgar, Cheltenham, pp.135–56.

Dunning, J.H. (1979), 'Explaining Changing Patterns of International Production: in Defence of an Eclectic Theory', *Oxford Bulletin of Economics and Statistics*, vol.41, pp.269–95.

Dunning, J.H. (1980), 'A note on Intra-Industry Foreign Direct Investment', *Banca Nazionale del Lavoro Quarterly Review*, vol.34, December.

Dunning, J.H. (1988), 'The eclectic paradigm of international production; a restatement and some possible extensions', *Journal of International Business Studies*, vol.19, no.1, pp.6–12.

Dunning, J.H. (1993), *The Globalisation of Business; the challenge of the 1990s*, Routledge, London.

Dunning, J.H. and Cantwell, J. (1987), *IRM Directory of Statistics of International Investment and Production*, Macmillan, London.

Durán-Herrera, J.J. (1992), 'Cross Direct Investment and Technological Capability of Spanish Domestic Firms', in J. Cantwell, (ed.), *Multinational Investment in Modern Europe*, Edward Elgar, Aldershot, pp.214–55.

Duroselle, J.B. (1987), 'L'Europe dans l'Historiographie 1815–1914', in A. Rijksbaron *et al.* (eds), *Europe from a Cultural Perspective*, Nijgh en Van Ditmar, The Hague, pp.31–2.

Dustmann, C. (1996), 'Return Migration: the European experience', *Economic Policy*, vol.2, pp.215–50.

ECJ (1985), *Judgement of the Court of 22 May 1985*, in Case 13/83 European Parliament vs. Council of the European Community.

Edwards, S. (1999), 'How effective are capital controls?', *Journal of Economic Perspectives*, vol.13, no.4, pp.65–84.

Edye, D. (1987), *Immigrant Labour and Government Policy*, Gower, Aldershot.

Eijffinger, S. and de Haan, J. (1996), 'The political economy of central bank independence', *Special Papers in International Economics*, no.19, Princeton University, Princeton, NJ.

Eijffinger, S. W. and de Haan, J. (2000), *European Monetary and Fiscal Policy*, Oxford University Press, Oxford.

El-Agraa, A.M. and Jones, A.J. (1981), *Theory of Customs Unions*, Philip Allan, Oxford.

Eliasson, G. (1984), 'The Micro Foundations of Industrial Policy', in A. Jacquemin (ed.), *European Industry: Public Policy and Corporate Strategy*, CEPS, Clarendon, Oxford, pp.295–326.

Eliassen, K. A. and Sjovaag, M. (eds) (1999), *European Telecommunications Liberalisation*, Routledge, London.

Emerson, M. (1977), 'The finances of the European Community: a case study in embryonic fiscal federalism', in W. Oates, (ed.), *The Political Economy of Fiscal Federalism*, Lexington, Mass., pp.129–72.

Emerson, M., Aujean, M., Catinat, M., Goybet, P. and Jacquemin, A. (1988), 'The Economics of 1992; An Assessment of the Potential Economic Effects of Completing the Internal Market of the European Community', *European Economy*, no.35/3, pp.5–222.

Erdmenger, J. (1981), *The European Community Transport Policy*, Gower, Aldershot.

Erkel Rousse, H. and Melitz, J. (1995), 'New empirical evidence on the costs of monetary union', *CEPR Discussion Paper*, no.1169.

Ethier, W.J. (1998), 'The new regionalism', *The Economic Journal*, vol.108, pp.1149–61.

Eurostat (1974), *Statistics of Energy*, Special Nr 4, Luxemburg.

Eurostat (1983), *Monthly Bulletin of Foreign Trade*, special issue 1958–1982, Luxemburg.

Eurostat (1985), *Foreign Population and Foreign Employees in the Community*, Luxemburg.

Eurostat (1987), *Employment and Unemployment*, Theme 3, Series C, Luxemburg.

Eurostat (1992), *International Trade in Services, 1979–1988*, Series 6D, Luxemburg.

Eurostat (1995), *Labour Force Survey*, Luxemburg.

Eurostat (several years), *Electricity Prices*, Luxemburg.

Faber, M. and Breyer, F. (1980), 'Eine ökonomische Analyse konstitutioneller Aspekte der Europäischen Integration', *Jahrbuch für Sozialwissenschaft*, vol.31, pp.213–27.

Fatas, A. (1997), 'EMU: countries or regions? Lessons from the EMS experience', *CEPR Discussion Papers*, no.1558, London.

Feldstein, M. and Horioka, C. (1980), 'Domestic Savings and International Capital Flows', *The Economic Journal*, vol.90, pp.314–29.

Ferndandez, A., Arrunada, B. and Gonzalez, M. (2000), 'Quasi integration in less than truckload trucking', in C. Menard (ed.), *Institutions, contracts, organisations (perspectives from new institutional economics)*, Edward Elgar, Cheltenham, pp.293–312.

Fernandez, R. (1997), 'Returns to regionalism: an evaluation of non-traditional gains from RTAs', *CEPR Discussion Papers*, no.1634, CEPR, London.

Ferner, A. and Hyman, R. (eds) (1992), *Industrial Relations in the New Europe*, Blackwell, Oxford.

Findlay, R. (1982), 'International Distributive Justice, a Trade-Theoretic Approach', *Journal of International Economics*, vol.13, pp.1–14.

Finsinger, J. and Pauly, M.V. (eds) (1986), *The Economics of Insurance Regulation*, Macmillan, Basingstoke.

Finsinger, J., Hammond, E. and Tapp, J. (1985), *Insurance: Competition on Regulation, a Comparative Study*, The Institute for Fiscal Studies, London.

Fischer, P. and Straubhaar, T. (1996), *Migration and economic integration in the Nordic common labour market*, Nord (Nordic Council of Ministers), Copenhagen.

Fisher, M.R. (1966), *Wage Determination in an Integrating Europe*, Sythoff, Leiden.

Fisher, S. (1987), 'International Macro-Economic Policy Coordination', *NBER Working Paper* no.2244, NBER, Cambridge, Massachusetts.

Fleming, M. (1971), 'On Exchange Rate Unification', *Economic Journal*, vol.81, pp.467–88.

Forte, F. (1977), 'Principles for the Assignment of Public Economic Functions in a Setting of Multi-Layer Government, EC', *Report of the (McDougall) Study Group on the role of Public Finance in European Integration*, vol.II, Collection of Studies of Economics and Finances, Series no.B 13, Brussels.

Francko, L.G. (1976), *The European Multinationals; a Renewed Challenge to American and British Business*, Harper and Row, London.

François, J.F., McDonald, B. and Nordstrom, H. (1996), 'A user's guide to the Uruguay round assessments', *Working Paper*, no.ERAD 96.003 WTO.

Frankel, J.A. (1989), 'Quantifying International Capital Mobility in the 1980's', *NBER Working Paper*, 2856, NBER, Cambridge, Massachusetts.

Frankel, J.A. and Rose, A.K. (1998), 'The endogeneity of the optimum currency area criteria', *The Economic Journal*, vol.108, pp.1009–25.

Franzmeyer, F. (1982), *Approaches to Industrial Policy within the EC and its Impact on European Integration*, Gower, Aldershot.

Franzmeyer, F., Hrubesch, P., Seidel, B. and Weise, Ch. (1991), *The Regional Impact of Community Policies*, EP, Luxemburg.

Fratianni, M. (1995), 'Variable integration in the European Union', in *CEIS: Il 'Cantiere' Europa: vincoli e opportunita*, Porto Cervo, pp.95–120.

Frey, B. (1985), 'The Political Economy of Protection', in D. Greenaway (ed.), *Current Issues in International Trade*, Macmillan, London, pp.139–57.

Frey, B. and Eichenberger, R. (1997), 'FOCJ: creating a single European market for governments', in D. Schmidtchen and Cooter, R. (eds), *Constitutional Law and Economics of the European Union*, Edward Elgar, Cheltenham, pp.195–216.

Frey, B. and Schneider, F. (1984), 'International Political Economy, a Rising Field', *Economia Internazionale*, vol.37, no.3–4, pp.308–47.

Friedberg, R.M. and Hunt, J. (1995), 'The impact of immigrants on host country wages, employment and growth', *Journal of Economic Perspectives*, vol.9, no.2, pp.23–44.

Friedman, M. and Friedman, R. (1980), *Free to Choose, a Personal Statement*, Harcourt Brace Jovanovich, New York, p.154.

Fries, T. (1984), 'Uncertainty as a possible rationale for Customs Unions', *Journal of International Economics*, vol.17, no.3/4, pp.347–57.

Frisch, H. (1983), 'Theories of Inflation', *Cambridge Surveys of Economic Literature*, Cambridge University Press, Cambridge.

Fuente, A. de la and Vives, X. (1995), 'Infrastructure and education as instruments of regional policy; evidence from Spain', *Economic Policy*, vol.20, pp.13–51.

Fujita, M., Mallampally, P. and Sauvant, K.P. (1997), 'European Union direct investment in developing Asia: and developing Asia direct investment in the European Union', *Transnational Corporations*, vol.6, no.1, pp.83–100.

Fukao, M. and Hanazaki, M. (1987), 'Internationalisation of Financial Markets and the Allocation of Capital', *OECD Economic Studies*, no.8, pp.35–92.

Gaab, W., Granziol, M.J. and Horner, M. (1986), 'On Some International Parity Conditions: an Empirical Investigation', *European Economic Review*, vol.30, no.3, pp.683–713.

Gardner, E.H. (1992), 'Taxes on capital income; a survey', in G. Kopits (ed.), *Tax Harmonization in the European Community: policy issues and analysis*, IMF occasional paper 94, Washington, pp.52–71.

Geroski, P. and Jacquemin, A. (1984), 'Large Firms in the European Corporate Economy and Industrial Policy in the 1980s', in A. Jacquemin (ed.), *European Industry: Public Policy and Corporate Strategy*, CEPS, Clarendon, Oxford, pp.343–67.

Geroski, P. and Jacquemin, A. (1985), 'Industrial Change, Barriers to Mobility and European Industrial Policy', *Economic Policy*, vol.1, no.1, pp.170–218.

Gialloreto, L. (1988), *Strategic Airline Management*, Pitman, London.

Giavazzi, F. and Pagano, M. (1986), 'The Advantages of Tying one's Hands; EMS Discipline and Central Bank Credibility', *European Economic Review*, vol.28, pp.1055–82.

Giersch, H. (1949), 'Economic Union between Nations and the Location of Industries', *Review of Economic Studies*, vol.17, pp.87–97.

Giersch, H. (1987), *Internal and External Liberalisation for Faster Growth: Economic Papers*, Commission of EC, Brussels.

Giovannini, A. (1989), 'National Tax Systems versus the European Capital Market', *Economic Policy*, pp.346–86.

Glachant, J-M. and Finon, D. (2000), 'Why do the European Union's electricity industries continue to differ? A new institutional analysis', in C. Menard (ed.), *Institutions, contracts, organisations (perspectives from new institutional economics)*, Edward Elgar, Cheltenham, pp.313–34.

Glass, A.J. and Saggi, K. (1999), 'FDI policies under shared factor markets', *Journal of International Economics*, vol.49, pp.309–32.

Glejser, H. (1972), 'Empirical Evidence on Comparative Cost Theory from the European Common Market Experience', *European Economic Review*, vol.163, pp.247–59.

Golombek, R., Hoel, M. and Vislie, J. (eds) (1987), *Natural Gas Markets and Contracts*, North-Holland, Amsterdam.

Gomes, L. (1987), *Foreign Trade and the National Economy; Mercantilist and Classical Perspectives*, Macmillan, London.

Gordon, J. (1992), 'An analysis of the EC Structural Funds', in G. Kopits (ed.), *Tax Harmonization in the European Community: policy issues and analysis*, IMF occasional paper 94, Washington, pp.92–104.

Gordon, R.H. (1983), 'An Optimal Taxation Approach to Fiscal Federalism', *Quarterly Journal of Economics*, vol.48, no.4, pp.567–86.

Graham, E.M. (1992), 'Direct Investments between the US and the EC, Post 1986 and Pre 1992', in J. Cantwell (ed.), *Multinational Investment in Modern Europe*, Edward Elgar, Aldershot, pp.46–70.

Grauwe, P. de (1975), 'Conditions for Monetary Integration, a Geometric Interpretation', *Weltwirtschaftliches Archiv*, vol.3, pp.634–44.

Grauwe, P. de (1987), 'International Trade and Economic Growth in the European Monetary System', *European Economic Review*, vol.31, pp.389–98.

Grauwe, P. de (1992), *The Economics of Monetary Integration*, Oxford University Press, Oxford.

Grauwe, P. de (1996), 'Monetary union and convergence economics', *European Economic Review*, vol.40, pp.1091–101.

Grauwe, P. de (2000), *Economics of Monetary Union*, 4th edn, Oxford University Press, Oxford.

Grauwe, P. de and Aksov, Y. (1999), 'Are Central European Countries part of the European Optimum Currency Area?' in: P. de Grauwe and V. Lavra (eds), *Inclusion of Central European Countries in the European Monetary Union*, Kluwer, Dordrecht, pp.13–36.

Greenaway, D. (1983), *International Trade Policy, from Tariffs to the New Protectionism*, Macmillan, London.

Greenaway, D. (1987), 'Intra-Industry Trade, Intra-Firm Trade and European Integration; Evidence, Gains and Policy Aspects', *Journal of Common Market Studies*, vol.26, no.2, pp.153–72.

Greenaway, D. and Milner, C. (1986), *The Economics of Intra-Industry Trade*, Basil Blackwell, Oxford.

Gremmen, H. (1985), 'Testing Factor Price Equalisation in the EC: An Alternative Approach', *Journal of Common Market Studies*, vol.23, no.3, pp.277–86.

Griffiths, B. (1975), *Invisible Barriers to Invisible Trade*, Macmillan, London.

Grinols, E.J. (1984), 'A Thorn in the Lion's Paw; Has Britain Paid Too Much for Common Market Membership?', *Journal of International Economics*, vol.16, pp.271–93.

Gros, D. (1987), 'On the Volatility of Exchange Rates: a Test of Monetary and Portfolio Balance Models of Exchange Rate Determination', *Economic Working Document*, vol.32, CEPS, Brussels.

Gros, D. (1989), 'Paradigms for the Monetary Union of Europe', *Journal of Common Market Studies*, vol.27, no.3, pp.219–30.

Gros, D. (1996), 'A Reconsideration of the Optimum Currency Area Approach: The Role of External Shocks and Labour Mobility', *National Institute Economic Review*, October, pp.108–17.

Gros, D. and Thygesen, N. (1998), *European Monetary Integration*, 2nd ed., Longman, London.

Gros, D., Blanchard, O., Emerson, M., Mayer, T., St Paul, G., Sinn, H. and Tabellini, G. (1999), *Macro Economic Policy in the First Year of Euroland*, CEPS, Brussels.

Grubel, H.G. (1974), 'Taxation and the Rates of Return from some US Assets Holdings Abroad', *Journal of Political Economy*, vol.82, pp.469–87.

Grubel, H.G. (1981), *International Economics*, Irwin, Homewood, Illinois.

Grubel, H.G. (1994), 'The economics of international labor and capital flows', in H. Giersch (ed.), *Economic Aspects of International Migration*, Springer, Berlin, pp.75–92.

Grubel, H.G. and Lloyd, P. (1975), *Intra-Industry Trade: the Theory and Measurement of International Trade in Differentiated Products*, Macmillan, London.

Gual, J. (1993), 'An Econometric Analysis of Price Differentials in the EEC Automobile Market', *Applied Economics*, vol.25, pp.599–607.

Guieu, P. and Bonnet, C. (1987), 'Completion of the Internal Market and Indirect Taxation', *Journal of Common Market Studies*, vol.25, no.3, pp.209–23.

Gwilliam, K.M., Petriccione, S., Voigt, F. and Zighera, J.A. (1973), 'Criteria for the Coordination of Investments in Transport Infrastructure', *The EEC Studies, Transport Series Nr 3*, Brussels.

Haaland, J. (1990), 'Assessing the Effects of EC Integration on EFTA Countries; the Position of Norway and Sweden', *Journal of Common Market Studies*, vol.28, no..4, pp.379–400.

Haaland, J. and Norman, V. (1992), *Global Production Effects of European Integration*, paper for the CEPR Conference Paris.

Haas, E.B. (1958), *The Uniting of Europe; Political, Social and Economic Forces 1950–1957*, Stevens, London.

Haisken-De New, J.P. (1996), *Migration and the inter-industry wage structure in Germany*, Springer, Berlin.

Hajnal, P.I. (1989), *The Seven Power Summit*, Documents Kraus, New York.

Hall, G. (ed.) (1986), *European Industrial Policy*, Croom Helm, London.

Hall, R. and van der Wee, D. (1992), 'Community regional policies for the 1990s', *Regional Studies*, vol.26, no.4, pp.399–404.

Hamada, K. (1985), *The Political Economy of International Monetary Interdependence*, Cambridge University Press, Cambridge.

Hammar, T. (1985), *European Immigration Policy*, Cambridge University Press, Cambridge.

Hanlon, P. (1999), 'Global Airlines: Competition in a Transnational Industry', 2nd edn, Butterworth/Heinemann, Oxford

Hantrais, L. (1995), *Social Policy in the European Union*, Macmillan, Basingstoke.

Hart, P., Ledger, G., Roe, M. and Smith, B. (1992), *Shipping Policy in the European Community*, Avebury, Aldershot.

Hartley, K. (1987), 'Public Procurement and Competitiveness: a Community Market for Military Hardware and Technology?', *Journal of Common Market Studies*, vol.25, no.3, pp.237–47.

Hartmann, P. (1998), 'Structural policy and multi level governance in the EC', in A.W. Cafruny and G.G. Rosenthal (eds), *The State of the European Community: the Maastricht Debate and Beyond*, Longman, Harlow, pp.391–410.

Hatzius, J. (2000), 'Foreign direct investment and factor demand elasticities', *European Economic Review*, vol.44, pp.117–43.

Hawtrey, R. (1947), *The Gold Standard in Theory and Practice*, Longmans, London.

Heidhues, T., Josling, T., Ritson, C. *et al.* (1978), 'Common Prices and Europe's Farm Policy', *Thames Essays*, no.13, Trade Policy Research Centre, London.

Heijke, J.A.M. and Klaassen, L.H. (1979), 'Human Reactions to Spatial Diversity,

Mobility in Regional Labour Markets', in H. Folmer and J. Oosterhaven (eds), *Spatial Inequalities and Regional Development*, Nijhoff, The Hague, pp.117–30.

Helg, R. and Ranci, P. (1988), 'Economies of Scale and the Integration of the EC, the Case of Italy', in *Research into the Cost of Non-Europe, Basic Findings*, vol.2, CEC, Luxemburg, pp.205–85.

Helleman, S. and Hens, L. (1999), 'Towards a monetary model for the euro-USD exchange rate', in W. Meeusen (ed.), *Economic Policy in the European Union: Current Perspectives*, Edward Elgar, Cheltenham, pp.103–120.

Helpman, E. and Krugman, P.R. (1985), *Market Structure and Foreign Trade: Increasing Returns, Imperfect Competition and the International Economy*, Wheatsheaf, Brighton.

Hennart, J.F. (1983), 'The Political Economy of Comparative Growth Rates; the Case of France', in D. Mueller (ed.), *The Political Economy of Growth*, Yale University Press, New Haven, pp.176–203.

Henrekson, M., Torstenson, J. and Torstenson, R. (1997), 'Growth effects of European integration', *European Economic Review*, vol.41, pp.1537–57.

Henry, P. (1981), *Study of the Regional Impact of the Common Agricultural Policy*, CEC, Luxemburg.

Herbst, L. (1986), 'Die Zeitgenössische Integrationstheorie und die Anfänge der Europäischen Einigung 1947–1950', *Vierteljahreshefte für Zeitgeschichte*, II, vol.34, pp.161–204.

Hewitt, A. (1984), 'The Lomé Conventions: Entering a Second Decade', *Journal of Common Market Studies*, vol.23, no.2, pp.95–115.

Heylen, F. and Poeck, A. van (1995), 'National Labour Market Institutions and the European Economic and Monetary Integration Process', *Journal of Common Market Studies*, vol.33, no.4, pp.573–95.

Hill, B.E. and Ingersent, K.A. (1982), *The Economic Analysis of Agriculture*, 2nd edn, Heinemann, London.

Hine, R.C. (1985), *The Political Economy of European Trade*, Wheatsheaf, Brighton.

Hine, R.C. (1992), *The Political Economy of Agricultural Trade*, Edward Elgar, Aldershot.

Hirsch, S. (1974), 'Hypothesis Regarding Trade Between Developing and Industrial Countries', in H. Giersch (ed.), *The International Division of Labour*, Mohr, Tübingen, pp.65–82.

Hirsch, S. (1981), 'Peace Making and Economic Interdependence', *The World Economy*, vol.4, pp.407–17.

Hirschmann, A.O. (1981), 'Three Uses of Political Economy in Analysing European Integration', in *Essays in Trespassing; Economics to Politics and Beyond*, Cambridge University Press, Cambridge, pp.266–84.

Hocking, R. (1980), 'Trade in Motorcars between the Major European Producers', *Economic Journal*, vol.90, pp.504–19.

Hodgson, G.M. (1988), *Economics and Institutions*, Polity Press, Cambridge.

Hodgson, G.M., Samuels, W.J. and Tool, M.C. (eds) (1994), *The Elgar Companion to Institutional and Evolutionary Economics*, Edward Elgar, Aldershot.

Hoekman, B. and Djankov, S. (1996), 'The European union's Mediterranean Free Trade initiative', *The World Economy*, vol.19, no.4, pp.387–406.

Hoekman, B.M. and Kostecki, M. (1996), *The Political Economy of the World Trading System; from GATT to WTO*, Oxford University Press, Oxford.

Hoeller, P. and Louppe, M.O. (1994), 'The EC's internal market; implementation and economic effects', *OECD Economic Studies*, no.23, Paris.

Holden, M. (1994), *The Common Fisheries Policy; origin, evaluation and future*, Blackwell, Oxford.

Holloway, J. (1981), *Social Policy Harmonisation in the European Community*, Gower, Aldershot.

Holtfrerich, C.-L. (1989), 'The Monetary Unification Process in Nineteenth-Century

Germany', in M. de Cecco and A. Giovannini (eds), *A European Central Bank?*, Cambridge University Press, Cambridge, pp.216–41.

Hudson, R. and Schamp, E.W. (eds) (1995), *Towards a new map of automobile manufacturing in Europe; new production concepts and spatial restructuring*, Springer, Heidelberg.

Hudson, R. and Williams, A. (1986), *The United Kingdom*, Harper and Row, London.

Hufbauer, G.C. (1968), 'The Commodity Composition of Trade in Manufactured Goods', *Conference on Technology and Competition in International Trade*, NBER, New York.

Hufbauer, G.C. (1990), 'An Overview', in G.C. Hufbauer (ed.), *Europe 1992; An American Perspective*, Brookings Institution, Washington.

Hufbauer, G.C. and Scott, J.J. (1985), *Economic Sanctions Reconsidered; History and Current Policy*, Institute for International Economics, Washington.

Hulsink, W. (1999), *Privatisation and Liberalisation in European Telecommunications: Comparing Britain, the Netherlands and France*, Routledge, London.

Hymer, S. (1996), *The International Operations of National Firms: A Study of Direct Foreign Investment (originally published in 1976)*, MIT Press, Cambridge, Mass.

IBRD (1985), *World Development Report*, Oxford University Press, New York.

IEE (1978), *La Charte Sociale Européenne: Dix Années d'Application*, Editions de l'Université, Brussels.

IFO (1989), 'An empirical assessment of factors shaping regional competitiveness in problem regions', mimeo, Munich.

ILO (1956), *Social Aspects of European Economic Cooperation*, report by a group of experts, Geneva.

IMF (1984), *Exchange Rate Volatility and World Trade*, IMF occasional paper, no.28.

Ingersent, K.A. and Rayner, A.J. (1999), *Agricultural Policy in Western Europe and the United States*, Edward Elgar, Cheltenham.

Ingo, W. (1985), 'Barriers to Trade in Banking and Financial Services', *Thames Essays*, no.41, Trade Policy Research Centre, London.

Ingram, J.C. (1973), 'The Case for European Monetary Integration', *Essays in International Finance*, no.98, Princeton University, Princeton, NJ.

Ishiyama, Y. (1975), 'The Theory of Optimum Currency Areas, a Survey', *IMF Staff Papers*, vol.22, pp.344–83.

Jacquemin, A. (1979), *Economie Industrielle Européenne; Structures de Marché et Stratégies d'Entreprises*, 2nd edn, Dunod, Paris.

Jacquemin, A. (1982), 'Imperfect Market Structure and International Trade, Some Recent Research', *Kyklos*, vol.35, pp.73–93.

Jacquemin, A. (1991), *Merger and Competition Policy in the European Community*, Blackwell, Oxford.

Jacquemin, A. and de Jong, H.W. (1977), *European Industrial Organisation*, Macmillan, London.

Jacquemin, A. and Sapir, A. (1988), 'European Integration or World Integration?', *Weltwirtschaftliches Archiv*, vol.124, pp.127–39.

Jacquemin, A. and Sapir, A. (1991), 'Europe post-1992; internal and external liberalisation', *American Economic Review*, vol.81, no.2, pp.166–70.

Jacquemin, A., and Sapir, A. (1995), 'Is a European hard core credible? A statistical analysis', *CEPR discussion paper series*, no.1242, Centre for Economic Policy Research, London.

Jacquemin, A. and Wright, D. (1993), *The European Challenges Post 1992; Shaping Factors, Shaping Actors*, Edward Elgar, Aldershot.

Jensen, W.G. (1983), *Energy in Europe 1945–1980*, Fouls, London.

Johnson, H.G. (1958), 'The Gains from Freer Trade in Europe, an Estimate', *Manchester School*, vol.26, no.3, pp.247–55.

Johnson, H. (1965), 'An economic theory of protectionism, tariff bargaining and the formation of customs unions', *Journal of Political Economy*, vol.73, pp.256–83.

Johnston, R.B. (1983), *The Economics of the Euromarket, History, Theory and Policy*, Macmillan, London.

Jones, K. (1984), 'The Political Economy of Voluntary Export Restraint Agreements', *Kyklos*, vol.37, pp.82–101.

Jong, H.W. de (1981), *Dynamische Markttheorie*, Stenfert Kroese, Leiden.

Jong, H.W. de (1987), 'Market Structures in the European Economic Community', in M. Macmillen, D.G. Mayes and P. van Veen (eds), *European Integration and Industry*, Tilburg University Press, Tilburg, pp.40–89.

Jong, M.W. de (1993), 'Service industries; innovation and internationalization', in H.W. de Jong (ed.), *The Structure of European Industry*, 3rd edn, Kluwer, Dordrecht, pp.337–66.

Jong, H.W. de (1993a), 'Market Structures in the EEC', in H.W. de Jong (ed.), *The Structure of European Industry*, 3rd edn, Kluwer, Dordrecht, pp.1–42.

Jong, H.W. de (ed.) (1993b), *The Structure of European Industry*, 3rd edn, Kluwer, Dordrecht.

Kaelble, H. (1986), *Sozialgeschichte der Europäischen Integration, 1880–1980*, Freie Universität, Berlin.

Kaempfer, W.H. and Loewenberg, A.D. (1992), *International Economic Sanctions; a Public Choice Approach*, Westview Press, Boulder, Colorado.

Kahler, M. (1995), *International Institutions and the Political Economy of Integration*, Brookings Institution, Washington.

Kaldor, N. (1966), *The Causes of the Slow Growth of the United Kingdom*, Cambridge University Press, Cambridge.

Kane, D.R. (1982), *The Euro-Dollar Market and the Years of Crisis*, Croom Helm, London.

Karsenty, G. (1999), *Just How Big are the Stakes? An Assessment of Trade in Services by Mode of Supply*, World Trade Organisation, Geneva.

Kauppinen, T. (ed.) (1998), *The Impact of EMU on Industrial Relations in the European Union*, Finnish Labour Relations Association, Publication no 9, Helsinki.

Kawai, M. (1992), 'Optimum currency areas', in P. Newman, M. Milgate and J. Eatwell (eds), *The New Palgrave Dictionary of Money and Finance*, Macmillan, London.

Kay, J. and Keene, M. (1987), 'Alcohol and Tobacco Taxes, Criteria for Harmonisation', in S. Cnossen (ed.), *Tax Coordination in the European Community*, Kluwer, Deventer, pp.85–112.

Kayser, B. (1972), *Cyclically Determined Homeward Flows of Migrant Workers*, OECD, Paris.

Keely, C.B. and Tran, B.N. (1989), 'Remittances from Labour Migration: Evaluations, Performance and Implications', *International Migration Review*, vol.23, no.3, pp.500–25.

Keen, M. and Smith, S. (1996), 'The future of value added in the European Union', *Economic Policy; a European Forum*, vol.23, pp.373–420.

Kennedy Brenner, C. (1979), *Foreign Workers and Immigration Policy*, OECD/DC, Paris.

Kennedy, P. (1988), *The Rise and Fall of the Great Powers*, Fontana Press, London.

Kenwood, A.G. and Lougheed, A.L. (1999), *The Growth of the International Economy 1820–2000: An Introductory Text*, 4th edn, Routledge, London.

Keohane, R.O. and Hoffmann, S. (1991), 'Institutional Change in Europe in the 1980's', in R.O. Keohane and S. Hoffmann (eds), *The New European Community, Decision Making and Institutional Change*, Westview Press, Boulder, Colorado, pp.1–39.

Keynes, J.M. (1936), *The General Theory of Employment, Interest and Money*, Harcourt, Brace & Co., New York.

Kindleberger, C.P. (1987), *International Capital Movements*, Cambridge University Press, Cambridge.

Kindleberger, C.P. *et al.* (1979), *Migration, Growth and Development*, OECD, Paris.

Klaassen, L.H. and Drewe, P. (1973), *Migration Policy in Europe*, Saxon House, Farnborough.

Klaassen, L.H. and Molle, W.T.M. (eds) (1982), *Industrial Migration and Mobility in the European Community*, Gower, Aldershot.

Klein, L. (1985), 'Trade and Sectoral Adjustment Policy Problems', in T. Peeters, P. Praet and P. Reding (eds), *International Trade and Exchange Rates in the Late Eighties*, North-Holland, Amsterdam, pp.111–30.

Kock, K. (1969), *International Trade Policy and the GATT, 1947–1967*, Almquist and Wicksell, Stockholm.

Koedijk, K. and Kremers, J. (1996), 'Market opening, regulation and growth in Europe', *Economic Policy; a European Forum*, vol.23, pp.443–67.

Koekkoek, K.A. and Mennes, L.B.M. (1988), 'Some Potential Effects of Liberalising the Multi-Fibre Arrangement', in L.B.M. Mennes and J. Kol (eds), *European Trade Policies and the Developing World*, Croom Helm, Beckenham, pp.187–213.

Koekkoek, K.A., Kuyvenhoven, A. and Molle, W. (1990), 'Europe 1992 and the Developing Countries, an Overview', *Journal of Common Market Studies*, vol.29, no.2, pp.111–31.

Koester, U. (1977), 'The Redistributional Effects of the Common Agricultural Financial System', *European Review of Agricultural Economics*, vol.4, no.4, pp.321–45.

Koester, U. and Tangermann, S. (1976), *Alternative der Agrarpolitik*, Hiltrup, Münster.

Kol, J. (1987), 'Exports from Developing Countries; Some Facts and Scope', *European Economic Review*, vol.31, pp.466–74.

Kol, J. (1988), *The Measurement of Intra-Industry Trade*, Erasmus University Press, Rotterdam.

Kol, J. and Kuypers, B. (1996), *The cost for consumers and taxpayers of the Common Agricultural Policy of the European Union; the case of the Netherlands*, Erasmus University Press, Rotterdam.

Kolvenbach, W. and Hanau, P. (1988), *Handbook on European Employee Co-Management*, Kluwer, Deventer.

Kool, C. and Olie, R. (1997), 'De EMU als fusieproces' (The EMU as a merger process), *ESB*, vol.82, no.4111, pp.495–98.

Kottis, A. (1985), 'Female/Male Earnings Differentials in the Founder Countries of the EEC; an Econometric Investigation', *De Economist*, vol.132, no.2, pp.204–23.

Kozma, F. (1982), *Economic Integration and Economic Strategy*, Nijhoff, The Hague.

Krägenau, H. (1987), *Internationale Direktinvestitionen*, IFW, Weltarchiv, Hamburg.

Krauss, H.B. (1979), *The New Protectionism, the Welfare State and International Trade*, Basil Blackwell, Oxford.

Krauss, L.B. (1968), *European Integration and the US*, Brookings Institution, Washington.

Kreinin, M.E. (1973), 'The Static Effects of EEC Enlargement on Trade Flows', *Southern Economic Journal*, vol.39, pp.559–68.

Krugman, P. (1979), 'A Model of Innovation, Technology Transfer, and the World Distribution of Income', *Journal of Political Economy*, vol.87, pp.253–67.

Krugman, P. (1980), 'Scale economies: product differentiation and the pattern of trade', *American Economic Review*, vol.70, no.5, pp.950–59.

Krugman, P. (1986), *Strategic Trade Policy and the New International Economics*, MIT Press, Cambridge, Mass.

Krugman, P. (1991), *Geography and Trade*, MIT Press, Cambridge, Mass.

Krugman, P. and Venables, A.J. (1995), 'Globalization and the inequality of nations', *NBER Working Paper*, no.5098, Washington.

Kuznets, S. (1966), *Modern Economic Growth; Rates, Structure and Spread*, Yale University Press, New Haven.

Laffan, B. (1983), 'Policy Implementation in the European Community: The European Social Fund as a Case Study', *Journal of Common Market Studies*, vol.21, no.4, pp.389–408.

Lamfalussy, A. (1981), 'Changing Attitudes towards Capital Movements', in F. Cairncross (ed.), *Changing Perceptions of Economic Policy*, Methuen, London, pp.194–217.

Landesmann, M.A. and Petit, P. (1995), 'International trade in producer services', *The Service Industries Journal*, vol.15, no.2, pp.123–61.

Langhammer, K.J. and Sapir, A. (1987), *Economic Impact of Generalised Tariff Preferences*, TPRC, Gower, Aldershot.

Lannes, X. (1956), 'International Mobility of Manpower in Western Europe' (I + II), *International Labour Review*, vol.73, pp.1–24 and 135–51.

Lattre, A. de (1985), 'Floating, Uncertainty and the Real Sector', in L. Tsoukalis (ed.), *The Political Economy of International Money: In Search of a New Order*, Sage, London, pp.71–103.

Laudati, L.L. (1998), 'Impact of community competition law on member state competition law', in S. Martin (ed.), *Competition Policies in Europe*, North-Holland, Amsterdam, pp.381–408.

Lawton, T.C. ed. (1999), *European Industrial Policy and Competitiveness*, Macmillan, Basingstoke.

Layard, R., Nickell, S.J. and Jackman, R. (1991), *Unemployment*, Oxford University Press, Oxford.

Lebergott, S. (1947), 'Wage Structures', *Review of Economics and Statistics*, vol.29, pp.247–85.

Lebon, A. and Falchi, G. (1980), 'New Developments in Intra-European Migration Since 1974', *International Migration Review*, vol.14, no.4, pp.539–73.

Lemaitre, P. and Goybet, C. (1984), *Multinational Companies in the EEC* (IRM Multinational Report no.1), John Wiley, Chichester.

Lemmen, J.J.G. and Eijffinger, S.C.W. (1993), 'The Degree of Financial Integration in the European Community', *De Economist*, vol.141, no.2, pp.189–213.

Lemmen, J.J.G. and Eijffinger, S.C.W. (1996), 'The fundamental determinants of financial integration in the European Union', *Weltwirtschaftliches Archiv*, vol.132, no.3, pp.432–456.

Levi, M. (1981), *International Finance; Financial Management and the International Economy*, McGraw-Hill, New York.

Lindbeck, A. (1981), 'Industrial Policy as an Issue of the Economic Environment', *The World Economy*, vol.4, no.4.

Linder, S.B. (1961), *An Essay on Trade and Transformation*, Almquist and Wicksell, Uppsala.

Lindert, P. (1986), *International Economics*, 8th edn, Irwin, Homewood, Illinois.

Linnemann, H. (1966), *An Econometric Study of International Trade Flows*, North-Holland, Amsterdam.

Lipgens, W., Loth, W. and Milward, A. (1982), *A History of European Integration, vol.1, 1945–1947, The Formation of the European Unity Movement*, Clarendon and Oxford University Press, London and New York.

Lipsey, R.G. (1960), 'The Theory of Customs Unions: a General Survey', *Economic Journal*, vol.70, pp.496–513.

Lloyd, P.J. (1982), '3 x 3 Theory of Customs Unions', *Journal of International Economics*, vol.12, pp.41–63.

Lloyd, P.J. (1992), 'Regionalisation and World Trade', *OECD Economic Studies*, vol.18, pp.7–34.

Locksey, G. and Ward, T. (1979), 'Concentration in Manufacturing in the EC', *Cambridge Journal of Economics*, vol.3, no.1, pp.91–7.

Löffelholz, H.D. von (1992), *Der Beitrag der Ausländer zum wirtschaftlichem Wohlstand in der BRD*, mimeo, RWI, Essen.

Long, F. (1980), *The Political Economy of EEC Relations*, Pergamon, Oxford.

Lopandic, D. (1986), 'The European Community and Comecon', *Review of International Affairs*, vol.876, no.3, pp.12–14.

Lucas, N. (1977), *Energy and the European Communities*, Europa Publications, London.

Lucas, N. (1985), *Western European Energy Policies, a Comparative Study*, Oxford University Press, Oxford.

Ludlow, P. (1982), *The Making of the European Monetary System*, Butterworth, London.

Lundberg, L. (1992), 'European Economic Integration and the Nordic Countries' Trade', *Journal of Common Market Studies*, vol.30, no.2, pp.157–73.

Lunn, J. (1980), 'Determinants of US investment in the EEC; Further Evidence', *European Economic Review*, vol.24, pp.93–101.

MAAREC (1999), *Corporate Effective Tax Rates in the European Union*, Maastricht.

MacDougall, G.D.A. *et al.* (1977), *Report of the Study Group on the Role of Public Finance in European Integration*, CEC, Economy and Finance Series, vol.1, General Report, Brussels.

Machlup, F. (1977), *A History of Thought on Economic Integration*, Macmillan, London.

McKinnon, R. (1963), 'Optimum Currency Areas', *American Economic Review*, vol.53, pp.717–25.

MacLaughlin, A.M. and Maloney, W.A. (1999), *The European Automobile Industry: Multilevel Governance, Policy and Politics*, Routledge, London.

MacMillan, M.J. (1982), 'The Economic Effects of International Migration; a Survey', *Journal of Common Market Studies*, vol.20, no.3, pp.245–67.

MacNamus, J. (1972), 'The theory of the international firm', in G. Paquet (ed.), *The Multinational Firm and the Nation State*, Collier, Macmillan, pp.66–93.

Magnifico, G. (1985), *Regional Imbalances and National Economic Performance*, Office of Official Publications of the EC, Luxemburg, pp.85–95.

Mahe, L.P. and Ortalo-Magne, F. (1999), 'Five proposals for a European model of the countryside', *Economic Policy: A European Forum*, vol.28, pp.89–134.

Maillet, P. (1977), *The Construction of a European Community*, Praeger, New York.

Maillet, P. and Rollet, Ph. (1986), 'L'Insertion de l'Europe dans la Division Internationale du Travail; Appréciations et Suggestions', *Revue du Marché Commun*, no.299, pp.371–86.

Majone, G. (1996), *Regulating Europe*, Routledge, London.

Malcor, R. (1970), 'Problèmes Posés par l'Application Pratique d'une Tarification pour l'Usage des Infrastructures Routières', *The EEC Studies*, Transport Series no.2, Brussels.

Maloney, J. and Macmillen, M. (1999), 'Do currency unions grow too large for their own good?', *The Economic Journal*, vol.109, pp.572–87.

Mark, N.C. (1985a), 'Some Evidence on the International Inequality of Real Interest Rates', *Journal of International Money and Finance*, vol.4, no.2, pp.189–208.

Mark, N.C. (1985b), 'A Note on International Real Interest Differentials', *Review of Economics and Statistics*, vol.67, no.4, pp.681–4.

Marks, F., Scharpf, F.W., Schmitter, P.C. and Streeck, W. (1996), *Governance in the European Union*, Sage, London.

Marks, G. (1993), 'Structural policy and multi level governance in the EC', in A.W. Cafruny and G.G. Rosenthal (eds), *The State of the European Community: the Maastricht Debate and Beyond*, Longman, Harlow, pp.391–40.

Marks, G. (1996), *Governance in the European Union*, Sage, London.

Markusen, J.R. (1983), 'Factor Movements and Commodity Trade as Complements', *Journal of International Economics*, vol.14, pp.341–56.

Markusen, J.R. and Venables, A. (1995), *Multinational Firms and the New Trade Theory*, NBER working paper, no.5036.

Martin, J.P. (1998), 'What works among active labour market policies: evidence from OECD countries' experiences', *OECD, Occasional papers*, no.35, Paris.

Martin, P. (1996), 'A sequential approach to regional integration: the European Union and Central and Eastern Europe', *European Journal of Political Economy*, vol.12, pp.581–98.

Martin, P.H. and Rogers, C.A. (2000), 'Long-term growth and short-term economic instability', *European Economic Review*, vol.44, pp.359–81.

Martin, S. (ed.) (1999), *Competition Policies in Europe*, North-Holland, Amsterdam.

Marques-Mendes, A.J. (1986a), 'The Contribution of the European Community to Economic Growth', *Journal of Common Market Studies*, vol.24, no.4, pp.261–77.

Marques-Mendes, A.J. (1986b), *Economic Integration and Growth in Europe*, Croom Helm, London.

Masson, P. (1996), 'Fiscal dimensions of EMU', *The Economic Journal*, vol.106, no.437, pp.996–1004.

Mathias, P. and Davis, J.A. (1991), *Innovation and Technology in Europe; from the Eighteenth Century to the Present Day*, Basil Blackwell, Oxford.

Mathieson, D.J. and Rojas-Suarez, L. (1994), 'Capital controls and capital account liberalisation in industrial countries', in L. Leiderman and A. Razin (eds), *Capital Mobility; The impact on consumption, investment and growth*, Cambridge University Press, Cambridge.

Matthews, A. (1985), *The Common Agricultural Policy and the Less Developed Countries*, Gill and Macmillan, Dublin.

Matusz, S.J. and Tarr, D.G. (1999), 'Adjusting to trade policy reform', *Policy Research Working Paper*, no.2142, World Bank, Washington.

Mayes, D. (1978), 'The Effects of Economic Integration on Trade', *Journal of Common Market Studies*, vol.17, no.1, pp.1–25.

Maynard, G. and Ryckeghem, W. van (1976), 'Why Inflation Rates Differ, a Critical Examination of the Structural Hypothesis', in H. Frisch (ed.), *Inflation in Small Countries*, Springer, Berlin, pp.47–72.

Meade, J.E. (1955), *The Theory of Customs Unions*, North-Holland, Amsterdam.

Meester, G. and Strijker, D. (1985), *Het Europees Landbouwbeleid voorbij de Scheidslijn van Zelfvoorziening* (WRR, V46), State Publishing Office, The Hague.

Meiklejohn, R. (1999), 'An international competition policy, do we need it? Is it feasible?', *The World Economy*, Vol.22, pp.1233–49.

Menil, G. de (1999), 'Real capital market integration in the EU; how far has it gone? What will the effect of the euro be?', *Economic Policy: A European Forum*, vol.28, pp.167–204.

Messerlin, P.A. (1988), 'The EC Anti-Dumping Regulations; a First Economic Appraisal 1980–1985', paper presented to the First International Seminar on International Economics, Oxford, August 1988.

Messerlin, P.A. (1992), 'Trade Policies in France', in D. Salvatore (ed.), *National Trade Policies, Handbook of Comparative Economic Policies*, vol.2, Greenwood Press, New York.

Messerlin, P.A. (1993), 'Services in EEC; the European Community as a World Trade Partner', *European Economy*, no.52, pp.129–56.

Messerlin, P.A. (1999), *Measuring the Cost of Protection in Europe*, Institute for International Economics, Washington.

Messerlin, P.A. and Becuwe, S. (1986), 'Intra-Industry Trade in the Long Term; the French Case 1850–1913', in D. Greenaway and P.K.M. Tharakan (eds), *Imperfect Competition and International Trade*, Wheatsheaf, Brighton, pp.191–216.

Meyer, F.W. and Willgerodt, H. (1956), 'Der Wirtschaftspolitische Aussagewert Internationaler Lohnvergleiche', in *Internationale Lohngefaelle, Wirtschaftspolitische Folgerungen, und Statistische Problematik*, Bundesministerium für Wirtschaftspolitische Zusammenarbeit, Deutscher Bundesverlag, Bonn.

Meyer, G. (1973), *Problems of Trade Policy*, Oxford University Press, London.

Mihailovic, K. (1976), 'Migration and the Integration of Labour Markets', in F. Machlup (ed.), *Economic Integration, Worldwide, Regional, Sectoral*, Macmillan, London, pp.163–86.

Miller, M.H. and Spencer, J.E. (1977), 'The Static Economic Effects of the UK joining the EEC, a General Equilibrium Approach', *Review of Economic Studies*, vol.44, pp.71–93.

Mishalani, P. *et al.* (1981), 'The Pyramid of Privilege', in C. Stevens (ed.), *The EEC and the Third World, a Survey I*, Hodder and Stoughton and ODI/IDS, London, pp.60–82.

Mishan, E.J. (1982), *Introduction to Political Economy*, Hutchinson, London.

Mishkin, F.S. (1984a), 'The Real Interest Rate; a Multicountry Empirical Study', *Canadian Journal of Economics*, vol.17, no.2, pp.283–311.

Mishkin, F.S. (1984b), 'Are Real Interest Rates Equal Across Countries? An Empirical Investigation of International Parity Conditions', *Journal of Finance*, vol.39, no.5, pp.1345–57.

Mitchell, B. (1981), *European Historical Statistics 1750–1975*, 2nd edn, Sythoff/Noordhoff, Alphen a/d Rijn.

Mitrany, D. (1966), *A Working Peace System*, Quadrangle Books, Chicago (reprint from earlier book of 1940s).

Modigliani, F. (1996), 'The shameful rate of unemployment in the EMS: causes and cures', *De Economist*, vol.144, no.3, pp.363–96.

Molina, J.L.M. de and García Perea, P. (1992), 'European Economic Integration from the Standpoint of Spanish Labour Market Problems', in David W. Marsden (ed.), *Pay and Employment in the New Europe*, Billing and Sons, Worcester, pp.99–122.

Molle, W., Sleijpen, O. and Van Heukelen, M. (1993), 'The Impact of an Economic and Monetary Union on Social and Economic Cohesion; Analysis and Ensuing Policy Implications', in K. Gretschmann (ed.), *Economic and Monetary Union; Implications for National Policy Makers*, EIPA, Maastricht, pp.217–43.

Molle, W.T.M. (1983a), *Industrial Location and Regional Development in the European Community, the FLEUR Model*, Gower, Aldershot.

Molle, W.T.M. (1983b), 'Technological Change and Regional Development in Europe (Theory, Empirics, Policy)', *Papers and Proceedings of the Regional Science Association*, European Congress, pp.23–38.

Molle, W.T.M. (1985), '"1992", De Europese interne markt voltoooid?' ("1992" Will the European Single Market be completed?), *Economische Statistische Berichten*, vol.70, p.837.

Molle, W.T.M. (1986), 'Regional Impact of Welfare State Policies in the European Community', in J.H.P. Paelinck (ed.), *Human Behaviour in Geographical Space*, Gower, Aldershot, pp.77–90.

Molle, W.T.M. (1989), 'De Europese Gemeenschap in 2000' (the European Community in 2000), *Economisch Statistische Berichten*, vol.74, pp.271–1273.

Molle, W.T.M. (1990), 'Will the Completion of the Internal Market Lead to Regional Divergence?', in H. Siebert (ed.), *The Completion of the Internal Market*, Institut für Weltwirtschaft, Kiel.

Molle, W.T.M. (1993), 'Oil Refining and Petrochemical Industry', in H.W. de Jong (ed.), *The Structure of European Industry*, 3rd edn, Kluwer, Dordrecht, pp.43–63.

Molle, W.T.M. (1996), 'The contribution of international aid to the long term solution of the European migration problem', in D. Corry (ed.), *Economics and European Migration Policy*, IPPR, London, pp.50–75.

Molle, W.T.M. (1997), 'The Regional Economic Structure of the European Union: an Analysis of Long-Term Developments', in K. Peschel (ed.), *Regional Growth and Regional Policy within the Framework of European Integration*, Physica-Verlag, Heidelberg, pp.66–86.

Molle, W.T.M. and Boeckhout (1995), 'Economic disparity under conditions of integration; a long term view of the European case', *Papers in Regional Science, the Journal of the RSA*, vol.74, no.2, pp.105–123.

Molle, W.T.M. and Cappellin, R. (eds) (1988), *Regional Impact of Community Policies in Europe*, Avebury, Aldershot.

Molle, W.T.M., de Koning, J. and Zandvliet, Ch. (1992), 'Can Foreign Aid Reduce East–West Migration in Europe; with Special Reference to Poland?', *ILO Working Paper 67*, Geneva.

Molle, W.T.M., with the assistance of Van Holst, B. and Smit, H. (1980), *Regional Disparity and Economic Development in the European Community*, Saxon House, Farnborough.

Molle, W.T.M. and van Mourik, A. (1987), 'Economic Means of a Common European Foreign Policy', in J.K. de Vree, P. Coffey and R.H. Lauwaars (eds), *Towards a European Foreign Policy*, Nijhoff, Dordrecht, pp.165–92.

Molle, W.T.M. and van Mourik, A. (1988), 'International Movements of Labour under Conditions of Economic Integration; the Case of Western Europe', *Journal of Common Market Studies*, vol.26, no.3, pp.317–42.

Molle, W.T.M. and van Mourik, A. (1989a), 'A Static Explanatory Model of International Labour Migration to and in Western Europe', in I. Gordon and A. Thirlwall (eds), *European Factor Mobility, Trends and Convergences*, Macmillan, London, pp.30–52.

Molle, W.T.M. and van Mourik, A. (eds) (1989b), *Wage Structures in the European Community, Convergence or Divergence?*, Gower, Aldershot.

Molle, W.T.M. and Wever, E. (1983), *Oil Refineries and Petrochemical Industries in Western Europe*, Gower, Aldershot.

Monnet, J. (1976), *Mémoires*, Fayard, Paris.

Monti, M. (1996), '"Monti memorandum" on fiscality', *Europe Documents*, no.1981, Luxemburg.

Moore, M.O. (1998), 'European steel policies in the 1980s: hindering technological innovation and market structure change', *Weltwirtschaftliches Archiv*, vol.134, no.1, pp.42–68.

Moravcsik, A. (1993), 'Preferences and Power in the European Community: A Liberal Intergovernmentalist Approach', *Journal of Common Market Studies*, vol.31, no.4, pp.473–524.

Moravscik, A. (1998), *The Choice for Europe: Social Purpose and State Power from Messina to Maastricht*, UCL Press, London.

Morsink, R.L.A. (1998), *Foreign Direct Investment and Corporate Networking: A Framework for Spatial Analysis of Investment Conditions*, Edward Elgar, Cheltenham.

Morsink, R. and Molle, W.T.M. (1991), *Direct Investment and Monetary Integration, European Economy*, special edition, no.1, pp.36–55.

Mortensen, J. (1992), 'The Allocation of Savings in a Liberalised European Capital Market', in A. Steinherr (ed.), *The New European Financial Market Place*, Longman, London, pp.208–20.

Moss, J. (1982), *The Lomé Conventions and their Implications for the US*, Westview Press, Boulder, Colorado.

Motta, M. and Norman, G. (1996), 'Does economic integration cause foreign direct investment?', *International Economic Review*, vol.37, no.4, pp.757–83.

Moulaert, F. and Derykere, Ph. (1982), 'The Employment of Migrant Workers in West Germany and Belgium', *International Migration Quarterly*, vol.2, pp.178–97.

Mourik, A. van (1987), 'Testing Factor Price Equalisation in the EC: An Alternative Approach: A Comment', *Journal of Common Market Studies*, vol.26, no.1, pp.79–86.

Mourik, A. van (1989), 'Countries, a Neo-Classical Model of International Wage Differentials', in W.T.M. Molle and A. van Mourik (eds), *Wage Differentials in the European Community, Convergence or Divergence?*, Gower, Aldershot, pp.83–103.

Mourik, A. van (1993), 'Wages and European Integration', PhD, RL, Maastricht.

Mueller, C.F. (1980), *The Economics of Labor Migration, a Behavioral Analysis*, Academic Press, New York.

Mueller, D. (1981), 'Competitive Performance and Trade within the EEC, Generalisations from Several Case Studies with Specific Reference to the West German Economy', *Zeitschrift für die Gesamte Staatswissenschaften*, vol.137, no.3, pp.638–63.

Mueller, D.C. (ed.) (1980), *The Determinants and Effects of Mergers; an International Comparison*, Oelgeschlager, Cambridge, Mass.

Mueller, D.C. (ed.) (1983), *The Political Economy of Growth*, Yale University Press, New Haven.

Mueller, D.C. (1989), *Public Choice II*, Cambridge University Press, Cambridge.

Mundell, R.A. (1957), 'International Trade and Factor Mobility', *American Economic Review*, vol.47, no.3, pp.321–35.

Mundell, R.A. (1961), 'A Theory of Optimum Currency Areas', *American Economic Review*, vol.53, pp.657–64.

Muntendam, J. (1987), 'Philips in the World, a View of a Multinational on Resource Allocation', in B. van der Knaap and E. Wever (eds), *New Technology and Regional Development*, Croom Helm, London, pp.136–44.

Murfin, A. (1987), 'Price Discrimination and Tax Differences in the European Motor Industry', in S. Cnossen (ed.), *Tax Coordination in the European Community*, Kluwer, Deventer, pp.171–95.

Murrell, P. (1983), 'The Comparative Structure of Growth in West Germany and British Manufacturing Industries', in D. Mueller (ed.), *The Political Economy of Growth*, Yale University Press, New Haven, pp.109–32.

Musgrave, R.A. and Musgrave, P. (1989), *Public Finance in Theory and Practice*, McGraw-Hill, New York.

Myrdal, G. (1956), *An International Economy, Problem and Prospects*, Harper and Bros, New York.

Myrdal, G. (1957), *Economic Theory and Underdeveloped Regions*, Duckworth and Co., London.

Neary, P. (1987), 'Tariffs, Quotas and VER With and Without Internationally Mobile Capital', paper to the European Economic Association Conference, Copenhagen.

Neary, P. and Ruane, F.P. (1984), 'International Capital Mobility, Shadow Prices and the Cost of Protection', *Working Paper 32*, Centre of Economic Research, University College Publication, Dublin.

NEI/E&Y (1992), 'New location factors for mobile investment in Europe', *CEC Regional Development Studies*, no.6, Brussels.

Neumark, F. *et al.* (1963), 'Report of the Fiscal and Financial Committee', *The EEC Reports on Tax Harmonisation*, International Bureau of Fiscal Documentation, Amsterdam.

Neven, D., Nuttall, R. and Seabright, P. (1993), *Merger in Daylight; the Economics and Politics of European Merger Control*, CEPR, London.

NIESR (1991), *A New Strategy for Economic and Social Cohesion after 1992*, London.

NIESR (1996), *Capital Market Liberalization in Europe*, London.

Noël, E. (1988), 'Working Together; the Institutions of the European Community', *European Documentation*, Luxemburg.

Norman, V. (1989), 'EFTA and the Internal European market', *Economic Policy*, vol.2, pp.424–65.

Norman, V. (1991), '1992 and EFTA', in L.A. Winters and A. Venables (eds), *European Integration, Trade and Industry*, Cambridge University Press, Cambridge, pp.120–41.

Oates, W. (1972), *Fiscal Federalism*, Harcourt, New York.

Oberender, P. and Rüter, G. (1993), 'The Steel Industry, a Crisis of Adaptation', in H.W. de Jong (ed.), *The Structure of European Industry*, 3rd edn, Kluwer, Dordrecht, pp.65–89.

Odagiri, H. (1986), 'Industrial Policy in Theory and Reality', in H.W. de Jong and W.G. Shepherd (eds), *Mainstreams in Industrial Organisation*, Book II, pp.387–412.

OECD (1964), *Industrial Statistics 1900–1962*, Paris.

OECD (1965), *Wages and Labour Mobility*, Paris.

OECD (1966), *Energy Policy*, Paris.

OECD (1968), *Capital Market Study*, five vols, Paris.

OECD (1973), *Oil, the Present Situation and Future Prospects*, Paris.

OECD (1978), *The Migratory Chain*, Paris.

OECD (1979), *International Direct Investment; Policies, Procedures and Practices*, Paris.

OECD (1980), *Controls on International Capital Movements; the Experience with Controls on International Portfolio Operations in Shares and Bonds*, Paris.

OECD (1981b), *Regulations Affecting International Banking Operations*, 2 vols, Paris.

OECD (1982a), *Controls on International Capital Movements, the Experience with Controls on International Financial Credits, Loans and Deposits*, Paris.

OECD (1982b), *Code of Liberalisation of Capital Movements*, Paris.

OECD (1982c), *Controls and Impediments Affectinq Inward Direct Investment in OECD Member Countries*, Paris.

OECD (1983a), *International Trade in Services; Insurance: Identification and Analysis of Obstacles*, Paris.

OECD (1983b), *The Implications of Different Means of Agricultural Income Support*, Paris.

OECD (1984a), *International Trade in Services; Banking: Identification and Analysis of Obstacles*, Paris.

OECD (1984b), *Merger Policies and Recent Trends in Mergers*, Paris.

OECD (1985b), *Tourism Policy and International Tourism*, Paris.

OECD (1985c), *Cost and Benefits of Protection*, Paris.

OECD (1986a), *International Trade in Services; Audiovisual Works*, Paris.

OECD (1986b), *SOPEMI; Continuous Reporting System on Migration*, Paris (also 1973–86).

OECD (1987a), 'Science and Technology', *Newsletter* no.10, Paris.

OECD (1987c), *Recent Trends in International Direct Investment*, Paris.

OECD (1987d), *National Policies and Agricultural Trade*, Paris.

OECD (1987e), *The Cost of Restricting Imports; the Automobile Industry*, Paris.

OECD (1987f), *Energy Policies and Programmes of IEA Countries*, 1986 Review, Paris.

OECD (1987g), *Energy Balances of OECD countries 1970–1985*, Paris.

OECD (1991), *Taxing Profits in a Global Economy: Domestic and International Issues*, Paris.

OECD (1992), *Trends in International Migration*, SOPEMI, Paris.

OECD (1993a), *The Changing Course of International Migration*, Paris.

OECD (1993b), *Employment Outlook*, July, Paris.

OECD (1994a), *Migration and Development, new partnerships for cooperation*, Paris.

OECD (1994b), *The OECD Jobs Study, Evidence and Explanations*, Part II: The Adjustment Potential of the Labour Market, Paris.

OECD (1994c), 'Labour standards and economic integration', *Employment Outlook*, July, Paris, pp.137–66.
OECD (1995a), *Code of Liberalization of Capital Movements*, Paris.
OECD (1995b), *Introduction to the Codes of Liberalization*, Paris.
OECD (1995c), *Code of Liberalization of Current Invisible Operations*, Paris.
OECD (1995d), *The OECD Jobs Study: Investment, Productivity and Employment*, Paris.
OECD (1995e), *Economic Outlook*, no.58, Paris.
OECD (1996), *Agricultural Policies, Markets and Trade in OECD Countries; Monitoring and Evaluation*, Paris.
OECD (1998a), *Value Added Taxes in Central and Eastern European countries: A Comparative Survey and Evaluation*, Paris.
OECD (1998b), 'Public financial management and fiscal goals', *Working Paper*, ECO/CPE/WP/1 (98)10.
OECD (1999), *EMU: Facts, Challenges and Policies*, Paris.
Okun, A. (1975), *Equality and Efficiency; the Big Trade Off*, Brookings Institution, Washington.
Olie, R.L. (1996), *European Transnational Mergers*, Universiteit Maastricht, Maastricht.
Oliveira Martins, J. (1994), 'Market structure, trade and industry wages', *OECD Economic Studies*, no.22, Paris.
Olofsdotter, K. and Torstensson, J. (1998), 'Economic integration, market size and the welfare effects of trade liberalisation', *Weltwirtschaftliches Archiv*, vol.134, no.2, pp.302–19.
Olson, M. (1965), *The Logic of Collective Action*, Harvard University Press, Cambridge, Mass.
Olson, M. (1983), *The Rise and Decline of Nations (Economic Growth, Stagflation and Social Rigidities)*, Yale University Press, New Haven.
Oort, C.J. (1975), *Study of the Possible Solutions for Allocating the Deficit which may Occur in a System of Charging for the Use of Infrastructures Aiming at Budgetary Equilibrium*, CEC, Brussels.
Owen, N. (1983), *Economies of Scale, Competitiveness and Trade Patterns within the European Community*, Clarendon, Oxford.
Ozawa, T. (1992), 'Cross Investments between Japan and the EC. Income Similarity, Technological Congruity and Economics of Scope', in J. Cantwell (ed.), *Multinational Investment in Modern Europe*, Edward Elgar, Aldershot, pp.13–45.
Padoa-Schioppa, T. *et al.* (1987), *Europe in the 1990's; Efficiency, Stability and Equity; a Strategy for the Evolution of the Economic System of the European Community*, Oxford University Press, Oxford.
Page, S. (1981), 'The Revival of Protectionism and its Consequences for Europe', *Journal of Common Market Studies*, vol.20, no.1, pp.17–40.
Pain, N. and Young, G. (1996), 'Tax competition and the pattern of European direct investment', Paper of the institute of Fiscal Studies Conference on Public Policy and the Location of Economic Activity, London.
Palmer, M. and Lambert, J. *et al.* (1968), *European Unity; a Survey of the European Organisations*, PEP, Unwin University Books, London.
Papadimetriou, D.G. (1978), 'European Labour Migration (Consequences for the Countries of Workers' Origin)', *International Studies Quarterly*, vol.22, no.3, pp.377–408.
Pearson, M. and Smith, S. (1992), *The European Carbon Tax; an Assessment of the European Commission Proposals*, Institute of Fiscal Studies, London.
Pedler, R.H. and Schaefer, G.F. (eds) (1996), *Shaping European Law and Policy; the role of the committees and comitology in the political process*, EIPA, Maastricht.
Pedler, R.H. and van Schendelen, M.P.C.M. (eds) (1994), *Lobbying the European Union; Companies, Trade Associations and Issue Groups*, Dartmouth, Aldershot.

Peeters, T., Praet, P. and Reding, P. (eds) (1985), *International Trade and Exchange Rates in the Late Eighties*, North-Holland, Amsterdam.

Pejovich, S. (1998), *Economic Analysis of Institutions and Systems*, rev. 2nd edn, Kluwer, Dordrecht.

Pelkmans, J. (1980), 'Economic Theories of Integration Revisited', *Journal of Common Market Studies*, vol.18, no.4, pp.333–54.

Pelkmans, J. (1982), 'The Assignment of Public Functions in Economic Integration', *Journal of Common Market Studies*, vol.21, no.1, pp.97–121.

Pelkmans, J. (1983), 'European Direct Investments in the European Community', *Journal of European Integration*, vol.7, no.1, pp.41–70.

Pelkmans, J. (1984), *Market Integration in the European Community*, Nijhoff, The Hague.

Pelkmans, J. (ed.) (1985), *Can the CAP be Reformed?*, EIPA, Maastricht.

Pelkmans, J. (1986), 'Completing the Internal Market for Industrial Products', CEC, Brussels.

Pelkmans, J. (1991), 'Towards Economic Union', in P. Ludlow (ed.), *Setting EC Priorities 1991–92*, CEPS/Brasseys, London.

Pelkmans, J. (1997), *European Integration: Methods and Economic Analysis*, Longman, Harlow, New York.

Pelkmans, J. and Vanheukelen, M. (1988), 'The Internal Markets of North America. Fragmentation and Integration in the US and Canada, Research on the "Cost of Non-Europe", Basic Findings', CEC, vol.16, Luxemburg.

Pelkmans, J. and Vollebergh, A. (1986), 'The Traditional Approach to Technical Harmonisation: Accomplishments and Deficiencies', in J. Pelkmans and M. Vanheukelen (eds), *Coming to Grips with the Internal Market*, EIPA, Maastricht, pp.9–30.

Pelkmans, J. and Winters, L.A. (1988), *Europe's Domestic Market*, Routledge, London.

Perée, E. and Steinherr, A. (1989), 'Exchange Rate Uncertainty and Foreign Trade', *European Economic Review*, vol.33, pp.1241–64.

Perotti, R. (1996), 'Fiscal Consolidation in Europe: Composition Matters', *The American Economic Review*, vol.86, no.2, pp.105–10.

Pertek, J. (1992), *General Recognition of Diplomas and Free Movement of Professionals*, EIPA, Maastricht.

Peschel, K. (1985), 'Spatial Structures in International Trade; an Analysis of Long-Term Developments', *Papers of the Regional Science Association*, vol.58, pp.97–111.

Peschel, K. (1999), *The development of integration areas in Europe*, mimeo, IRF, Christian Albrecht Universitaet, Kiel.

Petit, M. *et al.* (1987), *The Agricultural Policy Formation in the European Community; The Birth of Milk Quotas and the CAP Reform*, Elsevier, Amsterdam.

Petith, H.C. (1977), 'European Integration and the Terms of Trade', *Economic Journal*, vol.87, pp.262–72.

Petrochilos, G.A. (1989), *Foreign Direct Investment and the Development Process*, Avebury, Aldershot.

Phelps-Brown, H. (1977), *The Inequality of Pay*, Oxford University Press, Oxford.

Philip, A.B. (1978), 'The Integration of Financial Markets in Western Europe', *Journal of Common Market Studies*, vol.16, pp.302–22.

Phylaktis, K. and Wood, G.E. (1984), 'An Analytical and Taxonomic Framework for the Study of Exchange Controls', in J. Black and G.S. Dorrance (eds), *Problems of International Finance*, St Martin's Press, New York, pp.149–66.

Pinder, J. (1986), 'The Political Economy of Integration in Europe, Policies and Institutions in East and West', *Journal of Common Market Studies*, vol.24, no.1, September, pp.1–14.

Pinder, J. (1991), *European Community, the Building of a Union*, Oxford University Press, Oxford.

Pirenne, H. (1927), *Les Villes du Moyen-âge*, Lamertin, Brussels.

Pischken, J.-S. and Velling, J. (1994), 'Wage and employment effects of immigration to Germany', *CEPR discussion paper 935*, London.

Polachek, S.W. (1980), 'Conflict and Trade', *Journal of Conflict Resolution*, vol.24, pp.55–78.

Pollard, S. (1981a), *Peaceful Conquest, the Industrialisation of Europe 1760–1970*, Oxford University Press, Oxford.

Pollard, S. (1981b), *The Integration of the European Economy since 1815*, George Allen and Unwin, London.

Pomfret, R. (1986), *Mediterranean Policy of the European Community; a Study of Discrimination in Trade*, Macmillan, London.

Pool, B. (1990), 'The Creation of the Internal Market in Insurance', CEC, Luxemburg.

Poon, J. and Pandit, K. (1996), 'The geographic structure of cross-national trade flows and region states', *Regional Studies*, vol.303, pp.273–85.

Pratten, C. (1988), 'A Survey of the Economies of Scale', *Research into the Cost of Non-Europe; Basic Findings*, vol.2, Luxemburg, pp.11–165.

Prest, A.R. (1983), 'Fiscal Policy', in P. Coffey, (ed.), *Main Economic Policy Areas of the EEC*, 2nd edn, M. Nijhoff, The Hague, pp.59–90.

Preston, L.E. and Windsor, D. (1997), *The Rules of the Game in the Global Economy: Policy Regimes for International Business*, 2nd edn, Kluwer, Boston.

Price Waterhouse (1988), 'The Cost of non-Europe in Financial Services', *Research into the Cost of Non-Europe; Basic Findings*, vol.9, CEC, Brussels.

Priore, H.J. (ed.) (1979), *Unemployment and Inflation; Institutionalists' and Structuralists' Views*, Sharpe, White Plains, New York.

Pryor, F. (1972), 'An International Comparison of Concentration Ratios', *Review of Economics and Statistics*, vol.54, no.2, pp.130–40.

Puchala, D.J. (1984), *Fiscal Harmonisation in the European Communities, National Policies and International Cooperation*, Pinter, London.

Pugh, G., Tyrall, D. and Tarnawa, L. (1999), 'Exchange rate variability international trade and the single currency debate: a survey', in W. Meeusen (ed.), *Economic Policy in the European Union: Current Perspectives*, Edward Elgar, Cheltenham.

Pugliese, E. (1992), 'The New International Migration and Changes in the Labour Market', *Labour*, vol.6, no.1, pp.165–79.

Reder, M.W. (1962), *Wage Differentials, Theory and Measurement*, Princeton, NJ.

Redmond, J. (ed.) (1992), *The External Relations of the European Community; the International Response to 1992*, St Martin's Press, New York.

Redor, D. (1992), *Wage Inequalities in East and West*, Cambridge University Press, Cambridge/New York.

Rees, R. and Kessner, E. (1999), 'Regulation and efficiency in European insurance markets', *Economic Policy: A European Forum*, vol.29, pp.365–400.

Resnick, S. and Truman, E. (1975), 'An Empirical Examination of Bilateral Trade in Europe', in B. Balassa (ed.), *European Economic Integration*, North-Holland, Amsterdam, pp.41–78.

Richardson, J. (1987), *A Subsectoral Approach to Services Trade Theory*, SWF Pergamon, Oxford.

Ricq, C. (1983), 'Frontier Workers in Europe', in M. Anderson (ed.), *Frontier Regions in Europe*, Frank Cass, London, pp.98–108.

Riemsdijk, J.F. van (1972), 'A System of Direct Compensation Payments to Farmers as a Means of Reconciling Short Run to Long Run Interests', *European Review of Agricultural Economics*, vol.1, no.2, pp.161–89.

Rietbergen, T. van (1999), *The Internationalization of European Insurance Groups*, KNAW/FRWUU, Utrecht.

Rijksbaron, A., Roobol, W.H. and Weisglas, M. (eds) (1987), *Europe from a Cultural Perspective. Historiography and Perceptions*, Nijgh and Van Ditmar, The Hague.

Ritson, C. (ed.) (1978), 'The Lomé Convention and the CAP', *Commonwealth Economic Papers*, no.12, Commonwealth Secretariat, London.

Robson, P. (1988), *The Economics of International Integration*, 3rd edn, Allen and Unwin, London.

Rogers, J.H., Hufbauer, G.C. and Wada, E. (2001), 'Price level convergence and inflation in Europe', *Working paper 01.1*, Institute for International Economics, Washington.

Rogoff, K. (1999), 'Monetary models of dollar/yen/euro nominal exchange rates: dead or undead?', *The Economic Journal*, vol.109, pp.655–59.

Rollet, P. (1984), *Spécialisation Internationale et Intégration Economique et Monétaire dans les Pays CEE*, CREI, Lille.

Rollo, J.M.C. and Warwick, K.S. (1979), 'The CAP and Resource Flows among EEC Member States', *Working Paper no.27*, Government Economic Service, London.

Rose, A.K. (2000), 'One market, one money: the effect of common currencies on trade', *Economic Policy: A European Forum*, vol.30, pp.7–47.

Rose, R. *et al.* (1985), *Public Employment in Western Nations*, Cambridge University Press, Cambridge.

Rosecrance, R. (1984), *The Rise of the Trading State: Commerce and Conquest in the Modern World*, Basic Books, New York.

Rothwell, R. and Zegveld, W. (1981), *Industrial Innovation and Public Policy; Preparing for the 1980s and 1990s*, Pinter, London.

Rubalcaba-Bermejo, L. (1999), *Business Services in European Industry: Growth, Employment and Competitiveness*, CEC, Luxemburg.

Rubin, J. and Thygesen, N. (1996), 'Monetary union and the outsiders: a cointegration–codependence analysis of business cycles in Europe', *Economie Appliquée*, vol.XLIX, no.3, pp.123–71.

Ruding, O. *et al.* (1992), *Conclusions and Recommendations of the Committee of Independent Experts on Company Taxation*, OOPEC, Luxemburg.

Rugman, A.M. (ed.) (1982), *New Theories of the Multinational Enterprise*, Croom Helm, London.

Ruigrok, W. and Tulder, R. van (1995), *The Logic of International Restructuring*, Routledge, London.

Sachs, J. (1980), 'Wages, Flexible Exchange Rates and Macro-Economic Policy', *Quarterly Journal of Economics*, vol.94, pp.731–47.

Sala-I-Martin, X. (1996), 'Regional cohesion: evidence and theories of regional growth and convergence', *European Economic Review*, vol.40, pp.1325–52.

Salt, J. (1976), 'International Labour Migration, the Geographical Pattern of Demand', in J. Salt and H. Clout (eds), *Migration in Post-War Europe, Geographical Essays*, Oxford University Press, Oxford, pp.126–67.

Salvatori, D. (1991), 'The Automobile Industry', in D. Mayes (ed.), *The European Challenge, Industry's Response to the 1992 Programme*, Harvester Wheatsheaf, London, pp.28–90.

Sampson, A. (1977), *The Seven Sisters*, Corgi, London.

Sannucci, V. (1989), 'The establishment of a Central Bank; Italy in the nineteenth century' in M. de Cecco and A. Giovannini (eds), *A European Central Bank?*, Cambridge University Press, Cambridge, pp.244–74.

Sapir, A. (1989), 'Does 1992 Come Before or After 1990? on Regional versus Multilateral Integration', in R. Jones and A.O. Krueger (eds), *The Political Economy of International Trade*, Basil Blackwell, Oxford, pp.197–222.

Sapir, A. (1992), 'Regional integration in Europe', *Economic Journal*, vol.102, pp.1491–1506.

Sapir, A. (1997), 'Domino effects in West European trade 1960–1992', *Discussion Paper, No.1576*, CEPR, London.

Sapir, A. (2000), 'Trade regionalism in Europe: towards an integrated approach', *Journal of Common Market Studies*, vol.38, no.1, pp.151–62.

Saunders, C. and Marsden, D. (1981), *Pay Inequalities in the European Communities*, Butterworths, London.

Saunders, P. and Klau, F. (1985), 'The Role of the Public Sector, Causes and Consequences of the Growth of Government', *OECD Economic Studies*, no.4, pp.1–239.

Scaperlanda, A.E. (1967), 'The EEC and US Foreign Investment; Some Empirical Evidence', *Economic Journal*, vol.77, pp.22–6.

Scaperlanda, A.E. and Mauer, L.J. (1969), 'The Determinants of US Direct Investment in the EEC', *American Economic Review*, vol.59, pp.558–68.

Scharpf, F.P. (1999), *Governing in Europe: Effective and Democratic?* Oxford University Press, Oxford.

Schendelen, M.P.C.M. van (1984), 'The European Parliament; Political Influence is more than Legal Powers', *Journal of European Integration*, vol.8, pp.59–76.

Schendelen, M.P.C.M. van (1993), *National Public and Private EC Lobbying*, Dartmouth, Aldershot.

Schendelen, M.P.C.M. van (1998), *EU Committees as Influential Policy Makers*, Ashgate, Aldershot.

Scherer, F. (1974), 'The Determinants of Multi-Plants Operations in Six Nations and Twelve Industries', *Kyklos*, vol.27, no.1, pp.124–39.

Scherer, F.M. (2000), *Competition Policy, Domestic and International*, Edward Elgar, Cheltenham.

Schippers, J.J. and Siegers, J.J. (1986), 'Womens' Relative Wage Rate in the Netherlands, 1950–1983; a Test of Alternative Discrimination Theories', *De Economist*, vol.134, no.2, pp.165–80.

Schmidtchen, D. and Cooter, R. (1997), *Constitutional Law and Economics of the European Union*, Edward Elgar, Cheltenham.

Schmitz, A. (1970), 'The Impact of Trade Blocks on Foreign Direct Investments', *Economic Journal*, vol.80, pp.724–31.

Schmitz, A. and Bieri, J. (1972), 'EEC-Tariff and US Direct Investment', *European Economic Review*, vol.3, pp.259–70.

Schulze, G.G. (2000), *The political economy of capital controls*, Cambridge University Press, Cambridge.

Schwalbach, J. (1988), 'Economies of Scale and Intra-Community Trade', in *Research into the Cost of Non-Europe, Basic Findings*, vol.2, CEC, Brussels, pp.167–204.

Schwarze, J. (1987), 'Towards a European Foreign Policy; Legal Aspects', in J.K. de Vree, P. Coffey and R.H. Lauwaars (eds), *Towards a European Foreign Policy*, Nijhoff, Dordrecht, pp.69–97.

Scitovsky, T. (1958), *Economic Theory and Western European Integration*, Allen and Unwin, London.

Scott, N. (1967), *Towards a Framework for Analysing the Cost and Benefits of Labour Migration*, Institute for International Labour Studies, Bulletin, Geneva, February.

Seers, D., Schaffer, B. and Kiljunen, M.L. (1979), *Underdeveloped Europe: Studies in Core-Periphery Relations*, Harvester Press, Hassocks, Sussex.

Seers, D., Vaitsos, C. and Kiljunen, M.L. (1980), *Integration and Unequal Development, The Experience of the EC*, St Martin's Press, New York.

Segré, C. *et al.* (1966), *The Development of a European Capital Market*, CEC, Brussels.

Seidel, B. (1983), *Wage Policy and European Integration*, Gower, Aldershot.

Seifert, W.G., Achleiter, A.K., Mattern, F., Streit, C.C. and Voth, H.J. (2000), *European capital markets*, Macmillan Business, London.

Sellekaerts, W. (1973), 'How Meaningful are Empirical Studies on Trade Creation and Trade Diversion?', *Weltwirtschaftliches Archiv*, vol.109, no.4, pp.519–51.

SER (1992), *Migratie, Arbeidsmarkt en Sociale Zekerheid*, Den Haag.

Sexton, J.J., Walsh, B.M., Hannan, D.F. and McMahon, D. (1991), *The Economic and Social Implications of Emigration*, NESC, Dublin.

Shapiro, C. and Varian, H.R. (1999), *Information Rules: A Strategic Guide to the Network Economy*, Harvard BS Press, Boston.

Sharp, M. (ed.) (1985), *Europe and the New Technologies, Six Case Studies in Innovation and Adjustment*, Pinter, London.

Shaw, R.W. and Simpson, P. (1987), *Competition Policy; Theory and Practice in Western Economies*, Wheatsheaf, Brighton.

Shepherd, W.G. (1985), *Public Policies Towards Business*, 7th edn, Irwin, Homewood, Illinois.

Shlaim, A. and Yannopoulos, G.N. (1976), *The EC and the Mediterranean Countries*, Cambridge University Press, Cambridge.

Siebert, H. (ed.) (1994), *Migration; a Challenge for Europe*, Mohr, Tübingen.

Simões, V.C. (1992), 'European Integration and the Pattern of FDI Flows in Portugal', in J. Cantwell (ed.), *Multinational Investment in Modern Europe*, Edward Elgar, Aldershot, pp.256–97.

Simon, J.L. (1989), *The Economic Consequences of Immigration*, Basil Blackwell, Oxford.

Sleuwaegen, L. (1987), 'Multinationals, the European Community and Belgium; Recent Developments', *Journal of Common Market Studies*, vol.26, no.2, pp.255–72.

Sleuwaegen, L. (1993), 'Road Haulage', *European Economy/Social Europe*, no.3, pp.211–50.

Sleuwaegen, L. and Yamawaki, H. (1988), 'European Common Market: Structure and Performance', *European Economic Review*, vol.32, pp.1451–75.

Smith, A. and Venables, A.J. (1988), 'Completing the Internal Market in the EC, some Industry Simulations', *European Economic Review*, vol.32, pp.1501–25.

Söderston, B. (1980), *International Economics*, 2nd edn, Macmillan, London.

Soete, L. (1987), 'The Impact of Technological Innovation on International Trade Patterns: the Evidence Reconsidered', *Research Policy*, pp.101–30.

Spaak, P.H. *et al.* (1956), *Rapport des Chefs de Délégation aux Ministres des Affaires Etrangères*, Brussels.

Spannent, (1991), *Direct Investment of the European Community*, Eurostat, Luxemburg.

Spencer, S. (ed.) (1994), *Immigration as an Economic Asset; the German Experience*, IPPR, London.

Steinherr, A. (1984), 'Convergence and Coordination of Macro-Economic Policies: Some Basic Issues', *European Economy*, no.20, pp.71–110.

Steinherr, A. (1985), 'Competitiveness and Exchange Rates; some Policy Issues for Europe?', in T. Peeters, P. Praet and P. Reding (eds), *International Trade and Exchange Rates in the Late Eighties*, North-Holland, Amsterdam, pp.163–90.

Steinherr, A. (1994), *30 years of European Monetary Integration; from the Werner Plan to the EMS*, Longman, London.

Steinle, W. (1988), 'Social Policy', in W. Molle and R. Cappellin (eds), *Regional Impact of Community Policies in Europe*, Avebury, Aldershot, pp.108–23.

Stevens, C. (ed.) (1981), *EEC and the Third World; a Survey*, Hodder and Stoughton, London.

Stokman, A.C.J. (1995), 'Effects of exchange rate risk on intra-EC trade', *De Economist*, vol.143, no.1, pp.41–54.

Stopford, J.M. and Baden-Fuller, Ch. (1987), 'Regional Level Competition in a Mature Industry; the Case of European Domestic Appliances', *Journal of Common Market Studies*, vol.26, no.2, pp.173–92.

Strauss, R. (1983), 'Economic Effects of Monetary Compensatory Amounts', *Journal of Common Market Studies*, vol.21, no.3, pp.261–81.

Streit, M.E. and Voigt, S. (1997), 'Towards ever closer union – or ever larger? Or both? Entry to the European Union from the perspective of constitutional economics', in D. Schmidtchen and R. Cooter (eds), *Constitutional Law and Economics of the European Union*, Edward Elgar, Cheltenham, pp.223–48.

Strijker, D. and de Veer, J. (1988), 'Agriculture', in W. Molle and R. Cappellin (eds), *Regional Impact of Community Policies in Europe*, Avebury, Aldershot, pp.23–44.

Swoboda, A. (ed.) (1976), 'Capital Movements and their Control', in *IUHEI,CEI*, no.3, Sythoff, Leiden.

Talbot, R.B. (1977), 'The European Community's Regional Fund', *Progress in Planning*, vol.8, no.3, pp.183–281.

Tangermann, S. (1984), 'Guarantee Thresholds, a Device for Solving the CAP Surplus Problem?', *European Review of Agricultural Economics*, vol.11, no.2, pp.159–68.

Tangermann, S. (1995), 'Eastward enlargement of the EU; will agricultural policy be an obstacle?', *Intereconomics*, vol.30(b), pp.277–84.

Tangermann, S. (1999), 'Europe's agricultural policies and the Millennium Round', *The World Economy*, vol.22, no.9, pp.1155–79.

Tapp, J. (1986), 'Regulation of the UK Insurance Industry', in J. Finsinger and J. Pauly (eds), *The Economics of Insurance Regulation*, Macmillan, Basingstoke, pp.27–64.

Tarditi, S. (1984), 'La Crise de la PAC: un Point de Vue Italien', *Economie Rurale*, vol.163, pp.28–33.

Teulings, A.W.M. (1984), 'The Internationalisation Squeeze: Double Capital Movement and Job Transfer within Philips Worldwide', *Environment and Planning*, A, vol.16, pp.597–614.

Tharakan, P.K.M. (ed.) (1983), *Intra-Industry Trade; Empirical and Methodological Aspects*, North-Holland, Amsterdam.

Tharakan, P.K.M. (1988), 'The Sector/Country Incidence of Anti-Dumping and Countervailing Duty Cases in the EC', in L.B.M. Mennes and J. Kol (eds), *European Trade Policies and the Developing World*, Croom Helm, Beckenham, pp.94–135.

Thomsen, S. and Nicolaides, Ph. (1991), *The Evolution of Japanese Direct Investments in Europe*, Harvester Wheatsheaf, Brighton.

Thornton, J. (1992), 'Interest Rates in Domestic and Eurocurrency Markets', *Applied Economics*, vol.24, pp.1103–5.

Thygesen, N. (1990), 'The Benefits and Costs of Currency Unification', in H. Siebert (ed.), *The Completion of the Internal Market*, IWW/Mohr, Tübingen, pp.347–75.

Tichy, G. (1992), 'The European Neutrals', in S. Borner and H. Grubel (eds), *The European Community after 1992. Perspectives from the Outsiders*, Macmillan, London, pp.165–91.

Tims, W. (1987), 'EC Agricultural Policies and the Developing Countries', in L.B.M. Mennes and J. Kol (eds), *European Trade Policies and the Developing World*, Croom Helm, Beckenham, pp.135–87.

Tinbergen, J. (1953), *Report on Problems Raised by the Different Turnover Tax Systems Applied within the Common Market*, ECSC, Luxemburg.

Tinbergen, J. (1954), *International Economic Integration*, Elsevier, Amsterdam.

Tinbergen, J. (1959), 'Customs Unions, Influence of their Size on their Effect', *Selected Papers*, North-Holland, Amsterdam, pp.152–64.

Tinbergen, J. (1965), *International Economic Integration*, 2nd edn, Elsevier, Amsterdam.

Tinbergen, J. (1991), 'The Velocity of Integration', *De Economist*, vol.139, no.1, pp.1–11.

Tinbergen, J. and Fischer, D. (1987), *Warfare and Welfare, Integrating Security Policy into Socio-Economic Policy*, Wheatsheaf, Brighton.

Tironi, E. (1982), 'Customs Union Theory in the Presence of Foreign Firms', *Oxford Economic Papers*, vol.34, pp.150–71.

Torsten, P. (1995), 'European Monetary Union and labour markets; what to expect?', *International Labour Review*, vol.134, no.3, pp.315–32.

Toulemon, R. and Flory, J. (1974), *Une Politique Industrielle pour l'Europe*, PUF, Paris.

Tovias, A. (1978), 'Differential country size as an incentive to the proliferation of trading blocks', *Journal of Common Market Studies*, vol.16, no.3, pp.246–66.

Tovias, A. (1982), 'Testing Factor Price Equalisation in the EEC', *Journal of Common Market Studies*, vol.20, pp.165–81.

Tovias, A. (1990), 'The Impact of Liberalising Government Procurement Policies of Individual EC Countries on Trade with Non-Members', *Weltwirtschaftliches Archiv*, vol.126, no.4, pp.722–36.

Tovias, A. (1991), 'A Survey of the Theory of Economic Integration', *Journal of European Integration*, vol.XV, no.1, pp.5–23.

Tucker, K. and Sundberg, M. (1988), *International Trade in Services*, Routledge, London.

Tulder, R. van and Ruigrok, W. (1997), 'The nature of institutional change: managing rival dependencies', in A. Amin and J. Hausner (eds), *Beyond Markets and Hierarchy: Interactive Governance and Social Complexity*, Edward Elgar, Cheltenham, pp.129–58.

Tyers, R. (1994), 'The Cairns Group perspective', in K.A. Ingersent, A.J. Rayner and R.C. Hine (eds), *Agriculture in the Uruguay Round*, London, Macmillan, pp.88–110.

UN (1979), *Labour Supply and Migration in Europe; Demographic Dimensions 1950–1975 and Prospects*, UN/ECE, Geneva.

UN (1980), *Tendencies and Characteristics of International Migration since 1950*, Geneva.

UN/ECE (1967), *Incomes in Postwar Europe: Economic Survey of Europe in 1965*, part 2, Geneva.

UN/ECE (1977), *Intra-European Temporary Migration of Labour, its Consequences for Trade, Investment and Industrial Co-operation*, TRADER 341, Geneva.

UN/ECE (1980), *Economic Role of Women in the ECE Region*, Chapter 4, Geneva.

UNCTAD (1983), *Protectionism and Structural Adjustment; Production and Trade in Services, Policies and their Underlying Factors bearing upon International Service Transactions*, Geneva.

Ungerer, H. *et al.* (1986), 'The European Monetary System, Recent Developments', *Occasional Paper*, no.48, IMF, Washington.

UNIPEDE (1982), 'Influence des Prix sur la Consommation d'Electricité', *Rapport du Groupe 60.02*, Brussels.

UNIPEDE (1985), *Compte Rendu d'Activités du Groupe d'Experts pour l'Etude de l'Influence entre Prix et Consommation de l'Electricité*, Athens.

Urban, G. (1983), 'Theoretical Justification for Industrial Policy', in F.G. Adams and C.R. Klein (eds), *Industrial Policies for Growth and Competitiveness: an Economic Perspective*, Heath, Lexington Mass, pp.21–40.

USDL (1989), 'The Effects of Immigration on the US Economy and Labor Market', *Migration, Policy and Research*, report 1, Bureau of International Labor Affairs, Washington.

Valdés, A. and Zietz, J. (1995), 'Distortions in world food markets in the wake of GATT; evidence and policy implications', *World Development*, vol.23, no.6, pp.913–26.

Vandamme, J. (ed.) (1986), *New Dimensions in European Social Policy*, TEPSA, Croom Helm, London.

Van den Bergh, P. *et al.* (1987), 'Deregulering van de Internationale Financiële Stromen en Valutastelsel', in Auctores Varii, *Sociaal-Economische Deregulering*, 130e Vlaams Economisch Congres, pp.843–78.

Vanhove, N. and Klaassen, L.H. (1987), *Regional Policy, a European Approach*, 2nd edn, Gower, Aldershot.

Van Meerhaeghe, M.A.G. (1998), *International Economic Institutions*, 7th edn, Kluwer, Dordrecht.

Vassille, L. (1989), 'Similarity among Countries; an International Comparison Based on Data from the 1978/79 Survey'; and 'Industries; the Role of Productivity, Skill and Other Factors', in W. Molle and A. van Mourik (eds), *Wage Differentials in the European Community, Convergence or Divergence?*, Gower, Aldershot, pp.65–83 and 139–63.

Vaubel, R. (1986), 'A public choice approach to international organisation', *Public Choice*, vol.51, pp.39–57.

Vaubel, R. (1994), 'The public choice analysis of European integration: a survey', *European Journal of Political Economy*, vol.10, pp.227–49.

Vaubel, R. (1996), 'Constitutional safeguards against centralisation in federal states; an international cross section analysis', *Constitutional Political Economy*, vol.7, pp.79–102.

Venables, A. (1987), 'Customs Union and Tariff Reform under Imperfect Competition', *European Economic Review*, vol.31, pp.103–10.

Verdoorn, P.J. (1952), 'Welke zijn de Achtergronden en Vooruitzichten van de Economische Integratie in Europa en welke Gevolgen zou deze Integratie hebben, met name voor de Welvaart in Nederland?', *Overdruk no.22*, Centraal Planbureau, The Hague.

Verdoorn, P.J. and Schwartz, A.N.R. (1972), 'Two Alternative Estimates of the Effects of EEC and EFTA on the Pattern of Trade', *European Economic Review*, vol.3, no.3, pp.291–335.

Vernon, R. (1966), 'International Investment and International Trade in the Product Cycle', *Quarterly Journal of Economics*, vol.80, pp.190–207.

Vernon, R. (1979), 'The product cycle hypothesis in a new international environment', *Oxford Bulletin of Economics and Statistics*, vol.41, no.4, pp.255–67.

Verrijn Stuart, G.M. *et al.* (1965), 'Europees Kapitaalverkeer en Europese Kapitaalmarkt', *European Monographs*, no.5, Kluwer, Deventer.

Viaene, J.M. (1982), 'A Customs Union between Spain and the EEC', *European Economic Review*, vol.18, pp.345–68.

Vickerman, R. and Armstrong, H.W. (eds) (1995), *Convergence and Divergence among European Regions*, Pion, London.

Viñals, J. (1994), 'Building a monetary union in Europe: is it worthwhile, where do we stand, and where are we going?', *CEPR Occasional Paper*, no.15, Centre for Economic Policy Research, London.

Viner, J. (1950), *The Customs Union Issue*, Stevens and Sons, London.

Voigt, F., Zachcial, M. and Rath, A. (1986), 'Regulation and Modal Split in the International Freight Transport of the EC', mimeo, University of Bonn, CEC, Brussels.

Völker, E. (1983), 'The Major Instruments of the CCP', in J.H. Bourgeois *et al.* (eds), *Protectionism and the European Community*, Kluwer, Antwerp, pp.17–49.

Vosgerau H.J. (1989), *New Institutional Arrangements for the World Economy*, Springer, Berlin.

Vromen, J.J. (1995), *Economic Evolution: An Enquiry into the Foundations of New Institutional Economics*, Routledge, London.

Waelbroeck, J. (1976), 'Measuring the Degree of Progress of Economic Integration', in F. Machlup (ed.), *Economic Integration, Worldwide, Regional, Sectoral*, Macmillan, London, pp.89–99.

Wallace, H., Caporaso, J.A., Schampf, F.W. and Moravcsik, A. (1999), 'Review section: the choice for Europe: social purpose and state power from Messina to Maastricht', *Journal of European Public Policy*, vol.6, no.1, pp.155–79.

Ward, E. (1986), 'A European Foreign Policy', *International Affairs*, no.4, pp.573–82.

Weiss, F.D. (1987), 'A Political Economy of European Community Trade Policy against the LDCs', *European Economic Review*, vol.31, pp.457–65.

Werner, P. *et al.* (1970), 'Report to the Council, Commission on the Realisation by Stages of the Economic and Monetary Union in the Community', *Bulletin of the EC II*, Supplement.

Wessels, W. (1997), 'An ever closer fusion? A dynamic macropolitical view on integration processes', *Journal of Common Market Studies*, vol.35, no.2, pp.267–99.

Weyman-Jones, T.G. (1986), *Energy in Europe; Issues and Policies*, Methuen, London.

Whalley, J. (1979), 'Uniform Domestic Tax Rates, Trade Distortions and Economic Integration', *Journal of Public Economics*, vol.11, pp.213–21 (see also the further debate in *JPE*, December 1981, pp.379–90).

Whalley, J. (1985), *Trade Liberalisation among Major World Trading Areas*, MIT Press, Cambridge, Massachusetts.

Whichart, O.G. (1981), 'Trends in the US Direct Investment Position Abroad, 1950–1979', US Department of Commerce, *Survey of Current Business*, vol.61, no.2, pp.39–56.

Winters, L.A. (1997), 'What can European experience teach developing countries about integration?', *The World Economy*, vol.20, no.7, pp.889–911.

Wilke, M. and Wallace, H. (1990), 'Subsidiarity, Approaches to Power Sharing in the EC', *Royal Institute of International Affairs*, Discussion Papers no.27, London.

Wilkins, M. (1986), 'The History of European Multinationals, a New Look', *Journal of European Economic History*, vol.15, no.3, pp.483–510.

Williamson, J. (1976), 'The Implication of European Monetary Integration for the Peripheral Areas', in J. Vaizey (ed.), *Economic Sovereignty and Regional Policy*, Gill and Macmillan, Dublin, pp.105–21.

Williamson, J. and Bottrill, A. (1971), 'The Impact of Customs Unions on Trade in Manufactures', *Oxford Economic Papers*, vol.23, pp.323–51, reprinted in M. Kraus (ed.) (1973), *The Economics of Integration*, Allen and Unwin, London, pp.118–51.

Williamson, O.E. (1985), *The Economic Institutions of Capitalism*, The Free Press, New York.

Wilson, K. and Dussen, J. van der (eds) (1995), *The History of the Idea of Europe*, Routledge, London.

Winsemius, A. (1939), *Economische Aspecten der Internationale Migratie*, Bohn, Haarlem.

Winter-Ebmer, R. and Zweimueller, J. (1996), 'Immigration and the earnings of young native workers', *Oxford Economic Papers*, vol.48, pp.473–91.

Winters, L.A. (1985), 'Separability and the Modelling of International Economic Integration', *European Economic Review*, vol.27, pp.335–53.

Winters, A.L. (1987), 'Britain in Europe: a Survey of Quantitative Trade Studies', *Journal of Common Market Studies*, vol.25.

Winters, L.A. (1990), 'The so-called "non-economic" objectives of agricultural support', in *OECD Economic Studies no.3*, pp.237–66.

Winters, L.A. (1997), 'What can European Experience teach developing countries about integration?', *The World Economy*, vol.20, no.7, pp.889–912.

Wittelloostuyn, A. van and Maks, J.A.H. (1988), 'Workable Competition and the Common Market', *European Journal of Political Economy*, vol.16, pp.1–19.

Wolf, Ch. (1987), 'Market and Non-Market Failures; Comparison and Assessment', *Journal of Public Policy*, vol.7, no.1, pp.43–70.

Wolf, M. (1988), 'An Unholy Alliance: the European Community and Developing Countries in the International Trading System', in L.B.M. Mennes and J. Kol (eds), *European Trade Policies and the Developing World*, Croom Helm, Beckenham, pp.31–57.

Wonnacott, P. and Wonnacott, R. (1981), 'Is Unilateral Tariff Reduction Preferable to a Customs Union? The Curious Case of the Missing Foreign Tariffs', *American Economic Review*, vol.71, pp.704–14.

Woolly, P. (1974), 'Integration of Capital Markets', in G. Denton (ed.), *Economic and Monetary Union in Europe*, Croom Helm, London, pp.23–55.

WTO (1996), *Annual Report 1996, vol.1, special topic: trade and foreign investment*, Geneva.

WTO (2000), *Annual Report*, World Trade Organisation, Geneva.

Yannopoulos, G.N. (1985), 'The Impact of the European Economic Community on East–West Trade in Europe', *University of Reading Discussion Papers in Economics*, Series A, no.165.

Yannopoulos, G.N. (1990), 'Foreign Direct Investment and European Integration; the evidence from the formative years of the European Community', *Journal of Common Market Studies*, vol.28, no.4, pp.235–57.

Young, C. (1972), 'Association with the EEC; Economic Aspects of the Trade Relationship', *Journal of Common Market Studies*, vol.11, no.2, pp.120–35.

Young, O.R. (1993), *The International Political Economy and International Institutions*, Edward Elgar, Cheltenham.

Ypersele, J. van and Koene, J.C. (1985), 'The European Monetary System; Origins, Operation and Outlook', *CEC Series European Perspectives*, Luxemburg.

Yuill, D. *et al.* (1999), *European Regional Incentives*, 18th edn, Bowker/Saur, London.

Zietz, J. and Valdés, A. (1986), 'The potential benefits to LDCs of trade liberalization in beef and sugar by industrialized countries', in *Weltwirtschaftliches Archiv*, vol.122, pp.93–112.

Zimmermann, K.F. (1995), 'Tackling the European migration problem', *Journal of Economic Perspectives*, vol.9, no.2, pp.45–62.

Zippel, W. (1985), 'Die Bedeutung einer Harmonisierung der Einzelstaatlichen Verkehrspolitiken im Hinblick auf den Integrationsprozess', in F. Voigt and H. Witte (eds), *Integrationswirkungen von Verkehrssystemen und ihre Bedeutung für die EG*, Duncker und Humblot, Berlin, pp.21–35.

Zodrow, G.R. (1983), *Local Provision of Public Services: the Tiebout Model after Twenty-five Years*, Academic Press, New York.

Index